Reims

NORTHEAST FRANCE

Troyes

Dijon

CENTRAL FRANCE
AND THE ALPS

Lyon

Grenoble

THE SOUTH OF FRANCE

Ajaccio

DK TRAVEL GUIDES

FRANCE

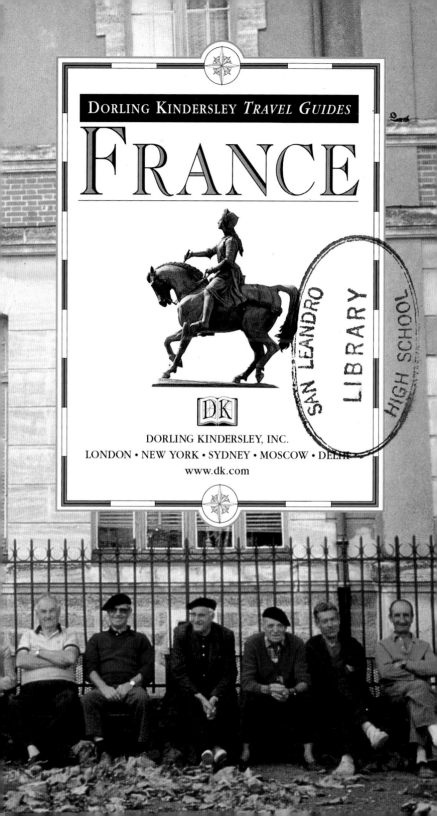

DORLING KINDERSLEY *TRAVEL GUIDES*

FRANCE

DK

DORLING KINDERSLEY, INC.

LONDON • NEW YORK • SYDNEY • MOSCOW • DELHI

www.dk.com

DORLING KINDERSLEY, INC.

www.dk.com

PROJECT EDITOR Rosemary Bailey
ART EDITOR Janis Utton
EDITORS Tanya Colbourne, Fiona Morgan,
Anna Streiffert, Celia Woolfrey
US EDITORS Laaren Brown, Mary Ann Lynch, Mary Sutherland
DESIGNERS Joy FitzSimmons, Erika Lang, Clare Sullivan

MAIN CONTRIBUTORS
John Ardagh, Rosemary Bailey, Judith Fayard, Lisa Gerard-Sharp,
Colin Jones, Alister Kershaw, Alec Lobrano, Anthony Roberts,
Alan Tillier, Nigel Tisdall

PHOTOGRAPHERS
Max Alexander, Neil Lukas, John Parker, Kim Sayer

ILLUSTRATORS
Stephen Conlin, John Lawrence, Maltings Partnership,
John Woodcock

Reproduced by Colourscan (Singapore)
Printed and bound by South China Printing Co Ltd

First American Edition, 1994
8 10 9 7

Published in the United States
by Dorling Kindersley, Inc.,
95 Madison Avenue, New York, NY 10016
Reprinted with revisions 1996, 1997, 1998, 1999, 2000

Copyright © 1994, 2000 Dorling Kindersley Limited, London

Library of Congress Cataloging-in-Publication Data

France -- 1st American ed.
p. cm. -- (Eyewitness travel guides)
Includes index
ISBN 1–56458–646–4
1. France -- Guidebooks. I. Series.
DC20.F715 1994   94–15654
914.404'839--dc20   CIP

THROUGHOUT THIS BOOK, FLOORS ARE REFERRED TO IN ACCORDANCE WITH
EUROPEAN USAGE, I.E., THE "FIRST FLOOR" IS ONE FLIGHT UP.

**The information in every
Dorling Kindersley Travel Guide is checked annually**.
Every effort has been made to ensure that this book is as up-to-
date as possible at the time of going to press. Some details,
however, such as telephone numbers, opening hours, prices,
gallery hanging arrangements and travel information are liable to
change. The publishers cannot accept responsibility for any
consequences arising from the use of this book. We value the
views and suggestions of our readers very highly. Please write to:
Editorial Director, Dorling Kindersley Travel Guides,
Dorling Kindersley, 9 Henrietta Street, London WC2E 8PS.

CONTENTS

Bust of Charlemagne

INTRODUCING FRANCE

PARIS AND ILE DE FRANCE

The fishing village of St-Jean-de-Luz in the Pyrenees

Grape harvest in Alsace

Palais des Papes, Avignon

HOW TO USE THIS GUIDE

THIS GUIDE helps you get the most from your visit to France. It provides expert recommendations and detailed practical information. *Introducing France* maps the country and sets it in its historical and cultural context. The 15 regional chapters, plus *Paris and Ile de France*, describe important sights, with maps, pictures and illustrations. Throughout, features cover topics from food and wine to culture and beaches. Restaurant and hotel recommendations can be found in *Travelers' Needs*. The *Survival Guide* has tips on everything from the French telephone system to transportation.

PARIS AND ILE DE FRANCE

The center of Paris has been divided into five sightseeing areas. Each has its own chapter, which opens with a list of the sights described. A separate section covers Ile de France. All sights are numbered and plotted on an area map. The detailed information for each sight follows the map's numerical order, making sights easy to locate within the chapter.

Sights at a Glance lists the chapter's sights by category: Churches; Museums and Galleries; Historic Buildings; Squares and Gardens.

All pages relating to Paris and Ile de France have green thumb tabs.

A locator map shows where you are in relation to other areas of the city center.

1 Area Map
For easy reference, the sights are numbered and located on a map. Sights in the city center are also shown on the Paris Street Finder *on pages 146–59.*

2 Street-by-Street Map
This gives a bird's-eye view of the key areas in each chapter.

A suggested route for a walk is shown in red.

Stars indicate the sights that no visitor should miss.

3 Detailed information
The sights in Paris and Ile de France are described individually. Addresses, telephone numbers, opening hours and information on admission charges and wheelchair access are also provided for each entry.

THE MASSIF CENTRAL

1 Introduction
The landscape, history and character of each region are described here, showing how the area has developed over the centuries and what it offers to the visitor today.

FRANCE AREA BY AREA
Apart from Paris and Ile de France, France has been divided into 15 regions, each of which has a separate chapter. The most interesting towns and places to visit have been numbered on a *Pictorial Map.*

Each area of France can be quickly identified by its color coding, shown on the inside front cover.

2 Pictorial Map
This shows the road network and gives an illustrated overview of the whole region. All interesting places to visit are numbered, and there are also useful tips on getting around the region by car and train.

3 Detailed information
All the important towns and other places to visit are described individually. They are listed in order, following the numbering on the Pictorial Map. Within each town or city, there is detailed information on important buildings and other sights.

Story boxes highlight noteworthy features of the top sights.

For all the top sights, a Visitor's Checklist provides the practical information you will need to plan your visit.

4 France's top sights
These are given two or more full pages. Historic buildings are dissected to reveal their interiors. The most interesting towns or city centers are shown in a bird's-eye view, with sights pointed out and described.

INTRODUCING
FRANCE

Putting France on the Map

F RANCE, ONE OF THE LARGEST countries in Europe, has airline connections with most cities in the world. Paris is the major transportation hub, with two international airports; others include Bordeaux, Lille, Lyon, Nice and Toulouse. There are good, high-speed rail links with the rest of Europe, and a network of efficient highways. A number of ferry routes cross the Mediterranean to Corsica and beyond. Cross-Channel ferries serve several ports, with the Channel Tunnel providing an alternative link by rail.

Europe
France, known as the "Hexagon" because of its six-sided shape, is bordered by six countries: Spain south across the Pyrenees; Italy and Switzerland beyond the Alps; Luxembourg and Belgium to the north; and Germany on the other side of the Rhine. The United Kingdom lies across the English Channel (La Manche).

KEY

⛴	Ferry service
✈	International airport
═	Highway
═	Main road
—	Railroad

0 kilometers 100

0 miles 100

Greater Paris

The capital of France, Paris is situated in Ile de France. Greater Paris has over 9 million inhabitants, 2.1 million of whom live in Ville de Paris within the Périphérique (beltway).

Regional France

France has a population of over 56 million, and receives over 44 million visitors a year. It covers an area of 543,965 sq km (210,025 sq miles). Paris is the largest city, followed by Lyon, Marseille and the Lille-Lens-Valenciennes urban area. The Loire, Seine, Garonne and Rhône are the longest of France's many rivers. This book divides the country into 15 regions, plus a separate section for Paris and Ile de France, although officially France comprises 22 *régions*.

GETTING AROUND

In spite of its size, France is relatively easy to travel around. There is a well-organized rail network, and traveling times are considerably shortened between towns with a high-speed TGV link *(see p635)*. Most highways have expensive tolls but are fast and efficient for longer distances. Smaller roads are usually a more interesting way to discover the country's varied landscape *(pp638–40)*, and they are almost invariably well maintained and marked.

KEY

━━━ Highway

━━━ Major road

━━━ Minor road

0 kilometers   100

0 miles   100

Eyewitness France Regions

Each of the chapters in this guide has a color code. The chapters are grouped into five sections – Northeast France, Western France, Central France and the Alps, Southwest France and the South of France – plus Paris and Ile de France.

KEY TO COLOR-CODING

Paris and Ile de France

Northeast France

Le Nord and Picardy

Champagne

Alsace and Lorraine

Western France

Normandy

Brittany

The Loire Valley

Central France and the Alps

Burgundy and Franche-Comté

Massif Central

The Rhône Valley and French Alps

Southwest France

Poitou and Aquitaine

Périgord, Quercy and Gascony

The Pyrenees

The South of France

Languedoc-Roussillon

Provence and the Côte d'Azur

Corsica

CORSICA

Corsica

Situated 193 km (120 miles) from the Côte d'Azur, Corsica can be reached by ferry or air. Covering an area of 8,680 sq km (3,350 sq miles), it is the third-largest island in the Mediterranean.

A PORTRAIT OF FRANCE

HE FRENCH THEMSELVES *are the best advocates for visiting France, convinced that their way of life is best, and that their country is the most civilized on earth. The food and wine are justly celebrated. French literature, art, cinema, and architecture can be both profound and provocative. Offering both cerebral and sensual experiences, France is a country where anyone can feel at home.*

France's landscape ranges from high mountain plateaus to lush farmland, traditional villages to chic boulevards. Its regional identities are equally diverse. The country belongs to both northern and southern Europe, and encompasses Brittany with its Celtic maritime heritage, the Mediterranean sunbelt, Germanic Alsace-Lorraine, and the hardy mountain regions of the Auvergne and the Pyrenees. Paris is at the heart of it all, with its aloof, brusque citizens and intense tempo. Other cities range from Lille, the huge industrial center in the north, to Marseille, the biggest port on the Mediterranean. The differences between north and south, country and city are

Marianne, symbol of France

well established and, in fact, cherished, despite the determination of the more progressive French to link their country by TGV (high-speed train) and the home databank service, Minitel. High-tech advances like these have provoked a strong opposite reaction: as life in France becomes more city-based and industrialized, so too, there are those working to safeguard the old, traditional ways and to protect rural life.

The idea of life in the country – *douceur de vivre* (the Good Life), long tables set in the sun for the wine and anecdotes to flow – is as seductive as ever for residents and visitors alike. Nevertheless, the rural way of life has been changing. Whereas in 1945 one

A high-speed TGV *(train à grande vitesse)*, linking Paris with the provinces

◁ **Café life in St-Tropez, one of the country's many pleasures** person in three worked in farming, today it is only one in 16. France's main exports used to be luxury goods like perfumes and Cognac; today, such exports have been overtaken by cars, telecommunications equipment, nuclear power stations and fighter aircraft.

People remain firmly committed to their roots, however, and often keep

The popular *moto* (scooter)

a place in the country where they go for vacations or retirement. On average, there are more French people who have second homes than any other nationality; and in many areas such as Provence, the dying villages have been finding a new life as chic summer residences for Parisians and foreigners. Many artists and arti-

Chanel chic

sans from the towns now go to live and work in the country; or entrepreneurs set up factory workshops there, more feasible in the age of the fax machine and the computer.

Social changes have also followed the decline in influence of the Catholic Church. Today only 14 percent of the population attend mass regularly. Nearly half of all couples live together before marriage, and many never marry at all. Abortion is now legal.

Women, once treated as second-class citizens, have won legal equality in the last 30 years; in 1991 Edith Cresson was the first

woman to be appointed Prime Minister of France. Nevertheless, in France as in the rest of Europe, in politics, industry and big business there is still a reluctance to give senior posts to women. A flirtatious gallantry exists between the sexes, even in public and office life, and influential feminists take care to remain "feminine." Within the family, the old parental authoritarianism has waned; in schools, the harsh discipline has given way to a freer atmosphere – trends resulting from the May 1968 political uprising that marked France so deeply *(see p63)*.

SOCIAL CUSTOMS AND POLITICS

French social life, except between close friends, has always been marked by formality – cheek kissing and handshakes, the use of titles *("Bonjour, Monsieur le President")*, the infrequent use of Christian names, the preference for the formal *vous* rather than the intimate *tu*. However, this has been changing among the younger generation, who

The May 1968 uprising, a catalyst for profound change in France

Farming in Alsace-Lorraine

will now call you by your Christian name, and who use *tu* even at work. Standards of dress have become much more informal, too, though the French are still very concerned about dressing well, and they judge others by their clothes: they prefer an elegantly casual Cardin sweater to an ill-fitting formal suit.

Formality lingers on elsewhere, however, and France remains very legalistic – whether you are buying a house, exporting an antique or getting divorced. But the French also display a charming insouciance about their famous red tape. Rules and laws are there to be ingeniously evaded, twisted or made more human. This sport of avoiding bureaucracy has a name of its own, *le système D*, to be accompanied with a shrug and a smile. For example, since 1992 a new law requires non-smoking areas in public places, even in the most nicotine-stained of tiny bars – but no one really minds if the law is not always rigidly followed.

Today, the old sharp Left/Right ideological divide that used to dominate French politics is giving way to a more gentle, center-focused consensus. This has been fostered by François Mitterrand, who was reelected president for another seven years in 1988 and has left more of a mark on French politics than any postwar politician since de Gaulle. However, the Republican spirit is still evident in recent confrontations, most notably in the burning down of the Rennes Parliament building in 1993. The upper bourgeoisie still holds much of the real power in France, through both state and business appointments; the once-powerful Communist Party is in steep decline. As in other European countries, there has recently been increased support for the far right. High unemployment – France's worst social problem today – has led to growing racism against black immigrants, many of whom are from former French colonies in North Africa.

Charles de Gaulle

CULTURE AND THE ARTS

Culture is taken seriously in France, and writers, intellectuals, artists and fashion designers are held in high social esteem. As a result, the state financed

Designer Thierry Mugler at the Paris collections

a large network of provincial arts centers in the 1960s, and has traditionally given subsidies that have allowed experimentation in art and design. The French remain justly proud of their own serious cinematic tradition, and are determined to defend it against the tide of Hollywood films. Other areas – from the music industry to the French language itself – are subject to the same protectionist attitudes.

Avant-garde art and literature and modern architecture all enjoy strong patronage in France. Some of the more exciting architectural projects range from the striking new buildings in Paris – the Louvre pyramid and La Grande Arche at La Défense – to the postmodern housing projects of Nîmes, Montpellier and Marseille in the south.

Traditional Breton costumes, worn for festivals and *pardons*

MODERN LIFE

The Government's eagerness to stimulate technology has brought innovations such as the Minitel, the videotext databank service, free to many homes. The Minitel can be used as a telephone directory, for booking plane or theater tickets, and for a huge range of communications services. In some ways, the French are already in the 21st century, but remain ambivalent about modernism: they are conservative in many of their tastes and habits.

It will be interesting to see how long after the introduction of the Euro French citizens continue to calculate in Francs, seeing that many have barely accepted the new Franc introduced in 1960. And the French still refuse to stagger their summer vacations, concentrating on the peak period of late July and August, when they take to the roads and coastal resorts.

Modernity has brought some major changes to daily life. For example,

A view through the base of La Grande Arche, part of the huge business complex on the edge of Paris

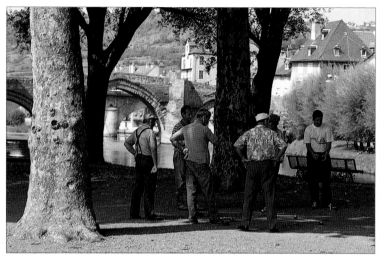

The traditional game of *boules* or *pétanque*, still extremely popular – especially in the south

France has Europe's largest hyper-markets, which have been steadily ousting the local grocery or corner store. Though American in inspiration, these remain French in what they sell: a long delicatessen counter can

have a wonderful display of 100 or so French cheeses and *charcuterie* (pre-pared meats), while the huge range of fresh vegetables, fruits and herbs is a tribute to their role in French cuisine.

Southern produce: melons, peaches and apricots

However, under modern pressures, eating habits have been changing in a curious way. The French used to eat well every day as a matter of course. Today they are in a hurry, and for most meals of the week they will eat simply – either a quick fried steak or pasta dish at home, or a snack in town (hence the wave of fast-food places that have sprung up, in defiance of French tradition). But meals still remain an important part of French leisure activity – not just for the food and wines themselves, though these

are perhaps the world's best, but also for the pleasure of lengthy, unhurried meals and good conversation around a table, among family or friends. They will reserve their gastronomy for the once-or-twice-a-week special occasion – a dinner party, or a superior meal in a restaurant with a loved one, or the extended family Sunday lunch, which remains an important French ritual. It is at these times that the French zest for life is at its most exuberant.

Remote farm – a nostalgic reminder of rural life

The Classic French Menu

THE TRADITIONAL French meal consists of at least three courses. *Les entrées* or *hors d'oeuvre* (appetizers) include soups, egg dishes, salads or *charcuterie*, such as sliced sausage or ham. For *les plats* (main courses), fish or meat is served often with sauce, and accompanied by potatoes, rice or pasta, and vegetables. Cheese comes before dessert, which can include sorbets, fruit tarts or *pâtisserie*. A fixed-price menu is the cheapest option. For more information on French restaurants, see pp576–9.

Soupe à l'oignon *is a favorite in bistros. Croutons, grated cheese and sometimes egg yolk are added to the onion soup.*

Fish soup

Endive salad with diced fried bacon

Goat's cheese melted on toast with salad

Omelette with herbs

Oeufs en Cocotte *are prepared by baking eggs, cream and butter in a china ramekin. They may be sprinkled with fresh herbs and garnished with mushrooms.*

Fried sole served with melted butter

Pike dumplings in a cream sauce

Coquilles Saint-Jacques *are plump sea scallops. They are cooked simply in a little butter. Their orange tails, containing edible roe, are delicious.*

Minced beef with potato purée

Steak with pepper sauce

Veal stew enriched with egg and cream

Breast of duck

Pork chop

Veal sweetbreads

Hors d'Oeuvre

Soupe de poissons

Soupe à l'oignon

Salade frisée aux lardons

Crottin chaud en salade

Omelette aux fines herbes

Oeufs en cocotte

Poissons

Sole Meunière

Quenelles de brochet

Coquilles St Jacques

Viandes

Hachis parmentier

Noisettes d'agneau

Bifteck au poivre

Blanquette de veau

Magret de canard

Côte de porc

Ris de veau

Coq au vin

Noisettes d'Agneau *are small, tender lamb cutlets, sautéed in butter and served rare with mushrooms and herb-and-garlic butter.*

Coq au vin *is one of the best-known French dishes, made of chicken braised in a sauce of red wine, herbs, garlic, pearl onions and button mushrooms.*

BREAKFAST

The French rarely eat cereal, eggs or meat for breakfast, so assorted breads spread with butter and jams are the morning choice. These include *croissants*: flaky, buttery crescent-shaped pastries; a piece of *baguette* (the classic long thin loaf), which is split in half and spread with butter and jam to create a *tartine*; *pain au chocolat*: a buttery square roll with a melted tablet of chocolate inside; and *brioche*, an airy muffin-shaped, egg-enriched yeast bread. This is washed down with coffee or tea and, in some cafés, a glass of red wine, which is said to be good for digestion. The most common form of coffee at breakfast is *café au lait*, espresso coffee served with warm milk.

Croissants

Brioches

Pains au chocolat

Menu à 100F.

Fixed-price menu of the day

Crudités
Raw vegetables

Salade de tomates
Sliced tomatoes in vinaigrette dressing

Escargots à la bourguignonne
Snails in garlic butter

Cuisses de grenouilles
Frogs' legs in garlic butter

Matelote d'anguilles et de carpe
A stew of eel and carp

Entrecôte Bercy

Pintade rôtie garnie
Roast guinea hen

Andouillettes
Small tripe sausages

Fromage ou Desserts

Entrecôte Bercy *is rib steak served with a white wine sauce, named after Quai de Bercy in Paris where wine was unloaded.*

Fromage

DESSERTS

Tarte aux myrtilles

Pêche Melba

Crème caramel
Egg custard with a caramel sauce

Ile flottante
Meringues floating in a creamy custard sauce

Crêpes flambées
Sugared crêpes flamed in a liqueur

Gâteau St Honoré
Chocolate cake, named for the patron saint of pastry cooks

The cheese board *may include goat's, cow's and sheep's milk cheeses, to be eaten with bread or a knife and fork.*

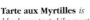

Tarte aux Myrtilles *is blueberry tart. Like most French fruit tarts, it consists of a shallow shortbread crust filled with fruit.*

Pêche Melba *is peaches, ice cream and raspberry sauce, created by famed chef Escoffier for the singer Dame Nellie Melba.*

The Wine of France

WINEMAKING IN FRANCE dates back to pre-Roman times, although it was the Romans who disseminated the culture of the vine and the practice of winemaking throughout the country. The range, quality and reputation of the fine wines of Bordeaux, Burgundy, the Rhône, and Champagne in particular have made them rôle models the world over. France's everyday wines can be highly enjoyable too, and there are also good wines now emerging from the southern regions.

Picker's hod

Traditional vineyard cultivation

WINE REGIONS

Each of the 10 principal wine-producing regions has its own identity, based on grape varieties, climate and local culture. *Appellation contrôlée* laws guarantee a wine's origins and style.

Reims
Paris
Marne
Strasbourg
Loire
Nantes
Tours
Dijon
Clermont-Ferrand
Lyon
Dordogne
Bordeaux
Rhône
Garonne
Pau
Toulouse
Marseille
Perpignan

0 kilometers 150
0 miles 150

KEY

☐	Bordeaux
☐	Burgundy
☐	Champagne
☐	Alsace
☐	Loire
☐	Provence
☐	Jura and Savoie
☐	The Southwest
☐	Languedoc-Roussillon
☐	Rhône

HOW TO READ A WINE LABEL

Even the simplest label will provide a key to the wine's flavor and quality. It will bear the name of the wine and its producer, its vintage if there is one, and whether it comes from a strictly defined area (*appellation contrôlée* or VDQS) or is a more general *vin de pays* or *vin de table*. It may also have a regional grading, as with the *crus classés* in Bordeaux. The shape and color of the bottle is also a guide. Most good-quality wine is bottled in green glass, which helps to protect it from light.

The property or producer

Château-bottled, rather than a blend from a merchant or grower's cooperative

MIS EN BOUTEILLE AU CHÂTEAU
CHÂTEAU MARGAUX
GRAND VIN
1985
PREMIER GRAND CRU CLASSÉ
MARGAUX
APPELLATION MARGAUX CONTRÔLÉE
S.C.A. CHATEAU MARGAUX PROPRIETAIRE A MARGAUX - FRANCE

Pictures may be realistic or fanciful

Capacity of the bottle

The vintage, from the French word *vendange*, or harvest

The wine's *appellation contrôlée*

How Wine is Made

Wine is the product of the juice of freshly picked grapes, after natural or cultured yeasts have converted the grape sugars into alcohol during the fermentation process. The yeasts, or lees, are normally filtered out before bottling.

WHITE WINE   RED WINE

Newly harvested grapes, whether red or white, are first lightly crushed to bring the sugar-rich juices into contact with the yeasts in the grape skins' "bloom."

Old wine press

Red wine gets its backbone from tannins present in red grape skins. The stems also contain tannins, but of a harsher kind; most winemakers de-stem most or all of their red grapes before they are pressed.

Tanks for maceration

Crusher and de-stemmer

For young white wines and some reds (e.g. simple Beaujolais) that do not gain complexity from aging, the crushed grape juice may be steeped, or macerated, with the grape skins for a few hours to add aroma and flavor.

White wine uses only lightly pressed juice for the freshest and fruitiest flavors. For red wine, the grapes are pressed again more thoroughly, and this vin de presse, rich in tannins and other flavor elements, can be blended back into the wine as needed.

Press

Fermentation is a natural process, but can be unpredictable; nowadays, many growers use cultured yeasts and hygienic, temperature-controlled stainless-steel tanks to control fermentation and ensure consistent results.

Wines that do not require aging may be filtered straight into their bottles, but barrels are used to age many finer wines. The flavors imparted by the oak are an integral part of many wines' identities – for example, the "wood-shavings" character of red Bordeaux.

Fermentation vat

Oak casks

Different shades of glass identify the wine regions

Bottle shapes typical of red Bordeaux (left) and Burgundy

Artists in France

Aʀᴛɪsᴛs ʜᴀᴠᴇ always been inspired by France, especially since landscape became a legitimate subject for art in the 19th century. Art and tourism have been closely linked for more than a century. The establishment of artists' colonies in Brittany, the forest of Fontainebleau and the south of France did much to make these areas attractive to visitors. Today, one of the pleasures of touring the countryside is seeing the landscapes made famous in paintings.

Follower of *the French Classical tradition of landscape painting, Jean-Baptiste-Camille Corot recorded* The Belfry of Douai *(1871).*

Le Nord and Picardy

Gustave Courbet, *socialist and leader of the Realist School of painting, captured this famous coastal town in* The Cliffs at Etretat after a Storm *(1869).*

Normandy

Paris and Ile de France

Brittany

Loire Valley

Emile Bernard *was fascinated by the wild, almost primitive character of the Breton landscape and the individuality of its inhabitants. He was one of the community of artists based in Pont Aven. His* La Ronde Bretonne *(1892) portrays local Celtic customs.*

Poitou and Aquitaine

Neo-Impressionist *artist and exponent of Pointillism, Paul Signac indulged his love of maritime subjects on the coasts of France. Entrance to the Port at La Rochelle (1921) shows his use of myriad dots of color to represent nature.*

Périgord, Quercy and Gascony

Pyrenees

Languedoc Roussillon

Théodore Rousseau, *the leading light of the Barbizon School (see p171) of landscape painters, visited the Auvergne in 1830. It was here that he began to paint "en plein air" (in the open air). The results are seen in this sensitively observed scene,* Sunset, Auvergne *(c.1830).*

In his **Eiffel Tower** *(1926) Robert Delaunay investigated the abstract qualities of color. His wife, artist Sonia Delaunay, said, "The Eiffel Tower and the Universe were one and the same to him."*

A few months before his tragic death in July 1890, Vincent Van Gogh painted the Church at Auvers. *He noted that the building "appears to have a violet-hued blue color; pure cobalt."*

Scenes from *everyday life were realistically rendered by Gustave Courbet, as here in* Young Ladies of the Village Giving Alms to a Cow Girl in a Valley near Ornans *(1851–2).*

Alsace and
Lorraine

Champagne

Maurice Utrillo *painted this village scene,* The Church of Saint Bernard in Summer *(1924), while staying at his mother's home. The somber tone and emptiness reflect his unhappy life.*

Burgundy and
Franche-Comté

The Massif
Central

The Rhône Valley
and French Alps

Provence and
the Côte d'Azur

Landscape at Collioure
(1905) depicts the vivid colors of this little Catalan fishing village. It was here that Henri Matisse founded the art movement of the Fauves, or "Wild Beasts," who used exceptionally bright, expressive colors.

The French Riviera *attracted many artists (see pp462–3). Raoul Dufy particularly appreciated its pleasures, seen in this typical scene of blue skies and palm trees,* La Jetée Promenade à Nice *(1928).*

0 kilometers   100

0 miles   100

Writers in France

Monument to Baudelaire

WRITERS AND INTELLECTUALS traditionally enjoy great prestige in France. One of the most august of French institutions is the Academie Française, whose 40 members, most of them writers, have pronounced on national events and have, on occasion, held public office.

The work of many French novelists is deeply rooted in their native area, ranging from the Normandy of Gustave Flaubert to Jean Giono's Provence. In addition to their literary merit, these novels provide a unique guide to France's regional identities.

THE NOVEL

The farmland of the Beauce, where Zola based his novel, *La Terre*

Colette's house in Burgundy

THE FIRST great French writer was Rabelais in the 16th century, a boisterous, life-affirming satirist *(see p285)*. Many writers in the Age of Enlightenment that followed emphasized the classic tradition of reason,

Marcel Proust, author of *Remembrance of Things Past*

clarity and objectivity in their work. The 19th century was the golden age of the French humanist novel, producing Balzac, with his vast fresco of contemporary society; Stendhal, a fierce critic of the frailties of ambition in *Scarlet and Black*; and Victor Hugo, known for epics such as *Les Misérables*. George Sand broke ground with her novels such as *The Devil's Pool*, which depicted peasant life, albeit in an idealized way. In the same century, Flaubert produced his masterwork *Madame Bovary*, a study of provincialism and misplaced romanticism. In contrast, Zola wrote *Germinal, La Terre* and other studies of lower-class life.

Marcel Proust combined a poetic evocation of his boyhood with a portrait of high society in his long novel

Remembrance of Things Past. Others have also written poetically about their childhood, including Alain-Fournier in *Le Grand Meaulnes* and Colette in *My Mother's House*.

A new kind of novel emerged after World War I. Jean Giono's *Joy of Man's Desiring* and François Mauriac's masterly *Thérèse Desqueyroux* explored the impact of landscape upon human character. Mauriac, and also George Bernanos in his *Diary of a Country Priest*, used lone spiritual struggle as a theme. The free-thinker André Gide was another leading writer of the interwar years with his *Strait is the Gate* and the autobiographical *If it Die*.

In the last 40 years, Alain Robbe-Grillet and others have promoted an experimental style known as the Nouveau Roman, subordinating character and plot to detailed physical description. Critics of the style feel that it has contributed to the recent decline of the novel.

Hugo's novel *Les Misérables*, made into a musical in the 1980s

THEATER

THE THREE classic playwrights of French literature, Racine, Molière and Corneille, lived in the 17th century. Molière's comedies satirized the vanities and foibles of human nature. Corneille and Racine wrote noble verse tragedies. They were followed in the 18th century by Marivaux, writer of romantic comedies, and Beaumarchais, whose *Barber of Seville* and *Marriage of Figaro* later became operas.

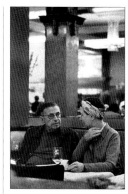

Molière, the 17th-century dramatist

Victor Hugo's dramas were the most vigorous product of the 19th century. The exceptional dramatists of the 20th century range from Jean Anouilh, author of urbane philosophical comedies, to Jean Genet, ex-convict critic of the establishment. In the 1960s, Eugene Ionesco from Romania and Samuel Beckett from Ireland were among the pioneers of a new genre, the "theater of the absurd." Since then, no major playwrights have emerged, but experimental work flourishes in state-subsidized theater companies.

POETRY

THE GREATEST of early French poets was Ronsard, who wrote sonnets about nature and love in the 16th century. Lamartine, a major poet of the early 19th century, also took nature as one of his themes (his poem *Le Lac* laments a lost love). Later the same century, Baudelaire *(Les Fleurs du mal)* and Rimbaud *(Le Bateau Ivre)* were considered provocative in their day. Nobel prizewinner in 1904, Frédéric Mistral wrote in his native Provençal tongue. The greatest poet of the 20th century is considered to be Paul Valéry, whose work is profoundly philosophical.

PHILOSOPHY

FRANCE has produced a large number of leading philosophers in the European humanist tradition. One of

Novels by Albert Camus, who won the Nobel Prize in 1957

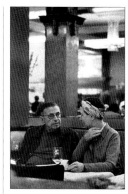

Sartre and de Beauvoir in La Coupole restaurant in Paris, 1969

the first was Montaigne in the 16th century, an inspired moralist who established the essay as an art form. Then came Descartes, the master of logic, and the philosopher Pascal. The 18th century produced two great figures – Voltaire, the supreme liberal, and Rousseau, who preached the harmonizing influence of living close to nature.

In the 20th century an element of philosophy entered the French novel, in the work of Sartre, de Beauvoir and Camus. Sartre led the existentialist movement in Paris in the early 1940s with his novel *Nausea* and his treatise *Being and Nothingness*. Camus' novel about alienation, *The Outsider*, was equally influential.

Barthes and Foucault were among the structuralists who followed. Their radical ideas dominated the Paris intellectual scene in the 1970s and 1980s.

FOREIGN WRITERS

Many foreign writers have visited and been inspired by France, from Petrarch in 14th-century Avignon to Goethe in Alsace in 1770–71. The Riviera attracted many English writers, including Somerset Maugham, Katharine Mansfield and Graham Greene. In 1919 the American Sylvia Beach opened the first Shakespeare and Company bookstore in Paris, which became a cultural center for expatriate writers. In 1922 she was the first to publish James Joyce's masterwork, *Ulysses*.

Hemingway with Sylvia Beach and friends, Paris 1923

Romanesque and Gothic Architecture in France

FRANCE IS RICH in medieval architecture, ranging from small Romanesque churches to great Gothic cathedrals. As the country emerged from the Dark Ages in the 11th century, there was a surge in Romanesque building, based on the Roman model of thick walls, round arches and heavy vaults. French architects improved this basic structure, leading to the flowering of Gothic in the 13th century. Pointed arches and flying buttresses were the key features that allowed for much taller buildings with larger windows.

LOCATOR MAP

① *Romanesque abbeys & churches*

⑬ *Gothic cathedrals*

ROMANESQUE FEATURES

The plan of Angoulême shows the cross shape and the rounded eastern apse typical of Romanesque architecture.

Transept · Apse · Crossing

A section of Le Puy reveals a high barrel-vaulted nave with round arches and low side aisles. Light could enter through windows in the side aisles and the central lantern tower.

Central lantern tower · Side aisle · Vaulted nave

The massive walls of the nave bays of St-Etienne support a three-story structure of arcades, a gallery and clerestory.

Gallery · Clerestory · Arcades

GOTHIC FEATURES

The plan of Amiens shows the nave and apse flanked by a continuous row of chapels.

Lady chapel · Apsidal chapel · Apse · Double-aisled nave

A section of Beauvais shows how the nave could be raised to staggering heights thanks to exterior support from flying buttresses.

Buttress · Rib vault · Flying buttresses

Pointed arches withstood greater stress, permitting larger windows as in the nave at Reims.

Triforium · Tracery · Pointed arch

WHERE TO FIND ROMANESQUE ARCHITECTURE

1. St-Etienne, Caen *p244*
2. Mont-St-Michel, Normandy *p248*
3. St-Pierre, Angoulême *p409*
4. Notre-Dame, Le Puy *p355*
5. St-Pierre, Moissac *pp432–3*
6. St-Sernin, Toulouse *pp436–7*
7. Ste-Foy, Conques *pp356–7*
8. Sacré-Coeur, Paray-le-Monial *p335*
9. St-Philibert, Tournus *p334*
10. St-Etienne, Nevers *p328*
11. Ste-Madeleine, Vézelay *pp326–7*
12. Marmoutier, Saverne *p223*

WHERE TO FIND GOTHIC ARCHITECTURE

13. Notre-Dame, Strasbourg *p221*
14. Notre-Dame, Reims *pp202–3*
15. Notre-Dame, Laon *p195*
16. Notre-Dame, Amiens *pp192–3*
17. St-Pierre, Beauvais *p190*
18. St-Denis, Ile-de-France *p162*
19. Sainte-Chapelle, Paris *pp80–81*
20. Notre-Dame, Paris *p82–3*
21. Notre-Dame, Chartres *pp298–301*
22. St-Etienne, Bourges *p303*

Central tower
Entrance arches
Lateral tower
Tiered apse
Apsidal chapel
Ambulatory

The west façade of Marmoutier Abbey, *with its towers, narrow windows and small portal, has a fortified appearance.*

The east end of Nevers *has a rounded apse surrounded by a semicircular ambulatory and radiating chapels. The chapels were added to provide space for altars.*

Stepped tower
Sculpted portal
Rose
Apse
Buttress
Chapel

The west façade of Laon *has decorative, sculpted portals and a rose window characteristic of Gothic style.*

The east end of Beauvais, *with its delicate buttresses topped by pinnacles, is the culmination of High Gothic.*

TERMS USED IN THIS GUIDE

Basilica: Early church with two aisles and nave lit from above by clerestory windows.

Clerestory: A row of windows illuminating the nave from above the aisle roof.

 Rose: Circular window, often stained glass.

Buttress: Mass of masonry built to support a wall.

 Flying buttress: An arched support transmitting thrust of the weight downward.

Portal: Monumental entrance to a building, often decorated.

 Tympanum: Decorated space, often carved, over a door or window lintel.

Vault: Arched stone ceiling.

Transept: Two wings of a cruciform church at right angles to the nave.

Crossing: Center of cruciform where transept crosses nave.

Lantern: Turret with windows to illuminate interior, often with cupola (domed ceiling).

Triforium: Middle story between arcades and clerestory.

Apse: Termination of the church, often rounded.

Ambulatory: Aisle running around east end, passing behind the sanctuary.

Arcade: Set of arches and supporting columns.

Rib vault: Vault supported by projecting ribs of stone.

 Gargoyle: Carved grotesque figure, often a water spout.

Tracery: Ornamental carved stone pattern within Gothic window.

Flamboyant Gothic: Carved stone tracery resembling flames.

 Capital: Top of a column, usually carved.

Rural Architecture

FRENCH FARMHOUSES ARE ENTIRELY products of the soil, built of stone, clay or wood, depending on what materials are found locally. As the topography changes so does the architecture, from the steeply sloped roofs covered in flat tiles in the north to the broad canal-tiled roofs of the south.

Despite this rich regional diversity, French farmhouses fall into three basic categories: the *maison bloc,* where house and outbuildings share the same roof; the high house, with living quarters upstairs and livestock or wine cellar below; and courtyard farmsteads, their buildings set around a central court.

Shuttered window in Alsace

Symmetrical façade

Wood from local forests

The chalet *is typical of the Jura, Alps and Vosges mountains. The* maison bloc *housed both family and livestock throughout the winter. Gaps between the gable planks allowed air to circulate around crops stored in the loft, and an earth ramp behind gave wagons access. Many lofts also had a threshing floor.*

Half-timbered houses *are typical of Normandy, Alsace, Champagne, Picardy, the Landes and Basque country. The filling between the timbers was wattle and daub or in some cases brick, but it is the arrangement of the smaller posts, different in each region, that best expresses the local style.*

Normandy wood structure

Flat-tiled roof

Dovecote with flat tiles

Raised stone foundations

Steps to front door

Animals or wine housed here

The high house *is most prominent in the southeast, and is normally built of stone with an exterior stone staircase and upstairs porch. Wine growers' barrels could be stored on the ground floor without hoisting, or livestock stabled there. High houses in the Lot Valley often boast a dovecote.*

The long house is the oldest form of maison bloc, *with family and livestock at opposite ends of the building – originally one room. In this Breton version, separate doorways lead to house and stable. A dividing wall became common only in the 19th century.*

Local stone

Slate roof

Entrance to lodging

Stable entrance

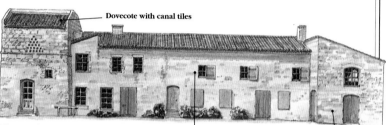

Dovecote with canal tiles

The word "mas" *generally refers to any Provençal farmhouse. In the Camargue and the Crau, it is a farmstead for large-scale sheep farming built in an "agglomerated" style: the outbuildings, although attached to one another, are of different heights. Often, a dovecote is included.*

Ocher and beige colors of the south

Rendered façade

Pebble and brick wall

Half-timber and brick

Compressed cob: *pisé*

Sun-dried adobe bricks

Pebbles in lime mortar

Brick, flint and chalk

WALLS

Limestone, granite, sandstone and pebbles were all used for building walls. But if no stone was available, clay was dug for infilling half-timbered houses, as wattle and daub. The alternative was to use a cob mixture *(pisé)*, pressed into blocks in a process called *banchange*. Adobe (sundried brick) was also used, but fired brick was fairly rare as it was expensive to bake. Still, brick was sometimes used as trim or combined with chalk or pebbles in a "composite" walling. Walls were generally rendered with mortar.

Flat terra-cotta tiles in colors of local sand

Pantiles, used in Flanders and Picardy

Canal clay tiles typical of the south

ROOFING

Two roof styles distinguish the north and south. Northern roofs are steeply pitched, so that any rainwater runs off easily. In the south, roofs are covered with canal clay tiles, and more gently sloped to prevent the tiles from sliding off.

FRANCE THROUGH THE YEAR

THE FRENCH, with their farming roots, are deeply aware of the changing seasons, and the mild climate means they can celebrate outdoors most of the year. History and tradition are honored with *fêtes*, such as Bastille Day (July 14). For culture lovers, thousands of arts festivals are held in various locations, from the huge Avignon Theater Festival down to small village events. Large national sports events, such as the Tour de France bicycle race, are featured annual events. There are also festivals throughout the year, featuring every kind of food and wine. In high season in the summer, the cities empty and locals and tourists flock to the beaches and countryside.

SPRING

FRANCE'S OUTDOOR life resumes in spring, terrace cafés filling up in the sunshine. Easter is a time of Catholic processions and concerts of sacred music. The Cannes Film Festival in May is the best known of the season's many conventions and trade fairs.

MARCH

Tinta' Mars *(all month)*, Langres. Cabaret and musical evenings at various venues.
International Dog-sled Championships *(second week)*, Chamrousse.
Montbéliard Chocolate Carnival *(usually second week)*.
Grenoble Jazz Festival *(Mar 18–27)*. Jazz concerts.
Wine Sales of the Hospices *(last weekend)*, Nuits-St-

Formula One racing at the Monaco Grand Prix

La Bravade procession honoring Saint Torpes in St-Tropez

Rugby ball

Georges, Burgandy.
Musical Flower Show *(end Mar–May)*, Epinal.

APRIL

Six Nations Rugby Tournament, Parc des Princes, Paris.
Good Friday penitential processions Sartène *(see p533)*, Perpignan *(see p474)* and Holy Week processions all over France.
Passion Plays *(Easter)*, reenactments of the Crucifixion throughout France. **Bourges Spring Festival** *(third week, see p303)*.
Europa Jazz Festival *(last two weeks)*, Le Mans. Young

Spring asparagus

jazz musicians from all over the world come to play.
Horse riding: International Competition *(last week)*, Saumur.
International Paris Fair *(end Apr–first week May)*, Parc des Expositions, Paris. Crafts and art exhibits.
Joan of Arc Festival *(end Apr–early May)*, Orléans *(see p302)*.
Foire de Paris *(end Apr)*, Paris Expo.

MAY

Asparagus harvest, notably in the Loire Valley.
International Grand Prix de Monaco *(Ascension weekend, see p520)*.

Oloron-Ste-Marie Agricultural Fair *(May 1, see p445).*
Paris International Marathon *(mid-May)*, from place du Concorde to Château de Vincennes.
La Bravade *(May 16–18)*, St-Tropez *(see p506).*
Cannes Film Festival *(second and third week).*
International Sailing Week *(third week)*, La Rochelle.
Gypsy Pilgrimage *(May 24–26)*, Stes-Maries-de-la-Mer *(see p500).*
Festival d'Amiens *(last week).* Jazz and world music at various locations.

Fête de Transhumance *(end of May).* Herds are taken up to summer pastures.
Nîmes Feria *(end May)*, bullfights and street music

Traditional movement of animals to summer pastures

festival *(see p486).*
Grandes Eaux Musicales *(May–Oct, Sundays)*, Versailles. Classical music in the grounds of the château.

SUMMER

THE FRENCH vacation season begins in mid-July, with the return to work and school *(la rentrée)* in early September. Beaches, marinas and campsites are all full to bursting. Every village has its *fête* and there are countless festivals and sports events.

JUNE

French Tennis Open *(last week May – first week Jun)*, Stade Roland Garros, Paris.
Strasbourg International Music Festival *(until Jul).*
Puy-du-Fou Pageant *(Jun–Sep)*, 18th-century village

The rose season in full bloom

brought to life in the park at Les Epesses, Vendée.
Le Mans 24-Hour Automobile Race *(third weekend, see p281).*
Rose Show *(Jun 21)*, Bois de Boulogne, Paris.
Fête de St-Jean *(Jun 24)*, music, bonfires and fireworks all over France.
Tarasque Festival *(last week)*, Tarascon *(see p497).*

JULY

Aix Festival *(all month)*, Aix-en-Provence *(see p501).*
Avignon Theater Festival *(all month, see p493).*
Eté Girondin *(until Aug).* Jazz concerts throughout Aquitaine *(see p411).*

Bullfighting in Mont-de-Marsan

Tombées de la Nuit *(first week)*, Rennes. Arts festival.
Troménie *(Jul 11)*, Locronan. Procession of penitents *(see p263).*
Comminges Festival *(mid-Jul–end Aug, see p452).*
Foix Medieval Festival *(mid-Jul–mid Aug, see p453).*
JVC Grand Parade du Jazz *(mid-Jul)*, Nice.
Mont-de-Marsan Feria *(third week).* Bullfights and music *(see p415).*
International Jazz Festival *(second half)*, Antibes and Juan-les-Pins *(see p511).*
Jazz Vienne *(first two weeks)*, Vienne *(see p372).*
Sète Festival *(second and third weeks, see p482).*
Tour de France bicycle race *(third week).* The grand finale takes place on the Champs-Elysées, Paris.

Cyclists in the final stage of the Tour de France cycle race

Vacationers on a crowded beach in Cannes on the Côte d'Azur

AUGUST

Peak tourist season
(Aug 1–15).
Lourdes Pilgrimage
(Palm Sun to Aug 15, see p449).
International Organ Festival *(Jul–Sep)*, organ recitals in Chartres cathedral.
Pablo Casals Festival *(end Jul–mid-Aug)*, Prades *(see p470).*

Avignon Theater Festival performer

Fête de la Véraison *(first or second weekend)*, medieval celebration of fruit harvest, Châteauneuf-du-Pape *(see p494).*
Parade of Lavender Floats *(first or second weekend)*, Digne *(see p507).*
Interceltic Festival *(second week)*, traditional Celtic arts, crafts and music, Lorient *(see p405).*
"Feria" – Bullfight *(mid-Aug)*, Dax *(see p415).*
St-Jean-Pied-de-Port-Basque Fête *(mid-Aug, see p444).*
Son et Lumière (sound and light) displays in historic buildings everywhere and August 15 fireworks.
International Sardana Festival *(third weekend)*, Céret *(see p472).*

AUTUMN

IN WINE REGIONS, the grape harvest is the occasion for much gregarious jollity, and every wine village celebrates with a wine festival. When the new wine is ready in November there are more festivities. The hunting season begins – hunters are out everywhere. In the south-west, small migrating birds are trapped in nets, often to the fury of ecologists.

Ceremony for the Induction of new Chevaliers at the Hospice de Beaune

SEPTEMBER

Festival de l'Ile de France *(weekends, until mid-Oct)*, Classical and jazz concerts.
Picardy Cathedral Festival *(mid-Sep)*, classical concerts in the region's cathedrals.
"Musicades" *(first two weeks)*, Lyon. Classical music concerts.
Le Puy "Roi de l'Oiseau," *(third week)*, Renaissance-style festival *(see p355).*
Grape harvest, wine regions throughout France.

OCTOBER

Pottery-makers Festival *(first weekend)*, Lyon.
Prix de l'Arc de Triomphe *(first Sun)*, Horse racing at Longchamp, Paris.
Espelette Red Pepper Festival *(last weekend, see p443)*, in the Basque region.
Walnut season, throughout Périgord region.

Classical cello

NOVEMBER

Dijon International Food and Wine Festival *(first two weeks)*. Traditional gastronomic fair.
Apple Festival *(mid-Nov)*, Le Havre.
Wine Sales and Les Trois Glorieuses *(third weekend)*, Beaune *(see p336).*
Truffle season *(until Mar)*, Périgord, Quercy and Provence.

WINTER

AT CHRISTMAS, traditional nativity plays are held in churches and there are fairs and markets throughout France. In the Alps and the Pyrenees, and even the Vosges and Massif Central, the ski slopes are crowded. In Flanders and Nice, carnivals take place before Lent.

Christmas wreath

DECEMBER

Men's International Skiing Competition *(mid-Dec)*, Val d'Isère. Most important skiing competition of the year.

JANUARY

Château de Thoiry Music Festival *(all year)*, concerts of every kind of music.
Abbaye de Fontevraud Season of Music *(until Jun, see p284)*.

Downhill skier on the slopes in the French Alps

Monte-Carlo Rally *(usually mid-Jan, see p520)*.
Limoux Carnival *(until Mar)*. Street festival held since the Middle Ages.

FEBRUARY

Découvertes *(first week)*, Grand Palais. International art show for new artists.
Lemon Festival *(mid-Feb–Mar)*, Menton *(see p519)*.
Nice Carnival and the Battle of Flowers *(late Feb–early Mar, see p516)*.
International Jazz Festival *(mid–end Feb)*, Cannes.

The Taj Mahal re-created at the Lemon Festival in Menton

Celebrating the Nice Carnival and the Battle of Flowers

Bastille Day parade past the Arc de Triomphe

PUBLIC HOLIDAYS

New Year's Day (Jan 1)
Easter Sunday and Monday
Ascension Day (sixth Thursday after Easter)
Whit Monday (second Monday after Ascension)
Labor Day (May 1)
VE Day (May 8)
Bastille Day (Jul 14)
Assumption Day (Aug 15)
All Saints' Day (Nov 1)
Remembrance Day (Nov 11)
Christmas Day (Dec 25)

The Climate of France

SET ON EUROPE'S western edge, France has a varied, temperate climate. An Atlantic influence prevails in the north-west, with westerly sea winds bringing humidity and warm winters. The east experiences Continental temperature extremes, with frosty, clear winters and often stormy summers. The south enjoys a Mediterranean climate, with hot, dry summers and mild winters punctuated by violent winds.

PARIS AND ILE DE FRANCE

°F				
		75	61	
	58	59	49	44
	44			36
☼	6 hrs	8 hrs	4.5 hrs	2 hrs
☂	2 in	2.25 in	2.25 in	2.25 in
month	Apr	Jul	Oct	Jan

Average monthly maximum temperature

Average monthly minimum temperature

Average daily hours of sunshine

Average monthly rainfall

NORMANDY

°F				
		71	61	
	55	55	46	46
	41			36
☼	5.5 hrs	7 hrs	4 hrs	2 hrs
☂	1.75 in	2 in	2.75 in	2.5 in
month	Apr	Jul	Oct	Jan

LOIRE VALLEY

°F				
		76	64	
	59	57	48	47
	43			37
☼	6 hrs	8.5 hrs	4.5 hrs	2.5 hrs
☂	2 in	1.75 in	3 in	3.5 in
month	Apr	Jul	Oct	Jan

BRITTANY

°F				
		75	63	
	58	55	47	46
	42			36
☼	6 hrs	8 hrs	4.5 hrs	2 hrs
☂	1.75 in	1.5 in	2.5 in	2.5 in
month	Apr	Jul	Oct	Jan

POITOU AND AQUITAINE

°F				
		79	66	
	62	58	48	49
	44			37
☼	6.5 hrs	9 hrs	5.5 hrs	2.5 hrs
☂	2.75 in	1.75 in	3.5 in	4 in
month	Apr	Jul	Oct	Jan

PYRENEES

°F				
		77	66	
	59	56	46	50
	41			33
☼	5 hrs	7.5 hrs	5.5 hrs	3.5 hrs
☂	3.75 in	2.5 in	3 in	3.75 in
month	Apr	Jul	Oct	Jan

PÉRIGORD, QUERCY AND GASCONY

°F				
		81	66	
	62	58	48	47
	43			36
☼	6 hrs	9 hrs	4.5 hrs	2.5 hrs
☂	2.25 in	2 in	2.25 in	2.5 in
month	Apr	Jul	Oct	Jan

Le Havre

PAR

Rennes

Tours

Nantes

Bordeaux

Montauban

Biarritz

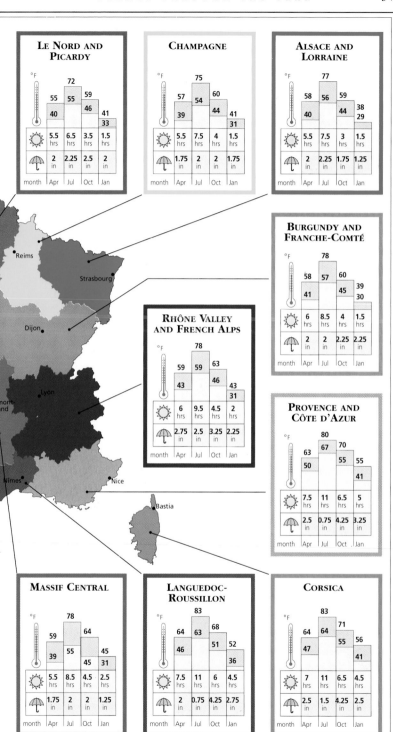

LE NORD AND PICARDY

°F		72		
	55	55	59	
	40		46	41
				33
☼	5.5 hrs	6.5 hrs	3.5 hrs	1.5 hrs
☂	2 in	2.25 in	2.5 in	2 in
month	Apr	Jul	Oct	Jan

CHAMPAGNE

°F		75		
	57	54	60	
	39		44	41
				31
☼	5.5 hrs	7.5 hrs	4 hrs	1.5 hrs
☂	1.75 in	2 in	2 in	1.75 in
month	Apr	Jul	Oct	Jan

ALSACE AND LORRAINE

°F		77		
	58	56	59	
	40		44	38
				29
☼	5.5 hrs	7.5 hrs	3 hrs	1.5 hrs
☂	2 in	2.25 in	1.75 in	1.25 in
month	Apr	Jul	Oct	Jan

BURGUNDY AND FRANCHE-COMTÉ

°F		78		
	58	57	60	
	41		45	39
				30
☼	6 hrs	8.5 hrs	4 hrs	1.5 hrs
☂	2 in	2 in	2.25 in	2.25 in
month	Apr	Jul	Oct	Jan

RHÔNE VALLEY AND FRENCH ALPS

°F		78		
	59	59	63	
	43		46	43
				31
☼	6 hrs	9.5 hrs	4.5 hrs	2 hrs
☂	2.75 in	2.5 in	3.25 in	2.25 in
month	Apr	Jul	Oct	Jan

PROVENCE AND CÔTE D'AZUR

°F		80		
	63	67	70	
	50		55	55
				41
☼	7.5 hrs	11 hrs	6.5 hrs	5 hrs
☂	2.5 in	0.75 in	4.25 in	3.25 in
month	Apr	Jul	Oct	Jan

MASSIF CENTRAL

°F		78		
	59		64	
	39	55		45
			45	31
☼	5.5 hrs	8.5 hrs	4.5 hrs	2.5 hrs
☂	1.75 in	2 in	2 in	1.25 in
month	Apr	Jul	Oct	Jan

LANGUEDOC-ROUSSILLON

°F		83		
	64	63	68	
	46		51	52
				36
☼	7.5 hrs	11 hrs	6 hrs	4.5 hrs
☂	2 in	0.75 in	4.25 in	2.75 in
month	Apr	Jul	Oct	Jan

CORSICA

°F		83		
	64	64	71	
	47		55	56
				41
☼	7 hrs	11 hrs	6.5 hrs	4.5 hrs
☂	2.5 in	1.5 in	4.25 in	2.5 in
month	Apr	Jul	Oct	Jan

Reims

Strasbourg

Dijon

Lyon

Clermont-Ferrand

Nîmes

Nice

Bastia

THE HISTORY OF FRANCE

THE ONLY European country to face both the North Sea and the Mediterranean, France has been subject to a particularly rich variety of cultural influences. Though famous for the rootedness of its peasant population, it has also been a European melting pot, from before the arrival of the Celtic Gauls in the centuries before Christ, through to the Mediterranean immigrations of the 20th century.

Fleur-de-lys, the royal emblem

Roman conquest by Julius Caesar had an enduring impact, but from the 4th and 5th centuries AD, waves of Barbarian invaders destroyed much of the Roman legacy. The Germanic Franks provided political leadership in the following centuries, but when their line died out in the late 10th century, France was socially and politically fragmented.

THE FORMATION OF FRANCE

The Capetian dynasty gradually pieced France together over the Middle Ages, a period of great economic prosperity and cultural vitality. The Black Death and the Hundred Years' War brought setbacks, and the dynasty's power was seriously threatened by the rival Burgundian dukes. France recovered, however, and flourished during the Renaissance, followed by the grandeur of Louis XIV's reign. During the Enlightenment, in the 18th century, French culture and institutions were the envy of Europe.

The Revolution of 1789 ended the absolute monarchy and introduced major social and institutional reforms, many of which were endorsed and consolidated by Napoleon. Yet the Revolution also inaugurated the instability that has remained a hallmark of French politics: since 1789, France has known five republics, two empires and three brands of royal power, plus the Vichy government during World War II.

Modernization in the 19th and 20th centuries proved a slow process. Railroads, the military service and radical educational reforms were crucial in forming a sense of French identity among the citizens.

Rivalry with Germany dominated French politics for most of the late 19th and early 20th centuries. The population losses in World War I were traumatic for France, and so was its occupation by Germany from 1940–44. Yet since 1945, the two countries have proved the backbone of the developing European Union.

Inlaid marble tabletop showing the map of France in 1684

◁ *La République,* painted by Charles Landelle in 1848

Prehistoric France

THE EARLIEST TRACES of human life in France date back to around 2 million BC. From around 40,000 BC, *Homo sapiens* lived an itinerant existence as hunters and gatherers. Around 6000 BC, following the end of the Ice Age, a major shift in lifestyle occurred, as people settled down to herd animals and cultivate crops. The advent of metalworking allowed more effective tools and weapons to be developed. The Iron Age is associated particularly with the Celts, who arrived from the east during the first millennium BC. A more complex social hierarchy developed, consisting of warriors, farmers, artisans and druids (Celtic priests).

Bronze Age vase, Brittany

FRANCE IN 8000 BC

☐ *Former coastline*

☐ *Present-day land mass*

Carnac Stone Alignments *(4500–4000 BC) The purpose of the extensive networks of megaliths around Carnac (see p268) remains obscure. They possibly served in pagan rituals or as an astronomical calendar.*

These carvings of horses' heads were found in the Pyrenees and date from around 9000 BC.

The mammoth, here carved from animal bone, was a thick-coated giant that died out after the end of the Ice Age.

Cro-Magnon Man *This skull, dating to c.25,000 BC, was discovered at Cro-Magnon in the Dordogne in 1868. In comparison with most of his predecessors, Cro-Magnon Man was tall, robust and had a large head. He differed only marginally from us.*

PREHISTORIC ART
The rich deposits of cave art in France have only been recognized as authentic for just over a century. They include wall paintings and sketches as well as various engraved objects. Venus figurines, carved with flint tools, probably had ritual and religious rather than erotic purposes.

TIMELINE

2,000,000 BC Early hominid societies

30,000 Cro-Magnon Man

Painting of bulls in Lascaux

2,000,000 BC	30,000	25,000	20,000

400,000 Discovery of fire by *Homo erectus*

28,000 The first Venus sculptures, possibly representing fertility goddesses

Primitive stone tool

THE HISTORY OF FRANCE

Doorway, Roquepertuse
Religion was an important part of Celtic life. The Celts made a cult of severed heads – presumably of their enemies – as seen in this sanctuary doorway dating from the 3rd century BC.

The prehistoric hunter's quarry is here represented by a flock of chamois (goatlike antelopes) carved on bone.

This carved bone, found in Laugerie Basse in the Dordogne, shows a bison chased by a man with a spear.

This highly stylized female figure, a Venus figurine found in southwest France, was carved from mammoth tusk in around 20,000 BC.

The Lascaux cave paintings in Périgord *(see p424)* are among the best in the world. Other cave decoration is found around Les Eyzies *(pp424–5)*, at the Vallée des Merveilles near Tendes in the Alpes-Maritimes *(p519)* and in the Grotte du Pech Merle in the Lot Valley *(p428)*. The intriguing menhirs at Filitosa in Corsica *(pp532–3)* are about 4,000 years old.

The Lascaux cave paintings, dating from 16,000–14,000 BC, include images of bulls and mammoths.

Copper Ax *(c.2000 BC)*
Copper tools preceded the arrival of the stronger and more malleable bronze alloy. Iron was to prove the toughest and most useful metal of all.

Bronze Armor
Bronze and Iron Age people were highly warlike. The Celtic Gauls were feared even by Romans. Their protective armor, such as this breastplate dating from 750–475 BC, was light but reasonably effective.

15,000 Hunters live on wandering herds of mammoth, rhinoceros and reindeer. Art includes the Lascaux caves and Val Camonica/Mont Bego engravings	**7000– 4500** Neolithic revolution: farming, megaliths and menhir stone sculptures	**600** Greek colony at Marseille. Mediterranean luxury goods exchanged for tin, copper, iron and slaves. Early urban development

15,000	10,000	5,000

10,000 End of Ice Age. More regions become inhabitable

10,000–6000 Mammoth herds disappear and hunters must rely on animals of the forest, including wild boar and aurochs

1200–700 Arrival of the Celts during the Bronze and Iron Ages

500 Celtic nobles bury their dead with riches such as the Vix treasure *(see p324)*

Celtic helmet

Roman Gaul

THE ROMANS HAD ANNEXED the southern fringe of France by 125–121 BC. Julius Caesar brought the rest of Gaul under Roman control in the Gallic Wars (58–51 BC). The province of Gaul prospered: it developed good communications, a network of cities crammed with public buildings and leisure facilities such as baths and amphitheaters, while in the countryside large villas were established. By the 3rd century AD, however, barbarian raids from Germany were causing increasing havoc. From the 5th century barbarians began to settle throughout Gaul.

Roman mosaic from Vienne

FRANCE IN 58 BC

☐ *Roman Gaul*

Emperor Augustus, who was considered a living God, was worshiped at this altar.

Roman Dolce Vita
The Romans brought material comfort and luxury, and wine production became widespread. This 19th-century painting by Couture conveys a contemporary view of Roman decadence.

Vercingetorix
The Celtic chieftain Vercingetorix was Julius Caesar's greatest military opponent. This bronze statue is at Alise-Sainte-Reine (see p324), the Gauls' final stand in 51 BC.

LA TURBIE

This impressive monument near Monaco was erected in 6 BC by the Roman Senate. It celebrates Augustus's victory over the Alpine tribes in 14–13 BC. Badly pillaged for its stone, it was only partly restored in 1935.

TIMELINE

125–121 BC Roman colonization of Southern Gaul

31 BC Frontiers of the Three Gauls (*Gallia Celtica, Gallia Aquitania* and *Gallia Belgica*) established by Augustus

Augustus

200 BC	100	0	AD 100

58–51 BC Julius Caesar's Gallic Wars result in establishment of Roman Gaul

Julius Caesar

52–51 BC Vercingetorix revolt

16 BC Maison Carrée built in Nîmes (see pp486–7)

AD 43 Lugdunum (Lyon) established as capital of the Three Gauls

Dancing Girl
Celtic art continued, uninfluenced by Roman naturalistic ideals. This bronze statuette of a young woman dates from the 1st–2nd century AD.

A statue of Augustus was placed at the top of the original monument.

Enameled Brooch
This decorative Gallo-Roman brooch dates from the second half of the 1st century BC.

WHERE TO SEE GALLO-ROMAN FRANCE

Gallo-Roman remains are to be found all over France, many of them in Provence. In addition to La Turbie *(see p519)*, there is the Roman amphitheater in Arles *(p475)* and the theater and triumphal arch in Orange *(p492)*. Elsewhere, there are ruins at Autun in Burgundy *(p329)*, the Temple d'Auguste et Livie in Vienne *(p372)*, Les Arènes at Nîmes *(pp486–7)* and fragments of Vesunna in Périgueux *(p424)*.

Les Arènes in Nîmes, *built at the end of the 1st century AD, is still in use today.*

The Claudian Tables
In AD 48, Emperor Claudius persuaded the Senate to allow Gauls full Roman citizenship. The grateful Gauls recorded the event on stone tables, found at Lyon.

The 44 tribes subjugated by Augustus are listed on an inscription, with a dedication to the emperor.

Emperor Augustus
Augustus, the first Roman Emperor (27 BC–AD 14), upheld the Pax Romana, a peace agreement that allowed the Gauls to concentrate on culture rather than war.

AD 177 First execution of Christian martyrs, Lyon. Sainte Blandine is thrown to the lions, who refuse to harm her

Sainte Blandine

360 Julian, prefect of Gaul, proclaimed Roman Emperor. Lutetia changes name to Paris

200	300	400

275 First Barbarian raids

313 Christianity officially recognized as religion under the rule of Constantine, the first Christian emperor

406 Barbarian invasion from the east. Settlement of the Franks and Germanic tribes

476 Overthrow of the last Roman emperor leads to end of the western Roman Empire

The Monastic Realm

THE COLLAPSE of the Roman Empire led to a period of instability and invasions. Both the Frankish Merovingian dynasty (486–751) and the Carolingians (751–987) were unable to bring more than spasmodic periods of political calm. Throughout this turbulent period, the Church provided an element of continuity. As centers for Christian scholars and artists, the monasteries helped to restore the values of the ancient world. They also developed farming and viticulture; and some became extremely powerful, dominating the country economically as well as spiritually.

9th-century gold chalice

FRANCE IN 751

☐ *Carolingian Empire*

Stable with lay brethren's quarters above

Charlemagne *(742–814)*
The greatest of Carolingian rulers, Charlemagne created an empire based on strictly autocratic rule. Powerful and charismatic, he could neither read nor write.

Bakery

The great infirmary hall could accommodate about 100 patients. It was flanked by the Lady Chapel.

Saint Benedict
Saint Benedict established the Benedictine rule: monks were to divide their time between work and prayer.

CLUNY MONASTERY
The Benedictine abbey of Cluny *(see p335)* was founded in 910 with the aim of major monastic reforms. This major religious center, here shown as a reconstruction (after Conant), had great influence over hundreds of monasteries throughout Europe.

TIMELINE

481 Clovis the Frank becomes first Merovingian king

507 Paris made capital of the Frankish kingdom

c.590 Saint Colombanus introduces Irish monasticism to France

732 Battle of Poitiers: Charles Martel repulses Arab invasion

500 | **600** | **700**

496 Conversion of Clovis, king of the Franks, to Christianity

628–37 Dagobert I, the last effective ruler of the Merovingian dynasty, brings temporary unity to the Frankish kingdom

Dagobert I

751 Pepin becomes first king of the Carolingian dynasty

Baptism of Clovis
The Frankish chieftain Clovis was the first barbarian ruler to convert to Christianity. He was baptized in Reims in 496.

The abbey church, begun in 1088, was the largest church in Europe before St. Peter's was built in Rome in the 16th century.

Cemetery chapel

WHERE TO SEE MONASTIC FRANCE

The monastic realm has survived in austere Cistercian abbeys in Burgundy, such as Fontenay *(see pp322–3)*. Little remains of Cluny, but some of the superb capitals can still be admired *(p335)*. The best way to experience monastic France might be to retrace the **Cluny capitals** steps of medieval pilgrims and visit the monastic centers on the route to Santiago de Compostela *(pp390–91)*, such as Vézelay *(pp326–7)*, Le Puy *(pp354–5)*, Conques *(pp358–9)*, Moissac *(pp432–3)* and St-Sernin in Toulouse *(pp436–7)*.

Monastic Arts
In scriptoriums, talented artists dedicated their time to the meticulous art of illuminating and copying manuscripts for the libraries.

Monastic Labor
Monks of the Cistercian rule were renowned for their commitment to manual labor such as cultivating the land and producing wine and liqueurs.

1096 First Crusade

1066 Conquest of England by the Normans

Carolingian soldiers

987 Hugh Capet, first Capetian ruler

| 800 | 900 | 1000 |

843 Treaty of Verdun: division of the Carolingian Empire into three parts including West Francia

910 Foundation of the Benedictine monastery of Cluny

1077 Bayeux tapestry

800 Coronation of Charlemagne as Holy Roman Emperor

William the Conqueror steering his ship on the Bayeux tapestry

Gothic France

FRANCE IN 1270
☐ *Royal territory*
▨ *Other fiefs*

Tʜᴇ ɢᴏᴛʜɪᴄ ꜱᴛʏʟᴇ, epitomized by soaring cathedrals (*see pp28–9*), emerged in the 12th century at a time of growing prosperity and scholarship, crusades and an increasingly dominant monarchy. The rival French and Burgundian courts (*see p333*) became models of fashion and etiquette for all of Europe. *Chansons des gestes* (epic poems) performed by troubadours celebrated the code of chivalry.

Medieval knights in combat

FRANCE IN 1270
☐ *Royal territory*
▨ *Other fiefs*

Ciborium of Alpais
Alpais, a renowned 12th-century goldsmith in Limoges, made this superb ciborium, used to hold wafers for the Holy Communion.

Winch to lift stone sections

Courtly Love
According to the code of chivalry, knights dedicated their service to an ideal but unapproachable lady. Courtesy and romance were introduced in art and music.

The king supervised the building of the cathedral, accompanied by the architect.

Draper's Window
The textile trade benefited from the era of urban prosperity. This stained-glass window in a church in Semur-en-Auxois (see p325) shows wool washers at work.

TIMELINE

c.1100 First edition of the epic poem *Chanson de Roland*

1117 Secret marriage of the scholar Abelard and his student Héloïse. Her uncle, canon Filibert, does not approve and forces him to become a monk while she retires as a nun

1154 Angevin Empire created by Anglo-Norman dynasty starting with Henry Plantagenet, a Count of Anjou and King of England (as Henry II)

| 1100 | 1125 | 1150 | 1175 |

1115 Saint Bernard founds the Cistercian Abbey at Clairvaux

1120 Rebuilding of the Abbey of St-Denis; birth of the Gothic style

King Philip Augustus, who adopted the fleur-de-lys emblem

1180–1223 Reign of Philip Augustus

The Crusades
In an attempt to win back the Holy Land from the Turks, Philip Augustus set out on the Third Crusade (1189) alongside England's Richard the Lion-Heart and Holy Roman Emperor Frederick Barbarossa.

Lacelike sculpture adorned the façades of the Gothic cathedrals.

Stonemasons cut stones on site.

ELEANOR OF AQUITAINE

Strong-willed and vivacious Eleanor, duchess of independent Aquitaine, contributed to the conflict between France and England. In 1137 she married the pious Louis VII of France. Returning from a crusade, Louis found that their marriage had broken down. After the annulment in 1152, Eleanor married Henry of Anjou, taking her duchy with her. Two years later Henry successfully claimed the throne of England. Aquitaine came under English rule, and thus the Angevin Empire began.

Eleanor of Aquitaine and Henry II are buried in Fontevraud (p284).

St. Bernard *(1090–1153) Key figure of the Cistercian rule and counselor to the pope, St. Bernard preached rigorous simplicity of life.*

Holy Relic
Throughout the Middle Ages most churches could boast at least one saint's relic. The cult of relics brought pilgrims and more riches.

THE BUILDING OF A CATHEDRAL
In affluent, mercantile towns, skilled masons constructed towering Gothic cathedrals of revolutionary design, such as Chartres *(see pp298–301)* and Amiens *(pp192–3)*. With their improbable height and lightness, they were a testimony to both faith and prosperity.

Louis IX on his death bed

1226 Louis IX crowned king

1270 Death of Louis IX at Tunis in the Eighth Crusade

1305 Papacy established in Avignon

1200	1225	1250	1275	1300

1214 Battle of Bouvines. Philip Augustus begins to drive the English out of France

1259 Normandy, Maine, Anjou and Poitou acquired from England

1285 Philip the Fair crowned

1297 Louis IX is canonized, becoming Saint Louis

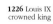

The Hundred Years' War

Public execution, in Froissart's 14th-century chronicle

T HE HUNDRED YEARS' WAR (1337–1453), pitting England against France for control of French land, had devastating effects. The damage of warfare was amplified by frequent famines and the ravages of bubonic plague in the wake of the Black Death in 1348. France came close to being permanently partitioned by the king of England and the duke of Burgundy. In 1429–30 the young Joan of Arc helped rally France's fortunes, and within a generation the English had been driven out of France.

FRANCE IN 1429

☐ *France*

▨ *Anglo-Burgundy*

Angels with trumpets announce the Last Judgment.

Men of War

One of the reasons men enlisted as soldiers was hope for plunder. Both the French and English armies lived off the land, at the expense of the peasantry.

The elect, springing resurrected from their graves, are ushered into heaven.

The Black Death

The plague of 1348–52 caused 4–5 million deaths, about 25 percent of the French population. For want of medicines people had to put their faith in prayers and holy processions.

TIMELINE

1346 Battle of Crécy: French defeated by English

1328 Philip VI, first Valois monarch

1356 French defeat at Battle of Poitiers

14th-century flame-thro[w]

1325	1350	1375

1337 Start of the Hundred Years' War

Plague victims

1348–52 The Black Death

1358 Bourgeois uprising in Paris led by Etienne Marcel. The Jacquerie peasant uprising in Northern France

Medieval Medicine

The state of the heavens was widely held to influence earthly conditions, such as health, and a diagnosis based on the zodiac was considered reliable. The standby cure for all sorts of ailments was bloodletting.

English Longbow

The king's troops fought against England, but the individual French duchies supported whichever side seemed more favorable. In the confused battles, English bowmen excelled. Their longbows caused chaos among the hordes of mounted French chivalry.

Christ as Supreme Judge is flanked by angels bearing the instruments of the Passion.

Archangel Michael, resplendent with peacock wings, holds the judgment scales. The weight of sinners outbalances the elect.

John the Baptist is accompanied by the 12 apostles and the Virgin Mary, dressed in blue.

The damned, with hideously twisted faces, fall into Hell.

THE LAST JUDGMENT

With war, plague and famine as constant visitors, many people feared that the end of the world was nigh. Religious paintings, such as the great 15th-century altar screen by Rogier van der Weyden in the Hôtel-Dieu in Beaune *(see pp336–7)*, reflected the moral fervor of the time.

Attack on Heresy

The general anxiety spilled over into anti-Semitic pogroms and attacks on alleged heretics, who were burned at the stake.

1415 Battle of Agincourt. French defeat by Henry V of England

1411 *Les Très Riches Heures du Duc du Berry* prayer book, by Paul and Jean de Limbourg *(see p194)*

1419 Charles VI of France makes Henry V of England his heir

1429 Intervention of Joan of Arc: Charles VII crowned king

1431 Joan of Arc burned at stake as witch by the English

1453 End of the Hundred Years' War. Only Calais remains in English hands

1400	1425	1450

Joan of Arc

Renaissance France

As a result of the French invasion of Italy in 1494, the ideals and aesthetic of the Italian Renaissance spread to France, reaching their height during the reign of François I. Known as a true Renaissance prince, he was skilled in letters and art as well as sports and war. He invited Italian artists, such as Leonardo and Cellini, to his court and enjoyed Rabelais' bawdy stories. Another highly influential Italian was Catherine de' Medici (1519–89). Widow of Henri II, she virtually ruled France through her sons, François II, Charles IX and Henri III. She was also one of the major players in the Wars of Religion (1562–93) between Catholics and Protestants, which divided the nobility and tore the country to pieces.

Masked lute-player

FRANCE IN 1527

☐ *Royal territory*

▨ *Other fiefs*

The corner towers are a Gothic feature transformed by Italian lightness of touch into pure decoration.

Galerie François I, Fontainebleau
The artists of the School of Fontainebleau blended late Italian Renaissance style with French elements.

Power Behind the Throne
Catherine de' Medici dominated French politics from 1559–89.

AZAY-LE-RIDEAU

One of the loveliest of the Loire châteaux, Azay was begun in 1518 *(see p286)*. Italian influences are visible, and it is clear that this is a dwelling meant for pleasure rather than defense.

TIMELINE

1470 First printing presses established in France

Prototype tank by Leonardo da Vinci

1519 Leonardo da Vinci dies in the arms of François I at the French court in Amboise

1536 Calvin's *Institutes of the Christian Religion* leads to a new form of Protestantism

1470	1480	1490	1500	1510	1520	1530

1477 Final defeat of the Dukes of Burgundy, who sought to establish a middle kingdom between France and Germany

1494–1559 France and Austria fight over Italian territories in the Italian Wars

1515 Reign of François I begins

Golden coin showing the fleur-de-lys and the salamander of François I

Gold Pomander
Pomanders containing sweet-smelling herbs and spices such as cinnamon were carried in times of plague to ward off the bad air held responsible for contagion.

The staircase was in the new Italian fashion with double flights of steps rather than a spiral.

Ballroom with Flemish tapestries

The Red Room

New France
French expansion and quest for colonies started with Cartier's expedition to Canada in 1534 (see p272).

WHERE TO SEE RENAISSANCE FRANCE

In Paris, many churches and the impressive place des Vosges *(see p87)* date from the Renaissance. There are countless 16th-century châteaux in the Loire and Burgundy. Among the finest are Chenonceau *(pp288–9)* and Tanlay *(p321)*. Salers *(p353)* is a virtually intact Renaissance town. The historic center of Toulouse *(p436)* has many elegant Renaissance palaces.

This fireplace *stands in François I's room at Château de Chenonceau.*

François I and the Italian Influence
François I, here receiving Raphael's painting The Holy Family *in 1518, collected Italian art at Fontainebleau. Among the favored painters were Michelangelo, Leonardo and Titian.*

1540	1550	1560	1570	1580	1590	1600

1539 Edict of Villers Cotterets makes French the official language of state

1559 Treaty of Cateau–Cambrésis ends the Italian Wars

1562 Wars of Religion between Catholics and Protestants start

1572 Massacre of Protestants on St. Bartholomew's Eve in Paris

St. Bartholomew's Eve Massacre

1589 Henry III murdered. The Huguenot Henry IV becomes first Bourbon king of France

1593 Henry IV converts to Catholicism and ends the Wars of Religion

1598 Edict of Nantes: tolerance for Protestantism

1608 Foundation of Quebec

The Grand Siècle

**Emblem of
the Sun King**

THE END OF THE RELIGIOUS WARS heralded a
period of exceptional French influence
and power. The cardinal ministers
Richelieu and Mazarin paved the way for
Louis XIV's absolute monarchy. Political
development was matched by artistic styles
of unprecedented brilliance: enormous
Baroque edifices, the drama of Molière
and Racine, and the music of Lully.
Versailles *(see pp164–7)*, built under the
supervision of Louis' capable finance minister Colbert,
was the glory of Europe, but its cost and Louis XIV's
endless wars proved expensive for the French state
and led to widespread misery by the end of his reign.

FRANCE IN 1661

☐ *Royal territory*

☐ *Avignon (papal enclave)*

**Madame (married to
Monsieur) as Flora**

Molière *(1622–73)*
*Actor-playwright Molière performed
many plays for Louis XIV and his court,
though some of his satires were
banned. After his death, his company
became the basis of the French state
theater, the Comédie Française.*

**Monsieur, the
king's brother**

Madame de Maintenon
*In 1684,
following the
death of his
first wife,
Marie-Thérèse,
Louis secretly
married his
mistress Mme. de
Maintenon, then
aged 49.*

THE SUN KING AND HIS FAMILY
Claiming to be monarch by divine right, Louis XIV
commanded court painter Jean Nocret to devise this
allegorical scene in 1665. Surrounded by his family,
the king appears as the sun god Apollo.

TIMELINE

1610–17 Marie de' Medici acts as Regent for Louis XIII	*Cardinal Richelieu*	**1634** Foundation of the literary society Académie Française	**1642–3** Death of Louis XIII and Cardinal Richelieu. Accession of Louis XIV with Mazarin as principal minister
	1624 Cardinal Richelieu becomes principal minister		

1610	1620	1630	1640	1650

1617 Louis XIII accedes at the age of 17	**1631** Foundation of *La Gazette*, France's first newspaper	**1637** Descartes' *Discourse on Method*	**1648–52** The Fronde: French civil wars
		1635 Richelieu actively involves France in the Thirty Years' War	

Louis XIV's Book of Hours
After a lively and libertine youth, Louis became increasingly religious. His Book of Hours (1688–93) is in Musée Condé (see p195).

Royal Wedding
Louis XIII and Anne of Austria were married in 1615. After his death, Anne became regent for the young Louis XIV with Cardinal Mazarin as minister.

Baroque Figurine
The royal glory was reflected in the arts. This objet d'art *features a Christ in jasper on a pedestal decorated with gilded cherubs and rich enameling.*

Louis XIV as Apollo

Anne of Austria as Cybele

The dauphin (the king's son)

Grande Mademoiselle, the king's cousin, as Diana

Queen Marie-Thérèse as Juno

WHERE TO SEE ARCHITECTURE OF THE GRAND SIÈCLE

Paris boasts many imposing Grand Siècle buildings, such as the Hôtel des Invalides *(see p110)*, the Dôme church *(p111)* and the Palais du Luxembourg *(pp122–3)*, but the Château de Versailles *(pp164–7)* is the ultimate example of the flamboyance of the period. Reminders of this glory include the sumptuous Palais Lascaris in Nice *(p518)* and the Corderie Royale in Rochefort *(p407)*. At the same time, military architect Vauban constructed mighty citadels, such as Neuf-Brisach *(see p216)*.

Versailles's *interior is a typical example of the gilded Baroque style.*

Playwright Jean Racine (1639–99)

1661 Death of Mazarin: Louis XIV becomes his own principal minister

1662 Colbert, finance minister, reforms finances and the economy

1680 Creation of the theater Comédie Française

1685 Revocation of the Edict of Nantes of 1598: Protestantism banned

1682 Royal court moves to Versailles

1686 Opening of the Café Procope (first coffeehouse in Paris)

1689 Major wars of Louis XIV begin

1709 Last great famine in French history

1660	1670	1680	1690	1700

17th-century cannon

Enlightenment and Revolution

Plate of Louis XVI's execution

IN THE 18TH CENTURY, Enlightenment philosophers such as Voltaire and Rousseau redefined man's place within a framework of natural principles, thus challenging the old aristocratic order. Their essays were read across Europe and even in the American colonies. But although France exported worldly items as well as ideas, the state's increasing debts brought social turmoil, triggering the 1789 Revolution. Under the motto "Freedom, Equality, Fraternity," the new Republic and its reforms had a far-reaching impact on the rest of Europe.

FRANCE IN 1789

☐ *Royal France*

▨ *Avignon (papal enclave)*

Voltaire *(1694–1778)*
Voltaire, master of satire, wrote numerous essays and the novel Candide. *His fierce critiques sometimes forced him into exile abroad.*

Jacobin Club

National Assembly

The Guillotine
This infamous invention was introduced in 1792 as a humane alternative to other forms of capital punishment, which had usually involved torture.

Place de la Révolution
(see p94) is where Louis XVI's execution took place in 1793.

The Tuileries

Café Le Procope was the haunt of Voltaire and Rousseau.

Palais Royal
The private residence of the Duke of Orléans, the Palais Royal (see p95) became a center of revolutionary agitation from 1789. It was also the site of several printing presses.

TIMELINE

1715 Death of Louis XIV, accession of Louis XV		**1743–64** Mme. de Pompadour, Louis XV's favorite, uses her influence to support artists and philosophers during her time at court

1715	**1725**	**1735**	**1745**	**1755**

1720 Last outbreak of plague in France: population of Marseilles decimated

Physician's protective costume worn during the plague

1751 Publication of the first volume of Diderot's *Encyclopedia*

1756–63 Seven Years' War: France loses Canada and other colonial possessions

Revolutionary Symbols
The motifs of the Revolution, such as the blue, white and red of the tricolor, even appeared on wallpaper in the 1790s.

Queen Marie-Antoinette
Marie-Antoinette's frivolous behavior helped discredit the monarchy. She was held in the Conciergerie and brought to the guillotine in 1793.

The Marais, earlier an aristocratic area, fell into decay as a result of the Revolution.

Bastille

REVOLUTIONARY PARIS

From 1789, Paris housed numerous political clubs, such as the left-wing Jacobins, and many revolutionary newspapers. The war tune "La Marseillaise," introduced by volunteers from the south, was soon heard everywhere.

WHERE TO SEE 18TH-CENTURY FRANCE

The Palais de l'Elysée, built in 1718 (see p104), is an outstanding example of 18th-century Parisian architecture. Examples across France include the curious Saline Royale in Arc-et-Senans (p340), the Grand Théâtre in Bordeaux (p412), the elegant mansions in Condom (p430) and the merchants' houses in Ciboure (p443). The Château de Laàs in Sauveterre de Béarn is a feast of 18th-century art and furniture (p448).

The Grand Théâtre in Bordeaux
is an excellent example of elegant
18th-century architecture.

Revolutionary Calendar
A new calendar was introduced, the months named after seasonal events. This engraving shows Messidor, the month of harvest.

1768 Annexation of Corsica

1789 Storming of the Bastille, and establishment of constitutional monarchy: abolition of feudalism

1783 First balloon ascent, by the Montgolfier brothers

Model of the Bastille

1765	1775	1785	1795

1774 Accession of Louis XVI

Electors' card for the Convention of 1792

1794 Overthrow of Robespierre and end of the Terror

1762 Rousseau's *Emile* and the *Social Contract*

1778–83 France aids the 13 colonies in the American Revolution

1792 Overthrow of Louis XVI: establishment of First Republic

Napoleonic France

TWO GENERATIONS of Napoleons dominated France from 1800 to 1870. Napoleon Bonaparte took the title of Emperor Napoleon I. He extended his empire throughout most of western Europe, placing his brothers and sisters on the thrones of conquered countries. Defeated in 1814 and replaced by the restored Bourbon dynasty, followed by the 1830 Revolution and the so-called July Monarchy, the Napoleonic clan made a comeback after 1848. Napoleon I's nephew, Louis Napoleon, became President of the Second Republic, then made himself emperor as Napoleon III. During his reign, Paris was modernized and the industrial transformation of France began.

Légion d'Honneur

EUROPE IN 1812

☐ *Napoleonic rule*

☐ *Dependent states*

The laurel crown of the Roman emperors

Napoleon, as First Consul, is crowned by Chronos, the God of Time.

Musée du Louvre
The museum had opened in 1792, but it flourished during Napoleon's reign. He took a personal interest in both acquisitions and organization.

The revolutionary tricolor flag was kept throughout the empire.

Imperial Insignia
Napoleon I created a new titled aristocracy, who were allowed coats of arms. Only his, however, was permitted a crown. The eagle symbol was adopted in 1800, an evocation of Imperial Rome.

Légion d'Honneur medal

TIMELINE

Josephine's bed at Malmaison

1804 Napoleon crowned as Emperor. Napoleonic Civil Code established

1800 Establishment of the Bank of France

1809 Josephine and Napoleon divorce. She retains Château Malmaison (*see p163*)

1814 Defeat of Napoleon by the Allies (England, Russia, Austria and Prussia). Napoleon exiled to Elba

1800	1810	1820

1801–3 Treaty of Amiens brings temporary peace to Europe

1802 Establishment of the Légion d'Honneur

1806 Arc de Triomphe commissioned

1803 Resumption of wars to create the Napoleonic Empire

1815 The "Hundred Days": Napoleon returns from Elba, is defeated at Waterloo and exiled to St. Helena

July Revolution
Three days of street fighting in July 1830 ended unpopular Bourbon rule.

The Napoleons
This imaginary group portrait depicts Napoleon I (seated), his son "Napoleon II" – who never ruled (right) – Napoleon's nephew Louis Napoleon (Napoleon III) and the latter's young son.

The Civil Code, created by Napoleon, is here shown as a tablet.

Napoleon on Campaign
A dashing general in the late 1790s, Napoleon remained a remarkable military commander throughout his reign.

EMPIRE FASHION

Greek and Roman ideals were evident in architecture, furniture, design and fashion. Women wore light, Classical tunics, the most daring with one shoulder or more bare. David and Gérard were the fashionable portraitists, while Delacroix and Géricault created many Romantic masterpieces.

NAPOLEONIC GLORY

Though professing himself a true revolutionary, Napoleon developed a taste for imperial pomp. However, he also achieved some long-lasting reforms such as the Civil Code, the new school system and the Bank of France.

Madame Récamier *held a popular salon and was renowned for her beauty and wit. David painted her in 1800.*

1830	1840	1850	1860

1832 Cholera epidemics begin

1838 Daguerre experiments with photography

1851 Coup d'état by Louis Napoleon

1848 Revolution of 1848: end of July Monarchy and establishment of the Second Republic

1852 Louis Napoleon crowned as Emperor Napoleon III

1830 Revolution of 1830: Bourbon Charles X replaced by the July Monarchy of King Louis-Philippe

1840 Large-scale railroad building

1853 Modernization of Paris by Haussmann

1857 Baudelaire *(Les Fleurs du Mal)* and Flaubert *(Mme. Bovary)* prosecuted for public immorality

1859–60 Annexation of Nice and Savoy

Train on the Paris – St-Germain line

The Belle Epoque

THE DECADES before World War I became the *Belle Epoque* for the French, remembered as a golden era forever past. Nevertheless, this was a politically turbulent time, with working-class militancy, organized socialist movements and the Dreyfus Affair polarizing the country between Left and anti-semitic Right. New inventions such as electricity and vaccination against disease made life easier at all social levels. The cultural scene thrived and took new forms with Impressionism and Art Nouveau, the realist novels of Gustave Flaubert and Emile Zola, cabaret and cancan and, in 1895, the birth of the movie theater.

Art Nouveau vase by Lalique

FRANCE IN 1871

☐ *Under Third Republic*
▨ *Alsace and Lorraine*

Universal Exhibition
The 1889 Paris exhibition was attended by 3.2 million people. Engineer Eiffel's breathtaking iron structure dominated the exhibition and caused great controversy at the time.

Statue of Apollo by Aimé Millet

Stage

Copper-green roofed cupola

Backstage area

Peugeot Car *(1899)*
The car and bicycle brought new freedom, becoming a part of people's leisure time. Peugeot, Renault and Citroën were all founded before World War I.

The auditorium decorated in gold and purple seated over 2,000 guests.

TIMELINE

1869 Opening of the Suez Canal, built by Ferdinand de Lesseps

Woman on the barricades in 1871

1871 The Paris Commune leads to the Third Republic

1880s Scramble for colonies in Africa and Asia begins

1889 Universal Exhibition in Paris; Eiffel Tower built

1865	1870	1875	1880	1885	1890

1870–71 Franco-Prussian War: defeat and overthrow of Napoleon III; France cedes Alsace and Lorraine to Germany

1881–6 Reforms in education by Jules Ferry

1874 Impressionist movement begins

1885 Pasteur produces vaccine for rabies, the first tested on a human

1890 Peugeot constructs one of the earliest automobiles

Poster Art
The poster was revolutionized by Art Nouveau, with designs by Alphonse Mucha particularly popular. This one from 1897 is for beer, the beverage of the lost Alsace and Lorraine, which became a "patriotic" drink.

Staircase at the Opera
The grand staircase had colored marble columns and a frescoed ceiling. As this painting by Beroud from 1887 shows, it soon became a showcase for high society.

WHERE TO SEE THE BELLE EPOQUE

Belle Epoque buildings include the Negresco Hotel, Nice *(see p516)*, the Grand Casino in Monte-Carlo *(p520)* and the Palais Hotel in Biarritz *(p442)*. The Musée d'Orsay in Paris *(pp116–17)* exhibits Art Nouveau objects and furniture.

Guimard's Metro entrance is a typical example of the elegant, swirling lines of Art Nouveau.

Emperor's
pavilion

Grand Foyer with
balconies and lavishly
decorated ceiling

Grand staircase

OPÉRA GARNIER
Founded by Napoleon III in 1862, the new opera was opened to great public acclaim in 1875 and became a focus of Belle Epoque social life. Designed by Charles Garnier, its extravagant exterior was matched by its sumptuous interior decor.

The Divine Sarah
Actress Sarah Bernhardt (1844–1923) worked in all theatrical genres, dominating the Paris stage.

1895 First movie shown by the Lumière brothers

Caricature of Zola

1894–1906 The alleged treason of Dreyfus sparks the Dreyfus Affair, involving the author Zola among others

1909 Blériot flies the Channel

1918 Armistice ends the war

1917 Mutinies in the army suppressed by Pétain

1916 Battle of Verdun

1895	1900	1905	1910	1915

1905 Official separation of church and state

1913 Publication of Proust's first volume of *Remembrance of Things Past*

1898 Marie and Pierre Curie discover radium

1914 World War I breaks out

French recruit, 1916

1919 Treaty of Versailles

Avant-Garde France

DESPITE THE DEVASTATION wrought by two world wars, France retained its international renown as a center for the avant garde. Paris in particular was a magnet for experimental writers, artists and musicians. The cafés were full of American authors and jazz musicians, French surrealists and filmmakers. The French Riviera also attracted colonies of artists and writers, from Matisse and Picasso to Hemingway and F. Scott Fitzgerald, along with the wealthy industrialists and aristocrats arriving in automobiles or the famous Train Bleu. And from 1936, paid vacations meant that the working classes could also enjoy the new fashion for sunbathing.

FRANCE IN 1919

☐ *French territory*

African Gods of Creation

Art Deco 1925
The International Exhibition in Paris in 1925 launched the Art Deco style: geometrical shapes and utilitarian designs, adapted for mass production.

Dancers in heavy cardboard costumes

The Jazz Age
Paris welcomed American jazz musicians, such as Sidney Bechet in 1925 and Dizzy Gillespie (left), co-founder of Bebop, in the 1940s.

Citroën Goddess *(1956)*
This elegant model became an icon of the new French consumerism evident in the 1950s and '60s.

The costumes and scenery by the Cubist Léger were striking and made to look partly mechanical.

TIMELINE

1920 French Communist Party founded. Publication of Tristan Tzara's *Dadaist Manifesto*

1928 Premiere of *Un Chien Andalou* by Luis Buñuel and Salvador Dalí

Air France airplane, 1937

1933 Air France begins operation

1937 Premiere of *La Grande Illusion* by Jean Renoir

1920

1930

1924 Olympic Games in Paris. André Breton publishes the *Surrealist Manifesto*

Detail of poster for the 1924 Olympics

1936–38 The "Popular Front": radical social program introduced, including paid vacations

1929–39 The Depression

1938 Munich Conference: height of appeasement

Coco Chanel (1883–1971)
*Chanel, here photographed by
Man Ray, revolutionized fashion
in the 1920s with her elegant
but comfortable clothes.*

WORLD WAR II

Following the collapse of the
Third Republic in 1940, Paris
and the north and west parts of
France were occupied by the
Germans until the Liberation in
1944. Southeast France formed
the collaborationist Vichy state,
led by Marshal Pétain and
Pierre Laval. Meanwhile, the
Free French movement was
led by Charles de Gaulle, with
Jean Moulin coordinating the
operations of the many
different Resistance factions.

Par Avion
*France pioneered the use of
airmail, starting in 1927.*

First
Man and
Woman

*German soldiers liked to pose
in front of the Eiffel Tower during
the occupation of Paris.*

LA REVUE DES
FOLIES-BERGERE
1926-1927

LA CRÉATION DU MONDE (1923)
Artistic experimentation thrived in the early
20th century. *La Création du Monde* by Les
Ballets Suédois had costumes by Léger and
music by Milhaud. Diaghilev's Ballets Russes
also competed for avant-garde artists such as
Picabia, Cocteau, Satie and Sonia Delaunay.

The African theme
was based on text
by Blaise Cendrars.

Josephine Baker (1906–75)
*The music hall flourished in the
1920s with Mistinguett and Josephine
Baker as its undisputed queens.*

1940 German offensive:
the Fall of France. Vichy
government led by Pétain

1949 Establishment of
NATO. Founding of the
Council of Europe

1958 5th Republic begins under
President de Gaulle

1942 The whole of France
controlled by Germany

1956 Late in her career, Edith Piaf crowns
her success at Carnegie Hall, New York

1940		1950

1944 D-Day: Allied
landings in Normandy

1946 Sartre establishes
Les Temps Modernes.
First Cannes Film Festival

1954 France withdraws
from Indo-China after
Battle of Dien Bien Phu.
Start of Algerian
insurrection

1939 Declaration of
World War II

1945 End of the war.
Votes for women

Modern France

AFTER THE 1950s, the traditional foundations of French society changed: the number of peasant farmers plummeted, old industries decayed, jobs in the service sector and high-technology industries grew dramatically, and the French came to enjoy the benefits of mass culture and widespread consumerism. High prestige projects, such as Concorde, TGV, La Défense and the Pompidou Center, brought international acclaim. Efforts for European integration and the inauguration of the Channel Tunnel aim toward closer relations with France's neighbors.

Lemon squeezer by Philippe Starck

FRANCE TODAY

☐ *France*

▨ *European Union*

Pompidou Center *(1977)*
The Pompidou Center's controversial building changed the aspect of the historic quarter of Beaubourg. A major arts center, it has re-vitalized the formerly rundown area (see pp88–9).

La Grande Arche was opened in 1989 to commemorate the bicentenary of the Revolution.

Shopping center

New Wave Film
Directors like Godard and Truffaut launched a refreshing, personal style of films, such as Jules et Jim *(1961).*

LA DÉFENSE
The huge modernist business center at La Défense *(see p126)*, on the edge of Paris, was developed in the 1960s and has become a prime site for the headquarters of major multinational companies.

TIMELINE

1960 First French atomic bomb. Decolonization of black Africa	**1963** First French nuclear power station		**1968** May demonstrations	**1973** Extension of the Common Market (EU) from six to nine states
		1966 France leaves NATO	**1969** Pompidou replaces de Gaulle as president	**1974** Giscard d'Estaing elected president
1960			**1970**	
1962 Evian agreements lead to Algerian independence	**1965** First French satellite		**1970** Charles de Gaulle dies	**1976** First commercial flight for Concorde airplane
	1967 Common Agricultural Policy, subsidizing Europe's farmers		**1977** Jacques Chirac first mayor of Paris since 1871. Opening of the Pompidou Center	

EU Flag
France has been one of the leading forces in the European Union ever since the move toward closer European collaboration began in the 1950s.

TGV
The TGV (Train à Grande Vitesse) is one of the world's fastest trains (see pp634–5). It typifies the French government's commitment to high technology and improved communications.

The Fiat Tower
is one of Europe's tallest towers, at a height of 178 m (584 ft).

Fashion by Lacroix
Despite less demand for haute couture, Paris is still a major fashion center. The designs shown on the catwalk, here by Christian Lacroix, remain proof of the world-renowned skills of French designers.

MAY 1968

The events of May 1968 began as a political revolt by left-wing students against the Establishment and had a profound influence on French society. Around 9 million workers, and leading intellectuals like Jean-Paul Sartre, joined the rebellion, demanding better pay, better study conditions and the overhaul of traditional values and institutions.

***Student riots** starting in Nanterre, just outside Paris, sparked widespread rioting and industrial unrest in France.*

Palais de la Défense was built first and houses the center for industry.

1980 Giverny, Monet's garden, opens to the public *(see p256)*

1989 Bicentennial celebration of the French Revolution

1991 Edith Cresson is first woman prime minister

1995 Jacques Chirac is president

1998 France hosts and wins the soccer World Cup

1980

1990

2000

1981 Mitterrand becomes president and heads Socialist governments 1981–6

François Mitterrand

1987 Mitterrand and Thatcher sign agreement for Channel Tunnel. Trial in Lyons of ex-SS Officer Klaus Barbie

1994 Channel Tunnel opens

1996 France mourns Mitterrand, who dies after a long illness

1997 Socialist Lionel Jospin becomes prime minister in landslide victory

Kings and Emperors of France

Following the breakup of the Roman Empire, the Frankish king Clovis consolidated the Merovingian dynasty. It was followed by the Carolingians, and, from the 10th century, by Capetian rulers. The Capetians established royal power, which passed to the Valois branch in the 14th century, and then to the Bourbons in the late 16th century, following the Wars of Religion. The Revolution of 1789 seemed to end the Bourbon dynasty, but it made a brief comeback in 1814–30. The 19th century was dominated by the Bonapartes, Napoleon I and Napoleon III. Since the overthrow of Napoleon III in 1870, France has been a republic.

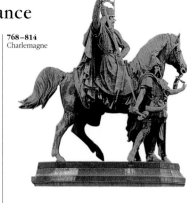

768–814 Charlemagne

954–986 Lothaire

898–929 Charles III, the Simple

884–888 Charles II, the Fat

879–882 Louis III

840–877 Charles I, the Bald

1137–80 Louis VII

987–996 Hugh Capet

1031–60 Henri I

1060–1108 Philippe I

743–751 Childéric III

716–721 Chilpéric II

695–711 Childebert II

674–691 Thierri III

655–668 Clothaire III

628–637 Dagobert I

566–584 Chilpéric I

558–562 Clothaire I

447–458 Merovich

458–482 Childéric I

400	500	600	700	800	900	1000	1100
MEROVINGIAN DYNASTY				CAROLINGIAN DYNASTY		CAPETIAN DYNASTY	
400	500	600	700	800	900	1000	1100

751–768 Pépin the Short

721–737 Thierri IV

711–716 Dagobert III

691–695 Clovis III

668–674 Childéric II

637–655 Clovis II

584–628 Clothaire II

562–566 Caribert

511–558 Childebert I

996–1031 Robert II, the Pious

986–987 Louis V

936–954 Louis IV, the Foreigner

888–898 Odo, Count of Paris

882–884 Carloman

877–879 Louis II, the Stammerer

814–840 Louis I, the Pious

482–511 Clovis I

1108–37 Louis VI, the Fat

1226–70 Louis IX
(St. Louis)

1515–47 François I

1498–1515 Louis XII,
Father of his People

1483–98 Charles VIII

1422–61 Charles VII, the
Victorious

1270–85 Philippe III

1547–59 Henri II

1285–1314 Philippe
IV, the Fair

1559–60 François II

1316–22
Philippe V

1610–43 Louis XIII

1328–50
Philippe VI

1643–1715 Louis
XIV, the Sun King

1774–92 Louis XVI

1804–14
Napoleon I

1200	1300	1400	1500	1600	1700	1800

VALOIS DYNASTY — **BOURBON DYNASTY**

1200	1300	1400	1500	1600	1700	1800

1314–16
Louis X

1380–1422
Charles VI,
the Fool

1560–74
Charles IX

1814–24
Louis XVIII

1574–89
Henri III

1824–30
Charles X

1322–28
Charles IV, the
Fair

1364–80
Charles V,
the Wise

1589–1610
Henri IV

1830–48
Louis-Philippe I

1852–70
Napoleon III

1350–64 Jean II,
the Good

1223–6 Louis VIII

1180–1223 Philip Augustus

1461–83 Louis XI, the Spider

1715–74
Louis XV

PARIS AND ILE DE FRANCE

Introducing Paris and Ile de France

THE FRENCH CAPITAL is rich in museums, art galleries and monuments. The Louvre, Eiffel Tower and Pompidou Center are among the most popular sights. Surrounding Paris, the Ile de France takes in 12,000 sq km (4,600 sq miles) of busy suburbs and commuter towns punctuated by châteaux, the most celebrated being Versailles. Farther out, suburbia gives way to farmland, forests and the magnificent palace of Fontainebleau.

Arc de Triomphe

Opéra Garnier

CHAMPS-ELYSEES AND INVALIDES
Pages 100–11

Eiffel Tower

Musée d'Orsay

The Eiffel Tower, *designed for the Universal Exhibition of 1889, scandalized contemporary critics but is now the capital's most famous landmark* (see p109).

The Musée d'Orsay, *opened in 1986, was created from a late 19th-century railroad station* (see pp116–17). *It houses a magnificent collection of 19th- and early 20th-century art, including Jean-Baptiste Carpeaux's* Four Quarters of the World (1867–72).

ILE DE FRANCE
Pages 160–71

Versailles

Fontainebleau

0 kilometers   25

0 miles   25

**TUILERIES
AND OPERA**
Pages 90–99

The Louvre

Pompidou Center

**ILE DE LA CITÉ,
MARAIS AND
BEAUBOURG**
Pages 76–89

Notre-Dame

THE LEFT BANK
Pages 112–23

Musée de Cluny

0 kilometers   1

0 miles   0.5

The Pompidou Center
*(1977) is as famous for
its novel inside-out design
as it is for masterpieces
by Picasso, Matisse and
Miró* (see pp88–9).

***Notre-Dame**, a stunning example of Gothic archi-
tecture begun in 1163, took two centuries and armies
of medieval workers to complete* (see pp82–3). *Architect
Viollet-le-Duc designed the spire in the 19th century.*

A RIVER VIEW
OF PARIS

Sculpture on the Pont Alexandre III

THE REMARKABLE French music-hall star Mistinguett described the Seine as a "pretty blonde with laughing eyes." The river most certainly has a beguiling quality, but the relationship that exists between it and the city of Paris is far more than one of flirtation.

No other European city defines itself by its river in the same way as Paris. The Seine is the essential point of reference to the city: distances are measured from it, street numbers determined by it, and it divides the capital into two distinct areas, the Right Bank on the north side of the river and the Left Bank on the south side. These are as well-defined as any of the official boundaries. The city is also divided historically: the east is linked to the city's ancient roots, and the west to the 19th–20th centuries.

Practically every building of note in Paris is either along the riverbank or within a stone's throw of it. The quays are lined by fine bourgeois apartments, magnificent town houses, world-renowned museums and striking monuments.

Above all, the river is very much alive. For centuries, fleets of small boats used it, but motorized land traffic stifled this once-bustling scene. Today, the river is busy with commercial barges and massive *bateaux-mouches* – pleasure boats carrying sightseers up and down the river.

The Latin Quarter Quayside is on the left bank of the Seine. Associated with institutes of learning since the Middle Ages, it acquired its name from the early Latin-speaking students.

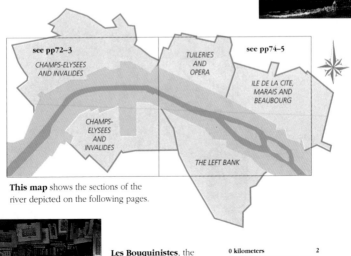

see pp72–3

CHAMPS-ELYSEES AND INVALIDES

TUILERIES AND OPERA

see pp74–5

ILE DE LA CITE, MARAIS AND BEAUBOURG

CHAMPS-ELYSEES AND INVALIDES

THE LEFT BANK

This map shows the sections of the river depicted on the following pages.

Les Bouquinistes, the bookstalls on the riverbanks, are treasure troves of secondhand books and prints, and perfect for an afternoon's browsing.

0 kilometers		2
0 miles	1	

KEY

▢ Illustrated area

◁ **Pont Alexandre III, encrusted with exuberant statuary**

From Pont de Grenelle to Pont de la Concorde

THE GRAND monuments along this stretch of the river are remnants of the Napoleonic era and the Industrial Revolution. The elegance of the Eiffel Tower, the Petit Palais and the Grand Palais is matched by more recent buildings, such as the Palais de Chaillot and the skyscrapers on the Left Bank.

Palais de Chaillot
Built for the 1937 Exhibition, the striking colonnaded wings house four museums, a theater and a movie theater (p106).

The Palais de Tokyo forms part of the Film Library. Figures by Bourdelle adorn it.

The Pont Bir-Hakeim has a dynamic statue by Wederkinch rising at its north end.

Bateaux Parisiens Tour Eiffel

Trocadéro **M**

Vedettes de Paris Ile de France

Passerelle

Maison de Radio France is an imposing circular building, designed in 1960, which houses studios as well as a radio museum.

Passy **M**

Pont d'Iéna

Eiffel Tower
This is Paris's most identifiable landmark (p109).

RER **Champ de Mars Tour Eiffel**

Pont de Bir-Hakeim

RER **Prés. Kennedy Radio France**

The Statue of Liberty was given to the city in 1885. It faces west, toward the original statue in New York.

Pont de Grenelle

KEY

M	Metro station
RER	RER station
▣	Batobus stop
▬	River trip boarding point

Grand Palais
Major exhibitions and a science museum are based here (p105).

Petit Palais
Now the Paris museum of fine arts, this was first designed as a companion to the Grand Palais (p104).

The Zouave, a statue on the central pier, is a useful gauge for checking flood levels.

The Liberty Flame is a memorial to the fighters of the French Resistance during World War II.

The Assemblée Nationale Palais-Bourbon was originally built for Louis XIV's daughter. It has accommodated the lower house of the French Parliament since 1830.

Dôme Church
The majestic gilded dome (p111) *is here seen from Pont Alexandre III. Napoleon's tomb is installed in the crypt.*

Pont Alexandre III
Flamboyant statuary decorates Paris's most ornate bridge (p105).

From Pont de la Concorde to Pont de Sully

THE HISTORIC heart of Paris lies on the banks and islands of the east river. At its center is the Ile de la Cité, a natural stepping stone across the Seine and the cultural core of medieval Paris. Today, it is still vital to Parisian life.

Jardin des Tuileries
These are laid out in the formal style (pp94–5).

Musée du Louvre
Before becoming the world's greatest museum and home to the Mona Lisa, *this was Europe's largest royal palace* (pp96–9).

Pont de la Concorde

Assemblée Nationale

Pont Solférino

Quai d'Orsay

Pont Royal

Pont du Carrousel

Pont des Arts

Musée de l'Orangerie
An important collection of 19th-century paintings is on display here (p94).

Musée d'Orsay
This converted railroad station houses Paris's outstanding collection of Impressionist art (pp116–17).

Bateaux Vedettes du Pont Neuf

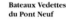

BATOBUS

The Batobus shuttle service departs May–Sep: 10am–7pm (9pm Jul & Aug) daily, every 25 min. Board at:
Eiffel Tower. Map 6 D3. Ⓜ Bir Hakeim.
Musée d'Orsay. Map 8 D2. Ⓜ Assemblée Nationale.
Louvre. Map 8 D2. Ⓜ Palais Royal-Musée du Louvre.
Hôtel de Ville. Map 9 B4. Ⓜ Hôtel de Ville.
Notre-Dame. Map 9 B4. Ⓜ Saint-Michel.
Saint-Germain des Prés. Map 8 E3.
Ⓜ Saint-Germain des Prés.

The Pont des Arts
was Paris's first cast-iron bridge. Completed in 1804, it took two years to build.

Hôtel des Monnaies, the Mint, was built in 1778, and has an extensive coin and medallion collection in its old milling halls.

How to Take a Seine Cruise

Vedettes du Pont Neuf

Bateaux Vedettes Pont Neuf Seine Cruise

The boarding point is: **Square du Vert-Galant** (Pont Neuf). **Map** 8 F3. 01 53 00 98 98. M *Pont Neuf.* RER *Châtelet.* 24, 27, 58, 67, 70, 72, 74, 75. **Departures** *Apr–Oct: 10:30am, 11:15am, noon, (every 45 min), 1:30pm–6:30pm, 9–10:30pm (every 30 min) daily; Nov–Mar: 10:30am, 11:15am, noon, 2–5:45pm, daily (every 30 min);* **Duration** *1 hr.*

BATEAUX-MOUCHES

Bateaux Mouches Seine Cruise

The boarding point is: **Pont de l'Alma. Map** 6 F1. 01 42 25 96 10. M *Alma-Marceau.* RER *Pont de l'Alma.* 42, 63, 72, 80, 92. **Departures** *Mar–Nov: 10am–11pm daily (every 30 min); Nov–Mar: 11am, 2:30pm, 4pm, 9pm (extra departures Sat, Sun & public hols).* **Duration** *1 hr 15 min.* **Lunch cruise** *Mar–Nov: 1pm Tue–Sun.* **Dinner cruise** *8:30pm daily.* Bâteaux Mouches are the largest cruise boats.

ILE de FRANCE

Vedettes de Paris Ile de France Seine Cruise

The boarding point is: **Pont d'Iéna. Map** 6 D2. 01 47 05 71 29. M *Bir Hakeim.* RER *Champ-de-Mars–Tour Eiffel.* 22, 30, 32, 44, 63, 69, 72, 82, 87. **Departures** *May–Oct: 10am–11pm daily (every 30 min); Nov–Apr: 11am–8pm Mon–Fri (every hour); 11am–8pm Sat, Sun (every 30 min).* **Duration** *1 hr.* Vedettes are small boats which allow passengers to view the surroundings through glass walls.

BATEAUX PARISIENS

Bateaux Parisiens Tour Eiffel Seine Cruise

The boarding point is: **Pont d'Iéna. Map** 6 D2. 01 44 11 33 44. M *Trocadéro, Bir Hakeim.* RER *Champ-de-Mars–Tour Eiffel.* 42, 82, 72. **Departures** *Easter–Oct: 10am–10:30pm daily (every 30 min); Nov–Easter: 10am–9pm daily (every hour).* **Lunch cruise** *1pm daily.* **Dinner cruise** *8:30pm daily.* **Duration** *2 hr 30 min. Jacket and tie.* Bateaux Parisiens are a more luxurious version of Bateaux Mouches.

Ile de la Cité
This tiny island on the Seine was first inhabited around 200 BC by a Celtic tribe known as the Parisii (pp78–9).

Conciergerie
During the Revolution, this building, with its distinctive towers, became notorious as a prison (p79).

The Ile St-Louis has been a desirable address since the 17th century, when its elegant houses were built.

Notre-Dame
This towering cathedral surveys the river (pp82–3).

Bateaux Parisiens

ILE DE LA CITÉ, MARAIS AND BEAUBOURG

THE RIGHT BANK is dominated by the modernistic Forum des Halles and Pompidou Center in the Beaubourg. These are Paris's most thriving public areas, with millions of tourists, shoppers and students flowing between them. Young people flock to Les Halles, shopping for the latest street fashions beneath the concrete and glass bubbles of the underground arcades. All roads from Les Halles appear to lead to the Pompidou Center, an avant-garde assembly of pipes, ducts and cables housing the Musée National d'Art Moderne. The smaller streets around the center are full of art galleries housed in crooked, gabled buildings.

The motto of the city of Paris

The neighboring Marais was abandoned by its royal residents during the 1789 Revolution, and it descended into architectural wasteland before being rescued in the 1960s. It has since become a very fashionable address, though small cafés, bakeries and artisans still survive in its streets.

Notre-Dame cathedral, the Palais de Justice and Sainte-Chapelle continue to draw tourists to the Ile de la Cité, despite extensive redevelopment of the island in the last century. At the eastern end, a bridge connects with the Ile St-Louis, a former swampy pastureland transformed into a residential area with lovely, tree-lined quays.

SIGHTS AT A GLANCE

Museums and Galleries
Crypte Archéologique ⑤
Hôtel de Sens ⑧
Hôtel de Soubise ⑭
Maison de Victor Hugo ⑱
Musée Carnavalet ⑯
Musée Picasso ⑮
Pompidou Center pp88–9 ⑬

Historic Buildings
Conciergerie ②
Hôtel de Ville ⑩
Palais de Justice ③
Tour St-Jacques ⑪

Squares
Place de la Bastille ⑲
Place des Vosges ⑰

Churches
Notre-Dame pp82–3 ⑥
Sainte-Chapelle ④
St-Eustache ⑫
St-Gervais–St-Protais ⑨
St-Louis-en-l'Ile ⑦

Bridges
Pont Neuf ①

GETTING THERE
Metro stations in the area include Châtelet, Hôtel-de-Ville and Cité. Bus routes 47 and 29 serve Beaubourg and the Marais respectively. Several bus routes cross Ile de la Cité and Ile St-Louis.

KEY
	Street-by-Street map *pp78–9*
	Street-by-Street map *pp84–5*
M	Metro station
◎	Batobus boarding point
P	Parking
RER	RER station

0 meters 500
0 yards 500

◁ **View of the Pont Neuf and Ile de la Cité from the Pont des Arts**

Street-by-Street: Ile de la Cité

T HE ORIGINS OF PARIS are on the Ile de la
Cité, the boat-shaped island on the
Seine first inhabited by Celtic tribes in the
3rd century BC. One tribe, the Parisii,
eventually gave its name to the city. The
island offered a convenient river crossing
on the route between northern and
southern Gaul and was easily defended.
In later centuries, the settlement was
expanded by the Romans, the Franks
and the Capetian kings to form the
nucleus of today's city.

Remains of the first buildings can
still be seen today in the
archaeological crypt of the
great medieval cathedral of
Notre-Dame. At the other
end of the island is Sainte-
Chapelle, another
Gothic masterpiece.

★ **Conciergerie**
*This sinister-looking building was the country's
main prison during the Revolution* ❷

**The Marché aux Fleurs et
Oiseaux** in place Louis-Lépine is
one of the largest flower
markets in Paris, with
birds and pets for
sale on Sundays.

Metro Cité

To Pont Neuf

★ **Sainte-Chapelle**
*A jewel of Gothic
architecture, Sainte-
Chapelle is famous for its
magnificent stained-glass
windows* ❹

Palais de Justice
*With a history spanning
over 16 centuries, the old
palace is today a massive
complex of law courts* ❸

Point Zéro
marks the spot
from which all
road distances
are measured
in France.

CRYPTE
DU
PARVIS

Crypte Archéologique
*Deep under the square lie remnants of
houses dating back 2,000 years* ❺

To Latin Quarter

STAR SIGHTS
★ **Notre-Dame**
★ **Sainte-Chapelle**
★ **Conciergerie**

KEY

– – – Suggested route

Hôtel Dieu, a large hospital serving central Paris, was founded in AD 651 by St. Landry, Bishop of Paris.

LOCATOR MAP
See Street Finder maps 8, 9

★ **Notre-Dame**
This cathedral is a superb example of French medieval architecture ❻

Musée Notre-Dame, founded in 1951, contains exhibits and documents commemorating the great events in Notre-Dame's history.

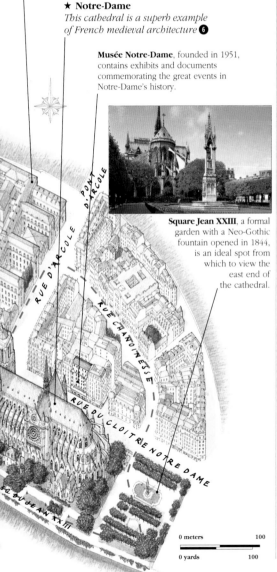

Square Jean XXIII, a formal garden with a Neo-Gothic fountain opened in 1844, is an ideal spot from which to view the east end of the cathedral.

0 meters 100
0 yards 100

Pont Neuf, the city's oldest bridge

Pont Neuf ❶

75001. **Map** 8 F3. Ⓜ *Pont Neuf, Cité.*

DESPITE ITS NAME (New Bridge), this bridge is the oldest in Paris and has been immortalized by major literary and artistic figures. The first stone was laid by Henri III in 1578, but it was Henri IV (whose statue stands at the center) who inaugurated it and gave it its name in 1607.

Conciergerie ❷

1 quai de l'Horloge 75001. **Map** 9 A3. 🎬 *01 53 73 78 50.* Ⓜ *Cité.* **Open** *Apr–Sep: 9:30am–6:30pm daily; Oct–Mar: 10am–5pm daily (last adm: 30 mins before closing).* **Closed** *Jan 1, May 1, Nov 1 & 11, Dec 25.* 🔖 📷 📹 *11am, 3pm daily.* 🔲

FORMING PART of the huge Palais de Justice, the historic Conciergerie served as a prison from 1391–1914. Henry IV's assassin, François Ravaillac, was imprisoned and tortured here in 1610.

During the Revolution, the building was packed with over 4,000 prisoners. Its most celebrated inmate was Marie-Antoinette, who was held in a tiny cell until her execution in 1793. Others included Charlotte Corday, who stabbed Revolutionary leader Marat while he bathed.

The Conciergerie has a superb four-aisled Gothic hall, where guards of the royal household once lived. Renovated during the 19th century, the building retains its 11th-century torture chamber and the 14th-century clock tower.

A sculptured relief on the Palais de Justice

Palais de Justice ❸

4 boulevard du Palais (entrance by
the Cour de Mai) 75001. **Map** 9 A3.
📞 01 44 32 50 00. Ⓜ Cité.
Open 9am–6pm daily.

Tⁿʰⁱˢ HUGE BLOCK of buildings making up the law
courts of Paris stretches the
entire width of the Ile de la
Cité. It is a splendid sight
with its Gothic towers lining
the quays. The site has been
occupied since Roman times
when it was the governors'
residence. It was the seat of
royal power until Charles V
moved the court to the Marais
following a bloody revolt
in 1358. In April 1793, the
notorious Revolutionary
Tribunal began dispensing
justice from the Première
Chambre Civile, or first civil
chamber. Today, the site
embodies Napoleon's great
legacy – the French judicial
system. Trials are usually public
and tourists are welcome.

Crypte Archéologique ❺

1 place du Parvis Notre-Dame 75004.
Map 9 A4. 📞 01 43 29 83 51. Ⓜ Cité.
Open Apr–Sep: 10am–5:30pm daily;
Oct–Mar: 10am–5pm daily. **Closed** Jan
1, May 1, Nov 1 & 11, Dec 25.

Sⁱᵀᵁᴬᵀᴱᴰ BENEATH the *parvis*
(main square) of Notre-Dame
and stretching 120 m (393 ft)
underground, the crypt was
opened in 1980 as Paris's
museum of archaeology.
Exhibits include streets and
houses from the Gallo-Roman
period, sections of Lutetia's
3rd-century BC wall, and
remains of the cathedral.
Models explain the development of Paris from a settlement
of the Parisii, the 3rd-century
Celtic tribe who named the city.

Notre-Dame ❻

See pp82–3.

Sainte-Chapelle ❹

4 boulevard du Palais 75001.
Map 9 A3. 📞 01 53 73 78 50. Ⓜ
Cité. **Open** Apr–Sep: 9:30am–6:30pm
daily; Oct–Mar: 10am–5pm daily.
Closed Jan 1, May 1, Nov 1 & 11,
Dec 25.

Eᵀʰᴱᴿᴱᴬᴸ ᴬᴺᴰ MAGICAL,
Sainte-Chapelle has
been hailed as one of
the greatest architectural
masterpieces of the
Western world. In the
Middle Ages the devout
likened this church to
"a gateway to heaven."
No visitor can fail to
be transported by the
blaze of light created
by the 15 magnificent
stained-glass windows,
separated by pencil-like
columns soaring 15 m
(50 ft) to the star-studded
roof. The windows
portray more than 1,000
biblical scenes in a
kaleidoscope of red,
gold, green and blue.
Starting from the left
near the entrance and
proceeding clockwise,
you can trace the
scriptures from Genesis
through to the Crucifixion
and the Apocalypse.
The chapel was built in 1248
by Louis IX to house what was
believed to be Christ's Crown
of Thorns and fragments of
the True Cross (now in the
treasury at Notre-Dame). The
king, who was canonized for
his good works, purchased
these relics from the Emperor
of Constantinople, paying
three times more for them than
for the entire construction of
Sainte-Chapelle.
The building actually
consists of two separate
chapels. The somber
lower chapel was used
by servants and lower
court officials, while the
exquisite upper chapel,
reached by means of a
narrow spiral staircase,
was reserved for the roy-
al family and its courtiers.
A discreetly placed win-
dow enabled the king to
take part in the celebra-
tions unobserved.
During the Revolution
the building was badly
damaged and became a
warehouse for storing
flour. It was renovated a
century later by architect
Viollet-le-Duc.
Today, evening con-
certs of classical music
are held regularly in the
chapel, taking advantage
of its superb acoustics.

The magnificent interior of Sainte-Chapelle

St-Louis-en-l'Ile ⑦

19 bis rue St-Louis-en-l'Ile 75004.
Map 9 C4. ☎ *01 46 34 11 60.* Ⓜ *Pont Marie.* **Open** *8am–noon, 3–7pm Tue–Sun.* **Closed** *public hols.* ⒪

THE CONSTRUCTION of this church was begun in 1664 from plans by the royal architect Louis Le Vau, who lived on the island. It was completed and consecrated in 1726. Among its outstanding exterior features are the 1741 iron clock at the entrance and the pierced iron spire.

The interior, in the Baroque style, is richly decorated with gilding and marble. There is a statue of St. Louis holding a crusader's sword. A plaque in the north aisle, given in 1926, bears the inscription "in grateful memory of St. Louis in whose honor the City of St. Louis, Missouri, USA is named." The church is also associated with Carthage Cathedral in Tunisia, where St. Louis is buried.

The interior of St-Louis-en-l'Ile

Hôtel de Sens ⑧

1 rue du Figuier 75004. **Map** 9 C4. ☎ *01 42 78 14 60.* Ⓜ *Pont-Marie.* **Open** *1:30–8:30pm Tue–Fri; 10am–8:30pm Sat.* **Closed** *public hols.*

ONE OF ONLY a handful of medieval buildings still standing in Paris, the Hôtel de Sens is home to the Forney arts library. During the period of the Catholic League in the 16th century, it was turned into a fortified mansion and occupied by the Bourbons, the Guises and Cardinal de Pellevé.

St-Gervais– St-Protais ⑨

Place St-Gervais 75004. **Map** 9 B3. ☎ *01 48 87 32 02.* Ⓜ *Hôtel de Ville.* **Open** *6am–9pm daily.*

NAMED AFTER Gervase and Protase, two Roman soldiers martyred by the Emperor Nero, the origins of this magnificent church go back to the 6th century. It boasts the earliest Classical façade in Paris, dating from 1621 and with a triple-tiered arrangement of Doric, Ionic and Corinthian columns.

Behind the façade lies a late Gothic church renowned for its association with religious music. It was for this church's organ that François Couperin (1668–1733) composed his two masses.

UPPER CHAPEL WINDOWS

1 Genesis
2 Exodus
3 Numbers
4 Deuteronomy: Joshua
5 Judges
6 *left* Isaiah *right* Rod of Jesse
7 *left* St. John the Evangelist *right* Childhood of Christ
8 Christ's Passion
9 *left* St. John the Baptist *right* Story of Daniel
10 Ezekiel
11 *left* Jeremiah *right* Tobiah
12 Judith and Job
13 Esther
14 Book of Kings
15 Story of the Relics
16 Rose Window: The Apocalypse

The spire rises 75 m (245 ft) into the air.

The stained-glass windows of the upper chapel constitute a vast illustrated Bible.

The upper chapel was reserved for the royal family and its entourage.

The Crown of Thorns adorns the chapel's pinnacle.

The Rose Window tells the biblical story of the Apocalypse in 86 panels of stained glass.

The lower chapel was used by servants and commoners.

Main portals

Notre-Dame ❻

No OTHER BUILDING epitomizes the history of Paris more than Notre-Dame. Built on the site of a Roman temple, the cathedral was commissioned by Bishop de Sully in 1159. The first stone was laid in 1163, marking the start of two centuries of toil by armies of Gothic architects and medieval craftsmen. It has been witness to great events of French history ever since, including the coronations of Henry VI in 1422 and Napoleon Bonaparte in 1804. During the Revolution, the building was desecrated and rechristened the Temple of Reason. Extensive renovations (including the addition of the spire and gargoyles) were carried out in the 19th century by architect Viollet-le-Duc.

★ **West Façade**
The beautifully proportioned west façade is a masterpiece of French Gothic architecture.

387 steps lead to the top of the south tower, where the famous Emmanuel bell is housed.

★ **Galerie des Chimères**
The cathedral's legendary gargoyles (chimères) gaze menacingly from the cathedral's ledge.

★ **West Rose Window**
This window depicts the Virgin in a medallion of rich reds and blues.

STAR FEATURES

★ **West Façade and Portals**

★ **Flying Buttresses**

★ **Rose Windows**

★ **Galerie des Chimères**

The Kings' Gallery features 28 stone images of the kings of Judah.

Portal of the Virgin
The Virgin surrounded by saints and kings is a fine composition of 13th-century statues.

★ Flying Buttresses
Jean Ravy's spectacular flying buttresses at the east end of the cathedral have a span of 15 m (50 ft).

The spire, designed by Viollet-le-Duc, soars to a height of 90 m (295 ft).

View of Interior
The view from the main entrance takes in the high-vaulted central nave, choir and high altar.

The transept was built at the start of Philippe-Auguste's reign, in the 13th century.

The treasury houses the cathedral's religious treasures, including ancient manuscripts and reliquaries.

★ South Rose Window
This south façade window, with its central depiction of Christ, is an impressive 13 m (43 ft) high.

The "Mays" Paintings
These religious paintings, by Charles Le Brun and Le Sueur, among others, were presented by the Paris guilds every May 1 from 1630 to 1707.

Street-by-Street: The Marais

Once an area of marshland (*marais* means swamp), the Marais grew steadily in importance from the 14th century, by virtue of its proximity to the Louvre, the preferred residence of Charles V. Its heyday was in the 17th century, when it became a fashionable area for the moneyed classes.

They built many grand and sumptuous mansions, the *hôtels* that still dot the Marais today. Many of these buildings have been restored and turned into museums.

To the Pompidou Center

★ **Musée Picasso**
The palatial home of a 17th-century salt-tax collector is the setting for the most extensive collection of Picassos in the world ❶⑤

Rue des Francs-Bourgeois, built in 1334, was named after the *francs* – almshouses for the poor at Nos. 34 and 36.

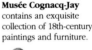

Musée Cognacq-Jay contains an exquisite collection of 18th-century paintings and furniture.

Hôtel de Lamoignon was built in 1584 and houses Paris's historical library.

Rue des Rosiers, in the heart of the Jewish quarter, is lined with 18th-century houses, shops and restaurants serving hot pastrami and borscht.

★ **Musée Carnavalet**
Occupying two large mansions, this museum covers the history of Paris from Roman times ❶⑥

KEY

– – – Suggested route

0 meters 100

0 yards 100

★ **Place des Vosges**
*This enchanting square is
an oasis of peace and
tranquility* ⑰

LOCATOR MAP
See Street Finder maps 9, 10

Maison de Victor Hugo
Author of Les Misérables, *Victor Hugo
lived at No. 6 place des Vosges, now
a museum of his life and work* ⑱

**To Metro Sully
Morland**

Hôtel de Sully, with its
orangerie and courtyard, is an
elegant Renaissance mansion.

Hôtel de Ville ⑩

4 place de l'Hôtel de Ville 75004.
Map 9 B3. 📞 *01 42 76 50 49.*
Ⓜ *Hôtel-de-Ville.* **Admission** *by
group guided tour only (call to
arrange).* **Closed** *public hols, official
functions (call to check).* ♿

H OME OF THE city council,
the Hôtel de Ville is a
19th-century reconstruction of
the 17th-century town hall
burned down by insurgents of
the Paris Commune in 1871.
It is a highly ornate example
of Third Republic architecture,
with elaborate stonework,
turrets and statues overlooking
a pedestrianized square.

The 16th-century Tour St-Jacques

Tour St-Jacques ⑪

Square de la Tour St-Jacques 75004.
Map 9 A3. Ⓜ *Châtelet.* **Not open**
to the public.

T HIS IMPOSING late Gothic
tower, dating from 1522, is
all that remains of a medieval
church used as a rendezvous
by pilgrims setting out for
Compostela in Spain. The
building was destroyed by
revolutionaries in 1797.
Earlier, Blaise Pascal, the
17th-century philosopher,
mathematician, physicist and
writer, used the tower for
barometric experiments. His
statue stands at the base of
the tower, which is now used
as a meteorological station.

St-Eustache ⑫

Place du Jour 75001.
Map 9 A1. 🦻 01 42 36 31 05.
Ⓜ️ *Les Halles.* 🚇 *Châtelet-Les-Halles.*
Open *9am–7pm daily.*

WITH ITS GOTHIC PLAN and
Renaissance decoration,
St-Eustache is one of Paris's
most beautiful churches. Its
massive interior is modeled
on Notre-Dame, with five naves
and side and radial chapels.
The 105 years (1532–1637) it
took to complete the church
saw the flowering of the
Renaissance style, which is
evident in the magnificent
arches, pillars and columns.
   St-Eustache has been the
setting for many ceremonial
events, including the baptisms
of Cardinal Richelieu and
Madame de Pompadour, and
the funerals of fabulist La
Fontaine, Colbert (prime minister of Louis XIV), 17th-
century dramatist Molière,
composer Rameau and

St-Eustache and sculptured head,
l'Ecoute, by Henri de Miller

revolutionary orator Mirabeau.
It was here that Berlioz first
performed his *Te Deum* in
1855 and Liszt his *Messe
Solenelle* in 1866. Today,
talented choir groups perform
here regularly and organ recitals are held in June and July.

Pompidou Center ⑬

See pp88–9.

Hôtel de Soubise ⑭

60 rue des Francs-Bourgeois 75003.
Map 9 C2. 🦻 01 40 27 60 96.
Ⓜ️ *Rambuteau.* **Open** *noon–6:45pm
Wed–Mon.* **Closed** *public hols.*

THIS IMPOSING MANSION, built
from 1705 to 1709 for the
Princesse de Rohan, is one of
two main buildings housing the
national archives (the other
one being the Hôtel de Rohan).
It boasts a majestic courtyard
and 18th-century interior decoration by some of the best-
known artists of the time.
   Natoire's *rocaille* work on the
Oval Salon, the Princess's bedchamber, can be admired in the
museum of French history now
housed here. Other exhibits
include Napoleon's will, in
which he asks for his remains
to be returned to France.

Musée Picasso ⑮

Hôtel Salé, 5 rue de Thorigny.
Map 10 D2. 🦻 01 42 71 25 21. Ⓜ️
St-Sébastien Froissart. **Open** *Oct–Mar:
9:30am–5:30pm Wed–Mon; Apr–Sep:
9:30am–6pm Wed–Mon.* **Closed** *Jan
1, Dec 25.* 🎫 📷 ♿ 🎟️ *by appt*

UPON THE DEATH OF the
Spanish-born artist Pablo
Picasso (1881–1973), who
lived most of his life in France,
the French State inherited one-
quarter of his works in lieu of
death taxes. It used them to
establish the Musée Picasso,
which opened in 1986. The
museum is housed in the
beautifully restored Hôtel Salé,
one of the loveliest buildings
in the Marais. It was built in
1656 for Aubert de Fontenay,
collector of the dreaded salt
tax (*salé* means "salty").
   Comprising over 200
paintings, 158 sculptures, 88
ceramic works and some 3,000
sketches and engravings, this
unique collection shows the
enormous range and variety
of Picasso's work, including
examples from his Blue, Pink
and Cubist periods.
   Highlights to watch for are
his Blue period *Self-portrait,*

Woman Reading (1932) by
Pablo Picasso

painted at age 20; studies for
his masterpiece *Les Demoiselles
d'Avignon; Still Life with Caned
Chair,* which introduced collage
to Cubism; the Neo-Classical
Pipes of Pan; and
The Crucifixion.
   Also exhibited
are works from
Picasso's private art
collection, including
paintings by Rousseau,
Renoir, Cézanne, Braque,
Balthus, Miró and Matisse.

First floor

Entrance

Basement

Musée Carnavalet ⓰

23 rue de Sevigné 75003. **Map** 10 D3.
☎ 01 42 72 21 13. Ⓜ St-Paul.
Open 10am–5:40pm Tue–Sun.
Closed public hols. 🎟 📷
🎫 1:30pm Tue, 2:15pm Sun.

DEVOTED TO the history of Paris since Roman times, this vast museum occupies

A magnificent 17th-century ceiling painting by Charles Le Brun

KEY TO FLOORPLAN

⬜	Paintings
⬜	Illustrations
⬜	Sculpture garden
⬜	Ceramics
⬜	Non-exhibition space

GALLERY GUIDE

The collection is mainly presented in chronological order, starting on the first floor with the Blue and Pink periods, Cubist and Neo-Classical works. The ground floor displays works from the late 1920s to the late 1930s, and from the mid-1950s to 1973. Ceramics, illustrations and work from the war years are in the basement.

Ground floor

🚻 **Entrance**

two adjoining mansions. They include entire decorated rooms with gilded paneling, furniture and *objets d'art*; many works of art, such as paintings and sculptures of prominent personalities; and engravings showing Paris being built.

The main building is the Hôtel Carnavalet, built as a town house in 1548 by Nicolas Dupuis. The literary hostess Madame de Sévigné lived here between 1677 and 1696, entertaining the intelligentsia of the day and writing her celebrated *Lettres*. Many of her possessions are in the first-floor exhibit covering the Louis XIV era.

The 17th-century Hôtel le Peletier, opened in 1989, features superb reconstructions of early 20th-century interiors. Artifacts from the Revolution and Napoleonic era are on display, and reconstructed interiors include Proust's bedroom.

Place des Vosges ⓱

75003, 75004. **Map** 10 D3.
Ⓜ Bastille, St-Paul.

THIS PERFECTLY symmetrical square, laid out in 1605 by Henri IV, is considered among the most beautiful in the world by Parisians and visitors alike. Thirty-six houses, nine on each side, are built over arcades that today accommodate antiques shops and fashionable cafés. The square has been the scene of many historical events over the centuries, including a three-day tournament in celebration of the marriage of Louis XIII to Anne of Austria in 1615.

Maison de Victor Hugo ⓲

6 place des Vosges 75004. **Map** 10 D4.
☎ 01 42 72 10 16. Ⓜ Bastille.
Open 10am–5:40pm Tue–Sun.
Closed public hols. 🎟 🎫 by appt.

THE FRENCH POET, dramatist and novelist lived on the second floor of the former Hôtel Rohan-Guéménée, the

largest house on the square, from 1832 to 1848. It was here that he wrote most of *Les Misérables* and completed other famous works. On display are reconstructions of some of the rooms in which he lived, complete with his desk, the furniture he made, his pen-and-ink drawings and mementos from the crucially important periods of his life, from his childhood to his exile between 1852 and 1870.

Marble bust of Victor Hugo by Auguste Rodin

Place de la Bastille ⓳

75004. **Map** 10 E4. Ⓜ Bastille.

NOTHING REMAINS of the infamous prison stormed by the revolutionary mob on July 14, 1789, the event that sparked the French Revolution.

The 52-m (170-ft) Colonne de Juillet stands in the middle of the traffic-clogged square to honor the victims of the July Revolution of 1830. On the south side of the square (at 120 rue de Lyon) is the 2,700-seat Opéra Bastille, completed in 1989, the bicentennial of the French Revolution.

The "genius of liberty" statue on top of the Colonne de Juillet

Pompidou Center ⑬

THE POMPIDOU IS LIKE a building turned inside out: escalators, elevators, air and water ducts, and even the massive steel struts that make up the building's skeleton are all on the outside. This allowed architects Richard Rogers, Renzo Piano, and Gianfranco Franchini, to create a flexible exhibition space. Artists featured in the museum include Matisse, Picasso, Miró, and Pollock, representing such schools as Fauvism, Cubism, and Surrealism. Outside in the Piazza, large crowds gather to watch the street performers. The Pompidou has been completely renovated for the new Millennium.

KEY

☐ Exhibition space

☐ Nonexhibition space

This riotous jumble of glass and steel, known as Beaubourg, is Paris's top tourist attraction, built in 1977 and drawing over seven million visitors a year.

Mobile on Two Planes (1955)
20th-century American artist Alexander Calder introduced the mobile as an art form.

To the Atelier Brancusi ↙

GALLERY GUIDE

The permanent collections are on the fifth and fourth levels: works from 1905–60 are on the former, contemporary art on the latter. The first and sixth levels are for changing exhibitions; the second and third house a library. The lower levels make up "The Forum," the focal public area, with a performance center, movie theater, and children's workshop.

Sorrow of the King (1952)
This collage was created by Matisse using gouache-painted paper cutouts.

Portrait of the Journalist Sylvia von Harden *(1926) The surgical precision of Otto Dix's style makes this a harsh caricature.*

Man with a Guitar *(1914) Braque, along with Picasso, developed the Cubist technique of presenting many different views of the subject in one picture.*

With the Black Arc *(1912) The transition to Abstraction, one of the major art forms of the 20th century, can be seen in the works of Wassily Kandinsky.*

VISITORS' CHECKLIST

Centre d'Art et de Culture Georges Pompidou, Pl G Pompidou. **Map** 9 B2. **C** *01 44 78 12 33.* **M** *Rambuteau, Châtelet, Hôtel de Ville.* *21, 29, 38, 47, 58, 69, 70, 72, 74, 75, 76, 81, 85, 96.* **RER** *Châtelet-Les-Halles.* **P** *Centre G Pompidou.* **Open** *noon–10pm Mon, Wed–Fri, 10am–10pm Sat, Sun.* **Closed** *May Day public hol.* **Atelier Brancusi open** *noon–10pm Mon–Fri; 10am–10pm Sat, Sun & public hols.* **www.cnac-gp.fr**

Picasso Fountain
This fountain, which was inaugurated in 1983, is in the Place Igor Stravinsky near the Pompidou Centre. It was designed by sculptors Jean Tinguely and Niki de Saint Phalle, both of whom are represented in the Pompidou Centre.

BRANCUSI WORKSHOP

The Atelier Brancusi, on the rue Rambuteau side of the piazza, is a reconstruction of the workshop of the Romanian-born artist Constantin Brancusi (1876–1957), who lived and worked in Paris. He bequeathed his entire collection of works to the French state on condition that his workshop be rebuilt as it was. The wide range of exhibits includes more than 200 sculptures and plinths, 1600 photographs, and the tools Brancusi used in his work. Also featured are some of his more personal items such as documents, pieces of furniture, and his book collection.

Interior of the Brancusi workshop, designed by Renzo Piano

TUILERIES AND OPÉRA

THE 19TH-CENTURY grandeur of Baron Haussmann's *grands boulevards* offsets the bustle of bankers, theater-goers, sightseers and shoppers who frequent the area around the Opéra. A profusion of shops and department stores, ranging from the exclusively expensive to the popular, draws the crowds. Much of the area's older character is found in the early 19th-century shopping arcades, with elaborate steel and glass roofs. They are known as *galeries,* or *passages,* and were restored to their former glory in the 1970s. Galerie Vivienne, the most impressive, has an elaborate, patterned mosaic floor. The passage des Panoramas, passage Verdeau and the tiny passage des Princes are more old-style Parisian. These streets abound with food shops of all kinds,

Lamppost of vestal virgin outside the Opéra

noted for their mouthwatering displays of expensive jams, spices, pâtés, mustards and sauces.

The Tuileries area lies between the Opéra and the river, bounded by the vast place de la Concorde in the west and the Louvre to the east. The Louvre palace combines one of the world's greatest art collections with I.M. Pei's avant-garde glass pyramid. Elegant squares and formal gardens give the area its special character. Monuments to monarchy and the arts coexist with modern luxury at its most ostentatious. Place Vendôme, home to exquisite jewelry shops and the luxurious Ritz Hotel, is a heady mix of the wealthy and the chic. Parallel to the Jardin des Tuileries are two of Paris's foremost shopping streets, the rue de Rivoli and rue St-Honoré, full of expensive boutiques, bookshops and five-star hotels.

SIGHTS AT A GLANCE

Museums and Galleries
Galerie National du Jeu de Paume ❻
Musée des Arts Décoratifs ⓫
Musée Grévin ❸
Musée du Louvre pp96–9 ⓮
Musée de l'Orangerie ❽

Squares, Parks and Gardens
Jardin des Tuileries ❾
Place de la Concorde ❼
Place Vendôme ❺

Monuments
Arc de Triomphe du Carrousel ⓬

Historic Buildings
Opéra de Paris Garnier ❷
Palais Royal ⓭

Churches
La Madeleine ❶
St-Roch ❿

Shops
Les Galeries ❹

GETTING THERE
This area is well served by the metro system, with stations at Tuileries, Pyramides, Palais Royal, Madeleine and Opéra, among others. Bus routes 24 and 72 pass along quai des Tuileries and quai du Louvre, while routes 21, 27 and 29 serve avenue de l'Opéra.

KEY

▨	Street-by-Street map *pp92–3*
M	Metro station
P	Parking

0 meters   500
0 yards   500

◁ **View of the place de la Concorde and the Obelisk**

Street-by-Street: Opéra Quarter

IT HAS BEEN SAID that the whole world will pass you by if you sit for long enough at the Café de la Paix (opposite the Opéra Garnier). During the day, the area is a center of commerce, tourism and shopping, with mammoth department stores lining the *grands boulevards.* In the evening, the clubs and theaters attract a totally different crowd, and the cafés along boulevard des Capucines throb with life.

Statue by Gurnery on the Opéra

★ **Opéra Garnier**
Dating from 1875, the grandiose opera house has come to symbolize the opulence of the Second Empire ❷

STAR SIGHTS

★ **La Madeleine**

★ **Opéra Garnier**

No. 26 place de la Madeleine is home to Fauchon, the most exclusive gourmet food shop in Paris.

RUE TRONCHET

RUE VIGNON

RUE GODOT DE MAUROY

RUE CAUMARTIN

RUE AUBER

RUE EDOUARD VII

PL DE LA MADELEINE

BLVD DES CAPUCINES

BLVD DE LA MADELEINE

Ⓜ **Metro Madeleine**

★ **La Madeleine**
The original model of the Madeleine can be seen at the Musée Carnavalet
(see p87) ❶

Boulevard des Capucines
(No. 14) is where the Lumière brothers staged the first public screening of a movie on December 28, 1895.

LOCATOR MAP
See Street Finder
maps 4, 7, 8

Musée de l'Opéra
contains the scores of every ballet and opera performed at the Opéra, and memorabilia ranging from Nijinsky's dancing shoes to Pavlova's tiara.

PL DIACHILEV

SCRIBE

Metro
Opéra

PL DE
L'OPÉRA

Place de l'Opéra was designed by Baron Haussmann and is one of Paris's busiest intersections.

RUE DAUNOU

KEY

- - - Suggested route

0 meters 100
0 yards 100

Marochetti's *Mary Magdalene Ascending to Heaven* in La Madeleine

La Madeleine ❶

Place de la Madeleine 75008.
Map 3 C5. 01 44 51 69 00.
Madeleine. **Open** 7:30am–7pm
Mon–Sat, 7:45am–7pm Sun.

MODELED AFTER a Greek temple, La Madeleine was begun in 1764 but not consecrated until 1845. Before that, there were proposals to turn it into a stock exchange, a bank, a theater, a railroad station, or yet another monument to Napoleon.

A colonnade of Corinthian columns encircles the building and supports a sculptured frieze. The inside is crowned by three ceiling domes and lavishly decorated with fine sculptures, rose marble and gilt.

Opéra de Paris Garnier ❷

Place de l'Opéra 75009. **Map** 4 DF.
01 40 01 22 63. Opéra. **Open**
10am–5pm daily. **Closed** public hols.

SOMETIMES COMPARED to a giant wedding cake, this extravagant building was designed by Charles Garnier for Napoleon III in 1862. The Prussian War and the 1871 uprising delayed the opening of the building till 1875.

The Opéra is famous for its Grand Staircase made of white Carrara marble, towered over by a huge chandelier. It is also renowned for its five-tiered auditorium in red velvet and gold, with a false ceiling painted by Chagall in 1964.

Though operas are performed in the Opéra Bastille, the Opéra Garnier is still Paris's unrivaled center for ballet.

Musée Grévin ❸

10 boulevard Montmartre 75009.
Map 4 F4. 01 47 70 85 05.
rue Montmartre. **Open** 1–7pm
daily, 10am–7pm school
vacs.

FOUNDED IN 1882, this museum is now a Paris landmark, on a par with Madame Tussauds in London. It shows important historical scenes such as Louis XIV at Versailles and the arrest of Louis XVI. Figures from the arts, politics, film and sports are also on

Sign outside the
Musée Grévin

display. On the first floor, there is a holography museum devoted to optical tricks. The museum also houses a 320-seat theater.

Les Galeries ❹

75002. **Map** 4 F5. Bourse.

THE EARLY 19th-century glass-roofed shopping arcades (known as *galeries* or *passages*) are concentrated between boulevard Montmartre and rue St-Marc. They house an eclectic mixture of small shops selling everything from designer jewelry to rare books and art supplies. One of the most charming is the Galerie Vivienne (off the rue Vivienne or the rue des Petits Champs), with its mosaic floor and excellent tearoom.

Place Vendôme 5

75001. **Map** 8 D1. **M** *Tuileries.*

Perhaps the best example of 18th-century elegance in the city, the architect Jules Hardouin-Mansart's royal square was begun in 1698. The original plan was to house academies and embassies behind its arcaded façades, but instead bankers moved in and created sumptuous mansions for themselves. The square's most famous residents include Frédéric Chopin, who died here in 1849 at No. 12, and César Ritz, who established his famous hotel at No. 15 in 1898.

Monet's *Waterlilies (Nymphéas)* on display in the Musée de l'Orangerie

Galerie National du Jeu de Paume 6

Jardin des Tuileries, place de la Concorde 75008. **Map** 7 C1.
☎ *01 47 03 12 50.* **☎** *01 42 60 69 69.*
M *Concorde.* **Open** *noon–9:30pm Tue, noon–7pm Wed–Fri, 10am–7pm Sat & Sun.* **Closed** *Jan 1, May 1 & Dec 25.*

The Jeu de Paume – literally "game of the palm" – was built as two royal tennis courts by Napoleon III in 1851. When the game's popularity waned, the courts were converted into a gallery devoted to French Impressionist art. In 1986, the collection was moved to the Musée d'Orsay across the river *(see pp116–17).* The Jeu de Paume now exhibits contemporary art.

Place de la Concorde 7

75008. **Map** 7 C1. **M** *Concorde.*

One of Europe's most magnificent and historic squares, covering over 20 acres, the place de la Concorde was a swamp

until the mid-18th century. It became the place Louis XV in 1775, when royal architect Jacques-Ange Gabriel was asked by the king to design a suitable setting for an equestrian statue of himself.

The monument, which lasted here less than 20 years, was replaced by the guillotine (the Black Widow, as it came to be known), and the square was renamed place de la Révolution. On January 21, 1793, Louis XVI was beheaded, followed by over 1,300 other victims including Marie Antoinette, Madame du Barry, Charlotte Corday (Marat's assassin) and revolutionary leaders Danton and Robespierre.

The blood-soaked square was optimistically renamed place de la Concorde after the Reign of Terror finally came to an end in 1794. A few decades later, the 3,200-year-old Luxor obelisk was presented to King Louis-Philippe as a gift from the viceroy of Egypt (who also donated Cleopatra's Needle in London).

Flanking the rue Royale on the north side of the square are two of Gabriel's Neo-Classical mansions – the Hôtel de la Marine and the exclusive Hôtel Crillon.

The 3,200-year-old obelisk from Luxor

Musée de l'Orangerie 8

Jardin des Tuileries, place de la Concorde 75008. **Map** 7 C1.
☎ *01 42 97 48 16.* **M** *Concorde.*
Closed *for renovation until 2001.*

Paintings from Claude Monet's crowning work, representing part of his waterlily series, fill the two oval ground floor rooms. Known as the *Nymphéas,* most of the canvases were painted between 1899 and 1921 in his garden at Giverny, near Paris.

This superb work is complemented by the Walter-Guillaume collection, including 24 canvases by Renoir, notably *Young Girls at the Piano;* dramatic works by Soutine; and 14 Cézannes, including *The Red Rock.* Picasso is represented by early works, including *The Female Bathers,* and Rousseau by 9 paintings, notably *The Wedding* and *Old Junier's Cart.* Other outstanding works are by Sisley, Derain, Modigliani and Utrillo.

Jardin des Tuileries 9

75001. **Map** 8 D1. **M** *Tuileries, Concorde.*

These neo-classical gardens once belonged to the Palais des Tuileries, which the Communards razed to the ground in 1871. They were laid out in the 17th century by André Le Nôtre, who created the broad central avenue and topiary arranged in geometric designs. One of the most popular open spaces in the city, the Tuileries is a lovely spot for a picnic or leisurely stroll.

St-Roch ⓾

296 rue St-Honoré 75001. **Map** 8 E1.
C 01 42 44 13 20. **M** Tuileries.
Open 8:15am–7:30pm daily.
Closed non-religious public hols.

THIS HUGE CHURCH was designed by Jacques Lemercier, architect of the Louvre, and its foundation stone was laid by Louis XIV in 1653. It is a treasure house of religious art, much of it from now-vanished churches and monasteries, and contains the tombs of the playwright Pierre Corneille, the royal gardener André Le Nôtre and the philosopher Denis Diderot.

Vien's *St. Denis Preaching to the Gauls* (1767) in St-Roch

Musée des Arts Décoratifs ⓫

Palais du Louvre, 109 rue de Rivoli 75001. **Map** 8 E2. **C** 01 44 55 57 50.
M Palais Royal, Tuileries. **Open** 11am–6pm Tue, Thu, Fri; 11am–9pm Wed; 10am–6pm Sat & Sun. **Library closed** until 2001.

OCCUPYING THE northwest wing of the Palais du Louvre, this museum offers a fascinating potpourri of decorative art and domestic design

The Buren Columns in the main courtyard of the Palais Royal

from the Middle Ages to the present day. The Art Nouveau and Art Deco rooms, include a reconstruction of the Left Bank home of couturier Jeanne Lanvin. Other floors show Louis XIV, XV and XVI styles of decoration and furniture. Contemporary designers such as Jean-Michel Wilmotte, Philippe Starck and Andrée Putman are also represented.

Arc de Triomphe du Carrousel ⓬

Place du Carrousel 75001.
Map 8 E2. **M** Palais Royal.

THIS ROSE-MARBLE ARCH was built by Napoleon to celebrate various military triumphs, including the Battle of Austerlitz in 1805. The crowning statues, added in 1828, are copies of the famous Horses of St. Mark's that Napoleon stole from Venice, and that he was subsequently forced to return following his defeat at Waterloo in 1815.

Palais Royal ⓭

Place du Palais Royal 75001.
Map 8 E1. **M** Palais Royal.
Buildings closed to the public.

THIS FORMER royal palace has had a turbulent history. It was built by Cardinal Richelieu in the early 17th century, passing to the Crown on his death and becoming the childhood home of Louis XIV. Under the 18th-century royal dukes of Orléans, it became the epicenter of brilliant gatherings, interspersed with periods of gambling and debauchery. It was from here that the clarion call to revolution roused the mobs to storm the Bastille on July 14, 1789.

The southern section of the building now houses the Councils of State and the Ministry of Culture. Just west of the palace at 2 rue de Richelieu is the Comédie Française, established by Louis XIV in 1680. Luxury shops occupy the rear section of the palace, where artists such as Colette and Cocteau once lived.

The Arc de Triomphe du Carrousel crowned by Victory riding a chariot

Musée du Louvre ⑭

T HE MUSEE DU LOUVRE, containing one
of the most important art collections
in the world, has a history dating from
medieval times. Built as a fortress in
1190 by King Philippe-Auguste to
protect Paris against Viking raids,
it lost its keep and dungeon in the
reign of François I, who replaced
it with a Renaissance-style
building. Thereafter, four
centuries of French kings
and emperors improved
and enlarged it. As part
of a major restoration
project, completed
in 1998, the Louvre
has made many
important new
acquisitions.

**The Louvre's east façade, facing
St-Germain l'Auxerrois**

**The Jardin du
Carrousel** was once
the grand approach to the
Tuileries Palace, which was set
ablaze in 1871 by insurgents of
the Paris Commune.

BUILDING THE LOUVRE

Over many centuries the
Louvre was enlarged by a
succession of French rulers,
shown below with their dates.

**The new Carrousel
du Louvre** underground
visitors' complex (1993),
with galleries, shops,
restrooms, parking and
an information desk, lies
beneath the Arc de
Triomphe du Carrousel.

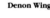

Denon Wing

Pyramid entrance

The inverted glass pyramid
brings light to the subterranean
complex, echoing the museum's
new main entrance in the Cour
Napoléon.

MAJOR ALTERATIONS

☐ Reign of François I (1515–47)

☐ Catherine de' Medici (about 1560)

▨ Reign of Henri IV (1589–1610)

▨ Reign of Louis XIII (1610–43)

☐ Reign of Louis XIV (1643–1715)

▨ Reign of Napoleon I (1804–15)

▨ Reign of Napoleon III (1852–70)

☐ I.M. Pei (1989) (architect)

★ **Arc de Triomphe
du Carrousel**
*This triumphal arch was
built to celebrate Napoleon's
military victories in 1805.*

STAR FEATURES

★ **Perrault Colonnade**

★ **Medieval Moats**

★ **Arc de Triomphe
du Carrousel**

THE GLASS PYRAMID

Plans for the modernization and expansion of the Louvre were first conceived in 1981. They included the transfer of the Ministry of Finance from the Richelieu wing of the Louvre to new offices elsewhere, as well

as a new main entrance designed by architect I.M. Pei in 1989. Made of metal and glass, the pyramid enables the visitor to see the buildings around the palace, while allowing light down into the underground visitors' reception area.

VISITORS' CHECKLIST

Map 8 E2. ⌂ 01 40 20 53 17.
ℹ 01 40 20 51 51. Ⓜ Palais
Royal, Musée du Louvre. 🚌 21,
27, 39, 48, 68, 69, 72, 95. 🚇
Châtelet-Les-Halles. 🅾 Louvre.
🅿 Carrousel du Louvre (entrance
via avenue du General Lemmonier);
place du Louvre, rue St-Honoré.
Museum open 9am–6pm
Thu–Sun (last adm: 5:30pm);
9am–9:45pm Mon & Wed (last
adm: 9:30pm). **Hall Napoléon**
(including History of the Louvre,
Medieval Louvre, auditorium,
temporary exhibitions, restaurants,
bookstore) **open** 9am–10pm
Wed–Mon. **Closed** most public
hols. 🎟 (half price after 3pm and
all day Sun. Free 1st Sun of month).
♿ partial. 📷 (every day except
Sun) call 01 40 20 57 60. 🍴
www.louvre.fr

Cour Marly is the glass-roofed courtyard that now houses the *Marly Horses* (see p99).

Richelieu Wing

Cour Puget

Hall Napoléon is situated under the pyramid.

Cour Khorsabad

Sully Wing

Cour Carrée

★ **Perrault's Colonnade**
The east façade, with its majestic rows of columns, was built by Claude Perrault, who worked on the Louvre with Louis Le Vau in the mid-17th century.

The Salle des Caryatides
is named after the four monumental statues created by Jean Goujon in 1550 to support the upper gallery. Built for Henri II, it is the oldest room in the palace.

Cour Napoléon

The Louvre of Charles V
In about 1360, Charles V transformed Philippe-Auguste's old fortress, with its distinctive tower and keep, into a royal residence.

★ **Medieval Moats**
The base of the twin towers and the drawbridge support of Philippe-Auguste's fortress can be seen in the excavated area.

Exploring the Louvre's Collection

D UE TO THE VAST SIZE of the Louvre's collection, it is useful to set a few viewing priorities before starting. The collection of European paintings (1400–1848) is comprehensive, with over half the works by French artists. The extensively renovated departments of Oriental, Egyptian, Etruscan, and Roman antiquities feature numerous new acquisitions and rare treasures. The varied display of *objets d'art* includes furniture and jewelry.

The Raft of the Medusa (1819)
by Théodore Géricault

EUROPEAN PAINTING: 1400 TO 1848

P AINTING FROM northern Europe (Flemish, Dutch, German and English) is well covered. One of the earliest Flemish works is Jan van Eyck's *Madonna of the Chancellor Rolin* (about 1435), which shows the Chancellor of Burgundy kneeling in prayer before the Virgin and Child. Hieronymus Bosch's *Ship of Fools* (1500) is a satirical account of the futility of human existence.

Mona Lisa (about 1504) by
Leonardo da Vinci

In the Dutch collection, Rembrandt's *Self-portrait*, his *Disciples at Emmaus* (1648) and *Bathsheba* (1654) are examples of the artist's genius.

The three major German painters of the 15th and 16th centuries are represented by important works. There is a youthful *Self-portrait* (1493) by Albrecht Dürer, a *Venus* (1529) by Lucas Cranach and a portrait of the great humanist scholar Erasmus by Hans Holbein.

The museum's collection of Italian paintings is large, covering the period from 1200 to 1800. The father figures of the early Renaissance, Cimabue and Giotto, are here, as is Fra Angelico, with his *Coronation of the Virgin* (1435), and Pisanello, with his delightful *Portrait of Ginevra d'Este* (about 1435). Several paintings by Leonardo da Vinci are on display, for instance the *Virgin with the Infant Jesus and St. Anne* which is as enchanting as his *Mona Lisa*.

The Louvre's fine collection of French painting ranges from the 14th century to 1848.

Paintings after this date are housed in the Musée d'Orsay *(see pp116–17)*. Outstanding is Enguerrand Quarton's *Villeneuve-les-Avignon Pietà* (1455). The great 18th-century painter of melancholy, J.A. Watteau, is represented, as is J.H. Fragonard, master of the Rococo, whose delightfully frivolous subjects are evident in *The Bathers* from 1770.

EUROPEAN SCULPTURE: 1100 TO 1848

E ARLY FLEMISH and German sculpture in the collection includes such masterpieces as Tilman Riemenschneider's *Virgin of the Annunciation,* from the end of the 15th century, and a life-size nude figure of the penitent Mary Magdalen by Gregor Erhart (early 16th century). An important work of Flemish sculpture is Adrian de Vries's long-limbed *Mercury and Psyche* from 1593, which was originally made for the court of Rudolph II in Prague.

The French section opens with early Romanesque works, such as the figure of Christ by a 12th-century Burgundian sculptor, and a head of St. Peter. With its eight black-hooded mourners, the late 15th-century tomb of Philippe Pot (a high-ranking official in Burgundy) is one of the more unusual pieces. Diane de Poitiers, Henri II's mistress, had a large figure of her namesake Diana, goddess of the hunt, installed in the courtyard of her castle west of Paris. It is now in the Louvre.

**The tomb of Philippe Pot (late 15th century) by
Antoine le Moiturier**

**The celebrated *Marly Horses*
(1745) by Guillaume Coustou**

The works of French sculptor
Pierre Puget (1620–94) have
been assembled in the Cour
Puget. They include a figure of
Milo of Crotona, the Greek ath-
lete who got his hands caught
in the cleft of a tree stump and
was eaten by a lion. The wild
horses of Marly now stand in
the Cour Marly, surrounded by
other masterpieces of French
sculpture, including Jean-
Antoine Houdon's early 19th-
century busts of famous men
such as Diderot and Voltaire.

The collection of Italian
sculpture includes such splendid exhibits as Michelangelo's
Slaves and Benvenuto Cellini's
Fontainebleau *Nymph*.

ORIENTAL, EGYPTIAN, GREEK, ETRUSCAN AND ROMAN ANTIQUITIES

A SUBSTANTIAL overhaul of the
Louvre has boosted its
collection of antiquities, which
range from the Neolithic period to the fall of the Roman
Empire. Among the new ex-
hibits are Greek and Roman
glassware dating from the 6th
century BC. Important works
of Mesopotamian art include
one of the world's oldest legal
documents, a basalt block
bearing the code of the
Babylonian King Hammurabi,
dating from about 1700 BC.

The warlike Assyrians are
represented by delicate carvings and a spectacular reconstruction of part of Sargon II's
(722–705 BC) palace with its
winged bulls. A fine example
of Persian art is the enameled
brickwork depicting the king
of Persia's personal guard of
archers (5th century BC).

Most Egyptian art was
made for the dead, who
were provided with the
things they needed for the
afterlife. Examples include
the lifelike funeral
portraits, such as the
Squatting Scribe, and
several sculptures of
married couples.

The departments of
Greek, Roman and
Etruscan antiquities
contain a vast array of
fragments, among them
some exceptional
pieces. There is a
geometric head from
the Cyclades (2700
BC) and an elegant
swan-necked bowl
hammered out of a
gold sheet (2500 BC).
The two most famous
Greek marble statues,
the *Winged Victory of
Samothrace* and the
Venus de Milo,
both belong to
the Hellenistic
period (late 3rd to
2nd century BC),
when more
natural-looking
human forms were produced.

The undisputed star of the
Etruscan collection is the
terracotta sarcophagus of a
married couple who look as
though they are attending an
eternal banquet, while the
highlight of the Roman section
is a 2nd-century
bronze head of
the Emperor
Hadrian.

**Venus de Milo
(Greece, late 3rd–early
2nd century BC)**

**Squatting Scribe (about 2500 BC), a lifelike
Egyptian funeral sculpture**

OBJETS D'ART

T HE CATCH-ALL term *objets
d'art* (art objects) covers a
vast range of items: jewelry,
furniture, clocks, watches,
sundials, tapestries, miniatures,
silver and glassware, cutlery,
Byzantine and Parisian carved
ivory, Limoges enamels,
porcelain, French and
Italian stoneware, rugs,
snuffboxes, scientific
instruments and
armor. The Louvre
has well over 8,000
pieces, from many
ages and regions.

Many of these
precious objects came
from the Abbey of
St-Denis, where the
kings of France were
crowned. The treasures
include a serpentine
stone plate from the 1st
century AD with a 9th-
century border of gold
and precious stones; a
porphyry vase that
Suger, Abbot of St-
Denis, had mounted in
gold in the shape of an
eagle; and the golden
scepter made for
King Charles V in
about 1380.

The French crown
jewels include the coronation
crowns of Louis XV and
Napoleon, scepters, swords
and other accessories of the
coronation ceremonies. On
display also is the Regent, one
of the purest diamonds in the
world, which Louis XV wore
at his coronation in 1722.

One window room is taken
up with a series of tapestries
called the *Hunts of Maximilian,*
originally executed for
Emperor Charles V in 1530.
The large collection of French
furniture ranges from the 16th
to the 19th centuries and is
assembled by period, or in
rooms devoted to donations
by distinguished collectors.
On display are pieces
by such exceptionally
prominent furniture-
makers as André-
Charles Boulle, cabinet-
maker to Louis XIV,
who worked at the
Louvre in the late 17th
to mid-18th centuries.

CHAMPS-ELYSÉES
AND INVALIDES

THE RIVER SEINE bisects this area, much of which is built on a monumental scale, from the imposing 18th-century buildings of Les Invalides to the Art Nouveau avenues surrounding the Eiffel Tower. Two of Paris's grandest thoroughfares dominate the neighborhood to the north of the Seine: the Champs-Elysées has many chic hotels and shops but today is more down-

**Ornate lamppost on
Pont Alexandre III**

scale; and the rue du Faubourg St-Honoré boasts the heavily guarded Palais de l'Elysée. The village of Chaillot was absorbed into the city in the 19th century, and many of its opulent Second Empire mansions are now embassies or company headquarters. Streets around the place du Trocadéro and the Neo-Classical Palais de Chaillot are packed full of museums and elegant cafés.

SIGHTS AT A GLANCE

Historic Buildings and Streets
Avenue des Champs-Elysées ❷
Champ-de-Mars ⓰
Ecole Militaire ⓱
Hôtel des Invalides ⓳
Les Egouts ⓭
No. 29 Avenue Rapp ⓯
Palais de l'Elysée ❸

Museums and Galleries
Grand Palais ❺
Musée de l'Armée ⓴
Musée d'Art Moderne de la Ville de Paris ❼
Musée de la Mode et du Costume Palais Galliera ❽

Musée National des Arts Asiatiques Guimet ❾
Musée National d'Ennery ⓾
Musée Rodin ㉓
Palais de Chaillot ⓬
Petit Palais ❹

Churches
Dôme Church ㉒
Sainte-Clothilde ㉔
St-Louis-des-Invalides ㉑

Monuments and Fountains
Arc de Triomphe ❶
Eiffel Tower p109 ⓮
Fontaine des Quatre Saisons ㉕

Modern Architecture
UNESCO ⓲

Gardens
Jardins du Trocadéro ⓫

Bridges
Pont Alexandre III ❻

GETTING THERE

Metro stations in this area include Etoile, Trocadéro and Champs-Elysées. Bus routes 42 and 73 serve the Champs-Elysées; routes 87 and 69 serve avenue de Suffren and rue St-Dominique, respectively.

KEY

	Street-by-Street map *pp102–3*
M	Metro station
RER	RER station
⃝	Batobus boarding point
P	Car park

0 meters   500
0 yards   500

Street-by-Street: Champs-Elysées

THE FORMAL GARDENS that line the Champs-Elysées from the place de la Concorde to the Rond-Point have changed little since they were laid out by the architect Jacques Hittorff in 1838. The gardens were used as the setting for the World's Fair of 1855, which included the Palais de l'Industrie, Paris's response to London's Crystal Palace. The Palais was later replaced by the Grand Palais and the Petit Palais, which was created as a showpiece of the Third Republic for the Universal Exhibition of 1900. They sit on either side of an impressive vista that stretches from the place Clémenceau across the elegant curve of the Pont Alexandre III, with its four strong anchoring columns, to the Invalides.

Théâtre du Rond Point, an original Champs-Elysées building, is home to the Marcel-Maréchal Company.

Metro Franklin D. Roosevelt

★ **Avenue des Champs-Elysées**
This was the setting for the victory parades following the two World Wars ❷

★ **Grand Palais**
Designed by Charles Girault and built between 1897 and 1900, this elaborate exhibition hall, with its splendid glass dome, is frequently used for major exhibitions ❺

The Lasserre restaurant is decorated in the style of a luxury ocean liner dating from the 1930s.

Palais de la Découverte, a museum of scientific discovery, was originally opened in the Grand Palais for the World's Fair of 1937.

STAR SIGHTS

★ Avenue des Champs-Elysées

★ Grand Palais

★ Petit Palais

KEY

– – – Suggested route

0 meters   100

0 yards   100

The Jardins des Champs-Elysées, with their fountains, flower beds and pleasure pavilions, have been a popular spot since the 19th century.

CHAMPS-ELYSEES AND INVALIDES

LOCATOR MAP
See Street Finder maps
2, 3, 6, 7

Metro
Champs-
Elysées-
Clémenceau

To place
de la
Concorde

★ **Petit Palais**
The art collections of the city of Paris are housed here. They contain artifacts ranging from antique sculptures to landscape painters of the Barbizon school ❹

To the Invalides

Pont Alexandre III
This highly ornate, single-span structure symbolizes the optimism of the Belle Epoque at the turn of the century ❻

The east façade of the Arc de Triomphe

Arc de Triomphe ❶

Place Charles de Gaulle. **Map** 2 D4.
📞 *01 55 37 73 77.* **Open** *Apr–Sep: 9:30am–11pm daily; Oct–Mar: 10am–10:30pm daily.* **Closed** *public hols.*

AFTER HIS greatest victory, the Battle of Austerlitz in 1805, Napoleon promised his men they would "go home beneath triumphal arches." The first stone of what was to become the world's most famous triumphal arch was laid the following year. But disruptions to architect Jean Chalgrin's plans, combined with the demise of Napoleonic power delayed the completion of the bridge until 1836. Standing 50 m (164 ft) high, the Arc is encrusted with flamboyant reliefs, shields, and sculptures. The viewing platform offers fascinating views of the city.

On November 11, 1920, the body of the Unknown Soldier was placed beneath the arch to commemorate the dead of World War I, and the eternal flame is lit every evening.

High relief by J.P. Corot, celebrating the Triumph of Napoleon

BARON HAUSSMANN

A lawyer by training and civil servant by profession, Georges-Eugène Haussmann (1809–91) was appointed Prefect of the Seine in 1852 by Napoleon III. For 17 years Haussmann was responsible for the urban modernization of Paris. With a team of the best architects and engineers of the day, he demolished the crowded, insanitary streets of the medieval city and created a well-ventilated and ordered capital within a geometrical grid. The new plan involved redesigning the area at one end of the Champs-Elysées and creating a star of 12 avenues which were centered around the new Arc de Triomphe.

Arc de Triomphe

12 avenues forming a star (*étoile*)

Place de l'Etoile

Avenue des Champs-Elysées ❷

75008. **Map** 3 A5. **M** *Franklin D. Roosevelt, George V.*

Paris's most well-known and popular thoroughfare was a desolate marshland until about 1667, when the master landscape-garden designer André Le Nôtre (*see p169*) created a tree-lined avenue that he named the Champs-Elysées. It has been the "triumphal way" ever since the home-coming of Napoleon's body from St. Helena in 1840. Today, it is an ideal place to stop for a drink and observe the charm of Parisian life.

Elysée guard

Palais de l'Elysée ❸

55 rue du Faubourg-St-Honoré 75008. **Map** 3 B5. **M** *St-Philippe-du-Roule.* **Not open** to the public.

Set amid splendid English-style gardens, the Elysée Palace was built in 1718 by Molet and has been the official residence of the President of the Republic since 1873. The palace has seen many changes over the centuries: Louis XV's mistress, Madame de Pompadour, had the site enlarged to suit her lavish lifestyle. It became a public entertainment park after the Revolution. In the 19th century it was occupied by Napoleon's sister, Caroline, and her husband, Murat. Two delightful rooms have been preserved from this period. General de Gaulle used to give press conferences in the Hall of Mirrors. Today, the President's apartments, with furniture by designer Philippe Starck, can be found on the first floor, in their English-style garden setting, opposite the rue de l'Elysée.

Petit Palais ❹

Av Winston Churchill 75008. **Map** 7 B1. **◖** *01 42 65 12 73.* **M** *Champs-Elysées-Clémenceau.* **Open** *10am–5:40pm Tue–Sun.* **Closed** *public hols.* 🗓 📷 ♿

Built for the Universal Exhibition in 1900, to stage a major display of French art, this jewel of a building now houses the Musée des Beaux-Arts de la Ville de Paris. The architect, Charles Girault, arranged the palace around a semicircular

GRAND PALAIS

Exhibition space   Iron supports

Pont Alexandre III, built between 1896–1900 for the Universal Exhibition

courtyard and garden, similar in style to the Grand Palais. The exhibits, which were donated by private collectors, are divided into sections. These include the Dutuit Collection of medieval and Renaissance *objets d'art*, paintings and drawings; the Tuck Collection of 18th-century furniture and *objets d'art*; and the City of Paris

collection, with work by such artists as Ingres, Delacroix and Courbet, and the landscape painters of the Barbizon School.

Grand Palais ❺

Porte A, avenue Eisenhower 75008.
Map 7 A1. 🗓 01 44 13 17 30.
Ⓜ *Champs-Elysées-Clémenceau.*
Open 10am–8pm (10pm Wed)
Wed–Mon. **Closed** public hols. 🅰

THE EXTERIOR of this huge palace combines an imposing Classical stone façade with a riot of Art Nouveau ironwork. It was built at the same time as the Petit Palais opposite, and has a splendid glass roof and bronze statues of flying horses and chariots at its four corners. The building looks most dramatic at night, when the glass roof glows with the lights from inside and the statues are silhouetted against the sky. The Great Hall and glass cupola can be seen from the interior during temporary exhibitions, which are held in the Galeries Nationales du Grand Palais. The Salon des Antiquaires is temporarily closed for restoration.

Entrance to the Petit Palais

Pont Alexandre III ❻

75008. **Map** 7 A1. Ⓜ *Champs-Elysées-Clémenceau.*

THIS IS PARIS'S prettiest bridge, with exuberant Art Nouveau decoration of gilt and bronze lamps, cupids and cherubs, nymphs and winged horses at either end. It was built between 1896 and 1900 to commemorate the 1892 French-Russian alliance, and in time for the Universal Exhibition in 1900. Pont Alexandre III was named after Tsar Alexander III (father of Nicholas II), who laid the foundation stone in October 1896.

The style of the bridge reflects that of the Grand Palais, to which it leads on the Right Bank. The construction of the bridge is a marvel of 19th-century engineering. It consists of a 6-meter-high (18 ft) single-span steel arch across the Seine. The design was subject to strict controls that prevented the bridge from obscuring the view of the Champs-Elysées or the Invalides, so today you can still enjoy the magnificent views from here.

Great Hall

Glass cupola

Quadriga (chariot and four horses) by Récipon

Musée d'Art Moderne de la Ville de Paris ❼

11 avenue du Président-Wilson 75116. **Map** 6 E1. ☎ 01 53 67 40 00. Ⓜ Iéna. **Open** 10am–6:45pm Sat, Sun; 10am–5:30pm Tue–Fri. **Closed** public hols.

THIS MUSEUM covers trends in 20th-century art and is located in the east wing of the Palais de Tokyo. The Fauves and Cubists are well represented here. Highlights include Raoul Dufy's gigantic mural *The Spirit of Electricity*, (created for the 1937 World's Fair), and Matisse's *The Dance*

(1932). Also exhibited here is a collection of Art Deco furniture from the period 1920–37.

Musée de la Mode et du Costume Palais Galliera ❽

10 av Pierre 1er de Serbie 75116. **Map** 6 D1. ☎ 01 47 20 85 23. Ⓜ Iéna, Alma–Marceau. **Open** 10am–6pm Tue–Sun, but call to check as only open for two exhibitions per year. **Closed** public hols.

DEVOTED TO the evolution of fashion, this museum is housed in the Renaissance-style palace built for the Duchesse

Maria de Ferrari Galliera in 1892. The collection includes more than 100,000 outfits and fashion accessories, from the 18th century to the present day. Donations have been made by such fashionable women as Baronne Hélène de Rothschild and Princess Grace of Monaco. Eminent couturiers such as Balmain and Balenciaga have donated their designs to the museum.

Because they are often extremely fragile, the fashion exhibits are displayed in rotation, usually in two major exhibitions each year. These shows can highlight a particular couturier's career or explore a single theme.

Trocadéro fountains in front of the Palais de Chaillot

Jardins du Trocadéro ⓫

75016. **Map** 6 D2. Ⓜ Trocadéro.

THESE BEAUTIFUL gardens cover 25 acres. Their centerpiece is a long, rectangular ornamental pool, bordered by stone and bronze-gilt statues, which looks spectacular at night when the fountains are illuminated. The statues include *Woman* by Georges Braque and *Horse* by Georges Lucien Guyot. On either side of the pool, the slopes of the Chaillot hill lead gently down to the Seine and the Pont d'Iéna. There is a freshwater aquarium in the northeast corner of the gardens, which are richly laid out with trees, walkways, small streams and bridges.

Palais de Chaillot ⓬

17 place du Trocadéro 75016. **Map** 5 C2. Ⓜ Trocadéro. **Open** 9:45am–5:15pm Wed–Mon. **Closed** public hols. **Cinémathèque Française** open for screenings: ☎ 01 56 26 01 01.

THE PALAIS, with its huge, curved colonnaded wings, each culminating in a vast pavilion, houses four museums, a theater and a cinema. Designed in Neo-Classical style for the 1937 Paris Exhibition by Azéma, Louis-Auguste Boileau and Jacques Carlu, it is adorned with sculptures and bas-reliefs. On the walls of the pavilions are gold inscriptions which were written by the poet and essayist Paul Valéry.

The *parvis*, or square, situated between the two pavilions is highly decorated with bronze sculptures, ornamental pools

and shooting fountains. On the terrace in front of the *parvis* stand two impressive bronzes, *Apollo* by Henri Bouchard and *Hercules* by Pommier. Steps lead down from the terrace to the Théâtre National de Chaillot, which, after World War II, enjoyed fame for its avant-garde productions.

The basement of the palace houses Paris's main film institute, the Cinémathèque Française, founded by Henri Langlois in 1936. One of the areas devastated by a fire in 1997, the institute has been restored and screens a daily-changing schedule of film classics. Still under renovation after the fire, the Musée du Cinéma Henri Langlois, also here, exhibits a large collection of artifacts dating back to the origins of photography and cinema.

Musée National des Arts Asiatiques Guimet 9

6 place d'Iéna 75116. **Map** 6 D1.
01 45 05 00 98. **M** Iéna. **Closed**
for restoration until 2000. New galleries opened at 19 avenue
d'Iéna (call to check opening hours).

ONE OF THE WORLD'S leading museums of Asian art, the Guimet has the finest collection of Cambodian (Khmer) art in the West. It was originally set up in Lyon in 1879 by the industrialist and Orientalist Emile Guimet and moved to Paris in 1884. It includes an Asian research center.

Buddha head from Musée Guimet

Musée National d'Ennery 10

59 avenue Foch 75016. **Map** 1 B5.
01 45 53 57 96. **M** Porte Dauphine. **Closed** for refurbishment until further notice.

THIS MANSION, which dates from the Second Empire period, contains two highly personal museums of precious *objets d'art*. Adolphe d'Ennery, the 19th-century dramatist and collector of Far Eastern art, assembled this array of Chinese and Japanese figures, ceramic boxes, ornaments and furniture, dating from the 17th to the 19th century.

PALAIS DE CHAILLOT

Théâtre National de Chaillot

Musée des Monuments Français

Place du Trocadéro

Musée de la Marine

Musée de l'Homme

Cinémathèque Française

Musée du Cinéma Henri Langlois

Palais de Chaillot

Jardins du Trocadéro

Trocadéro Fountains

In the east wing is the Musée des Monuments Français, designed in 1882 by Viollet-le-Duc. This museum plots the history of French monumental art, from pre-Roman times to the 19th century. The Musée de l'Homme in the west wing portrays the history and development of humankind. Highlights include a mummy from the Incas and a rich African section. Also in the west wing is the Musée de la Marine, devoted to French naval history.

Some of these museums are due to move eventually to the nearby Palais de Tokyo, but the Palais de Chaillot will still be worth a visit, if only for the view of the Eiffel Tower.

Les Egouts ⑬

In front of 93 quai d'Orsay 75007.
Map 6 F2. ⓕ *01 53 68 27 81 (in
English).* Ⓜ *Pont-de-l'Alma.* **Open**
*11am–4pm (5pm in summer)
Sat–Wed.* ♿

ONE OF BARON HAUSSMANN'S
finest achievements, the
majority of Paris's sewers
(égouts) date from the Second
Empire. If laid end to end the
2,100 km (1,300 miles) of
sewers would stretch from
Paris to Istanbul. They are a
popular tourist attraction. All
tours have been limited to a
small area around the quai
d'Orsay entrance and are now
on foot. A sewer museum has
been established here where
visitors can discover the
mysteries of underground
Paris. There are also displays
showing how the machinery
used in the sewers has
changed over the years.

Eiffel Tower ⑭

See p109.

No. 29 Avenue Rapp ⑮

75005. **Map** 6 E2. Ⓜ *Pont-de-
l'Alma.*

A PRIME EXAMPLE of Art
Nouveau architecture, No.
29 avenue Rapp won its
designer, Jules Lavirotte, first
prize at the Concours des

**Original Art Nouveau doorway at
No. 29 avenue Rapp**

Façades de la Ville de Paris in
1901. Its ceramics and
brickwork are decorated with
animal and flower motifs
intermingling with female
figures. These are super-
imposed on a multicolored
sandstone base to produce a
façade that is deliberately
erotic and was certainly
subversive in its day. Also
worth visiting nearby is
Lavirotte's building, complete
with watchtower, which can
be found in the square Rapp.

Champ-de-Mars ⑯

75007. **Map** 6 E3. Ⓜ *Ecole-Militaire.*
ⓇⒺⓇ *Champ-de-Mars–Tour-Eiffel.*

THE VAST GARDENS stretching
from the Eiffel Tower to
the Ecole Militaire (Military
School) were originally a
parade ground for
young officer cadets.
The area has
since been used
for horse racing,
hot-air ballooning
and mass
ceremonies to
celebrate the
anniversary of the
Revolution on July
14. The first
ceremony was
held in 1790, in the
presence of a glum,
captive, Louis XVI.
Mammoth exhibitions were
held here in the late 19th
century, among them the
1889 World's Fair, for which
the Eiffel Tower was erected.

**A Paris balloon
ascent**

Ecole Militaire ⑰

1 place Joffre 75007. **Map** 6 F4.
Ⓜ *Ecole-Militaire.* **Visits** *by special
permission only – contact the
Commandant in writing.*

THE ROYAL MILITARY academy
of Louis XV was founded
in 1751 to educate 500 sons of
impoverished officers. Louis XV
and Madame de Pompadour
commissioned architect
Jacques-Ange Gabriel to design
a building that would rival
Louis XVI's Hôtel des Invalides.
Financing the building became
a problem, so a lottery was
authorized and a tax was
raised on playing cards.

**A 1751 engraving showing the
planning of the Ecole Militaire**

One of the main features
is the central pavilion – a
magnificent example of the
French Classical style, with
ten Corinthian columns
and a quadrangular
dome. Four
figures adorn the
entablature frieze,
symbolizing
France, Victory,
Force and Peace.
An early cadet at
the academy was
Napoleon, whose
graduation report
stated that "he could
go far if the circum-
stances are right."

UNESCO ⑱

7 place de Fontenoy 75007.
Map 6 F5. ⓕ *01 45 68 10 60 (in
English).* Ⓜ *Ségur, Cambronne.*
Open *9:30am– 12:30pm, 2:30–6pm
Mon–Fri.* **Closed** *public hols & during
conference sessions.* ♿

THIS IS the headquarters of
the United Nations
Educational, Scientific and
Cultural Organization
(UNESCO). The aim of the
organization is to contribute
to international peace and
security through education,
science and culture.
UNESCO is a treasure trove
of modern art, including an
enormous mural by Picasso,
ceramics designed by Joan
Miró and sculptures by Henry
Moore. Another attractive
feature is the quiet Japanese
garden designed by Nogushi.

Eiffel Tower ⑭

Eiffel Tower seen from the Trocadéro

Built for the Universal Exhibition of 1889, and to commemorate the centennial of the Revolution, the 319-m (1,046-ft) Eiffel Tower (Tour Eiffel) was meant to be a temporary addition to Paris's skyline. Designed by Gustave Eiffel, it was fiercely decried by 19th-century aesthetes. It stood as the world's tallest building until 1931, when New York's Empire State Building was completed.

VISITORS' CHECKLIST

Champ-de-Mars–Tour Eiffel. **Map** 6 D3. ☎ *01 44 11 23 11.* Ⓜ *Bir Hakeim.* 🚌 *42, 69, 72, 82, 87, 91 to Champ-de-Mars.* RER *Champ-de- Mars.* ◯ *Tour Eiffel.* **Open** *Sep–Jun: 9:30am– 11pm; Jul & Aug: 9am–mid- night.* 🎟 ⚬ ♿ 🍴

The third level, 276 m (899 ft) above the ground, can hold 400 people at a time.

★ Viewing Gallery
On a clear day it is possible to see for 72 km (45 miles), including a distant view of Chartres Cathedral.

DARING FEATS

The tower has always inspired crazy stunts. In 1912, Reichelt, a Parisian tailor, attempted to fly from the parapet with only a cape for wings. He plunged to his death in front of a large crowd.

Stuntman Reichelt

STAR FEATURES

★ Eiffel Bust

★ Viewing Gallery

The double-decker elevators have a limited capacity, and during the tourist season there can be long waits for the elevators. The trip up is not for those who fear heights.

The second level is at 115 m (376 ft), 359 steps above the first level, or a few minutes ride in the elevator.

Cineiffel
This small audiovisual museum shows historical film footage of the tower.

Jules Verne restaurant is rated highly in Paris, offering not only superb food, but a breathtaking panoramic view.

★ Eiffel Bust

The achievement of Eiffel (1832–1923) was honored by Antoine Bourdelle, who placed this bust under the tower in 1923.

The first level, is 57 m (187 ft) high. Take the elevator or walk up 345 steps. There's a post office here.

LES INVALIDES

Musée de l'Armée   Hôtel des Invalides   Cour d'Honneur

Musée de l'Ordre de la Libération   Musée des Plans-Reliefs   Dôme Church   St-Louis-des-Invalides

Hôtel des Invalides ⑲

75007. **Map** 7 A3. **C** *01 44 42 37 70.* **M** *Latour-Maubourg, Varenne.* **Open** *10am–6pm (5pm winter) daily.* **Closed** *Jan 1, May 1, Nov 1, Dec 25.*

THIS IMPOSING building, from which the area takes its name, was commissioned by Louis XIV in 1671 for his wounded and homeless veterans, many of whom had become beggars. Designed by Libéral Bruand, it was completed in 1676 by Jules Hardouin-Mansart. He later incorporated the Dôme Church, with its glittering golden roof, which was built as Louis XIV's private chapel. Nearly 6,000 soldiers once lived here. Today there are fewer than 100. The harmonious Classical façade is one of the most impressive sights in Paris, a masterpiece of French 17th-century architecture. The entire ensemble is vast, brimming with architectural and historical splendor. The building houses the Musée de l'Armée and the Musée de l'Ordre de la Libération. This was set up to honor feats of heroism during World War II under the leadership of Charles de Gaulle. The story is told using documents, photographs and mementos. The Musée des Plans-Reliefs in the right wing houses a large collection of detailed military models of French forts and fortified towns considered top secret until the 1950s. Bruand's Cour d'Honneur is still used for military parades.

Musée de l'Armée ⑳

Hôtel des Invalides 75007. **Map** 7 A3. **C** *01 44 42 37 72.* **M** *Latour-Maubourg, Varenne.* **Open** *10am–6pm (5pm winter) daily.* **Closed** *Jan 1, May 1, Nov 1, Dec 25.*

THIS IS ONE of the most comprehensive museums of military history in the world, with exhibits ranging from the Stone Age to World War II. It is housed in two galleries, situated on either side of the magnificent courtyard of the Hôtel des Invalides.

Among the vast collection is an exhibit recalling the victories and defeats of France through history, dedicated mainly to the Napoleonic era. Uniforms, weapons and models are on display, as well as the emperor's death mask and stuffed horse, Vizier. Other exhibits include François I's ivory hunting horns, Oriental arms from China, Japan and Turkey, and a model of the 1944 Normandy landing.

St-Louis-des-Invalides ㉑

Hôtel des Invalides 75007. **Map** 7 A3. **M** *Varenne, Latour-Maubourg.* **C** *01 44 42 37 65.* **Open** *9:30am–5pm (4:30pm winter) daily.*

ALSO KNOWN AS the "soldiers' church," this is the chapel of the Hôtel des Invalides. It was built from 1679 to 1708

The façade of the Musée de l'Armée

Altar of St-Louis-des-Invalides with banners seized in battle

by Jules Hardouin-Mansart, according to Bruand's design. The stark, Classical interior is well-proportioned, designed in the shape of a Greek cross.

There is a fine 17th-century organ, built by Alexandre Thierry, on which the first performance of Berlioz's *Requiem* was given on December 5 1837. More than 200 musicians and choristers participated in the concert.

Dôme Church ②

Hôtel des Invalides, avenue de Tourville. **Map** 7 A3. 01 44 42 37 72. Latour-Maubourg, Varenne. 28, 49, 63, 69, 82, 83, 87, 92 to Les Invalides. Invalides. Tour Eiffel. **Open** Oct–Mar: 10am–5pm; Apr–Sep: 10am–6pm daily. **Closed** Jan 1, May 1, Jun 17, Nov 1, Dec 25.

JULES HARDOUIN-MANSART was asked in 1676 by the Sun King, Louis XIV, to build the Dôme Church to complement the existing buildings of the Invalides military refuge, designed by Libéral Bruand, and to reflect the splendor of his reign. The Dôme was to be reserved for the exclusive use of the Sun King and as the location of royal tombs.

The resulting masterpiece is one of the greatest examples of 17th-century French architecture, the period known as the *grand siècle*. After Louis XIV's death, plans to bury the royal family in the church were abandoned; it became a monument to Bourbon glory.

The main attraction has to be the tomb of Napoleon; 20 years after his death on the island of St. Helena, his body was returned to France on the authority of Louis-Philippe. His remains were installed in the crypt, encased in six coffins within an enormous red porphyry sarcophagus, resting on a pedestal of green granite. His son and brothers, Jerôme and Joseph, are also entombed in the crypt.

Marshal Foch, commander of the Allied troops during World War I, is buried here. There is also a memorial to Sébastien le Prestre de Vauban, Louis XIV's military architect.

Dôme Church with cupola, first gilded in 1715

Musée Rodin ②

77 rue de Varenne 75007. **Map** 7 B3. 01 47 05 01 34. Varenne. **Open** 9:30am–5:45pm (4:45pm winter) Tue–Sun. **Closed** Jan 1, May 1, Dec 25. restricted.

AUGUSTE RODIN (1840–1917), widely regarded as one of the greatest French sculptors, lived and worked in the Hôtel Biron, an elegant 18th-century mansion, from 1908 until his death. In return for a state-owned flat and studio, Rodin left his work to the nation, and it is now exhibited here. Some of his most celebrated sculptures are on display in the garden: *The Burghers of Calais, The Thinker, The Gates of Hell (see p116)* and *Balzac*.

The indoor exhibits are arranged in chronological order, spanning Rodin's entire career. Highlights of the collection include *The Kiss* and *Eve*.

Sainte-Clothilde ②

12 rue Martignac 75007. **Map** 7 B3. 01 44 18 62 64. Solférino, Varenne, Invalides. **Open** 8am–7pm daily.

DESIGNED BY the German-born architect Franz Christian Gau and built in 1846–56, this Neo-Gothic church was inspired by the mid-19th-century enthusiasm for the Middle Ages, made fashionable by such writers as Victor Hugo. The church is noted for its imposing twin towers, clearly visible from across the Seine.

The interior decoration includes wall paintings by James Pradier and stained-glass windows with scenes relating to the patron saint of the church. The composer César Franck was organist here from 1858 to 1890.

Fontaine des Quatre Saisons ②

57–59 rue de Grenelle 75007. **Map** 7 C4. rue du Bac.

THE EMINENT sculptor Edmé Bouchardon was commissioned in 1739 to design an attractive and practical fountain to supply water to the wealthy who lived around the boulevard Raspail. It is decorated with large allegorical figures of the city of Paris and bas-reliefs of the four seasons.

In the house behind the fountain (No. 59) lived Alfred de Musset, the 19th-century novelist.

Rodin's *The Thinker* in museum garden

THE LEFT BANK

THE LEFT BANK has long been associated with poets, philosophers, artists and radical thinkers of all kinds. It still has its share of bohemian street life and pavement cafés, but the smart set has moved in, patronizing Yves St-Laurent and the exclusive interior design shops in rue Jacob.

The Latin Quarter is the ancient area lying between the Seine and Luxembourg Gardens, and is today filled with bookstores, art galleries and cafés. The boulevard St-Michel, bordering the Latin quarter and St-Germain-des-Prés, has slowly given way to commerce, and is full of

Clock in the Musée d'Orsay

fast-food places and cheap shops. The surrounding maze of narrow, cobbled streets has retained its character, with ethnic shops and avant-garde theaters dominated by the façade of the Sorbonne, France's first university, built in 1253.

Many Parisians dream of living near the Luxembourg Gardens, a quiet area with charming old streets, gateways and elaborate gardens full of paths, lawns and tree-lined avenues. Students come here to chat, and on warm days, old men still meet underneath the chestnut trees to play chess or the traditional French game of *boules*.

SIGHTS AT A GLANCE

GETTING THERE

This area is served by metro stations at St-Germain-des-Prés, St-Michel and St-Sulpice, among others, with RER stations at Musée d'Orsay and Luxembourg. Bus routes 24, 63 and 87 serve boulevard St-Germain; route 38 serves boulevard St-Michel.

KEY

▨	Street-by-Street map *pp114–15*
▨	Street-by-Street map *pp120–21*
▨	Street-by-Street map *pp122–3*
M	Metro station
RER	RER station
P	Parking
◻	Batobus boarding point

◁ **Jardin du Luxembourg with Panthéon**

Street-by-Street: St-Germain-des-Prés

Organ grinder in St-Germain

AFTER WORLD WAR II, St-Germain-des-Prés became synonymous with intellectual life centered on bars and cafés. Philosophers, writers, actors and musicians mingled in the cellar nightspots and brasseries, where existentialist philosophy co-existed with American jazz.

The area is now more upscale than in the heyday of Jean-Paul Sartre and Simone de Beauvoir, the enigmatic singer Juliette Greco and the New Wave filmmakers. However, the writers are still around, enjoying the pleasures of sitting in Les Deux Magots, Café de Flore and other haunts. The 17th-century buildings have survived, but signs of change are evident in the affluent shops dealing in antiques, books and fashion.

Les Deux Magots became a focus of bohemian and literary activity in the 1920s.

Café de Flore, the former favorite haunt of Jean-Paul Sartre, Simone de Beauvoir and other French intellectuals, still has a classic Art Deco interior.

Brasserie Lipp, decorated with colorful ceramics, is a renowned brasserie frequented by politicians.

RUE DU DRAGON

RUE DU SABOT

RUE DE RENNES

RUE BONAPARTE

BLVD ST

RUE DU FOUR

Metro St-Germain-des-Prés

★ **St-Germain-des-Prés**
The philosopher René Descartes is among the notables buried here in Paris's oldest church ❺

★ **Boulevard St-Germain**
Café terraces, boutiques, movies, restaurants and bookstores characterize the central section of the Left Bank's main street ❷

STAR SIGHTS

★ **St-Germain-des-Prés**

★ **Boulevard St-Germain**

★ **Musée Delacroix**

KEY

– – – Suggested route

LOCATOR MAP
See Street Finder maps 7, 8

TUILERIES
ILE DE LA CITE, MARAIS AND BEAUBOURG
Seine
INVALIDES
THE LEFT BANK

★ **Musée Delacroix**
The home of the Romantic painter Eugène Delacroix (1798–1863) is now a museum devoted to his art ❻

Palais Abbatial was the residence of abbots from 1586 till the 1789 Revolution.

Rue de Buci was for centuries an important street and the site of some Real Tennis courts. It now holds a lively market.

RUE MAZARINE

RUE DE BUCI

RUE DIDEROT LE BATEAU

GERMAIN

RUE DE SEINE

RUE DE L'ANCIENNE COMEDIE

RUE DE MONTFAUCON

RUE PELIBIEN

RUE MABILLON

CARREFOUR DE L'ODEON

Metro Odéon

M

Metro Mabillon

| 0 meters | 100 |
| 0 yards | 100 |

Musée d'Orsay ❶

See pp116–17.

Boulevard St-Germain ❷

75006, 75007. **Map** 8 D4.
Ⓜ Solférino, Rue du Bac, St-Germain-des-Prés, Mabillon, Odéon.

THE LEFT BANK'S most celebrated thoroughfare curves across three districts from the Ile St-Louis to the Pont de la Concorde. The architecture is homogeneous because the boulevard was another of Baron Haussmann's bold strokes of 19th-century urban planning, but it encompasses a wide range of different lifestyles, from bohemian to bourgeois.

Starting from the east, it passes Musée de Cluny and the Sorbonne. It is most lively from boulevard St-Michel to St-Germain-des-Prés, with its café culture.

Quai Voltaire ❸

75006, 75007. **Map** 8 D3.
Ⓜ Rue du Bac.

THE QUAI VOLTAIRE is now home to some of the most important antiques dealers in Paris. Many famous people have lived in the attractive 18th-century houses, among them Voltaire at No. 27 and Richard Wagner, Jean Sibelius and Oscar Wilde at No. 19.

VOLTAIRE
NE A PARIS
LE 21 NOVEMBRE 1694
EST MORT
DANS CETTE MAISON
LE 30 MAI 1778

Plaque marking the house in quai Voltaire where Voltaire died in 1778

Musée d'Orsay ❶

IN 1986, 47 YEARS AFTER it had closed as a mainline railroad station, Victor Laloux's superb turn-of-the-century building reopened as the Musée d'Orsay. Originally built as the Orléans railroad terminus in the heart of Paris, it narrowly avoided demolition in the 1970s. During its conversion to a museum, much of the original architecture was retained. The new museum presents the rich diversity of visual arts from 1848 to 1914 and explains the social, political and technological context in which they were created. Most of the exhibits are paintings and sculptures, but there are also displays of furniture, the decorative arts and the newspaper and motion picture industries.

Young Dancer of Fourteen (1881) by Edgar Dégas

The Gates of Hell (1880–1917)
Rodin included figures that he had already created, such as The Thinker *and* The Kiss, *in this famous gateway.*

Dancing at the Moulin de la Galette (1876)
To capture the light filtering through the trees, Renoir painted this colorful picture outdoors.

The Dance (1867–8)
Carpeaux's dynamic sculpture caused a scandal when it was first unveiled in 1869.

KEY TO FLOORPLAN

☐ Architecture & Decorative Arts	☐ Naturalism and Symbolism
☐ Sculpture	☐ Art Nouveau
☐ Painting before 1870	☐ Temporary exhibitions
☐ Impressionism	☐ Non-exhibition space
☐ Neo-Impressionism	

Doctor Paul Gachet *(1890)*
*This portrait by Van Gogh is
one of three and was painted
the same year the artist died.*

GALLERY GUIDE

*The ground floor has works
from the mid- to late 19th
century. The middle level
features Art Nouveau
decorative art and late
19th- to early 20th-
century paintings
and sculptures. The
upper level has
Impressionist and Neo-
Impressionist art.*

Upper
level

Middle level

Entrance

Ground floor

Shop entrance

VISITORS' CHECKLIST

1 rue de Bellechasse. **Map** 8 D2.
C *01 40 49 48 14.* **M** *Solférino.*
24, 68, 69, 84 to Quai A.
France; 73 to Rue Solférino; 63,
83, 84, 94 to Bd St-Germain.
RER *Musée d'Orsay.* **O** *Musée
d'Orsay.* **P** *Quai d'Anatole
France.* **Open** Jun–Sep: 9am–
6pm Tue–Sun (9:45pm Thu);
Oct–May: 10am–6pm Tue–Sat
(9:45pm Thu), 9am–6pm Sun.
Closed Jan 1, May 1, Dec 25.

EXPLORING THE MUSÉE D'ORSAY

Many of the paintings in
the Musée d'Orsay came
from the Louvre and the
Impressionist collection
once in the Jeu de Paume.
Paintings from before 1870
are on the ground floor,
presided over by Thomas
Couture's massive *Romans
of Decadence.* Neo-Classical
masterpieces, such as Ingres'
La Source, hang near
Romantic works such as
Delacroix's turbulent *Tiger
Hunt.* These exotic visions
contrast with Realist works
by Courbet and others and
early canvases by Degas
and Manet, including the
latter's famous *Olympia.*

The museum's central aisle
overflows with sculpture,
from Daumier's satirical busts
of members of parliament
to Carpeaux's exuberant
The Dance and Rodin's *The
Gates of Hell.* Decorative
arts and architecture are on
the middle level, where
there is also a display of Art
Nouveau – sinuous lines

**Blue Waterlilies (1919) by
Claude Monet**

characterize Lalique's
jewelry and glassware and
the designs of Hector
Guimard, who produced
the characteristic curved
entrances of the Paris metro.

Among the many high-
lights of the Impressionist
rooms on the upper level
are Monet's *Rouen Cathedral*
series *(see p257)* and Renoir's
joyful *Moulin de la Galette.*
The Post-Impressionist
collection includes the *Eglise
d'Auvers* by Van Gogh;
works by Cézanne; Seurat's
pointillist compositions such
as *Le Cirque;* Gauguin's
highly-colored Symbolist
works; Toulouse-Lautrec's
depictions
of Parisian
women and
nightlife; and
Rousseau's
charmingly
naive dream
world. Among
the highlights
of the post-
1900 display
is Matisse's
*Luxe, Calme
et Volupté.*

Le Déjeuner sur l'Herbe (1863) by Edouard Manet

The façade of the Ecole Nationale Supérieure des Beaux Arts

Ecole Nationale Supérieure des Beaux Arts ❹

14 rue Bonaparte 75006. **Map** 8 E3. 📞 01 47 03 52 15. Ⓜ St-Germain-des-Prés. **Open** for tours only: 2pm, 2:30pm, 3pm Mon. 🎥 by appt.

THE MAIN FRENCH school of fine arts has an enviable position at the corner of the rue Bonaparte and the riverside quai Malaquais. It is housed in several buildings, the most imposing being the 19th-century Palais des Etudes. A host of budding French and foreign painters and architects have crossed the large courtyard, which contains a 17th-century chapel, to study in the ateliers of the school. Young American architects, in particular, have come here to study over the past century.

St-Germain-des-Prés ❺

3 place St-Germain-des-Prés 75006. **Map** 8 E4. 📞 01 43 25 41 71. Ⓜ St-Germain-des-Prés. **Open** 7am–8pm daily.

THIS IS THE OLDEST CHURCH in Paris, originating in 542 as a basilica to house holy relics. It became an immensely powerful Benedictine abbey, rebuilt in the 11th century, but most of it was destroyed by fire in 1794. Major restoration took place in the 19th century. One of the three original towers survives, housing one of the oldest belfries in France. The interior of the church is an interesting mix of architectural styles, with 6th-century marble columns, Gothic vaulting and Romanesque arches. Famous tombs include that of 17th-century philosopher René Descartes.

Musée Eugène Delacroix ❻

6 rue de Fürstenberg 75006. **Map** 8 E4. 📞 01 44 41 86 50. Ⓜ St-Germain-des-Prés. **Open** 9:30am–5pm Wed–Mon. 🎥 📷 🛈

THE LEADING nonconformist Romantic painter Eugène Delacroix lived and worked here from 1857 till his death in 1863. Here, he painted *The Entombment of Christ* and *The Way to Calvary* (which now hang in the museum). He also created superb murals for the Chapel of the Holy Angels in the nearby St-Sulpice church.

The apartment and garden studio has a portrait of Georges Sand, Delacroix self-portraits and sketches. There are also temporary exhibitions.

Jacob Wrestling with the Angel by Delacroix, in St-Sulpice (*see p123*)

Rue de l'Odéon ❼

75006. **Map** 8 F5. Ⓜ Odéon.

OPENED IN 1779 to improve access to the Odéon theater, this was the first street in Paris to have pavements with gutters, and it still has many 18th-century houses.

Sylvia Beach's bookstore, the original Shakespeare & Company, stood at No. 12 from 1921 to 1940. It was a magnet for writers like James Joyce, Ezra Pound and Hemingway.

Musée de Cluny ❽

6 place Paul-Painlevé. **Map** 9 A5. 📞 01 53 73 78 00. Ⓜ Cluny, St-Michel, Odéon. Ⓡ St-Michel. **Open** 9:15am–5:45pm Wed–Mon. **Closed** Jan 1, Nov 1, Dec 25. 🎥 📷

THE MUSEUM, now officially known as the Musée National du Moyen Age – Thermes de Cluny, offers a unique combination of Gallo-

Stone heads of the Kings of Judah carved around 1220

St-Séverin ❾

1 rue-des-Prêtres-St-Séverin 75005. **Map** 9 A4. 📞 01 42 34 93 50. Ⓜ St-Michel. **Open** 11am–7:45pm Mon–Fri, 11am–8pm Sat, 9am–9pm Sun.

ST-SEVERIN, one of the most beautiful churches in Paris, is named after a 6th-century hermit. It is a perfect example of the Flamboyant Gothic style. Construction finished in the early 16th century and included a remarkable double aisle encircling the chancel. In the garden stands the church's medieval gable-roofed charnel house.

Gargoyles adorning the gables of the Flamboyant Gothic St-Séverin

The School woodcarving (English, early 16th century)

LADY WITH THE UNICORN TAPESTRIES

These six outstanding tapestries are fine examples of the *millefleurs* style. Developed in the 15th and early 16th centuries, the style is noted for its graceful depiction of animals and people and its fresh and harmonious colors.

The poetic elegance of a unicorn on the sixth tapestry

Roman ruins, incorporated into a medieval mansion, and one of the world's finest collections of medieval art and crafts. The museum's name came from the Abbot of Cluny in Burgundy, Pierre de Chalus, who bought the ruins in 1330. The present building was erected from 1485–98.

Among the star exhibits are the tapestries, remarkable for their quality, age and state of preservation. The highlight of the sculpture section is the Gallery of the Kings, while one of Cluny's most precious items, the Golden Rose of Basel from 1330, is found in the collection of jewelry and metalwork. Other parts of the collection include stained glass, woodcarvings, Books of Hours and enamelwork.

St-Julien-le-Pauvre ⑩

1 rue St-Julien-le-Pauvre 75005. **Map** 9 A4. 01 43 29 09 09. St-Michel. St-Michel. **Open** 10am–1:30pm, 3–7pm daily.

THE CHURCH is one of the oldest in Paris, dating from between 1165 and 1220. The university held its official meetings in the church until 1524, when a student protest created so much damage that university meetings were barred from the church by parliament. It has belonged to the Melchite sect of the Greek Orthodox Church since 1889 and is now the setting for classical and religious concerts.

La Sorbonne ⑪

47 rue des Ecoles 75005. **Map** 9 A5. 01 40 46 22 11. Cluny-La Sorbonne, Maubert-Mutualité. only by appt. Write to Service des Visites.

THE SORBONNE, seat of the University of Paris until 1969, was established in 1253 by Robert de Sorbon, confessor to Louis IX, for 16 poor scholars to study theology. From these modest origins, the college became the center of scholastic theology. In 1469, three printing machines were brought from Mainz, and the first printing house in France was founded. The college's opposition to liberal 18th-century philosophical ideas led to its suppression during the Revolution. It was re-established by Napoleon in 1806, and the 17th-century buildings replaced. In 1969, the Sorbonne split into 13 separate universities, but the building still holds some lectures.

ST-ETIENNE-DU-MONT

16th-century belfry tower

Rood screen

St-Etienne-du-Mont ⑫

Place Ste-Geneviève 75005. **Map** 13 A1. 01 43 54 11 79. Cardinal Lemoine. **Open** 8am–noon, 2–7pm Mon–Sat, 9am–noon, 3–7pm Sun. **Closed** public hols, Mon during Jul–Aug.

THIS REMARKABLE church houses the shrine of Saint Geneviève, patron saint of Paris, and the remains of the great literary figures Racine and Pascal. Some parts are Gothic while others date from the Renaissance, including the rood screen.

Medieval window

Street-by-Street: Latin Quarter

SINCE THE MIDDLE AGES, this riverside quarter has been dominated by the Sorbonne, and acquired its name from the early Latin-speaking students. It dates back to the Roman town across from the Ile de la Cité; at that time the rue St-Jacques was one of the main roads out of Paris. The area is generally associated with artists, intellectuals and a bohemian way of life; it also has a history of political unrest. In 1871, the place St-Michel became the center of the Paris Commune, and in May 1968 it was a site of student uprisings. Today, the eastern half has become sufficiently chic, however, to house members of the Establishment.

Latin jazz

★ **St-Séverin**
Begun in the 13th century, this church took three centuries to build and is a fine example of the Flamboyant Gothic style **9**

Metro St-Michel

Boulevard St-Michel, or Boul'Mich as it is affectionately known by locals, is a lively mélange of cafés, bookstores and clothes shops, with nightclubs and experimental cinemas nearby.

Metro Cluny La Sorbonne

0 meters   100
0 yards   100

★ **Musée de Cluny**
One of the finest collections of medieval art in the world is kept here in a superb late 15th-century building, incorporating the ruins of Gallo-Roman baths **8**

KEY

– – – Suggested route

LOCATOR MAP

See Street Finder maps 8, 9, 12, 13

★ **St-Julien-le-Pauvre**
Rebuilt in the 17th century, this church was used to store animal feed in the Revolution ⑩

Metro
Maubert
Mutualité

STAR SIGHTS

★ **Musée de Cluny**

★ **St-Séverin**

★ **St-Julien-le-Pauvre**

Panthéon ⑬

Place du Panthéon 7500. **Map** 13 A1.
C *01 44 32 18 00.* **M** *Maubert-Mutualité, Cardinal-Lemoine.* **Open** *Oct–Mar: 10am–6:15pm; Apr–Sep: 9:30am–6:30pm; daily.* **Closed** *Jan 1, May 1, Nov 11, Dec 25.*

W HEN LOUIS XV recovered from a desperate illness in 1744, he was so grateful to be alive that he conceived a magnificent church to honor Saint Geneviève, the patron saint of Paris. The French architect Jacques-Germain Soufflot, planned the church in Neo-Classical style. Work began in 1764 and was completed in 1790 under the control of Guillaume Rondelet,

The Panthéon Interior
The interior has four aisles arranged in the shape of a Greek cross, from the center of which the great dome rises.

ten years after Soufflot's death. But with the Revolution underway, the church was soon turned into a pantheon – a monument housing the tombs of France's great heroes. Napoleon returned it to the Church in 1806, but it was secularized and then desecularized once more before finally being made a civic building in 1885.

The façade, inspired by the Rome Pantheon, is decorated with a pediment relief by David d'Angers, depicting the mother country granting laurels to her great men. Among those resting here are Voltaire, Rousseau, and Zola. Also here are the ashes of Pierre and Marie Curie and André Malraux.

Iron-Framed Dome
The fresco in the dome's stone cupola represents the Glorification of Sainte Geneviève, *commissioned by Napoleon in 1811.*

The dome lantern

The dome galleries

Entrance

Crypt
Under the building, the vast crypt divides into galleries flanked by Doric columns. Many French notables rest here, including Voltaire and Emile Zola.

Street-by-Street: Luxembourg Quarter

Sᴉᴛᴜᴀᴛᴇᴅ ᴏɴʟʏ ᴀ ꜰᴇᴡ sᴛᴇᴘs from the bustle of St-Germain-des-Prés, this graceful and historic area offers a peaceful haven in the heart of a modern city. The Jardin du Luxembourg and Palais du Luxembourg dominate the surroundings. The gardens became fully open to the public in the 19th century under the ownership of the Comte de Provence (later to become Louis XVIII), when, for a small fee, visitors could come in and feast on fruit from the orchard. Today, the gardens, palace and old houses on the streets to the north remain unspoiled and attract many visitors.

To St-Germain-des-Prés

STAR SIGHTS

★ St-Sulpice

★ Palais du Luxembourg

Place St-Sulpice, ringed by flowering chestnut trees, was begun in 1754.

★ St-Sulpice
This huge Classical church, by six different architects, took over a century to build ⓯

RUE HENRI DE JOUVENEL / RUE FÉROU

RUE SERVANDONI

RUE GARANCIÈRE

RUE DE TOURNON

Jardin du Luxembourg is a popular garden where people come to relax, sunbathe, sail boats in the pond or admire the many beautiful statues erected in the 19th century.

RUE DE VAUGIRARD

0 meters	100
0 yards	100

★ Palais du Luxembourg
First built as a royal residence, the palace has been used for various purposes, from prison to Luftwaffe headquarters. This garden façade was added in 1841 ⓮

KEY

– – – Suggested route

LOCATOR MAP
See Street Finder maps 8, 12, 13

Fontaine de Médicis is a 17th-century fountain in the style of an Italian grotto. It is thought to have been designed by Salomon de Brosse.

Saint Geneviève, patron saint of Paris, whose prayers saved Paris from the Huns in AD 451, is honored by this statue by Michel-Louis Victor in 1845.

Palais du Luxembourg ⑭

15 rue de Vaugirard 75006. **Map** 8 E5. ⬛ *01 42 34 20 00.* Ⓜ *Odéon.* ⬛ *Luxembourg.* **Visits** organized first Sun of each month through the Caisse Nationale de Monuments. ⬛ *01 44 61 20 89. Apply in advance.* 🖼

NOW THE HOME of the French Senate, this palace was built to remind Marie de' Médici, widow of Henri IV, of her native Florence. By the time it was finished (1631), she had been banished from Paris, but it remained a royal palace until the Revolution. Since then the palace has been used briefly as a prison, and, in World War II, it served as headquarters for the German Luftwaffe.
    It was designed by Salomon de Brosse in the style of the Pitti Palace in Florence.

St-Sulpice ⑮

Place St-Sulpice 75006. **Map** 8 E5. ⬛ *01 46 33 21 78.* Ⓜ *St-Sulpice.* **Open** 8:30am–7:30pm daily. 📷

THIS HUGE and imposing church was started in 1646 and took more than a century to finish. The result is a simple façade with two tiers of elegant columns and two mismatched towers at the ends. Large arched windows fill the vast interior with light.
    In the side chapel to the right are murals by Eugène Delacroix, including *Jacob Wrestling with the Angel (see p118)* and *Heliodorus Driven from the Temple.*

The Classical two-story west front of St-Sulpice with its two towers

Carpeaux's fountain sculpture

Fontaine de l'Observatoire ⑯

Place Ernest Denis, avenue de l'Observatoire 7500. **Map** 12 E2. ⬛ *Port Royal.*

SITUATED AT THE southern tip of the Jardin du Luxembourg, this is one of the finest fountains in Paris. The central sculpture, by Jean-Baptiste Carpeaux, was erected in 1873. Made of bronze, it has four women holding aloft a globe representing four continents – the fifth, Oceania, was left out for reasons of symmetry. There are some subsidiary figures, including dolphins, horses and a turtle.

Val-de-Grâce ⑰

1 place Alphonse-Laveran 75005. **Map** 12 F2. ⬛ *01 40 51 51 92.* ⬛ *Port Royal.* **Open** noon–6pm Tue, Wed, Sat, Sun. 🖼

THIS IS ONE of the most beautiful churches in France, built for Anne of Austria (wife of Louis XIII) in gratitude for the birth of her son. Young Louis XIV himself laid the first stone in 1645.
    The church is noted for its lead-and-gilt dome. In the cupola is Pierre Mignard's enormous fresco, with over 200 triple-life-size figures. The six huge, twisted marble columns that frame the altar are similar to those made by Bernini for St. Peter's in Rome.

FARTHER AFIELD

MANY OF PARIS'S famous sights are slightly out of the city center. Montmartre, long a mecca for artists and writers, still retains much of its bohemian atmosphere, and Montparnasse is full of bustling cafés and theater crowds. The famous Cimetière du Père Lachaise numbers Chopin, Oscar Wilde and Jim Morrison among its dead, and, along with the parks and gardens, provides a tranquil escape from sightseeing. Modern architecture can be seen at Fondation Le Corbusier and La Défense, and there is a huge selection of museums to visit. To the northeast, the science museum at La Villette provides an educational family outing.

SIGHTS AT A GLANCE

Museums and Galleries
Musée de Cristal de Baccarat **9**
Musée Gustave Moreau **8**
Musée Marmottan **5**
Musée National d'Histoire Naturelle **23**
Museum National des Arts Africains et Océaniens **19**

Churches and Mosques
Mosquée de Paris/Institut musulman **26**
Sacré-Coeur **11**
St-Alexandre-Nevsky **6**

Parks and Gardens
Bois de Boulogne **2**
Jardin des Plantes **24**
Parc André Citroën **27**
Parc des Buttes-Chaumont **17**

Parc Monceau **7**
Parc Montsouris **22**

Modern Architecture
La Défense **1**
Fondation Le Corbusier **3**
Institut du Monde Arabe **25**

Historic Districts
Canal St-Martin **16**
Montmartre pp128–9 **10**
Montparnasse **28**

Cemeteries
Cimetière de Montmartre **13**
Cimetière du Montparnasse **29**
Cimetière du Père Lachaise **18**

Markets
Marché aux Puces de St-Ouen **14**

Historic Buildings and Streets
Bibliothèque Nationale de France **21**
Catacombes **30**
Château de Vincennes **20**
Moulin Rouge **12**
Rue La Fontaine **4**

Theme Parks
Cité des Sciences et de l'Industrie pp132–3 **15**

KEY

| | Main sightseeing area |

| ▬▬ | Major roads |

0 kilometers   4

0 miles   2

FARTHER AFIELD

◁ **The narrow rue St-Rustique winding up the hill to Sacré-Coeur**

West of the City

La Défense ❶

La Grande Arche. **(** 01 49 07 27 27. **RER** La Défense. **Open** 10am–6pm daily. 🖼 See **The History of France** pp62–3.

Tнıs sкʏscraper business city on the western edge of Paris is the largest office development in Europe. La Grande Arche is an enormous hollow cube large enough to contain Notre-Dame cathedral. Designed by Danish architect Otto von Spreckelsen in the late 1980s, the arch houses an exhibition gallery and a conference center, and offers a superb view over the city.

La Grande Arche in La Défense

Bois de Boulogne ❷

75016. **M** Porte Maillot, Porte Dauphine, Porte d'Auteuil, Sablons. **Open** 24 hrs daily. 🖼 to specialized gardens and museum. &

Located between the western edges of Paris and the Seine River, this 865-ha (2,137-acre) park offers a vast belt of greenery for strolling, cycling, riding, boating, picnicking or spending a day at the races. The Bois de Boulogne was once part of the immense Forêt du Rouvre. In the mid-19th century Napoleon III had the Bois designed and landscaped by Baron Haussmann along the lines of Hyde Park in London. Several self-contained parks within

the forest include the Pré Catelan and the Bagatelle gardens, with architectural follies and an 18th-century villa famous for its rose garden. The villa was built in just 64 days as the result of a bet between the Comte d'Artois and Marie Antoinette.

By day the Bois is busy with families, joggers and walkers, but after dark it is notoriously seedy – and best avoided.

Fondation Le Corbusier ❸

8–10 square du Docteur-Blanche 75016. **(** 01 42 88 41 53. **M** Jasmin. **Open** 10am–12:30pm, 1:30–6pm Mon–Fri. **Closed** public hols, Aug, Dec 24–Jan 2. 🖼

In a quiet corner of Auteuil stand the villas La Roche and Jeanneret, the first two Parisian houses built by the brilliant and influential 20th-century architect Charles-Edouard Jeanneret, better known as Le Corbusier. Built at the start of the 1920s, they demonstrate his revolutionary use of white concrete in Cubist forms. Rooms flow into each other, allowing maximum light and volume, and the houses stand on stilts with windows along their entire length. Villa La Roche was owned by the art patron Raoul La Roche. Today, both villas serve as a documentation center on Le Corbusier where lectures on his work are given.

An Art Nouveau window in the rue la Fontaine

Rue la Fontaine ❹

75016. **Map** 5 A4. **M** Michel-Ange Auteuil, Jasmin. **RER** Radio-France.

The rue la fontaine and surrounding streets act as a showcase for some of the most exciting early 20th-century, low-cost architecture, featuring sinuous decorative detail. At No. 14 stands the Castel Béranger, which firmly established the reputation of architect Hector Guimard. He went on to design the city's Art Nouveau metro entrances.

Musée Marmottan ❺

2 rue Louis Boilly 75016. **(** 01 44 96 50 33. **M** Muette. **Open** 10am–5pm Tue–Sun. **Closed** Jan 1, May 1, Dec 25. 🖼 &

The museum was created in the 19th-century mansion of the famous art historian Paul Marmottan in 1932. He bequeathed his house, plus his Renaissance, Consular and First Empire paintings and furniture, to the Institut de France.

In 1971 the museum acquired one of the world's most important collections of work by Impressionist painter Claude Monet, at the bequest of his son, Michel. Some of Monet's most famous paintings are here, including *Impression – Sunrise*

A landscaped island in the Bois de Boulogne

(from which came the term "Impressionist"), a painting of Rouen Cathedral *(see p257)* and several from the *Water-lilies* series *(see p94)*. Also on show is the body of work painted at Giverny during the last years of Monet's life. This includes paintings such as *The Japanese Bridge* and *The Weeping Willow*. The wild, expressive brushstrokes and iridescent colors make these some of the museum's most powerful works.

Part of Monet's personal art collection was passed on to the museum, including work by fellow Impressionists Camille Pissarro, Pierre-Auguste Renoir and Alfred Sisley. The museum also displays medieval illuminated manuscripts and 16th-century Burgundian tapestries.

Colonnade beside the *naumachia* basin in Parc Monceau

North of the City

St-Alexandre-Nevsky Cathedral

St-Alexandre-Nevsky ❻

12 rue Daru 75008. **Map** 2 F3.
🇨 01 42 27 37 34. Ⓜ *Courcelles, Ternes.* **Open** 3–5pm Tue, Fri, Sun.

THIS IMPOSING Russian Orthodox cathedral, with its five golden-copper domes, signals the presence of a large Russian community in Paris. Designed by members of the St. Petersburg Fine Arts Academy and financed jointly by Tsar Alexander II and the local Russian community, the cathedral was completed in 1861. Inside, a wall of icons divides the church in two.

The Greek-cross plan and the rich interior mosaics and frescoes are Neo-Byzantine in style, while the exterior and gilt domes are traditional Russian Orthodox in design.

Parc Monceau ❼

Bd de Courcelles 75017. **Map** 3 A3.
🇨 01 42 27 08 64. Ⓜ *Monceau.*
Open 7am–9pm daily (10pm summer).

THIS GREEN HAVEN dates back to 1778, when the Duc de Chartres commissioned the painter-writer and amateur landscape designer Louis Carmontelle to create a magnificent garden. The result was an exotic landscape full of architectural follies in the English and German style.

Over the years the land changed hands and in 1852 was acquired by the state and made into a chic public park. A few of the original features still remain. Among them is the *naumachia* basin – an ornamental version of a Roman pool used for simulating naval battles.

Musée Gustave Moreau ❽

14 rue de la Rochefoucauld 75009.
Map 4 E3. 🇨 01 48 74 38 50.
Ⓜ *Trinité.* **Open** 11am–5:15pm Mon & Wed, 10am–12:45pm, 2–5:15pm Thu–Sun. **Closed** some public hols. 🎟

THE SYMBOLIST painter Gustave Moreau (1826–98), known for his symbolic works depicting biblical and mythological fantasies, lived and worked in this handsome town house at the end of the 19th century. *Jupiter and Semele,* one of the artist's outstanding works, is displayed here, along with other major paintings and some of the 7,000 drawings and 1,000 oils and watercolors that Moreau bequeathed to the state.

Musée de Cristal de Baccarat ❾

30 bis rue de Paradis 75010.
🇨 01 47 70 64 30. Ⓜ *Château d'Eau, Poissonnières.* **Open** 10am–6pm Mon–Sat. **Closed** public hols. 🎟 📷 🎟 by appt.

THE RUE DE PARADIS has a number of glass and ceramics retailers, including the Baccarat company, founded in 1764 in Lorraine. The Musée de Cristal is beside the Baccarat showroom and displays over 1,200 articles made by the company. These include services created for the royal and imperial courts of Europe and many of the best pieces produced in the workshops.

Also on display are some of the techniques for shaping the crystal ware. These are as intricate as the finished work itself.

Le Vase d'Abyssinie, made of Baccarat crystal and bronze

Montmartre ⑩

Tʜᴇ sᴛᴇᴇᴘ *butte* (hill) of Montmartre has been associated with artists for 200 years. Théodore Géricault and Camille Corot came here at the start of the 19th century, and in the 20th century Maurice Utrillo immortalized the streets in his works. Today, street artists thrive predominantly on the tourist trade, but much of the area still preserves its villagey, sometimes seedy, prewar atmosphere. The name of the area is ascribed to martyrs tortured and killed in the area around AD 250, hence *mons martyrium*.

Streetside painter

Montmartre Vineyard
This is the last Parisian vineyard. The harvest is celebrated on the first Saturday in October.

Metro
Lamarck
Caulaincourt

Au Lapin Agile
"The Agile Rabbit," once a literary haunt, is now one of the city's best-known nightclubs.

A la Mère Catherine
This was a favorite restaurant of Russian cossacks. They would shout "Bistro!" (meaning "quick") – which gave the bistro its name.

Espace Montmartre Salvador Dalí
Some 330 works by the Surrealist painter and sculptor are on display here.

Place du Tertre
The tourist center of Montmartre is full of portraitists. Artists first exhibited in the square in the 19th century.

Kᴇʏ

— — — Suggested route

| 0 meters | 100 |
| 0 yards | 100 |

Musée de Montmartre
The work of many artists who lived in the area is displayed here: Portrait of a Woman *(1918) is by the Italian painter and sculptor Amedeo Modigliani.*

LOCATOR MAP
See Street Finder maps 3, 4

TUILERIES AND OPERA
BEAUBOURG

Sacré-Coeur
This Neo-Romanesque church, started in the 1870s and completed in 1914, contains many treasures, such as this figure of the Virgin Mary and Child *(1896) by P. Brunet* **⓫**

St-Pierre de Montmartre
This is an early Parisian church with origins dating back to the 6th century.

RUE DU MONT-CENIS
RUE DU CHEVALIER
RUE DU CARDINAL GUIBERT
RUE LAMARCK
RUE PAUL ALBERT
PL DU PARVIS DU SACRE COEUR
RUE AZAIS
RUE ST ELEUTHERE
RUE DU CARDINAL DUBOIS
GABRIELLE
RUE CH NODIER
RTHE
RUE CHAPE
SQ DE WILLETTE
PL ST-PIERRE
RUE TARDIEU
RUE STEINKERQUE

To metro Anvers

The funiculaire, or cable car, at the end of the rue Foyatier takes you to the foot of the basilica of the Sacré-Coeur. Metro tickets are valid for it.

Square Willette lies below the forecourt of the Sacré-Coeur. It is laid out on the side of the hill in a series of descending terraces with lawns, shrubs, trees and flower beds.

Musée d'Art Naïf Max Fourny
Almost 600 examples of naive art are housed here, including The Wall *(1944) by F. Tremblot.*

Sacré-Coeur ⓫

35 rue de Chevalier 75018. **Map 4 F1.** 01 53 41 89 00. **M** *Abbesses (then take the funiculaire to the steps of the Sacré-Coeur), Anvers, Barbès-Rochechouart, Château-Rouge, Lamarck-Caulaincourt.* 30, 54, 80, 85. **Basilica open** 6:45am–10:30pm daily. **Dome and crypt open** 9am–7pm daily (6pm winter). **for crypt and dome.** *restricted.*

THE SACRE-COEUR basilica, dedicated to the Sacred Heart of Christ, was built as a result of a private religious vow made at the outbreak of the Franco-Prussian war. Two businessmen, Alexandre Legentil and Rohault de Fleury, promised to finance the basilica should France be spared from assault. Despite the war and the Siege of Paris, invasion was averted and work began in 1875 to Paul Abadie's designs. The result has never been considered particularly graceful, but the basilica is vast and impressive, and is one of France's most important Roman Catholic buildings.

The stained glass gallery affords a view of the whole interior.

The ovoid dome is the second-highest point in Paris, after the Eiffel Tower.

The Great Mosaic of Christ (1912–22), by Luc Olivier Merson, dominates the chancel vault.

Bronze doors in the portico show the Last Supper and other biblical scenes.

The crypt vaults house a chapel containing Alexandre Legentil's heart in a stone urn.

Moulin Rouge ⓬

82 bd de Clichy 75018. **Map** 4 E1. 01 53 09 82 82. **M** *Blanche.* **Open** 9pm–1am daily. *See **Entertainment in Paris** p141.*

BUILT IN 1885, the Moulin Rouge was turned into a dance hall in 1900; only the red sails outside date from the original nightclub. Henri de Toulouse-Lautrec immortalized the wild cancan shows in his drawings, and the high-kicking routines continue today in glittering, Las Vegas-style revues.

Cimetière de Montmartre ⓭

20 avenue Rachel 75018. **Map** 4 D1. 01 43 87 64 24. **M** *Place de Clichy.* **Open** 8am–6pm Mon–Sat, 9am–6pm Sun.

THIS HAS been the resting place for many luminaries of the creative arts since the beginning of the 19th century.

The composers Hector Berlioz and Jacques Offenbach (who wrote the famous cancan tune), Russian dancer Waslaw Nijinsky, and film director François Truffaut are just a few of the famous people who have been buried here over the years.

There is also a Montmartre cemetery near square Roland-Dorgelès, known as the St-Vincent cemetery. This is where the French painter Maurice Utrillo is buried.

African stall in the Marché aux Puces de St-Ouen

Marché aux Puces de St-Ouen ⓮

Rue des Rosiers, St-Ouen 75018. **M** *Porte-de-Clignancourt.* **Open** 7am–6pm Sat–Mon. *See **Shops and Markets** p138.*

THIS IS THE OLDEST and largest of the Paris flea markets, covering 6 ha (15 acres) near the Porte de Clignancourt. In the 19th century, rag merchants and tramps would gather outside the fortifications that marked the city limits and offer their wares for sale. Today the area is divided into separate markets and is well-known for its heavy Second Empire furniture and ornaments. Although there are few bargains to be had, this does not deter the huge weekend crowds.

Cité des Sciences et de l'Industrie ⓯

See pp132–3.

Canal St-Martin ⑯

M *Jaurès, J Bonsergent, Goncourt.*

A WALK ALONG THE QUAYS on either side of the Canal St-Martin gives a glimpse of how this thriving, industrial, working-class area of the city looked at the end of the 19th century. The 5-km (3-mile) canal, opened in 1825, provided a shortcut for river traffic between loops of the Seine. A smattering of brick-and-iron factories and warehouses survive from this time along the Quai de Jemmapes. Here, too, you will find the legendary Hôtel du Nord, which featured in Marcel Carné's 1930s film of the same name. The canal itself is quietly busy with barges and anglers; around it the tree-lined quays, iron footbridges and public gardens are ideal for a leisurely stroll.

Boats moored at Port de l'Arsenal

Parc des Buttes-Chaumont ⑰

Rue Manin 75019 (access from Rue Armand Carrel). **C** *01 53 35 89 35.* M *Botzaris, Buttes-Chaumont.* **Open** *6:45am–9pm (11pm summer) daily.*

F OR MANY THIS is the most pleasant and unexpected park in Paris. Urban planner

Baron Haussmann converted the hilly site from a garbage dump and quarry with gallows at the foot, to English-style gardens in the 1860s. His partner on the project was landscape architect Adolphe Alphand, who became chief organizer of a vast 1860s program to provide the pavement-lined Parisian avenues with benches, streetlights, newspaper kiosks and urinals.

Others involved in the creation of this highly praised park were the engineer Darcel and the landscape gardener Barillet-Deschamps. They created a lake, made an island with real and artificial rocks, gave it a Roman-style temple and added a waterfall, streams, and footbridges leading to the island. Today, in summer, visitors will also find boating facilities, donkey rides and sun worshipers on the beautifully kept lawns.

East of the City

Cimetière du Père Lachaise ⑱

16 rue du Repos. **C** *01 43 70 70 33.* M *Père Lachaise, Alexandre Dumas.* **Open** *8am–5:30pm daily.*

P ARIS'S most prestigious cemetery is set on a wooded hill overlooking the city. The land was once owned by

Père de la Chaise, Louis XIV's confessor, but it was bought by order of Napoleon in 1803 to create a completely new cemetery. This became so popular with the Parisian bourgeoisie that the boundaries were extended six times during the 19th century. Here are buried celebrities such as

the writer Honoré de Balzac and the composer Frédéric Chopin and, more recently, the singer Jim Morrison and the actors Simone Signoret and Yves Montand.

Simone Signoret and Yves Montand

Oscar Wilde

The Columbarium

Marcel Proust

Allan Kardec

Edith Piaf

Victor Noir

Molière

Elizabeth Demidoff

Sarah Bernhardt

Théodore Géricault

Monument aux Morts

François Raspail

Frédéric Chopin

Main entrance

Jim Morrison

Cité des Sciences et de l'Industrie ⓯

THIS HUGELY popular science and technology museum occupies the largest of the old Villette slaughterhouses, which now form part of a massive urban park. Architect Adrien Fainsilber has created an imaginative interplay of light, vegetation, and water in the high-tech, five-story building, which soars 40 m (133 ft) high, stretching over 7 acres. At the museum's heart is the Explora exhibit, a fascinating guide to the worlds of science and technology. Visitors can play computerized games on space, the earth and ocean, computers, and sound. On other levels there are theaters, a science newsroom, a library, and shops.

Modern folly in the Parc de la Villette

★ Planetarium
In this 260-seat auditorium, special effects projectors and the latest sound systems create exciting images of the stars and planets.

Starball
The Planetarium's 10,000 lenses reproduce images of the sky as it is viewed by astronauts beyond the earth's atmosphere.

★ Ariane
Rocket displays explain how astronauts are sent into space and include an example of the European rocket Ariane.

Entrance from the west

370-seat auditorium

Hemispheric screen

Main lobby

LA GÉODE

This giant entertainment sphere houses a huge hemispherical movie screen, 1,000 sq m (11,000 sq ft), showing films on nature, travel, and space.

The moat was designed by Fainsilber so that natural light could penetrate into the lower levels of the building.

The main hall has a vast, cathedral-like atmosphere, with its soaring network of shafts, bridges, escalators and balconies.

STAR EXHIBITS

★ **Planetarium**

★ **Ariane**

★ **La Géode**

VISITORS' CHECKLIST

30 av Corentin-Cariou 75019.
📞 01 40 05 80 00. Ⓜ Porte de
la Villette. 🚌 150, 152, 250A to
Porte de la Villette. 🅿 on site.
Open 9am–6pm (7pm Sun)
Tue–Sun (last adm: 5:30pm). 🈵
♿ **Concerts. Films, videos.
Conference center. Library.**

Cupolas
*The two glazed domes,
17 m (56 ft) in diameter,
filter the flow of natural
light into the main hall.*

The greenhouses are
square hothouses, 32 m
(105 ft) high and wide,
linking the park to the
building.

Mirage Aircraft
*A full-size model of the
French-built jet fighter is one
of the exhibits illustrating
advances in technology.*

To La Géode

Walkways
*The walkways cross the
encircling moat to link the
various floors of the museum
to the Géode and the park.*

Children's Science City
*In this lively, extensive area, children can
experiment and play with machines that
show how scientific principles work.*

Bibliothèque Nationale de France

Museum National des Arts Africains et Océaniens ⑲

293 avenue Daumesnil 75012.
【 01 44 74 84 80. Ⓜ Porte Dorée.
Open 10am–5:30pm Wed–Mon,
12:30–6pm Sat, Sun. **Closed** May.1
🅥 ⅋ restricted.

THIS MUSEUM IS housed in
an Art Deco building de-
signed by architects Albert La-
prade and Léon Jaussely for
the city's grand colonial exhibition in 1931. Inside is a remarkable collection of African
and Australasian art, including
antelope masks from Mali,
Moroccan jewelry, Aborigine
bark paintings, and African
wood and copper figures on
the themes of life and death.

Château de Vincennes ⑳

Avenue de Paris 94300 Vincennes.
【 01 43 28 15 48. Ⓜ Château de
Vincennes. 🆁🅴🆁 Vincennes. **Open**
Oct–Mar: 10am–5pm daily (last
adm 4:15pm); Apr–Sep: 10am–6pm
daily. **Chapel open** 🅥 only.

THE CHATEAU de Vincennes
was the permanent royal
residence until the 17th century, before the court moved
to Versailles. The royal chambers and beautiful Gothic
chapel are all worth seeing;
so is the large, impressive
museum in the medieval keep.
Beyond the château moat is
the Bois de Vincennes. Once
a royal hunting ground, it is
now a landscaped forest with
lakes and cascades, and a zoo.

Bibliothèque Nationale de France ㉑

Quai François-Mauriac 75013.
🄵 01 53 79 59 59. Ⓜ Quai de la
Gare. **Open** 10am–8pm Tue–Sat,
noon–7pm Sun. **Closed** public hols
& 2 weeks mid-Sep. 🅥 ⅋

THESE FOUR great book-
shaped towers house ten
million volumes. The reference and research libraries, in
the central podium, offer over
400,000 titles. Other resources
include digitized illustrations,
sound archives, and CD-ROMs.

South of the City

Parc Montsouris ㉒

Bd Jourdan 75014. 【 01 45 88 28 60.
Ⓜ Porte d'Orléans. 🆁🅴🆁 Cité Univer-
sitaire. **Open** 7:30am–7pm daily.

THIS ENGLISH-STYLE park, the
second largest in Paris, was
laid out by the landscape architect Adolphe Alphand from
1865–1878. With its restaurant,
lawns, and lake – home to a
variety of birds – it is popular
with students and children.

Skull of the reptile dimetrodon

Musée National d'Histoire Naturelle ㉓

2 rue Buffon 75005. **Map** 14 D1. 【
01 40 79 30 00. Ⓜ Jussieu, Austerlitz.
Open 10am–5pm Wed–Mon. **Closed**
public hols. 🅥 ⅋ restricted.

THE NATURAL HISTORY Museum
is organized into four
departments, with a new
evolution gallery planned. The
paleontology section features
skeletons, casts of various
animals, and an exhibition
showing the evolution of the

vertebrate skeleton. Paleo-
botany is devoted to plant
fossils, and mineralogy to
rocks and gemstones. On
display in the entomology
department are some of the
world's oldest insect fossils.
The museum bookshop is
in the house where the
naturalist Buffon lived from
1772 until his death in 1788.

Jardin des Plantes ㉔

57 rue Cuvier 75005. **Map** 13 C1.
Ⓜ Jussieu, Austerlitz. **Open**
9am–6pm (5pm winter) daily.

THE BOTANICAL gardens were
established in 1626 when
Jean Hérouard and Guy de la
Brosse, Louis XIII's physicians,
obtained permission to found
a royal medicinal herb garden.
A school of botany, natural
history, and pharmacy followed, and the garden opened to
the public in 1640. One of the
city's great parks, it contains a
natural history museum,
botanical school, and zoo.
The park has an alpine
garden with plants from
Corsica, Morocco, the Alps,
and the Himalayas, and an
unrivaled display of herbaceous and wild plants, as
well as beautiful vistas and
walkways flanked by ancient
statues. The Cedar of Lebanon
here, originally from Britain's
Kew Gardens, was the first to
be planted in France.

Rue Mouffetard, one of several markets near Jardin des Plantes

Institut du Monde Arabe

1 rue des Fossés St-Bernard 75005.
Map 9 C5. **[** 01 40 51 38 38.
M Jussieu, Cardinal-Lemoine.
**Museum & temporary exhibitions
open** 10am–6pm Tue–Sun. **Library
open** 1–8pm Tue–Sat.

THIS MAGNIFICENT modern
building was designed by
French architect Jean Nouvel,
and cleverly combines high-
tech details with the spirit of
traditional Arab architecture.
   On the seventh floor there
is a comprehensive display
of Islamic works of art from
the 9th to the 19th centuries
including glassware, ceramics,
and sculpture. The highlight
of the museum is the fine
collection of *astrolabes*, the
much-prized tool used by the
ancient Arabic astronomers.

Mosquée de Paris/Institut musulman

Place du Puits de l'Ermite 75005.
[01 45 35 97 33. **M** Place
Monge. **Open** 9am–noon, 1–6pm
Sat–Thu. **Closed** Muslim hols.

BUILT IN THE 1920s in the
Hispano-Moorish style,
these buildings are the spiritual center for Paris's Muslim
community and the home of
the Grand Imam. Once used
solely by scholars, the mosque
has expanded over the years
and now houses the best Turkish baths in the city, a restaurant, and beautiful *salon de thé*.

Parc André Citroën

Rue Balard 75015. **M** Javel, Balard.
Open 7:30am– dusk Mon–Fri,
9am–dusk Sat, Sun & public hols.

DESIGNED BY both land-
scapers and architects, this
park is a fascinating blend of
styles, ranging from wildflower
meadow in the north to sophisticated monochrome mineral and sculpture gardens in
the southern section. Modern
water sculptures dot the park.

Institut du Monde Arabe, covered with photosensitive light screens

Tour Montparnasse

Montparnasse

75014 & 75015. **Map** 11 & 12.
M Vavin, Raspail, Edgar Quinet.

THE NAME Montparnasse
was first used ironically
in the 17th century, when art
students performed their work
on a "mount" of rubble left
over from quarrying.
In ancient Greece, Mount
Parnassus was dedicated to
poetry, music, and beauty.
By the 19th century, crowds
were drawn to the local
cabarets and bars by duty-
free prices. The mixture of
art and high living was particularly potent in the 1920s
and 1930s when Hemingway,
Picasso, Cocteau, Giacometti,
Matisse, and Modigliani were
"Montparnos," as the residents
were called. This epoch ended
with World War II. The modern *quartier* is dominated
by the much-hated Tour
Montparnasse, visible from
all over Paris, and vast office
developments.

Cimetière du Montparnasse

3 bd Edgar Quinet. **Map** 12 D3. **[** 01
44 10 86 50. **M** Edgar Quinet. **Open**
8am–6pm Mon–Fri, 8:30am–6pm Sat,
9am–6pm Sun (5:30pm in winter).

MONTPARNASSE cemetery
opened in 1824 and fast
became a chic burial place.
Among those buried here are
Serge Gainsbourg, Charles
Baudelaire, Left-Bank personalities Jean-Paul Sartre and
Simone de Beauvoir, and Guy
de Maupassant.

Catacombes

1 place Denfert-Rochereau 75014.
Map 12 E3. **[** 01 43 22 47 63.
M Denfert-Rochereau. **Open** 2–
4pm Tue–Fri, 9–11am, 2–4pm Sat
& Sun. **Closed** public hols.

A LONG SERIES of quarry
tunnels built in Roman
times, the catacombs are now
lined with ancient bones and
skulls. Thousands of rotting
corpses were transported
here in the 1780s to absorb
the excess from the unsanitary
Les Halles cemetery.

**Skulls and bones stored in the
catacombs**

SHOPS AND MARKETS

OR MANY PEOPLE, Paris epitomizes luxury and good living. Exquisitely dressed men and women sip wine by the banks of the Seine against the backdrop of splendid French architecture, or shop at small specialized stores. The least expensive way of joining the chic set is to create French style with accessories or costume jewelry. Alternatively, try shopping in the January or July sales. If your budget allows, take the opportunity to buy world-famous Parisian fashions, or feast on the wonderful gourmet delicacies, displayed with consummate artistry. Parisian shopping streets and markets are the ideal place to indulge in the French custom of strolling for the express purpose of seeing and being seen. For up-to-the-minute high fashion, the rue du Faubourg-St-Honoré is hard to beat, with its exquisite couture window displays. Browsing around the bookstands along the Seine is another favorite French pastime. A brief survey of some of the best and most famous places to shop follows.

Shopping in avenue de Montaigne

OPENING HOURS

SHOPS GENERALLY OPEN from 9:30am to 7pm, Monday to Saturday. Markets and local shops close on Mondays and some places also close for the month of August.

PAYMENT AND VAT

TRAVELER'S CHECKS, VISA, MasterCard and American Express are widely accepted. Prices will normally include sales tax (TVA), which varies from 5% to 25%. Non-EU residents are entitled to a refund, provided you spend at least F2,000 in one shop and are staying in France for under six months. Fill in a form (*bordereau de détaxe* or *bordereau de vente*) and give it to customs when you leave the country. For further information on how to pay for goods, *see pp620–21*.

WOMEN'S FASHIONS

PARIS IS THE HOME of haute couture. Original haute couture garments, as opposed to imitations and adaptations, are one-of-a-kind creations designed by the 23 couture houses listed with the Fédération Française de la Couture. The rules governing the classification "haute couture" are fairly strict, and many of the world's top designers, such as Claude Montana and Karl Lagerfeld, are not included on this prestigious list. Astronomical prices put haute couture beyond the reach of most pockets, yet it still remains the lifeblood and

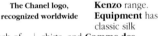

The Chanel logo, recognized worldwide

focus of the French fashion industry. Most couture houses are on or near rue du Faubourg-St-Honoré, including **Chanel**, **Christian Lacroix**, **Guy Laroche**, **Nina Ricci**, **Yves Saint Laurent** and **Christian Dior**.

Hermès has classic country chic, and no one can resist **MaxMara**'s Italian elegance or a **Giorgio Armani** suit. **Karl Lagerfeld** designs for Chanel and has created his own sleek line. If your wardrobe lacks color, try the exotic **Kenzo** range. **Equipment** has classic silk shirts, and **Comme des Garçons** has avant-garde, quirky clothes for both sexes.

THE CENTER OF PARIS COUTURE

The couture houses are concentrated on the Right Bank, around rue du Faubourg-St-Honoré and avenue Montaigne.

Yves Saint Laurent
Guy Laroche
Nina Ricci
Hermès
Givenchy
Christian Dior
Chanel

AVENUE GEORGE V · RUE FRANÇOIS · AVE DES CHAMPS ELYSÉES · ROND POINT · COURS ALBERT I · COURS LA REINE · RUE DU FAUBOURG · ST-HONORE · PLACE DE LA CONCORDE

For accessories to complete the look, **Cartier** and **Christian Lacroix** are hard to beat.

Nearby rue Jean-Jacques Rousseau is now a prime shopping area. The eccentric but celebrated designer **Jean-Paul Gaultier** has a shop at Les Halles shopping center, as does **Agnès B**, whose clothes combine the vary latest chic with comfort. There are also inexpensive outlets selling copies of new designs in the center. Rue des Rosiers in the Marais is full of new designers – try **Lolita Lempicka** or you may be tempted by the more daring **Azzedine Alaïa**.

La Samaritaine department store in Beaubourg and Les Halles

Kenzo designerwear in the place des Victoires

MEN'S CLOTHES

MEN DON'T HAVE the luxury of haute couture dressing; their choice is limited to ready-to-wear, but most of the big name womenswear designers also produce a line for men, although they tend to be rather expensive. A good example is **Gianni Versace**, with his classic Italian clothes for men.

On the Right Bank, the household name designers include the stylish **Giorgio Armani**, **Pierre Cardin**, **Yves Saint Laurent** and **Lanvin**, who is particularly popular for his beautifully made leather accessories. Across the Seine, **Francesco Smalto**'s elegant creations are bought by the likes of Jean-Paul Belmondo, and for those who are not afraid to make a bold fashion statement, there is **Yohji Yamamoto**.

DEPARTMENT STORES

IF TIME IS SHORT and you want to make all your purchases under one roof, try the *grands magasins* (department stores), all of which have restaurants as well. Most still operate a ticket system for selling goods. The assistant writes a ticket for goods from a single boutique, which you take to a cashier to be validated. You then return to the assistant to pick up your purchase. This can be time-consuming, so shop early in the day and avoid Saturdays. Be assertive, as the French don't pay attention to lines!

Au Printemps is huge, with separate buildings for menswear, household goods and women's and children's clothes. Fashion shows are held on Tuesdays at 10am (also on Fridays in summer). The beauty department, with a vast perfume selection, is definitely worth a visit.

Cartier, one of the world's most exclusive stores

Au Bon Marché, on the Left Bank, was the first department store in Paris and is the most chic, with a good food hall. **Galeries Lafayette** has a wide range of clothes at all price levels. Fashion shows are held at 11am on Wednesdays and also on Fridays in summer. **La Samaritaine** is one of the oldest shops in Paris, and full of bargains. It includes a sportswear shop and has good sales on household goods and furnishings. The store has a panoramic view of the Seine from the restaurant (closed in winter).

ART AND ANTIQUES

YOU CAN BUY art and antiques from shops and galleries of established reputations, or from flea markets and avant-garde galleries.

To avoid paying duty, you will need a certificate of authenticity when exporting *objets d'art* over 20 years old and any goods over a century old worth more than F1,000,000. Seek professional advice and declare the item at customs if in doubt.

Many of the prestigious antique shops and galleries are near the rue St-Honoré, including **Le Louvre des Antiquaires**, which comprises 250 different shops. On the Left Bank is the Carré Rive Gauche, an organization of 30 antiques dealers. Here, **Didier Aaron** is an international expert on the 17th and 18th centuries. Two galleries worth a visit are **Artcurial**, for books and prints, and **Lavignes-Bastille**.

CHILDREN

THE CITY has many appealing toy shops, including one of the world's most famous, **Au Nain Bleu**, situated in rue du Faubourg-St-Honoré. Unfortunately, the toys tend to be rather expensive, so a visit to the store is best kept as a special treat.

There is no shortage of children's fashion in Paris, in all styles and price ranges. A good place to start is the rue du Jour in Beaubourg and Les Halles, which has a number of children's boutiques. Many designers of adult clothes also have boutiques for children, including **Kenzo**, **Baby Dior** and **Agnès B**. Prices can be extremely high, though. Ready-to-wear chains such as **Bonpoint** sell chic, expensive, but well-made clothes, and the shops are also conveniently located. Perhaps not surprisingly, the best-selling children's garments at **Tartine et Chocolat** on rue du Faubourg-St-Honoré are overalls.

For little feet, **Froment-Leroyer** offers the best all-around classics.

Characters from the Tintin series, Au Nain Bleu toy shop

BOOKS, NEWSPAPERS AND MAGAZINES

ENGLISH AND AMERICAN publications are found at large magazine stands and some bookstores. If French is no obstacle, weeklies *Pariscope* and *L'Officiel des Spectacles* have comprehensive listings.

Two English-language newspapers are published in France: the *International Herald Tribune*, a daily, and *The European*, a weekly. The monthly *Boulevard* and the

Bookstall at Vanves market

bi-weekly *France–US Contacts* are both published in English.

Some large department stores have a book department, and there are many English-language bookstores such as **WH Smith**, **Brentano**, and **Village Voice**. **Gibert Joseph** is a French-language bookstore selling general and educational books, while **La Hune** specializes in art, design, cinema, fashion, and photography. **Tea and Tattered Pages** is a British secondhand bookstore.

Elegantly packaged produce from Fauchon

FOOD AND WINE

PARIS'S GASTRONOMIC treats include *foie gras*, *charcuterie*, cheese and wine. Some streets positively overflow with food shops – try rue Montorgueil or rue Rambuteau, which has a marvelous row of fishmongers, delicatessens and shops selling prepared food. Charcuteries such as **Fauchon**, in place Madeleine, and the basement of **Au Bon Marché** department store sell cheese, snails, truffles, caviar and regional produce. **L'établissement Poilâne** sells perhaps the only bread in Paris known by the name of its baker. Be prepared for big crowds on weekends and around 4pm when a fresh batch comes out of the oven.

Chocolate is another French obsession. **Christian Constant**'s low-sugar creations, well-known to connoisseurs, are made from pure cocoa. **Barthélemy** in the rue de Grenelle has exceptional Roquefort. **Caves Taillevent**, an enormous wine cellar with some of Paris's most expensive wine, is worth a tour.

MARKETS

THE FRENCH still shop daily, hence food markets are always packed. Most fruit and vegetable markets are open from around 8am to 1pm and from 4pm to 7pm Tuesday to Saturday, and 9am to 1pm Sunday. Watch out for rotten produce – buy products loose, not in boxes. A little language is useful for specifying *pas trop mûr* (not too ripe), or *pour manger ce soir* (to be eaten tonight). The newly renovated **Marché St-Germain** is a good bet for Italian, Mexican, Greek, Asian and organic produce. The **Rue Lepic** fruit and vegetable market, close to Montmartre, is at its most lively on weekends. The **Rue Poncelet** food market is worth a trip for its variety of bakeries, pâtisseries and charcuteries. **Rue de Seine** and **Rue de Buci** have florists and two excellent pâtisseries.

Paris's biggest and best-known flea market is the **Marché aux Puces de St-Ouen**. Divided into separate markets, it specializes in furniture, antiques, old jewelry and secondhand clothes. The smaller **Marché de la Porte de Vanves** has good-quality bric-a-brac – get there early for the best choice.

Lionel Poilâne's bread bearing his trademark – a square

DIRECTORY

WOMEN'S FASHION

Agnès B
6 rue de Jour 75001.
Map 9 A1.
01 45 08 56 56.

Azzedine Alaïa
7 rue de Moussy 75004.
Map 9 C3.
01 40 27 85 58.

Cartier
13 rue de la Paix 75002.
Map 4 D5.
01 42 61 58 56.

Chanel
42 av Montaigne 75008.
Map 3 A5.
01 47 20 84 45.

Christian Dior
30 av Montaigne 75008.
Map 6 F1.
01 40 73 54 44.

Christian Lacroix
29 av Montaigne 75008.
Map 3 B5.
01 42 68 69 50.

Comme des Garçons
40–42 rue Etienne-Marcel 75002.
Map 9 A1.
01 42 33 05 21.

Equipment
46 rue Etienne-Marcel 75002.
Map 9 A1.
01 40 26 17 84.

Giorgio Armani
6 pl Vendôme 75001.
Map 4 D5.
01 42 61 55 09.

Guy Laroche
30 rue du Faubourg-St-Honoré 75008.
Map 3 C5.
01 40 06 01 70.

Jean-Paul Gaultier
6 rue Vivienne 75002.
Map 8 F1.
01 42 86 05 05.

Hermès
24 rue du Faubourg-St-Honoré 75008.
Map 3 C5.
01 40 17 47 17.

Kenzo
3 pl des Victoires 75001.
Map 8 F1.
01 40 39 72 03.

Lolita Lempicka
3 bis rue des Rosiers 75004.
Map 9 C3.
01 48 87 09 67.

MaxMara
37 rue du Four 75006.
Map 8 D4.
01 43 29 91 10.

Nina Ricci
39 av Montaigne 75008.
Map 6 F1.
01 49 52 56 00.

Yves Saint Laurent
5 av Marceau 75016.
Map 6 E1.
01 44 31 64 00.

MEN'S CLOTHES

Francesco Smalto
44 rue François 1er 75008. **Map** 2 F5.
01 47 20 70 63.

Gianni Versace
62 rue du Faubourg-St-Honoré 75008. **Map** 3 C5.
01 47 42 88 02.

Lanvin
32 rue Marbeuf 75008.
Map 4 F5.
01 53 75 02 20.

Pierre Cardin
27 av Marigny 75008.
Map 3 B5.
01 42 66 64 74.

Yohji Yamamoto
3 rue de Grenelle 75006.
Map 8 D4.
01 45 44 29 32.

DEPARTMENT STORES

Au Bon Marché
22 rue de Sèvres 75007.
Map 7 C5.
01 44 39 80 00.

Au Printemps
64 bd Haussman 75009.
Map 4 D4.
01 42 82 50 00.

Galeries Lafayette
40 bd Haussmann 75009.
Map 4 E4.
01 42 82 34 56.

La Samaritaine
19 rue de la Monnaie 75001. **Map** 8 F2.
01 40 41 20 20.

ART AND ANTIQUES

Artcurial
9 av Matignon 75008.
Map 3 A5.
01 42 99 16 16.

Le Louvre des Antiquaires
2 pl du Palais-Royal 75001. **Map** 8 F2.
01 42 94 27 00.

Didier Aaron
118 rue du Faubourg-St-Honoré 75008. **Map** 3 C5.
01 47 42 47 34.

Lavignes-Bastille
27 rue de Charonne 75011. **Map** 10 F4.
01 47 00 88 18.

CHILDREN

Au Nain Bleu
406–410 rue St-Honoré 75008. Map 3 C5.
01 42 60 39 01.

Baby Dior
28 av Montaigne 75008.
Map 6 F1.
01 40 73 55 44.

Bonpoint
15 rue Royale 75008.
Map 3 C5.
01 47 42 52 63.

Froment-Leroyer
7 rue Vavin 75006.
Map 12 E1.
01 43 54 33 15.

Tartine et Chocolat
105 rue du Faubourg-St-Honoré 75008. **Map** 3 B5.
01 45 62 44 04.

BOOKS

Brentano
37 av de l'Opera 75002.
Map 4 E5.
01 42 61 52 50.

Gibert Joseph
26 bd St-Michel 75006.
Map 8 F5.
01 44 41 88 88.

La Hune
170 bd St-Germain 75006. **Map** 8 D4.
01 45 48 35 85.

Tea and Tattered Pages
24 rue Mayet 75006.
Map 11 B1.
01 40 65 94 35.

Village Voice
6 rue Princesse 75006.
Map 8 E1.
01 46 33 36 47.

WH Smith
248 rue de Rivoli 75001.
Map 7 C1.
01 44 77 88 99.

FOOD AND WINE

Barthélemy
51 rue de Grenelle 7007.
Map 8 D4.
01 45 48 56 75.

Caves Taillevent
199 rue du Faubourg-St-Honoré 75008. **Map** 2 F3.
01 45 61 14 09.

Christian Constant
37 rue d'Assas 75006.
Map 12 E1.
01 53 63 15 15.

L'établissement Poilâne
8 rue du Cherche-Midi 75006. **Map** 8 D4.
01 45 48 42 59.

Fauchon
26 pl de la Madeleine 75008. **Map** 3 C5.
01 47 42 60 11.

MARKETS

Marché St-Germain
Rue Mabillon and rue Lobineau 75005.
Map 8 E4.

Rue Lepic
75018. **Map** 4 F1.

Rue Poncelet
75017. **Map** 2 E3.

Marché de la Porte de Vanves
Av Georges-Lafenestre & av Marc-Sangnier 75014.

Marché aux Puces de St-Ouen
Rue des Rosiers, St-Ouen 75018.

Rue de Seine and Rue de Buci
75006. **Map** 8 E4.

ENTERTAINMENT IN PARIS

WHETHER YOUR preference is for classical drama, avant-garde theater, ballet, opera or jazz, movies or dancing the night away, Paris has it all. There is plenty of free entertainment, too, from the street performers outside the Pompidou Center to musicians found all over the city and in the metros.

Parisians themselves like nothing better than strolling along the boulevards or sitting at a sidewalk café

nursing a drink as they watch the world go by. If, however, you're looking for the ultimate "Gay Paree" experience, you can take in any of the celebrated nightclubs.

For fans of spectator sports there is tennis, the Tour de France or horse racing. Fitness centers and gyms cater to the more active. And for those disposed to more leisurely pursuits, there is always a game of lawn bowling (boules) to be played in the park.

The glass façade of the Bastille Opéra

BOOKING TICKETS

DEPENDING on the event, tickets can often be bought at the door, but for popular events it is wiser to purchase tickets in advance at the **FNAC** chain or **Virgin Megastore**. Theater box offices open daily from about 11am–7pm. Most accept credit card bookings by telephone. The **Kiosque Théâtre** sells leftover tickets for up to half the price the day of performance.

THEATER

FROM THE GRANDEUR of the Comédie Française to slapstick farce and avant-garde drama, theater is flourishing in Paris. Founded in 1680 by royal decree, the Comédie Française is the bastion of French theater, aiming to keep classical drama in the public eye and to perform works by the best modern playwrights. Formerly the second theater of the Comédie Française, the **Odéon Théâtre de l'Europe** now specializes in plays from

other countries, performed in their original language. In an underground auditorium in the Art Deco Palais de Chaillot, the **Théâtre National de Chaillot** stages lively productions of European classics. The **Théâtre National de la Colline** specializes in contemporary dramas.

Among the most important of the serious independents is the **Comédie des Champs-Elysées**, while for over 100 years, the **Palais Royal** has been the temple of risqué farce. The café theaters such as **Théâtre d'Edgar** and **Au Bec Fin** are good places for seeing new talent.

In the summer, street theater thrives in tourist areas such as the Pompidou Center, Les Halles and St-Germain-des-Prés. Outdoor performances of Shakespeare and classic French plays are given at the Shakespeare Garden in the Bois de Boulogne.

CLASSICAL MUSIC

THE MUSIC SCENE in Paris has never been so busy. There are many first-class venues with an excellent range of opera, classical and contemporary music productions.

Opened in 1989, the ultramodern 2,700-seat **Opéra de Paris Bastille** stages classic and modern operas. The showcase for productions from outside France is the **Opéra Comique**, which also specializes in operettas.

The **Salle Pleyel** is Paris's principal concert hall and home of the Orchestre de Paris. Both the **Théâtre des Champs-Elysées** and the **Auditorium du Châtelet** are recommended for their varied, high-quality events. The main venues for chamber music and recitals

LISTINGS MAGAZINES

Pariscope and *L'Officiel des Spectacles* are two of the best listings magazines in Paris. Published every Wednesday, you can pick them up at any newsstand. *Le Figaro* also has a good listings section on Wednesdays. *Boulevard* is published every 3 months in English, and is available at newsstands or W.H. Smith (*see p139*).

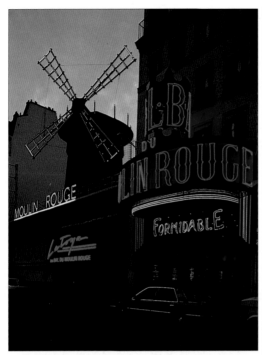

The famous silhouette of the Moulin Rouge nightclub

are the **Théâtre de la Ville** and the **Salle Gaveau**. Paris's newest spot is the **Cité de la Musique** in the Parc de la Villette. It is home to the renowned contemporary music group, the Ensemble InterContemporain, directed by Pierre Boulez.

DANCE

THE FRENCH are very vocal in their appreciation or dislike of dance, and those who fail to please are subjected to boos, hisses and mass walkouts in mid-performance.

The opulent **Opéra Garnier** has performance space for 450 artists and is home to the Ballet de l'Opéra de Paris, which has earned a reputation as one of the best classical ballet companies in the world. Government support has helped the **Théâtre de la Ville** to become Paris's most important venue for modern dance, with subsidies keeping ticket costs relatively low.

The **Maison des Arts de Créteil** stages famous overseas companies, as well as its own much-praised productions.

CLUBS AND CABARET

MUSIC IN PARIS CLUBS tends to follow the trends set in the US and Britain. Only a few clubs, such as **Balajo**, once frequented by Edith Piaf, and the ultra-hip **Folies Pigalle**, a former strip joint, are genuinely up-to-the-minute with their music.

La Locomotive attracts a mixed crowd to its three-level mainstream house nights. **Les Bains** is the old standby nightspot attracting fashion and show business people.

For a more Latin touch, try **La Java**. The dance floor of this club, where Edith Piaf once performed, now sways to Cuban and Brazilian sounds.

When it comes to picking a cabaret, the rule of thumb is simple: the better known places are best. The **Folies-Bergères** is the oldest music hall in Paris and probably the most famous in the world. It is closely rivaled by the **Lido** and the **Moulin Rouge**, birthplace of the cancan. **Paradis Latin** is the most "French" cabaret in the city. It presents variety acts whose sketches are enlivened by remarkable special effects and scenery.

ROCK, JAZZ AND WORLD MUSIC

THE TOP international acts are usually to be found at the enormous arenas such as **Palais Omnisports de Paris-Bercy** or the **Zénith**. For a more intimate atmosphere, the legendary **Olympia** has assigned seating and good acoustics. To hear indigenous rock groups like Les Negresses Vertes and Mano Negra, go to **La Cigale** or **Elysée-Montmartre** in the Pigalle area.

Jazz-crazy Paris has innumerable packed clubs where the best talent in the world can be heard on any evening. All the great jazz musicians have performed at **New Morning**, which also hosts African, Brazilian and other sounds. For Dixieland, go to **Le Petit Journal St-Michael**.

World music and jazz lovers alike can see leading acts and dance until dawn at the excellent **Chapelle des Lombards**.

La Locomotive, a huge disco on three levels

FILM

PARIS IS THE WORLD'S capital of film appreciation. It was the cradle of the cinematograph nearly 100 years ago. Then in the late 1950s and early 1960s, the city nurtured that very Parisian vanguard movement, the New Wave, when film directors such as François Truffaut and Jean-Luc Godard revolutionized the way films were made and perceived.

There are now more than 300 screens within the city limits, distributed among 100 theaters. Most are concentrated in movie belts, which enjoy the added appeal of nearby restaurants and shops. The Champs-Elysées has the densest movie theater strip in town, where you can see the latest Hollywood smash or French *auteur* triumph, as well as classic reissues.

In the vicinity of the Opéra de Paris Garnier, the movie theaters in the Grands Boulevards include two notable landmarks: the 2,800-seat **Le Grand Rex**, with its Baroque decor, and the **Max Linder Panorama**, which was completely refurbished in the 1980s. The place de Clichy is the last Parisian stronghold of Pathé, while the newest hub of Right Bank movies is in the Forum des Halles shopping mall. The largest screen in France, except for a special screen at **La Géode**, is the new **Gaumont** flagship in the place d'Italie district.

On the Left Bank, Odéon-St-Germain-des-Prés has taken over from the Latin Quarter as the city's heartland for art and repertory film theaters.

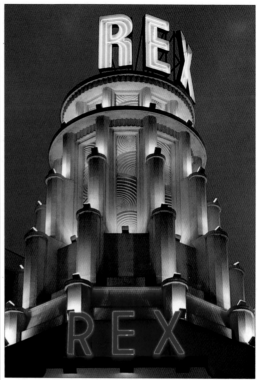

The dome of the 2,800-seat Le Grand Rex movie theater

SPORT

PARIS IS HOST to some of the foremost sporting events in the world. City-wide frenzy sweeps Paris when the Tour de France bicycle race finishes there in July. From late May to mid-June, Parisians live and breathe tennis during the **Roland Garros** national tennis championship. The Prix de l'Arc de Triomphe, held at the **Hippodrome de Longchamp** on the first Sunday in October, provides the opportunity to see the rich in all their finery as well as first-class flat horse-racing.

The **Palais Omnisports de Paris-Bercy** is the venue for a vast range of events, including the Paris tennis open, the six-day cycling race, showjumping, martial arts and rock concerts. **Parc des Princes** is home to Paris's top soccer team, Paris St-Germain.

THE CELEBRATED CAFÉS OF PARIS

One of the most enduring images of Paris is the Left Bank café scene, where great artists, writers and eminent intellectuals consorted. Before World War I, hordes of Russian revolutionaries, including Lenin and Trotsky, whiled away their days in the Rotonde and the Dôme in Montparnasse. In the 1920s, Surrealists dominated café life. Later came the American writers led by Ernest Hemingway and F. Scott Fitzgerald, whose haunts included La Coupole. After World War II, Jean-Paul Sartre and other Existentialists shifted the cultural scene northward to St-Germain.

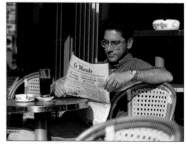

Newspaper reading remains a typical café pastime

DIRECTORY

BOOKING TICKETS

FNAC
26–30 av des Ternes
75017. **Map** 2 D3.
01 44 09 18 00.

Forum Les Halles, 1–7 rue
Pierre Lescot 75001.
Map 9 A2.
01 40 41 40 00.

Virgin Megastore
52–60 av des Champs-
Elysées 75008. **Map** 2 F5.
01 49 53 50 00.

Kiosque Théâtre
15 pl de la Madeleine
75008. **Map** 3 C5.

THEATER

Au Bec Fin
6 rue Thérèse 75001.
Map 8 E1.
01 42 96 29 35.

**Comédie des
Champs-Elysées**
15 av Montaigne 75008.
Map 6 F1.
01 53 23 99 19.

Comédie Française
Place Colette 75001.
Map 8 E1.
01 44 58 15 15.

**Odéon Théâtre de
l'Europe**
Pl de l'Odéon 75006.
Map 8 F5.
01 44 41 36 36.

Palais Royal
38 rue Montpensier
75001. **Map** 8 E1.
01 42 97 59 81.

Théâtre d'Edgar
58 bd Edgar-Quinet
75014.
Map 12 D2.
01 42 79 97 97.

**Théâtre National
de Chaillot**
1 pl du Trocadéro
75016.
Map 5 C2.
01 53 65 30 00.

**Théâtre National
de la Colline**
15 rue Malte-Brun
75020.
01 44 62 52 52.

CLASSICAL MUSIC

**Auditorium du
Châtelet**
(Auditorium des Halles)
Forum des Halles, Porte
St-Eustache.
Map 9 A2.
01 42 28 28 40.

Cité de la Musique
221 av Jean-Jaurès 75019.
01 44 84 44 84.

Opéra Comique
(Salle Favart) 5 rue Favart
75002. **Map** 4 F5.
01 42 44 45 46.

**Opéra de Paris
Bastille**
120 rue de Lyon 75012.
Map 10 E4.
08 36 69 78 68.

Salle Gaveau
45 rue la Boétie 75008.
Map 3 B4.
01 49 53 05 07.

Salle Pleyel
252 rue du Faubourg St-
Honoré 75008. **Map** 2 E3.
01 45 61 53 00.

**Théâtre des
Champs-Elysées**
15 av Montaigne 75008.
Map 6 F1.
01 49 52 50 50.

Théâtre de la Ville
2 pl du Châtelet 75004.
Map 9 A3.
01 42 74 22 77.

DANCE

**Maison des Arts de
Créteil**
Pl Salvador Allende 94000
Créteil.
01 45 13 19 19.

Opéra Garnier
Pl de l'Opera 75009.
Map 4 E5.
01 40 01 17 89.

Théâtre de la Ville
(See Classical Music.)

CLUBS AND
CABARET

Les Bains
7 rue du Bourg-L'Abbé
75003. **Map** 9 B1.
01 48 87 01 80.

Balajo
9 rue de Lappe 75011.
Map 10 E4.
01 47 00 07 87.

Folies-Bergères
32 rue Richer 75009.
01 44 79 98 98.

Folies Pigalle
11 pl Pigalle 75009.
Map 4 E2.
01 48 78 25 56.

La Java
105 rue du Faubourg-du-
Temple 75010.
01 42 02 20 52.

La Locomotive
90 bd de Clichy 75018.
Map 4 D1.
01 53 41 88 88.

Lido
116 bis av des Champs-
Elysées 75008. **Map** 2 E4.
01 40 76 56 10.

Moulin Rouge
82 bd de Clichy 75018.
Map 4 E1.
01 46 06 00 19.

Paradis Latin
28 rue du Cardinal-Lemoine
75005. **Map** 9 B5.
01 43 25 28 28.

ROCK, JAZZ AND
WORLD MUSIC

**Chapelle des
Lombards**
19 rue de Lappe 75011.
Map 10 F4.
01 43 57 24 24.

La Cigale
120 bd Rochechouart
75018. **Map** 4 F2.
01 42 23 15 15.

Elysée-Montmartre
72 bd Rochechouart
75018. **Map** 4 F2.
01 44 92 45 45.

New Morning
7–9 rue des Petites-Ecuries
75010.
01 45 23 51 41.

Olympia
28 bd des Capucines
75009. **Map** 4 D5.
01 47 42 25 49.

**Palais Omnisports
de Paris-Bercy**
8 bd de Bercy 75012.
Map 14 F2.
01 44 68 44 68.

**Le Petit Journal St-
Michel**
71 bd St-Michel
75005.**Map** 12 F1.
01 43 26 28 59.

Zénith
211 av de Jean-Jaurès
75019.
01 42 08 60 00.

FILM

Gaumont Gobelins
58 & 73 av des Gobelins
75013. **Map** 13 B4.
01 47 07 55 88.

La Géode
26 av Corentin-Cariou
75019.
01 40 05 80 00.

Le Grand Rex
1 bd Poissonnière
75002.
01 42 36 83 93.

**Max Linder
Panorama**
24 bd Poissonnière 75009.
01 48 24 88 88.

SPORT

**Hippodrome de
Longchamp**
Bois de Boulogne 75016.
01 44 30 75 00.

**Palais Omnisports
de Paris-Bercy**
(See Rock, Jazz and World
Music.)

Parc des Princes
24 rue du Commandant-
Guilbaud 75016.
01 42 88 02 76.

**Stade Roland
Garros**
2 av Gordon-Bennett
75016.
01 47 43 48 00.

PARIS STREET FINDER

THE MAP REFERENCES given for sights, shops and entertainment venues described in the Paris section of the guide refer to the maps on the following pages. Map references are also given for Paris hotels (see pp540–44) and restaurants (pp580–84), and for useful addresses in the Travelers' Needs and Survival Guide sections at the back of the book. The maps include not only the main sightseeing areas but also the most important districts for hotels, restaurants, shopping and entertainment venues. The key map below shows the area of Paris covered by the Street Finder, with the arrondissement numbers for the various districts. The symbols used for sights and other features on the Street Finder maps are listed opposite.

Paris is divided into 20 arrondissements, outlined in orange and numbered on this map.

| 0 kilometers | 1 |
| 0 miles | 0.5 |

KEY

-- Arrondissement boundary

How the Map References Work

The first figure tells you which *Street Finder* map to turn to.

Hôtel de Ville ⓾

4 place de l'Hôtel-de-Ville 75004.
Map 9 B3. 【 42 76 50 49.
Ⓜ *Hôtel-de-Ville.* **Open** 10:30am Mon
for tours in French, leaving from the
info office at 29 rue de Rivoli. **Closed**
public hols, official functions. ♿

The letter and number give the grid reference. Letters go across the map's top and bottom; numbers on its sides.

The map continues on page 13 of the *Street Finder.*

Key to Street Finder

	Major sight
	Other sight
	Other building
Ⓜ	Metro station
RER	RER station
	Bus terminus
	Riverboat boarding point
P	Parking
	Tourist information
	Hospital with emergency room
	Police station
	Church
	Synagogue
⊠	Post office
	Railroad line
	Autoroute
	One-way street
	Pedestrianized street
«130	House number (main street)

Scale of Map Pages

0 meters   200
                              1:12,000
0 yards   200

ILE DE FRANCE

SET AT THE HEART OF FRANCE, with Paris as its hub, Ile de France extends well beyond the densely populated suburbs of the city. Its rich countryside incorporates a historic royal region of monumental splendor central to *"la gloire de la France."*

The region became a favorite with French royalty after François I transformed Fontainebleau into a Renaissance palace in 1528. Louis XIV kept the Ile de France as the political axis of the country when he started building Versailles in 1661. This Classical château, created by the combined genius of Le Nôtre, Le Vau, Le Brun and Jules Hardouin-Mansart, is France's most visited sight. It stands as a monument to the power of the Sun King and is still used for state occasions. Rambouillet, closely linked with Louis XVI, is now the summer residence of the French president, while Malmaison was the favorite home of Empress Josephine. To the north, the Château d'Ecouen offers a showcase of Renaissance life, and to the south, Vaux-le-Vicomte boasts some of the loveliest formal gardens in France.

Nourished by the Seine and Marne rivers, the Ile de France is a patchwork of chalky plains, wheatfields and forests. The serene, poplar-lined avenues and rustic charm of the region have been an inspiration to painters such as Corot, Rousseau, Pissarro and Cézanne.

SIGHTS AT A GLANCE

Châteaux and Museums
Château de Dampierre **8**
Château de Fontainebleau **13**
Château de Malmaison **5**
Château de Rambouillet **9**
Château de Sceaux **7**
Château Vaux-le-Vicomte **11**
Château de Versailles **6**
Musée National de la
    Renaissance **2**

Towns
Provins **12**
St-Germain-en-Laye **4**

Abbeys and Churches
Abbaye de Royaumont **1**
Basilique St-Denis **3**

Theme Parks
Disneyland Paris **10**

KEY

☐ Greater Paris

☐ Central Paris

✈ International airport

▭ Highway

▭ Major road

▭ Minor road

0 kilometers   20

0 miles   10

ILE DE FRANCE

◁ **Magnificent formal gardens at the Château Vaux-le-Vicomte**

The vaulted Gothic refectory of Abbaye de Royaumont

Abbaye de Royaumont ❶

Fondation Royaumont, Asnières-sur-Oise, Val-d'Oise. **[** 01 30 35 59 00. **Open** daily. 📷 **&** restricted. 📷 call 01 30 35 59 91. **Concerts.**

SET AMONG WOODS "near water and far from man-kind," 30 km (20 miles) north of Paris, Royaumont is the finest Cistercian abbey in the Ile de France. Chosen for its remoteness, the abbey's stark stonework and simplicity of line reflect the austere teachings of St. Bernard. However, unlike his Burgundian abbeys, Royaumont was founded in 1228 by Louis IX and his mother, Blanche de Castille. "St. Louis" showered the abbey with riches and chose it as a royal burial site.

The abbey retained its royal links until the Revolution, when much of it was destroyed. It was then a cotton mill and orphanage until its revival as a cultural center. The original pillars still remain, along with a gravity-defying corner tower and the largest Cistercian cloisters in France, which enclose a charming Classical garden. The monastic quarters border one side of the cloisters.

The Château de Royaumont, erected as the abbot's palace on the eve of the Revolution, is set apart and resembles an Italianate villa. A stroll around the grounds will reveal the monks' workshops, woods, ponds and Cistercian canals.

The abbey is sometimes used for concerts: phone the Fondation Royaumont for details.

Musée National de la Renaissance ❷

Chateau d'Ecouen, Val-d'Oise. **[** 01 34 38 38 50. **Open** Wed–Mon. **Closed** Jan 1, May 1, Dec 25. 📷 **&**

THIS IMPOSING moated château is curiously adrift, halfway between St-Denis and Royaumont. Now a Renaissance museum, Ecouen's magnificent quadrilateral exterior provides an authentic setting for an impressive collection of paintings, tapestries, coffers, carved doors and staircases salvaged from other 16th-century châteaux.

Ecouen was built in 1538 for Anne de Montmorency, advisor to François I and commander in chief of his armies. As the second most powerful person in the kingdom, he employed Ecole de Fontainebleau artists and craftsmen to adorn his palace. Their influence is apparent in the ravishing painted fireplaces, depicting biblical and Classical themes in mysterious landscapes. The most striking room is the chapel, containing a minstrels' gallery and vaulted ceilings painted with the Montmorency coat of arms.

Upstairs, a long gallery contains one of the finest series of 16th-century tapestries in France. Equally compelling are the princely apartments, the Renaissance tiled floors, the library of illuminated manuscripts, a collection of vivid ceramics from Lyon, Nevers, Venice and Faenza and Iznik, and a display of early mathematical instruments and watches.

Since the ground floor is open in the morning and the second floor in the afternoon, lunching at Ecouen is advised.

Basilique St-Denis ❸

1 rue de la Légion d'Honneur, St-Denis. Seine-St-Denis. **Open** daily. **Closed** Jan 1, May 1, Nov 1 & 11, Dec 25. 📷 **&**

ACCORDING TO LEGEND, the decapitated St. Denis struggled here, clutching his head, and an abbey was erected to commemorate the martyred bishop. Following the burial of Dagobert I in the basilica in 638, a royal link with St-Denis began, which was to span 12 centuries. Most French kings were entombed in St-Denis, and all the queens of France were crowned here.

The elegant, early Gothic basilica rests on Carolingian and Romanesque crypts. Of the medieval effigies, the most impressive are of Charles V (1364) and a 12th-century likeness in enameled copper of Blanche de France with her dog.

The masklike serenity of these effigies is in sharp

Statue of Louis XVI at St-Denis

The west wing of Musée National de la Renaissance

The Renaissance tomb of Louis XII and Anne de Bretagne in St-Denis

contrast to the graphically realistic Renaissance portrayal of agony present in the grotesque mausoleum of Louis XII and Anne de Bretagne. Both are represented as naked figures in the tabernacle, their faces eerily captured at the moment of death. Above the mausoleum, effigies of the finely dressed royal couple contemplate their own nakedness. As a reflection of humanity in the face of death, the basilica's tombs have few rivals.

St-Germain-en-Laye ❹

Yvelines. 🚶 41,000. 🚇 🚌 🛈
Maison Claude Debussy, 38 rue au Pain. 📞 *01 34 51 05 12.*
🎪 *Tue, Fri & Sun.*

DOMINATING the place Général de Gaulle in this chic suburb is the legendary Château de St-Germain, birthplace of Louis XIV.

Louis VI built the original stronghold in 1122 but only the keep and St-Louis chapel remain. Under François I and Henri II, the medieval upper tiers were demolished, leaving a moated pentagon. Henri IV built the pavilion and terraces that run down to the Seine, and Louis XIV had Le Nôtre landscape the gardens before leaving for Versailles in 1682.

Today the château houses the **Musée des Antiquités Nationales**, which exhibits archaeological finds from prehistory to the Middle Ages. Created by Napoleon III, the collection includes a 22,000-year-old carved female, a megalithic tomb, a bronze helmet from the 3rd century BC and Celtic jewelry. The finest treasure is the Gallo-Roman mosaic pavement.

🏛 Musée des Antiquités Nationales

Château de St-Germain-en-Laye.
📞 *01 34 51 53 65.* **Open** *Wed–Mon.*
📷 ♿

Château de Malmaison ❺

Rueil-Malmaison, Hauts-de-Seine.
📞 *01 41 29 05 55.* **Open** *9:30am–12:30pm, 1:30–5:45pm Wed–Fri, 10am–6:30pm Sat & Sun (6pm in winter).* 📷 ♿ *restricted.*

SITUATED 15 km (9 miles) west of Paris, Richelieu's 17th-century estate is now best known for its Napoleonic associations. Bought by Josephine as a retreat from the formality of the Emperor's residences at the Tuileries and Fontainebleau, it still has charming rural grounds. While Josephine loved this country manor, Napoleon scorned the front entrance as fit only for servants. Instead, he had a curious drawbridge built at the back of the château.

The finest rooms are the frescoed and vaulted library, the canopied campaign room, and the sunny Salon de Musique, hung with paintings from Josephine's private collection. Contrast Napoleon's restrained yellow canopied bedroom with the bedchamber in which Josephine died. Many of the rooms overlook the romantic "English" gardens and the famous rose garden which was cultivated by Josephine after her divorce.

Memorabilia abound, from Imperial eagles to David's moody portrait of Napoleon, or Gérard's painting of the languid Josephine reclining on a chaise longue.

Château Bois Préau, set in the wooded grounds, houses a museum dedicated to Napoleon's exile and death.

Empress Josephine's bed at Château de Malmaison

Château de Versailles ⑥

THE PRESENT PALACE, started by Louis XIV in 1668, grew around Louis XIII's original hunting lodge. Architect Louis Le Vau built the first section, which expanded into an enlarged courtyard. From 1678, Jules Hardouin-Mansart added north and south wings and the Hall of Mirrors. He also designed the chapel, completed in 1710. The Opera House (L'Opéra) was added by Louis XV in 1770. André Le Nôtre enlarged the gardens and broke the monotony of the symmetrical layout with expanses of water and creative use of uneven ground. Opposite the château is the Musée des Carrosses, housing a collection of royal carriages.

Garden statue of a flautist

★ Formal Gardens
Geometric paths and shrubs are features of the gardens.

The Orangery was built beneath the Parterre du Midi to house exotic plants in winter.

Fountain of Latona
Four marble basins rise to Balthazar Marsy's statue of the goddess Latona.

Water Parterre

★ Château
Under Louis XIV, Versailles became the center of political power in France.

Dragon Fountain
The fountain's centerpiece is a winged monster.

The King's garden features a mirror pool in the 19th-century garden created by Louis XVIII.

Colonnade
Mansart designed this circle of marble arches in 1685.

VISITORS' CHECKLIST

Versailles, Yvelines. 01 30 84 74 00. 171 from Paris. RER Versailles Rive Gauche. Versailles Chantiers, Versailles Rive Droite. **Château open** Oct– Apr: 9am–5pm Tue–Sun; May– Sep: 9am–6pm Tue–Sun. **Grand Trianon & Petit Trianon open** Oct–Apr: 10am–noon, 2pm–5pm Tue–Fri, 10am–5pm Sat & Sun; May–Sep: 10am–6pm Tue–Sun (last adm: 30 mins before closing). **Musée des Carrosses open** summer: 12:30–6pm Sat & Sun; winter: 9:30am–12:30pm, 2–5pm Sat & Sun.

The Grand Canal was the setting for Louis XIV's boating parties.

Petit Trianon
Built in 1762 as a retreat for Louis XV, this small château became a favorite with Marie Antoinette.

Fountain of Neptune
Groups of sculptures spray spectacular jets of water in Le Nôtre's 17th-century garden.

★ **Grand Trianon**
Louis XIV built this small palace of stone and pink marble in 1687 to escape the rigors of court life, and to enjoy the company of Madame de Maintenon.

STAR FEATURES

★ **Château**

★ **Formal Gardens**

★ **Grand Trianon**

Inside the Château de Versailles

The SUMPTUOUS main apartments are on the first floor of this vast château complex. Around the Marble Courtyard are the private apartments of the king and queen. On the garden side are the state apartments where official court life took place. These were richly decorated by Charles Le Brun with colored marble, stone and wood carvings, murals, velvet, silver and gilded furniture. Beginning with the Salon d'Hercule, each state room is dedicated to an Olympian deity. The climax is the Hall of Mirrors, where 17 great mirrors face tall arched windows.

KEY TO FLOORPLAN

- South wing
- Coronation room
- Madame de Maintenon's apartments
- Queen's apartments and private suite
- State apartments
- King's apartments and private suite
- North wing
- Non-exhibition space

★ Queen's Bedroom
In this room the queens of France gave birth to the royal children in public view.

The Marble Courtyard is overlooked by a gilded balcony.

Entrance

The Salon du Sacre is adorned with huge paintings of Napoleon by Jacques-Louis David.

Entrance

★ Salon de Vénus
A statue of Louis XIV stands amid the rich marble decor of this room.

Stairs to ground floor reception area

★ Chapelle Royale
The chapel's first floor was reserved for the royal family and the ground floor for the court. The beautiful interior is decorated with Corinthian columns and white marble, gilding and Baroque murals.

STAR FEATURES

- **★ Chapelle Royale**
- **★ Salon de Vénus**
- **★ Hall of Mirrors**
- **★ Queen's Bedroom**

★ Hall of Mirrors
*Great state occasions were held in
this room stretching 70 m (233 ft)
along the west façade. Here, in
1919, the Treaty of Versailles was
ratified, ending World War I.*

Oeil-de-Boeuf

The King's Bedroom
is where Louis XIV
died in 1715.

**The Cabinet du
Conseil** was used by
the king to receive his
ministers and family.

Salon de la Guerre
*The room's theme of
war is reinforced by
Antoine Coysevox's
stuccoed relief of Louis
XIV riding to victory.*

**Louis XVI's
library** features
Neo-Classical
paneling and
the king's
terrestrial globe.

Salon d'Apollon
*Designed by Le Brun
and dedicated to the
god Apollo, this was
Louis XIV's throne
room. A copy of
Hyacinthe Rigaud's
famous portrait of
the king (1701)
hangs here.*

Salon d'Hercule

TIMELINE

1667 Grand Canal begun	*Louis XV*		**1793** Louis XVI and Marie Antoinette executed	**1833** Louis-Philippe turns the château into a museum
1668 Construction of new château by Le Vau	**1722** 12-year-old Louis XV occupies Versailles			

1650	1700	1750	1800	1850

1671 Interior decoration by Le Brun begun	**1715** Death of Louis XIV. Versailles abandoned by court	**1789** King and queen forced to leave Versailles for Paris		
1661 Louis XIV enlarges château	**1682** Louis XIV and Marie-Thérèse move to Versailles	**1774** Louis XVI and Marie Antoinette live at Versailles	**1919** Treaty of Versailles signed on June 28	

Château de Sceaux ❼

Sceaux, Hauts-de-Seine. 📞 01 46 61 06 71. **Open** Wed–Mon. **Closed** public hols.

THE PARC DE SCEAUX, bounded by elegant villas, is an appealing mixture of formal gardens, woods and water, featuring Classical gardens designed by Le Nôtre. The gardens use water to great effect, with tiered waterfalls and fountains presenting a moving staircase that cascades into an octagonal basin. This feeds into the Grand Canal and offers a poplar-lined view to the Pavillon de Hanovre. This elegant pavilion is one of several that adorn the park, which also contains Mansart's Classical Orangerie. Today this is the setting for exhibitions and, in summer, classical music concerts.

Built for Colbert in 1670, the original château was demolished and rebuilt in Louis XIII style in 1856. The stylish fake contains the Musée de l'Ile de France, which celebrates the landscapes, châteaux and history of the region through paintings, furniture, sculpture and ceramics.

Château de Dampierre ❽

Dampierre-en-Yvelines, Yvelines. 📞 01 30 52 53 24. **Open** Apr–mid-Oct: daily pm. restricted.

AFTER VERSAILLES and Rambouillet, Dampierre is the most celebrated château southwest of Paris. Built in

1675 for the Duc de Chevreuse, the exterior of the château is a harmonious composition of rose-colored brick and cool stone, designed by Hardouin-Mansart.

By contrast, the interior sumptuously evokes Versailles, particularly in the royal apartments and the Louis XIV dining room. The grandest room is the frescoed Salle des Fêtes, remodeled in the 19th century in triumphal Roman style. The rooms overlook gardens landscaped around a canal by Le Nôtre.

Château de Rambouillet

Château de Rambouillet ❾

Rambouillet, Yvelines. 📞 01 34 94 28 79. **Open** Wed–Mon. **Closed** Jan 1, May 1, Nov 1 & 11, Dec 25, and when president in residence.

THE CHATEAU borders the deep Forêt de Rambouillet, once the favorite royal hunting ground. This ivy-covered red-brick château, flanked by five stone towers, is curious rather than beautiful. Adopted as a feudal castle, country estate, royal palace and Imperial residence, it reflects a composite of French royal history. Since 1897, it has been the president's official summer residence.

Inside, oak-paneled rooms are adorned with Empire-style furnishings and Aubusson tapestries. The main façade overlooks Classical parterres. Nearby is the Queen's Dairy, given by Louis XVI to Marie Antoinette so that she could play milkmaid.

Environs
About 28 km (17 miles) north on the D11 is the **Château de Thoiry**, which has a large zoo of around 800 animals in its grounds and an innovative play area for children.

Disneyland Paris ❿

Marne-la-Vallée, Seine-et-Marne. 📞 01 60 30 60 30. **Open** daily. Marne-la-Valée-Chessy. TGV from Lille or Lyon. from Charles de Gaulle and Orly airports.

THE RESORT covers 600 ha (1,500 acres) of which the theme park covers 40 ha (99 acres). The park is divided into five themes: Frontierland, Adventureland, Main Street USA, Fantasyland and Discoveryland. Although themes rely heavily on Hollywood nostalgia, Disneyland Paris has tried to give this park a European touch. The resort's rides include Space Mountain which tests even the sturdiest of dispositions.

Minnie Mouse

Château Vaux-le-Vicomte ⓫

Maincy, Seine-et-Marne. 📞 01 64 14 41 90. **Open** mid-Mar–Nov 11: daily.

SET NORTH OF MELUN, not far from Fontainebleau, the château enjoys a peaceful rural location. Nicolas Fouquet, a

ANDRÉ LE NÔTRE

As the greatest French landscape gardener, Le Nôtre (1613–1700) created masterpieces in château gardens all over France. His Classical vision shaped many in the Ile de France, such as those at Dampierre, Sceaux and Vaux-le-Vicomte. At Vaux he perfected the concept of the *jardin à la française*: avenues framed by statues and box hedges; water gardens with fountains and ornate pools; graceful terraces and geometrical parterres "embroidered" with motifs. His genius lay in architectural orchestration and a sense of symmetry, typified by the sweeping vistas of Versailles, his greatest triumph.

Provins ⑫

Seine-et-Marne. 👥 *12,000.* 🚏 🚍
ℹ️ *Chemin de Villecran (01 64 60 26 26).* 🛒 *Sat.*

AS A ROMAN OUTPOST, Provins commanded the border of Ile de France and Champagne. Today, it offers a coherent vision of the medieval world. Ville Haute, the upper town, is clustered within high 12th-century ramparts, complete with crenelations and defensive ditches. The ramparts to the west are the best preserved. Here, between the fortified gateways of Porte de Jouy and Porte St-Jean, the fortifications are dotted with square, round and rectangular towers.

The town is dominated by Tour César, a keep with four corner turrets and a pyramid-shaped roof. The moat and fortifications were added by the English during the Hundred Years' War. A guard-room leads to a gallery and views over the place du Chatel, a dusty square of medieval gabled houses, and the Grange aux Dîmes to the endless wheatfields beyond.

Provins is proud of its crimson roses. Every June, a floral celebration is held in the riverside rose garden, marked by a medieval festival.

powerful court financier to Louis XIV, challenged the architect Le Vau and the decorator Le Brun to create the most sumptuous palace of the day. The result, one of the greatest 17th-century French châteaux, surpassed Fouquet's dreams. However, it also led to his downfall. Louis and his ministers were so enraged – because its luxury cast the royal palaces into the shade – that they arrested Fouquet and confiscated all his estates.

As befits Fouquet's grand tastes, the interior is a gilded banquet of frescoes, stucco, caryatids and giant busts. The Salon des Muses boasts Le Brun's magnificent frescoed ceiling of dancing nymphs and poetic sphinxes. La Grande Chambre Carrée is decorated in Louis XIII style with paneled walls and an impressive triumphal frieze, evoking Rome. Unlike Versailles or even Fontainebleau, its many rooms feel touchingly intimate and the scale is not overwhelming.

Yet Vaux-le-Vicomte's continuing fame is due to André Le Nôtre's stunning gardens, the finest in the Ile de France. The landscape designer's early training as a painter is evident in the magnificent succession of terraces, ornamental lakes and fountains, which descend to a formal canal.

Château Vaux-le-Vicomte seen across the gardens designed by Le Nôtre

Château de Fontainebleau ⓭

Ceiling detail from the Salle de Bal

FONTAINEBLEAU is not the product of a single vision, but a bewildering cluster of styles from different periods. Louis VII built an abbey here that was consecrated by Thomas à Beckett in 1169. A medieval tower survives, but the present château harks back to François I. Originally drawn by the local hunting, the Renaissance king created a decorative château modeled on Florentine and Roman styles.

Fontainebleau's abiding charm comes from its relative informality and spectacular forest setting. While impossible to cover in a day, the *grands appartements* provide a sumptuous introduction to this royal palace.

Ground floor

Jardin de Diane
Now more romantic than Classical, the garden features a bronze fountain of Diana as huntress.

★ Escalier du Fer-à-Cheval
This imposing horseshoe-shaped staircase by Jean Androuet du Cerceau, built in 1634, lies at the end of Cour du Cheval Blanc. Its ingenious design allowed carriages to pass beneath the two arches.

KEY TO FLOOR PLAN

☐ Petits Appartements

☐ Galerie des Cerfs

☐ Musée Chinois

☐ Musée Napoléon

☐ Grands Appartements

☐ Salle Renaissance

☐ Appartements de Madame de Maintenon

☐ Grands Appartements des Souverains

☐ Escalier de la Reine/ Appartements des Chasses

☐ Chapelle de la Trinité

☐ Appartement Intérieur de l'Empereur

Cour du Cheval Blanc was once a simple enclosed courtyard. It was transformed by Napoleon I into the main approach to the château.

Museum entrance

STAR FEATURES

★ **Escalier du Fer-à-Cheval**

★ **Salle de Bal**

★ **Galerie François I**

The Jardin Anglais is a romantic "English" garden, planted with cypress and plantain trees. It was re-designed in the 19th century.

Porte Dorée
Originally a feudal gate-house, this was transformed into the entrance pavilion to the forest by Gilles Le Breton for François I.

Cour Oval

First floor

VISITORS' CHECKLIST

Seine-et-Marne. **[** *01 60 71 50 70.* **Open** *9:30am–12:30pm, 2–5pm Wed–Mon.* **Closed** *Jan 1, May 1, Dec 25.*

★ **Salle de Bal**
The Renaissance ballroom, de-signed by Primaticcio (1552), was finished under Henri II. His emblems adorn the walnut cof-fered ceiling, forming a pattern reflected in the parquet floor.

The Appartements de Napol-eon I house his grandiose throne in the Emperor's Salle du Trône, formerly the Chambre du Roi.

Cour de la Fontaine

★ **Galerie François I**
This gilded gallery is a tribute to the Italian artists in the Ecole de Fontainebleau. Rosso Fiorentino's allegorical frescoes pay homage to the king's wish to create "a second Rome."

Chapelle de la Sainte Trinité was designed by Henri II in 1550. The chapel acquired its vaulted and frescoed ceiling under Henri IV and was completed by Louis XIII.

THE BARBIZON SCHOOL

Artists have been drawn to the glades of Fontainebleau since the 1840s, when a group of landscape painters, determined to paint only from nature, formed around Théodore Rousseau and Millet. They settled in the hamlet of Barbizon where, today, Rousseau's workshop is a museum dedicated to the Ecole de Barbizon.

Spring at Barbizon, **painted by Jean-François Millet (1814–75)**

NORTHEAST
FRANCE

Introducing Northeast France

THE FLAT, OPEN PLAINS of the Northeast are bordered by the Vosges Mountains and the forests of the Ardennes. Apart from the somber battle memorials, the area is best known for the fine wines of Champagne and Alsace, and for some of France's finest Gothic cathedrals. Its traditional coal, steel and textile industries have declined but wheat and wine production prosper, and the Channel Tunnel promises economic revival. This map shows some of the many interesting sights in the area.

Amiens Cathedral *is renowned for its fine wood carvings and its nave, the highest in France (see pp192–3).*

Amiens Cathedral

LE NORD AND PICARDY
(See pp182–95)

Beauvais Cathedral

Château de Compiègne

Reir Cathe

The pride of Beauvais *is its Gothic cathedral and astronomical clock (see p190), which escaped heavy bombing during World War II.*

Half-timbered houses *and Renaissance mansions line the streets and alleys of Troyes' Old Town (see p206), rebuilt after the great fire in 1524. Its cathedral has remarkable stained-glass windows.*

Troyes Cathedra

The legacy of World War I *is strong in this area of former battlefields. The Douaumont Memorial outside Verdun (see pp180–81), with its 15,000 graves, is only one of many memorials and cemeteries here.*

Haut-Koenigsbourg, *a castle rebuilt in Neo-Gothic style by Kaiser Wilhelm II when Alsace-Lorraine was under German rule, is one of Alsace's most popular attractions (see p218).*

Strasbourg*, seat of the European Council, has a fine Gothic cathedral (see pp220–21) surrounded by delightful historic buildings.*

Douaumont Memorial

Porte Chaussée, Verdun

Place Stanislas, Nancy

Strasbourg Cathedral

CHAMPAGNE
(See pp196–207)

ALSACE AND LORRAINE
(See pp208–23)

Haut-Koenigsbourg

0 kilometers   50

0 miles   50

Regional Food: Northeast France

Visitors to Boulogne, Le Touquet and Calais know the northeast best for its sea catch. Besides heaped platters of *fruits de mer*, a plate of steamed mussels and french fries is one of the pleasures of this coast. A giant waffle dusted with sugar completes the meal.

Hops, used to make the local beer, grow inland, along with fields of chicory. Both hops and chicory are served as vegetables. Alsace and Lorraine share in the tradition of beer-making – beer is commonly used in cooking in Lorraine, while Riesling wine is more popular in Alsace. Alsatian cooking centers around *charcuterie* (cooked meats), culminating in the classic *choucroute garnie* (sauerkraut with pork and sausages).

Rich cakes and tarts are also popular, especially the *kougelhopf*, a ring-shaped cake studded with raisins, currants and almonds, and sometimes soaked in Kirsch.

Potato salad with sausage *reveals the German influence in robust Alsatian fare. This dish is usually served warm.*

Herrings, *found along the northeast coast of France, are popular grilled or cured, and served with potatoes.*

Brioche *is a buttery, egg-enriched bread. In Alsace, various brioches are associated with festivals –* neujohweka *are eaten on New Year's Day, and on St. Nicholas Day (Dec 6) bakers make small brioche figures called* bonshommes.

Bacon

Frankfurter

Pâté en croûte *is cooked in a pastry case. The pastry keeps the pâté moist and faintly pink while it is baked in the oven.*

Sauerkraut

Boiled potatoes

Pork belly

Choucroute garnie *is an earthy dish of sauerkraut with bacon, cured pork loin or knuckle, and fresh and smoked sausages – among them* boudin noir *(black pudding),* saucisse de Strasbourg *(a plump frankfurter) and* boudin blanc *(white pork sausage). It should be accompanied by boiled potatoes and strong* moutarde de Meaux, *along with a glass of chilled Alsatian Riesling wine.*

Pea soup, *also known as* Potage St-Germain, *is made with fresh peas, which abound in the market gardens of Amiens.*

Truite Ardennaise, *pan-fried trout with smoked ham and cream, is an old-time classic from the Ardennes region.*

Zewelwai *or onion quiche is a tart made with a filling of onions, eggs and cream, typical of Lorraine.*

Porc aux deux pommes *is the quintessential Alsatian dish, consisting of pork served with potatoes and apples.*

Ardennes ham, *cured in the traditional local method, takes its name from the area. It is then salted and cold-smoked.*

Carbonnade *is a beef stew braised in beer; the name derives from "carbon," when the meat was grilled over coals.*

Tarte Alsacienne *is a fruit- and custard-filled tart, often made with yeasted dough instead of shortbread pastry.*

Madeleines *are tea cakes made famous by Marcel Proust in* Remembrance of Things Past.

Rum babas *are rum and sugar syrup-soaked yeast pastries baked in individual molds.*

Macaroons *are almond meringue biscuits, a specialty of Nancy, capital of Lorraine.*

Brie de Meaux

Munster

Coulommiers

DRINKS

Beer is often drunk with meals in the northeast. Traditional methods of beer-making are still followed by big breweries such as Kronenbourg, as well as many smaller breweries.

Savenne   **Kronenbourg**   **Bière de Garde**

CHEESES

In addition to the familiar Brie de Meaux and tangy Munster of Alsace, the northeast has many lesser known but equally flavorful cheeses such as the pungent Maroilles, Vieux Lille, Boulette d'Avesnes, Dauphin, Rollot and Coulommiers.

France's Wine Regions: Champagne

Giant carved barrel, Épernay

Since its fabled "invention" by the monk Dom Pérignon in the 17th century, no other wine has rivaled champagne as the symbol of luxury and celebration. Most champagne is non-vintage: the skill of the blenders *(see p200)*, using reserves of older wines, creates consistent excellence year after year. The "big names" *(grandes marques)* command the prestige and the prices here; however, many small growers and cooperatives also produce excellent-value wines. Along with vintage champagnes, made only in the best years, they are well worth seeking out.

LOCATOR MAP

◻ *Champagne wine region*

Grapes going for pressing, Montagne de Reims

WINE REGIONS

Champagne is a compact wine region, largely in the French *département* of the Marne. Certain areas within it are particularly identified with certain styles of wine. The Aube is famous not only for champagne but also for pricey and eccentric still wine, Rosé des Riceys.

[Map of Champagne region showing: Soissons, Château Thierry, La Ferté-sous-Jouarre, Nogent-sur-Seine, Petit Morin, Grand Morin, with roads N3, A4, D1, RD33]

KEY FACTS ABOUT CHAMPAGNE

 Location and Climate
The cool, marginal climate creates the quality that other sparkling wines strive for, but seldom achieve. Chalky soils and east- and north-facing aspects help produce the relatively high acidity champagne needs.

Grape Varieties
Three varieties are grown, red **Pinot Noir** and **Pinot Meunier**, and white **Chardonnay**. Most champagne is a blend of all three, though Blanc de Blancs is 100 per cent Chardonnay and Blanc de Noirs, although white, is made only from red grapes.

 Good Producers
Grandes Marques: Bollinger, Krug, Louis Roederer, Pol Roger, Deutz, Billecart-Salmon, Veuve Clicquot, Charles Heidsieck, Taittinger, Ruinart, Laurent Perrier.
Négociants, cooperatives and growers: A. Bonnet, Boizel, Bricout, Drappier, Ployez-Jacquemart, Union Champagne, Cattier, Gimmonet, Andre Jacquart, Jacques Selosses, Chartogne-Taillet, Alfred Gratien, Emile Hamm, Albert Beerens, Vilmart.

Good Vintages
1996, 1990, 1989, 1988, 1985, 1983.

BOLLINGER *Special Cuvée* BRUT *Champagne* *Ay France*

From a name *famous even to nonwine lovers, this is in the classic* brut *(dry) style; only* brut non dosage *or* brut sauvage *is drier.*

KEY

◻	Champagne *appellation* area
◻	Vallée de la Marne district
◻	Montagne de Reims district
◻	Côte de Sézanne district
◻	Côte des Blancs district
◻	Aube district

0 kilometers   15

0 miles   15

Champagne Charlie
*was immortalized in
a British music-hall
song as a high-living,
devil-may-care figure.*

Meticulously laid out vineyards of a champagne château

Pink champagne, *often with
hints of soft fruit flavors,
makes perfect summer
drinking; it normally gains
its color from the blending of
red and white wines.*

BRUT ROSÉ
Billecart-Salmon
Mareuil sur Aÿ
Champagne

CHAMPAGNE DEUTZ
Maison Deutz et Geldermann
FONDÉE EN 1838
BLANC DE BLANCS 1982   AY-CHAMPAGNE
PRODUCE OF FRANCE

From the respected
*house of Deutz, this vin-
tage Blanc de Blancs is
champagne in a lighter
style, from a year in
which the Chardonnay
ripened to perfection.*

Champagne blender

CHAMPAGNE
Canard-Duchêne
DEMI-SEC

For those who *prefer
a less dry champagne,
a demi-sec, like this
wine from Canard-
Duchêne, makes the
ideal choice.*

Map labels

Vesle
Ardre
Vesle
REIMS
N51
N44
Verzenay • • Beaumont-sur-Vesle
Verzy
Bouzy
Marne
Aÿ-Champagne
Épernay • Chouilly
Cramant • • Avize
Oger • Le Mesnil-sur-Oger
Vertus •
• Bergères-lès-Vertus
RD33
N51
N77
RD77
Ste-Menehould •
A4
Châlons-en-Champagne
N44
Vitry-le-François •
N4   N4
ézanne
N77
Aube
Arcis-sur-Aube •
RD396
• Romilly-sur-Seine
Seine
Brienne-le-Château •
TROYES
N19
• Bar-sur-Aube
N77   N71   Bar-sur-Seine •
Aube
Les Riceys •   Seine

The Battle of the Somme

THE MANY CEMETERIES that cover the Somme region serve as poignant reminders of the mass slaughter that took place on the Western Front in World War I (which ended with the Armistice on November 11, 1918). Between July 1 and November 21, 1916, the Allied forces lost more than 600,000 men and the Germans at least 465,000. The Battle of the Somme, a series of campaigns conducted by British and French armies against fortified positions held by the Germans, relieved the hard-pressed French at Verdun; but hopes of a breakthrough never materialized, and the Allies only managed to advance 16 km (10 miles).

British World War I soldier

LOCATOR MAP

☐ *Somme battlefield*

Beaumont Hamel Memorial Park, a tribute to the Royal Newfoundland Regiment, features a huge bronze caribou.

Thiepval Memorial was designed by Sir Edwin Lutyens. It dominates the landscape of Thiepval, one of the most hard-fought areas of the battle, appropriately chosen as a memorial to the 73,412 British soldiers with no known grave.

Albert was the site of heavy bombardment by German artillery in 1916. Today, the town is a convenient center for visiting the battlefields. The Albert Basilique, with its leaning Virgin statue, was damaged but is now restored. It was a landmark for thousands of troops.

Lochnager Mine Crater, formed by the largest of the British mines exploded on July 1, 1916, lies on the ridge by La Boiselle.

The British Tank Memorial, on the main road from Albert to Bapaume, commemorates the first use of tanks in warfare on September 15, 1916. The attack was a limited success; World War I tanks were too slow and unreliable to transform warfare and it continued to be fought mainly by heavy artillery and machine guns.

Propaganda in World War I was employed by both sides to maintain support at home. This French postcard has an especially popular image. It shows a dying soldier kissing the flag, under the tender gaze of a ministering nurse, affirming his faith in the cause as he breathes his last breath.

Delville Wood South African Memorial and Museum show the importance of Commonwealth forces in the Somme.

VISITORS' CHECKLIST

D929, D938 from Albert. ℹ️ *9 rue Gambetta, Albert.* 📞 *03 22 75 16 42.* **Albert Basilique, Beaumont Hamel Memorial Park, Thiepval, La Boiselle, Delville Wood and Pozières memorials open** *daily.* **Ulster Tower open** *May–Sep (by appt).* **South African Memorial Museum**, Delville Wood, Longueval. 📞 *03 22 85 02 17.* **Open** *Feb–mid-Dec: Tue–Sun.* **Closed** *public hols.* ♿ **Historial de Péronne** 📞 *03 22 83 14 18.* **Open** *May–Sep: daily; Oct–Apr: Tue–Sun.* **Closed** *mid-Dec–mid-Jan.* 📷 ♿ 📹

Poppies were one of the few plants to grow on the battlefield. Ghengis Khan brought the first white poppy from China and, according to legend, it turned red after battle. Today poppies are a symbol of remembrance.

KEY

☐ Allied forces

☐ German forces

☐ Front Line before July 1, 1916

☐ Front Line progress July–September 1916

☐ Front Line progress September–November 1916

0 kilometers   5

0 miles   5

Bapaume

Flers

Morval

Ginchy

Maurepas

aricourt

Péronne

The Front Line trenches stretched from the North Sea to the Swiss frontier; only by keeping underground could men survive the terrible conditions. Trenches remain in a few areas, including the Beaumont Hamel Park.

LE NORD
AND PICARDY

···

PAS DE CALAIS · NORD · SOMME · OISE · AISNE

BENEATH THE MODERN SKIN *of France's northernmost region, the sights and monuments bear witness to the triumphs and turbulence of its past: soaring Gothic cathedrals, stately châteaux along the Oise River and the battlefields and memorials of World War I.*

The Channel ports of Dunkerque, Calais and Boulogne and the refined resort of Le Touquet are the focal points along a busy coastline that stretches from the Somme estuary to the Belgian frontier. Boulogne has a genuine maritime flavor, and the white cliffs running from here to Calais provide the most dramatic scenery along the Côte d'Opale.

Flemish culture holds sway along the border with Belgium: an unfamiliar France of windmills and canals where the local taste is for beer, savory stews and festivals with gallivanting giants. Lille is the dominant city here, a sprawling modern metropolis with a lively historic heart and an excellent art museum. To the southwest, the grace of Flemish architecture is handsomely displayed in the central squares of Arras, the capital of Artois.

From here to the Somme Valley, the legacy of World War I, with its memorial cemeteries and poppy-strewn battlefields, makes for compelling viewing.

Cathedrals are the main appeal of Picardy. In Amiens, its capital, Cathédrale Notre-Dame is a pinnacle of the Gothic style – its magnificence echoed by the dizzying achievements at Beauvais farther south. Splendid cathedrals in Noyon, Senlis and the delightful hilltop town of Laon chart the evolution of the Gothic. Closer to Paris, two châteaux command attention. Chantilly, the epicenter of French equestrianism, boasts gardens by Le Nôtre and a 19th-century château housing copious art treasures. Compiègne, bordered by a large and inviting forest, plays host to a lavish royal palace favored by French rulers from Louis XV to Napoleon III.

Memorial cemetery in Vallée de la Somme, an area still haunted by the memory of World War I

◁ Catamarans on the busy beach of Le Touquet Paris-Plage

Exploring Le Nord and Picardy

As THE GATEWAY to England and Belgium, this northern corner of France is buzzing with businesses and industries, with the large, Euro-oriented city of Lille offering great culture as well as a new hi-tech district. Yet peace and quiet is never far away. The coast between the historic port of Boulogne-sur-Mer and the Vallée de la Somme has a rich birdlife and is perfect for a relaxing seaside visit. Inland, the many Gothic cathedrals such as Amiens and Beauvais make an impressive tour, and the World War I battlefields and memorials provide an important insight into 20th-century history. Farther south, the grand châteaux at Compiègne and Chantilly – which has the fascinating Musée Condé – are easily visited en route to or from Paris.

To Osten

DUNKERQUE ④

CALAIS ③

CÔTE D'OPALE

⑥

FLANDRE MARITIME

BOULOGNE-SUR-MER ②

ST-OMER ⑤

BÉTHU

Lys

① *LE TOUQUET*

FORÊT DE CRÉCY

ABBEVILLE ⑨

VALLÉE DE LA SOMME

To Dieppe

Somme ⑩ *AMIENS*

BEAUVAIS ⑪

Oise

CHANTILLY ⑯ *SENL* ⑮

PARC ASTÉRI

To Paris

Key

▬	Highway
▬	Major road
▬	Minor road
▬	Scenic route
∼	River
☀	Viewing point

0 kilometers   25

0 miles   25

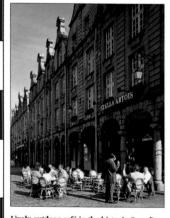

**Lively outdoor café in the historic Grand'
Place in the heart of Arras**

SIGHTS AT A GLANCE

The meandering waters in the Vallée de la Somme

GETTING AROUND

Principal road and rail connections run between Paris and the cross-Channel ports of Boulogne, Calais and Dunkerque, and to the Channel Tunnel at Sangatte. There are good links with Lille and Belgium along the A1 autoroute and by TGV train – Lille is a major TGV hub. Amiens has bus service to most major cities in the region and to Paris. The A26 autoroute runs from Calais to Troyes via Arras and Laon. Also known as the *Autoroute des Anglais,* it is a good alternative if you want to avoid Paris when driving south. There is an international airport at Lille.

Poppies, the symbol of World War I battlefields, in Vallée de la Somme

Le Touquet beach at low tide

Le Touquet ❶

Pas de Calais. ⚐ 6,000. ⛴ 🚉 🚌
🛈 Palais de l'Europe (03 21 06 72 00).
🛍 Thu & Sat (Jun–mid-Sep: also Mon).

PROPERLY KNOWN as Le Touquet Paris-Plage, this resort was created in the 19th century and became fashionable with the rich and famous between the two World Wars.

A vast pine forest, planted in 1855, spreads around the town, sheltering stately villas. To the west, a grid of stylish hotels, vacation residences and sophisticated shops and restaurants borders a long, sandy beach. A racecourse and a casino help retain Le Touquet's affluent atmosphere, complemented by seaside amusements and sports facilities, including horseback-riding, golf and land yachting.

Farther inland, the hilltop town of **Montreuil** has lime-washed 17th-century houses, abundant restaurants and a tree-shaded rampart walk.

Boulogne-sur-Mer ❷

Pas de Calais. ⚐ 44,000. 🚉 🚌 ⛴
🛈 Forum Jean Woël, quai de la Poste (03 21 31 68 38). 🛍 Wed & Sat.

AN IMPORTANT fishing port and popular cross-Channel terminus, Boulogne rewards its visitors well. Its historical attractions come neatly boxed in a walled Haute Ville, with the Porte des Dunes opening onto a 17th–19th-century ensemble of Palais de Justice,

Bibliothèque and Hôtel de Ville in **place de la Résistance**.

The 19th-century **Basilique Notre-Dame** is capped by a huge dome visible for miles around. Inside, a bejeweled wooden statue represents Boulogne's patroness, Notre-Dame de Boulogne. She is wearing a *soleil*, a radiant headdress also worn by the women of the town during the *Grande Procession* held annually in her honor. Nearby, the powerful moated 13th-century **Château**, built for the counts of Boulogne, is now a well-organized historical museum.

In the center of town, shops, hotels and fish restaurants line the quai Gambetta on the east bank of the Liane River. To the north lie Boulogne's beach and **Nausicaa**, a spectacular and innovative aquarium and sea center.

North of the town, the **Colonne de la Grande Armée** was erected in 1841 as a monument to Napoleon I's planned invasion of England in 1803–5. From the top there is a panoramic view along the coast toward Calais. This is the most scenic stretch of the Côte d'Opale (Opal Coast),

with the windblown headlands of **Cap Gris-Nez** and **Cap Blanc-Nez** offering extensive views across the Channel.

🏯 **Château**
Rue de Bernet. 📞 03 21 10 02 20.
Open Wed–Mon. **Closed** Jan 1, May 1, Dec 25. 🎫
🐠 **Nausicaa**
Bd Sainte-Beuve. 📞 03 21 30 99 99.
Open daily. **Closed** 2 weeks in Jan, Jan 1, Dec 25. 🎫 ♿

Calais ❸

Pas de Calais. ⚐ 80,000. 🚉 🚌 ⛴
🛈 12 bd Clémenceau (03 21 96 62 40). 🛍 Wed, Thu & Sat.

CALAIS IS A BUSY cross-Channel port to the west. Clumsily rebuilt after World War II, it seems to have little to offer at first sight.

The **Musée des Beaux Arts et de la Dentelle**, however, has works by the Dutch and Flemish Schools, and recalls the town's lace-making industry. Also on display are studies for Auguste Rodin's famous statue *The Burghers of Calais* (1895). This monument stands outside the

The windswept Cap Blanc-Nez on the Côte d'Opale

The Burghers of Calais by Auguste Rodin (1895)

Musée Portuaire

9 quai de la Citadelle. **C** *03 28 63 33 39.* **Open** *Wed–Mon.* **Closed** *Jan 1, May 1, Dec 25.*

Musée des Beaux Arts

Place du Général de Gaulle. **C** *03 28 59 21 65.* **Open** *Wed–Mon.* **Closed** *some public hols.*

Musée d'Art Contemporain

Avenue des Bains. **C** *03 28 59 21 65.* **Open** *Wed–Mon.* **Closed** *some public hols.*

rebuilt Flemish Renaissance-style Hôtel de Ville in the southern part of town. It celebrates an event during Edward III's siege of Calais in 1347, when six burghers offered their lives to save the town. Their livesz were later spared.

Musée de la Guerre, housed in a battle-scarred German blockhouse, offers a detailed account of local events during World War II.

Musée des Beaux Arts et de la Dentelle

25 rue Richelieu. **C** *03 21 46 48 40.* **Open** *Wed–Mon (Sun pm).* **Closed** *public hols.*

Musée de la Guerre

Parc Saint Pierre. **C** *03 21 34 21 57.* **Open** *Feb–Nov: Wed–Mon.*

Dunkerque ❹

Nord. 🏘 *70,000.* 🚆 🚌 🚢 **i** *4 place Général de Gaulle (03 28 66 79 21).* 🚌 *Wed & Sat.*

DUNKERQUE is a major port and industrial center with a cross-Channel ferry terminal to the west. Place du Minck, with fresh fish stalls, is a good starting point for exploring the port, by foot or boat. A stroll along the Bassin du Commerce leads to **Musée Portuaire**, celebrating the port's maritime past and present.

In the town center, a statue commemorates the local hero, 17th-century corsair Jean Bart, who lies buried in **Eglise St-Eloi**. The belfry (1440) offers views and a Jean Bart tune.

Musée des Beaux Arts has an exhibition of the dramatic evacuation of 350,000 British and French troops in 1940. Also on display are works by artists Vasarely and César.

To the northeast, near Malo-les-Bains, the **Musée d'Art Contemporain** features ceramics and glassware.

The port at Dunkerque

St-Omer ❺

Pas de Calais. 🏘 *15,000.* 🚆 🚌 **i** *bd Pierre Guillain (03 21 98 08 51).* 🚌 *Sat.*

REFINED and old-fashioned St-Omer seems untouched by the war. Pilasters adorn the elegant 17th- and 18th-century houses lining the cobbled streets. Among them is **Hôtel Sandelin**, built in 1777, now a museum of fine and decorative arts. The **Cathédrale Notre-Dame**, features original 13th-century tiles and a huge Classical organ. Nearby, the **Bibliothèque Municipale** contains rare manuscripts and early books from the Abbaye St-Bertin, a ruined 15th-century abbey east of St-Omer.

Hôtel Sandelin

14 rue Carnot. **C** *03 21 38 00 94.* **Open** *Wed–Sun.* **Closed** *public hols.* *ground floor only.*

Bibliothèque Municipale

40 rue Gambetta. **C** *03 21 38 35 08.* **Open** *Tue–Sat.* **Closed** *public hols.*

CHANNEL CROSSINGS

Calais is only 36 km (22 miles) southeast of the English coast, and crossing the waters of the Channel – which the French know as La Manche (the Sleeve) – has inspired many intrepid exploits. The first crossing by balloon was in 1785 by Jean Pierre Blanchard; Captain M. Webb made the first swim in 1875; and Louis Blériot's pioneering flight followed in 1909. Plans for an undersea tunnel, first laid as early as 1751, were finally achieved in 1994 with the opening of a rail link between Sangatte and Folkestone.

Children watching Louis Blériot taking off, 1909

Flandre Maritime ❻

Nord. 🚉 Lille. 🚌 Bergues.
🚢 Dunkerque. 🛈 Bergues, La
Mairie (03 28 68 60 44).

SOUTH OF DUNKERQUE lies a
flat, agricultural plain with
narrow waterways and expan-
sive skies – an archetypal
Flemish landscape with canals,
cyclists and ancient windmills.
The **Noordmeulen**, built just
north of Hondschoote in 1127,
is thought to be the oldest
windmill in Europe.

From Hondschoote the D3
follows the Canal de la Basse
Colme west to Bergues, a
fortified wool town with fine
16th–17th-century Flemish
works in its **Musée Municipal**.
Farther south, the hilltop
town of **Cassel** has a cobbled
Grande Place with 16th–18th-
century buildings, and views
across Flanders and Belgium
from its Jardin Public.

🏛 Musée Municipal

1 rue du Mont de Piété, Bergues.
📞 03 28 68 13 30. **Open** Feb–Dec:
Wed–Mon. 🖼

Lille ❼

Nord. 🚶 175,000. 🚉 🚌 🛈
Palais Rihour (03 20 21 94 21). 🚢 daily.

LILLE IS THE CAPITAL of Le Nord
and the most important
city in northern France. Close
to the Belgian border, it is
the heart of a conurbation of

**Flower stands in the arcades of
the Vieille Bourse in Lille**

Musicians in place du Général de Gaulle, in the heart of Vieux Lille

industrial estates, suburbs and
new towns with over a million
inhabitants. Lille is set to play
a pivotal role in the new
barrier-free Europe – a high-
tech business district is under
construction, known as
EuraLille and served by its
own rail station, Lille-Europe.

The city's charm lies in its
historic center, Vieux Lille – a
vibrant concentration of
cobbled squares and narrow
streets packed with stylish
shops, cafés and restaurants.
Place du Général de Gaulle
forms its hub, bordered by
the impressive façades of
the Art Deco **Voix du Nord**
newspaper offices and the
17th-century **Vieille Bourse**
(Old Exchange). To the east
lie the imposing **Nouvelle
Bourse** (New Exchange) and
the **Opéra**, both built at the
start of the 20th century.

For an overview of the Lille
region, ascend the belfry of
the city's 1920s town hall.

♿ Hospice Comtesse

32 rue de la Monnaie. 📞 03 20 49 50
90. **Open** Wed–Mon. **Closed** Jan 1,
May 1, Jul 14, Nov 1, Dec 25. 🖼
♿ restricted.

A hospital was first founded
here in 1237. Today its 15th-
and 17th-century buildings are
used for exhibitions. The Sick
Room (1470) has a splendid
barrel-vaulted ceiling and in
the Community Wing is a
beautiful Delft-tiled kitchen. The
hospice also has a collection
of ancient musical instruments.

🏛 Musée des Beaux Arts

Pl de la République. 📞 03 20 06 78
00. **Open** Wed–Mon. 🖼 ♿
One of the best art collections
outside Paris, the museum is
strong on Flemish works, including Rubens and Van Dyck.
Other highlights are *Paradise
and Hell* by Dirk Bouts, Van
Goyen's *The Skaters*, Goya's
The Letter, Delacroix's *Médée*
as well as works by Courbet
and Impressionist paintings.

Arras ❽

Pas de Calais. 👥 42,000. 🚉 🚌
ℹ️ Hôtel de Ville, place des Héros
(03 21 51 26 95). **Open** Wed–Mon.

T HE CENTER of Arras, capital
of the Artois region, is
graced by two picturesque
cobbled squares enclosed by
155 houses with 17th-century
Flemish-style façades. A
triumph of postwar recon-
struction, each residence in the
Grand' Place and the smaller
Place des Héros has a slightly
varying design, with some
original shop signs still visible.

A monumental **Hôtel de
Ville** rebuilt in the Flamboyant
Gothic style stands at the
west end of place des Héros
– in the foyer are two giants,
Colas Dédé and Jacqueline,
who swagger around the
town during local festivals.
From the basement you
can take an elevator up to
the belfry, which offers
superb views, or take a
guided tour into the
labyrinth of underground
passages below Arras.
These were cut in the
limestone as early as the
10th century. They
have often
served as
shelter, and
during World War I
as a subterranean
army camp.

The huge Abbaye
St-Vaast includes an
18th–19th-century
Neo-Classical cathedral
and the **Musée des Beaux-
Arts**. The museum contains
some fine medieval sculpture
including a pair of beautifully

**Roadside shrine,
Somme Valley**

carved 13th-century angels.
Among other exhibits are a
local *arras* (hanging tapestry),
and 19th-century works by the
School of Arras, a group of
realist landscape painters
influenced by Corot.

🏛 **Hôtel de Ville**
Pl des Héros. 📞 03 21 51 26 95.
Open daily. **Closed** Jan 1, Dec 25. 📷
🏛 **Musée des Beaux Arts**
22 rue Paul Doumer. 📞 03 21 71 26
43. **Open** Wed–Mon. **Closed** public
hols. 📷

Vallée de la Somme ❾

Somme. 🚉 🚌 🚗 Amiens.
ℹ️ Péronne (03 22 84 42 38).

M EANDERING west from St-
Quentin to St-Valéry-sur-
Somme, the river Somme
acts as a natural guide
through northern Picardy.
Its name is well known
from the battles fought here
during World War I (see
pp180–81). For a thought-
provoking introduction, visit
the **Historial de la Grande
Guerre**, which makes
imaginative use of
archive film, posters,
weapons, toys and
the savage art
of Otto Dix.
From
Péronne
west to
Amiens (see
p190), small lakes
and wooded
islands make the Somme
Valley an attractive area for
camping, walking and fishing.
In summer a small steam train

Boating on the Somme

offers scenic rides between
Froissy and Dompierre.

West of Amiens lies **Samara**,
the largest archaeological park
in France. Adopting Amiens's
Gallo-Roman name, the park
has realistic reconstructions
of prehistoric dwellings. Exhibitions explain primitive crafts
like flintcutting, dyeing and
corngrinding. There are also
botanical gardens.

Farther downstream, **Abbeville** is worth a stop for the
time-battered Eglise St-Vulfran.
Begun in 1488, it has a Flamboyant Gothic west front with
beautiful door panels carved
in the 16th century.

From here the Canal de la
Somme guides the river to
St-Valery-sur-Somme. This
fishing port-cum-resort has a
Haute Ville with partly preserved ramparts and a tree-
shaded seaside promenade.

A pleasant way to enjoy the
sea, sand and marsh landscape
of the bay is to take the little
train that loops between
Cayeux-sur-Mer and Le Crotoy
during the summer. Bird-
watchers can visit the **Maison
de l'Oiseau** on the D3 toward Cayeux-sur-Mer and
the **Parc Ornithologique de
Marquenterre** at St-Quentin-
en-Tourmont north of the bay.

🏛 **Historial de la Grande
Guerre**
Château de Péronne. 📞 03 22 83 14
18. **Open** Oct–Apr: Tue–Sun; May–
Sep: daily. **Closed** Nov 1.
📷 ♿ 🛍
🏛 **Samara**
La Chaussée-Tirancourt. 📞 03 22 51 82
83. **Open** Jan–mid-Dec: daily. 📷 ♿

16th-century carvings on Eglise St-Vulfran in Abbeville, Somme Valley

Amiens ❿

Somme. 🏛 *130,000.* ▢ ▢
ℹ *6 bis rue Duseval (03 22 71 60
51).* ➤ *Wed & Sat.*

THERE IS MORE to Amiens, the
capital of Picardy, than its
Cathédrale Notre-Dame *(see
pp192–3).* The picturesque
quarter of St-Leu is a pedestrianized area of low houses and
flower-lined canals with waterside restaurants, bars and
artisans' shops. Farther east are
Les Hortillonages, a colorful
patchwork of marshland
market gardens, once tended
by farmers using punts and
now a protected natural site.

Musée de Picardie displays
medieval religious sculpture
and 19th-century marble and
bronze statues. Among its fine
range of 16th–20th-century
paintings are a remarkable set
of 16th-century group portraits,
commissioned annually as an
offering to the cathedral. To
the south lies the circus created
by author Jules Verne (1828–
1905). His home, **Maison à la
Tour**, is now a documentation
center. **Musée d'Art Local et
d'Histoire Régionale** has
exhibits of furniture and
objets d'art from the region.

🏛 **Musée de Picardie**
48 rue de la République. 【 *03 22 97
14 00.* **Open** daily. **Closed** Jan 1, May
1, Nov 1 & 11, Dec 25. 📷 ♿
🏛 **Musée d'Art Local et
d'Histoire Régionale**
36 rue V Hugo. 【 *03 22 97 14 00.*
Open Easter–Sep: Thu–Sun; Oct–
Easter: Sun. **Closed** Jan 1, May 1,
Nov 1 & 11, Dec 25. 📷 ♿

The clock depicts
Christ surrounded by
the 12 apostles.

Mechanical figures
perform scenes from
the Last Judgment.

**Clock
showing
age of the
world**

**Solstice
indicator**

Astronomical clock in Beauvais cathedral

Beauvais ⓫

Oise. 🏛 *56,000.* ▲ ▢ ▢
ℹ *1 rue Beauregard (03 44 15 30 30).*
➤ *Wed & Sat.*

HEAVILY BOMBED in World
War II, Beauvais is now a
modern town with one out-
standing jewel. **Cathédrale St-
Pierre** is a poignant, neck-
cricking finale to the vaulting
ambition that created the great
Gothic cathedrals. In 1227
work began on a building
designed to soar above all predecessors, but the roof of the
chancel caved in twice from
lack of support before its
completion in the early 14th
century. Delayed by wars and
inadequate funds, the transept
was not completed until 1550.
In 1573 its crossing collapsed
after a tower and spire were
added. What remains today is
nevertheless a masterpiece,
rising 48 m (157 ft) high.
In the transept much of the
original 16th-century stained
glass survives, while near the
north door is a 90,000-part
astronomical clock assembled
in the 1860s. What would
have been the nave is still
occupied by the remnants of
a 10th-century church known
as the Basse-Oeuvre.

The former Bishop's Palace
is now home to the **Musée
Départemental de l'Oise**.
The collection includes
archaeological finds, medieval
sculpture, tapestries and local
ceramics. Beauvais has a long
tradition of tapestry manufacturing, and examples from

VIOLLET-LE-DUC

The renowned architectural theorist Viollet-le-Duc (1814–79)
was the first to fully appreciate Gothic architecture. His
1854 dictionary of architecture celebrated medieval building
techniques, showing that the
arches and tracery of Gothic
cathedrals were solutions
to architectural problems,
not mere decoration. His
restoration work included
Château de Pierrefonds,
Notre-Dame in Paris
(see pp82–3) and Car-
cassonne *(see pp478–9).*

**Medieval architects, as
drawn by Viollet-le-Duc**

the French national collection are shown in the **Galerie Nationale de la Tapisserie**.

🏛 **Musée Départemental de l'Oise**
Ancien Palais Episcopal, 1 rue du Musée. 📞 *03 44 11 43 83*. **Open** *Wed–Mon. Closed Jan 1, Easter, Mon, Whit Mon, May 1, Dec 25.* 🚫
🏛 **Galerie Nationale de la Tapisserie**
22 Rue St-Pierre. 📞 *03 44 05 14 28.* **Open** *Tue–Sun (call to check).* 🚫

Noyon ⓬

Oise. 🏠 *15,000.* 🚉 ℹ️ *place de l'Hôtel de Ville (03 44 44 21 88).* 🛒 *Wed & Sat, first Tue of each month.*

Noyon has long been a religious center. The **Cathédrale de Notre-Dame**, dating from 1150, is the fifth to be built on this site and was completed by 1290. It provides a harmonious example of the transition from Romanesque to Gothic style. A local history museum, the **Musée du Noyonnais**, occupies part of the former Bishop's Palace, and at the cathedral's east end is a rare half-timbered chapter library built in 1506.

Jean Calvin, the Protestant theologian and one of the leaders of the Reformation, was born here in 1509 and is commemorated in the small **Musée Jean Calvin**.

🏛 **Musée du Noyonnais**
Ancien Palais Episcopal, 7 rue de l'Evêché. 📞 *03 44 09 43 41.* **Open** *Wed–Mon. Closed Jan 1, Nov 11, Dec 25.* 🚫 ♿

The rib-vaulted nave of Cathédrale de Notre-Dame, Noyon

Path through Forêt de Compiègne

Compiègne ⓭

Oise. 🏠 *50,000.* 🚉 🚌 ℹ️ *Hôtel de Ville (03 44 40 01 00).* 🛒 *Wed & Sat.*

Compiègne is where Joan of Arc was captured by the Burgundians in 1430. A 16th-century Hôtel de Ville with a towering belfry rules over the center, but the town is most famous for its royal **château**.

Designed as a summer residence for Louis XV by Jacques Ange Gabriel, the château was completed by Louis XVI, restored by Napoleon and later became a favorite residence of Napoleon III and Empress Eugénie. Guided tours of the imperial apartments progress through stately and private chambers, such as the sumptuous bedrooms of Napoleon I and Marie-Louise.

Within the château, the Musée du Second Empire and Musée de l'Impératrice display furniture, portraits and memorabilia, while the Musée de la Voiture is an entertaining assembly of historic carriages, bicycles and early automobiles.

South and east of the town, the old hunting grounds of **Forêt de Compiègne** spread as far as Pierrefonds, with ample space for walks and picnics beneath its oaks and beeches. East of the D130, Les Beaux Monts provide majestic views back to the château.

The Clairière de l'Armistice, north of the N31, marks the spot where the armistice of World War I was signed on November 11, 1918. The small **Musée Wagon de l'Armistice**

contains a replica of the train car where the ceremony took place, which was used again in World War II by Hitler as a humiliating venue for the signing of the French surrender on June 22, 1940.

♣ **Château de Compiègne**
Place du Général de Gaulle. 📞 *03 44 38 47 00.* **Open** *Wed–Mon. Closed Jan 1, May 1, Nov 1, Dec 25.* 🚫 ♿
🏛 **Musée Wagon de l'Armistice**
Clairière de l'Armistice (in direction of Soissons). 📞 *03 44 85 14 18.* **Open** *Wed–Mon. Closed Jan 1, Dec 25.* 🚫

Château de Pierrefonds

Château de Pierrefonds ⓮

Oise. 📞 *03 44 42 72 72.* **Open** *daily. Closed Jan 1, May 1, Nov 1, Dec 25.* 🚫

The immense Château de Pierrefonds dominates the small village below. A mighty castle was constructed here by Louis d'Orléans in the 14th century, but by 1813 it had become a picturesque ruin, which Napoleon I purchased for less than 3,000 francs.

In 1857, Napoleon III commissioned the architect Viollet-le-Duc to restore it, and in 1884 Pierrefonds was reborn as an imperial residence. The exterior, with its moat, drawbridge, towers and double sentry walks, is a diligent reconstruction of medieval military architecture. The interior, by contrast, is enlivened by the romantic fancies of Viollet-le-Duc and his patron. There are guided tours and a historical exhibition.

Amiens Cathedral

WORK ON THE LARGEST cathedral in France started in 1220, financed by profits from the cultivation of woad, a plant valued for its blue dye. It was built to house the head of St. John the Baptist, brought back from the Crusades in 1206 and a magnet for pilgrims. It is still displayed in the Treasury. Within 50 years Notre-Dame was complete, a masterpiece of engineering – Gothic architecture carried to a bold extreme. Restored in the 1850s by Viollet-le-Duc *(see p190)*, and having miraculously survived two world wars, the cathedral is famous for its rich array of statues and reliefs, which inspired John Ruskin's *The Bible of Amiens* in 1884.

★ **West Front**
The King's Gallery, a row of 22 colossal statues repre-senting the kings of France, spans the west front. The statues are also thought to symbolize the kings of Judah.

St. Firmin Portal is decorated with figures and scenes from the life of St. Firmin, the martyr who brought Christianity to Picardy and became the first bishop of Amiens.

The calendar shows signs from the zodiac, with the corresponding monthly labors below. It depicts everyday life in the 13th century.

Weeping Angel
Sculpted by Nicolas Blasset in 1628, this sentimental statue in the ambulatory became a popular image during World War I.

STAR FEATURES
★ **West Front**
★ **Nave**
★ **Choir Stalls**
★ **Choir Screens**

Central Portal
Scenes from the Last Judg-ment decorate the tympanum, with the Beau Dieu, a statue of Christ, between the doors.

Towers

Two towers of unequal height frame the west front. The south tower was completed in 1366, the north in 1402. The spire was replaced twice, in 1627 and 1887.

VISITORS' CHECKLIST

Cathédrale Notre-Dame, place Notre-Dame. 03 22 71 60 50. **Open** Apr–Oct: 8:30am–7pm; Nov–Mar: 9am–noon, 2–5pm (6pm Sat). **Closed** last Sun of Sep, Dec 23. 9am, 10:15am, 11:30am, 6pm Sun.

The Flamboyant tracery of the rose window was created in the 16th century.

A double row comprising 22 elegant flying buttresses supports the construction.

★ **Nave**

Soaring 42 m (138 ft) high, with support from 126 slender pillars, the brightly illuminated interior of Notre-Dame is a hymn to the vertical.

★ **Choir Stalls**

The 110 oak choir stalls (1508–19) are delicately carved with 4,000 biblical, mythical and contemporary figures.

★ **Choir Screens**

Vivid scenes from the lives of St. Firmin and St. John, carved in the 15th–16th centuries, adorn the ambulatory.

The flooring was laid down in 1288 and reassembled in the late 19th century. The faithful followed its labyrinthine shape on their knees.

Senlis ⑮

Oise. 🏘 16,000. 🚌 ℹ️ place du Parvis Notre-Dame (03 44 53 06 40). 🛒 Tue & Fri.

SENLIS, 10 km (6 miles) east of Chantilly, is worth visiting for its Gothic cathedral and the well-preserved historic streets in the old town that surround it. **Cathédrale Notre-Dame** was constructed during the second half of the 12th century, and the sculpted central doorway of its west front, depicting the Assumption of the Virgin, influenced later cathedrals such as Amiens (*see pp192–3*). The spire of the south tower dates from the 13th century, while the Flamboyant south transept, built in the mid-16th century, makes an ornate contrast with the austerity of earlier years. Opposite the west front, a gateway leads to the ruins of the Château Royal and its gardens. Here the **Musée de la Vénerie**, housed in a former priory, celebrates hunting through paintings, old weapons and trophies.

The **Musée d'Art** recalls the town's Gallo-Roman past and also has an excellent collection of early Gothic sculpture.

🏛 **Musée de la Vénerie**
Château Royal, place du Parvis Notre-Dame. ☎ 03 44 53 00 80 ext. 1315.
Open Thu–Mon, Tue pm.
Closed May 1. 🚫 📷 obligatory.
🏛 **Musée d'Art**
Ancien Evêché, 2 place Notre-Dame. ☎ 03 44 53 00 80 ext. 1247.
Open Wed pm – Mon. **Closed** May 1. 🚫

Les Très Riches Heures du Duc de Berry, on display in Chantilly

Chantilly ⑯

Oise. 🏘 11,000. 🚌 🚇 ℹ️ 23 avenue du Maréchal Joffre (03 44 57 08 58). 🛒 Wed & Sat.

THE HORSE-RACING CAPITAL of France, Chantilly offers a classy combination of château, park and forest that has long made it a popular excursion.

With origins from Gallo-Roman times, the château of today started to take shape in 1528, when the famous Anne de Montmorency, constable of France, had the old fortress replaced and added the Petit Château. During the time of the Great Prince of Condé (1621–86), renovation work continued and Le Nôtre created a park and fountains that made even Louis XIV jealous.

Destroyed in the Revolution, the Grand Château was again

CHANTILLY HORSE RACING

Chantilly is the capital of thoroughbred racing in France, a shrine to the long-standing love affair between the French upper classes and the world of horses. It was the firm belief of Prince Louis-Henri de Bourbon, creator of Chantilly's monumental Grandes Ecuries, that he would one day be reincarnated as a horse. Horse racing was introduced from England around 1830 and soon became very popular. The first official race meeting was held here in 1834, and today around 3,000 horses are trained in the surrounding forests and countryside. Every June, Chantilly becomes the focus of the social and flat racing season when top riders and their thoroughbreds compete for its two historic trophies, the Prix du Jockey-Club and Prix de Diane-Hermès.

Prix Equipage de Hermès, one of many prestigious races at Chantilly

rebuilt and its receptions and hunting parties became crowded by the fashionable high society of the 1820s–30s. It was finally replaced by a Renaissance-style château in the late 19th century.

Today the Grand Château and the Petit Château form the **Musée Condé**, displaying art treasures collected by its last private owner, the Duke of Aumale. These include work by Raphael, Botticelli, Poussin and Ingres, and an entertaining gallery of 16th-century portraits by the Clouet brothers. Among the most precious items is the famous 15th-century illuminated manuscript *Les Très Riches Heures du Duc de Berry;* reproductions are on display. You can also tour the stately apartments, with decorative conceits ranging from frolicking monkeys to triumphant battles.

Both châteaux are somewhat upstaged by the magnificent stables (Grandes Ecuries), an equestrian palace designed by Jean Aubert in 1719 that could accommodate 240 horses and 500 dogs. Adjacent to the hippodrome, it is occupied by the **Musée Vivant du Cheval**, presenting various breeds of horses and ponies as well as riding displays.

🏛 **Musée Condé**
Château de Chantilly. 📞 03 44 62 62 62. **Open** Wed–Mon. 🎫

🐎 **Musée Vivant du Cheval**
Grandes Ecuries du Prince de Condé, Chantilly. 📞 03 44 57 40 40. **Open** Wed–Mon. 🎫 ♿

Parc Astérix ⑰

Plailly. 📞 03 36 68 30 10. **Open** Apr–Aug: daily, Sep–Oct: Wed, Sat, Sun. **Closed** Some Mon & Fri in May & June (call to check). 🎫 ♿

A SHORT DRIVE north of Charles de Gaulle Airport on the A1 Autoroute stands a fortified Gallo-Roman encampment with its own customs controls, currency, Menhir FM radio station and security staff wearing plastic-winged helmets. This atmospheric theme park, very popular with families, gives visitors a real feeling for the comic-strip heroes created by Goscinny and Uderzo.

A stroll along Via Antiqua reveals architecture and souvenirs from Asterix's journeys, while the Asterix Village and the Roman camp are reconstructions from the cartoons. Fairground thrills range from high-speed water rides – strictly for the adventurous – to more sedate old-fashioned merry-go-rounds.

Rue de Paris represents Paris through the centuries, including the construction of Notre-Dame in Paris and the heroic exploits of the Three Musketeers. Souvenir shops are never very far away.

Asterix with friends, Parc Astérix

Laon ⑱

Aisne. 🏠 36,000. 🚉 ℹ️ *pl du Parvis de la Cathédrale (03 23 20 28 62).* 🔄 *Thu & Sat.*

THE CAPITAL of the Aisne *département*, Laon occupies a dramatic site on top of a long, narrow ridge surrounded by wide plains.

The pedestrianized rue Châtelaine, a major shopping street in Laon

Rose window in the 13th-century Cathédrale de Notre-Dame, Laon

The old town, on top of the mount, is best approached by Poma, an automated cable car that swings up from the railroad station to the place du Général Leclerc.

The pedestrianized rue Châtelaine leads to Laon's splendid **Cathédrale de Notre-Dame**. Completed in 1235, the cathedral lost two of its original seven towers in the Revolution but remains an impressive monument to the early Gothic style.

Notable details include the deep porches of the west façade, the four-story nave, and the carved Renaissance screens enclosing its side chapels. The immense 13th-century rose window in the apse beautifully represents the Glorification of the Church. Protruding from the cathedral's western towers are statues paying tribute to the oxen used to haul stone for its construction.

The rest of medieval Laon rewards casual strolling: a promenade rings the 16th-century **Citadelle** farther east, while to the south you can follow the ramparts past the Porte d'Ardon and Porte des Chenizelles to **Eglise St-Martin**, with good views back over the rooftops to the cathedral from rue Thibesard.

South of Laon is Chemin des Dames, named after Louis XV's daughters, who used to take this route. It is more often remembered as a World War I battlefield, now lined with cemeteries and memorials.

CHAMPAGNE

MARNE · ARDENNES · AUBE · HAUTE-MARNE

C HAMPAGNE IS A NAME *of great resonance, conjuring up images of celebration and the world-famous cathedral in Reims. Yet beyond the glamour lies an unspoiled rural area of strikingly contrasting landscapes: the rolling plains of Champagne, giving way to lakes and water meadows to the south, and the dense forests and hills of the Ardennes in the north.*

The so-called "sacred triangle of Champagne," linking Épernay, Reims and Châlons-en-Champagne, is like a magnet for wine lovers. Here, the experience of drinking fine champagne is enhanced by gourmet meals of stuffed trout, Ardennes ham and the famous sausages called *andouillettes*.

The well-marked *route touristique du champagne* wends its way through vineyards toward endless cereal plains stretching southward to the "lake district," an area of oak forests, water meadows and streams.

On the border between France and Belgium lies the Ardennes, named after the Celtic word for deep forest. This wild border land of dramatic valleys, deciduous forests and hills is cut by the meanderings of the Meuse River. Border fortifications include the vast citadel of Sedan and the star-shaped bastion of Rocroi, as well as the Maginot Line outposts built before World War II.

The Ardennes may offer appealing countryside but Champagne is culturally superior, with impressive towns and their painstakingly restored historic centers. It has some striking churches, from the Gothic majesty of Reims Cathedral to the rustic charm of its typical wooden *champenois* churches. These feature vivid stained-glass windows by the famous School of Troyes, whose subtle craftsmanship seems to typify the appeal of this quiet region.

Timber-framed *champenois* church at Lac du Der-Chantecoq

◁ Cathédrale St-Etienne in Châlons-en-Champagne

Exploring Champagne

CHAMPAGNE draws wine lovers to the sacred triangle between Reims, Epernay and Châlons-en-Champagne, but the region also attracts culture lovers to its great churches, notably Reims Cathedral. Reims abounds in gastronomic restaurants but Troyes, the former capital of Champagne, makes the most delightful base. Although much of Champagne is flat, the wild and wooded Ardennes to the north attracts walkers and nature lovers. North of Reims, the Ardennes Canal can be explored by barge or pleasure boat from Rethel; to the south, water sports are popular on the lakes east of Troyes.

Fishing by a canal in Montier-en-Der near Lac du Der-Chantecoq

GETTING AROUND

International flights to the Reims-Champagne airport usually involve changing planes in Paris. By road, Reims, the main focus for visitors, is easily reached along the A4 highway from Alsace or Paris. The train from Paris takes 90 minutes. Rail transportation within the region is reasonably good and so are the roads.

The subtleties of the wine-growing landscape can be explored from Reims along the many signposted roads marked "Route de Champagne."

Windmill at Verzenay, Parc Naturel de la Montagne de Reims

A *grande marque* champagne from Reims

SIGHTS AT A GLANCE

Argonne ⑦
Châlons-en-Champagne ⑨
Charleville-Mézières ⑤
Chaumont ⑪
Épernay ②
L'Épine ⑧
Langres ⑫
Reims ①
Rocroi ④
Sedan ⑥
Troyes ⑩
Vallée de la Meuse ③

The Old Town in Monthermé in Vallée de la Meuse, encircled by the river

KEY

	Highway
	Major road
	Minor road
	Scenic route
	River
☼	Viewing point

0 kilometers   25

0 miles   25

Gilded reliquary (1896), with body of St. Remi, in Basilique St-Remi, Reims

Reims ❶

Marne. 🏠 185,000. ✈ 🚇 🚍
ℹ 2 rue Guillaume de Machault
(03 26 77 45 25). 🛒 daily.

RENOWNED the world over from countless champagne labels, Reims is home to some of the best-known *grandes marques*. But the city has another, much earlier, claim to fame: since the 11th century, all the kings of France have come to this "city of coronations" to be crowned in its remarkable Gothic **Cathédrale Notre-Dame** (*see pp202–3*).

Although World War II bombing destroyed much of Reims's architectural coherence, there are some remarkable monuments here. The **Crypto-portique**, part of the forum, and Porte Mars, a triumphal Augustan arch, recall the city's Roman past. In 1945, the German surrender was taken in the **Musée de la Reddition** in Eisenhower's French headquarters during World War II. **Musée des Beaux Arts** houses a fine collection of 15th- and 16th-century canvases depicting biblical scenes; portraits by the Cranachs; *The Death of Marat* by David, and more than 20 landscapes by Corot. Also featured are the Barbizon School, Impressionists and modern masters.

In 1996 Reims was the venue for celebrations marking the 1,500-year anniversary of the baptism, in the cathedral, of Clovis, the first King of the Franks.

🏛 Ancien Collège des Jésuites & Planetarium

1 place Museux. ☎ 03 26 85 51 50.
College open daily. **Closed** public hols.
Planetarium open Sat & Sun. 🈲
Founded in 1606, this college was a hospice until 1976. Nowadays its 300-year-old

vines, Romanesque wine cellars and Baroque interior play their part as atmospheric film sets, notably for the film of Zola's *Germinal* (1992) and *Queen Margot* (1993), starring Isabelle Adjani. Highlights include the refectory's marquetry ceiling and the kitchen, the only room where fireplaces were allowed in an austere Jesuit establishment. A double spiral staircase leads to a Baroque library topped by a ceiling like an upturned boat. Housed in the same building since 1979 is the **Planetarium** with views of the sky from everywhere in the world.

🏛 Basilique St-Remi

Place de Lenoncourt. **Open** daily. ♿
Now marooned in a modern quarter, this Benedictine abbey church, the oldest church in Reims, began as a Carolingian

Porte Mars, a reminder of Reims in Roman times

MÉTHODE CHAMPENOISE

To produce its characteristic bubbles, champagne has to undergo a process of double fermentation.
• **First fermentation:** The base wine, made from rather acidic grapes, is fermented at 68°–72°F in either stainless steel tanks or, traditionally, in oak barrels. It is then siphoned off from the sediment and kept at colder temperatures to clear completely, before being drawn off and blended with wines from other areas and years (except in the case of vintage champagne). The wine is bottled and the *liqueur de tirage* (sugar, wine and yeast) is added.
• **Second fermentation:** The bottles are stored for a year or more in cool, chalky cellars. The yeast converts the sugar to alcohol and carbon dioxide, which produces the sparkle, and the yeast cells die leaving a deposit. To remove this, the inverted bottles are turned and tapped daily to shift the deposits into the neck of the bottle (*remuage*). Finally, the deposits are expelled by the process known as *dégorgement*, and a bit of sugar (*liqueur d'expédition*) is added to adjust the sweetness before the final cork is inserted.

Champagne Mumm of Reims

basilica dedicated to Saint Remi (440–533). Inside, an Early Gothic choir and radiating chapels can be seen, as well as sculpted Romanesque capitals in the north transept.

⬦ Musée St-Remi
53 rue Simon. **(** 03 26 85 23 36. **Open** daily, pm only. **Closed** Jan 1, May 1, Jul 14, Nov 1 & 11, Dec 25.
Set in the former abbey, the adjoining museum encloses the original Gothic chapter house within its cloistered 17th-century shell. On display in the museum are archaeo-logical artifacts, 15th-century tapestries depicting the life of Saint Remi, and a varied collection of weapons dating from the 16th–19th centuries.

Épernay ❷

Marne. 🏠 28,000. 🚊 🚌 🛈 7 av de Champagne (03 26 53 33 00). 🗓 Wed, Sat & Sun.

Tʜᴇ sᴏʟᴇ ʀᴇᴀsᴏɴ for visiting Épernay is to burrow into the chalky *caves* and taste the champagne. This rather undis-tinguished town dominates the champagne industry, and has the highest per capita income in France. As proof, the avenue de Champagne quarter abounds in mock-

Statue of Dom Perignon at Moët

Renaissance mansions. **Moët et Chandon**, dating back to 1743, is the largest and slickest *maison*, the star of the Moët-Hennessy stable.

The group also owns other brands, such as Ruinart, Dom Perignon, Pommery, Mercier and even Parfums Dior. When the recession took the fizz out of Champagne in 1993, Moët took the step of making a number of people redundant and provoked the first ever

strike in the industry. The cellars of Moët and **Mercier** are both based in avenue de Champagne, and either is well worth a visit. Mercier has the distinction of displaying a giant cask created for the 1889 Paris Exhibition, and takes visitors trundling through the *caves* in an electric train.

De Castellane, in avenue de Verdun, offers a more personalized tour, complete with a chance to taste their champagne.

🏛 Moët et Chandon
20 avenue de Champagne. **(** 03 26 51 20 00. **Open** mid-Nov–mid-Mar: Mon–Fri.
🏛 Mercier
70 avenue de Champagne. **(** 03 26 51 22 22. **Open** Mar–Nov: daily; Dec–Feb: Thu–Mon. **Closed** Dec 25–Jan 1.
🏛 De Castellane
57 rue de Verdun. **(** 03 26 51 19 11. **Open** Apr–Oct: daily.

Dégorgement *is the final removal of the yeast deposits from the bottle. The neck of the bottle is plunged in freezing brine and the frozen block of sediment is then removed.*

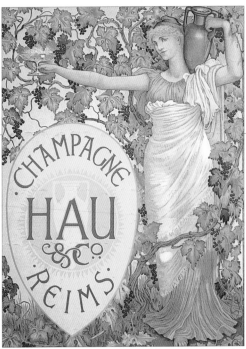

Seductive marketing *of champagne since the last century has ensured its continuing success.*

The bubbles in champagne *are produced during the second fermentation. Ageing for several years or more improves the quality of champagne.*

Reims Cathedral

THE MAGNIFICENT GOTHIC Cathédrale Notre-Dame at Reims is noted for its harmony and monumentality. A cathedral has stood on this site since 401 but the present building was begun in 1211. Reims has been the backdrop for coronations from medieval times till 1825, when Charles X was crowned. The coronation of Charles VII here in 1429 was attended by Joan of Arc. During the Revolution, the rood screen and windows were destroyed but the stonework survived. World War I damage was finally fully restored in 1996, to coincide with the 1,500th anniversary of the baptism of Clovis, King of the Franks, at Reims, which was considered the first coronation of a French king.

★ **Great Rose Window**
Best seen at sunset, the 13th-century window shows the Virgin surrounded by the apostles and angel musicians. It is set within a larger window, a feature common in 13th-century architecture.

The Nave
Compared with the nave at Chartres (see pp298–301), Reims is taller. Its elegant capitals are decorated with naturalistic floral motifs such as ivy and berries.

WEST FAÇADE

SOUTH FAÇADE

★ **Smiling Angel**
Rich in statuary, Reims is often called "the cathedral of angels." Situated above the left (north) portal, this enigmatic angel with unfurled wings is the most celebrated of the many that grace the building.

★ **Gallery of the Kings**
The harmonious west façade, decorated with over 2,300 statues, is the most notable feature at Reims. Fifty-six stone effigies of French kings form the Gallery of the Kings.

PALAIS DU TAU

The archbishop's palace adjoining the cathedral is named after its T-shaped design, based on early episcopal crosses. (Tau is Greek for T.) The palace, built in 1690 by Mansart and Robert de Cotte, encloses a Gothic chapel and the 15th-century Salle du Tau, rooms associated with French coronations. On the eve of a coronation, the future king spent the night in the palace. After being crowned in the cathedral, he held a magnificent banquet in the palace. The Salle du Tau, or banquet hall, is the finest room in the palace, with a magnificent barrel-vaulted ceiling and walls hung with 15th-century Arras

tapestries. The palace now houses a museum of statuary and tapestries from the cathedral, including a 15th-century tapestry of the baptism of Clovis, the first Christian king.

Salle du Tau – the banquet hall

VISITORS' CHECKLIST

Cathédrale Notre-Dame, place du Cardinal Luçon. (03 26 47 55 34. **Open** 7:30am–7:30pm daily. ✝ 8am & 7pm Mon–Fri; 9am, 10:15am & noon Sun.
Palais du Tau (03 26 47 81 79. **Open** daily. **Closed** Jan 1, May 1, Nov 1 & 11, Dec 25.

Apse Gallery
The restored claire-voie (open work) gallery on the apse is crowned by statues of mythological beasts.

The radiating chapels of the apse are supported by flying buttresses and adorned with octagonal pinnacles.

South transept

The clerestory windows pioneered Gothic tracery by dividing the lights with slender bars of stone, creating a decorative, intersecting pattern.

APSE

SIDE SECTION

Pinnacles on the flying buttresses shelter guardian angels, symbolic protectors of the cathedral.

STAR FEATURES

★ **Gallery of the Kings**

★ **Smiling Angel**

★ **Great Rose Window**

Chagall Window
The windows in the axial chapel were designed by the 20th-century artist Marc Chagall and made by local craftsmen. This one depicts the Crucifixion and the Sacrifice of Isaac.

The *sentier touristique*, a walk along the ramparts of Rocroi

Vallée de la Meuse ❸

Ardennes. 🚆 *Revin*. 🛈 *Revin (03 24 40 19 59).*

THE MEUSE meanders through the Ardennes among spectacular scenery of wild gorges, woods and warped rock formations of granite or schist.

Dramatically situated on a double meander of the Meuse, **Revin** is an unremarkable town in an exceptional site, with the Vieille Ville enfolded in the north bend. From the quay, you can see wooded **Mont Malgré Tout** and a route dotted with observation points and steep trails. Just south is **Dames de la Meuse**, a rocky outcrop over the river gorge.

Monthermé lies on two banks, with the Vieille Ville clustered on the charming left bank. The rocky gorges around **Roche à Sept Heures** on the far bank entice climbers and ramblers. Farther on is **Rocher des Quatre Fils d'Aymon**, a ridge whose jagged crest suggests the silhouette of four legendary local horsemen.

Rocroi ❹

Ardennes. 🏚 *2,600.* 🚆 🛈 *place d'Armes (03 24 54 20 06).* 🛒 *Tue.*

SET ON the Ardennes plateau, the star-shaped citadel of Rocroi was originally built under Henri II in 1555, and later made impregnable by Vauban in 1675 *(see p216).*

The main attraction is the *sentier touristique,* a walk along the ramparts beginning in the Porte de France, the southern gateway. The nature preserve at Rièzes is home to orchids and carnivorous plants.

Charleville-Mézières ❺

Ardennes. 🏚 *57,000.* 🚆 🚌 🛈 *4 place Ducal (03 24 32 44 80).* 🛒 *Tue, Thu & Sat.*

KNOWN AS the gateway to the Ardennes, this riverside ford was originally two towns. The somber medieval citadel of Mézières merged with the neat Classical town of Charleville in 1966. Mézières has irregular slate-covered houses curving around a bend in the Meuse. Battered fortifications and gateways are visible from avenue de St-Julien. Tucked into the ramparts is the much-remodeled Gothic **Notre-Dame de l'Espérance**.

The centerpiece of Charleville is **place Ducale**, a model of Louis XIII urban planning,

echoing place des Vosges in Paris *(see p87)*. The poet Arthur Rimbaud was born nearby in 1854. His modest birthplace at No. 12 rue Thiers is still there, along with his childhood home on the Meuse at 7 quai Arthur Rimbaud.

Just along the quayside is the Vieux Moulin, the town house whose view inspired *Le Bateau ivre*, Rimbaud's greatest poem. Inside is the small **Musée Rimbaud**, with manuscripts and photographs by the poet.

🏛 Musée Rimbaud
Quai Arthur Rimbaud. 📞 *03 24 32 44 65.* **Open** *Tue–Sun.* **Closed** *Jan 1, May 1, Dec 25.* 🖼

Sedan ❻

Ardennes. 🏚 *22,000.* 🚆 🚌 🛈 *Château Fort, place du Château (03 24 27 73 73).* 🛒 *Wed & Sat.*

JUST TO THE EAST of Charleville is the **Château de Sedan**, the largest fortified castle in the whole of Europe. There has been a bastion on these slopes since the 11th century, but each Ardennes conflict has meant a new tier of defenses for Sedan.

In 1870, during the Franco-Prussian War, with 700 Prussian cannons turned on Sedan, Napoleon III surrendered, and 83,000 French prisoners were deported to Prussia. In May 1940, after capturing Sedan, German forces reached the French coast a week later.

The seven-story bastion contains sections dating from medieval times to the 16th

The 19th-century poet Rimbaud, whose birthplace was Charleville

century. Highlights of any visit are the ramparts, the 16th-century fortifications and the magnificent 15th-century eaves in one tower. A jumbled **Musée du Château**, that is located in the south wing has a section devoted to military campaigns.

The bastion is surrounded by 17th-century slate-roofed houses which hug the banks of the Meuse. These reflect the city's earlier prosperity as a Huguenot stronghold.

🏛 **Musée du Château**
1 place du Château. ☎ 03 24 27 73 75. **Open** Mar–Oct: Tue–Sun. 🖼

Environs
Farther south is **Fort de Vitry-la-Ferté**, one of the few forts on the Maginot line to have come into direct and devastating combat with the enemy in 1940.

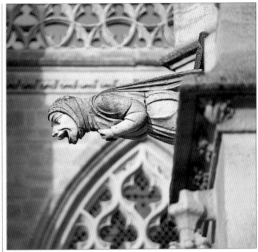

Gargoyle on Basilique de Notre-Dame de l'Epine

Courtyard inside the heavily fortified Château de Sedan

Argonne ❼

Ardennes & Meuse. 🚌 Vouziers. ℹ Sainte-Menehould (03 26 60 85 83).

EAST OF REIMS, the Argonne is a compact region of picturesque valleys and forests, a countryside dotted with priories, trenches and war cemeteries.

As a wooded border between the rival bishoprics of Champagne and Lorraine, the Argonne was home to abbeys and priories. Now ruined, the Benedictine abbey of **Beaulieu-en-Argonne** boasts a fine wine press and has forest views. Just north is **Les Islettes**, known for its faïence pottery and tiles. The hilly terrain here was a battleground during the Franco-Prussian War and lay on the Western front in World War I. The disputed territory of **Butte de Vauquois**, north of Les Islettes, bears a war memorial.

L'Épine ❽

Marne. 🚶 650. 🚌

L'ÉPINE IS WORTH visiting if only for a glimpse of the **Basilique de Notre-Dame de l'Épine**, surrounded by wheatfields. Designed on the scale of a cathedral, this 15th-century Flamboyant Gothic church has been a pilgrimage site, especially in summer, since medieval times. Even French kings have come here to venerate a "miraculous" statue of the Virgin.

On the façade, three gabled portals are offset by floating tracery, a gauzy effect reminiscent of Reims cathedral. All around are gruesome gargoyles symbolizing evil spirits and deadly sins, chased out by the holy presence within. Unfortunately, the most risqué sculptures were destroyed, judged obscene by 19th-century puritans. The subdued Gothic interior contains a 15th-century rood screen and the venerated statue of the Virgin.

CHAMPAGNE TIMBER CHURCHES

Skirting Lac du Der-Chantecoq lies a region of woodland, water meadows and characteristic Romanesque and Renaissance timber-framed churches with curious pointed gables and *caquetoirs*, rickety wooden porches. Many have intimate and often beautifully carved interiors with stained-glass windows designed in the vivid colors of the School of Troyes. Rural roads link churches in Bailly-le-Franc, Chatillon-sur-Broué, Lentilles, Vignory, Outines, Chavanges and Montier-en-Der.

16th-century timber church in Lentilles

Châlons-en-Champagne ●

Marne. ▓ 48,000. 🚊 🚌
🚩 3 quai des Arts (03 26 65 17 89).
🚩 Wed & Sat.

ENCIRCLED BY the Marne River and minor canals, Châlons' sleepy bourgeois charm is made up of half-timbered houses and gardens mirrored in canals. Nearby are vineyards producing Blanc de Blancs.

From quai de Notre-Dame there are views of old bridges and the Romanesque towers of **Notre-Dame-en-Vaux**, a masterpiece of Romanesque-Gothic. Behind the church is a well-restored medieval quarter and the **Musée du Cloître de Notre-Dame-en-Vaux**, containing the original Romanesque cloisters.

Cathédrale St-Etienne, by the canal, is a Gothic affair with a Baroque portal, Romanesque crypt and vivid medieval windows. Beyond is **Le Petit Jard**, riverside gardens overlooking the Château du Marché, a turreted toll-gate built by Henri IV. The neighboring place de la République has lively bars and restaurants.

🏛 **Musée du Cloître de Notre-Dame-en-Vaux**
Rue Nicolas Durand. 📞 03 26 64 03 87. **Open** Wed–Mon. **Closed** Jan 1, May 1, Nov 1 & 11, Dec 25. 🈴

Troyes ●

Aube. ▓ 60,000. 🚊 🚌 🚩 16 bd Carnot (03 25 82 62 50). 🚩 Sat.

TROYES IS A DELIGHT, a city of magnificent Gothic churches and charming 16th-century courtyards, in a historic center shaped like a champagne cork. The city is famous for its heritage of stained glass and sausages (andouillettes), its knitwear industry and factory outlets.

The battered Flamboyant Gothic west front of the **Cathédrale St-Pierre-et-St-Paul** opens onto a splendid vaulted interior. The nave is bathed in mauvish-red rays from the 16th-century rose

Statuary in Troyes' Cathédrale St-Pierre-et-St-Paul

window, complemented by the discreet turquoise of the Tree of Jesse window and the intense blue of the medieval windows of the apse.

Nearby, **Eglise St-Nizier** glitters in the faded quarter behind the cathedral, with its shimmering tiled Burgundian roof. Inside, it is lit by windows in a range of warm mauves and soothing blues.

The harmonious Gothic **Basilique St-Urbain** boasts grand flying buttresses (and fine windows, although these are currently undergoing restoration). **Eglise Ste-Madeleine** is noted for its elaborate 16th-century rood screen resembling lacy

Rue Larivey, a typical street with half-timbered houses, in Troyes

foliage, grapes and figs. Beyond is a wall of windows in browns, reds and blues. The ruelle des Chats, which is a quaint covered passageway, connects rue Charbonnet and rue Champeaux.

Set in one of the best-preserved quarters, **Eglise St-Pantaléon** faces a Renaissance mansion. A Gothic and Renaissance interior houses an imposing collection of 16th-century statuary and severe grisaille windows.

🏛 **Musée d'Art Moderne**
Palais Episcopal, place St-Pierre. 📞 03 25 76 26 80. **Open** Wed–Mon. **Closed** public hols. 🈴 🅿
Beside the cathedral, the former episcopal palace is now a museum of modern art, with a sculpture by Rodin and an especially fine collection of Fauvist paintings, as well as other modern art.

🏛 **Hotel du Petit Louvre**
Rue de la Montée St-Pierre. **Courtyard only open** daily.
Set off quai Dampierre, this newly restored hôtel particulier boasts a fish-scale roof, medieval tower, Renaissance courtyard, staircase and well. The highlight is a façade adorned with quizzical multi-colored faces.

Environs

The city's green playground, **Lac et Forêt d'Orient**, is 25 km (15 miles) east of Troyes. The forest is dotted with marshes, nature reserves and smaller lakes. Lac d'Orient, a large artificial lake, is popular for sailing, and there's water-skiing on Lac Amance and fishing at Lac du Temple.

Chaumont ⑪

Haute-Marne. 🏔 29,000. 🚉 🚌
ℹ place du Général de Gaulle (03 25 03 80 80). 🏛 Wed & Sat.

As the former residence of the Counts of Champagne, this feudal town enjoyed great prestige in the 13th century. On the far side of a ravine, the old town is on a rocky spur, with the Palais de Justice and the medieval castle keep dominating.

The keep, is a reminder that this quiet administrative center had a formidable past. This impression is confirmed by the Renaissance town houses which are bulging with *tourelles d'escaliers*, turreted staircases.

Basilique St-Jean-Baptiste, a gray stone Champenois church, is the most remarkable monument in Chaumont. The interior is enlivened by a spider's web of vaulting, a striking turreted staircase and Renaissance galleries. Near the entrance is a tiny chapel containing an unsettling *Mise au Tombeau* (1471), an intense multicolored stone group of 10 mourners gathered around Christ laid out on a shroud in his tomb. In the left transept is a bizarre but beguiling *Tree of Jesse*. On this ill-lit Renaissance stone relief, a family tree sprouts from the sleeping Jesus, who slumbers unawares – much like Chaumont itself.

Environs

Twenty-three kilometers (14 miles) northwest of Chaumont, **Colombey-les-Deux-Eglises** will forever be associated with General Charles de Gaulle. The de Gaulles bought their home, **La Boisserie**, in 1933, but

Cathédrale St-Mammès in Langres

had to abandon it during the war, when it was badly damaged. After its restoration, de Gaulle would return to La Boisserie from Paris on weekends to write his memoirs and plan comebacks. He eventually died here on November 9, 1970. The house is now a museum, with memorabilia from his life.

In the village churchyard, the General and President of France lies in a simple tomb. However, a giant granite cross of Lorraine, erected in 1972, dominates the skyline – a grandiose memorial more in keeping with de Gaulle's notion of *la gloire*.

🏛 La Boisserie

Colombey-les-Deux-Eglises. 📞 03 25 01 52 52. **Open** Mar–Dec: Wed–Mon. **Closed** Dec 25. 🎦 🚫

Langres ⑫

Haute-Marne. 🏔 10,000. 🚉 🚌
ℹ square O Lahalle (03 25 87 67 67). 🏛 Fri.

Set on a rocky spur, Langres lies beyond Chaumont, in the backwaters of southern Champagne. This ancient bishopric was one of the gateways to Burgundy and the birthplace of the encyclopedist, Denis Diderot (1713–84). Langres promotes itself as a land of springs, claiming that its proximity to the sources of the Seine and Marne grant it mystical powers.

Virtually the whole town is enclosed by medieval ramparts, Langres' undoubted attraction. A succession of towers and parapets provides glimpses of romantic town gates, sculpted Renaissance mansions and dim alleys. From the ramparts stretch panoramic views of the Marne Valley, the Langres plateau, the Vosges, and, on a clear day, even Mont Blanc.

Near Porte Henri IV stands the much-remodeled **Cathédrale St-Mammès**. The gloomy vaulted interior, in Burgundian Romanesque style, is redeemed by the sculpted capitals in the apse, reputedly taken from a temple of Jupiter.

Langres runs a lively summer season, featuring re-creations of a Renaissance tavern and the Nightwatchmen's Round, a folkloric evening stroll.

Memorial to General de Gaulle at Colombey-les-Deux-Eglises

ALSACE AND LORRAINE

....

MEURTHE-ET-MOSELLE · MEUSE · MOSELLE · BAS-RHIN
HAUT-RHIN · VOSGES

As border regions, Alsace and Lorraine have been fought over for centuries by France and Germany, their beleaguered past recalled by many military strongholds and cemeteries. But today, peace pervades the region, with its pastel-painted villages, fortified towns and sleepy vineyards.

At the northeast frontier of France, bordered by the Rhine, Alsace forms a fertile watershed between the mountains of the Vosges and the Black Forest in Germany. Lorraine, with its gentle rolling landscape on the other side of the mountains, is the poorer cousin but appears more overtly French in character.

EMBATTLED TERRITORY

Caught in the wars between France and Germany, Alsace and Lorraine have changed nationality four times since 1871. Centuries of strife have made border citadels of Metz, Toul and Verdun in Lorraine, while Alsace abounds with castles, from the pastiche folly of Haut-Koenigsbourg to Saverne's ruined fortress, built to guard a strategic pass in the Vosges. However, the area has a strong identity of its own, taking pride in local costumes, traditions and dialects. In Alsace, Route du Vin vineyards nudge pretty villages in the Vosges foothills. Strasbourg, the capital, is a cosmopolitan city with a 16th-century center, while Nancy, Lorraine's historic capital, represents elegant 18th-century architecture and town planning.

Much of the attraction of this region lies in its cuisine. Lorraine offers beer and quiche lorraine. In Alsace, cozy *winstubs*, or wine cellars, serve sauerkraut and flowery white wines, such as Riesling and Gewürztraminer.

Villagers enjoying the view from their window in Hunspach, north of Strasbourg in the northern Vosges

◁ Half-timbered houses with flower-clad balconies along the Route du Vin in Alsace

Exploring Alsace and Lorraine

VISITORS SEEKING ART and architecture will be amply rewarded by the charming medieval towns and excellent city museums of the region. Undiscovered Lorraine is the place to clamber over military citadels, walk in unspoiled countryside and unwind at relaxing spas. By contrast, Alsace offers magnificent forests and rugged mountain drives in the Vosges; quaint villages; and rich wines. The Route du Vin *(see pp222–3)* is one of the region's many scenic routes. It is particularly popular during the wine harvest festivities but is worth visiting in any season.

SIGHTS AT A GLANCE

To Luxembourg

To Reims

To Paris
Troyes

To Dijon

KEY

	Highway
	Major road
	Minor road
	Scenic route
∼	River
✲	Viewing point

Field of sunflowers just outside the village of Turckheim

The picturesque village of Riquewihr on the Route du Vin

GETTING AROUND

There is an international airport at Strasbourg and just across the border is Geneva Airport. If you are reliant on public transportation, Strasbourg, Colmar and Nancy make the best bases. There are good road and rail links between these towns and to Switzerland and Germany. The spectacular journey over the Vosges and along the Route du Vin is best made by car or on tours from Colmar or Strasbourg.

To Karlsruhe
Mannheim

BETSCHDORF

HAGUENAU

SAVERNE

STRASBOURG

OBERNAI

SÉLESTAT

CHÂTEAU DU
HAUT-KOENIGSBOURG

RIBEAUVILLÉ

RIQUEWIHR

COLMAR

GÉRARDMER

ÉGUISHEIM

NEUF-BRISACH

GUEBWILLER

ÉPINAL

CERNAY

MULHOUSE

To Besançon

To Basel
Bern
Zurich

0 kilometers   20

0 miles   10

The Ossuaire de Douaumont, a sentinel for the regiments of crosses on the battlefields of Verdun

Verdun ●

Meuse. ▲ 23,000. ▭ ▭ **i** place de la Nation (03 29 86 14 18). ➤ Fri.

THICK WALLS, drawbridges and gateways bear witness to Verdun's militaristic past. Based strategically at the mouth of the Meuse and near the border, it has almost inevitably been caught up in countless wars over the centuries. In 1916, Verdun became the symbol of French resistance when over 400,000 Frenchmen trying to defend the citadel.

The crenelated **Porte Chaussée**, a medieval river gateway, still guards the eastern entrance to the town and is the most impressive of the remaining fortifications.

Although battered by war damage, the **Citadelle de Verdun** retains its 12th-century tower, the only relic from the original abbey that Louis XIV's architect, Vauban, incorporated into his new military design. Now a war museum, the **Musée de la Citadelle Militaire**, it recreates through an audio-visual display Verdun's role in World War I. The citadel case-mates come to life as grim trenches, and the presentation ends by showing how the "Unknown Soldier" was chosen for the symbolic tomb under the Arc de Triomphe in Paris (see p103).

The **Cathédrale de Notre-Dame**, perched on high, looks dramatic, but the impression is marred by the clumsiness of its remodeling. The Rhenish cathedral retains Romanesque elements, from a tympanum showing Christ in Majesty to sculptures of Adam and Eve that are visible from the medieval cloisters. In the 18th century, the Romanesque sections were bricked up in deference to prevailing Baroque taste, but they were exposed once again by the bombardments of 1916.

Environs

It is Verdun's fate to be forever associated with the horrors of 1916–17. The harrowing battlefields of Verdun lie north of the city, on both banks of the Meuse. Because the villages in the area were razed, little now remains except the trenches and a few forts. The landscape is now littered with somber memorials, most notably the **Ossuaire de Douaumont**, a repository for the unidentified remains of 130,000 French and German soldiers of World War I.

� **Musée de la Citadelle Militaire**

La Citadelle. **[** 03 29 86 14 18. **Open** daily. **Closed** Jan 1, Dec 25. 🎥 🖾

The 16th-century cloisters of Eglise St-Gengoult in Toul

Toul ❷

Meurthe-et-Moselle. ▲ 18,000. ▭ ▭ **i** parvis de la Cathédrale (03 83 64 11 69). ➤ Wed & Fri.

LYING WITHIN dark forests west of Nancy, the octag-onal fortress city of Toul is encircled by the Moselle and the Canal de la Marne. Along with Verdun and Metz, Toul was one of the 4th-century bishoprics. In the early 18th century, Vauban built the cita-del, from which the ring of defensive waterways, the octagonal city ramparts and the **Porte de Metz** remain.

The **Cathédrale St-Etienne**, begun in the 13th century, took over 300 years to build and thus reflects a composite of styles, with Flamboyant Gothic predominating. It suf-fered damage in World War II, but the purity of the Champ-enois style has survived, notably in the arched, high-galleried interior. The imposing Flamboyant Gothic façade is flanked by octagonal towers. Other highlights are the two Renaissance chapels close to the transepts and the vast Champenois cloisters, decorated with sculpted foliage and stone gargoyles.

The Gothic façade of **Eglise St-Gengoult** is flanked by towers and adorned by Gothic stained-glass windows depic-ting the life of St. Gengoult.

Rue du Général-Gengoult, behind the church, contains a group of sculpted Renais-sance houses, and just north of the city are vineyards that produce the local "gray" Côtes de Toul wines.

Environs
Accessible from either Metz or
Toul, the vast **Parc Régional
de Lorraine** takes in red-tiled
cottages, vineyards, forests,
cropland, *chaumes* (high
pastureland), marshes and
lakes. Inns in the area are
especially noted for
their quiche lorraine
and *potée lorraine*,
a bacon casserole.

Jupiter Slaying a Monster on the
Column of Merten in La Cour d'Or

Metz ❸

Moselle. 🏠 124,000. 🚆 🚌 🚍
ℹ️ place d'Armes (03 87 55 53 76).
🛒 Tue, Thu & Sat.

A N AUSTERE yet appealing city,
Metz sits at the confluence
of the Moselle and the Seille.
Twenty bridges crisscross the
rivers and canals, and there
are pleasant walks along the
banks. This Gallo-Roman city,
now the capital of Lorraine,
has always been a pawn in
the game of border chess –
annexed by Germany in 1870,
regained by France in 1918.
  Set on a hill above the
Moselle, the **Cathédrale St-
Etienne** overlooks the historic
center. The Gothic exterior
flaunts impressive flying
buttresses and long-necked
gargoyles. Inside, stained-
glass windows, from Gothic
to modern, including some
by Chagall, present walls of
shimmering light.
  To the northwest of the
cathedral, a narrow wooden
bridge leads across to the
island of Petit Saulcy, where
the oldest French theater is
still in use. Located on the
other side of the cathedral, the
Porte des Allemands,

spanning a river, more
resembles a medieval castle
because of its bridge,
defensive towers and 13th-
century gate with pepper
mill-shaped towers.
  In the Vieille Ville, place
St-Louis is a delightful square
bordered by lofty, arcaded
14th-century mansions. **Eglise
St-Pierre-aux-Nonnains**
claims to be one of the oldest
churches in France. The
external walls and the ruined
façade date from Roman times,
while much of the rest belongs
to the 7th-century convent
that occupied the site. Nearby
is the frescoed 13th-century
Chapelle des Templiers,
built by the Knights Templar.

🏛 Musée de la Cour d'Or
2 rue du Haut-Poirier. 📞 03 87 75 10
18. **Open** daily. **Closed** some public
hols. 🖼
Also known as the Musée d'Art
et d'Histoire, this fascinating
collection is set in the Petits-
Carmes, a deconsecrated
17th-century monastery incorporating Gallo-Roman thermal
baths and a medieval tithe
barn. On display are Merovingian stone carvings, Gothic
painted ceilings, and German,
Flemish and French paintings.

WHITE STORKS

Until recently, the white
stork, traditionally a symbol
of good fortune, was a
frequent sight in northeast
France. White storks spend
the winter in Africa, but
migrate north to breed.
However, the gradual
draining of marshy ground
and pesticides and electric
cables have threatened
their survival here. A
program to reintroduce
them to the area has set
up breeding centers, as at
Molsheim and Turckheim,
which means these striking
birds can once again be
seen in Alsace-Lorraine.

The 13th-century Chapelle des Templiers, with restored frescoes, in Metz

Place Stanislas in Nancy, with statue of Stanislas Leczinski, Duke of Lorraine and father-in-law of Louis XV

Nancy ④

Meurthe-et-Moselle. 🚉 *102,000.*
✈ 🚉 🚌 🛈 *14 place Stanislas
(03 83 35 22 41).* 🛒 *Tue–Sat.*

LORRAINE'S HISTORIC capital
backs onto the Canal du
Marne and the Meurthe River.
In the 18th century, Stanislas
Leczinski, Duke of Lorraine
(*see p292*), embellished Nancy
beyond recognition, making it
a model of the golden age of
18th-century town planning.

The second golden age was
at the turn of this century,
when glassmaker Emile Gallé
founded the Ecole de Nancy,
a forerunner of the Art
Nouveau movement in France.

Nancy's principal and most
renowned landmark is **place
Stanislas**. Laid out in the
1750s, this elegantly proportioned square is enclosed by
highly ornate gilded wrought-
iron gates and railings, a hallmark of the city. Lining the
square are pavilions, including the Hôtel de Ville (town
hall) and stylish restaurants.

An Arc de Triomphe leads
to place de la Carrière, a
gracious, tree-lined square. At
the far end, flanked by semicircular arcades, is the Gothic
Palais du Gouvernement.
Next door in the Parc de la

Pépinière is Rodin's statue of
Claude Lorrain, the landscape
painter, born near Nancy.

The Grande Rue provides a
glimpse of medieval Nancy.
Of the original fortifications
only the Porte de la Craffe,
which was used as a prison
after the Revolution, remains.

🏠 Eglise et Couvent des Cordeliers et Musée Régional des Arts et Traditions Populaires

64 & 66 Grande Rue. 🅒 *03 83 32 18
74.* **Open** *Wed–Mon.* **Closed** *Jan 1,
May 1, Jul 14, Nov 1, Dec 25.* 🖼
The Dukes of Lorraine are
buried in the crypt, and the
adjoining converted monastery
contains the Musée Régional
des Arts et Traditions Populaires, covering folklore,
furniture, costumes and crafts.

🏛 Musée des Beaux Arts

3 place Stanislas. 🅒 *03 83 85 30 72.*
Open *Wed–Mon.* **Closed** *for
renovation until 1999.* 🖼
The fine arts museum is noted
for Delacroix's dramatic *Death
of Charles the Bold at Nancy*
(1833), as well as for pastoral
scenes by Poussin and Claude
Lorrain. On the ground floor
are 19th- and 20th-century
paintings by artists including
Manet, Monet, Berthe Morisot,
Utrillo, Dufy and Modigliani.

🏛 Musée Historique Lorraine

Palais Ducal, 64 Grande Rue. 🅒 *03 83
32 18 74.* **Open** *Wed–Mon.* **Closed**
Jan 1, May 1, Jul 14, Nov 1, Dec 25. 🖼
The museum of the history of
Lorraine has a rich collection
of archaeological finds, sculptures and paintings, including
two by Georges de la Tour.

🏛 Musée de l'Ecole de Nancy

36–38 rue de Sergent Blandan.
🅒 *03 83 40 14 86.* **Open**
Wed–Sun, Mon pm. **Closed** *Jan 1,
May 1, Jul 14, Nov 1, Dec 25.* 🖼
Exhibits in reconstructed Art
Nouveau settings include
furniture, fabrics and jewelry,
as well as the fanciful glassware of Emile Gallé, founder
of the Ecole de Nancy.

Arc de Triomphe in place Stanislas,
leading to place de la Carrière

Vosges landscape seen from the Route des Crêtes

THE ROUTE DES CRÊTES

This strategic mountain road (83 km/50 miles
long) connects the Vosges Valley from Col du
Bonhomme to Cernay, east of Thann, often
through woodland. Hugging the western side
of the Vosges, the Route des Crêtes was
created during World War I to prevent the
Germans from observing French troop
movements. When not shrouded in mist,
there are breathtaking views over Lorraine
from its many "crests" (*crêtes*).

Gérardmer ❺

Vosges. 🏠 *10,000.* 🚌 🚆 **i** *place des Déportés (03 29 27 27 27).* 🔴 *Thu & Sat.*

NESTLING ON the Lorraine side of the Vosges, on the shore of a magnificent lake stretching out before it, Gérardmer is a setting rather than a city. In November 1944, just before its liberation, Gérardmer was razed by the Nazi scorched-earth policy, but has since been reconstructed. Saw mills and woodcarving remain local trades, though tourism is fast replacing the textile industry.

Gérardmer is now a popular vacation resort. In winter, the steep slopes of the Vosges Cristallines around the town turn it into a ski resort, while the lake is used for water sports in summer. The town's attractions also include lakeside walks and boat trips, as well as Géromée cheese, similar to the more famous Munster, from just over the Alsatian border. Gérardmer also boasts the oldest tourist information office in the country, dating from 1875.

Yet, ultimately, it is the scenic drives and mountain hikes in the Vosges that attract adventurous visitors. Most leave the lakeside bowl to head for the Alsatian border via the magnificent **Route des Crêtes**, which can be joined at the mountain pass of Col de la Schlucht.

Re-creating village crafts in Ecomusée d'Alsace in Ungersheim

Mulhouse ❻

Haut Rhin. 🏠 *109,000.* ✈ 🚆 🚌 **i** *9 av du Maréchal Foch (03 89 35 48 48).* 🔴 *Tue, Thu & Sat.*

CLOSE TO the Swiss border, Mulhouse is primarily an industrial city, badly damaged in World War II. However, there are numerous technical museums and shopping galleries, as well as Alsatian taverns and Swiss wine bars. Most visitors use the city as a base for exploring the rolling hills of the Sundgau on the Swiss border.

Of the museums, **Musée de l'Impression sur Etoffes**, at 14 rue Jean-Jaques Henner, is devoted to textiles and fabric painting, while **Musée Français du Chemin de Fer**, at 2 rue Alfred Glehn, has a collection of steam and electric locomotives. **Musée National de l'Automobile**, at 192 avenue de Colmar, boasts over 100 Bugattis, plus several Mercedes and Ferraris and Charlie Chaplin's Rolls Royce. The place de la République, the liveliest part of town, has a **Musée Historique**, in the Renaissance former town hall.

Alsatian black pig in Ecomusée d'Alsace in Ungersheim

Environs
At Ungersheim, north of Mulhouse, the **Ecomusée d'Alsace** consists of rural settings transplanted here to preserve and display the region's heritage. The 12th-century fortified house from Mulhouse is a dramatic building, complete with Gothic garden. Farms are run along traditional lines, with livestock such as the Alsatian black pig. Rural crafts can be seen in their original settings.

🏛 **Ecomusée d'Alsace**
Chemin du Grosswald.
(*03 89 74 44 74.* **Open** *daily.* 🖼 👤

The lake at Gérardmer, offering sports and leisure activities

Guebwiller 🄼

Haut Rhin. 🄼 11,000. 🚌 🛈 73 rue de la République (03 89 76 10 63). 🛒 Tue & Fri.

SURROUNDED BY vineyards and flower-filled valleys, Guebwiller is known as "the gateway to the valley of flowers." However, as an industrial town producing textiles and machine tools, it feels cut off from its rural setting. The houses are digni-fied, but the *caves* and churches make it worth a visit.

Set on a pretty square, **Eglise Notre-Dame** combines Baroque theatricality with Neo-Classical elegance, while **Eglise des Dominicains** boasts Gothic frescoes and a fine rood screen. **Eglise St-Léger**, the richly ornamented Romanesque church, is the most rewarding, especially the façade, triple porch and portal.

Eglise St-Léger in Guebwiller

Environs

The scenic Lauch Valley, north-west of Guebwiller, is known as "Le Florival" because of its flowers and foliage. **Lauten-bach** is used as a starting point for hikes through this recog-nized *zone de tranquillité*. The village has a pink Roman-esque church, whose portal depicts human passion and the battle between Good and Evil. The square leads to the river, a small dam, a *lavoir* (public washing place) and houses overhanging the water.

Neuf-Brisach 🄼

Haut Rhin. 🄼 2,100. 🚌 🛈 Palais du Gouverneur, 6 place d'Armes (03 89 72 56 66). 🛒 1st & 3rd Mon of each month.

SITUATED NEAR the German border, this octagonal citadel is the military strategist Vauban's masterpiece. Built between 1698 and 1707, the citadel forms a typical star-shaped pattern, with symmetrical towers enclosing 48 equal squares. In the center, from where straight streets radiate for ease of defense, is

THE CITADEL OF NEUF-BRISACH

Porte de Bâle

The outer ring of defenses was built around two moats.

Place d'Armes, once the parade ground, provided the innermost refuge.

Porte de Strasbourg was originally protected by a draw-bridge.

Bastion

The fortress is divided into 48 *îlots* or squares.

The fortress walls are 9 m (30 ft) high and 4.5 m (14.5 ft) wide at their base.

The Porte de Belfort houses the Musée Vauban. A walk links Porte de Belfort with Porte de Colmar.

Porte de Colmar

The celebrated Isenheim altarpiece by Matthias Grünewald in Colmar

the place d'Armes and the Eglise St-Louis, which was added in 1731–6. It was Vauban's usual homage to his patron, Louis XIV, implying that the church was dedicated to the Sun King, rather than the saint.

The Porte de Belfort houses the **Musée Vauban**, which includes a model of the town, showing the outlying defenses, now concealed by woodland. They represent Vauban's barrier to the fortress and it is to his credit that the citadel was never taken.

🏛 **Musée Vauban**
Place Porte de Belfort. [03 89 72 56 66. **Open** Apr–Oct: Wed–Mon; Nov–Mar: groups only by appt. 🎫 ♿

Eguisheim ⓿

Haut Rhin. 🏙 1,500. 🚌 🛈 22a Grand'Rue (03 89 23 40 33).

E GUISHEIM is a most exquisite small town, laid out within three concentric rings of ramparts. Curled up within these 13th-century walls, the ensemble of austere fortifications and domestic elegance makes for a surprisingly harmonious whole.

In the center of town is the octagonal feudal **castle** of the Counts of Eguisheim. A Renaissance fountain in front has the statue of Bruno Eguisheim, born here in 1002. He became Pope Léon IX and was later canonized.

The Grand'Rue is lined with half-timbered houses, many showing their construction

date. Close to the castle is the **Marbacherhof**, a monastic tithe barn and cornhall. On a neighboring square, the modern parish church retains the original Romanesque sculpted tympanum.

The rest of the town has its share of Hansel-and-Gretel atmosphere, while inviting courtyards offer tastings of *grands crus*. From rue de Hautvilliers, outside the ramparts, a marked path leads through scenic vineyards.

Colmar ⓾

Haut Rhin. 🏙 65,000. 🚉 🚌 🛈 4 rue d'Unterlinden (03 89 20 68 92). 🛒 Wed, Thu & Sat.

C OLMAR IS THE BEST-preserved city in Alsace. As a trading post and river port, Colmar had its heyday in the 16th century, when wine merchants shipped their wine along the waterways running through the picturesque canal quarter,

now known as **Petite Venise**. "Little Venice" is best seen on a leisurely boat trip that takes you from the tanners' quarter to the rue des Tanneurs. The adjoining place de l'Alsacienne Douane is dominated by the **Koïfhüs**, a galleried customs house with a Burgundian tiled roof, overlooking half-timbered pastel houses that sport sculpted pillars.

Nearby, the place de la Cathédrale quarter is full of 16th-century houses with picturesque hanging signs. **Eglise St-Martin**, essentially Gothic, has a noted south portal. Just to the west, the place des Dominicains, with cafés, is dwarfed by the Gothic **Eglise Dominicains**. Inside is *La Vierge au Buisson de Roses* (1473), the glittering red and gold "Virgin of the Rose-bush" by Martin Schongauer, a renowned Alsatian painter and native of Colmar.

Place d'Unterlinden, the adjoining square, has the **Musée d'Unterlinden**. Set in a Dominican monastery, it displays early Rhenish paintings. The highlight is the Isenheim altarpiece. A master-piece of emotional intensity, it is part of an early 16th-century Alsatian panel painting by Matthias Grünewald.

In the historic center, the quaint rue des Têtes has the former wine exchange, a Renaissance town house known as the Maison des Têtes because of the grimacing heads on the gabled façade. And in rue Mercière, **Maison Pfister**, with its slender stair turret and galleried flower-decked façade, has come to typify the city.

Along the quai de la Poissonerie in the Petite Venise area of Colmar

Riquewihr ⓫

Haut Rhin. ᚋ 1,100. 🔲
ℹ 2 rue de 1ère Armée (03 89 49
08 40). 🚌 Fri.

VINEYARDS RUN right up to
the ramparts of Riquewihr,
the prettiest village on the
Route du Vin (see pp222–3).
Deeply pragmatic, Riquewihr
winemakers plant roses at the
end of each row of vines –
both for their pretty effect
and as early detectors of
parasites. The village belonged
to the Counts of Wurtemberg
until the Revolution and has
grown rich on wine, from
Tokay and Pinot Gris to
Gewürztraminer and Riesling.
Virtually an outdoor museum,
Riquewihr abounds in
cobbled alleys, geranium-clad
balconies, galleried courtyards,
romantic double ramparts and
watchtowers.

From the Hôtel de Ville, the
rue du Général de Gaulle
climbs gently past medieval
and Renaissance houses, half-
timbered, stone-clad or
corbelled. Oriel windows vie
with sculpted portals and
medieval sign boards. On the
right lies the idyllic **place des**

Trois Eglises. A passageway
leads through the ramparts to
the vineyards, stacked up on
the hill. Farther up lies the
Dolder, a 13th-century belfry,
followed by the **Tour Haute**,
marking the second tier of
ramparts. Beyond the gateway are **Cours des Bergers**,
gardens laid out around the
16th-century ramparts. The
picture-postcard image is only
challenged by the crowds in
summer or during the wine
harvest, when visitors outnumber the local population
several times over.

The pretty – and popular – village
of Riquewihr, set among vineyards

Ribeauvillé ⓬

Haut Rhin. ᚋ 4,800. 🚉 🔲
ℹ 1 Grand'Rue (03 89 73 62 22).
🚌 Sat.

OVERLOOKED by three ruined
castles, Ribeauvillé is
stiflingly prettified, as may be
expected from a popular
town on the Route du Vin.
This status is partly due to
healthy sales of the celebrated *grands crus* of Alsace,
especially Riesling. There are
ample opportunities for
tastings, particularly near the
park, in the lower part of
town (see pp222–3).

On the Grand'Rue (No. 14) is
the **Pfifferhüs**, the minstrels'
house, now a regional restaurant. As local cooks declare,
Ribeauvillé is the capital of the
kougelbopf, the light, almond-
flavored Alsatian cake.

Tortuous alleys wind past
steep-roofed artisans' and wine-
growers' houses in the upper
part of the town. Beyond are
Renaissance fountains, painted
façades and **St Grégoire-le-
Grand**, the Gothic parish
church. A marked path, which
begins in this part of town,
leads into the vineyards.

Château du Haut-Koenigsbourg ⓭

Orschwiller. 📞 03 88 82 45 82.
Call for opening times. 🈳 ⓫

LOOMING ABOVE the lovely
village of St-Hippolyte,
Haut-Koenigsbourg Castle,
the most popular attraction in
Alsace, dominates the horizon.
In 1114, the Swabian Emperor,
Frederick of Hohenstaufen,
built the first Teutonic castle
here, which was destroyed in
1462. Rebuilt and added to
under the Habsburgs, it
burned down in 1633. At the
end of the 19th century, Kaiser
Wilhelm II commissioned
Berlin architect Bodo Ebhardt
to restore the castle. The result
of his painstaking work was a
precise reconstruction of the
original building.

Despite a drawbridge, fierce
keep and rings of fortifications,
this warm sandstone hybrid is
too sophisticated for a feudal
château. The Cour d'Honneur
is a breathtaking re-creation,
with a pointed corner turret
and creaky arcaded galleries.
Within the castle are suitably
gloomy "Gothic" chambers and
airy "Renaissance" rooms. La
Grande Salle is the most
elaborate, with a Neo-Gothic
gallery and ornate paneling.
From the battlements,

almost 750 m (2,500 ft) above
the Alsace plain, stretches a
glorious Rhineland panorama,
bordered by the Black Forest
and the Alps. On the other
side are sweeping views,
from the high Vosges to
villages and vineyards
below.

Upper garden

West bastion

West wing

Outer walls

Chapelle St-Sébastien outside Dambach-la-Ville, along the Route du Vin

Sélestat **⑭**

Bas Rhin. 🏠 16,000. 🚉 🚌
ℹ️ *Commanderie Saint Jean, boulevard du Maréchal-Leclerc (03 88 58 87 20).* 🛒 *Tue.*

DURING THE RENAISSANCE, Sélestat was the intellectual center of Alsace, with a tradition of humanism fostered by Beatus Rhenanus, a friend of Erasmus. The famous **Bibliothèque Humaniste** has a magnificent collection of leather-bound editions of some of the earliest printed books and unique illuminated manuscripts. Nearby are the Cour des Prélats, a turreted ivy-covered mansion, and the Tour de l'Horloge, a medieval clock tower. **Eglise Ste-Foy** is 12th-century, with an octagonal bell tower. Opposite is **Eglise St-Georges**, glittering with green and red "Burgundian tiles."

🏛 **Bibliothèque Humaniste**
1 rue de la Bibliothèque.
📞 *03 88 92 03 24.*
Open *Jul–Aug: daily; Sep–Jun: Mon–Sat am.*
Closed *public hols.* ♿

Environs

Medieval **Dambach-la-Ville**, another pretty town, is linked to Andlau and red-tiled Itterswiller by a delightful rural road through vineyards.

Ebersmunster, a picturesque hamlet, has an onion-domed abbey church, whose Baroque interior is a sumptuous display of gilded stucco.

Obernai **⑮**

Bas Rhin. 🏠 10,000. 🚉 🚌
ℹ️ *place du Beffroi (03 88 95 64 13).* 🛒 *Tue & Thu.*

Young *Alsaciens* in traditional costume

AT THE NORTH END of the Route du Vin, Obernai retains a flavor of authentic Alsace: residents speak Alsatian, at festivities women wear traditional costume, and church services are well attended in the cavernous Neo-Gothic **Eglise St-Pierre-et-St-Paul**. The place du Marché is well preserved, and features the gabled **Halle aux Blés**, a 16th-century corn hall above a former butcher's shop, with a façade adorned with cows' and dragons' heads. Place de la Chapelle, the adjoining square, has a Renaissance fountain. The square is home to the 16th-century **Hôtel de Ville** and the **Kapellturm**, the galleried Gothic belfry. Side streets have Renaissance and medieval timber-framed houses. A stroll past the cafés on rue du Marché ends in a pleasant park by the ramparts.

Environs

Odile, Alsace's seventh-century patron saint, was born in Obernai but she is venerated on **Mont Sainte-Odile** to the west, where she is buried in the Chapelle Ste-Odile.

Molsheim, a former bishopric and fortified market town 10 km (6 miles) north, is noted for its attractive marketplace with fountain. The star attraction is the Metzig, a Renaissance-style butchers' guildhall, now the town hall.

North wing, with kitchens

South wing, with chapel

Entrance ramp to upper castle

Hostelry

Outer walls

Guardroom

Entrance

Well tower

Drawbridge within the walls of Château du Haut-Koenigsbourg

Strasbourg

Cathedral statue

HALFWAY BETWEEN PARIS and Prague, Strasbourg is often known, not surprisingly, as "the cross-roads of Europe." The city wears its European cosmopolitanism with ease – after all, its famous cathedral has catered to both Catholic and Protestant congregations – and, as one of the capitals of the European Union has sensibly located the futuristic European Parliament building just off the historic center. One way to see this, plus more traditional features of the city, is to take a boat trip along the waterways encircling the Old Town. On the way you will pass the Ponts-Couverts, covered bridges linked by medieval watchtowers that provide an observation point for the four Ill canals, and the scenic Petite France, once the tanners' district, dotted with mills and crisscrossed by bridges.

Barge on the canal

The central portal of the west façade of the cathedral

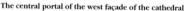

✝ Cathédrale Notre-Dame

A masterpiece of stone lace-work, the sandstone cathedral "rises like a most sublime, wide-arching tree of God," as Goethe marveled. Though construction began in the 11th century (the choir is Romanesque, the nave is Gothic), it ended only in 1439, with the completion of the west façade begun in 1277. The three portals are ornamented with statues. But the crowning glory is the kaleidoscope of the rose window. The south portal leads to the Gothic Pilier des Anges, or Pillar of Angels (built around 1230), set beside the Astronomical Clock: mechanical figures appear accompanied by chimes at 12:31pm. There are wonderful views over the city from the viewing platform, and on some summer evenings there are organ concerts.

In place de la Cathédrale, Maison Kammerzell, now a popular restaurant, was once a rich merchant's mansion and is the most elaborately carved in Alsace. The ground floor dates from 1467, the rest from 1589. From place du Château, behind the cathedral, a tourist "mini-train" passes the main sights in the historic center and Petite France.

🏛 Musée de l'Oeuvre de Notre-Dame

3 place du Château. 📞 03 88 52 50 00. **Open** Tue–Sun. **Closed** Jan 1, Good Fri, May 1, Nov 1, Dec 25. 🌀 & ground floor only.

The cathedral's impressive museum contains much of its original sculpture, as well as magnificent stained glass from the 11th century. A collection

IPE, the European Parliament building on the outskirts of the city center

VISITORS' CHECKLIST

Bas Rhin. 🏠 250,000. ✈ 12 km
(7.5 miles) SW Strasbourg.
🚉 place de la Gare (08 36 35
35 35). 🚌 place des Halles (03
88 77 70 70). 🛈 17 place de la
Cathédrale (03 88 52 28 28).
🕭 Mon–Sat. 🎼 Classical Music
Festival (Jun); Jazz Festival (Jun);
Musica, contemporary music
festival (mid-Sep–early-Oct).

STRASBOURG CITY CENTER

Cathédrale Notre-Dame ④
Maison Kammerzell ③
Musée Alsacien ⑦
Musée de l'Oeuvre
 de Notre-Dame ⑤
Palais des Rohan ⑥
Petite France ②
Ponts-Couverts ①

0 meters	250
0 yards	250

Bishops of Strasbourg. It
houses three museums: the
Musée des Beaux Arts; the
Musée Archéologique; and
the Musée des Arts
Décoratifs, which contains
the sumptuous State
Apartments and one of
the finest collections of
ceramics in France.
Nearby, in the old Customs
House, the Musée d'Art
Moderne has temp-
orary exhibitions
featuring works by
modern artists.

🏛 Musée Historique

3 place de la Grande Boucherie.
📞 03 88 52 50 00. **Closed** for
renovation until 1999. 🌅 🚹
The museum occupies the
cavernous 16th-century city
abattoir and focuses on Strasbourg's political, economic and
military history.

🏛 Musée Alsacien

23 quai St-Nicolas. 📞 03 88 35 55 36.
Open Wed–Mon. **Closed** Jan 1, Good
Fri, May 1, Nov 1, Dec 25. 🌅
Housed in a series of interconnecting Renaissance
buildings, the museum has
exhibits on local traditions
and popular arts and crafts.

of Medieval
and Renais-
sance Alsatian art
is displayed in an
intimate setting in this
somber gabled house.

🏛 Palais des Rohan

2 pl du Château. 📞 03 88 52 50 00.
Open Wed–Mon. **Musée d'Art
Moderne**, 5 rue du Château **open**
Wed–Mon. **Museums closed** Jan 1,
Good Fri, May 1, Nov 1 & 11, Dec 25.
🌅 🚹
Designed by the king's archi-
tect, Robert de Cotte, in 1730,
this grand Classical palace was
intended for the Prince-

KEY

🚤 Riverboat service

🅿 Parking

🛈 Tourist information

🕆 Church

**Ponts-Couverts with medieval
watchtowers over the canals**

The Alsace Route du Vin

MEANDERING over 180 km (110 miles) from Marlenheim to Thann, the picturesque wine route takes in historic towns with cobbled streets, medieval timber-framed houses and Renaissance fountains. Romantically appointed *winstubs*, or cellars, offer traditional *choucroute garnie* and flowery white Alsatian wines. Dedicated wine lovers could spend two or three days covering the route at leisure, or may want to make shorter trips in either direction to or from Colmar. For a refreshing contrast from the unremitting charm of the towns and villages, escape occasionally into *sentiers viticoles* – lovely paths through the vineyards themselves.

Alsatian wine master

Harvesting grapes in Alsace

MARLENHEIM

STRASBOURG →

Mont-Ste Odile

Andlau

Haut-Koenigsbourg

Sélestat

COLMAR

Rouffach

MULHOUSE

THANN

Molsheim ①
Renaissance building and Riesling vineyar vie for attention with Bugatti car museum.

Obernai ②
The galleried Kapellturm in the place du Marché dates from the 13th–16th centurie

Dambach-la-Ville ③
Vintner's carts now serve as decoration in this pretty medieval town renowned fc its *grand cru* Frankstein.

Ribeauvillé ④
Famed for its Riesling, th town celebrates Pipers' Day, the first Sunday in September, with a founta spouting free wine.

Riquewihr ⑤
A showcase of medieval anc Renaissance houses, this is o of France's most visited tow

Turckheim ⑥
Ancient buildings encirc place Turenne in this Renaissance town famou for its Brand wine.

Eguisheim ⑦
This ancient town ringed by medieval houses produces two *grands crus*, Eichberg (Oak Hill) and Pfersigberg (Peach Hill).

Guebwiller ⑧
Eglise St-Léger dates from the Middle Ages, when Guebwiller grew rich on wine. Today it is a busy textile town.

0 kilometers 5
0 miles 5

KEY

━━━ Wine route

〜〜 Other roads

ALSACE WINE

Alsace wines are usually aromatic, dry and full-bodied. All are white except Pinot Noir, used for light reds.

Late-harvested Alsatian classic

KEY FACTS

Location and climate
Protected by the Vosges, Alsace has a semi-continental, fairly dry, warm climate.

Grape varieties
Alsace wines are known simply by their grape variety. *Gewürztraminer*, with its exotic rose-petal character, is most typically Alsatian, although the *Riesling* is arguably the finest. *Muscat* is another aromatic variety. Spicy but less assertive than Gewürztraminer, *Pinot Gris* and the crisper, dry *Pinot Blanc* go well with food. *Pinot Noir* is the only red variety.

Lusciously rich, sweet, late-harvested wines are an Alsace specialty.

Best producers
Albert Boxler, Marcel Deiss, Marc Kreydenweiss, Bernard & Robert Schoffit, Kuentz-Bas, Domaine Weinbach, Josmeyer, Olivier Zind-Humbrecht, Charles Schléret, Domaines Schlumberger, Domaine Ostertag, Domaine Trimbach, Hugel & Fils, Cave de Turckheim.

Good vintages
1996, 1995, 1994, 1990, 1989, 1988.

The 12th-century chapel of the Château du Haut-Barr, near Saverne

Saverne 🟡

Bas Rhin. 🏠 10,300. 🚇 🚌 �ℹ 37 Grand Rue (03 88 91 80 47). 🗓 Tue, Thu & Sat am.

FRAMED BY HILLS, and situated on the Zorn River and the Marne-Rhine Canal, Saverne is a pretty sight. The town was a fief of the prince-bishops of Strasbourg, and its sandstone Château des Rohan was a favorite summer residence. Today, it houses the **Musée de la Ville de Saverne**, whose collection traces Saverne's past. On the far side of the château, the Grand'Rue is studded with restaurants and timber-framed Renaissance houses.

🏛 **Musée de la Ville de Saverne**
Château des Rohan. 📞 03 88 91 06 28. **Open** Mar–Nov: Wed–Mon; Dec–Feb: Sun. 🎫 ♿

Environs
To the southwest, perched on a rocky spur, the ruined **Château du Haut-Barr** – the "Eye of Alsace" – once commanded the vital pass of Col de Saverne.

In **Marmoutier**, 6 km (3.5 miles) south of Haut-Barr, is a renowned abbey church with a Romanesque-Lombard façade and octagonal towers.

Betschdorf 🟡

Bas Rhin. 🏠 3,600. ℹ La Mairie (03 88 54 48 00).

THE VIBRANT village of Betschdorf borders the Forêt de Haguenau, 45 km (27 miles) north of Strasbourg. Many residents occupy timber-framed houses dating from the 18th century, when pottery made the village prosperous. Generations of potters have passed down the knowledge of the characteristic blue-gray glaze to their sons, while the women have been entrusted with decorating it in cobalt blue. A pottery museum, with a workshop attached, displays rural

Betschdorf pottery

ceramics. Also worth visiting are the frescoed Gothic Niederbetschdorf church and the Lutheran Kuhlendorf church, the only timber-framed church in Alsace. Nearby is the Wacht, the former nightwatchmen's quarters. Betschdorf is a good place to try *tartes flambées* – hot, crispy bases topped with cheese or fruit.

Environs
Another pottery village, **Soufflenheim**, lies 10 km (6 miles) southeast. Its earth-colored pottery is usually painted with bold flowers.

WESTERN
FRANCE

Introducing Western France

THE WESTERN REGIONS of France have played very different historical roles, from the royal heartland of the Loire Valley to separatist Celtic Brittany. These are mainly rich farming regions, with fishing important along the coasts. Heavy industry and oil refineries are concentrated around Rouen and Le Havre. Visitors come for the wonderful beaches, quiet rural byways and the sumptuous Loire châteaux. This map shows the region's most celebrated sights.

The evocative silhouette of Mont-St-Michel has welcomed pilgrims since the 11th century. Today nearly one million visitors a year walk across the sands to the island abbey (see pp246–51).

Guimiliau Parish Close

Mont-St-Michel

BRITTANY
(See pp258–75)

Carnac Megaliths

The megaliths of Carnac are evidence of early settlers in Brittany. These ancient granite blocks, arranged in intriguing patterns, date to 4000 BC and are thought to have had a religious or astronomical significance (see p269).

The Bayeux Tapestry (see pp242–3) *shows William the Conqueror's invasion of England from the French point of view. Among its 58 scenes, key events such as the Battle of Hastings in 1066 are depicted with great vigor and finesse. Here, two of William's messengers are shown hurrying to meet him.*

Bayeux Tapestry

Rouen Cathedral

Château de Chambord *is the largest and most extravagant of the Loire châteaux (see pp292–3). François I transformed the original hunting lodge to a luxurious moated castle in 1519. Its splendor was completed by Louis XIV in 1685. Inside the 440 rooms are François' salamander emblem and 365 fireplaces, one for every day of the year.*

NORMANDY
(See pp236–57)

Chartres Cathedral

Le Mans Cathedral

Château de Chambord

Château de Villandry

Château de Chenonceau

THE LOIRE VALLEY
(See pp276–303)

0 kilometers   50

0 miles   50

Regional Food: Western France

Camembert cheese

WITH 480 KM (300 MILES) of coastline, Normandy cooking naturally draws on an abundance of fish and shellfish. Lambs graze on the salt marshes, giving the meat its slightly salty, distinctive flavor. Inland, dairy cattle produce rich milk for cream, cheese and butter. Calvados, the famous apple brandy, is derived from the apples that thrive here.

Seafood, salt-marsh lamb, cider, and cider *eau-de-vie* all cross the border into Breton cuisine, but particular to Brittany is fresh curd cheese or buttermilk with buckwheat *crêpes* – foods once regarded as humble but that have now become much sought-after ingredients of chic regional cuisine.

In the Loire Valley, the river is a source of tasty freshwater fish, and plump mushrooms are cultivated in caves along the riverbanks. The rich alluvial soils produce luscious vegetables, fruit, cheese and wine.

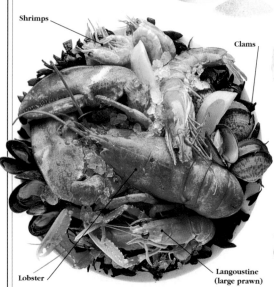

Pure sea salt crystals, seen glistening on the Guérande Peninsula of southeast Brittany, are raked in pans by farmers in the traditional way. This fine natural salt retains all its minerals and the unmistakable scent of the sea.

Shrimps

Clams

Lobster

Langoustine (large prawn)

Fruits de mer is a selection of local seafood which includes oysters, clams, mussels, crabs, langoustines, whelks (a type of snail), shrimps and periwinkles, often served on a great bed of ice and seaweed. Necessary accompaniments include lemons, shallot-and-vinegar sauce, chilled Muscadet, fresh rye bread and butter.

Moules marinières are mussels cooked in white wine, with onions, shallots, parsley and butter.

Oysters can be eaten raw straight from the shell or grilled quickly and served with a sauce.

Rillettes are chunks of pork or goose meat seasoned with herbs, cooked in lard and pounded to a paste.

Artichokes can be cooked in water or wine with herbs, stuffed, or served with herb or lemon-flavored butter.

Gigot d'agneau à la Bretonne *is roast lamb served with haricot beans simmered with tomatoes, garlic and onions.*

Salmon with beurre blanc, *a sauce of butter, wine and shallots, is a popular dish in both Brittany and the Loire.*

Tripe à la mode de Caen *is a Normandy dish of steamed tripe and vegetables cooked together very slowly in cider.*

Tarte tatin *is a caramelized upside-down apple tart, originally created at the Hôtel Tatin in the Loire Valley.*

Crêpes Suzettes, *one of Brittany's most famous dishes, is flavored with oranges and Grand Marnier liqueur.*

Galette biscuits *from Brittany are quite noticeably flavored with the slightly salty butter used in the regional cuisine.*

CHEESES

Some of France's finest cheeses come from Normandy – Camembert, pungent Livarot and creamy Pont-l'Evêque. Crottin de Chavignol from the Loire is one of the most popular *chèvres* (goat's cheeses).

Pont l'Eveque

Crottins de Chavignol

Livarot

Camembert

Benedictine   **Calvados**   **Cider**

DRINKS

In Normandy and most of Brittany, sparkling alcoholic and nonalcoholic cider is the local drink, an excellent accompaniment to savory *crêpes*. Much stronger is the apple brandy known as Calvados (*lambig* in Brittany). The herbal liqueur Benedictine was first concocted by a monk at Fécamp in 1510.

France's Wine Regions: the Loire

WITH A FEW EXCEPTIONS, the Loire is a region of good rather than great wines. The fertile agricultural soils of the meandering flatlands of the "Garden of France" are fine for fruit and vegetables, less so for the production of great wines. The cool, northern, Atlantic-influenced climate

Cabernet Franc, red grape of the Loire

nonetheless produces refreshing reds and summer rosés, aromatic white wines and attractively bracing sparkling wines. The white wines are very much in the majority here, and are usually intended for early consumption, so vintages in the Loire tend to matter less than in the classic red wine regions.

LOCATOR MAP

⬜ *Loire wine region*

The great sweet wine *of the Coteaux du Layon, Quarts de Chaume, is little-known outside France.*

QUARTS DE CHAUME
CHATEAU DE BELLE RIVE
APPELLATION QUARTS DE CHAUME CONTROLEE

Muscadet *with the words* sur lie *on the label has been aged on its "lees" (see p23), giving the wine more flavor and interest.*

CHATEAU du CLÉRAY
MUSCADET DE SÈVRE ET MAINE

WINE REGIONS

The Loire, flowing for some 1,000 km (620 miles), links the major wine areas of the Loire Valley. Near its source west of Burgundy, in the geographical center of France, lie Sancerre and Pouilly Fumé; the river flows west through Touraine and Anjou, finally reaching the coastal flats of the Pays Nantais, home of Muscadet.

• Châteaubriant
• Nozay
Erdre
Ancenis • ANGERS
Savennières •
St-Nazaire • *Loire* Chaume •
Faye
D'A
• Pornic • NANTES Bonnezeaux •
Cholet •
• Montaigu
Boulogne
Sèvre-Nantaise
Atlantique
La Roche-sur-Yon
Les Sables
D'Olonne
Sèvre-Niortaise
Part
Ni

Clos de l'Echo, Chinon, producer of fine, herbaceous red wine

KEY

⬜ Pays Nantais

⬜ Anjou-Saumur

⬜ Haut-Poitou

⬜ Touraine

⬜ Central Vineyards

0 kilometers   15

0 miles   15

*his red wine has been
nade using grapes from
ieilles vignes – the oldest
nd the best vines on the
rower's property.*

Red wine vineyards at Bourgueil

Vouvray *makes
still and sparkling
white wine, the
latter often aged
in chalk caves
very like those
in Champagne.*

LE MANS

N157

N23

Loir

N157

ORLEANS

N7

Vendôme

Loir

Loire

La Ferté-St-Aubin   Gien

Baugé

A10

Blois

A71

Sauldre

TOURS   Vouvray

Montlouis-sur-Loire

Aubigny-sur-Nère

Romorantin-Lanthenay

Cosne-Cours-
sur-Loire

ur

Bourgueil

Vienne

N76

Cher

Vierzon

Menetou-
Salon

Sancerre   Pouilly-su
Loire

pigny   Chinon

Loches   Valençay

Quincy

La Charité-
sur-Loire

Ste-Maure-
de-Touraine

A10

Indre

Reuilly

BOURGES

N143

N20

Auron

Cher

N7

Châtellerault

Creuse

Châteauroux

N149

Le Blanc

*A classic wine with a price to match,
Pouilly Fumé is revered for its
unique, smoky "gunflint" character.*

POITIERS

10

CLOS JOANNE D'ORON
Pouilly-Fumé

KEY FACTS ABOUT LOIRE WINES

Location and Climate
Fertile agricultural soils support
fruit, vegetables and cereals as
well as grapes. The climate is
cool, influenced by the nearby Atlantic,
giving the wines a refreshing acidity.

Grape Varieties
The **Muscadet** makes simple,
dry white wines. The ***Sauvignon***
makes gooseberryish, flinty dry
whites; it is at its finest in Sancerre and
Pouilly Fumé, but is also good in Touraine.
The **Chenin Blanc** makes dry and medium
Anjou, Savennières, Vouvray, Montlouis
and Saumur, sparkling Vouvray and Saumur,
and the famous sweet whites, Bonnezeaux,

Vouvray and Quarts de Chaume.
Summery reds are made from
the ***Gamay*** and the grassy,
herbaceous **Cabernet Franc**.

Good Producers
Muscadet: Sauvion, Guy Bossard,
Luneau. *Anjou, Savennieres,
Vouvray*: Richou, Domaine de la
Bizolière, Coulée de Serrant, Huet,
Domaine des Aubuissières, Bourillon-
Dorléans. *Touraine* (white): Domaine des
Acacias. *Saumur* (red): Filliatreau, Domaine
des Roches Neuves. *Chinon/Bourgueil* (red):
Joguet, Taluau, Druet. *Sancerre, Pouilly
Fumé, Ménétou-Salon*: Dagueneau, Reverdy,
Vacheron, Mellot, Henry Natter, Henry Pelle.

From Defense to Decoration

THE GREAT CHATEAUX of the Loire Valley gradually evolved from purely defensive structures to decorative palaces. With the introduction of firearms, castles lost their defensive function and comfort and taste predominated. Defensive elements like towers, battlements, moats and gatehouses were retained largely as symbols of rank and ancestry. Renaissance additions, like galleries and dormer windows, added elegance.

Salamander emblem of François 1

Slate and stone walls

Fortifications with towers removed

Circular tower, formerly defensive

Corbeled walkways, once useful in battle

Angers (see p281), *a fortress built from 1230– 40 by Louis IX, stands on a rocky hill in the town center. In 1585, Henri III removed the towers from 17 fortifications that were formerly 30 m (98 ft) high.*

Chaumont (see p296) *was rebuilt in 1498–1510 in Renaissance style by the Amboise family. Although it has a defensive appearance, with circular towers, corbeled walkways and a gatehouse, these features are mainly decorative. It was restored after 1875.*

Decorated turret

Azay-le-Rideau (see p286), *regarded as one of the most elegant and well-designed Renaissance châteaux , was built by finance minister Gilles Berthelot (1518–1527) and his wife Philippa Lesbahy. It is a mixture of traditional turrets with Renaissance pilasters and pinnacles. Most dramatic is the interior staircase with its three stories of twin bays and an intricately decorated pediment.*

Renaissance carved windows

Pilasters (columns)

Cylindrical tower

Dormer windows

Ussé (see p285) *was built in 1462 by Jean de Bueil as a fortress with parapets containing openings for missiles, battlements and gunloops. The Espinay family, chamberlains to both Louis XI and Charles VIII, bought the château and changed the walls overlooking the main court-yard to Renaissance style with dormer windows and pilasters. In the 17th century the north wing was demolished to create palatial terraces.*

Breton Traditions

BRITTANY WAS CHRISTENED Breiz Izel (Little Britain) by the migrants who fled here from Cornwall and Wales in the 5th and 6th centuries AD and imposed their customs, language and religion on the local Gauls. Brittany resisted Charlemagne, the Vikings, the Normans, English alliances and even French rule until 1532. Today, Breton is still taught in schools, and a busy calendar keeps Brittany in touch with its past and with other Celtic regions.

Bigouden lace headdresses

Breton music has strong Celtic links. Instruments like the biniou, similar to the bagpipes, and the oboelike bombarde are often heard at local festivals.

*A **pardon** is an annual religious festival honoring a local saint. The name derives from the granting of indulgences to pardon the sins of the past year. Some pardons, like those at Ste-Anne d'Auray and Ste-Anne-la-Palud, still attract thousands of pilgrims who carry banners and holy relics through the streets. Most pardons take place between April and September.*

Lace *coiffe* Felt hat Linen *coiffe* Small headdress

Wooden clogs

Embroidered apron

Baggy Breton trousers

Breton costumes, still seen at pardons and weddings, varied as each area had distinctive headdresses or coiffes. Artists like Gauguin often painted the costumes. There are good museum collections in Quimper (see p264) and Pont-l'Abbé in Pays Bigouden (see p263).

Brittany's Coastal Wildlife

Cliffs at the Pointe du Raz, Brittany

WITH ITS GRANITE CLIFFS, sweeping bays and deep estuaries, the Brittany coastline contains a wealth of different wildlife habitats. Parts of the coast have a tidal range of more than 50 m (150 ft), the highest in France, and this great variation in sea level divides marine life into several distinct zones. Most of the

Starfish region's famous shellfish, including mussels, clams and oysters, live on the lower shore, either on rocks or in muddy sand where they are submerged for most of the day. Higher zones are the preserve of limpets and barnacles and several kinds of seaweed that can survive out of the water for long periods. Above the sea, towering cliffs offer a nursery for seabirds and a foothold for many kinds of wildflowers.

The Ile de Bréhat at low tide

FEATURES OF THE COAST

This scene shows some of the wildlife habitats found on the Brittany coastline. When exploring the shore, make a note of the tide times, particularly if you plan to walk along the foot of the cliffs.

Salt-marsh flowers are at their best in late summer

Dunes, where marram grass grows, stabilize the sand.

Mud and sand are inhabited by clams and cockles that filter food from the water.

Rock stacks provide secure nurseries for nesting seabirds.

OYSTER BEDS

Like most marine mollusks, oysters begin their lives as tiny floating larvae. The first step in *ostréculture*, or oyster cultivation, consists of providing the larvae with somewhere to settle, which is usually a stack of submerged tiles. The developing oysters are later transferred to beds and left to mature before being collected for the market.

Oyster beds at Cancale

Clifftop turf often contains a narrow band of wildflowers sandwiched between fields and the sea.

Tidepools are flooded twice daily by the tide. They are inhabited by fish, mollusks, sea anemones and sponges.

COASTAL WILDLIFE

The structure of this shore determines the wildlife that lives on it. In a world beset by wind and waves, rocks provide solid anchorage for plants and a secure habitat for many small animals. Muddy sand is rich in nutrients, and has a greater abundance of life – although most of this is concealed beneath the surface.

Cliffs

The rock dove is a cliff-dwelling ancestor of the well-known city pigeon.

Thrift is a common spring flower, found on exposed ledges near the sea.

Rocks and Tidepools

Seaweed of many different varieties is exposed each day by the falling tide.

The limpet, a slow-moving creature, scrapes tiny plants from the rock surface.

The goby, with its sharp eyesight, dashes for cover at the first sign of movement above.

Crabs live at many different water depths. Some species are extremely good swimmers.

Mud and Sand

Cockles live in large numbers just beneath the surface of muddy sand.

The curlew has a forceps-like curved beak for extracting shellfish from mud and sand.

NORMANDY

EURE · SEINE-MARITIME · MANCHE · CALVADOS · ORNE

THE QUINTESSENTIAL IMAGE *of Normandy is of a lush, pastoral region of apple orchards and contented cows, cider and pungent cheeses – but this area also embraces the windswept beaches of the Cotentin and the wooded banks of the Seine Valley. Famous attractions include the great abbey churches of Caen, the mighty island of Mont-St-Michel and Monet's garden at Giverny.*

Normandy gets its name from the Viking Norsemen who sailed up the Seine River in the 9th century. Pillagers turned settlers, they made their capital at Rouen – today a cultured cathedral city seated in the eastern part of the region. Here the Seine meanders seaward past the ancient abbeys at Jumièges and St-Wandrille to a coast that became an outdoor studio for Impressionist painters during the mid- and late 19th century.

North of Rouen are the chalky cliffs of the Côte d'Albâtre. The mood softens at the port of Honfleur and the elegant resorts of the Côte Fleurie to the west. Inland lies the Pays d'Auge, with its half-timbered manor houses and patch-eyed cows. The western half of Normandy is predominantly rural, a *bocage* countryside of small, high-hedged fields with windbreaks composed of beech trees.

The modern city of Caen is worth visiting for its two great 11th-century abbey churches built by William the Conqueror and his queen, Matilda. Nearby in Bayeux, the story of William's invasion of England is told in detail by the town's famous tapestry. Memories of another invasion, the D-Day Landings of 1944, still linger along the Côte de Nacre and the Cotentin Peninsula. Thousands of Allied troops poured ashore onto these magnificent beaches in the closing stages of World War II. The Cotentin Peninsula is capped by the port of Cherbourg, still a strategic naval base. At its western foot stands one of France's greatest attractions: the monastery island of Mont-St-Michel.

Half-timbered manor house in the village of Beuvron-en-Auge, near Lisieux

◁ **Rich pastures and brown and white Norman cattle, the traditional wealth of the province**

Exploring Normandy

NORMANDY'S RICH HISTORICAL SIGHTS and diverse land-scape make it ideal for touring by car or bicycle. Rewarding coastal drives and good beaches can be found along the windswept Côte d'Albâtre and the Cotentin Peninsula. Farther south is one of France's most celebrated sights, Mont-St-Michel. Inland, follow the meandering lovely Seine Valley, passing cider orchards and half-timbered houses along the way, to visit historic Rouen and Monet's garden at Giverny.

Apple trees in blossom in the
Pays d'Auge

The **Côte d'Albâtre coastline**

SIGHTS AT A GLANCE

To Rennes

KEY

▬▬▬	Highway
▬▬▬	Major road
▭▭▭	Minor road
▬▬▬	Scenic route
～～	River
✳	Viewing point

GETTING AROUND

The A13 autoroute runs from Paris to Rouen and Caen, and there are main road and rail links to the cross-Channel ports of Dieppe, Le Havre, Caen (Ouistreham) and Cherbourg. Travel by public transportation beyond these arteries is limited. The region is threaded with minor roads, particularly delightful in the Pays d'Auge and Cotentin Peninsula. The principal airports are Rouen, Le Havre and Caen.

To Calais

DIEPPE
17

D925

CÔTE D'ALBÂTRE
16
D925

FORÊT D'EAWY

N29

N29

N15

BASSE-SEINE
18

PARC RÉGIONAL DE BROTONNE

LE HAVRE
15

ROUEN
19

LYONS-LA-FORÊT
To Reims

HONFLEUR
14

CÔTE FLEURIE
12

HAUTE-SEINE
20

A13 AUTOROUTE DE NORMANDIE

LES ANDELYS

PAYS D'AUGE
13

LISIEUX

GIVERNY
21

A13

N13

ÉVREUX
22

To Paris

ARGENTAN

N12

To Chartres

PARC RÉGIONAL DE NORMANDIE-MAINE

D955

↓ *To Le Mans*

0 kilometers   25

0 miles   25

The town of Les Andelys shrouded in mist

Rugged cliffs on the Cotentin Peninsula

Cotentin ①

Manche. ⛴ 🚉 🚌 🛳 *Cherbourg.*
ℹ️ *Cherbourg (02 33 93 52 02).*

Thrusting INTO the English
Channel, the Cotentin
Peninsula has a landscape
similar to Brittany's. Its long
sandy beaches are relatively
undeveloped, with wild and
windblown headlands around
Cap de la Hague and Nez de
Jobourg. The latter is a worthwhile goal for bird-watchers –
gannets and shearwaters fly
by in large numbers. Along
the east coast stretch the ex-
pansive sands of Utah Beach,
where American troops
landed as part of the Allied
invasion on June 6, 1944. Inland, Ste-Mère-Eglise commemorates these events with its
poignant **Musée des Troupes
Aéroportées** (Airborne
Troops Museum). Just outside
Ste-Mère-Eglise, the **Musée
de la Ferme du Cotentin**
offers an insight into rural life
in the early 1900s, while
farther north in the market
town of Valognes, the **Musée
Régional du Cidre et du
Calvados** celebrates the
thriving local talent for
making cider and Calvados.

Two fishing ports command
the peninsula's northeast
corner: Barfleur and St-Vaast-
la-Hougue, the latter famous
for oysters and a base for boat
trips to the Ile de Tatihou.
The Val de Saire is ideal for a
scenic drive, with the viewpoint at La Pernelle the best
place to survey the coast. On
the west side of the peninsula,

warmed by the Gulf Stream,
the resort of Barneville-
Carteret offers sandy beaches
and summer boat trips to the
Channel Islands. The low-
lying marshy landscape east
of Carentan forms the heart
of the Parc Régional des Marais
du Cotentin et du Bessin.

🏛 **Musée des Troupes
Aéroportées**
Place du 6 Juin, Ste-Mère-Eglise.
【 *02 33 41 41 35.* **Open** *Feb–Nov:
daily.* **Closed** *Dec–Jan.* 🎫 ♿

🏛 **Musée de la Ferme du
Cotentin**
Route de Beauvais, Ste-Mère-Eglise.
【 *02 33 41 30 25.* **Open** *Easter–Oct:
Wed–Mon (Jul & Aug: daily).* 🎫

🏛 **Musée Régional du Cidre
et du Calvados**
Rue du Petit-Versailles, Valognes.
【 *02 33 40 22 73.* **Open** *Apr–Sep:
Wed–Mon (Jul & Aug: daily).* **Closed**
Sun am. 🎫

Cherbourg ②

Manche. 🏘 *28,000.* ⛴ 🚉 🚌
🛳 ℹ️ *2 quai Alexandre III (02 33 93
52 02).* 🍴 *Tue, Thu & Sat.*

Cherbourg has been a
strategic port and naval
base since the mid-19th
century. The French Navy still
uses its harbors, along with
transatlantic ships and cross-
Channel ferries from England
and Ireland. For a commanding view over the port, drive
to the hilltop **Fort du Roule**,
which houses the **Musée de
la Libération**, recalling the
D-Day invasion and the
subsequent liberation of

Cherbourg. Most activity is
centered around the flower-
filled market square, place
Général de Gaulle, and along
shopping streets such as rue
Tour-Carrée and rue de la
Paix. The town's collection of
fine art is displayed in the
spacious **Musée Thomas-
Henry**, and includes some
enjoyable 17th-century Flemish
works, and portraits by Jean
François Millet, who was
born in the nearby village of
Gréville-Hague.

Parc Emmanuel Liais has
lovely small botanical gardens
and a densely packed **Musée
d'Histoire Naturelle**.

🏛 **Musée de la Libération**
Fort du Roule. 【 *02 33 20 14 12.* **Open**
Apr–Sep: daily; Oct–Mar: Tue–Sun.
Closed *Jan 1, Nov 1, Dec 25.* 🎫 ♿

🏛 **Musée Thomas-Henry**
Rue Vastel. 【 *02 33 23 02 23.* **Open**
Tue–Sun. **Closed** *public hols.* 🎫 ♿

🏛 **Musée d'Histoire
Naturelle**
Parc Emmanuel Liais, 9 rue de l'Abbaye.
【 *02 33 53 51 61.* **Open** *Tue–Sun.*
Closed *Sun am, public hols.* 🎫 ♿

Cherbourg town center

Coutances ③

Manche. 🏘 *12,000.* 🚉 🚌 ℹ️
place Georges Leclerc (02 33 45 17 79).
🍴 *Thu.*

From ROMAN TIMES until the
Revolution, the hilltop
town of Coutances was the
capital of the Cotentin. The
slender **Cathédrale Notre-
Dame**, a fine example of
Norman Gothic architecture,
was begun in the 1040s by
the local De Hauteville family,
with a soaring 41-m (135-ft)
lantern tower, and double
flying buttresses added in the
13th century. Also of interest
are the Gothic stained-glass
windows. Much of the town
was severely damaged during
World War II, but the cathedral,

the churches of St Nicholas and St Peter, and the beautiful public gardens with their rare plants, all survived.

The back of Coutances cathedral with its squat lantern tower

Granville ❹

Manche. 🏠 *13,000.* 🚌 🚏 🚢
🛈 *Mairie (02 33 91 30 00).*
🚢 *Wed & Sat.*

RAMPARTS enclose the upper town of Granville, which sits on a rocky spur overlooking the Baie du Mont-St-Michel. The walled town developed from fortifications built by the English in 1439 as part of their assault on Mont-St-Michel. Granville's long-established seafaring tradition is borne out by the **Musée de Vieux Granville**, found in the town gatehouse. The chapel walls of the **Eglise de Notre-Dame** are lined with tributes from local fishermen to their patroness Notre-Dame du Cap Lihou.

The lower town is an old-fashioned seaside resort with a casino, promenades and public gardens, and amusements such as an aquarium, a waxworks and a *Féerie du Coquillage* (Shell Wonderland). From the port, there are boat trips to the Iles Chausey, a scattering of low-lying granite islands that supplied the stone for the abbey of Mont-St-Michel.

🏛 **Musée de Vieux Granville**
2 rue Lecarpentier. 📞 *02 33 50 44 10.*
Open *Apr–Jun: Wed–Sun; Jul–Sep: Wed–Mon; Oct–Mar: Wed, Sat & Sun.* **Closed** *Jan 1, May 1, Nov 1 & 11, Dec 25.* 🎫

D-DAY LANDINGS

In the early hours of June 6, 1944, Allied forces began landing on the shores of Normandy, the first step in a long-planned invasion of German-occupied France, known as Operation Overlord. Parachutists were dropped near Ste-Mère-Eglise and Pegasus Bridge, and seaborne assaults were made along a string of code-named beaches. US troops landed on Utah and Omaha in the west, while British and Canadian troops, which included a contingent of Free French commandos, landed at Gold, Juno and Sword. Fifty years later, the beaches are still referred to by their code names.

American troops coming ashore during the Allied invasion of France

Pegasus Bridge, where the first French house was liberated, is a natural starting point for a tour around the sights and memorials. Farther west, evocative ruins of the artificial harbor towed across from England survive at Arromanches-les-Bains. There are British, German and American war cemeteries at La Cambe, Ranville and St-Laurent-sur-Mer. War museums at Bayeux, Caen, Ste-Mère-Eglise and Cherbourg provide background on D-Day and the ensuing Battle for Normandy.

ALLIED LANDINGS ON JUNE 6, 1944

Cherbourg
Douve
Le Havre
Seine
Ste-Mère-Eglise
UTAH
St-Laurent-sur-Mer
OMAHA
GOLD
JUNO
SWORD
Carentan
La Cambe
Arromanches-les-Bains
Bayeux
Pegasus Bridge
Vire
Ranville
St-Lô
Caen
Orne

KEY
American troops
British troops
Canadian troops
War cemetery
Parachute drop

0 kilometers 25
0 miles 25

By the end of D-Day, over 135,000 men had been brought ashore, with losses totaling around 10,000

Avranches

Manche. 🏠 *8,500.* �</> 🚌 ℹ *2 rue Général de Gaulle (02 33 58 00 22).* 🛒 *Sat.*

AVRANCHES has been a religious center since the 6th century and is the final stopping point for visitors to the abbey on Mont-St-Michel. The origins of the abbey lie in a vision experienced by Aubert, the Bishop of Avranches. One night in 708 the Archangel Michael touched his head and instructed him to build a church on the nearby island. Aubert's skull, with the finger-hole made by the angel, can be seen in the treasury of **St-Gervais** church in Avranches.

The best views of Mont-St-Michel are from the **Jardin des Plantes**. After the Revolution, 203 illuminated manuscripts were rescued from Mont-St-Michel's abbey; some can be seen at the **Musée Hôtel de Ville**. Nearby, the **Musée Municipal** introduces exhibits showing life in the Cotentin over the past centuries, with a model of Avranches cathedral, which was torn down in 1794.

🏛 **Musée Hôtel de Ville**
Place Littré. 📞 *02 33 89 29 40.* **Open** *Jun & Sep: Mon–Sat; Jul & Aug: daily.* 📷 ♿
🏛 **Musée Municipal**
Palais Episcopal, place Jean de Saint-Avit. 📞 *02 33 58 25 15.* **Open** *Easter–Jun & Sep: Wed–Mon; Jul & Aug: daily.* **Closed** *May 1.* 📷

Remains of Mulberry Harbor from World War II off the Côte de Nacre

Mont-St-Michel

See pp246–9.

Côte de Nacre

Calvados. ✈ *Caen.* 🚉 🚌 *Caen, Bayeux.* ⛴ *Caen-Ouistreham.* ℹ *Caen (02 31 27 14 14).*

THE STRETCH of coast between the mouths of the Orne and Vire rivers was dubbed the Côte de Nacre (Mother of Pearl Coast) in the 19th century. More recently it has become known as the site of the D-Day Landings, when Allied troops poured ashore at the start of Operation Overlord (*see p241*). The associated cemeteries, memorials and museums, and the remnants of the Mulberry Harbor at Arromanches-les-Bains, provide focal points for a visit. However, the coastline is equally popular as a summer vacation destination, offering long, sandy beaches with seaside resorts such as Courseulles-sur-Mer and Luc-sur-Mer. Both are less expensive and more relaxed than the resorts of the Côte Fleurie farther east.

Bayeux

Calvados. 🏠 *15,000.* 🚉 🚌 ℹ *Pont St-Jean (02 31 51 28 28).* 🛒 *Sat.*

BAYEUX was the first town to be liberated by the Allies in 1944 and fortunate to escape war damage. Today, an attractive nucleus of 17th–19th-century buildings remains around its central high streets, rue St-Martin and rue St-Jean.

BAYEUX TAPESTRY

A lively picture story justifying William the Conqueror's invasion of England, this 70-m-long (230-ft) embroidered hanging was probably commissioned by Bishop Odo of Bayeux. Offering insights into 11th-century life, and an action-packed account of the defeat of Harold, King of England, at the Battle of Hastings, the tapestry is valued as a work of art and as an entertaining historical document.

Harold's retinue sets off for France to inform William that Harold will succeed to the English throne.

Trees with interlacing branches are sometimes used to divide the tapestry's 58 scenes.

The latter, now pedestrianized, is lined with shops and cafés. Above the town rise the spires and domed lantern tower of the Gothic **Cathédrale Notre-Dame**. Beneath its harmoniously proportioned interior is an 11th-century crypt decorated with restored 15th-century frescoes of angels playing musical instruments. The original Romanesque church that stood here was consecrated in 1077, and it is likely that Bayeux's famous tapestry was commissioned for this occasion by one of its key characters, Bishop Odo.

The tapestry is displayed in a renovated seminary, **Centre Guillaume-le-Conquérant**, which gives a detailed audio-visual explanation of events leading up to the Norman conquest. On the southwest side of the highway circling the town, the **Musée Mémorial de la Bataille de Normandie** traces the events of the Battle of Normandy and includes an excellent film compilation made from World War II newsreels.

🏛 **Centre Guillaume-le-Conquérant**
Rue de Nesmond. 【 02 31 51 25 50.
Open daily. **Closed** Jan 1, Dec 25.
🚫 ♿
🏛 **Musée Mémorial de la Bataille de Normandie**
Boulevard Fabian-Ware. 【 02 31 92 93 41. **Open** daily. **Closed** Jan 1, last 2 weeks of Jan, Dec 25. 🚫 ♿

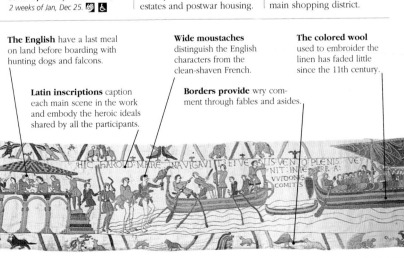

The Abbaye aux Hommes in Caen

Caen ❾

Calvados. 🏠 116,000. ✈ 🚌 🚉
🚇 🈯 place St-Pierre (02 31 27 14 14).
🗓 Fri & Sun.

IN THE MID-11TH century Caen became the favorite residence of William the Conqueror and Queen Matilda, and despite the destruction of three-quarters of the city during World War II, much remains of their creation. The monarchs built two great abbeys and a castle on the north bank of the Orne River, bequeathing Caen a core of historic interest worth looking for beyond its industrial estates and postwar housing.

Much-loved by the citizens of Caen, the **Eglise St-Pierre** was built on the south side of the castle in the 13th–14th centuries, with an impressively ornate Renaissance east end added in the early 16th century. The frequently copied 14th-century bell tower was destroyed in 1944 but has now been restored. To the east, rue du Vaugeux is the central street in Caen's small Vieux Quartier (Old Quarter). Now pedestrianized, the street still has some lovely half-timbered buildings. A walk west along rue St-Pierre or boulevard du Maréchal Leclerc leads to the city's main shopping district.

The English have a last meal on land before boarding with hunting dogs and falcons.

Wide moustaches distinguish the English characters from the clean-shaven French.

The colored wool used to embroider the linen has faded little since the 11th century.

Latin inscriptions caption each main scene in the work and embody the heroic ideals shared by all the participants.

Borders provide wry comment through fables and asides.

CAEN CITY CENTER

Abbaye-aux-Dames ⑥
Abbaye-aux-Hommes ①
Château ducal ③
Eglise St-Etienne ②
Eglise St-Pierre ④
La Trinité ⑤

KEY

🅿 Parking

ℹ Tourist information

✝ Church

0 meters 250

0 yards 250

🅰 Abbaye aux Hommes

Esplanade Jean-Marie Louvel. **Open** *daily. **Closed** Jan 1, Dec 25.* 📷 ♿ *obligatory.*
Work began on William's Abbey for Men in 1066 and was almost complete by his death 20 years later. The abbey church, **Eglise St-Etienne**, is a Norman Romanesque masterpiece, with a severe, unadorned west front crowned with 13th-century spires. The sparingly decorated nave was roofed in the early 12th century with stone vaulting that anticipates the Gothic style.

🅰 Abbaye aux Dames

Place de la Reine Mathilde. **Open** *daily. **Closed** Jan 1, Dec 25.* 📷 *obligatory.* ♿
Like William's Abbaye aux Hommes, Matilda's Abbey for Women also has a Norman Romanesque church, **La Trinité**, flanked by 18th-century buildings. Begun in 1060, it was consecrated six years later. Queen Matilda lies buried in the choir, and her beautifully restored abbey, with its creamy Caen stone, makes a serene and dignified mausoleum.

🏛 Château ducal

Esplanade du Château. **Musée des Beaux Arts** 📞 02 31 85 28 63. **Musée de Normandie** 📞 02 31 86 06 24. **Museums open** *Wed–Mon. **Closed** Jan 1, Easter, May 1, Ascension, Nov 1, Dec 25.* 📷 ♿
The ruins of Caen's castle offer spacious lawns, museums and rampart views over the city. An extensive fine art collection, strong on 17th-century French and Italian painting, is on exhibit in the **Musée des Beaux Arts**. The **Musée de Normandie** recalls traditional life in the region with displays and utensils – some dating from prehistoric times – on farming and lace.

🏛 Mémorial de Caen

Esplanade Dwight-Eisenhower. 📞 02 31 06 06 44. **Open** *mid-Jan–Dec: daily. **Closed** Dec 25.* 📷 ♿
In the northwest of Caen, close to the N13 highway, Mémorial is a museum dedicated to peace, placing the events of D-Day into the context of World War II and other conflicts of the 20th century. Opened in 1988, the museum uses a host of interactive and audiovisual techniques, including stunning compilations of archival and fictional film to explain the war's origins, document its horrors and consider the failed peace that followed.

Lush Orne Valley in the Suisse Normande

Suisse Normande ⑩

Calvados & Orne. 🚉 Caen. 🚌 🚌 Caen, Argentan. ℹ Putanges-Pont-Ecrepin (02 33 35 86 57).

THOUGH HARDLY LIKE the mountains of Switzerland, the cliffs and valleys carved out by the Orne River as it winds north to Caen have become a popular site for walking, climbing, camping and river sports. The area is also ideal for a lazy, rural drive. Its highest and most impressive point is the Oëtre Rock, off the D329, where you can look down over the dramatic gorges created by the Rouvre River.

Parc Régional de Normandie-Maine ⑪

Orne & Manche. 🚉 Alençon. 🚌 Argentan. ℹ Carrouges (02 33 27 40 62).

THE SOUTHERN FRINGES of central Normandy have been incorporated into France's largest regional park. Among the farmland and forests of oak and beech are several small towns. **Domfront** rests on a spur overlooking the Varenne River. The lakeside spa town **Bagnoles-de-l'Orne** offers a casino and sports facilities, while farther east, **Sées** has an attractive Gothic cathedral. The **Maison du Parc** at Carrouges provides information

Poster of Deauville, about 1930

on walks, horseback riding and cycling in the park.

🎨 Maison du Parc
Carrouges. 📞 02 33 81 75 75. **Open** Mon–Fri. **Closed** public hols.

Environs
Just north of the park, outside Mortrée, is the **Chateau d'O**, a moated Renaissance château with fine 17th-century frescoes. The **Haras du Pin** nearby is France's national stud, called "a horses' Versailles" for its grandeur and 17th-century architecture. Horse shows, dressage events and tours take place throughout the year.

Côte Fleurie ⑫

Calvados 🚉 🚌 Deauville. ℹ Deauville (02 31 14 40 00).

THE COTE FLEURIE (Flowery Coast) between Villerville and Cabourg has been planted with chic resorts that burst

into bloom every summer. **Trouville** was once a humble fishing village, but in the mid-19th century caught the attention of writers Gustave Flaubert and Alexandre Dumas. By the 1870s, Trouville had acquired grand hotels, a railroad station and pseudo-Swiss villas along the beachfront. It has, however, long been outclassed by its neighbor, **Deauville**, created by the Duc de Morny in the 1860s. This resort boasts a casino, racetracks, marinas and the famous beachside catwalk, Les Planches.

For something quieter, head west to smaller resorts such as Villers-sur-Mer or Houlgate. **Cabourg** farther west is dominated by the turn-of-the-century Grand Hôtel (see p551), where novelist Marcel Proust spent many summers. Proust used the resort as a model for the fictional Balbec in his novel *Remembrance of Things Past*.

Pays d'Auge ⑬

Calvados. 🚉 Deauville. 🚌 Lisieux. ℹ Lisieux (02 31 62 08 41).

INLAND from the Côte Fleurie, the Pays d'Auge is classic Normandy countryside, lushly woven with fields, wooded valleys, cider orchards, dairy farms and manor houses. Its capital is **Lisieux**, a cathedral town devoted to St. Thérèse of Lisieux, canonized in 1925, who attracts more than one million pilgrims each year. Lisieux is an obvious base for explor-ing the region, though nearby market towns, such as St-Pierre-sur-Dives and Orbec, are smaller and more attract-ive.

The best way to enjoy the Pays d'Auge is to sightsee around on its minor roads. Two marked tourist routes are devoted to cider and cheese, while splendid farmhouses, manors and châteaux testify to the wealth gained from this fertile land. Two typical manor houses that admit visitors are at **Crèvecoeur-en-Auge** and **St-Germain-de-Livet**, while the half-timbered village of **Beuvron-en-Auge**

APPLES AND CIDER

Apple orchards are a familiar feature of the Normandy countryside, and their fruit a fundamental ingredient in the region's gastronomic repertoire. No self-respecting pâtisserie would be without its *tarte normande* (apple tart), and every country lane seems to sport an *Ici Vente Cidre* (cider sold here) sign. Much of the harvest forms the raw material for cider and Calvados, an apple brandy aged in oak barrels for at least two years. Another local brew is made from pears, and known as *poiré* (perry).

Crops range from sour cider apples to sweet edible varieties

Mont-St-Michel ❻

The 10th-century abbey

The 11th-century abbey

The mid-18th-century abbey

SHROUDED BY MIST, engulfed by sea, soaring proudly above glistening sands – the silhouette of Mont-St-Michel is one of the most enchanting sights in France. Now linked to the mainland by a causeway, the island of Mont-Tombe (Tomb on the Hill) stands at the mouth of the Couesnon River, crowned by a fortified abbey that almost doubles its height. Lying strategically on the frontier between Normandy and Brittany, Mont-St-Michel grew from a humble 8th-century oratory to become a Benedictine monastery that had its greatest influence in the 12th and 13th centuries. Pilgrims known as *miquelots* journeyed from afar to honor the cult of St. Michael, and the monastery was a renowned center of medieval learning. After the Revolution, the abbey became a prison. It is now a national monument that draws some 850,000 visitors a year.

St. Michael

St-Aubert's Chapel

A small 15th-century chapel built on an outcrop of rock is dedicated to Aubert, the founder of Mont-St-Michel.

Gabriel Tower

★ Ramparts

English attacks during the Hundred Years' War led to the construction of fortified walls with imposing towers.

Entrance

TIMELINE

966 Benedictine abbey founded by Duke Richard I	**1211–28** Construction of La Merveille	**1434** Last assault by English forces. Ramparts surround the town	**1789** French Revolution: abbey becomes a political prison	**1874** Abbey declared a national monument	
					1922 Services again held in abbey church
700	**1000**	**1300**	**1600**	**1900**	
1017 Work on abbey church starts		**1516** Abbey falls into decline		**1877–9** Causeway built	**1895–7** Belfry, spire and statue of St. Michael added
708 St. Aubert builds an oratory on Mont-Tombe	**1067–70** Mont-St-Michel depicted in Bayeux Tapestry *Bayeux Tapestry detail*				**1969** Benedictine monks return

VISITORS' CHECKLIST

🚃 to Pontorson, then bus.
ℹ boulevard de l'Avancée
(02 33 60 14 30). 🎪 St-Michel
de Printemps (May).
Abbey 📞 02 33 89 80 00.
Open May–Sep: 9am–5:30pm;
Oct–Jun: 9:30am–4:30pm
(during school hols: 9:30am–
5pm). **Closed** Jan 1, May 1,
Nov 1, Nov 11, Dec 25.
📷 ✝ 12:15pm daily.
📷 📷

Tides of Mont-St-Michel
Extremely strong tides in the Baie du Mont-St-Michel act as a natural defense. They rise and fall with the lunar calendar and can reach speeds of 10 km/h (6 mph) in spring.

★ Abbey
Protected by high walls, the abbey and its church occupy an impregnable position on the island.

Gautier's Leap
At the top of the Inner Staircase, this terrace is named after a prisoner who leaped to his death.

Eglise St-Pierre

Liberty Tower

The Arcade Tower provided lodgings for the abbot's soldiers.

King's Tower

STAR FEATURES

★ Abbey

★ Ramparts

★ Grande Rue

★ Grande Rue
Now crowded with tourists and souvenir shops, the pilgrims' route, followed since the 12th century, climbs up past Eglise St-Pierre to the abbey gates.

The Abbey of Mont-St-Michel

THE PRESENT BUILDINGS bear witness to the time when the abbey served both as a Benedictine monastery and, for 73 years after the Revolution, as a political prison. In 1017 work began on a Romanesque church at the island's highest point, building over its 10th-century predecessor, now the Chapel of Our Lady Underground. A monastery built on three levels, La Merveille (The Miracle) was added to the church's north side in the early 13th century.

Cross in the choir

★ **Church**
Four bays of the Romanesque nave survive. Three were torn down in 1776, creating the West Terrace.

★ **La Merveille**
The Miracle is a Gothic masterpiece – a three-story monastic complex built in only 16 years.

Refectory
The monks had their meals in this long, narrow room, which is flooded with light through tall windows.

Knights' Room
The rib vaults and finely decorated capitals are typically Gothic.

CHURCH LEVEL

MIDDLE LEVEL

LOWER LEVEL

The Crypt of Thirty Candles is one of two 11th-century crypts built to support the transepts of the main church.

★ **Cloisters**
The cloisters with their elegant columns in staggered rows are a beautiful example of early 13th-century Anglo-Norman style.

VISITING THE ABBEY

The three levels of the abbey reflect the monastic hierarchy. The monks lived at the highest level, in an enclosed world of church, cloister and refectory. The abbot entertained his noble guests on the middle level. Soldiers and pilgrims further down on the social scale were received at the lowest level. Guided tours begin at the West Terrace at the church level and end in the almonry, where alms were dispensed to the poor. The almonry is now a bookstore and souvenir hall.

CHURCH LEVEL

- Cloister
- Refectory
- Abbey Church
- West Terrace
- Gautier's Leap
- Great Inner Staircase

MIDDLE LEVEL

- Knights' room
- Crypt of the Thirty Candles
- Guest room
- Our Lady Underground
- St. Etienne's Chapel
- St. Martin's Crypt
- Abbot's lodgings

Church Interior
A Flamboyant Gothic choir was built in 1446–1521, held up by crypts with massive supporting pillars.

LOWER LEVEL

- Cellar
- Almonry
- Abbey gardens
- Abbot's lodgings
- Guard's room

St. Martin's Crypt is an 11th-century barrel-vaulted chapel that preserves the austere forms of the original Romanesque abbey.

The abbot's lodgings were close to the abbey entrance, and he received prestigious visitors in the guest room. Poorer pilgrims were received in the almonry.

Benedictine Monks
Today a small monastic community lives in the abbey, continuing the religious traditions introduced by the Benedictines in 966.

STAR FEATURES

★ **Church**

★ **La Merveille**

★ **Cloisters**

Mont-St-Michel by night ▷

Honfleur

Calvados. 🏛 *8,400.* 🚉 *Deauville.* 🚌
ℹ️ *place Arthur Boudin (02 31 89 23 30).* 🚢 *Sat.*

A MAJOR DEFENSIVE PORT in the 15th century, Honfleur has blossomed into one of Normandy's most appealing harbors. At its heart is the Vieux Bassin (Old Dock). Constructed in the late 17th century, it is bordered on the western quayside by houses six or seven stories tall.

Honfleur became a center of artistic activity in the 19th century. Eugène Boudin, the seascape painter, was born here in 1824. Courbet, Sisley, Pissarro, Renoir and Cézanne all visited Honfleur, often meeting at the Ferme St-Siméon, which is now a luxury hotel. Painters still work from Honfleur's quayside and exhibit in the **Greniers à Sel**, two warehouses built in 1670 for storing salt. These lie to the east of the Vieux Bassin in an area known as l'Enclos, which made up the fortified heart of the town in the 13th century.

The **Musée de la Marine** displays mementos of Honfleur's nautical past, with a warren of Norman interiors next door in the former prison. To the west of the Vieux Bassin, is a wooden church in the place Ste-Catherine, built by ship's carpenters in the 15th century. The **Musée Eugène Boudin** documents the artistic appeal of Honfleur and the Seine estuary, with works ranging from Eugène Boudin

to Raoul Dufy. From here a steep walk, which is particularly enjoyable at sunset, leads to the hilltop chapel of **Notre-Dame de Grace**.

🏛 Greniers à Sel
Rue de la Ville/quai de la Tour.
🎫 *02 31 89 02 30.* **Open** *for guided tours, and during exhibitions (call for details).* 🎫 *obligatory, except during summer exhibitions.* 📷 ♿

🏛 Musée de la Marine
Quai St Etienne. 🎫 *02 31 89 14 12.* **Open** *mid-Feb–mid-Nov: Tue–Sun; Jul & Aug: daily.* **Closed** *May 1.* 📷 ♿

🏛 Musée Eugène Boudin
Place Erik Satie, rue de l'Homme de Bois. 🎫 *02 31 89 54 00.* **Open** *mid-Mar–Sep: Wed–Mon; Oct, Nov, Dec: Wed–Mon pm, Sat, Sun.* **Closed** *Jan–mid-Feb.* 📷 ♿

The quayside at Honfleur

Le Havre

Seine-Maritime. 🏛 *195,000.* ✈ 🚢
🚆 🚌 ℹ️ *186 bd Clemenceau (02 32 74 04 04).* 🚢 *Mon, Wed & Fri.*

S TRATEGICALLY positioned at the head of the Seine estuary, Le Havre (The Harbor) was created in 1517 by François I after the nearby port of Harfleur silted up.

During World War II it was virtually obliterated by Allied bombing, but despite the vast oil refineries and industrial zone which stands beside the port, it still has some appeal. Much of the city center was rebuilt in the 1950s and 1960s from designs by August Perret, whose towering **Eglise St-Joseph**, on boulevard François I, pierces the skyline in an emphatic manner. The **Musée Nalraux**, which has a stunning structure built entirely of glass and metal, has an exhilarating collection of works by the Le Havre-born artist Raoul Dufy.

🏛 Musée Nalraux
2 bd Clemenceau. 🎫 *02 35 19 62 62.* **Open** *Wed–Mon.*

Côte d'Albâtre

Seine-Maritime. 🚫 🚆 🚌 🚢
ℹ️ *Dieppe (02 35 14 40 60).*

T HE ALABASTER COAST gets its name from the chalky cliffs and milky waters that characterize the Normandy coastline between Le Havre and Le Tréport. It is best known for the **Falaise d'Aval** west of Etretat, eroded into an arch. The author Guy de Maupassant, born near Dieppe in 1850, compared these cliffs to an elephant dipping its trunk into the sea. From Etretat, a chain of coastal roads runs east across a switchback of breezy headlands and wooded valleys to Dieppe.

Fécamp is the only major town along this route. Its Benedictine abbey, now in ruins, was once an important pilgrimage center after a tree trunk containing drops of Christ's Blood was washed ashore here during the 7th century. This is enshrined in a reliquary at the entrance to the Lady Chapel of the abbey church, La Trinité.

The vast **Palais Bénédictine** is a mock Gothic and Renaissance homage to the ego of Alexander Le Grand, a local wine merchant who rediscovered the monks' recipe for Bénédictine, the famous herbal liqueur. Building of the palace began in 1880.

Woman with Parasol (1880) by Boudin in the Musée Eugène Boudin

The cliffs at Falaise d'Aval, famously likened to an elephant dipping its trunk into the sea

Today, it incorporates a distillery and an eccentric museum packed with art treasures and curios. The adjacent halls provide an aromatic account of the 27 herbs and spices that make up the elixir.

🏛 Palais Bénédictine

110 rue Alexandre Le Grand, Fécamp. 📞 02 35 10 26 10. **Open** daily. **Closed** Jan. 🎫 🛈

View of Dieppe from the château and museum above the town

Dieppe ⓱

Seine-Maritime. 🕌 40,000. ✕ 🚉 🚌 🛳 🛈 pont Jean Ango (02 35 14 40 60). 🚍 Tue, Thu & Sat.

Dieppe exploits a break in the chalky cliffs bordering the Pays de Caux, and has won historical prestige as a Channel fort, port and resort. Prosperity came during the 16th and 17th centuries, when local privateer Jean Ango raided the Portuguese and English fleets, and a trading post called Petit Dieppe was founded on the West African coast. At that time, Dieppe's population was almost double what it is today, and included a 300-strong community of craftsmen carving imported ivory. This maritime past is celebrated in the **Musée du Château**, housed in a 15th-century castle crowning the headland to the west of the seafront. Here you can see historical maps and model ships, a collection of Dieppe ivories, and paintings that evoke the town's development as a fashionable seaside resort during the 19th century. Dieppe had the beach closest to Paris, and it quickly responded to the developing passion for promenading, seawater cures and bathing.

Today, Dieppe's broad seafront includes lawns, seaside amusements and parking lots, and its liveliest streets surround the battle-scarred **Eglise St-Jacques** to the south. If the weather is poor, head for the **Cité de la Mer**, an exhibition center featuring models on maritime themes, and fun for children.

🏛 Musée du Château

📞 02 35 84 19 76. **Open** Jun–Sep: daily; Oct–May: Wed–Mon. **Closed** Jan 1, May 1, Nov 1, Dec 25. 🎫

🏛 Cité de la Mer

37 Rue de l'Asile Thomas. 📞 02 35 06 93 20. **Open** daily. 🎫 ♿

Basse-Seine ⓲

Seine-Maritime & Eure. ✈ Le Havre, Rouen. 🚉 🚌 Yvetot. 🛳 Le Havre. 🛈 Yvetot (02 35 95 08 40).

Meandering seaward from Rouen to Le Havre, the Seine River is crossed by three spectacular road bridges, the Pont de Brotonne and, farther west, the Pont de Tancarville.

The third bridge, the Pont de Normandie, was completed in 1995 and links Le Havre and Honfleur. The grace and daring of these modern bridges echoes the soaring aspirations of the abbeys, founded on the river's banks in the 7th and 8th centuries. The abbeys now provide good stepping stones for a tour of the Lower Seine Valley.

West of Rouen is the harmonious Eglise de St-Georges at **St-Martin-de-Boscherville** which, until the Revolution, was the church of a small walled abbey. Its 12th-century chapter house has remarkable biblical statues and carved capitals. From here the D62 highway runs south to the riverside village of La Bouille.

As you head northwest, an hourly car ferry at Mesnil-sous-Jumièges takes you over to the colossal ruins of the **Abbaye de Jumièges**. The abbey was founded in 654 and once housed 900 monks and 1,500 servants. The main abbey church dates from the 11th century; its consecration in 1067 was a major event, with William the Conqueror in attendance.

The D913 highway passes through oak and beech woods in the Parc Régional de Brotonne to the 7th-century **Abbaye de St-Wandrille**. The Musée de la Marine de Seine at **Caudebec-en-Caux** gives an engrossing account of life on this great river over the past 120 years.

Monk from Abbaye de St-Wandrille

Rouen ⑲

Founded at the lowest point where the Seine could be bridged, Rouen has prospered through maritime trade and industrialization to become a rich and cultured city. Despite the severe damage of World War II, the city boasts a wealth of historic sights on its right bank, all within walking distance of the central Cathédrale Notre-Dame, frequently painted by Monet. In turn a Celtic trading post, Roman garrison and Viking colony, Rouen became the capital of the Norman Duchy in 911. It was captured by Henry V in 1419 after a siege during the Hundred Years' War. In 1431, Joan of Arc was burned at the stake here in place du Vieux-Marché.

Rouen, a thriving port on the Seine River

Exploring Rouen

From the cathedral, the rue du Gros Horloge runs west under the city's Great Clock, to the place du Vieux Marché and its post-war Eglise Ste-Jeanne-d'Arc. Rue aux Juifs leads past the 15th-century Gothic **Palais de Justice**, once Normandy's parliament, to the chic shops and cafés around rue des Carmes. Farther east, between the St-Maclou and St-Ouen churches, are half-timbered houses in the rue Damiette and rue Eau de Robec. North, in place Général de Gaulle, is the 18th-century **Hôtel de Ville**.

🏛 **Cathédrale Notre-Dame**
This Gothic masterpiece is dominated by the famous west façade (*see p257*), painted

Cathédrale Notre-Dame, Rouen

by Monet, which is framed by two un-equal towers – the northern Tour St-Romain, and the later Tour du Beurre, supposedly paid for by a tax on butter consumption during Lent. Above the central lantern tower rises an 1876 Neo-Gothic spire, made from cast iron. Both the 13th-century northern Portail des Libraires and the 14th-century southern Portail de la Calende are worth seeing for their precise sculpting and delicate tracery, although they may be closed off for restoration. Many of the cathedral's riches can be seen by guided tour only. Highlights are the tomb of Richard the Lion-Heart, whose heart was buried here, and the unusual 11th-century semi-circular hall crypt, rediscovered in 1934.

KEY

P Parking

i Tourist information

🏛 Church

| 0 meters | 250 |
| 0 yards | 250 |

⛪ Eglise St-Maclou

This Flamboyant Gothic church has an elaborately decorated west façade with a five-bay porch and carved wooden doors depicting biblical scenes. Behind the church, its *aître*, or ossuary, is a rare surviving example of a medieval cemetery for the burial of plague victims. The timbers of its buildings, set around the quadrangle, are carved with a macabre array of grinning skulls, crossed bones, coffins, hourglasses, buckets, beds and grave-diggers' implements.

Pitcher, Musée de la Céramique

⛪ Eglise St-Ouen

Once part of a formidable Benedictine abbey, St-Ouen is a solid Gothic church with a lofty, unadorned interior made all the more beautiful by its restored 14th-century stained glass. Behind the church, there is a pleasant park which is an ideal spot for picnics.

🏛 Musée des Beaux Arts

Square Verdrel. 【 02 35 71 28 40.
Open *Wed–Mon.* **Closed** *public hols.*
The city's collection includes masterpieces by Caravaggio and Velázquez, and paintings by Normandy-born artists Théodore Géricault, Eugène Boudin and Raoul Dufy. Also on display is Monet's work entitled *Rouen Cathedral, The Portal, Gray Weather*.

🏛 Musée de la Céramique

Hôtel d'Hocqueville, 1 rue Faucon.
【 02 35 07 28 40. **Open** *Wed–Mon.*
Closed *public hols.*
Exhibits of 6,000 pieces of Rouen faïence – colorful glazed earthenware – together with other pieces of French and foreign china are displayed in a 17th-century town house. The works trace the history of Rouen faïence to its zenith in the 18th century.

🏛 Musée Le Secq des Tournelles

Rue Jacques-Villon. 【 02 35 82 42 92. **Open** *Wed–Mon.* **Closed** *public hols.*
Located in a 15th-century church, this wrought ironwork museum exhibits antique iron-mongery ranging from keys to corkscrews, Gallo-Roman spoons to mighty tavern signs.

🏛 Musée Flaubert

51 rue de Lecat. 【 02 35 15 59 95.
Open *Tue–Sat.* **Closed** *public hols.*
Flaubert's father was a surgeon at Rouen Hospital, and the house where the family lived combines mem-orabilia with an awesome – and occasionally gruesome – display of 17th–19th-century medical equipment.

AMIENS
RUE BEAUVOISINE
RUE DULONG
RUE JOYEUSE
RUE RICARD
RUE VERT BUISSON
RUE LOUIS
ACE DE LA ROUGEMARE
RUE DES MINIMES
LA SEILLE
RUE BOURG L'ABBE
PLACE DU GAL GAULLE
(11)
P
PLACE AMAND
(10)
RUE DES FAULX
PLACE DU LT AUBERT
RUE EAU DE ROBEC
RUE DAMETTE
RUE D'AMIENS
(9)
RUE GERICAULT
RUE HUGO
RUE VICTOR
RUE MARTAINVILLE
(8)
RUE E DUTUIT
RUE MOLIERE
ALSACE LORRAINE
Aéroport

SIGHTS AT A GLANCE

GUSTAVE FLAUBERT

The novelist Gustave Flaubert (1821–80) was born and raised in Rouen, and the city provides the backdrop for some memorable scenes in his masterpiece *Madame Bovary*.
Published in 1857, this realistic study of a country doctor's wife driven to despair by her love affairs provoked a scandal that made Flaubert's name. His famous stuffed green parrot, which can be seen in the Musée Flaubert, was always perched on his writing desk.

Flaubert's stuffed parrot

Château Gaillard and the village of Les Andelys, in a loop of the Seine River

Haute-Seine

Eure. 🚉 *Rouen.* 🚌 *Vernon, Val de Renvil.* 🚌 *Gisors, Les Andelys.* 🅸 *Les Andelys (02 32 54 41 93).*

SOUTHEAST OF ROUEN, the Seine River follows a convoluted course, with most points of interest on its north bank. At the center of the Forêt de Lyons, once the hunting ground for the Dukes of Normandy, is the country town of **Lyons-la-Forêt**, with half-timbered houses and an 18th-century covered market.

To the south, the D313 follows the gracefully curving Seine to the village of **Les Andelys**. Above it tower the ruins of Château Gaillard, which Richard the Lion-Heart, as king of England and duke of Normandy, built in 1197 to defend Rouen from the French. They eventually took the castle in 1204 by forcing a way in through the latrines.

Giverny ㉑

Eure. 🏘 *600.* 🅸 *36 rue Carnot, Vernon (02 32 51 39 60).*

IN 1883 the Impressionist painter Claude Monet rented a house in the small village of Giverny, and worked there until his death at the age of 86. The house, known as the **Fondation Claude Monet**, and its magnificent gardens are open to the public. The house is decorated in the original color schemes that Monet admired; the gardens are famous as the subject of some of the artist's best-loved studies. Only copies are on display in the small gallery, but there are outstanding original 19th- and 20th-century artworks in the **Musée d'Art Américain Giverny** nearby.

🏛 **Fondation Claude Monet**
Giverny, Gasny. 📞 *02 32 51 28 21.* **Open** *Apr–Oct: Tue–Sun.* 🈺
🏛 **Musée d'Art Américain Giverny**
99 rue Claude Monet, Giverny. 📞 *02 32 51 94 65.* **Open** *Apr–Oct: Tue–Sun.* 🈺 ♿

Évreux ㉒

Eure. 🏘 *55,000.* 🚌 🚌 🅸 *3 place du Général de Gaulle (02 32 24 04 43).* 🛒 *Wed & Sat.*

THOUGH CONSIDERABLY damaged in the war, Évreux is a pleasant cathedral town set in wide, agricultural plains. At its heart, the **Cathédrale Notre-Dame** is renowned for its 14th–15th-century stained glass. The building is predominantly Gothic, though Romanesque arches survive in the nave and Renaissance screens adorn its chapels. Next door, the former Bishop's Palace houses the **Musée Municipal**, with exhibits ranging from two Roman bronze statues of Jupiter and Apollo to fine 18th-century furniture and decorative art.

Monet's garden at Giverny, restored to its original profuse glory

Monet's Cathedral Series

In the 1890s, Claude Monet made almost 30 paintings of Rouen's cathedral, several of which are now in the Musée d'Orsay in Paris *(see pp116–17)*. He studied the effects of changing light on its façades, and described both the surface detail and huge bulk, putting color before contour. The archetypal Impressionist, Monet said he conceived this series when he watched the effects of light on a country church, "as the sun's rays slowly dissolved the mists . . . that wrapped the golden stone in an ideally vaporous envelope."

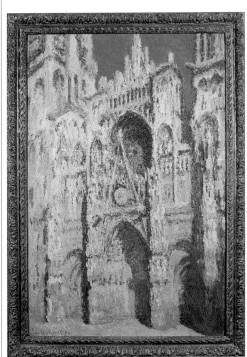

HARMONY IN BLUE AND GOLD *(1894)*

Monet selected a close vantage point for the series and especially liked this southwest view. The sun would cast afternoon shadows across the carved west front, accentuating the cavernous portals and the large rose window.

Monet's sketch, *one of many of Rouen, parallels the shimmering effect of the paintings.*

Harmony in Brown *(1894) is the only finished version of a frontal view of the west façade. Analysis has shown that it was begun as a southwest view, like the others.*

Harmony in Blue *(1894), compared with Harmony in Blue and Gold, shows the stone of the west façade farther softened by the diffuse light of a misty morning.*

The Portal, Gray Weather *(1894) was one of several canvases in the gray color group that showed the cathedral façade in the soft light of an overcast day.*

BRITTANY

FINISTÈRE · CÔTES D'ARMOR · MORBIHAN · ILLE-ET-VILAINE

JUTTING DEFIANTLY INTO THE ATLANTIC, France's northwest corner has long been culturally and geographically distinct from the rest of the country. Known to the Celts as Armorica, the land of the sea, Brittany's past swirls with the legends of drowned cities and Arthurian forests. Prehistoric megaliths arise mysteriously from land and sea, and the medieval is never far from the modern.

A long, jagged coastline is the region's great attraction. Magnificent beaches line its northern shore, swept clean by huge tides and interspersed with well-established seaside resorts, seasoned fishing ports and abundant oyster beds. The south coast is gentler, with wooded river valleys and a milder climate, while the west, being exposed to the Atlantic winds, has a drama that justifies its name: Finistère – "the End of the Earth."

Inland lies the Argoat – once the Land of the Forest, now a patchwork of undulating fields, woods and rolling moorland. Parc Régional d'Armorique occupies much of central Finistère, and it is in western Brittany that Breton culture remains most evident. In Quimper, and in the Pays Bigouden, crêpes and cider, traditional costumes and Celtic music are still a genuine part of the Breton lifestyle. Eastern Brittany has a more conventional appeal. Vannes, Dinan and Rennes, the Breton capital, have well-preserved medieval quarters where half-timbered buildings shelter inviting markets, shops, crêperies and restaurants. The walled port of St-Malo on the Côte d'Emeraude recalls the region's maritime prowess, while the remarkably intact castles at Fougères and Vitré are a reminder of the mighty border-fortresses that protected Brittany's eastern frontier before its final union with France in 1532.

Women dressed in traditional costume and *coiffe,* the typical Breton lace headdress

◁ Characteristic pink granite cliffs on the Côte de Granit Rose, northern Brittany

Exploring Brittany

IDEAL FOR A SEASIDE HOLIDAY, Brittany offers enjoyable drives along the headlands and beaches of the northern Côte d'Emeraude and Côte de Granit Rose, while the south coast boasts wooded valleys and the prehistoric sites of Carnac and the Golfe du Morbihan. The parish closes *(see pp266–7)* provide an intriguing insight into Breton culture, as does the cathedral town of Quimper. Be sure to visit the regional capital, Rennes, and the great castle at Fougères, and in summer take a boat trip to one of Brittany's islands.

SIGHTS AT A GLANCE

0 kilometers   25

0 miles   25

Lighthouse on the Île de Bréhat, Côte de Granit Rose

GETTING AROUND

Brittany's principal roads run from Rennes to Brest (N12), from Nantes to Quimper (N165), and from St-Malo to Rennes (N137). There are rail connections east–west and to the Channel ports of St-Malo and Roscoff, but north–south travel by public transportation is time consuming. Rennes and Brest have international airports, while others in the region are domestic or only have flights in summer.

ÎLE DE BRÉHAT

26 CÔTE D'ÉMERAUDE

DINARD

27

28 CANCALE

ST-MALO

MONT-ST-MICHEL

ST-BRIEUC

Caen

N176

29 DINAN

30 COMBOURG

FOUGÈRES 32

Rance

FORÊT DE RENNES

FORÊT DE PAIMPONT

25

RENNES 31

VITRÉ 33

PONTIVY

Le Mans

24 JOSSELIN

PLOËRMEL

VANNES

22

Nantes

23 GOLFE DU MORBIHAN

Vilaine

Nantes

KEY

Highway

Major road

Minor road

Scenic route

River

Viewing point

Half-timbered houses in the medieval part of Rennes

Île d'Ouessant **❶**

Finistère. ✈ *Ouessant (via Brest).*
🚂 *Brest, then boat.* 🚌 *Le Conquet,*
then boat. **ℹ** *place de l'Eglise,*
Lampaul (02 98 48 85 83).

A WELL-KNOWN Breton proverb
declares "He who sees
Ouessant sees blood." Also
known as Ushant, the island
is notorious among sailors for
its fierce storms and strong
currents. However, this most
westerly point of France has a
pleasant climate in summer
and, though often bleak and
stormy, can be surprisingly
mild in winter. Part of the Parc
Régional d'Armorique, the
windswept island is a popular
stopover for migrating birds.
These, along with a small seal
population, may be observed
from the Pern and Pen-ar-
Roc'h headlands.
   Two museums shed light on
the islands defiant history,
dogged by shipwreck and
tragedy. At Niou Uhella, the
Eco-Musée d'Ouessant has
furniture made from driftwood
and wrecks, often painted blue
and white in honor of the
Virgin Mary. Nearby, at Phare
du Créac'h, the **Musée des
Phares et Balises** explains
the history of Brittany's many
lighthouses and the daily life
of a lighthouse keeper.

🏛 Eco-Musée d'Ouessant
Niou Uhella. **【** *02 98 48 86 37.*
Open *Apr–Sep: daily; Oct–Mar:*
Tue–Sun (pm only). 📷 **&** *restricted.*
**🏛 Musée des Phares et
Balises**
Phare du Créac'h. **【** *02 98 48 80 70.*
Open *May–Sep: daily; Oct–Apr:*
Tue–Sun (pm only). 📷 **&**

Brest **❷**

Finistère. 🏙 *153,000.* 🛬 🚂 🚌 ⛴
ℹ *av Clémenceau (02 98 44 24 96).*
🚌 *daily.*

A NATURAL HARBOR protected
by the Presqu'île de
Crozon, Brest is France's
premiere naval port, with a
rich maritime history. Heavily
bombed during World War II,
it is now a modern commercial
city where cargo vessels and
fishing boats ply the waters.
There are extensive views of

Windswept moorlands near Ménez-Meur, Parc Régional d'Armorique

the Rade de Brest from the
Cours Dajot promenade. The
12th–17th-century **Château**
houses a naval museum with
a collection ranging from
historic maps and maritime
paintings to model ships,
carved wooden figureheads
and nautical instruments.
   Across the Penfeld River –
reached by Europe's largest
lifting bridge, the Pont de
Recouvrance – is the 16th-
century **Tour Tanguy**, which
has dioramas evoking old
Brest. Down by the Port de
Plaisance, **Océanopolis** is an
entertaining and educational
"sea center" with hands-on
exhibits, seals and aquariums.

♠ Château de Brest
【 *02 98 22 12 39.* **Open** *Wed–Mon.*
📷
♜ Tour Tanguy
Square Pierre Peron. **【** *02 98 00 88*
60. **Open** *Jun–Sep: daily; Oct–May:*
Wed, Thu, Sat & Sun pm only.
⚓ Océanopolis
Port de Plaisance du Moulin Blanc.
【 *02 98 34 40 40.* **Open** *daily.*
Closed *Sep–May: Mon pm* 📷 **&**

**Traditional boatbuilding at Le
Port-Musée, Douarnenez**

Parc Régional
d'Armorique **❸**

Finistère. 🛬 *Brest.* 🚂 *Chateaulin,*
Landernau. 🚌 *Le Faou, Huelgoat.*
ℹ *Saint-Éloy (02 98 21 90 69).*

T HE ARMORICAN Regional
Nature Park stretches west
from the moorlands of the
Monts d'Arrée to the Presqu'île
de Crozon and Ile d'Ouessant.
Within this protected area lies
a mixture of farmland, heaths,
remains of ancient oak forest
and wild, open spaces. The
park and its scenic coastline
are ideal for walking, riding
and touring by bicycle or car.
   Huelgoat is a good starting
point for inland walks, and
there are splendid views from
Ménez-Hom (300 m/1,082 ft).
   The main information center
for the park is at **Ménez-Meur**,
where there is a wooded estate
with wild and farm animals,
and a Breton horse museum.
Scattered around the park are
another nine small, theme
museums, some paying
tribute to country traditions
such as hunting, fishing and
tanning. Contemporary arts
and crafts are exhibited at
the **Maison des Artisans**
in Brasparts.
   The **Musée de l'Ecole
Rurale** at Trégarven re-creates
a rural school from the beginning of the 20th century,
while other museums are
devoted to subjects as diverse
as medieval monastic life,
ragpickers and the lifestyle
of a Breton country priest.

Douarnenez ❹

Finistère. 🏛 *16,700.* 🚌
🚶 *2 rue Docteur Mevel (02 98 92 13 35).* 🚌 *Mon–Sat.*

AT THE START of this century, Douarnenez used to be France's leading sardine port; today, it is still devoted to fishing, but is also a tourist resort, with beaches on both sides of the Pouldavid estuary.

Nearby lies the tiny **Île Tristan**, linked with the tragic love story of Tristan and Iseult. In the 16th century, it was the stronghold of a notorious brigand, La Fontenelle.

The picturesque **Port du Rosmeur** offers cafés, fish restaurants and boat trips around the bay, with a lively early morning *criée* (fish auction) held in the nearby Nouveau Port. The Port-Rhu has been turned into a floating museum, **Le Port-Rhu Musée**, with over 100 boats and several shipyards. Some of the larger vessels can be visited in tourist season.

🏛 **Le Port-Musée**
Place de l'Enfer. 📞 *02 98 92 65 20.*
Open *mid-Jun–Sep: daily; Oct–mid-Jun: Tue–Sun.* 🅿 ♿

Locronan's 15th-century Eglise St-Ronan, seen from the churchyard

Locronan ❺

Finistère. 🏛 *800.* 🚶 *place de la Mairie (02 98 91 70 14).*

DURING THE 15th–17th centuries, Locronan grew wealthy from the manufacture of sailcloth. After Louis XIV ended the Breton monopoly on this trade, the town declined – leaving an elegant ensemble of Renaissance

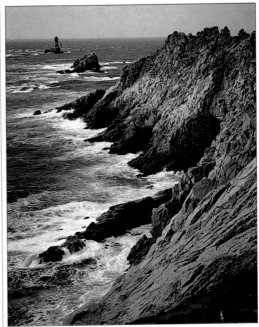

The awe-inspiring cliffs of Pointe du Raz

buildings that today attract huge numbers of visitors. In the town's central cobbled square stands a late 15th-century church dedicated to the Irish missionary St. Ronan. Down Rue Moal is the delightful **Chapelle Notre-Dame-de-Bonne-Nouvelle**, with a calvary and a fountain.

Every July, Locronan is the scene of a *Troménie,* a hilltop pilgrimage held in honor of St. Ronan. The more elaborate *Grande Troménie* takes place every six years.

Pointe du Raz ❻

Finistère. 🚉 *Quimper.* 🚌 *Quimper, then bus.* 🚶 *Audierne (02 98 70 12 20).*

THE DRAMATIC Pointe du Raz, almost 80 m (262 ft) high, is a narrow headland jutting into the Atlantic at the tip of Cap Sizun. The views of jagged rocks and pounding seas are breathtaking. Farther west lies the flat, treeless Ile de Sein and beyond that the lighthouse of Ar Men. Despite being only an average 1.5 m (5 ft) above sea level, Ile de

Sein is home to some 500 resolute inhabitants, and can be reached by boat from Audierne in an hour.

Pays Bigouden ❼

Finistère. 🚌 *Pont l'Abbé.* 🚶 *Pont l'Abbé (02 98 82 30 30).*

BRITTANY'S SOUTHWEST tip is known as the Pays Bigouden, a windy peninsula with proud and ancient traditions. The region is famous for the tall *coiffes* that are still worn by women at festivals and *pardons (see p233),* and there are many examples of these at the **Musée Bigouden**.

Along the Baie d'Audierne is a brooding landscape of weather-beaten hamlets and isolated chapels – the 15th-century calvary at **Notre-Dame-de-Tronoën** is the oldest in Brittany. There are invigorating sea views from **Pointe de la Torche** and from the **Eckmühl lighthouse**.

🏛 **Musée Bigouden**
Le Château, Pont l'Abbé. 📞 *02 98 66 09 09.* **Open** *Easter–May: Mon–Sat; Jun–Sep: daily.* **Closed** *May 1.* 🅿

Quimper ⓽

Finistère. 🏙 63,000. 🚄 🚌 🚗 🛳
ℹ place de la Résistance (02 98 53 04 05). 🗓 daily.

THE ANCIENT capital of Cornouaille, Quimper has a distinctly Breton character. Here you can find Breton language books and music for sale, buy a traditional costume or enjoy some of the best crêpes and cider in Brittany. Quimper gets its name from *kemper*, a Breton word meaning the confluence of two rivers, and the Steir and Odet still flow through this relaxed cathedral city.

West of the cathedral lies a pedestrianized area known as **Vieux Quimper**, full of shops, crêperies and half-timbered houses. Rue Kéréon is the main thoroughfare, with the place au Beurre and the picturesque *hôtel particuliers* (mansions) of rue des Gentilshommes to the north.

Quimper has been producing faïence, elegant hand-painted pottery, since 1690. The design often features decorative flowers and animals framed by blue and yellow borders. Originally created as wedding presents and heirlooms, faïence is today exported to collectors all over the world. In the southwest of the city lies the oldest factory, **Faïenceries HB-Henriot**, which is open to visitors from March to October.

🛈 Cathédrale St-Corentin

Quimper's cathedral is dedicated to the city's founder-bishop, St. Corentin. Begun in 1240, it is the earliest Gothic building in Lower Brittany, and was bizarrely constructed with the choir standing at a slight angle to the nave, perhaps to fit in with buildings that once stood behind. The two spires of the west façade were added in 1856. Between them is a statue of King Gradlon, the mythical founder of the

The Martyrdom of St. Triphine (1910) by Sérusier, Pont-Aven School

drowned city of Ys. After this deluge, he chose Quimper as his new capital and St. Corentin as his spiritual guide.

🏛 Musée des Beaux-Arts

40 place St-Corentin. 📞 02 98 95 45 20. **Open** Jul–Aug: daily; Sep–Jun: Wed–Mon. **Closed** most public hols; Nov–Mar: Sun am. 🎫 ♿

Quimper's art museum, one of the best in the region, was extensively restored in 1993. The collection is strong in late 19th- and early 20th-century artists, whose work – such as Jean-Eugène Buland's *Visite à Ste-Marie de Bénodet* – offers a valuable insight into the way visiting painters perpetuated a romantic view of Brittany. Also on exhibit are works by members of the Pont-Aven School and local artists J.J. Lemordant and Max Jacob.

Typical faïence plate from Quimper

🏛 Musée Departemental Breton

1 rue de Roi-Gradlon. 📞 02 98 95 21 60. **Open** Jun–Sep: daily; Oct–May: Tue–Sun. **Closed** public hols. 🎫 ♿

The 16th-century Bishop's Palace houses a well-presented collection of Breton costumes, furniture and faïence. Exhibits include elaborate *coiffes* from around Cornouaille, ornately carved box-beds and wardrobes, and turn-of-the-century tourist posters for Brittany.

Concarneau ⓽

Finistère. 🏙 19,000. 🚌 🛳
ℹ quai d'Aiguillon (02 98 97 01 44). 🗓 Mon & Fri.

AN IMPORTANT fishing port, Concarneau's principal attraction is its 14th-century **Ville Close** (walled town), built on an island in the harbor and completely encircled by massive lichen-covered granite ramparts. Access is by bridge from the place Jean Jaurès. Parts of the ramparts can be toured, and the narrow streets are full of shops and restaurants. The **Musée de la Pêche**, housed in the port's ancient barracks, explains the local techniques and history of sea-fishing.

🏛 Musée de la Pêche

Rue Vauban. 📞 02 98 97 10 20. **Open** daily. **Closed** Jan. 🎫 ♿

Fishing boats in Concarneau's busy harbor

Pont-Aven ⑩

Finistère. 🚊 *3,000*. 🚉 🛈 *place de l'Hôtel de Ville (02 98 06 04 70).* 🚌 *Tue.*

ONCE A MARKET town of "14 mills and 15 houses," Pont-Aven's picturesque location in the wooded Aven estuary made it attractive to many late 19th-century artists.

In 1888, Paul Gauguin, along with like-minded painters Emile Bernard and Paul Sérusier, developed a crude, colorful style of painting known as Synthetism. Drawing inspiration from the Breton landscape and its people, the Ecole de Pont-Aven (Pont-Aven School) worked here and in nearby Le Pouldu until 1896.

Today, the town remains devoted to art and has some 50 private galleries, along with the informative **Musée de Pont-Aven**, which documents the achievements of the Pont-Aven School. The surrounding woods proved inspirational to many visiting artists, and offer pleasant walks in their footsteps – one leads through the Bois d'Amour to the **Chapelle de Trémalo**, where the wooden Christ in Gauguin's *Le Christ Jaune* still hangs.

🏛 **Musée de Pont-Aven**
Pl de l'Hôtel de Ville. 📞 *02 98 06 14 43.* **Open** *daily.* **Closed** *between exhibitions.* 🖼 🚹

Notre-Dame-de-Kroaz-Baz, Roscoff

Le Pouldu ⑪

Finistère. 🚊 *4,000*. 🚉 🛈 *boulevard Charles Filiger (02 98 39 93 42).*

A QUIET PORT at the mouth of the River Laïta, Le Pouldu has a small beach and good walks. Its main attraction is **Maison de Marie Henry**, a reconstruction of the inn where Paul Gauguin and other artists stayed between 1889 and 1893. They covered every inch of the dining room, including the windowpanes, with self-portraits, caricatures and still-lifes. These were discovered in 1924 beneath layers of wallpaper.

🏛 **Maison de Marie Henry**
Rue des Grandes Sables. 📞 *02 98 39 98 51.* **Open** *Apr–May: Sat, Sun, public hols; Jun–Sep: Thu–Tue; July–Aug: daily.* 🖼

Roscoff ⑫

Finistère. 🚊 *3,700*. 🚉 🚉 🛳 🛈 *46 rue Gambetta (02 98 61 12 13).* 🚌 *Wed.*

ONCE A PIRATES' haunt, Roscoff is now a thriving Channel port and seaside resort. Signs of its wealthy seafaring past can be found in the old port, particularly along rue Amiral Réveillère and in place Lacaze-Duthiers. Here, the granite façades of the 16th- and 17th-century shipowners' mansions, and the weatherbeaten caravels and cannon decorating **Eglise Notre-Dame-de-Kroaz-Baz**, testify to the days when the pirates of Roscoff were as notorious as those of St-Malo (*see p272*). Notre-Dame, built in the early 16th century, has an elaborate lantern belfry.

Charles Perez Aquarium nearby is devoted to the weird and wonderful creatures that swim in the Channel. From the harbor, you can take a short boat trip to the peaceful **Ile de Batz**. Saltwater treatments are available at Roscoff's two thalassotherapy institutes. There is also a seaweed research center, Thalado. Near the Pointe de Bloscon there are colorful tropical gardens.

🐟 **Charles Perez Aquarium**
Place Georges Teissier. 📞 *02 98 29 23 23.* **Open** *Easter–Sep: daily;* 🖼 🚹 *restricted.*

PAUL GAUGUIN IN BRITTANY

Carving, Chapelle de Trémalo

Paul Gauguin's (1848–1903) story reads like a romantic novel. At the age of 35, he left his career as a stockbroker to become a fulltime painter. From 1886 to 1894, he lived and worked in Brittany, at Pont-Aven and Le Pouldu, where he painted the landscape and its people. He chose to concentrate on the intense, almost "primitive" quality of the Breton Catholic faith, attempting to convey it in his work. This is evident in *Le Christ Jaune* (Yellow Christ), inspired by a woodcarving in the Trémalo chapel. In Gauguin's painting, the Crucifixion is a reality in the midst of the contemporary Breton landscape, rather than a remote or symbolic event. This theme recurs in many of his paintings from the period, including *Jacob Wrestling with the Angel* (1888).

***Le Christ Jaune* (1889) by Paul Gauguin**

St-Thégonnec ⑬

Finistère. 🚌 *Open daily.* ♿

THIS IS ONE OF THE most complete parish closes in Brittany. Passing through its triumphal archway, the ossuary is to the left. The calvary, directly ahead, was built in 1610 and perfectly illustrates the extraordinary skills Breton sculptors developed as they worked with the local granite. Among the many animated figures surrounding the central cross, a small niche contains a statue of St. Thégonnec with a cart pulled by wolves.

Guimiliau ⑭

Finistère. **Open** daily. ♿

ALMOST 200 figures adorn Guimiliau's intensely decorated calvary (1581–88), many wearing 16th-century dress. Among them you can contemplate the legendary torment of Katell Gollet, a servant girl tortured by demons for stealing a consecrated wafer to please her lover. The church is dedicated to St. Miliau and has a richly decorated south porch. The baptistry's elaborately-carved oak canopy dates from 1675.

Font canopy from 1675, Guimiliau

Lampaul-Guimiliau ⑮

Finistère. **Open** daily. ♿

ENTERING THROUGH the monumental gate, the chapel and ossuary lie to the left, while the calvary is to the right. Here, however, it is the church that demands most attention. The interior is zealously painted and carved, including some naive scenes from the Passion depicted along the 16th-century rood beam dividing the nave and choir.

Parish Closes

REFLECTING THE RELIGIOUS FERVOR of the Bretons, the Enclos Paroissiaux (parish closes) were built during the 15th–18th centuries. At that time, Brittany had few urban centers but many wealthy rural settlements, which profited from maritime trading and the manufacture of cloth. Grand religious monuments, some taking over 200 years to complete, were built by small villages inspired by spiritual zeal and the more earthly desire to rival their neighbors. Some of the finest parish closes lie in the Elorn valley, linked by a well-marked Circuit des Enclos Paroissiaux.

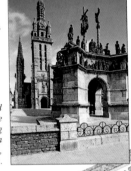

The enclosure, surrounded by a stone wall, is the hallowed area. By following the wall, visitors are drawn toward the triumphal arch, shown here in Pleyben.

The small cemetery reflects the size of the community that built these great churches.

GUIMILIAU PARISH CLOSE
The three essential features of a parish close are a triumphal gateway marking the entry into the hallowed enclosure, a calvary depicting scenes from the Passion and Crucifixion, and an ossuary beside the church porch.

The calvary is unique to Brittany, and may have been inspired by the crosses set on top of menhirs (see p269) by the early Christians. They provide a unique Bible lesson, often with the characters in 17th-century costumes, as in this example from St-Thégonnec.

Brittany's parish closes are mainly concentrated in the Elorn Valley. Along with St-Thégonnec, Guimiliau and Lampaul-Guimiliau, other parish closes to visit include Bodilis, La Martyre, La Roche-Maurice, Ploudiry, Sizun and Commana. Farther afield lie Plougastel-Doulas and Pleyben, while Guéhenno is in the Morbihan region.

Church interiors are usually adorned with depictions of local saints and scenes from their lives, along with ornately carved beams and furniture. This is the altarpiece in Guimiliau.

In the ossuary, bones exhumed from the cemetery were stored. Built close to the church entrance, the ossuary was considered a bridge between the living and the dead.

Church

South Porch

Calvary

Funeral Chapel

Field of the Dead

Triumphal Arch

The triumphal arch at St-Thégonnec, a monumental entrance, heralds the worshipper's arrival on sacred ground, like the righteous entering heaven.

Carvings in stone were created as biblical cartoons to instruct and inspire visitors. Their clear message is now often obscured by weather and lichen, but this one in St-Thégonnec is well preserved.

The chapel of Notre-Dame, perched on the cliffs above the beach of Port-Blanc, Côte de Granit Rose

Côte de Granit Rose ⑯

Côtes d'Armor. ✕ 🚉 🚌 *Lannion.*
ℹ️ *Lannion (02 96 46 41 00).*

THE COAST between Paimpol and Trébeurden is known as the Côte de Granit Rose because of its reddish-pink cliffs. These are best seen between Trégastel and Trébeurden, but the pink granite is also used as building material in the nearby towns. The stretch of coast between Trébeurden and Perros-Guirec is one of Brittany's most popular family vacation areas. Farther east are quieter beaches and coves, at **Trévou-Tréguignec** and **Port-Blanc**. Beyond the cathedral town of Tréguier, **Paimpol** is a working fishing port that once sent huge cod and whaling fleets to fish off Iceland and Newfoundland.

Tréguier ⑰

Côtes d'Armor. 👥 *2,900.*
ℹ️ *Hôtel de Ville (02 96 92 30 19).*
🅿️ *Wed.*

SET ON A HILL overlooking the estuary of the Jaundy and Guindy rivers, Tréguier stands apart from the seaside resorts of the Côte de Granit Rose. It is a typically Breton market town, content with its one major attraction, **Cathédrale St-Tugdual**, and makes few concessions to tourism. The cathedral, built in the 14th–15th centuries, is dedicated to the monk St.

Tugdual. It has three towers – one Romanesque, one Gothic and an 18th-century spire, pierced with holes in order to withstand strong winds.

Île de Bréhat ⑱

Côtes d'Armor. 🚌 🛥️ *Paimpol, then bus to Pointe de l'Arcouest (Mon–Sat in winter; daily in summer), then boat.* ℹ️ *Paimpol (02 96 20 83 16).*

A 15-MINUTE CROSSING from the Pointe de l'Arcouest, the Île de Bréhat is actually two islands, joined by a small bridge, which together are only 3.5 km (2.2 miles) long. With motorized traffic banned, and a climate mild enough for oleander, mimosa and a variety of fruit trees to flourish, it has a relaxing, pastoral atmosphere. Bicycle rentals and boat tours of the island are available in the main town, **Port-Clos**, and you can walk to the island's highest point, the **Chapelle St-Michel**.

Chapelle St-Michel, a landmark on Ile de Bréhat

Carnac ⑲

Morbihan. 👥 *4,400.* 🚌 ℹ️ *74 avenue des Druides (02 97 52 13 52).*

CARNAC IS ONE of the world's great prehistoric sites, with almost 3,000 menhirs in parallel rows north of the town center and an exceptional **Musée de Préhistoire**.
 In the town, the 17th-century **Eglise St-Cornély** is dedicated to St. Cornelius, patron saint of horned animals. Scenes from the saint's life are painted on its wooden ceiling. To the south, the long, sandy beach makes the town a popular seaside resort.

🏛️ **Musée de Préhistoire**
10 place de la Chapelle.
📞 *02 97 52 22 04.* **Open** *Wed–Mon.* **Closed** *Jan 1, May 1, Dec 25.*
📷 ♿

Presqu'île de Quiberon ⑳

Morbihan. ✕ *Quiberon (via Lorient).*
🚌 *Jul & Aug.* 🚌 🛥️ *Quiberon.* ℹ️ *Quiberon (02 97 50 07 84).*

ONCE AN ISLAND, the slender Quiberon peninsula has a bleak and windy west coast with sea-punished cliffs, known as the Côte Sauvage. The east is more benign, with sheltered beaches. At the southern tip of the peninsula is the fishing port and resort of **Quiberon**, departure point for the car ferry to Belle-Ile.
 In 1795, 10,000 Royalist troops were massacred here in an ill-fated attempt to reverse the French Revolution.

Brittany's Prehistoric Monuments

AT CARNAC, thousands of ancient granite rocks were arranged in mysterious lines and patterns by Megalithic tribes as early as 4000 BC. Their original purpose remains obscure: the significance was probably religious, but the precise patterns also suggest an early astronomical calendar. Celts, Romans and Christians have since adapted them to their own beliefs.

The Gavrinis Tumulus, Golfe du Morbihan

MEGALITHS

There are many different formations of megaliths, all with a particular purpose. Words from the Breton language, such as *men* (stone), *dole* (table) and *bir* (long), are still used to describe them.

Menhirs, *the most common megaliths, are upright stones, standing alone or arranged in lines. Those in circles are known as cromlechs.*

Dolmen, *two upright stones roofed by a third, were used as a burial chamber, such as the Merchant's Table at Locmariaquer.*

Allée couverte, *upright stones placed in a row and roofed to form a covered alley, can be seen at Carnac.*

A tumulus *is a dolmen covered with stones and soil to form a burial mound.*

KEY

▨	Megalithic sites
▨	Alignments

0 kilometers 10
0 miles 5

Brittany's major megalithic sites

BAIE DE QUIBERON

Gavrinis
Carnac
Quiberon

Alignment at Carnac

Menhirs of all shapes in a field near Carnac

Belle-Île-en-Mer ㉑

Morbihan. ✕ Quiberon (via Lorient).
⛴ from Quiberon. 🛈 Le Palais
(02 97 31 81 93).

BRITTANY's largest island lies
14 km (9 miles) south of
Quiberon and can be reached
in 45 minutes by car ferry
from Quiberon. Its coast
offers both rugged cliffs and
good beaches, while inland
lie exposed highlands inter-
sected by sheltered valleys.
In the main town, Le Palais,
stands the **Citadelle Vauban**,
a 16th-century star-shaped
fortress, and there are fine
walks and views along the
southern Côte Sauvage.

Cloisters of St-Pierre in Vannes

Vannes ㉒

Morbihan. 🏘 48,500. 🚊 🚌 🛈 1 rue
Thiers (02 97 47 24 34). 🛒 Wed & Sat.

STANDING AT THE HEAD of the
Golfe du Morbihan, Vannes
was the capital of the Veneti,
a seafaring Armorican tribe
defeated by Caesar in 56 BC.
In the 9th century, Nominoë,
the first Duke of Brittany,
made it his power base. The
city remained influential up
until the signing of the union
with France in 1532, when
Rennes became the Breton
capital. Today, it is a busy
commercial city with a well-
preserved medieval quarter,
and a good base for exploring
the Golfe du Morbihan.

The impressive eastern
walls of old Vannes can be
viewed from the promenade
de la Garenne. Two of the
city's old gates survive at
either end: Porte-Prison in the
north, and the southern Porte-

Breton seafarer, off Belle-Ile's coast

Poterne with a row of 17th-
century wash houses close by.

Walking up from Porte St-
Vincent, you find the city's
old market squares, still in
use today. The **place des
Lices** was once the scene of
medieval tournaments, and
the streets around the rue de
la Monnaie are full of well-
preserved 16th-century houses.

Begun in the 13th century,
Cathédrale St-Pierre has since
been drastically remodeled
and restored. The Chapel of
the Holy Sacrament houses
the revered tomb of Vincent
Ferrier, a Spanish saint who
died in Vannes in 1419.

Opposite the west front of
the cathedral, the old covered
market **La Cohue** (meaning
throng or hubbub) was once
the city's central meeting place.
Parts of the building date from
the 13th century, and a small
museum inside displays art
and artifacts relevant to the
history of Vannes and the
Golfe du Morbihan.

Housed in the 15th-century
Château Gaillard, the **Musée
d'Archéologie du Morbihan**

is a rich assembly of finds
from Morbihan's many
prehistoric sites, including
jewelry, pottery and
weapons. There is also a
gallery of medieval and
Renaissance *objets d'art*.

🏛 **Musée d'Archéologie du
Morbihan**
Château Gaillard, 2 rue Noé.
📞 02 97 42 59 80. **Open** Apr–Oct:
Mon–Sat; Nov–Mar: Mon–Sat pm.
Closed public hols. 📷

Environs
To the south of the city, the
Parc du Golfe is a park with
many amusements, a but-
terfly conservatory and an
aquarium with over 400
species of fish. Northeast of
Vannes, off the N166, lie the
romantic ruins of the 15th-
century **Tours d'Elven**.

Golfe du Morbihan ㉓

Morbihan. ✕ Lorient. 🚊 🚌 ⛴
Vannes. 🛈 Vannes (02 97 47 24 34).

MORBIHAN MEANS "little sea"
in Breton, an apt de-
scription for this landlocked
expanse of tidal water.
Connected to the Atlantic by
only a small channel between
the Locmariaquer and Rhuys
peninsulas, the gulf is dotted
with islands. Around 40 are
inhabited, with the **Ile d'Arz**
and the **Ile aux Moines** the
largest. These are served by
regular ferries from Conleau
and Port-Blanc, respectively.

Around the gulf several
small harbor towns thrive on
fishing, oyster cultivation and
tourism. There is a wealth of

The picturesque fishing port of Le Bono in Golfe du Morbihan

Young vacationers on the beach at Dinard, a classic seaside resort on the Emerald Coast

megalithic sites, notably the island of **Gavrinis** where a tumulus has been excavated to reveal extraordinary stone carvings *(see p269)*. There are boat trips to Gavrinis from Larmor-Baden and around the gulf from Locmariaquer, Auray, Vannes and Port-Navalo.

The medieval Château de Josselin on the banks of the River Oust

Josselin ㉔

Morbihan. 👥 *2,600.* 🚌 🛈 *place de la Congrégation (02 97 22 36 43).* 🛒 *Sat.*

OVERLOOKING the River Oust, Josselin is dominated by a medieval **Château** owned by the Rohan family since the end of the 13th century. Only four of its nine towers survive. The elaborate inner granite façade incorporates the letter "A" – a tribute to the much-loved Duchess Anne of Brittany (1477–1514), who presided over Brittany's "Golden Age." Tours are given of the 19th-century interior, and in the former stables is the Musée des Poupées, with 600 dolls. In the town, **Basilique Notre-Dame-du-Roncier** contains

the mausoleum of the castle's most famous owner and constable of France, Olivier de Clisson (1336–1407). West of Josselin at Kerguéhennec, the grounds of an 18th-century château have become a modern sculpture park.

⚓ **Château de Josselin**
🄲 *02 97 22 36 45.* **Open** *Apr–May & Oct: Wed, Sat, Sun & public hols, pm only; Jun & Sep: daily pm; Jul & Aug: daily.* 🖼️ ♿

Forêt de Paimpont ㉕

Ille-et-Vilaine. 🚂 *Rennes.* 🚌 *Nonfort sur Neu.* 🚌 *Rennes.* 🛈 *Piélan (02 99 06 86 07).*

ALSO KNOWN AS the Forêt de Brocéliande, this forest is a last remnant of the dense primeval woods that once covered much of Armorica. It has long been associated with the legends of King Arthur, and visitors still come to search for the magical

Legendary sorcerer Merlin and Viviane, the Lady of the Lake

spring where the sorcerer Merlin first met Viviane, the Lady of the Lake. The small village of **Paimpont** provides a good base for exploring both the forest and its myths.

Côte d'Emeraude ㉖

Ille et Vilaine & Côtes d'Armor.
✈️ *Dinard–St-Malo.* 🚌 🚌 🚢
🛈 *St-Malo (02 99 56 64 48).*

BETWEEN Le Val-André and the Pointe du Grouin near Cancale, sandy beaches, rocky headlands and classic seaside resorts stretch along Brittany's northern shore. Known as the Emerald Coast, its self-proclaimed Queen is the aristocratic resort of **Dinard**, "discovered" in the 1850s and still playing host to the international rich.

To its west, the summer holiday mood is sustained by such resorts as St-Jacut-de-la-Mer, St-Cast-le-Guildo, Sables d'Or-les-Pins and Erquy, all with tempting beaches. In the Baie de la Frênaye, the medieval **Fort La Latte** provides good views from its ancient watchtower, while the lighthouse that dominates **Cap Fréhel** nearby offers even more extensive panoramas.

East of Dinard, the D186 runs across the **Barrage de la Rance** to St-Malo. Built in 1966, it was the world's first dam to generate electricity using tidal power. Beyond St-Malo, coves and beaches surround La Guimorais, while around the Pointe du Grouin the seas are truly emerald.

SEAFARERS OF ST-MALO

St-Malo owes its wealth and reputation to the exploits of its mariners. In 1534 Jacques Cartier, born in nearby Rothéneuf, discovered the mouth of the St. Lawrence River in Canada and claimed the territory for France. It was Breton sailors who voyaged to South America in 1698 to colonize the Iles Malouines, known today as Las Malvinas, or the Falklands. By the 17th century, St-Malo was the largest port in France and famous for its corsairs – privateers licensed by the king to prey on foreign ships. The most illustrious were the swashbuckling René Duguay-Trouin (1673–1736), who captured Rio de Janeiro from the Portuguese in 1711, and the intrepid Robert Surcouf (1773–1827), whose ships hounded vessels of the British East India Company. The riches won by trade and piracy enabled St-Malo's ship-owners to build great mansions known as *malouinières*.

Explorer Jacques Cartier (1491–1557)

St-Malo ㉗

Ille-et-Vilaine. 🏘 49,000. ✈ 🚉
🚌 ⛴ 🛈 *esplanade St-Vincent*
(02 99 56 64 48). 🕒 *Mon–Sat.*

O NCE A FORTIFIED island, St-Malo stands in a commanding position at the mouth of the River Rance.

The city is named after Maclou, a Welsh monk who came here in the 6th century to spread the Christian message. During the 16th–19th centuries, the port won prosperity and power through the exploits of its seafarers. St-Malo was heavily bombed in 1944 but has since been scrupulously restored and is now a major port and ferry terminal as well as a resort.

Intra-muros, the old walled city, is encircled by ramparts that provide fine views of St-Malo and its offshore islands. Take the steps up by the **Porte St-Vincent** and walk clockwise, passing the mighty 15th-century **Grande Porte**.

Within the city is a web of narrow, cobbled streets with tall 18th-century buildings housing souvenir shops, seafood restaurants and crêperies. Rue Porcon-de-la-Barbinais leads to **Cathédrale St-Vincent**, whose somber 12th-century nave contrasts with the brilliant modern stained glass of the chancel. On cour La Houssaye, the 15th-century Maison de la Duchesse Anne has been carefully restored.

St-Malo seen at low tide through the gate of Fort National

⛪ Château de St-Malo

🎫 *02 99 40 71 57.* **Open**
Easter–Sep: daily; Oct–Easter: Tue–Sun.
Closed *Jan 1, Nov 1 & 11, Dec 25.* 🎫
St-Malo's castle dates from the 14th–15th centuries. The great keep, built in 1424, contains a museum of the city's history, including the adventures of its state-sponsored corsairs. From its watch towers, there is an impressive view of sea and coast. The adjacent tower, the Quic-en-Groigne, contains a museum of historical wax-works. Nearby, in the place Vauban, an aquarium has been built into the ramparts.

⛨ Fort National

Open *Easter–end Sep: daily at low tide.* 🎫
Constructed in 1689 by Louis XIV's famous military architect, Vauban, this fort can be reached on foot at low tide and offers good views of St-Malo and its ramparts. At low tide you can walk out to the island of **Grand Bé**. From the top there are great views along the whole of Côte d'Emeraude *(see p271)*. The St-Malo-born writer François-René de Chateaubriand is buried here.

⛨ Tour Solidor

St-Servan. 🎫 *02 99 40 71 58.*
Open *Easter–Sep: daily; Oct–Easter: Tue–Sun.* **Closed** *Jan 1, May 1, Nov 1 & 11, Dec 25.* 🎫
To the west of St-Malo in St-Servan, the three-towered Tour Solidor was built in 1382. Formerly a prison, it now houses an intriguing museum devoted to the ships and sailors that rounded Cape Horn, displaying ship models, logs and various instruments of a nautical flavor.

Environs

When the tide is out, good beaches are revealed around St-Malo and in the neighboring suburbs of St-Servan and Paramé. A regular passenger ferry runs across to Dinard *(see p271)* and the Channel Islands, and there are boat trips up the Rance to Dinan, and to the Iles Chausey, Ile de Cézembre and Cap Fréhel.

At Rothéneuf, you can visit the **Manoir Limoëlou**, home of the navigator Jacques Cartier. Nearby, on the coast, Les Rochers Sculptés is a beguiling array of granite

22f/Dz

Cancale oysters, prized for their
taste since Roman times

faces and figures carved into
the cliffs by a local priest,
Abbé Fouré, at the end of
the 19th century.

🏚 Manoir Limoëlou
Rue D Macdonald-Stuart, Limoëlou-
Rothéneuf. 【 02 99 40 97 73.
Open Jun–Aug: daily; Sep–May:
Mon–Fri. 🌀 🕭

Cancale ㉘

Ille-et-Vilaine. 🚶 5,000. 🚌
🈯 44 rue du Port (02 99 89 63 72).
🚌 Sun.

A SMALL PORT with views
across the Baie du Mont-
St-Michel, Cancale is entirely
devoted to the cultivation and
consumption of oysters. Prized
by the Romans, the acclaimed
flavor of Cancale's oysters is
said to derive from the strong
tides that wash over them
daily. You can survey the beds
from a *sentier des douaniers*
(coastguards' footpath, the
GR34) running along the cliffs.
  There are plenty of opportunities for sampling the local

specialty provided by a multi-
tude of bars and restaurants
along the busy quays of the
Port de la Houle, where the
fishing boats arrive at high
tide. Devotees should pay a
visit to the **Musée de
l'Huître et du Coquillage**.

**🏛 Musée de l'Huître et du
Coquillage**
Aurore. 【 02 99 89 69 99.
Open mid-Jun–mid-Sep: Mon–Fri. 🌀

Dinan ㉙

Côtes d'Armor. 🚶 12,800. 🚌 🚉
🈯 6 rue de l'Horloge (02 96 39 75 40).
🚌 Thu.

S ET ON A HILL overlooking
the wooded Rance valley,
Dinan is a modern market
town with a medieval heart.
Surrounded by ramparts,
the well-kept, half-timbered
houses and cobbled streets
of its Vieille Ville have an
impressive, unforced unity
best appreciated by climbing
to the top of its 15th-century
Tour d'Horloge, in rue de
l'Horloge. Nearby, **Basilique
St-Sauveur** contains the heart
of Dinan's most famous son,
the 14th-century warrior
Bertrand du Guesclin.
  Behind the church, Les
Jardins Anglais offer good
views of the River Rance and
the viaduct spanning it. A
short distance farther north,
the steep, geranium-decorated
rue du Jerzual winds down
through the 14th-century
town gate to the port. Once a
busy harbor from which
cloth was shipped, it is now a
quiet backwater where you

can take a pleasure cruise, or
follow a towpath walk around
to the restored 17th-century **le
prieuré St-Magloire** at Léhon.
  The **Musée-Château** houses
a small museum of local
history. Next to it is the 15th-
century **Tour de Coëtquen**.
From here, there are pleasant
walks beside the ramparts
along the promenade des
Petits Fossés and the promenade des Grands Fossés.

♠ Musée-Château
Château de la Duchesse Anne, rue
du Château. 【 02 96 39 45 20.
Open Jun–mid-Oct: daily; mid-Mar–
May, mid-Oct–mid-Nov: Wed–Mon;
Feb–mid-Mar, mid-Nov–Dec: Wed–
Mon am. **Closed** Dec 25. 🌀 🕭

Author and diplomat François-René
de Chateaubriand (1768–1848)

Combourg ㉚

Ille-et-Vilaine. 🚶 4,900. 🚌 🚉
🈯 place Albert Parent (02 99 73 13
93). 🚌 Mon.

A SMALL, SLEEPY town beside
a lake, Combourg is com-
pletely overshadowed by the
great, haunting **Château de
Combourg**, first built in the
11th century. The buildings
seen today date from the 14th
and 15th centuries. In 1761,
the château was bought by the
Comte de Chateaubriand, and
the melancholic childhood
spent there by his son, the
author and diplomat François-
René de Chateaubriand (1768–
1848), is candidly described in
his entertaining chronicle,
Mémoires d'Outre-Tombe.
  Empty after the Revolution,
the château was restored in the
late 19th century and is now
open for guided tours. In one
room are papers and furniture
relating to the life of François-
René de Chateaubriand.

♠ Château de Combourg
23 rue des Princes. 【 02 99 73 22 95.
Open Apr–Oct: Wed–Mon. 🌀

View over Dinan and the Gothic bridge crossing the River Rance

RENNES CITY CENTER

Cathédrale St-Pierre ②
Eglise St-Germain ⑧
Eglise St-Sauveur ③
Hôtel de Ville ④
Musée de Bretagne
  and Musée des
  Beaux Arts ⑨
Palais de Justice ⑥
Parc du Thabor ⑦
Portes
  Mordelaises ①
Opéra de
  Rennes ⑤

KEY

P Parking

i Tourist information

✚ Church

0 meters   250

0 yards   250

Rennes ㉛

Ille-et-Vilaine. 204,000. *rue St-Yves (02 99 79 01 98).* Tue–Sat.

Founded by the Gauls and colonized by the Romans, Rennes is strategically located where the Vilaine and Ille rivers meet. After Brittany's union with France in 1532, the town became regional capital. In 1720, a fire lasting for six days devastated the city. Today, a small part of the medieval city survives, together with the neat grid of 18th-century

The lively market at place des Lices in the heart of Rennes

buildings that arose from the ashes. Around this historic core are the tower blocks and hi-tech factories of modern Rennes – a confident provincial capital with two universities and a thriving cultural life.

Wandering through the streets that radiate from the place des Lices and the place Ste-Anne, it is easy to imagine what Rennes was like before the Great Fire. Now mostly pedestrianized, this area has become the city's youthful heart, with plenty of bars, crêperies and designer shops. At the western end of rue de la Monnaie stands the 15th-century **Portes Mordelaises**, once part of the city's ramparts.

Close by, **Cathédrale St-Pierre** was completed in 1844, the third on this site. Note the carved 16th-century Flemish altarpiece. Nearby is the 18th-century **Eglise St-Sauveur**. Just south of the attractive rue St-George, **Eglise St-Germain** has a typically Breton belfry and wooden vaulting. In the place de la Mairie stands the early 18th-century **Hôtel de Ville** and the Neo-Classical **Opéra de Rennes**. The **Parc du Thabor**, once part of a Benedictine monastery, is ideal for walks and picnics.

Half-timbered houses lining the narrow streets of old Rennes

✚ Palais de Justice

Place du Parlement. *Closed for restoration until at least 2000.*
Rennes' Law Courts, built in 1618–55 and designed by Salomon de Brosse, were the seat of the region's governing body until the Revolution.

Parts of the building were still used as criminal courts until it was severely damaged by fire during the riots over fish prices in February 1994. A restoration project will return its interior as well as exterior to their original state, including the unique coffered ceiling and gilded woodwork of the Grande Chambre.

🏛 Musée de Bretagne, Musée des Beaux Arts

20 quai Emile Zola. 📞 02 99 28 55 84 (Musée de Bretagne). 📞 02 99 28 55 85 (Musée des Beaux Arts). **Open** Wed–Mon. **Closed** public hols. 📷 ♿

The Musée de Bretagne, on the south bank of the Vilaine River, provides a stimulating introduction to Brittany's history. There are examples of traditional Breton furniture and costume, and displays on Brittany's prehistoric megaliths, the growth of Rennes, rural crafts and the fishing industry.

In the same building, the Musée des Beaux Arts has a wide-ranging collection of art from the 14th century to the present, including a room devoted to art on Breton themes. There are paintings by Gauguin, Bernard and other members of the Pont-Aven School (see p265), and three works by Picasso, including the lively *Baigneuse* painted at Dinard in 1928.

Environs

Just south of Rennes, the **Ecomusée du Pays de Rennes** traces the history of a local farm since the 17th century.

Some 16 km (10 miles) to the southeast of Rennes is **Châteaugiron**, a charming medieval village, with an imposing castle and houses preserving their wooden eaves.

🏛 Ecomusée du Pays de Rennes

Ferme de la Bintinais, route de Châtillon-sur-Seiche. 📞 02 99 51 38 15. **Open** mid-Jan–Feb: Wed–Mon. **Closed** Sat & Sun am, public hols. 📷 ♿

♣ Château de Châteaugiron

📞 02 99 37 89 02. **Open** Jul–Aug: daily; May–Jun & Sep: Sun pm. 📷

Fougères ㉜

Ille-et-Vilaine. 🏠 23,000. 🚌 🚊 1 place Aristide Briand (02 99 94 12 20). 🚉 Sat.

A FORTRESS TOWN close to the Breton border, Fougères rests on a hill overlooking the Nançon River. In the valley below, and still linked to the Haute Ville by a curtain of ancient ramparts, stands the mighty 11th–15th century

The mighty fortifications of Château de Fougères

Château de Fougères. To get a good overview of the château, go to the gardens of place aux Arbres behind the 16th-century **Eglise St-Léonard**. From here, you can descend to the river and the medieval houses around place du Marchix. The Flamboyant Gothic **Eglise St-Sulpice**, with its 18th-century wood-paneled interior and granite retables, is well worth visiting.

A walk around the castle's massive outer fortifications reveals the ambitious scale of its construction, with 13 towers and walls over 3 m (10 ft) thick. You can still climb the castle's ramparts and towers to get a feel of what it was like to live and fight within its staggered defenses. Much of the action in Balzac's novel *Les Chouans* (1829) takes place in and around Fougères and its castle.

♣ Château de Fougères

Place Pierre-Simon. 📞 02 99 99 79 59. **Open** Feb–Dec: daily. 📷

Overhanging timber-frame houses on rue Beaudrairie, Vitré

Vitré ㉝

Ill-et-Vilaine. 🏠 16,000. 🚌 🚊 place St-Yves (02 99 75 04 46). 🚉 Mon.

T HE FORTIFIED TOWN of Vitré is set high on a hill overlooking the Vilaine Valley. Its medieval **Château** is complete with pencil-point turrets and picturesque 15th–16th century buildings in attendance. The castle was rebuilt in the 14th–15th centuries and follows a triangular plan, with some of its ramparts walkable. There is a museum of local treasures in the Tour St-Laurent.

To the east, rue Beaudrairie and rue d'Embas have overhanging timber-frame houses with remarkable patterning.

The 15th–16th century **Cathédrale Notre-Dame**, built in Flamboyant Gothic style, has an elaborate south façade with an exterior stone pulpit. Farther along rue Notre-Dame, the promenade du Val skirts around the town's ramparts.

To the southeast of Vitré on the D88, the **Château des Rochers-Sévigné** was once the home of Mme. de Sévigné (1626–96), famous letter-writer and chronicler of life at the court of Louis XIV. The park, chapel and some of her rooms are open to the public.

♣ Château de Vitré

📞 02 99 75 04 54. **Open** Apr–Sep: daily. **Closed** Sat am, Sun am, Mon am. Jan 1, Easter, Nov 1, Dec 25. 📷

♣ Château des Rochers-Sévigné

📞 02 99 96 76 51. **Open** Apr–Sep: Mon pm–Fri. **Closed** Jan 1, Easter, Nov 1, Dec 25. 📷 ♿ restricted.

The Loire Valley

Indre · Indre-et-Loire · Loir-et-Cher · Loiret · Eure-et-Loir
Cher · Vendée · Maine-et-Loire · Loire-Atlantique · Sarthe

RENOWNED FOR ITS SUMPTUOUS CHATEAUX, *the relics of royal days gone by, the glorious valley of the Loire is rich in both history and architecture. Like the Loire River, this vast region runs through the heart of French life. Its sophisticated cities, luxuriant landscape and magnificent food and wine add up to a bourgeois paradise.*

The lush Loire Valley is supremely regal. Orléans was France's intellectual capital in the 13th century, attracting artists, poets and troubadours to the royal court. But the medieval court never stayed in one place for long, which led to the building of magnificent châteaux all along the Loire. Chambord and Chenonceau, the two greatest Renaissance châteaux, remain prestigious symbols of royal rule, resplendent within their ornamental gardens.

Due to its central location, culture and fine cuisine, Tours is the natural visitors' capital. Angers is a close second, but more authentic are the historic towns of Amboise, Blois, Saumur and Beaugency, strung out like jewels along the river. This is the classic Loire Valley, a château trail that embraces the Renaissance gardens of Villandry and the fairy-tale turrets of Azay-le-Rideau. Venture northward and the cathedral cities of Le Mans and Chartres reign supreme, their medieval centers bordered by Gallo-Roman walls. Nantes in the west is a breezy, forward-looking port and gateway to the Atlantic.

Southward, the windswept Vendée is edged by a wild, sandy coastline that is perfect for windsurfers and nature lovers alike. Inland, the Loire's more peaceful tributaries and the watery Sologne beg to be explored. Also ripe for discovery are troglodyte caves, sleepy hamlets and small Romanesque churches decorated with frescoes. Inviting inns offer game, fish and abundant fresh vegetables to be lingered over with a light white Vouvray wine or full-bodied Bourgueil. Overindulgence is no sin in this rich region.

The Loire River at Montsoreau, southeast of Saumur

◁ The fairytale Château de Saumur towering above the town and the Loire River

Exploring the Loire Valley

THE LUSH VALLEY LANDSCAPE, studded with France's greatest châteaux, is the main attraction. River cruises are available from Angers and Nantes, while the sandy Atlantic coast offers beach vacations. Peaceful country vacations can be had in the Vendée, and in the Loir and Indre valleys. Wine tours focus on Bourgueil, Chinon, Muscadet and Vouvray. The most charming bases are Amboise, Blois, Beaugency and Saumur, but culture-lovers are well-provided for throughout the region.

Countryside around Vouvray

To Caen

To Rennes
Brest

To Rennes
St-Malo

LAVAL

CHÂTEAUBRIANT

LE M

ANGERS

NANTES

LANGEAIS

SAUMUR

CLISSON

CHOLET

ÎLE DE NOIRMOUTIER

ABBAYE
DE FONTEVRA

MONTREUIL-BELLAY

To Poitie

ÎLE D'YEU

LA-ROCHE-SUR-YON

VENDÉE

LES SABLES D'OLONNE

KEY

	Highway
	Major road
	Minor road
	Scenic route
	River
	Viewing point

0 kilometers   25

0 miles   25

The 16th-century Château de
Villandry, set amid gardens

SIGHTS AT A GLANCE

A bridge over the Loire River pictured at dawn

GETTING AROUND

The region is well served by air, road and rail links. Nantes Airport has international flights, while Tours Airport serves Paris. Chartres, Le Mans, Angers and Nantes are reached from Paris by the A11, and the A10 links Orléans, Blois and Tours. The TGV train travels from Paris to Le Mans (1 hr); Tours (1 hr); Angers (90 min); and Nantes (2 hr). The smaller châteaux can be difficult to reach by public transportation, but tours are arranged at major tourist centers. For three or four people, car rental may be cheaper than public transportation.

Tomb of François II and his wife, Marguerite de Foix, in Cathédrale St-Pierre

Nantes ❶

Loire-Atlantique. 🏛 *260,000.*
✈ 🚊 🚌 🛈 *place du Commerce*
(02 40 20 60 00). 🚢 *daily.*

For centuries, Nantes disputed with Rennes over the title of capital of Brittany. Yet links with the Plantagenets and Henri IV also bound it to the "royal" Loire River. Since the 1790s it has officially ceased to be part of Brittany; though still Breton at heart, it is today capital of the Pays de la Loire.

Visually, Nantes is a city of variety, with high-tech towers overlooking the port, canals and Art Nouveau squares. Chic bars and restaurants cram the medieval nucleus, bounded by place St-Croix and the château.

The stark **Cathédrale St-Pierre**, started in 1434 but not completed until 1893, is notable for its sculpted Gothic portals and Renaissance tomb of François II, the last duke of Brittany. More impressive is the **Château des Ducs de Bretagne**, where Anne of Brittany was born in 1477 and where the Edict of Nantes was signed by Henri IV in 1598, granting Protestants religious freedom. Inside one wing of the castle is the **Musée des Salorges**, a naval museum that charts Nantes's colonial links and slave-trading activities in the 18th and 19th centuries. On display are Indian prints, a slave trader's study and a recreation of the bad conditions endured by the galley slaves.

♦ **Château des Ducs de Bretagne/Musée des Salorges**
Pl Marc Elder. 📞 *02 40 41 56 56.*
Open *Jul–Aug: daily; Sep–Jun:*
Wed–Mon. **Closed** *public hols.* 🎫

Environs
From Nantes, boats cruise the rivers Erdre and Sèvre, passing a succession of minor châteaux, Muscadet vineyards and gentle countryside.

Some 16 km (10 miles) southeast of Nantes is **Clisson**, a town razed to the ground during the Vendée Uprising of 1793, and later rebuilt along Italian lines, acquiring Neo-Classical villas, brick bell towers and red-tiled roofs. On a rocky spur overlooking the Sèvre River is the ruined 13th-century **Château de Clisson**, parts of which are under restoration.

♦ **Château de Clisson**
📞 *02 40 54 02 22.* **Open** *Wed–Mon.*
Closed *Christmas school vac.* 🎫

The Vendée ❷

Vendée and Maine-et-Loire.
✈ *Nantes.* 🚊 🚌 *La Roche-sur-Yon.*
🛈 *La Roche-sur-Yon (02 51 47 88 20).*

The counter-revolutionary movement that swept western France between 1793 and 1799 began as a series of uprisings in the Vendée, still an evocative name to the French. As a bastion of the ancien régime, the region rebelled against urban Republican values. But a violent massacre in 1793 left 80,000 royalists dead in one day as they tried to cross the Loire at St-Florent-le-Vieil. The Vendée farmers were staunch royalists, and, although they ultimately lost, the region remains colored by conservatism and religious fervor to this day.

1993 marked the bicentennial of the Vendée Uprising, which was commemorated by the opening of two new museums in Cholet and Challans. Other memorials include the war cemetery at the twice-besieged village of La Gaubretière and stained-glass windows in the parish church of Luc-sur-Boulogne.

Today, the tranquil Vendée welcomes "green" tourism. East and north of La Roche-sur-Yon lies the *bocage vendéen*, a wooded backwater with bridle paths and nature trails. The Atlantic coast between the Loire and Poitou is one of the cleanest and least explored in France, the only significant resort being **Les Sables d'Olonne**, which boasts a marina, a fort and the Vendée war museum. To

The harbor at Ile de Noirmoutier in the Vendée

the north, the marshy **Ile de Noirmoutier** is connected to the mainland at low tide via the Gois causeway.

Inland lies **Marais Poitevin** (*see p398*), its marshes home to bird sanctuaries and hamlets bordered by canals. Maillezais offers a Romanesque abbey as well as punting along the canals, while Chaillé-les-Marais has fine 17th-century churches. With the largest man-made waterways in France, this lush area is graced with the name Venise Verte (Green Venice).

The Apocalypse Tapestry in Angers

Angers ❸

Maine-et-Loire. 🏃 146,000. 🚗 🚉
🛈 pl Kennedy (02 41 23 51 11).
🛒 Wed, Sat.

Angers sees itself as the quintessential Loire city. It is the historic capital of Anjou, home of the Plantagenets and gateway to the Loire Valley.

Angers has a formidable 13th-century **château** (*see p232*). Inside is one of France's finest medieval tapestries, woven between 1375 and 1378. It tells the story of the Apocalypse, depicting battles between hydras and angels.

A short walk from the castle is the **Cathédrale St-Maurice**, noted for its Romanesque façade and 12th-century stained-glass windows. Close by, in place St-Croix, is the timber-framed **Maison d'Adam**, with carvings of the tree of life. The nearby **Musée David d'Angers**, housed in the glass-covered ruins of a 13th-century church, is a tribute to the eponymous 19th-century sculptor born in Angers. Across the Maine River, the Hôpital St-Jean, a hospital for the poor from 1174 to 1854, is today the home of the **Musée Jean Lurçat**. Its prize exhibit is the dramatic *Chant du Monde* tapestry created by Lurçat in 1957.

♣ **Château d'Angers**
📞 02 41 87 43 47. **Open** daily. **Closed** Jan 1, May 1, Nov 1 & 11, Dec 25. 🎫
🏛 **Musée David d'Angers**
33 bis rue Toussaint. 📞 02 41 87 21 03. **Open** mid-June–mid-Sep: daily; mid-Sep–mid-Jun: Tue–Sun. 🎫 🕭
🏛 **Musée Jean Lurçat**
4 boulevard Arago. 📞 02 41 24 18 45. **Open** mid-Jun–mid-Sep: daily; mid-Sep–mid-Jun: Tue–Sun. **Closed** public hols. 🎫 🕭

Environs
Within a 16-km (10-mile) radius of Angers lie the Classical **Château de Serrant** and the moated **Château du Plessis-Bourré**, a decorative pleasure dome encased in a feudal shell. For a quiet taste of the countryside, follow the Loire east along the sandbanks and dikes, enjoying the rustic fish restaurants and a vigorous game of *boule de fort* en route.

♣ **Château de Serrant**
St-Georges-sur-Loire. 📞 02 41 39 13 01. **Open** Jul–Aug: daily; Mar–Jun & Sep–Oct: Wed–Mon. 🎫
♣ **Château du Plessis-Bourré**
Ecuillé. 📞 02 41 32 06 01. **Open** Mar–Nov: Thu pm–Tue; Dec–Feb: groups by appt. 🎫

Le Mans ❹

Sarthe. 🏃 148,500. ✈ 🚗 🚉
🛈 Hôtel des Ursulines, rue de l'Etoile (02 43 28 17 22). 🛒 Wed, Fri & Sun.

Ever since Monsieur Bollée became the first designer to place an engine under a car hood, Le Mans has been synonymous with the motor trade. Bollée's son created an embryonic Grand Prix; ever since, the event (*see p33*) and associated **Musée de l'Automobile** have remained star attractions.

Stained-glass Ascension window in the Cathédrale St-Julien, Le Mans

Vieux Mans, the ancient fortified center, is surrounded by the greatest Gallo-Roman walls in France, best seen from the quai Louis Blanc. Once insalubrious and abandoned, the area has been extensively restored, and is now used as a period film set where epics such as *Cyrano de Bergerac* are filmed. Its pleasures lie in the Renaissance mansions, half-timbered houses, arcaded alleys and tiny courtyards. The crowning point is the Gothic **Cathédrale St-Julien**, borne aloft on flying buttresses, with its Romanesque portal rivaling that of Chartres. Inside, the Angevin nave opens into a Gothic choir, complemented by sculpted capitals and a 12th-century Ascension window.

🏛 **Musée de l'Automobile**
Circuit des 24 Heures du Mans.
📞 02 43 72 72 24. **Open** Jun–Sep: daily. 🎫 🕭

Le Mans racetrack: a 1933 print from the French magazine *Illustration*

Saumur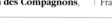

Maine-et-Loire. 32,000.
pl de la Bilange (02 41 40 20 60). Sat.

The Château de Saumur and spire of St-Pierre seen from the Loire

SAUMUR is celebrated for its fairy-tale château, cavalry school, mushrooms and sparkling wines. Its stone mansions recall the city's 17th-century heyday, when it was a bastion of Protestantism and vied with Angers as the intellectual capital of Anjou.

Towering high above both town and river is the turreted **Château de Saumur**. The present structure was started in the 14th century by Louis I of Anjou and remodeled a century later by his grandson, King René. A 90-minute guided tour covers porcelain and equestrian exhibits.

Saumur is predominantly a city of stone, but **place St-Pierre** boasts a number of well-restored, half-timbered houses and a medieval church containing 16th-century tapestries. Steps lead up to the galleried **Maison des Compagnons**,

King René's
coat of arms

the setting for Balzac's novel *Eugénie Grandet*.

On the south bank of the Loire in the western suburb of St-Hilaire-St-Florent is the **Ecole Nationale d'Equitation** (National Riding School), where the prestigious Cadre Noir puts on exciting equestrian shows for visitors.

The nearby **Musée du Champignon** organizes tours of the region's underground tufa caves, where 75 percent of the country's mushrooms are cultivated. Before returning to the town center, be sure to sample the local *méthode champenoise* sparkling wine – the best in France outside Champagne.

♠ **Château de Saumur**
02 41 40 24 40. **Open** Apr–Sep: daily; Oct–Mar: Wed–Mon. **Closed** Jan 1, Dec 25.

Ecole Nationale d'Equitation
St-Hilaire-St-Florent. 02 41 53 50 50. **Open** Apr–Sep: Mon–Sat am; Oct–Mar: by appt. **Closed** public hols.

♠ **Musée du Champignon**
St-Hilaire-St-Florent. 02 41 50 31 55. **Open** mid-Feb–mid-Nov: daily.

Environs
Downriver from Saumur is the lovely **Eglise de Cunault**, an 11th-century Romanesque abbey church with a fine west door and carved capitals.

Montreuil-Bellay ❻

Maine-et-Loire. 4,300. Saumur.
place du Concorde (02 41 52 32 39). Tue (Jun–Sep: Sun also).

SET ON THE Thouet River 17 km (11 miles) south of Saumur, Montreuil-Bellay is one of the region's most gracious small towns. It makes an ideal base for touring Anjou. Walled mansions overlook Gothic churches and the **Chapelle St-Jean**, an ancient hospice and pilgrimage center. A stroll along the riverbank leads past a priory, a miller's house and a city gate.

The imposing **Château de Montreuil-Bellay**, established in 1025, is a veritable fortress with its 13 interlocking towers, barbican and ramparts. A gracious 15th-century house lies beyond the fortified gateway, complete with vaulted medieval kitchen, ancient wine cellars (wine-tasting recommended), and an oratory decorated with 15th-century frescoes.

♠ **Château de Montreuil-Bellay**
02 41 52 33 06. **Open** Easter–Nov: Wed–Mon.

TROGLODYTE DWELLINGS

Some of the best troglodyte settlements in France have been carved out of the soft limestone (tufa) of the Loire Valley, especially around Saumur, Vouvray and along the Loir River. The caves, cut out of cliff-faces or dug underground, have been a source of cheap, secure accommodation for centuries. Today they are popular as *résidences secondaires*, or used for wine storage and mushroom growing. Some are now restaurants or hotels, and old quarries at Doué-la-Fontaine accommodate a zoo and a 15th-century amphitheater. At Rochemenier, near Saumur, is a well-preserved troglodyte village museum. A central pit is surrounded by a warren of caves, barns, wine cellars, dwellings and even a simple underground chapel.

Heralded by chimneys, the underground hamlet of nearby La Fosse is inhabited by one family that has made their eccentric home into a living museum open to visitors.

A typical troglodyte dwelling

Court Life in the Renaissance

Fʀᴀɴçᴏɪꜱ ɪ'ꜱ ʀᴇɪɢɴ, from 1515 to 1547, witnessed the pinnacle of the French Renaissance, characterized by an intense period of château-building and an interest in humanism and the arts. The itinerant court traveled between the pleasure palaces of Amboise, Blois and Chambord in the Loire. Days were devoted to hunting, falconry, *fêtes champêtres* (country festivals) or *jeu de paume*, a forerunner of tennis. Nights were given over to feasting, balls, poetry and romantic rendezvous.

Lute and mandolin music were much in vogue, as were Italian recitals and masquerades. Musicians played at the twice-weekly balls, where the pavane and galliard were danced.

The antics of François I's fools, Triboulet and Caillette, amused the court. Yet they were often mistreated: courtiers regularly nailed Caillette's ears to a post for fun, daring him to remain silent.

Rᴇɴᴀɪꜱꜱᴀɴᴄᴇ Fᴇᴀꜱᴛꜱ
Dinner usually took place before 7pm to the accompaniment of Italian music. Humanist texts were read aloud and the king's fools amused the courtiers.

Courtiers used their own knives at dinner. Forks were still rare, although their use was spreading from Italy.

A typical royal dinner comprised smoked eel, salted ham, veal pâté, egg and saffron soups, roast game and boiled meats, as well as fish dishes in lemon or gooseberry sauce.

The cost of lavish damask, satin and silk costumes often sent courtiers into debt.

Diane de Poitiers (1499–1566) became the mistress of the future Henri II when he was 12 years old. Two years later he married Catherine de' Medici, but Diane remained his favorite until his death.

Artists symbolized love in different ways during the Renaissance. Winged hearts charmingly perform the function here.

The Grand Moûtier cloisters

Abbaye de Fontevraud ❼

Maine-et-Loire. 🚌 *from Saumur.*
📞 *02 41 51 71 41.* **Open** *daily.* **Closed**
Jan 1, Nov 1 & 11, Dec 25. 🖼️ ♿

THE ABBAYE DE FONTEVRAUD is the largest and most remarkably intact medieval abbey in France. It was founded in the early 12th century by Robert d'Arbrissel, a visionary itinerant preacher who set up a Benedictine community of monks, nuns, nobles, lepers, vagabonds and repentant prostitutes.

TOUR EVRAUD

Pepperpot chimneys top the towers of the kitchen, restored in the 19th century.

Fireplace alcoves that look like side chapels housed the ovens.

THE PLANTAGENETS

The legendary counts of Anjou were named after the *genêt*, the sprig of broom Geoffrey Plantagenet wore in his cap. He married Matilda, daughter of England's Henry I. In 1154, when their son Henry – who had married Eleanor of Aquitaine (*see p47*) – acceded to the English throne, the Plantagenet dynasty of English kings was founded, fusing French and English destinies for 200 years.

Effigies of Henry II, Plantagenet king of England, and Eleanor of Aquitaine

The radical founder entrusted the running of the abbey to an abbess, usually from a noble family, and the abbey became a favorite sanctuary for the female aristocracy, including Eleanor of Aquitaine.

From 1804 to 1963 the abbey was used as a prison; since then the buildings have been painstakingly restored by the French government. Wandering around the abbey buildings, orangery and gardens gives a fascinating insight into monastic life. The focal point was the Romanesque

abbey church, consecrated in 1119. It boasts beautifully carved capitals and an immense single nave with four domes, the finest example of a cupola nave in France. Inside are the painted effigies of the Plantagenets dating from the early 13th century: Henry II of England, his redoubtable wife Queen Eleanor of Aquitaine, their Crusading son Richard the Lion-Heart and the sly Isabelle d'Angoulême, who poisoned her husband, King John.

The abbey's nuns lived around the Renaissance **Grand Moûtier cloisters**, forming one of the largest nunneries in France, and the leper colony's nurses were housed in the **St-Lazare priory**, now the atmospheric abbey hotel (*see p555*). Little remains of the monastic quarters, but the **St-Benoît hospital** survives. Most impressive is the octagonal kitchen with its fireplaces and chimneys in the **Tour Evraud**. Restored by Viollet-le-Duc in the 19th century, it is a rare example of secular Romanesque architecture.

The abbey, now an important arts center, regularly hosts concerts and exhibitions.

Chinon ❽

Indre-et-Loire. 🚶 *9,000.* 🚊 🚌 ℹ️ 1 *pl d'Hofheim (02 47 93 17 85).* 🛒 *Thu.*

THE CHATEAU DE CHINON is an important shrine in Joan of Arc country and, as such, wheedles francs from all passing pilgrims. It was here in 1429 that the saint first recognized the disguised dauphin (later Charles VII) and persuaded him to give her an

army in order to drive the English out of France. Before that, Chinon was the Plantagenet kings' favorite castle, and witnessed the death of Henry II. Although the **château** is now mostly in ruins, the ramparts are an impressive sight from the opposite bank of the Vienne River.

The town's bijou center is like a

Chinon's medieval summer pageant

medieval movie set. **Rue Voltaire**, lined with 15th- and 16th-century houses and once enclosed by the castle walls, represents a cross-section of Chinonais history. At No. 12 is the **Musée Animé du Vin**, where animated figures tell the story of winemaking. **No. 44** is a stone mansion where, in 1199, Richard the

Vineyard in the Chinon wine region

Lion-Heart is said to have died. The grandest mansion is the **Hôtel du Gouvernement**, with its double staircase and loggia. More charming is the **Maison Rouge** in the Grand Carroi, studded with a red-brick herringbone pattern.

The 15th-century **Hostellerie Gargantua**, where Rabelais's lawyer father once practiced, is now an agreeable inn *(see p555)*. The great Renaissance writer lived nearby, in the rue Jean-Jacques Rousseau.

The August medieval market is Chinon's most colorful pageant, when the town is given over to minstrels, strolling players, fire-eaters and jugglers.

🏛 Musée Animé du Vin
12 rue Voltaire. **[** *02 47 93 25 63.* **Open** *Apr–Sep: daily.* 🖼

Environs
Some 5 km (3 miles) southwest of Chinon is the rustic manor house of La Devinière, now the **Maison Rabelais**, where the 16th-century writer, priest and humanist scholar was born.

🏛 Maison Rabelais
Seuilly. **[** *02 47 95 91 18.* **Open** *daily.* **Closed** *Jan 1, Dec 25.* 🖼

Château d'Ussé ❾

Indre-et-Loire. 🚃 *Langeais, then taxi.* **[** *02 47 95 54 05.* **Open** *mid-Feb–mid-Nov: daily.* 🖼

THE FAIRY-TALE Château d'Ussé enjoys a bucolic setting overlooking watery meadows and the Indre River. Its romantic white turrets, pointed towers and chimneys inspired Charles Perrault's *Sleeping Beauty*.

Constructed in the 15th century, the castle was gradually transformed into an aristocratic château, which is still privately owned *(see p232)*. However, the sunless and musty interior is rather disappointing and the *Sleeping Beauty* tableaux are clumsily presented.

The château's delightful Renaissance chapel, framed by the oak forest of Chinon, has lost its Aubusson tapestries, but retains a lovely della Robbia terra-cotta *Virgin*.

Château de Langeais ❿

Indre-et-Loire. 🚃 *Langeais.*
[*02 47 96 72 60.* **Open** *daily.*
Closed *Dec 25.* 🖼

COMPARED with neighboring towns, Langeais is distinctly untouristy and has a welcoming, unpretentious feel. Its château is fiercely feudal, built strictly for defense with a drawbridge, portcullis and no concessions to the Renaissance. It was constructed by Louis XI in just five years, from 1465–9, with hardly an alteration since then. The ruins of an impressive keep, built by Foulques Nerra in AD 994, stand in the small château courtyard.

Unconvincing waxworks represent the marriage of Charles VIII and his childbride Anne of Brittany in 1491, a ceremony held in the Salle du Mariage. The room is decorated with intricate tiled floors, carved chests and a fine collection of 15th- and 16th-century Flemish and Aubusson tapestries.

FRANÇOIS RABELAIS

Rabelais, born in 1494, was a priest, doctor, diplomat and humanist scholar noted for his wisdom and tolerance. He is best remembered for his many ribald satires: *Pantagruel* and *Gargantua*, stories about a giant father and his son, were set around Chinon where Rabelais grew up.

Infant Pantagruel, depicted by Doré in 1854, was fed on the milk of 4,200 cows.

Château d'Azay-le-Rideau ⓫

Indre-et-Loire. 🚉 *Azay-le-Rideau.* 📞 *02 47 45 42 04.* **Open** *daily.* **Closed** *Jan 1, May 1, Nov 1 & 11, Dec 25.* 🎫

The Château de Villandry's *jardin d'ornament*

BALZAC CALLED Azay-le-Rideau "a multifaceted diamond set in the Indre." It is the most beguiling and feminine of Loire châteaux, created in the early 16th century by Philippa Lesbahy, wife of François I's corrupt finance minister. Although Azay is superficially Gothic (*see pp50–51, 232*), the turrets are purely decorative and the moats are picturesque pools. Azay was a pleasure palace, lived in during fine weather and deserted in winter. The illusion is sustained by a complex system of moats and weirs with Renaissance-style boats gliding across the waterlilies.

The interior is equally delightful – an airy, creaking mansion smelling faintly of cedarwood and full of lovingly re-created domestic detail. The period furniture, family portraits and exquisite tapestries confirm the impression of Azay as a Renaissance museum. Charming features include the portable Spanish cabinets and embroidered bed canopies. The four-story grand staircase is unusual for its time, being straight as opposed to spiral.

Wine-tasting opportunities in the village are a welcome reminder that vineyards are all around. Unlike most Loire villages, Azay is lively at night, thanks to the popularity of its poetic *son et lumière.*

Château de Villandry ⓬

Indre-et-Loire. 🚉 *Savonnières or Tours, then taxi.* 📞 *02 47 50 02 09.* **Château open** *mid-Feb–mid-Nov: daily; mid-Nov–mid-Feb: guided tours only.* **Gardens open** *daily.* 🎫

VILLANDRY was the last great Renaissance château built in the Loire Valley, a perfect example of 16th-century architecture. Its spectacular gardens were restored to their Renaissance splendor earlier this century by Dr. Joachim Carvallo, whose grandson continues his work unstintingly.

The result is a patchwork of sculpted shrubs and flowers on three levels: the kitchen garden (*jardin potager*), the ornamental garden (*jardin d'ornement*) and, on the highest level, the water garden (*jardin d'eau*). There are signs to explain the history and meaning behind each plant: the zucchini, for instance, symbolized fertility; cabbage, sexual and spiritual corruption. Plants were also prized for their medicinal prop-

erties: cabbage helped to cure hangovers, while pimento aided digestion. In the *jardin d'amour*, flowers depict the many faces of love: passionate, romantic, tragic and fickle. While tragic love is represented by crossed swords, fickleness is symbolized by yellow blooms.

A *chocolatier* in Tours

Tours ⓭

Indre-et-Loire. 🚶 *140,000.* ✈ 🚉 🚌 🅸 *78 rue Bernard Palissy (02 47 70 37 37).* 🛒 *Tue–Sun.*

TOURS IS THE MOST appealing of the major Loire cities, thanks to bourgeois prosperity, an intelligent restoration program and a lively university population. It is built on the site of a Roman town, and became an important center of Christianity in the 4th century under St. Martin, bishop of Tours. In 1461, Louis XI made the city the French capital, and it prospered on arms and fabrics. However, during Henri IV's reign the city lost favor with the monarchy, and the capital left Tours for Paris.

Bombarded by the Prussians in 1870, and bombed in World War II, Tours suffered extensive damage. By 1960, the middle classes had abandoned the historic center and

Château d'Azay-le-Rideau reflected in the Indre River

it became a slum, full of crumbling medieval masonry. Regeneration of the city has succeeded due to the popular policies of Jean Royer, mayor of Tours from 1958 to 1996.

The pedestrianized **place Plumereau** is Tours's most atmospheric quarter, set in the medieval heart of the city and full of cafés, boutiques and galleries. Streets such as rue Briçonnet reveal half-timbered façades, hidden courtyards and crooked towers. A gateway leads to place St-Pierre-le-Puellier, a square with sunken Gallo-Roman remains and a Romanesque church converted into a café. A few streets away in place de Châteauneuf lies the Romanesque **Tour Charlemagne**, all that remains of St. Martin's first church. West of here is the highly yuppified artisans' quarter, centered on the rue du Petit St-Martin.

The **Cathédrale St-Gatien**, in the eastern sector of the city, was begun in the early 13th century and completed in the 16th. Its Flamboyant Gothic façade is blackened and crumbling but still truly impressive, as are the medieval stained-glass windows.

Tours has several unusual museums. Considered the

Cathédrale St-Gatien in Tours

finest Renaissance building in Touraine, the **Hôtel Gouin** was a silk merchant's house and is now the archaeological museum, filled with medieval statuary. The **Musée des Beaux Arts**, set in the former episcopal palace, overlooks Classical gardens and a giant cedar of Lebanon. Its star exhibits are *The Resurrection* and *Christ in the Garden of Olives* by Mantegna, but more typical are the Loire landscapes and portraits. The **Historial de Touraine** in the nearby Château Royal is a perfect

introduction to the Loire, with 165 wax figures animating 15 centuries of local history.

Just west of here off rue Colbert is the **Eglise St-Julien**, whose Gothic monastic cells and chapterhouse contain a small wine museum and a crafts museum displaying the traditional work of the guilds.

🏛 **Hôtel Gouin**
25 rue du Commerce. ☎ *02 47 66 22 32.* **Open** *mid-Mar–Sep: daily; Feb–mid-Mar & Oct–Nov: Sat–Thu.* 🎫

🏛 **Musée des Beaux Arts**
18 place François Sicard.
☎ *02 47 05 68 73.* **Open** *Wed–Mon.* **Closed** *Jan 1, May 1, Jul 14, Nov 1, Nov 11, Dec 25.* 🎫

🏛 **Historial de Touraine**
Château Royal, 25 av André Malraux.
☎ *02 47 61 02 95.* **Open** *daily.* 🎫

Backgammon players in Tours's place Plumereau

TOURS TOWN CENTER

Cathédrale St-Gatien ⑤
Château Royal ④
Eglise St-Julien ③
Hôtel Gouin ②
Musée des Beaux Arts ⑥
Tour Charlemagne ①

AMBOISE
AVENUE ANDRÉ MALRAUX
PONT WILSON
Loire
PLACE ANATOLE FRANCE
AVENUE ANDRÉ MALRAUX
RUE DES TANNEURS
RUE DE CONSTANTINE
RUE COLBERT
RUE LAVOISIER
SAUMUR
R DE BRETONNEAU
RUE BRIÇONNET
PLACE ST PIERRE LE PUELLIER
RUE DU COMMERCE
RUE COLBERT
PLACE FRANÇOIS SICARD
PLACE PLUMEREAU
RUE DE CHANGE
PLACE DE LA RESISTANCE
RUE NATIONALE
RUE DE LA SCELLERIE
Office de Tourisme
PLACE DE CHATEAUNEUF
RUE DES HALLES
RUE MARCEAU
RUE DES HALLES
RUE EMILE ZOLA
PLACE DE LA PREFECTURE
PREFECTURE
RUE DES HALLES
RUE NERICAULT
RUE DESTOUCHES
RUE NATIONALE
RUE DE LA PREFECTURE
JARDIN DE LA PREFECTURE
PLACE GASTON PAILHOU
RUE GAMBETTA
Gare
Hôtel de Ville POITIERS
RUE DE CLOCHEVILLE

KEY

🅿 Parking
🕈 Church

0 meters 100
0 yards 100

Château de Chenonceau

Aromantic pleasure palace, Chenonceau was created from the Renaissance onward by a series of aristocratic women. A magnificent avenue bordered by plane trees leads to symmetrical gardens and the serene vision that Flaubert praised as "floating on air and water." The château stretches across the Cher River with a 60-m (197-ft) gallery built over a series of arches, its elegant beauty reflected in the languid waters. The grandeur continues inside with splendidly furnished rooms, airy bedchambers and fine paintings and tapestries.

Turreted Pavilion
This was built between 1513 and 1521 by Catherine Briçonnet and her husband, Thomas Bohier, over the foundations of an old water mill.

Chapelle
The chapel has a vaulted ceiling and pilasters sculpted with acanthus leaves and cockleshells. The stained glass, destroyed by a bomb in 1944, was replaced in 1953.

Catherine de' Medici's Gardens
Lavish court receptions and transvestite balls were held under Catherine's auspices.

TIMELINE

Catherine de' Medici

1533 Marriage of Catherine de' Medici (1519–89) to Henri II (1519–59). Chenonceau becomes a Loire royal palace

1559 Upon Henri's death, Catherine forces the disgraced Diane to accept the Château de Chaumont in exchange for Chenonceau

1789 Chenoncea is spared in the French Revolutio thanks to Madame Dupin

1500	1600	1700	1800

1575 Louise de Lorraine (1554–1601) marries Henri III, Catherine's third and favorite son

1547 Henri II offers Chenonceau to Diane de Poitiers, his lifelong mistress

1512 Thomas Bohier acquires medieval Chenonceau. His wife, Catherine Briçonnet, rebuilds it in Renaissance style

1730–99 Madame Dupin, a farmer-general's wife, makes Chenonceau a salon for writers and philosophers

1863 Madame Pelc restores the châtea its original s

Grande Galerie
The elegant gallery crowning the bridge is Florentine in style, created by Catherine de' Medici from 1570–76.

1913 The château is bought by the Menier family, the *chocolatiers* who still own it today

1941 Chenonceau chapel is damaged in a bombing raid

Diane de Poitiers

The Creation of Chenonceau

THE WOMEN RESPONSIBLE for Chenonceau each left their mark. Catherine Briçonnet, wife of the first owner, built the turreted pavilion and one of the first straight staircases in France here; Henri II's mistress, Diane de Poitiers, added the formal gardens and arched bridge over the Cher River; Catherine de' Medici transformed the bridge into an Italian-style gallery (having evicted Diane following her husband's death in 1559); Louise de Lorraine, bereaved wife of Henri III, inherited the château in 1590 and painted the ceilings black and white, the colors of royal mourning; Madame Dupin, a cultured 18th-century châtelaine, saved the château from destruction during the Revolution; and Madame Pelouze undertook a complete restoration in 1863.

Ground floor   First floor

CHÂTEAU GUIDE

The main living area was in the square-shaped turreted pavilion in the middle of the Cher River. Four principal rooms open off the Grande Galerie on the ground floor: the Salle des Gardes and the Chambre de Diane de Poitiers, both hung with 16th-century Flemish tapestries; the Chambre de François I, with a Van Loo painting; and the Salon Louis XIV. On the first floor, reached via the vestibule, are other sumptuous apartments including the Chambre de Catherine de' Medici and the Chambre de Vendôme.

1 Vestibule
2 Salle des Gardes
3 Chapelle
4 Terrasse
5 Librairie de Catherine de' Medici
6 Cabinet Vert
7 Chambre de Diane de Poitiers
8 Grande Galerie
9 Chambre de François I
10 Salon Louis XIV
11 Chambre des Cinq Reines
12 Cabinet des Estampes
13 Chambre de Catherine de' Medici
14 Chambre de Vendôme
15 Chambre de Gabrielle d'Estrée

Chambre de Catherine de' Medici

Vouvray ⑭

Indre-et-Loire. 🏘 *3,000.*
ℹ *Le Moirie (02 47 52 70 48).*
🗓 *Tue & Fri.*

JUST EAST OF TOURS is the village of Vouvray, home of the delicious white wine that Renaissance author Rabelais likened to taffeta. A visit to the **Ecomusée du Pays de Vouvray** wine museum rewards the visitor with a presentation and a film, followed by a wine tasting. If in Vouvray on a market day, buy a picnic lunch and head for the vineyards.

The star vineyard is **Huet**. In 1829 Sir Walter Scott sang the praises of the estate, toasting the dry white wines, the growers' quaint troglodyte homes hewn out of the rock, and the Gothic church in the vineyards. Little has changed in Vouvray. Huet's methods are still traditional, with wine fermented in oak barrels. Supported by local wine growers, Gaston Huet hit the headlines in 1990 with his protests against the building of tracks for the TGV train over Vouvray vineyards. A French compromise was eventually reached, and tunnels were built under the hilly vineyards.

The medieval town of Loches

🏛 **Ecomusée du Pays de Vouvray**
30 rue Victor Herault. 📞 *02 47 52 66 04.* **Open** *daily.* 🎟 ♿
🍷 **Huet**
Le Manoir du Haut-Lieu, 11–13 rue de la Croix-Buisée. 📞 *02 47 52 78 87.*
Open *Jul & Aug: Mon–Sat; Sep–Jun: by appt only.* **Closed** *public hols.* 🎟

Loches ⑮

Indre-et-Loire. 🏘 *7,000.* 🚉 🚌
ℹ *place de la Marne (02 47 59 07 98).*
🗓 *Wed & Sat.*

THIS UNSPOILED medieval town is slightly removed from the château trail in the Indre Valley. It is a backwater of late Gothic gateways and sculpted façades. Its impressive **Château** dominates the scene and boasts the deepest dungeons in the Loire. The building is associated with Charles VII and his beautiful mistress Agnès Sorel. It is also where Joan of Arc, after his historic victory in Orléans, pleaded with Charles to go to Reims and be crowned. Anne of Brittany's chapel is decorated with ermines (her emblem) and contains a poignant alabaster effigy of Agnès Sorel.

♠ **Château de Loches**
📞 *02 47 59 01 32.* **Open** *daily.*

THE HEROINE OF FRANCE

Joan of Arc is the quintessential French national heroine, a virginal warrior, a woman martyr, a French figurehead. Her divinely led campaign to "drive the English out of France" during the Hundred Years' War has inspired plays, poetry and films from Voltaire to Cecil B. de Mille. Responding to heavenly voices, she appeared on the scene as champion of the dauphin, the uncrowned Charles VII. He faced an Anglo-Burgundian alliance that held most of northern France, and had escaped to the royal châteaux on the Loire.

Joan convinced him of the importance of her mission, mustered the French troops and in May 1429 led them to victory over the English at Orléans. She then urged the dithering Charles to go to Reims to be crowned. However, in 1430 she was captured and handed over to the English. Accused of witchcraft, she was burned at the stake in Rouen in 1431 at the age of 19. Her legendary bravery and tragic martyrdom led to her canonization in 1920.

Earliest known drawing of Joan of Arc (1429)

Portrait of Joan of Arc *in the Maison Jeanne d'Arc in Orléans (see p302). She saved the city from the English on May 8, 1429, a date the Orléannais still celebrate annually.*

Montrésor ⑯

Indre-et-Loire. 🏠 380. 🛈 Grande Rue (02 47 92 71 04).

CLASSED "the most beautiful village in France," Montrésor does not disappoint. It is set on the Indrois River, in the loveliest valley in Touraine. Once a fief of the Cathédrale de Tours, the village became a Polish enclave in the 1840s. In 1849 a Polish nobleman, Count Branicki, bought the 15th-century **château**, built on the site of one of Foulques Nerra's

Farm building and poppy fields near the village of Montrésor

11th-century fortifications. It has remained in the family ever since, its interior virtually unchanged since Branicki's time.

🏰 **Château de Montrésor**
📞 02 47 92 60 04. **Open** Apr–Oct: daily. 📷 ✔ ♿

Château de Chenonceau ⑰

See pp288–9.

Amboise ⑱

Indre-et-Loire. 🏠 12,000. 🚉 🚌
🛈 Quai du Général de Gaulle (02 47 57 09 28). 🛒 Fri & Sun.

FEW BUILDINGS are more historically important than the **Château d'Amboise**. Louis XI lived here; Charles VIII was born and died here; François I and later Catherine de' Medici were regular visitors. The château was also the setting for the Amboise Conspiracy of 1560, an ill-fated Huguenot plot against François II. Visitors are shown where the corpses of 1,200 conspirators were hung from iron hooks on the façade of the château.

The **Tour des Minimes**, the château's original entrance, is

Amboise seen from the Loire

famous for its huge spiral ramp up which horsemen could ride to deliver provisions.

Perched on the ramparts is the Gothic **Chapelle St-Hubert**, believed to be Leonardo da Vinci's burial place. Under the patronage of François I, the artist spent the last years of his life in the nearby manor house of **Clos-Lucé**, whose cellars exhibit models of Leonardo's inventions constructed from his mechanical sketches.

🏰 **Château d'Amboise**
📞 02 47 57 00 98. **Open** daily. **Closed** Jan 1, Dec 25. 📷
🏛 **Clos-Lucé**
2 rue de Clos-Lucé. 📞 02 47 57 62 88. **Open** daily. **Closed** Jan 1, Dec 25. 📷

A romantic heroine, Joan of Arc was a popular subject for artists. This painting of her is by François Léon Benouville (1821–59).

***Burned at the stake** – a scene from* St. Joan, *Otto Preminger's 1957 epic film, which starred Jean Seberg.*

Château de Chambord ⑲

HENRY JAMES ONCE SAID, "Chambord is truly royal – royal in its great scale, its grand air, and its indifference to common considerations." The Loire's largest residence, brainchild of the extravagant François I, began as a hunting lodge in the Forêt de Boulogne. In 1519 the original building was razed and the creation of Chambord began, to a design probably initiated by Leonardo da Vinci. By 1537 the towers, keep and terraces had been completed by 1,800 men and two master masons. At one point, François suggested diverting the Loire to flow in front of his château, but he settled for redirecting the nearer Closson instead. His son Henry II continued his work, and Louis XIV completed the 440-roomed edifice in 1685.

The Château de Chambord with the Closson River, a tributary of the Loire, in the foreground

The chapel was begun by François I shortly before his death in 1547. Henri II added the second story and Louis XIV the roof.

The Salamander
François I chose the salamander as his enigmatic emblem. It appears over 800 times throughout the château.

★ **Roof Terraces**
This skyline of delicate cupolas has been likened to a miniature Oriental town. The roof terraces include a forest of elongated chimneys, miniature spires, shell-shaped domes and richly sculpted gables.

STAR FEATURES
★ **Roof Terraces**
★ **Vaulted Guardrooms**
★ **Grand Staircase**

The central keep (donjon), with its four circular towers, forms the nucleus of the château.

TIMELINE

1519–47 The Count of Blois' hunting lodge demolished by François I and the château created

1547–59 Henri II adds the west wing and second story of the chapel

1547 Upon François' death, the court leaves Chambord for Chenonceau and Blois

1500	1600	1700	1800	1900

1669–85 Louis XIV completes the building

1670 Molière's *Le Bourgeois Gentilhomme* staged at Chambord

1725–33 Inhabited by Stanislas Leczinski, exiled king of Poland who was made duke of Lorraine

1748 The Maréchal de Saxe acquires Chambord. Upon his death two years later, the château falls into decline

1840 Chambord declared a *Monument Historique*

1970s Giscard d'Estaing restores and refurnishes Chambord, and re-digs the moats

★ **Vaulted Guardrooms**
Arranged in the form of a Greek cross around the Grand Staircase, the vaulted guardrooms were once the setting for royal balls and plays. Their ceilings are decorated with François I's initials and salamander motif.

VISITORS' CHECKLIST

from Blois. 02 54 40 40 00. **Open** 9am–6:15pm daily (Jul–Aug until 6:45pm; Nov–Mar: 9am–5:15pm). Last adm: 30 min before closing. **Closed** Jan 1, May 1, Dec 25.

The lantern tower is 32 m (105 ft) high. Surmounting the terrace, it is supported by arched buttresses and crowned by a fleurs-de-lys.

François I's Bedchamber is where the king, hurt by a failed romance, scratched a message on a pane of glass: "*Souvent femme varie, bien fol est qui s'y fie.*" (Every woman is fickle, he who trusts one is a fool.)

Cabinet de François I
The king's barrel-vaulted study (cabinet) *in the outer north tower was turned into an oratory in the 18th century by Queen Catherine Opalinska, wife of Stanislas Leczinski (Louis XV's father-in-law).*

★ **Grand Staircase**
This innovative double-helix staircase was supposedly designed by Leonardo da Vinci. It ensures that the person going up and the person going down cannot meet.

Louis XIV's Bedchamber
Louis XIV's bedchamber lies within the Sun King's state apartments, the grandest quarters in the château.

Blois's Cathédrale St-Louis and Hôtel de Ville seen from across the Loire

Blois ⑳

Loir-et-Cher. 🏨 50,000. 🚊 🚌
🛈 Pavillon Anne de Bretagne, 3 av
Jean Laigret (02 54 90 41 41).
🗓 Tue, Thu, Sat & Sun.

ONCE A FIEF of the counts of
Blois, the town rose to
prominence as a royal domain
in the 15th century, retaining
its historic façades and refined
atmosphere to this day. Architectural interest abounds in
Vieux Blois, the hilly, partially
pedestrianized quarter enclosed
by the château, cathedral and
river. A well-signposted walking tour, the *route royale*, is
a gentle introduction to the
noble mansions and romantic
courtyards that grace the
Loire's most beguiling town.

Set back from the north
bank of the river, the **Château
de Blois** was the principal
royal residence until Henri IV
moved the court to Paris in
1598 – Louis XIV's creation
of Versailles (*see pp164–7*)
was to mark the final eclipse
of Blois. The château's four
contrasting wings make a har-

monious whole. The Salle des
Etats, the only part of the
building surviving from the
13th century, housed the
council and court, and is the
best-preserved Gothic hall in
the Loire. The adjoining late
15th-century Louis XII wing
infuses Gothic design with
Renaissance spirit, sealed with
the king's porcupine symbol
and motto: "From near and
afar, I can defend myself."

The 16th-century François I
wing is a masterpiece of the
French Renaissance, containing
a monumental spiral staircase
in an octagonal tower. By
contrast, the 17th-century
Gaston d'Orléans wing is a
model of Classical sobriety.

Blois is authentically furnished and hung with
paintings portraying its
troubled past. These
include a graphic
portrayal of the
murder of the Duc
de Guise in 1588.
Suspected of head-
ing a Catholic plot
against Henri III,
he was stabbed to

King Louis XII's porcupine symbol

death by guards in the king's
chamber. The most intriguing
room is Catherine de' Medici's
study, its walls containing 237
secret cabinets, full of jewels,
state papers and potions.

François I Staircase

*Built between 1515 and
1524, this octagonal
staircase is a master-
piece of the
early French
Renaissance.*

The gallery
provided an
ideal setting
for viewing
jousts and re-
ceptions held
in the inner
courtyard.

**François I's
salamander
motif** adorns
the openwork
balustrades.

The staircase
within the
tower slopes
appreciably
more steeply
than the
balustrades.

Louis XII wing of the Château de Blois

Dominating the eastern sector of the city, the **Cathédrale St-Louis** is a 17th-century reconstruction of a Gothic church that was almost completely destroyed by a hurricane in 1678. Behind the cathedral the former bishop's palace, built in 1725, has been used as the **Hôtel de Ville** (town hall) since 1940. The surrounding terraced gardens have lovely views over the city and river.

Place Louis-XII, the marketplace until the 18th century, is overlooked by splendid 17th-century façades, balconies and half-timbered houses. The finest is the **Maison des Acrobates**, carved with characters from medieval farces including acrobats and jugglers.

Rue Pierre de Blois, a quaint alley straddled by a Gothic passageway, winds downhill to the medieval Jewish ghetto. The dilapidated rue des Juifs boasts several distinguished *hôtels particuliers* (mansions), including the galleried **Hôtel de Condé**, with its Renaissance archway and courtyard. The most striking courtyard belongs to **Hôtel Belot**, a 16th-century mansion adorned with barrel-vaulted loggias and an external spiral staircase. The alley leads down to rue du Puits-Châtel, rich in Renaissance mansions.

Place Vauvert is the most charming square in Vieux Blois, bordered by restaurants and the galleried **Hôtel Sardini**, once owned by Renaissance bankers.

♣ Château de Blois
(*02 54 78 06 62.* **Open** *daily.*
Closed *Jan 1, Dec 25.* ⓩ

Covered Gothic passageway in rue Pierre de Blois

The nave of the abbey church of Notre-Dame in Beaugency

Beaugency ㉑

Loiret. 🏠 *7,000.* � � ℹ *3 pl de Docteur-Hyvernaud (02 38 44 54 42).* 🛒 *Sat.*

BEAUGENCY has long been the eastern gateway to the Loire. This compact medieval town makes a peaceful base for exploring the Orléanais region. Exceptionally for the Loire, it is possible to walk along the riverbanks and stone *levées*. At quai de l'Abbaye there is a good view of the 14th-century bridge, which, until modern times, was the only crossing point between Blois and Orléans. An obvious target for enemy attack, it was captured four times by the English during the Hundred Years' War before being retaken by Joan of Arc in 1429.

The center of town is dominated by a ruined 11th-century castle keep. It stands on **place St-Firmin**, along with a 16th-century bell tower (the church was destroyed in the Revolution) and an equestrian statue of Joan of Arc. The stone square is bordered by period houses, including the **Château Dunois**, a Renaissance manor house on the site of the feudal castle. It houses a regional museum featuring costumes, furniture, and antique toys.

Facing the Château Dunois is **Notre-Dame**, a Romanesque abbey church that witnessed the annulment of the marriage between Eleanor of Aquitaine and Louis VII in 1152, leaving Eleanor free to marry the future Henry II of England.

Nearby is the medieval clock tower in rue des Trois Marchands and, just beyond, the Gothic **Hôtel de Ville**, with its Renaissance façade adorned with the town arms. Equally charming are the streams in the nearby mill district, linking rue du Pont with rue du Rü.

♣ Château Dunois (Musée Régional de l'Orléanais)
Place Dunois. **(** *02 38 44 55 23.*
Open *Wed–Mon.* **Closed** *Jan 1, May 1, Dec 25.* ⓩ

Châteaux Tour of the Sologne

THE MYSTERIOUS SOLOGNE is a secretive landscape of woods and marshes edged by vineyards. Wine-lovers can indulge in tastings of Cheverny wine, accompanied by a dinner of succulent wild game from the region's forests, popular hunting grounds for centuries. The Sologne is a hunter's paradise and devotees of the sport can see the hounds used today, as well as hunting trophies of the past.

This ambling rural route takes in some of the Loire's most varied châteaux. The five on this tour – for which a couple of days is required – represent a delightful encapsulation of regional architecture. All styles are here, from feudal might to Renaissance grace and Classical elegance. Several are inhabited but can still be visited.

Château de Beauregard ②
Beauregard was built around 1520 as a hunting lodge for François I. It contains a gallery with 363 portraits of royalty.

Château de Chaumont ①
Chaumont is a feudal castle with Renaissance embellishments and lofty views over the Loire River *(see p232).*

| 0 kilometers | 5 |
| 0 miles | 5 |

KEY

▬▬ Tour route

══ Other roads

Pontlevoy

Vendôme ㉒

Loir-et-Cher. 🏛 18,000. 🚆 🚌
🛈 47 rue Poterie (02 54 77 05 07).
🗓 Fri & Sun.

ONCE AN IMPORTANT STOP for pilgrims en route to Compostela in Spain, Vendôme is now popular with modern pilgrims, thanks to the TGV rail service. Though a desirable address with Parisian commuters, the town still manages to retain its provincial charm. Vendôme's old stone buildings are encircled by the Loir River, its lush gardens and chic restaurants reflected in the water.

The town's greatest monument is the abbey church of **La Trinité**, founded in 1034. Its Romanesque bell tower (all that remains of the original structure) is overshadowed by the church portal, a masterpiece of Flamboyant Gothic tracery. The interior is embellished with Romanesque capitals and 14th-century choir stalls.

Commanding a rocky spur high above the Loir is the ruined **château**, built by the counts of Vendôme in the 13th and 14th centuries. Below is the watery **Parc Ronsard** with a medieval *lavoir*, a two-story laundry room. Leading downriver are delightful walks past willows, ruined towers, dams and mills.

Vendôme's native son Rochambeau, hero of the American Revolution

The Loir ㉓

Loir-et-Cher. 🚂 Tours. 🚆 🚌
Vendôme. 🛈 Montoire-sur-Loir
(02 54 85 00 29).

COMPARED WITH the royal Loire River, the tranquil Loir to the north has undeni-able charm. The stretch be-tween Vendôme and Trôo is the most rewarding, offering troglodyte caves *(see p282)*, walking trails, wine tasting, fishing and boat trips.

Les Roches-l'Evêque is a fortified village with cave dwellings carved into the cliffs. Just downstream is **Lavardin**, with its Romanesque church, half-timbered houses, Gothic bridge and a château ringed by ramparts. In **Montoire-sur-Loir**, the Chapelle St-Gilles boasts Romanesque frescoes in a former leper colony. **Trôo**, the next major village, is known for its Romanesque Eglise de St-Martin and a laby-rinth of troglodyte dwellings.

Château de Cour-Cheverny ③
Built in 1634, this Classical château still belongs to a descendant of the original owner. His 70 hounds, used for stag-hunting, are fed daily at 5pm.

Château de Villesavin ④
This intriguing but dilapidated Renaissance château possesses an authentic dovecote, complete with revolving ladder and space for 3,000 birds.

Château du Moulin ⑤
The "pearl of the Sologne" (1490) was built by a knight of Charles VIII.

ROMORANTIN-LANTHENAY →

St-Jacques-des-Guérets, facing the village of Trôo, has a frescoed Romanesque chapel, as does **Poncé-sur-le-Loir**, farther downstream. On the slopes are vineyards producing Jasnières and Côteaux du Vendômois. Wine tastings enliven sleepy **Poncé** and **La Chartre-sur-le-Loir**. The cliffs on the opposite bank are studded with caves, commonly used as wine cellars.

Northward, the **Forêt de Bercé** abounds with paths and streams, while to the west the small town of **Le Lude** sits on the south bank of the Loir, its romantic château combining fountains and fireworks in a magnificent *son et lumière*.

Some 20 km (12 miles) west of Le Lude lies the town of **La Flèche**, whose main attraction is the Prytanée National Militaire, originally a Jesuit college founded by Henri IV in 1604. Philosopher René Descartes was one of the college's earliest and most illustrious pupils.

Chartres ㉔

Eure-et-Loir. 🏠 42,000. 🚉 🚌
🅸 pl de la Cathédrale (02 37 21 50 00). 🛒 Sat.

CHARTRES MAY have the greatest Gothic cathedral in Europe *(see pp298–301)*, but the town's churches should not be ignored. The Benedictine abbey church of **St-Pierre** has lovely medieval stained-glass windows, while **St-Aignan** abuts 9th-century ramparts. By the river is the Romanesque **Eglise de St-André**, a deconsecrated church used for art exhibitions and jazz concerts. The **Musée des Beaux Arts**, beside the cathedral in the former episcopal palace, offers a fine collection of tapestries, Fragonard paintings and temporary exhibitions.

As one of the first urban conservation sites in France, Chartres is a success story. Quirky half-timbered houses abound along cobbled streets

One of the many washhouses along the Eure River

such as the rue des Ecuyers. Steep staircases known as *tertres* lead down to the Eure River, providing views of mills, medieval tanneries, humpback stone bridges, washhouses and the cathedral.

A major new onsite archaeological museum is being built by architect Richard Rogers to house ruins from the Gallo-Roman city, excavated in the shadow of the cathedral.

🏛 **Musée des Beaux Arts**
29 cloître Notre-Dame. ☎ 02 37 36 41 39. **Open** Wed–Mon. **Closed** Jan 1, May 1 & 8, Nov 1 & 11, Dec 25. 📷

Chartres Cathedral

ACCORDING TO ART HISTORIAN Emile Male, "Chartres is the mind of the Middle Ages manifest." Begun in 1020, the Romanesque cathedral was destroyed by fire in 1194. Only the north and south towers, south steeple, west portal and crypt remained; the sacred *Veil of the Virgin* relic was the sole treasure to survive. Peasant and lord alike helped to rebuild the church in just 25 years. Few alterations were made after 1250 and, fortunately, Chartres was unscathed by the Wars of Religion and the French Revolution. The result is a Gothic cathedral with a true "Bible in stone" reputation.

Part of the Vendôme Window

Elongated Statues
These statues on the Royal Portal represent Old Testament figures.

STAR FEATURES

★ **Stained-Glass Windows**

★ **South Porch**

★ **Royal Portal**

The taller of the two spires dates from the start of the 16th century. Flamboyant Gothic in style, it contrasts sharply with the solemnity of its Romanesque counterpart.

Gothic Nave
As wide as the Romanesque crypt below it, the nave reaches a lofty height of 37 m (121 ft).

★ **Royal Portal**
The central tympanum of the Royal Portal (1145–55) shows Christ in Majesty.

The lower half of the west front is a survivor of the original Romanesque church, the portal dating from the mid-12th century.

Labyrinth

THE LABYRINTH

The 13th-century labyrinth, inlaid in the nave floor, was a feature of most medieval cathedrals. As a penance, pilgrims used to follow the tortuous route on their knees, echoing the Way of the Cross. The journey of 262 m (851 ft), around 11 bands of broken concentric circles, took at least one hour to complete.

VISITORS' CHECKLIST

Pl de la Cathédrale. ☎ 02 37 21 75 02. **Open** 7:30am–7:15pm Mon–Sat; 8:30am Sun & public hols. ☦ 11:45am & 6pm Mon–Sat; 9:30am, 11am, 6pm Sun. 📷 ♿ 🎧 in English: noon & 2:45pm; French: 10:30am & 3pm.

Apsidal Chapel
This chapel houses the oldest cathedral treasure, the Veil of the Virgin *relic, which miraculously survived the fire of 1194. More artifacts can be found in the* St Piat Chapel.

Vaulted Ceiling
A network of ribs supports the vaulted ceiling.

★ **Stained-Glass Windows**
The windows cover a surface area of over 2,600 sq m (28,000 sq ft).

★ **South Porch**
Sculpture on the South Porch (1197–1209) reflects New Testament teaching.

The Crypt
This is the largest crypt in France, most of it dating from the early 11th century. It comprises two parallel galleries, a series of chapels and the 9th-century St. Lubin's vault.

The Stained Glass of Chartres

Donated by royalty, aristocracy and the merchant brotherhoods between 1210 and 1240, this glorious collection of stained glass is world-renowned. Over 150 windows illustrate biblical stories and daily life in the 13th century. During both World Wars the windows were dismantled piece by piece and removed for safety. There is an on-going program, begun in the 1970s, to restore the windows in the cathedral.

Stained glass above the apse

Redemption Window

Six scenes illustrate Christ's Passion *and death on the Cross (c.1210).*

★ Tree of Jesse

This 12th-century stained glass shows Christ's genealogy. The tree rises up from Jesse, father of David, at the bottom, to Christ enthroned at the top.

★ West Rose Window

This window (1215), with Christ seated in the center, shows the Last Judgment.

Key

1 Tree of Jesse	**12** Noah	**22** St. Anthony and St. Paul	**33** St. Theodore and St. Vincent
2 Incarnation	**13** St. John the Evangelist	**23** Blue Virgin	**34** St. Stephen
3 Passion and Resurrection	**14** Mary Magdalene	**24** Life of the Virgin	**35** St. Cheron
4 North Rose Window	**15** Good Samaritan and Adam and Eve	**25** Zodiac Window	**36** St. Thomas
5 West Rose Window	**16** Assumption	**26** St. Martin	**37** Peace Window
6 South Rose Window	**17** Vendôme Chapel Windows	**27** St. Thomas à Becket	**38** Modern Window
7 Redemption Window	**18** Miracles of Mary	**28** St. Margaret and St. Catherine	**39** Prodigal Son
8 St. Nicholas	**19** St. Apollinaris	**29** St. Nicholas	**40** Ezekiel and David
9 Joseph	**20** Modern Window	**30** St. Remy	**41** Aaron
10 St. Eustache	**21** St. Fulbert	**31** St. James the Greater	**42** Virgin and Child
11 St. Lubin		**32** Charlemagne	**43** Isaiah and Moses
			44 Daniel and Jeremiah

North Rose Window
This depicts the Glorification of the Virgin, *surrounded by the kings of Judah and the prophets (c.1230).*

GUIDE TO READING THE WINDOWS

Each window is divided into panels, which are usually read from left to right, bottom to top (earth to heaven). The number of figures or abstract shapes used is thought to be symbolic: three stands for the Church, while the number four symbolizes the material world or the four elements.

Mary and Child in the sacred mandorla (c.1150)

Two angels doing homage before the celestial throne

Christ's triumphal entry into Jerusalem on Palm Sunday

Upper panels of the Incarnation Window

6 South Rose Window
This illustrates the Apocalypse, *with* Christ in Majesty *(c.1225).*

STAR WINDOWS

★ **West Rose Window**

★ **Tree of Jesse**

★ **Blue Virgin Window**

★ **Blue Virgin Window**
The window's bottom panel depicts the conversion of water into wine by Christ at The Marriage at Cana.

ORLÉANS CITY CENTER

Cathédrale Sainte-Croix ④
Hôtel Groslot ②
Maison Jeanne
   d'Arc ①
Musée des
   Beaux Arts ③

KEY

P Parking

✝ Church

0 meters   250

0 yards   250

Orléans's Cathédrale Sainte-Croix

Orléans ㉕

Loiret. 🏘 150,000. ✕ 🚋 🚌
ℹ place Albert 1er (02 38 24 05 05).
🗓 Tue–Sun.

O RLÉANS has a royal and
republican tradition yet
feels curiously blank, despite its
Renaissance façades. However,
the city is not as soulless as it
seems, especially in its attach-
ment to Joan of Arc. It was
here that the Maid of Orléans
saved France from the English
in 1429 *(see p290)*. Since her

martyrdom at Rouen in 1431,
Joan remains a presence in
Orléans. Every April 29 and
May 7 and 8 her liberation of
the city is shown in a pageant
and a cathedral blessing.

Orléans's historic center was
badly damaged in World War
II, but much has been reconstructed, and the faded
grandeur lingers in Vieil
Orléans, the quarter bounded
by the cathedral, the Loire River
and the **place du Martroi**. The
latter, a Classical but windswept square, boasts lively
bars and an equestrian statue
of the city's heroine. Nearby,
the half-timbered **Maison
Jeanne d'Arc** was rebuilt
from period dwellings in 1965
on the site where Joan lodged
in 1429. Inside are audio-
visual re-creations of her life.

From place du Martroi, the
rue d'Escures leads past
Renaissance mansions to the
cathedral. **Hôtel Groslot** is the
grandest, a 16th-century red-
brick mansion where kings
Charles IX, Henri III and Henri
IV all stayed. The 17-year-old
François II died here in 1560
after attending a meeting of
the Estates General with his
child bride, Mary, later Queen

of Scots. The building served
as Orléans's town hall from
1790 to 1982. Its sumptuously
decorated interior contains
Joan of Arc memorabilia and
fine Renaissance paintings.

Virtually opposite the Hôtel
Groslot and alongside the new
town hall is the **Musée des
Beaux Arts**, displaying French
works from the 15th to the
20th century. Foreign painters,
including Tintoretto, Correggio,
Van Ruysdael and Velázquez,
are also represented.

The **Cathédrale Sainte-
Croix**, just to the south of the
museum, is an imposing
edifice that was begun in the
late 13th century, destroyed by
the Huguenots (Protestants) in
1568, and then rebuilt in supposedly Gothic style between
the 17th and 19th centuries.

🛕 **Hôtel Groslot**
Pl de l'Etape. 📞 02 38 79 22 30. **Open**
daily. **Closed** sporadically & May 8.
🏛 **Musée des Beaux Arts**
place Sainte-Croix. 📞 02 38 79 21
55. **Open** Tue–Sun. **Closed** Jan 1,
May 1, Nov 1, Dec 25. 🖼 ♿
🏛 **Maison Jeanne d'Arc**
3 place du Général de Gaulle. 📞 02 38
52 99 89. **Open** Tue–Sun. **Closed** Jan 1,
May 1, Dec 25; Nov–May: Sun am. 🖼

Joan of Arc stained-glass window in Orléans's Cathédrale Sainte-Croix

St-Benoît-sur-Loire ㉖

Loiret. 👥 2,000. ℹ️ La Mairie (02 38 35 79 00).

SITUATED ALONG the Loire River between Orléans and Gien, St-Benoît-sur-Loire boasts one of the finest Romanesque abbey churches in France, constructed between 1067 and 1108. It is all that survives of an important monastery founded in AD 650 and named after St. Benedict, patron saint of Europe. His relics were transported from Italy at the end of the 7th century.

The church's belfry porch is graced with carved capitals depicting biblical scenes. The nave is tall and light, and the choir floor is an amazing patchwork of marble. Daily services with Gregorian chant are open to the public.

Bourges ㉗

Cher. 👥 76,000. ✈️ 🚉 🚌
ℹ️ 21 rue Victor Hugo (02 48 23 02 60). 🛒 Thu–Sun.

THIS GALLO-ROMAN city retains its original walls but is best known as the city of Jacques Coeur, financier and foreign minister to Charles VII. The greatest merchant of the Middle Ages and a self-made man *par excellence*, it was in his capacity as an arms dealer that he established a tradition the city maintains to this day as the center of France's armaments industry.

Built over part of the walls, the **Palais Jacques Coeur** is a Gothic gem and a lasting memorial to its first master. It was finished in 1453, and incorporates Coeur's two emblems, scallop shells and hearts, as well as his punning family motto: *"A vaillan coeur, rien impossible"* – to the valiant heart, nothing is impossible. The obligatory tour reveals a barrel-vaulted gallery, a painted chapel and a chamber that housed Turkish baths.

Bourges also flourishes as a university town and cultural mecca, renowned for its spring festival of music and dance.

Rue Bourbonnoux leads to **St-Etienne**, the widest Gothic cathedral in France and the one most similar to Paris's Notre-Dame. The west façade has five sculpted portals, central one depicting an enthralling *Last Judgment*. In the choir are vivid 13th-century stained-glass windows presented by the guilds. The crypt holds the marble tomb of the 14th-century Duc de Berry, best known for commissioning the illuminated manuscript the *Très Riches Heures (see pp194–5)*. From the top of the north tower stretch views of the beautifully restored medieval quarter and the marshes beyond. Beside the cathedral is a magnificent tithe barn and the remains of the Gallo-Roman ramparts.

The **Jardin des Prés Fichaux**, set along the Yèvre River, contains pools, parterres and an open-air theater. On the northern edge of town lie the **Marais de Bourges**, some of the loveliest water meadows in France, best explored by flat-bottomed boat.

Stained-glass window in the Cathédrale St-Etienne

Statue of Jacques Coeur

♦ **Palais Jacques Coeur**
Rue Jacques Coeur. 📞 02 48 24 06 87.
Open daily. **Closed** Jan 1, May 1, Nov 1 & 11, Dec 25. 🏛️ 📷

Environs
About 22 miles (35 km) south of Bourges in the Berry region is the **Abbaye de Noirlac**. Founded in 1136, it is one of the best-preserved Cistercian abbeys in France.

Statue in the Jardin des Prés Fichaux

CENTRAL FRANCE AND THE ALPS

Introducing Central France and the Alps

THE GEOLOGICAL CONTRASTS of this region reflect its enormous variety, from the industrial and gastronomic metropolis of Lyon to the largely agricultural landscape of Burgundy. The mountains of the Massif Central and the Alps attract visitors for winter sports, superb walking and other outdoor activities. The major sights of this richly rewarding area, both natural and architectural, are shown here.

Basilique Ste-Madeleine, *the famous pilgrimage church crowning the hilltop village of Vézelay, is a masterpiece of Burgundian Romanesque. It is renowned for its vividly decorated tympanum and capitals (see pp326–7).*

The Abbaye de Ste-Foy *in the village of Conques (see pp356–7) is one of the great pilgrimage churches of France, with a fabulous treasury of medieval and Renaissance gold reliquaries.*

THE MASSIF CENTRAL
(See pp342–61)

Abbaye de Ste-Foy, Conques

The Gorges du Tarn *have some of France's most spectacular natural scenery. The road which follows the plunging course of the Tarn River gives dramatic viewing points along the canyon and across the limestone Causses (see pp360–61).*

***The Abbaye de Fontenay**, founded by Saint Bernard in the early 12th century, is the oldest Cistercian monastery in France (see pp322–3). This well-preserved Romanesque abbey is a perfect testimony to the severe ideal of the Cistercian life.*

Abbaye de Fontenay

...deleine, ...zelay

Palais des Ducs, Dijon

BURGUNDY AND FRANCHE-COMTÉ
(See pp316–41)

Théâtre Romain, Autun

Brou Abbey Church, Bourg-en-Bresse

Mont Blanc

Temple d'Auguste et Livie, Vienne

THE RHONE VALLEY AND FRENCH ALPS
(See pp362–81)

Le Puy

Palais Idéal du Facteur Cheval, Hauterives

Gorges du Tarn

0 kilometers 50
0 miles 50

Regional Food: Central France

Renowned for its gastronomic tradition, Lyon is the place to savor Lyonnais and Burgundian food at its best – from sophisticated three-star cuisine to the more robust, homey fare of the *"mères,"* the women cooks of Lyon. This eminent culinary flair is complemented by the wealth of fine local produce: the famed chicken from Bresse; prime lean beef from Charolais; ham from the Morvan hills; wild fowl and frogs from the marshes of the Dombes; fish from the Saône and the Rhône; and snails known as the "oysters of Burgundy." Franche-Comté and the Jura contribute to the regional repertoire with smoked sausages, farmhouse cheeses, walnut oil, and fish from glacier-fed lakes. In the Auvergne, regional fare features salted hams, pork, cheeses, potatoes, cabbage and lentils.

Pain d'epices

Oeufs en meurette *is a famous Burgundian dish of eggs poached in a red wine sauce with onions, mushrooms and bacon.*

Dijon mustard owes *its distinctive flavor to the combination of high quality mustard seeds, local wine, and* verjus *(the fermented juice of unripe grapes). A staple condiment in French households, the smooth and coarse-grained varieties are also used in cooking.*

Coarse-grained Dijon mustard

Smooth Dijon mustard

Rosette de Lyon *is the most famous of Lyon sausages. It is made of meat from leg of pork and served in chunky slices.*

Bacon

Mushrooms

Escargots à la Bourguignonne *are snails served with parsley and garlic butter. Small tongs are used to pluck the snails out of the shells.*

Beef

Wine sauce

Boeuf bourguignon, *the famous classic stew, is more refined than many other French stews. Burgundians prefer to use cuts of beef from Charolais cattle. The marinated meat is cooked slowly in Burgundy or Beaujolais wine until tender. Cubes of bacon, baby onions and mushrooms are then added.*

Falette *(stuffed breast of veal) is a specialty from the Auvergne. It can be served hot with braised cabbage, or cold with a salad.*

Minute steak Dijonnaise *is steak served in a cream and mustard sauce. Veal, rabbit and pork are also served in this way.*

Bresse chicken, *the appel-lation contrôlée chicken, is delicious served with a creamy sauce and wild morels.*

Andouillettes à la Lyonnaise *are tripe sausages stuffed with veal. Served with fried onions, they are typically Lyonnaise.*

Salt pork with lentils, *a specialty of the Auvergne, is salt-cured pork poached in wine with tiny green Puy lentils.*

Walnut and pear pie *is a double-crusted pie made with ground walnut pastry and filled with sliced pears.*

Cherry flan *or* **clafoutis** *is made with dark cherries covered in a batterlike dough and laced with kirsch, a cherry liqueur.*

CHEESES

Central France produces the richest selection of cheeses in France. These range from soft, tangy, brandy-soaked Epoisses from Burgundy and the Swiss-type cheeses of the Alps, used in fondue, to cheddarlike Cantal and blue-veined cheeses such as Roquefort.

Burgundy cheeses

Epoisses

Pipo Crem'

Bleu de Bresse

Alpine cheeses

Tomme au raisin

Raclette

Emmenthal Français

Vacherin

Massif Central cheeses

St-Nectaire

Roquefort

Fourme d'Ambert

Cantal

France's Wine Regions: Burgundy

Grape-picker's basket

BURGUNDY and its fine wines have inspired awe for centuries. The fame of the region's wines spread throughout Europe in the 14th century, under the Valois Dukes of Burgundy. After the French Revolution, Napoleonic laws of equal inheritance split vineyards into tiny fractions, resulting in a bewildering number of *appellations*. Even today, the classification system remains dauntingly complex. But despite its impenetrable image, this is must-see territory for the "serious" wine lover, with its rich vinous history and tradition and dazzling *grands crus*.

LOCATOR MAP

　▩ Burgundy wine region

Clos de Vougeot on the Côte de Nuits

WINE REGIONS

Between Chablis in the north and the Côte Chalonnaise and Mâconnais in the south is the Côte d'Or, incorporating Côte de Nuits and Côte de Beaune. The Beaujolais region *(see pp366–7)* lies below Mâcon.

PRINCIPAL WINE AREAS

Chablis

Auxerre •

DIJON

Beaune •

Chalons-sur-Saône

Mâcon

Villefranche-sur-Saône

LYON

KEY

□ Chablis

□ Côte de Nuits

□ Côte de Beaune

□ Côte Chalonnaise

▨ Mâconnais

▨ Beaujolais

0 kilometers　　50

0 miles　　　　50

KEY FACTS ABOUT BURGUNDY

Location and Climate
The continental climate (bleak winters and hot summers) can be very variable, making vintages a crucial quality factor. The best vineyards have chalky soil and face south or east.

Grape Varieties
Burgundy is at least relatively simple in its grape varieties. Red Burgundy is made from **Pinot Noir**, with its sweet flavors of raspberries, cherries and strawberries, while the **Gamay** makes red Mâcon and Beaujolais. **Chardonnay** is the principal white variety for Chablis and white Burgundy, though small amounts of **Aligoté** and **Pinot Blanc** are grown and the **Sauvignon** is a specialty of St. Bris.

Good Producers
White Burgundy: Jean-Marie Raveneau, René Dauvissat, La Chablisienne, Comtes Lafon, Guy Roulot, Etienne Sauzet, Pierre Morey, Louis Carillon, Jean-Marc Boillot, André Ramonet, Hubert Lamy, Jean-Marie Guffens-Heynen, Olivier Merlin, Louis Latour, Louis Jadot, Olivier Leflaive.
Red Burgundy: Denis Bachelet, Daniel Rion, Domaine Dujac, Armand Rousseau, Joseph Roty, De Montille, Domaine de la Pousse d'Or, Domaine de l'Arlot, Jean-Jacques Confuron, Robert Chevillon, Georges Roumier, Leroy, Drouhin.

Good Vintages
(Reds) 1990, 1989, 1988, 1985.
(Whites) 1992, 1990, 1989, 1986.

DIJON

So elaborate are Burgundy's
appellations *that individual
vineyards, like Clos la Roche,
may have their own brands.*

CLOS LA ROCHE

1986

DOMAINE DUJAC

Marsannay-la-Côte

Fixin

Grand cru *vineyards
are at the top of the
quality pyramid;
they also tend to
occupy the upper
slopes of the Côte d'Or.*

BOUCHARD PÈRE & FILS

RICHEBOURG

GRAND CRU

1985

Gevrey-Chambertin

Morey-St-Denis

Chambolle-Musigny

Vougeot

Vosne-Romanée

0 kilometers   5

0 miles   5

Nuits-St-Georges

NUITS·S·GEORGES

SES GRANDS VINS

SA CONFRÉRIE des CHEVALIERS du TASTEVIN

**Wine for the "knights
of the tasting cup"**

Pernand-Vergelesses

La Doix

Aloxe-Corton

Serrigny

Savigny-lès-Beaune

Chorey

BEAUNE

Pommard

Volnay

Monthelie

KEY

- Village *appellations*
- Côte de Nuits-Villages
- Hautes-Côtes de Nuits
- Hautes-Côtes de Beaune
- Côte de Beaune-Villages

Auxey-Duresses

Meursault

Blagny

St-Aubin

Puligny-Montrachet

Chassagne-Montrachet

ezize-lès-
Maranges

Santenay

Sampigny-lès-Maranges   Chagny

Cheilly-les-Maranges

Bouzeron

VINS DE BOURGOGNE

Puligny-Montrachet

Champ-Canet

*Burgundian villages have
often appropriated the name
of their most famous vineyard:
all the village wines of Puligny,
for example, can benefit from
the fame of Le Montrachet.*

THE CÔTE D'OR

The Côte de Nuits and Côte
de Beaune, together forming
the "golden" Côte d'Or *(see
p334),* meet at the historic
town of Beaune, which hosts
the most famous annual wine
auction in the world *(see
p336).* "Hautes-Côtes" and
"Villages" wines are made by
those not fortunate enough
to possess land in the starry
individual *appellations.*

Teams of grape-pickers at the vineyards of Nuits-St-Georges

The French Alps

IN ANY SEASON, the Alps are one of the most spectacular regions of France – a majestic mountain range stretching south from Lake Geneva almost to the Mediterranean, and climaxing in Europe's loftiest peak, the 4,800-m (15,770-ft) Mont Blanc. The area encompasses the old regions of Dauphiné and Savoie, once remote and independent (Savoie only became part of France in 1860). They have prospered since alpine holidays and skiing became popular during the last century, but are still very conscious of their distinct identity.

Children in traditional Savoie costumes

The Alpine landscape in winter: chalets and skiers on the slopes at Courchevel

WINTER

THE SKI SEASON usually starts just before Christmas, and finishes at the end of April. Most resorts offer both cross-country and downhill skiing, with many pistes (ski trails) linking two or more ski stations. The less energetic can enjoy the landscape from some of the highest cable cars (*téléphériques*) in the world.

Of the 100 or more French Alpine resorts, the most popular include **Chamonix-Mont Blanc**, the historic capital of Alpine skiing and site of the first Winter Olympics in 1924; **Megève**, which boasts one of the best ski schools in Europe; **Morzine**, a year-round resort on the Swiss border, adjacent to the modern, car-free resort of **Avoriaz**; modern **Albertville**, site of the 1992 Winter Olympics; **Les Trois Vallées**, which include glamorous

A cable car at Courchevel, part of Les Trois Vallées complex

A downhill skier at Val d'Isère

Courchevel and **Méribel**, and the lesser-known **Val Thorens/Les Ménuires**; **Tignes**, a year-round resort; **Les Arcs** and **La Plagne**, both custom built; and **Val d'Isère**, a favorite among the rich and famous.

ALPINE FLOWERS

In spring and early summer the pastures of the French Alps are ablaze with flowers. These include blue and yellow gentians, bellflowers, lilies, saxifrages and a variety of orchids. Steep mountain meadows cannot be farmed intensively, and the absence of fertilizers and weed killers enables wild flowers to flourish.

Spring gentian (*Gentiana verna*)

Martagon lily (*Lilium martagon*)

The French Alps in spring: flower-filled meadows bordered by dramatic white peaks

SPRING AND SUMMER

THE ALPINE summer season starts in late June, extending to early September – most resorts close in October and November

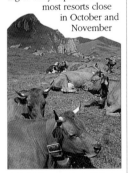

Belled dairy cows in an Alpine pasture

between the hiking and skiing seasons. After the spring thaw, flower-filled pastures, snow-fed mountain lakes and a huge number of marked trails make this area a hiker's paradise. In the Chamonix area alone there are over 310 km (195 miles) of hiking trails. The best known long-distance route is the **Tour du Mont Blanc**, a 10-day hike via France, Italy and Switzerland. The **GR5** traverses the entire Alps, passing through the **Parc National de la Vanoise** and **Parc Régional du Queyras** (*see p377*) to the south. *Téléphériques* give access to the higher trails, where the views are even more awesome. Be sure to bring plenty of warm,

waterproof clothing: the weather can change very quickly.

Many resorts are now concentrating on broadening their summer appeal – golf, tennis, mountain biking, horse riding, paragliding, canoeing, white water rafting, glacier skiing and mountain climbing are all widely available.

Mountain climbers scaling the heights around Mont Blanc

Geology of the Massif Central

THE MASSIF CENTRAL covers almost one-fifth of France and is over 250 million years old. Most of its peaks have been eroded to form a vast plateau split into deep valleys. The heart of the Massif consists of hard, igneous rocks like granite, with softer rocks such as limestone at its margins. Different rock types are reflected in the landscape and buildings; in the eroded Gorges du Tarn, the houses are built of russet-colored limestone. Massive granite farmhouses are a feature of Limousin, and Le Puy-en-Velay is known for its giant basalt pillars.

LOCATOR MAP

☐ *Extent of the Massif Central*

This granite portal is found in the Romanesque church at Moutier d'Ahun (see p346). Granite underlies much of the Massif Central.

Basalt *is a dark, fine-grained rock formed by volcanic lava. A common building stone in the Auvergne, it is often cut into blocks and bonded with lighter-colored mortar. In the medieval town of Salers (see p353), basalt was used for most of the buildings, including this one in the Grande Place.*

Montluçon

Moutier d'Ahun •

Limoges •

Clermont Ferrand

Dordogne

• Salers

Schist tiling *is featured on these roofs at Argentat. Schist is a crystalline rock that splits readily into layers. It is particularly common on the edge of the Massif, and provides an effective roofing material.*

• Argentat

Cère

Lot

Limestone walls *can be seen on houses in Espalion (see p356). Of all the rocks in the Massif Central, it is among the most easily worked. It splits readily and is soft enough to be cut into blocks with a handsaw. As with granite, its color and consistency vary from area to area.*

Mill

Tarn

| 0 kilometers | 50 |
| 0 miles | 50 |

Crystalized lava, *like this dramatic curtain of columns at Prades, formed when liquid basalt seeped through the surrounding rock and solidified to form giant crystals.*

KEY

	Sedimentary rock
	Surface volcanic rock
	Granite
	Metamorphic rock

evers

Loire

Saône

Lyon •

• St-Etienne

• Le-Puy-en-Velay

Rhône

Limestone plateaus (causses) *are typical of this region. Gorges, where rivers have cut through layers of this slightly soluble rock, run deep into the Massif Central.*

This mature landscape at Mont Aigoual is the highest point in the Cévennes (see p357), dividing rivers flowing into the Atlantic and the Mediterranean. Its granite and schist rocks show erosion.

RECOGNIZING ROCKS

Geologists divide rocks into three groups. Igneous rocks, like granite, are formed by volcanic activity and either extrude onto the surface or intrude into other rocks below ground. Sedimentary rocks are produced by sediment buildup. Metamorphic rocks have been transformed by heat or pressure.

SEDIMENTARY ROCK

Oolitic limestone often contains fossils and small amounts of quartz.

SURFACE VOLCANIC ROCK

Basalt, *which can form very thick sheets, is the most common lava rock.*

GRANITE

Pink granite, *a coarse-grained rock, is formed deep in the earth's crust.*

METAMORPHIC ROCK

Muscovite schist is a medium-grained mud or clay-based rock.

BURGUNDY AND FRANCHE-COMTÉ

···

YONNE · NIÈVRE · CÔTE D'OR · SAÔNE-ET-LOIRE
HAUTE-SAÔNE · DOUBS · JURA

URGUNDY CONSIDERS *itself the heart of France, a prosperous region with world-renowned wine, earthy but excellent cuisine and magnificent architecture. Franche-Comté to the east combines gentle farmland with lofty Alpine forests.*

Under the dukes of Valois, Burgundy was France's most powerful rival, with territory extending well beyond its present boundaries. By the 16th century, however, the duchy was ruled by governors appointed by the French king, but it still managed to keep its privileges and traditions. Once a part of Burgundy, Franche-Comté – the Free County – struggled to remain independent of the French crown, and was a province of the Holy Roman Empire until annexed by Louis XIV in 1674.

Burgundy is a wealthy region, a center of medieval religious faith that produced Romanesque masterpieces at Vézelay, Fontenay, and Cluny. Dijon is a splendid city, filled with the palaces of the old Burgundian nobility and a collection of great paintings and sculptures in the Musée des Beaux Arts. The vineyards of the Côte d'Or, the Côte de Beaune and Chablis yield some of the world's most venerated wines. Other richly varied landscapes – from the wild forests of the Morvan to the lush farmland of the Brionnais – produce snails, Bresse chickens and Charolais beef.

Franche-Comté has none of this opulence, though its capital, Besançon, is an elegant 17th-century city with a tradition of clockmaking. Topographically the Franche-Comté is divided in two, with gently rolling farmland in the Saône Valley and high Alpine scenery to the east. This forest country of Alpine torrents filled with trout is also the home of great cheeses, notably Vacherin and Comté, and of the well-known yellow wine of Arbois.

The prehistoric site of the Roche de Solutré near Mâcon

◁ **Vineyards at Santenay in the world-renowned Côte de Beaune district**

Exploring Burgundy and Franche-Comté

BURGUNDY IS FRANCE'S RICHEST province – historically, culturally, gastronomically and economically. This lush kernel of a once-great power possesses a concentration of unique Romanesque architecture in Fontenay and Vézelay, along with some of the world's most venerated wines. Dijon is a must for lovers of art, architecture and food. Franche-Comté is better suited for outdoor vacations, such as hiking and canoeing in wild scenery and crystal-clear rivers.

Burgundian riverscape near Fon

To Paris

SENS ①

TONNERRE ⑤ ⑥ CHÂTEAU DE TANLAY   CH. Su ⑧

AUXERRE ③   ④ CHABLIS   ⑦ CHÂTEAU D'ANCY-LE-FRANC

LA PUISAYE ②

ABBAYE DE FONTENAY ⑨

⑩ ST

AVALLON   ⑪

VÉZELAY ⑫   ⑬   SEMUR-EN-AUXOIS

MORVAN

⑭   ⑮ SAULIEU

LA CHARITÉ-SUR-LOIRE

PARC NATUREL RÉGIONAL DU MORVAN

CHÂTEAU CHINON

NEVERS   HAUT-FOLIN   ⑰ AUTUN

⑯

To Bourges

To Vichy Clermont-Ferrand

PARAY-LE-MONIAL ㉓

㉔

BRIONNAIS

KEY

▬▬	Highway
▬▬	Major road
▬▬	Minor road
▬▬	Scenic route
〰	River
☀	Viewing point

Distinctive Burgundian glazed roof tiles, Hôtel Aubriot in Dijon

SIGHTS AT A GLANCE

Wine harvest in Nuits-St-Georges, Côte d'Or

GETTING AROUND

Burgundy is well served by the A6 autoroute from Paris to Lyon and Marseille, which is joined by the A31 from Nancy and Dijon and the A36 from Besançon. Use the autoroutes to reach the main attractions if you are short of time; but if you have time and a taste for quiet country roads, those in Burgundy and Franche-Comté are among the most rewarding in France. The TGV links Dijon and Mâcon with Paris, Geneva and Marseille. Dijon is a major rail hub, also connecting other towns in the region. Dijon's international airport serves most European destinations.

0 kilometers   25

0 miles   25

Reliquary in the cathedral treasury at Sens

Sens ❶

Yonne. 👥 27,000. 🚊 🚌
🛈 place Jean-Jaurès (03 86 65 19 49). 🛒 Mon & Fri.

THE LITTLE TOWN of Sens, at the confluence of the rivers Yonne and Vanne, was important well before Caesar came to Gaul. Indeed, it was the Senones whose attempt to sack the Roman Capitol in 390 BC was so famously thwarted by a flock of geese.

The **Cathédrale St-Etienne** is Sens' outstanding glory. Begun before 1140, it is the oldest of the great Gothic cathedrals and its noble simplicity influenced many other churches. Louis IX (see p47) did the town the honor of getting married here in 1234.

The exquisite stained-glass windows from the 12th–16th centuries show biblical scenes, including the Tree of Jesse, and a tribute to Thomas à Becket who was exiled here. His liturgical robes can be seen in the rich treasury, now housed in the **Musée de la Cathédrale St-Etienne**. Among the other exhibits is a beautiful 11th-

century Byzantine coffer. The market held around the cathedral is excellent, and the town is renowned for its robust Burgundian fare.

🏛 **Musée de la Cathédrale St-Etienne**
Place de la Cathédrale. 📞 03 86 64 46 22. **Open** Jun–Sep: daily; Oct–May: Tue, Sat, Sun. 🚫 ♿

La Puisaye ❷

Yonne, Nièvre. 🚊 Auxerre, Clamecy, Bonny-sur-Loire, Cosne-Cours-sur-Loire. 🚌 St-Fargeau, St-Sauveur-en-Puisaye. 🛈 Maison de la Puisaye, St-Fargeau (03 86 74 15 72).

THE STRANGE, secret forest country of the Puisaye was immortalized by Colette (1873–1954), who was born at **St-Sauveur** in "a house that smiled only on its garden side . . .". The **Musée Collette**, housed in the town's 17th-century château, displays the writer's photographs, books, furniture and other objects.

The best way to explore the region is on foot or by bike around its watery woodlands, orchards and meadows, so unlike the rest of Burgundy. There are many interesting destinations, notably the 13th-century **Château de Ratilly** near St-Sauveur, with a pottery workshop and art exhibitions. More pottery can be seen in **St-Amand**, the center of Puisaye stoneware production. The pink-brick **Château de St-Fargeau** housed the exiled Grande Mademoiselle (see p53). The church in **La Ferté-Loupière** contains a 15th-

Colette in the 1880s at St-Sauveur

century Danse Macabre fresco, while the frescoes in Eglise St-Pierre in **Moutiers** show John the Baptist and the Creation.

🏛 **Musée Colette**
Château St-Sauveur-en-Puisay. 📞 03 86 45 61 95. **Open** Apr–Sep: Wed–Mon; Oct–Mar: Sat, Sun & public hols. 🚫

Auxerre ❸

Yonne. 👥 39,000. 🚊 🚌 🛈 1–2 quai de la République (03 86 52 06 19). 🛒 Tue & Fri.

BEAUTIFULLY SITUATED overlooking the Yonne River, Auxerre justly prides itself on a fine collection of churches, along with a charming pedestrianized main square, the place Charles-Surugue.

The Gothic **Cathédrale St-Etienne** took over three centuries to build and was completed in about 1560. It is famous for its intricate 13th-century stained glass. The choir, with its slender columns and colonettes, is the epitome of Gothic weightlessness and elegance, while the western portals are decorated with beautiful Flamboyant sculpture that has been sadly mutilated by war and weather. The Romanesque crypt is adorned with unique 11th–13th-century frescoes, including one depicting Christ on a white horse. The badly pillaged treasury is less impressive, but still has an interesting collection of beautifully illuminated manuscripts.

St. Germanus, mentor of St. Patrick and bishop of Auxerre

Château de St-Fargeau in the Puisaye region

in the 5th century, was buried at the former abbey church of **St-Germain**. The abbey was founded by Queen Clothilde, wife of Clovis *(see pp44–5)*, the first Christian king of France, and is a noted shrine. The crypt is partly Carolingian, with tombs and 11th–13th century frescoes. The former abbey houses the **Musée d'Art et d'Histoire** with an exhibition of Gallo-Roman finds from the region, witness to Auxerre's long history.

🏛 **Musée d'Art et d'Histoire**
2 place St-Germain. 📞 03 86 51 09 74. **Open** *Wed–Mon.* **Closed** *public hols.*

Medieval fresco in Cathédrale St-Etienne at Auxerre

Chablis ❹

Yonne. 👥 *2,300.* 🚉 ℹ️ *quai du Biez (03 86 42 80 80).* 🚌 *Sun.*

THERE CAN BE no question that Chablis tastes best in Chablis. Although this is one of the most famous wine

The intriguing spring of Fosse Dionne in Tonnerre

villages on earth, its narrow stone streets still have an air of sleepy prosperity. Saint Vincent, the patron saint of wine-growers, is celebrated by processions in February, attended by the wine brotherhood of Piliers Chablisiens.

Tonnerre ❺

Yonne. 👥 *6,000.* 🚉 🚌 ℹ️ *rue F-Nitteraud (03 86 55 14 48).* 🚌 *Sat.*

THE MYSTICAL, cloudy green spring of **Fosse Dionne** is a good reason to visit the small town of Tonnerre. An astonishing volume of water bursts up from the ground into an 18th-century washing site. Due to its depth and strong currents it has never been thoroughly explored, and local legend has it that a serpent lives on undisturbed at the bottom.

The **Hôtel-Dieu** is 150 years older than the Hôtel-Dieu in Beaune *(see p336–7)*.

It was founded by Margaret of Burgundy in 1293 to care for the poor. It lost its tiling during the Revolution, but the barrel-vaulted oak ceiling survived.

🏥 **Hôtel-Dieu**
Rue du Prieuré. 📞 03 86 55 33 00. **Open** *Easter–May & Oct: Sat, Sun & hols; Jun–Sep: Wed–Mon.*

Château de Tanlay ❻

Tanlay. 📞 *03 86 75 70 61.* **Open** *Apr–mid-Nov: Wed–Mon.*

THE MOATED Château de Tanlay is a beautiful example of French Renaissance, built in the mid-16th century. There is a *trompe l'oeil* in the Grande Galerie and, in the corner tower, an intriguing School of Fontainebleau painted ceiling. Its antique divinities represent famous Protestants and Catholics in the 16th century, such as Diane de Poitiers as Venus.

The Renaissance façade and *cour d'honneur* of Château de Tanlay

Abbaye de Fontenay **⑨**

THE TRANQUIL ABBEY of Fontenay is the oldest surviving Cistercian foundation in France and offers a rare insight into the Cistercian way of life. It represents the spirit of the order in the sublime gravity of its Romanesque church and its plain but elegant chapter house, in early Gothic style. The abbey was founded in 1118 by St. Bernard. Situated deep in the forest, it offered the peace and seclusion the Cistercians sought. Supported by the local aristocracy, the abbey began to thrive and remained in use until the Revolution when it was sold and converted into a paper mill. In 1906 the abbey came under new ownership and was restored to its original appearance.

Dovecote
A magnificent circular dovecote, built in the 13th century, is situated next to the kennel where the precious hunting dogs of the dukes of Burgundy were guarded by servants.

The 17th-century abbot's lodgings were built when the abbots were appointed by royal favor.

The bakehouse is no longer intact, but the 13th-century oven and chimney have survived.

The visitors' hostel is where weary wanderers and pilgrims were offered board and lodging by the monks.

★ Cloisters
For a 12th-century monk, a walk through the cloisters was an opportunity for meditation and provided shelter from the weather.

Warming Room

In the forge monks produced their own tools and hardware.

Fontenay "Prison"
It may be that this 15th-century building was actually used to lock up not local miscreants but important abbey archives, in order to protect them against damage by rats.

Scriptorium
Manuscripts were copied here. The adjacent warming room was used to warm chilled hands.

★ Abbey Church
Rich decoration has no place in this church from the 1140s. But the severe architectural forms, the warm color of the stone and the diffused light convey a grandeur of their own.

Dormitory
Monks slept in long rows on straw mattresses in this large, unheated room. The timberwork roof is from the late 15th century.

The herb garden was skillfully cultivated by the monks in order to grow healing herbs for medicines and potions.

STAR FEATURES

★ **Abbey Church**

★ **Cloisters**

Chapter house
Once a day, monks and abbot assembled in this room to discuss matters concerning the community. It derives much of its charm from the elegant 12th-century piers and ribbed vaults.

Infirmary

ST. BERNARD AND THE CISTERCIANS

In 1112 Bernard, a young Burgundian nobleman, joined the Cistercians. At the time the order was still obscure, founded 14 years earlier by a group of monks who wanted to turn their back on the elaborate lifestyle of Cluny *(see pp44–5)*, renounce the world and espouse poverty and simplicity of life. During Bernard's lifetime the Cistercians became one of the largest and most famous orders of its time. Part of this success was clearly due to Bernard's powerful personality and his skills as a writer, theologian and statesman. He reinforced the poverty rule, rejecting all forms of embellishment. In 1174, only 21 years after his death, he was canonized.

The Virgin Protecting the Cistercian Order, *by Jean Bellegambe*

Château d'Ancy-le-Franc 7

Ancy-le-Franc. 03 86 75 14 63.
Open Apr–mid-Nov: daily.
obligatory.

THE CLASSICAL Renaissance façade of Château d'Ancy-le-Franc gives an austere impression. Its inner courtyard, however, has a rich ornamentation. The château was built in the 1540s by the Italian Sebastiano Serlio, for the Duke of Clermont-Tonnerre. Most of the interior decorations were carried out by Primaticcio and other members of the Fontainebleau School *(see pp170–71)*. Diane de Poitiers, the duke's sister-in-law and mistress of Henry II, is portrayed in the *Chambre de Judith e Holophernes*.

In the outbuildings a vintage car and carriage museum displays over 80 vehicles.

The vase of Vix in the Musée du Châtillonnais, Châtillon-sur-Seine

Châtillon-sur-Seine 8

Côte d'Or. 6,850. place Marmont (03 80 91 13 19). Sat.

WORLD WAR II left Châtillon a smoking ruin, hence the town's resolutely modern aspect. But the past is still present in the **Musée du Châtillonnais**, where the magnificent Vix treasure is displayed. In 1953, the tomb of a Gaulish princess, dating from the 6th century BC, was discovered near Vix at Mont Lassois. The trove of jewelry and artifacts of Greek origin includes a stunning bronze vase, 164 cm (66 in) high and weighing 208 kg (459 lb).

The staid façade of Château d'Ancy-le-Franc

Another point of interest is the Romanesque **Eglise St-Vorles** containing an *Entombment* with Christ and mourners splendidly sculpted (1527).

At the nearby source of the Douix River, which runs into the Seine, is a beautiful grotto.

🏛 **Musée du Châtillonnais**
7 rue du Bourg. 03 80 91 24 67.
Open Wed–Mon. **Closed** Jan 1, May 1, Dec 25.

Abbaye de Fontenay 9

See pp322–3.

Alise-Ste-Reine 10

Côte d'Or. 670. Venarey-les-Laumes, 3 km (2 miles) (03 80 96 89 13).

MONT AUXOIS, above the little village of Alise-Ste-Reine, was the site of Caesar's final victory over the heroic Gaulish chieftain Vercingetorix

in 52 BC after a six-week siege *(see p42)*. The first excavations here were undertaken in the mid-19th century, and they uncovered the vestiges of a thriving Gallo-Roman town, with theater, forum and well laid-out street plan. The **Musée Alésia** has a collection of artifacts, jewelry and bronze figures from the site.

Alise is dominated by Aimé Millet's gigantic moustachioed statue of Vercingetorix, which was placed here in 1865 to commemorate the first excavations. Cynics feel that it bears a more than passing resemblance to Napoleon III, who sponsored the dig.

🏛 **Musée Alésia**
Rue de l'Hôpital. 03 80 96 10 95.
Open Apr–Nov 11: daily.

Environs
In the vicinity lies **Château de Bussy-Rabutin**. The spiteful 17th-century soldier and wit Roger de Bussy-Rabutin created its highly individualistic

Excavations at the Roman site near Alise-Ste-Reine

decor while exiled from Louis XIV's court. One room is dedicated to portraits of his many mistresses, as well as to some imaginary ones.

♣ **Château de Bussy-Rabutin**
Bussy-le-Grand. ◖ 03 80 96 00 03.
Open daily; Nov–Mar: Thu–Mon.
Closed Jan 1, May 1, Nov 1 & 11, Dec 25. ◢ ◢

Semur-en-Auxois ⓫

Côte d'Or. ♙ 4,500. ◰
◼ 2 place Gaveau (03 80 97 05 96).
◰ Thu & Sat.

Approached from the west, Semur-en-Auxois comes as a surprise on an otherwise uneventful road. Its massive round bastions built in the 14th century (one of them with an unnerving gash in it) suddenly appear, towering over the Pont Joly and the peaceful Armançon River.

The **Eglise Notre-Dame** dates from the 13th and 14th centuries, and was modeled on the cathedral of Auxerre. The fragile high walls had to be restored in the 15th and 19th centuries. The church houses significant artworks, from the tympanum showing the legend of Doubting Thomas on the north doorway, to the 15th-century *Entombment* by Antoine le Moiturier. The stained glass presents the legend of Sainte Barbara, and the work of different guilds, such as butchers and drapers.

Environs
The village of Epoisses is the site of the moated **Château d'Epoisses**, its 11th–18th-century construction blending medieval towers with fine Renaissance details, and a huge 15th-century dovecote. Epoisses is also the home of

Semur-en-Auxois by the Armançon River

one of Burgundy's most revered cheeses, to be sampled at the local café or *fromagerie*.

♣ **Château d'Epoisses**
Epoisses. ◖ 03 80 96 40 56. **Open** Jul–Aug: Wed–Mon (grounds: all year). ◢ ◢ ground floor only.

Vézelay ⓬

See pp326–7.

Avallon ⓭

Yonne. ♙ 8,600. ◰ ◰ ◼ 4 rue Bocquillot (03 86 34 14 19). ◰ Sat.

A fine old fortified town, Avallon is situated on a granite spur between two ravines by the Cousin River.

Avallon suffered much in the wars of Saracens, Normans, English and French, which accounts for its coldly defensive aspect. Today the town is quiet and quite beautiful, full of charming details. The principal monument is the 12th-century Romanesque **Eglise St-Lazare**, with two magnificent carved doorways. The larger of the two illustrates the signs of the zodiac, the labors of the month and the

Stained-glass window in Eglise Notre-Dame at Semur-en-Auxois

musicians of the Apocalypse. The nave is decorated with sophisticated acanthus capitals and polychrome statuary.

The **Musée de l'Avallonnais** has a wide-ranging collection. featuring an intricate Venus mosaic from the 2nd century AD, and Georges Rouault's (1871–1958) series of Expressionist etchings, the *Miserere*.

🏛 **Musée de l'Avallonnais**
Place de la Collégiale. ◖ 03 86 34 03 19. **Open** May–Oct: Wed–Mon. ◢

Environs
To the southwest of Avallon is the 12th-century Château de Bazoches, which was transformed into a military garrison by Vauban in the 17th century.

Miserere **by Georges Rouault in the Musée d'Avallonnais, Avallon**

Vézelay ⑫

THE GOLDEN GLOW of the Basilique Ste-Madeleine crowning Vézelay's hill is visible from afar. Tourists follow in the footsteps of medieval pilgrims, ascending the narrow street up to the former abbey church. In the 12th century, at the height of its glory, the abbey claimed to house relics of Mary Magdalene, and was also an important meeting point for pilgrims en route to Santiago de Compostela in Spain *(see pp390–91)*. Today its attraction lies in the Romanesque church with its magnificent sculpture and Gothic choir.

Decorated capital

View of Vézelay
The abbey dominates Vézelay's surroundings as it once dominated the religious and worldly affairs of the area.

Tour St-Michel was built in 1230–40. It derives its name from the statue of the archangel in the tower's southwest corner.

Nave of Ste-Madeleine
The nave was rebuilt between 1120–35, using alternate dark and light stone in the transverse arches.

Nave of Ste-Madeleine

The façade dates from 1150 and has a large 13th-century window. It was about to collapse when Viollet-le-Duc was commissioned to restore it according to old plans in 1840.

The narthex used to be a gathering point for medieval processions.

★ **Tympanum**
This masterpiece of sculpture (1120–35) shows Christ on His throne, stretching out His hands from which rays of light descend onto the apostles.

STAR FEATURES
★ **Tympanum**
★ **Capitals**

Tour St-Antoine was built at the same time as the choir, in the late 12th century. Its counterpart on the north side was never finished.

VISITORS' CHECKLIST

Basilique Ste-Madeleine, Vézelay.
03 86 33 39 50. Semizelles.
Open Apr–Oct: 6am– 8pm daily;
Nov–Mar: 7am–6pm. 7am,
12:30pm, 6pm, 6:30pm Tue–Fri;
8am, 12:30pm, 6pm, 6:30pm
Sat; 8am, 11am Sun.

The chapter house
and cloister are the
only parts remaining
from the 12th-century
monastic buildings.
Viollet-le-Duc rebuilt
the cloister and
restored the rib-
vaulted chapter house,
once a graceful
background for the
monks' daily
assemblies.

Crypt of Ste-Madeleine
*The Carolingian crypt houses relics
once thought to be Mary Magdalene's.
The vault was rebuilt in 1165.*

★ Capitals
*The capitals in the
nave and narthex
are exquisitely carved,
and provide a vivid
rendering of the stories
of Classical antiquity
and the Bible. The
master who created them
remains unknown.*

Choir of Ste-Madeleine
*The choir was rebuilt in the last quarter
of the 12th century in the then-modern
Gothic style of the Ile de France.*

Morvan, a region of rivers and forests, well-suited to fishing and other outdoor pursuits

Morvan ⑭

Yonne, Côte d'Or, Nièvre, Saône et Loire. ✈ Dijon. 🚉 Autun, Corbigny. 🚌 Château-Chinon, Saulieu, Avallon. ℹ️ Château-Chinon (03 86 85 06 58); Maison du Parc, St-Brisson (03 86 79 00).

MORVAN is a Celtic word meaning Black Mountain, which is a good description of this area seen from afar. The immense, sparsely inhabited plateau of granite and woodland appears suddenly in the center of the rich Burgundy hills and farmland. Stretching roughly north to south, it gains altitude as it proceeds southward, reaching a culminating point of 901 m (2,928 ft) at **Haut-Folin**.

The Morvan's two sources of natural wealth are abundant water and dense forests of oak, beech and conifer. In the old days lumber used to be floated out of the area to Paris via a network of lakes and rivers. Today it travels by truck, and the Yonne, Cousin and Cure rivers are instead used for recreation and the production of electricity.

The population continues to shrink, for the Morvan has always been a poor, remote area. Each of its largest towns, Château-Chinon in the center and Saulieu on the outskirts, has barely 3,000 inhabitants.

During World War II, the Morvan was a bastion of the French Resistance. Today a Regional Nature Park, its attraction is its wildness. Information on a wide variety of outdoor activities, including bicycling, canoeing, skiing, and horseback riding, is available at the Maison du Parc at St-Brisson, where there is also a **Musée de la Resistance**. There are plenty of short walking trails, in addition to two well-marked long distance paths: the GR13 (Vézelay to Autun) and the Tour du Morvan par les Grands Lacs.

🏛 **Musée de la Résistance**
Maison du Parc, St-Brisson. 📞 03 86 78 79 00. **Open** Apr–mid-Oct: daily. 📷 ♿

Saulieu ⑮

Côte d'Or. 🚶 2,900. 🚉 🚌 ℹ️ 24 rue d'Argentine (03 80 64 00 21 or 03 80 64 09 22). 🛍 Thu & Sat.

ON THE EDGE of the Morvan, Saulieu has been a shrine of Burgundian cooking ever since the 17th century. The town was then a stop on the Paris to Lyon coach road. Today the tradition is maintained by the world-famous chef Bernard Loiseau at the **Côte d'Or** restaurant (see p599). Yet there is more to Saulieu than ris de veau de lait braisé or poularde truffée à la vapeur. The Romanesque **Basilique St-Andoche**, built in the early 12th century, has decorated capitals with representations of the Flight into Egypt and a comical version of Balaam and his donkey waylaid by the Angel.

Nevers ⑯

Nièvre. 🚶 44,000. 🚉 🚌 ℹ️ Palais Ducal, rue Sabatier (03 86 68 46 00). 🛍 Sat.

LIKE ALL Burgundian towns fronting the Loire, Nevers should be approached from the west side of the river for a full appreciation of its noble site. Though lacking historical importance, the town has much to show. The Romanesque 11th-century **Eglise St-Etienne** has monolithic columns and a wreath of radiating chapels. In the crypt of the Gothic **Cathédrale St-Cyr** is a 15th-century sculpted Entombment. The contemporary stained-glass windows are also worth a look.

The overlordship of Nevers passed to the Italian Gonzaga family in the 16th century. The Gonzagas brought a school of artists skilled in the fine arts of faïence making and glassblowing. The industry has remained in the town, and the modern pottery, still in the traditional white, blue, yellow and green colors, is charming, with its curious trademark, the little green arabesque knot, or noeud

Nevers faïence vase

vert. The best place to view it is at the **Musée Municipal**, and the best place to buy it is the 17th-century **Faïencerie Montagnon** close by. The 12th-century **Porte du Croux** houses the **Musée Archéologique** with some remarkable Romanesque sculpture.

🏛 **Musée Municipal Frédéric Blandin**
Promenade des Remparts. 📞 *03 86 71 67 90.* **Open** *Wed–Mon.* 🏷

🏛 **Musée Archéologique**
Rue de la Porte-du-Croux. 📞 *03 86 59 17 85.* **Open** *Wed–Mon.* 🏷

Environs
Just south of Nevers, the 19th-century **Pont du Guetin** carries the Loire Canal majestically across the Allier River. The church at **St-Parize-le-Châtel** has a jolly Burgundian menagerie sculpted on the capitals of the crypt.

The *Temptation of Eve* in Autun

Autun ⓱

Saône-et-Loire. 🏠 *17,900.* 🚉 🚌
ℹ️ *2 av Charles de Gaulle (03 85 86 80 38).* 🛒 *Wed & Sun.*

A GUSTODUNUM, the town of Augustus, was founded in the late 1st century BC. It was a great center of learning,

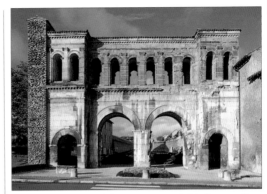

The imposing Porte St-André in Autun, once part of the Roman wall

with a population four times what it is today. Its theater, built in the 1st century AD, could seat 20,000 people.

Today Autun is still a delight, deserving gastronomic as well as cultural investigation.

The magical **Cathédrale St-Lazare** was built in the 12th century. It is special because of the genius of its sculptures, most of them by the mysterious 12th-century artist Gislebertus. He sculpted both the capitals inside and the glorious Last Judgment tympanum over the main portal. This masterpiece, called a "Romanesque Cézanne" by writer André Malraux, escaped notice and was saved from destruction during the Revolution because it had been plastered over in the 18th century. Inside, some of the capitals can be seen close up in a room in the tower. Look also for the sculpture of Pierre Jeannin

and his wife. Jeannin was the president of the Dijon parliament who prevented the Massacre of St. Bartholomew *(see pp50–51)* spreading to Burgundy with the immortal remark, "the commands of very angry monarchs should be obeyed very slowly."

The fine collection of medieval art at **Musée Rolin** includes the lovely bas relief *Temptation of Eve,* by Gislebertus. There is also the painted stone Virgin of Autun (15th century), and the *Nativity of Cardinal Rolin* by the Master of Moulins, from about 1480.

The monumental **Porte St-André,** the **Porte d'Arroux** and the ruins of the **Théâtre Romain** and the **Temple de Janus** are reminders of Autun's glorious Roman past.

🏛 **Musée Rolin**
5 rue des Bancs. 📞 *03 85 52 09 76.*
Open *Apr–Sep: Wed–Mon; Oct–Mar: Wed–Sun.* **Closed** *Jan 1, May 1, Jul 14, Nov 1 & 11, Dec 25.* 🏷

Remains of the Roman theater at Autun, dating from the 1st century AD

Street by Street: Dijon

T HE CENTER of Dijon is noted for its
architectural splendor – a legacy
from the Dukes of Burgundy *(see p333)*.
Wealthy parliament members also had
elegant *hôtels particuliers* built in the
17th–18th centuries. The capital of
Burgundy, Dijon today has a rich cultural
life and a renowned university. The
city's great art treasures are housed in
the Palais des Ducs. Dijon is also famous
for its mustard *(see p308)* and *pain
d'épice* (gingerbread), a reminder of the
town's position on the spice route. It
became a major rail hub during the 19th
century and now has a TGV link to Paris.

Hôtel de Vogüé
*This elegant 17th-century mansion is
decorated with Burgundian cabbages
and fruit garlands by Hugues Sambin.*

★ Notre-Dame
*This magnificent 13th-century
Gothic church has a façade
with gargoyles,
columns and
the popular
Jacquemart
clock. The
chouette (owl)
is reputed to
bring good
luck when
touched.*

Musée des Beaux Arts
*The collection of Flemish masters
here includes this 14th-century
triptych by Jacques de Baerze
and Melchior Broederlam.*

Place de la Libération was
created by Mansart in the 17th century.

★ Palais des Ducs
*The Dukes of Burgundy held court here, but
the building seen today was mainly built
in the 17th century for the parliament. It
now houses the Musée des Beaux Arts.*

Rue Verrerie
*This cobbled street in
the old merchants'
quarter is lined
with medieval half-
timbered houses.
Some have fine wood
carvings, such as
Nos. 8, 10 and 12.*

VISITORS' CHECKLIST

Côte d'Or. 🏠 151,000. ✈ 5 km
(3 miles) SSE Dijon. 🚌 🚉 Cours
de la Gare. 🛈 place Darcy
(03 80 44 11 44). 🍎 Tue, Fri &
Sat. 🎭 Florissimo (every 3 years:
1999, 2002, etc); Festival de
Musique (Jun); Fêtes de la Vigne
(Sep). **Hôtel de Vogüé** only
inner courtyard open to the
public. **Musée Magnin** (03 80
67 11 10) **open** Tue–Sun.
Closed some public hols. 🅰

★ St-Michel
*Begun in the 15th century
and completed in the 17th
century, St-Michel's façade
combines Flamboyant Gothic
with Renaissance details. On
the richly carved porch, angels
and biblical motifs mingle
with mythological themes.*

Musée Magnin
*A collection of French and
foreign 16th–19th-century
paintings are displayed
among period furniture in
this 17th-century mansion.*

Eglise St-Etienne dates
back to the 11th century
but has been rebuilt many
times. Its characteristic
lantern was added in 1686.

STAR SIGHTS

★ Palais des Ducs

★ Notre-Dame

★ St-Michel

KEY

– – – Suggested route

0 meters   100

0 yards   100

Well of Moses by Claus Sluter, in the Chartreuse de Champmol

Exploring Dijon

The center of Dijon is a warren of little streets well worth exploring. The rue des Forges, behind the Palais de Ducs, was the main street until the 18th century and is named after the jewelers and goldsmiths who had workshops there. The tourist office, housed in Hôtel Chambellan at No. 34, is Flamboyant Gothic with a stone spiral staircase and wooden galleries. At No. 38 the Maison Milsand, built in 1561, has a stone façade decorated by Hugues Sambin.

Rue Chaudronnerie has a number of houses of note, especially the Maison des Cariatides at No. 28, with ten fine stone-carved caryatids framing the windows. Place Darcy is lined with hotels and restaurants; the Jardin Darcy is delightful.

🏛 Musée des Beaux Arts

Place de la Ste-Chapelle. **📞** 03 80 74 52 70. **Open** Wed–Mon. **Closed** Jan 1, May 1, May 8, Jul 14, Nov 1 & 11, Dec 25. 🖼 ♿

Dijon's prestigious art collection is housed in the former Palais des Ducs (see p330). The Salle des Gardes on the first floor is dominated by the giant mausoleums of the dukes, with tombs sculpted by Claus Sluter (c.1345–1405). Other exhibits include two gilded Flemish retables and a portrait of Philip the Good by Rogier van der Weyden.

The art collection has many Dutch and Flemish masters and sculpture by Sluter and François Rude. There is also a large collection of Swiss and German primitives, 16th–18th century French paintings, and the Donation Granville of 19th- and 20th-century French art. Also note the vast ducal kitchens with six giant fireplaces, and the Tour Philippe le Bon, 46 m (150 ft) tall with a fine view of Burgundian tiled rooftops.

🔒 Cathédrale St-Benigne

Little remains of the 11th-century Benedictine abbey first founded in honor of St. Benigne, but beneath the Gothic church is a magnificent Romanesque crypt with a fine rotunda ringed by three circles of columns.

🏛 Musée Archéologique

5 rue du Docteur Maret. **📞** 03 80 30 88 54. **Open** Wed–Mon. **Closed** most public hols. 🖼

The museum is housed in the old dormitory of the Benedictine abbey of St-Benigne. The 11th-century chapterhouse, its stocky columns supporting a barrel-vaulted roof, houses a fine collection of Gallo-Roman sculpture. The ground floor, with its lovely fan vaulting, houses the famous head of Christ by Claus Sluter, originally from the Well of Moses.

⚜ Chartreuse de Champmol

1 bd Chanoine Kir. **Open** daily.

This was originally the site of a family necropolis built by Philip the Bold, destroyed during the Revolution. All that remains is a chapel doorway and the famous Well of Moses by Claus Sluter. It is now in the grounds of a psychiatric hospital east of Dijon train station, not very easy to find but definitely worth the effort. Despite its name, it is not a well, but a monument, its lower part probably originally surrounded by water. Sluter is renowned for his deeply cut carving, and this work, depicting six prophets, is exquisitely lifelike.

The tomb of Philip the Bold by Claus Sluter, now in the Salle des Gardes of the Musée des Beaux Arts

The Golden Age of Burgundy

WHILE THE FRENCH Capetian Dynasty fought in the Hundred Years' War *(see pp48–9)*, the dukes of Burgundy built up one of the most powerful states in Europe, which included Flanders and parts of Holland. From the time of Philip the Bold (1342–1404), the ducal court became a cultural force, supporting many of Europe's finest artists, such as painters Rogier Van der Weyden and the Van Eyck brothers and sculptor Claus Sluter. The duchy's dominions were, however, broken up after the death of Duke Charles the Bold in 1477.

The tomb of Philip the Bold in Dijon was made by the Flemish sculptor Claus Sluter, who was among the most brilliant artists of the Burgundian golden age. The dramatic realism of the mourners is one of the most striking features of this spectacular tomb, begun while the duke was still alive.

BURGUNDY IN 1477

▨ *Extent of the duchy at its peak*

THE MARRIAGE OF PHILIP THE GOOD

Philip the Good, duke from 1419–67, married Isabella of Portugal in 1430. This 17th-century copy of a painting by Van Eyck shows the sumptuous wedding feast, when Philip also inaugurated the chivalric Order of the Golden Fleece.

The dukes surrounded themselves with luxury, including fine gold and silverware.

Isabella of Portugal

The Duchess of Bedford, Philip's sister

Greyhounds were popular hunting animals at the Burgundian court.

Philip the Good is dressed in white ceremonial finery.

***Burgundian art**, such as this Franco-Flemish Book of Hours, reflected the Flemish origins of many of the dukes' favorite artists.*

***Dijon's Palais des Ducs** was rebuilt in 1450 by Philip the Good to reflect the glory of the Burgundian court, a center of art, chivalry and glorious feasts. Empty after Charles the Bold's death, it was reconstructed in the 17th century.*

Wine harvest in the vineyards of Nuits-St-Georges, part of the Côte d'Or district

Côte d'Or

Côte d'Or. 🚶 Dijon. 🚉 🚌 Dijon, Nuits-St-Georges, Beaune, Santenay. 🛈 Santenay (03 80 20 63 15: summer only); Beaune (03 80 26 21 30).

IN WINEMAKING TERMS, the Côte d'Or includes the Côte de Beaune and the Côte de Nuits in a nearly unbroken line of vines from Dijon to Santenay. Squeezed in between the flat plain of the Saône to the southeast and a plateau of rough woodland to the northwest, this narrow escarpment is about 50 km (30 miles) long. The grapes of the great Burgundy vineyards grow in the golden-reddish soil of the slope (hence the name).

The classification of the characteristics of the land is extremely technical and elaborate, but for the layman a rough rule of thumb might be that 95 percent of the best

Narrow street in Beaune's historic center

vines are on the uphill side of the N74 thoroughfare *(see pp310–11)*. The names on the signs haunt the dreams of wine lovers the world over: Gevrey-Chambertin, Vougeot, Chambolle-Musigny, Vosne-Romanée, Nuits-St-Georges, Aloxe-Corton, Meursault and Chassagne Montrachet.

Typical grape basket in the Musée du Vin de Bourgogne at Beaune

Beaune

Côte d'Or. 👥 22,000. 🚉 🚌 🛈 rue de l'Hôtel Dieu (03 80 26 21 30). 🛒 Sat & Wed.

THE OLD CENTER of Beaune, snug within its ramparts and encircling boulevards, is easy to explore on foot. Its indisputable treasure is the **Hôtel-Dieu** *(see pp336–7)*. The Hôtel des Ducs de Bourgogne, built in the 14th–16th centuries, houses the **Musée du Vin de Bourgogne**. The building, with its flamboyant façade, is as interesting as its display of traditional wine-making equipment.

Farther to the north lies the **Collégiale Notre-Dame**, begun in the early 12th century. Inside this mainly Romanesque church hang five very fine 15th-century woollen and silk tapestries. With hints

of early Renaissance style they delicately illustrate the life of the Virgin Mary in 19 scenes.

🏛 Musée du Vin de Bourgogne
Rue d'Enfer. 🕻 03 80 22 08 19.
Open Apr–Nov: daily; Dec–Mar: Wed–Mon. 🗓 ♿ ground floor only.

Tournus

Saône-et-Loire. 👥 7,400. 🚉 🚌 🛈 place Carnot (03 85 51 13 10). 🛒 Sat.

ONE OF BURGUNDY'S oldest and greatest Romanesque buildings is found in Tournus. The **Abbaye de St-Philibert** was founded by a group of monks from Noirmoutier who had been driven from their island by invading Normans in the 9th century, taking with them relics of their patron saint, Philibert. Rebuilt in the 10th–12th centuries, the well-fortified abbey church is made from lovely pale-pink stone.

Dovecote in Cormatin château gardens, Mâconnais

Nave of St-Philibert in Tournus

A narthex leads into the nave with its soaring pillars and black and white vaulting. The bones of St. Philibert can be seen in the choir, while in the niche on the south side is a 12th-century wood carving of Notre-Dame-la-Brune.

Environs
Southwest of Tournus lies the Mâconnais landscape of hills, vineyards, orchards, red-tiled farmhouses and Romanesque churches. **Brancion** is a pretty hill village; **Chapaize** has an 11th-century church; and there is a sumptuous Renaissance château at **Cormatin**. The village of **Taizé** is the center of a world-famous ecumenical community. To the north, **Chalon-sur-Saône** features old quarters and the Musée Niepce dedicated to the inventor of photography.

Cluny ㉒

Saône-et-Loire. ♔ 4,400. 🚗 ℹ 6 rue Mercière (03 85 59 05 34). 🚌 Sat.

T HE LITTLE TOWN of Cluny is overshadowed by the ruins of its great abbey. The **Ancienne Abbaye de Cluny** was once the most powerful monastic foundation in Europe (see pp44–5).

The abbey was founded by William the Pious, Duke of Aquitaine in 910. Within 200 years, Cluny had become the head of a major reforming order with monasteries all over Europe. Its abbots were considered as powerful as monarchs or popes, and four of them are

venerated as saints. By the 14th century, however, the system was in decline. The abbey was closed in 1790 and the church was later dismantled for building materials.

The guided tour presents the abbey remains, notably the Clocher de l'Eau Bénite (Holy Water Bell Tower), **Musée d'Art**, housed in the former abbot's palace, and its figured capitals displayed in the 13th-century flour storage. In town, don't miss the 12th-century **Eglise St-Marcel**.

Southwest of town, the chapel in **Berzé-la-Ville** is decorated with superb 12th-century frescoes, similar to those once seen at Cluny.

🏠 Ancienne Abbaye de Cluny
📞 03 85 59 12 79. **Open** daily. **Closed** Mar 1, May 1, Nov 11, Dec 25. 🖼️

🏛 Musée d'Art
Palais Jean de Bourbon. 📞 03 85 59 23 97. **Open** daily. **Closed** Jan 1, May 1, Nov 1 & 11, Dec 25. 🖼️ 🔵

Paray-le-Monial ㉓

Saône-et-Loire. ♔ 10,500. 🚗 🚉 ℹ 25 av Jean-Paul II (03 85 81 10 92). 🚌 Fri.

D EDICATED to the cult of the Sacred Heart of Jesus, the **Basilique du Sacré-Coeur** has made Paray-le-Monial one of the most important sites of pilgrimage in modern-day France. The cult was founded by Marguerite-Marie Alacoque who was born here in 1647, but it didn't develop until the 19th century. The church is a small version of the now lost abbey church of Cluny and features extraordinary harmony and purity in its Romanesque architecture.

The **Musée de la Faïence** in the cloister contains some remarkable examples of 19th-century Charolles porcelain with pastoral decorations.

Situated on place Guignaud is the ornate **Maison Jayet**, dating from the 16th century, which houses the town hall.

Basilique du Sacré-Coeur at Paray-le-Monial

Hôtel-Dieu

Christ-de-Pitié

AFTER THE HUNDRED Years' War, many of Beaune's inhabitants suffered the effects of poverty and famine. To remedy this, the chancellor, Nicolas Rolin, and his wife founded a hospice here in 1443, which was inspired by the architecture of Northern French hospitals. The Rolins provided an annual grant, and vines and saltworks for income. Today the hospice is considered a medieval jewel, with its superb geometric multi-colored Burgundian roof tiles. It houses two religious masterpieces: the *Christ-de-Pitié* statue, carved from wood, and Rogier van der Weyden's polyptych.

★ **Great Hall of the Poor**
The hall, with its carved, painted roof, has 28 four-poster beds, each one often used by several patients at a time. Meals were served from central tables.

Tribute to Rolin's Wife
A recurring motif features the entwined letters N and G, birds and stars, and the word "Seulle" referring to Rolin's wife Guigone, his "one and only."

Saint Hugues' Room
contains a painting of the saint curing two children. Frescoes by Isaac Moillon show the miracles of Christ.

Entrance

Saint Anne's Room has a tableau of nuns working in what was once the linen room, and a colorful feast-day tapestry.

ANNUAL CHARITY WINE AUCTION

On the third Sunday in November, Beaune's annual charity auction is the centerpiece of three days of festivities known as *Les Trois Glorieuses*. The banquet of the Con- frérie des Chevaliers du Tastevin is held on Saturday at the Château Clos de Vougeot. On Sunday the auction of wine from 151 acres of vineyards owned by nearby hospitals takes place. Its prices are the benchmark for the entire vintage. On Monday at La Paulée de Meursault there is a party where growers bring along bottles of their best vintages to enjoy.

Wine sold at the famous auction

STAR FEATURES

★ **Great Hall**

★ **Last Judgment Polyptych by Rogier van der Weyden**

Kitchen
The centerpiece of the kitchen is a Gothic fireplace with a dual hearth and a mechanical spit, made in 1698, which is turned by a wooden "robot."

VISITORS' CHECKLIST

Rue de L'Hôtel-Dieu, Beaune.
☎ 03 80 24 45 00. **Open**
Apr–mid-Nov: 9–6:30pm daily;
Dec–Mar: 9–11:30 am, 2–5pm
daily. 🖼 🎥 ✔
Wine Auction Les Halles
de Beaune (03 80 24 45 00).
Date 3rd Sunday in Nov.

Cour d'Honneur
The buildings of Hôtel-Dieu are arranged around a splendid central courtyard. This is flanked by a wooden gallery, above which rise high dormer windows topped by weather-vanes. The courtyard well is a fine example of Gothic wrought-iron work.

Glazed roof tiles, in a colorful geometric pattern, are the most dramatic feature of the Hôtel-Dieu.

Pharmacy
Such unusual potions as woodlouse powder, shrimps' eyes and vomit nut powder are stored in these Nevers pots. Nearby is a bronze mortar used to prepare the remedies.

St. Louis' Room

★ Last Judgment Polyptych
The naked figures shown in Rogier van der Weyden's 15th-century polyptych were briefly given clothing in the 19th century. At the same time, the altarpiece was cut in half so that the outer and inner panels could be seen together.

Château de Pierreclos in the Mâconnais region

Brionnais

Saône-et-Loire. ⚡ Mâcon.
▣ Paray-le-Monial, La Clayette.
▣ Paray-le-Monial, Anzy-le-Duc.
▪ Marcigny (03 85 25 39 06).

THE BRIONNAIS is a small and peaceful rural district, squeezed between the Loire River and the Beaujolais foothills in the far south of Burgundy.

Its agricultural staple is the white Charolais cow, which can be seen grazing everywhere. For a closer look at this regional symbol, visit the lively cattle market in **St-Christophe** early on Thursday mornings.

The area has an abundance of Romanesque churches, most of which are built of the local ocher-colored stone. The 11th-century church of **Anzy-le-Duc** has a majestic

Capital in St-Julien-de-Jonzy

three-tiered polygonal tower and exquisitely carved capitals. **Semur-en-Brionnais** was the birthplace of Cluny's famous abbot, St. Hugues. Its church is inspired by his great monastery. The church at **St-Julien-de-Jonzy** has a very finely carved tympanum.

A small town by the Genette River, **La Clayette** is graced by a château set in a lake. It is not open to the public, but has a vintage car museum and in summer is the setting for a son et lumière show.

Southeast of La Clayette the lonely **Montagne de Dun** rises just over 700 m (2,300 ft) and offers a panorama over the gentle, green Brionnais hills. This is some of the best picnic country in Burgundy, full of sleepy corners and quiet byways.

Mâcon ㉕

Saône-et-Loire. ⚡ 38,000. ▨ ▣
▣ ▪ 1 pl Saint Pierre (03 85 21 07 07). ▤ Sat.

AT THE FRONTIER between Burgundy and the south, Mâcon is an industrial town and wine center on the Saône.

The lack of churches is due to fervent anti-clericalism during the Revolution, when 14 were destroyed. A 17th-century convent has been turned into the **Musée des Ursulines**. Its collections include French and Flemish painting and an exhibition on the prehistoric site of Solutré. On the charming place aux Herbes, where the market is held, the **Maison de Bois** is a 15th-century wooden house covered with bizarre carvings.

🏛 **Musée des Ursulines**
Allée de Matisco. ▮ 03 85 39 90 38. **Open** Tue–Sat, Sun am. **Closed** most public hols. 🎟

Environs
The great **Roche de Solutré** rises dramatically above the Pouilly-Fuissé vineyards in the Mâconnais district (see p335). Below the rock, bones and flints from the Stone Ages have established it as an important archaeological site.

Mâconnais is also the land of the Romantic poet Lamartine (1790–1869). Born in Mâcon, he spent his childhood at Milly Lamartine and later lived at Château de St-Point. **Château de Pierreclos** is associated with his epic poem *Jocelyn*.

Charolais cattle grazing on the gentle hills of the Brionnais

Franche-Comté

A REGION OF WOODS and water, the Franche-Comté offers exceptional natural beauty combined with opportunities for canoeing, hiking and skiing. In addition to its interesting towns, this is a region to explore in the wild. Glorious scenery with grottoes and waterfalls are found all along the Vallée du Doubs. Farther south are the spectacular sources of the Lison and Loue rivers. The Reculées is an area of extraordinary formations of ridges and waterfalls such as Baume-les-Messieurs. In Région des Lacs, the silent, peaceful lakes are surrounded by mountain peaks and virgin forests.

Cascades du Hérisson ㉖

Pays-des-Lacs. 🛈 Clairvaux-les-Lacs (03 84 25 27 47).

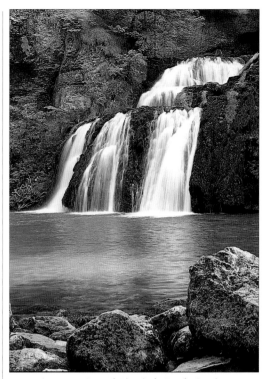

Nature at its purest at Source du Lison in the Franche-Comté

THE VILLAGE of Doucier, at the foot of the Pic de l'Aigle, is the start of the Hérisson River valley, one of the finest natural settings in the Jura. Park the car by the Moulin Jacquand windmill and walk up the trail through the woods to a spectacular waterfall, the 65-m (213-ft) Cascade de L'Eventail, and beyond to the equally impressive Cascade du Grand Saut. The walk, which takes about two hours there and back, is steep at times, and can be slippery so proper shoes are essential.

Arbois ㉗

Jura. 🏠 4,000. 🚌 🚆 🛈 10 rue de l'Hôtel de Ville (03 84 66 55 50). 🅿 Fri.

THE WINE TOWN of Arbois lies on the vine-covered banks of the Cuisance River. It is famous for its wines, especially the sherrylike *vin jaune* (yellow wine) of the district. On the north side of

the town is **Maison de Pasteur**, the preserved house and laboratory of the great practical scientist Louis Pasteur (1822–95), the first to test vaccines on humans.

Environs

Southeast of Dole is the 18th-century **Château d'Arlay**, with immaculately kept gardens

Dole ㉘

Jura. 🏠 27,000. 🚌 🚆 🛈 6 pl Grevy (03 84 72 11 22). 🅿 Tue, Thu & Sat.

THE BUSY TOWN of Dole lies where the Doubs meets the Rhine-Rhône Canal. The former capital of the Comté was always a symbol of the region's resistance to the French. The region had become used to relative independence under the Counts of Burgundy and then as part of the Holy Roman Empire. Though always French-speaking, its people did not appreciate the idea of the French absolute

monarchy and in 1636 endured a very long siege. The town finally submitted to Louis XIV first in 1668 and again in 1674.

There is a charming historic quarter in the center of town, full of winding alleys, houses dating back to the 15th century, and quiet inner courtyards. Place aux Fleurs offers an excellent view of this part of town and the mossy-roofed, 16th-century **Eglise Notre-Dame** with its high bell tower.

Virgin and Child on the north portal of Eglise Notre-Dame, Dole

The Saline Royale at Arc-et-Senans

Arc-et-Senans

Doubs. 1,300.
03 81 57 43 21.

DESIGNATED a world heritage site since 1982, the Saline Royale (royal salt works) at Arc-et-Senans were designed by the great French architect Claude-Nicolas Ledoux (1736–1806). He envisaged a development built in concentric circles around the main buildings. However, the only ones to be completed (in 1775) were the buildings used for salt production. Nevertheless, these show the staggering scale of Ledoux's idea: saltwater was to be piped from Salins-les-Bains nearby, and fuel to reduce it was to come from the Chaux Forest. The enterprise, which was never a financial success, was closed down in 1895, but the terrific buildings remain.

The **Musée Ledoux Lieu du Sel** displays intriguing models of the grand projects imagined by the visionary architect.

Musée Ledoux Lieu du Sel
Ancienne Saline Royale.
03 81 54 45 00. *Open daily.*
Closed Jan 1, Dec 25.

Champlitte

Haute Saône. 1,900. *La Mairie (03 84 67 68 78).*

AT A TIME when the rural farm life of the French countryside is fast disappearing, the **Musée des Arts et Traditions Populaires** in the small town of Champlitte has a special relevance. This museum of folk arts and

traditions (in a Renaissance château) was created by a local shepherd who collected objects and artifacts connected with disappearing local customs. One of the most poignant displays recalls the emigration of 400 inhabitants to Mexico in the mid-19th century.

Musée des Arts et Traditions Populaires
Place de l'Eglise. 03 84 67 82 00.
Open Jun–Aug: daily; Sep–May: Wed–Mon. *Closed* Jan 1, Nov 1, Dec 25.

Besançon

Doubs. 120,000.
2 place de la 1re Armée Française (03 81 80 92 55). Tue, Fri & Sun.

BESANÇON supplanted Dole as the capital of the Franche-Comté in the 17th century. It began as an ecclesiastical center and is now an industrial one, specializing in precision engineering. The stately architecture of the old town, often enriched with elegant wrought-iron work, is a 17th-century legacy.

A walk along the Grande Rue reveals varying aspects of the town's past. The **Palais Granvelle**, built for the Chancellor of the Holy Roman Emperor in 1534–42, has a beautiful Renaissance façade. Farther on are the birthplaces of the titanic novelist Victor Hugo (1802–85) at No. 140 and the Lumière brothers (*see p59*) at place Victor Hugo. Behind **Porte Noire**, a Roman arch, is the 12th-century Cathédrale St-Jean. In its bell tower is the extraordinary **Horloge Astronomique**, a

true symbol of Besançon's watchmaking past. Try to be there on the hour, when the figures pop out of the clock as if by magic.

The stunning **Musée des Beaux Arts et d'Archéologie** occupies the old corn market. Its collection includes works by Bellini, Cranach, Rubens, Fragonard, Boucher, Greuse, Ingres, Courbet, David, Goya, Matisse and Picasso.

Vauban's citadel, built on a strategic site overlooking the Doubs River, offers magnificent views and houses the intriguing **Musée Comtoise**, with a collection of local artifacts.

Horloge Astronomique
Rue de la Convention. 03 81 81 12 76. *Open* Apr–Sep: Wed–Mon; Oct–Dec, Feb–Mar: Thu–Mon. *Closed* Jan, May 1, Nov 1 & 11, Dec 25.

Musée des Beaux Arts et d'Archéologie
1 pl de la Révolution. 03 81 82 39 39. *Open* Wed–Mon. *Closed* Jan 1, May 1, Nov 1 & Dec 25. except Sun.

Musée Comtois
Rue des Fusillés de la Résistance, La Citadelle. 03 81 65 07 44. *Open daily. Closed* Jan 1, Dec 25.

The fantastic astronomical clock in Besançon, made in 1857–60

Ornans

Doubs. 4,300. *7 rue Pierre Vernier (03 81 62 21 50).*

THE GREAT Realist painter Gustave Courbet was born in Ornans in 1819. He painted the town in every possible light. His *Enterrement à Ornans* proved to be one of the most influential paintings

The striking Chapelle Notre-Dame-du-Haut by Le Corbusier at Ronchamp

of the 19th century. A stream of Courbet enthusiasts makes the pilgrimage to this delightful riverside town to see his grave and the paintings in his childhood home, now turned into the **Musée Courbet.**

🏛 Musée Courbet

Place Robert Fernier. 📞 03 81 62 23 30. **Open** Apr–Oct: daily; Nov–Mar: Wed–Mon. **Closed** Jan 1, May 1, Nov 1, Dec 25. 🖼

Environs
A canoeist's paradise, the **Vallée de la Loue** is the loveliest in the Jura. The D67 follows the river from Ornans eastward to Ouhans; from there it is only a 15-minute walk to its magnificent source. Various belvederes offer splendid views over the area.

Southwest of Ornans, the spectacular **Source du Lison** (*see p339*) is a 20-minute walk from Nans-sous-Ste-Anne.

Belfort ❸

Territoire de Belfort. 🏘 52,000. 🚉 🚌 🛈 2 bis rue Clemenceau (03 84 55 90 90). 🛒 daily.

THE SYMBOL of Belfort is an enormous pink sandstone lion. It was built (rather than carved) by Frédéric Bartholdi

(1834–1904), whose other major undertaking was the Statue of Liberty.

Belfort's immensely strong **citadel**, designed by Vauban under Louis XIV, withstood three sieges, in 1814, 1815 and 1870. Today this remarkable array of fortifications provides an interesting walk and extensive views of the surroundings. The **Musée d'Art et d'Histoire**, housed in some of the billets, displays models of the original fortifications as well as regional art and artifacts and contemporary exhibitions.

Ronchamp ❸

Haute Saône. 🏘 3,100. 🚌 🛈 place du 14 juillet (Apr–Nov: 03 84 63 50 82). 🛒 Sat.

LE COURBUSIER'S remarkable Chapelle Notre-Dame-du-Haut dominates this former miners' town. A sculpture rather than a building, its swelling concrete form was finalized in 1955. Light, shape and space form a successful unity in the interior.

There is also the **Musée de la Mine,** evoking the industry and the life of local miners.

Le Miroir d'Ornans in the Musée Courbet, Ornans

THE MASSIF CENTRAL

ALLIER · AVEYRON · CANTAL · CORRÈZE · CREUSE · HAUTE-LOIRE
HAUTE-VIENNE · LOZÈRE · PUY DE DÔME

THE MASSIF CENTRAL *is the keystone of France, holding the country together by the sheer force of its grandeur. It is surprisingly little known beyond its sprinkling of spas and the major cities of Clermont-Ferrand, Vichy and Limoges. This remarkable, remote and rugged region is one of France's best-kept secrets.*

The huge central plateau of ancient granite and crystalline rock that makes up the Massif Central embraces the dramatic landscapes of the Auvergne, Limousin, Aveyron and Lozère. Once a testing crossroads for pilgrims, and strung with giant volcanoes, it is a region of unsuspected richness, from the spectacular town of Le Puy-en-Velay, to the unique treasures of Conques.

With its crater lakes and hot springs, the Auvergne is the Massif Central's lush volcanic core, an outdoor paradise offering activities from hiking in summer to skiing in winter. It also has some of France's most beautiful Romanesque churches, medieval castles and Renaissance palaces. To the east are the mountain ranges of Forez, Livardois and Velay; to the west are the giant chains of extinct volcanoes – the Monts Dômes, Monts Dore and the Monts du Cantal. The Limousin, on the northwestern edge of the Massif Central, is gentler country, with green pastures and blissfully empty roads.

The Aveyron spreads into the southwest from the Aubrac Mountains, carrying with it the Lot, Aveyron and Tarn rivers through gorges and valleys with their cliffhanging villages. To the east in the Lozère are the Grands Causses, the vast, isolated uplands of the Cévennes. These barren plateaus give farmers a poor living, but have been a favorite place for adventurous travelers throughout the centuries.

La Bourboule, a spa town in the Monts Dore

◁ **The summit of Puy Mary, 1,787 m (5,863 ft), offering a superb view to walkers who attempt the ascent**

Exploring the Massif Central

NATURE IS AT ITS MOST MAGNIFICENT in the volcanic mountain ranges and wild river gorges of the Massif Central. This is a vast and unspoiled territory that offers spectacular sightseeing and every imaginable outdoor activity, with rafting, paragliding, canoeing and hiking among the many choices. There are hundreds of churches, châteaux and museums to nourish lovers of history, architecture and art; and good, hearty regional cooking and wonderful local wines for lovers of good living.

KEY

▬▬	Highway
▬▬	Major road
▬▬	Minor road
▬▬	Scenic route
∿	River
☆	Viewing point

0 kilometers   25

0 miles   25

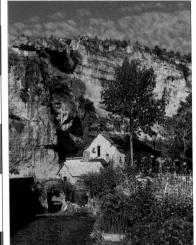

Limestone cliffs of the Gorges du Tarn

GETTING AROUND

There is good air and rail service connecting Paris with the major towns of Limoges, Clermont-Ferrand and Vichy. Within the region, many of the most interesting towns and sights are easily accessible only by car. Clermont-Ferrand, Issoire and Thiers are all close to major autoroutes, and Limoges to a good national road, the N20. Most minor roads are well kept, but allow for slow driving in the mountains. A few roads are vertiginous, especially the road to the summit of Puy Mary, which is breathtaking.

To Poitiers

LIMOGES

AUBUSSON

UZERCHE

TULLE

TURENNE

COLLONGES-LA-ROUGE

CONQ

To Toulouse Carcassonne

To Orléans

MOULINS ④

MONTLUÇON ③

CHÂTEAU DE LAPALISSE ⑤

VICHY ⑥

RIOM

MONTS DÔMES ⑫

CLERMONT-FERRAND ⑩

THIERS ⑦

ORCIVAL ⑪

ST-NECTAIRE ⑨

MONTS DORE ⑬

ISSOIRE ⑧

PARC NATUREL RÉGIONAL LIVRADOIS-FOREZ

PARC NATUREL RÉGIONAL DES VOLCANS D'AUVERGNE

LA CHAISE-DIEU ⑲

To St-Etienne Lyon

SALERS ⑰

MONTS DU CANTAL ⑱

AURILLAC

Gorges de la Truyère

LE PUY-EN-VELAY ⑳

VALLÉE DU LOT ㉑

RODEZ ㉓

MENDE

GORGES DU TARN ㉖

PARC NATIONAL DES CÉVENNES

To Avignon

CORNICHE DES CÉVENNES ㉔

MILLAU

GRANDS CAUSSES ㉕

To Montpellier

Fall view of the foothills of Puy Mary in the Monts du Cantal

IE NY SCAY QVEL REMEDDE METT
RE AVX OVELLES PVSSAYGE
COVRIR TOVES NE LES PVIS SE
COVRIS MIEVX MEVLT VALVT
DEVX ME DEMETRE
1577.

A Limoges enamel plaque, The Bad Shepherd

Limoges ❶

Haute-Vienne. 🏛 *140,000.* ✈ 🚍
🚌 **i** *bd de Fleurus (05 55 34 46 87).*
🛏 *daily.*

THE CAPITAL of the Limousin
has two hearts: the old
Cité, which grew up around
the cathedral on a plateau
overlooking the Vienne River,
and the rival château on an
adjacent rise, now the commercial center of the modern
city. The Cité was ravaged by
the Black Prince in 1370
during the Hundred Years'
War and never recovered;
today, it is a quiet place to
wander among half-timbered
houses and narrow streets.

The area was famous for
enamelwork in the Middle Ages
and Renaissance period, but it
was not until the 1770s, when
kaolin deposits were discovered
nearby, that Limoges became
synonymous with porcelain.
The legendary local ware is on
display at the superb **Musée
National Adrien-Dubouché**.
More than 10,000 exhibits, including early Greek and
Chinese pieces, trace the history of ceramics to the present

day. The **Musée Municipal
de l'Evêché** houses some 500
Limousin enamels.

🏛 Musée National Adrien-Dubouché

Place Winston Churchill.
【 *05 55 33 08 50.* **Open** *Wed–Mon.*
Closed *Jan 1, May 1, Dec 25.* 🈲

🏛 Musée Municipal de l'Evêché

Place de la Cathédrale. 【 *05 55 45
61 75.* **Open** *Jul, Aug: daily; Oct–Jun:
Wed–Mon.* **Closed** *Jan 1, May 1,
Nov 1 & 11, Dec 25.*

Environs

Intense Resistance activity in
the Limousin during World
War II led to severe reprisals
by the occupying army. On
June 10, 1944, at the village
of Oradour-sur-Glane, SS
troops burned alive the entire
population of 650. The ruins
have been kept as a shrine,
and a new village built next
to them. The lively town of
St-Junien, a glove-making
center since the Middle Ages,
has an intriguing 11th-century
church (the Collégiale St-
Junien) containing a statue of
Sainte Madeleine clothed entirely in her own blonde hair.

Aubusson ❷

Creuse. 🏛 *6,000.* 🚍 🚌 **i** *rue
Vieille (05 55 66 32 12).* 🛏 *Sat.*

AUBUSSON OWES its renown
to the exceptionally pure
waters of the Creuse, perfect
for making the delicately
colored dyes used for
tapestries and rugs. Tapestry
production was at its zenith in
the 16th and 17th centuries,
but by the end of the 18th
century, the Revolution and
patterned wallpaper had
swept away the clientele.

In the 1940s, Aubusson was
revived, largely due to the
artist Jean Lurçat, who persuaded other modern artists
to design for tapestry. The
**Musée Departemental de la
Tapisserie**, across the river
from the Old Town, displays
a permanent collection of these
modern works. Visitors are
welcome at the **Manufacture
St. Jean**, where they may
watch tapestries and custom-
made carpets being expertly
restored and made by hand.

🏛 Musée Departemental de la Tapisserie

Avenue des Lissiers. 【 *05 55 66 33
06.* **Open** *Wed–Mon.* 🈲 🈺

🏛 Manufacture St. Jean

3 rue St. Jean. 【 *05 55 66 10 08.*
Open *Mar–Oct: daily; Nov–Feb:
Mon–Fri.* **Closed** *Dec 23–Jan 1.* 🈲

Environs

A single street of 15th-century
houses and a Roman bridge
comprise **Moûtier-d'Ahun**,

**Tapestry restoration at the
Manufacture St. Jean in Aubusson**

Romanesque church at Moûtier-d'Ahun near Aubusson

tucked into the lush Creuse Valley. Vestiges of a Benedictine abbey still remain in the half-Romanesque, half-Gothic church with its elaborate stone portal. The choir has wooden stalls, for which it is worth paying a visit to the church. They are masterpieces of late 17th-century carving with intricately worked motifs of flora and fauna representing the different facets of Good and Evil in figurative form. There is a garden where the nave once was.

Montluçon ❸

Allier. 👥 *45,000.* ✈ 🚋 🚌 🛈 *5 Place Piquand (04 70 05 11 44).* 🛒 *Sat.*

MONTLUÇON is the economic center of the region, a small town with a medieval core. At its heart there is a Bourbon château. The **Musée des Instruments et des Musiques**, previously housed in the château, has closed for renovation. The **Musée d'Arts Décoratifs et Beaux Arts** has 19th- and 20th-century prints by local artists as well as displays of regional faïence. The 12th-century **Eglise de St-Pierre** is a surprise, with giant stone columns and a huge barrel-vaulted ceiling.

🏛 **Musée des Instruments et des Musiques Populaires**
Château des Ducs de Bourbon.
🅲 *04 70 02 56 57.* **Open** *Wed–Mon.*
Closed *public hols.*

Moulins ❹

Allier. 👥 *23,000.* 🚋 🚌 🛈 *place de l'Hôtel de Ville (04 70 44 14 14).* 🛒 *Tue & Fri.*

CAPITAL of the Bourbonnais and seat of the Bourbon Dukes since the 10th century, Moulins flourished during the early Renaissance and is now an appealing backwater.

Moulins' most celebrated sight is the Flamboyant Gothic **Cathédrale Notre-Dame**, where members of the Bourbon court appear amid the saints in the 15th- and 16th-century stained-glass windows.

The treasury contains a luminous 15th-century Virgin and Child triptych by the "Master of Moulins." Benefactors Pierre II, Duke of Bourbon, and his wife, Anne de Beaujeu, bedecked in embroidery and jewels, are shown being introduced to a less richly dressed Madonna in the central panel.

The tower keep and the single remaining wing of the Bourbon **Vieux Château** house a superb collection of sculpture, paintings and decorative art from the 12th to the 16th centuries.

🔒 **Cathédrale Notre-Dame**
Rue Louis Mantin. **Treasury open** *summer: daily.* 🎟 **Closed** *winter: Sun.*

Stained-glass windows at the Cathédrale Notre-Dame in Moulins

Château de Lapalisse ❺

Allier. ☎ 04 70 99 37 58, 04 70 55 01 12. **Open** Easter–Oct: Wed–Mon. 🖼️

IN THE EARLY 16th century, the Marshal of France, Jacques II de Chabannes, hired Florentine architects to reconstruct the feudal château-fort in Lapalisse, creating a refined Renaissance castle, inhabited ever since by his descendants. The *salon doré* (gilded room) has a beamed ceiling paneled in gold, and two huge 15th-century Flemish tapestries showing the Crusader Knight Godefroy de Bouillon and Greek hero Hector, two of the nine classic braves of chivalric legend.

Environs
From Lapalisse, the D480 leads up through the beautiful Besbre Valley past a handful of other small, well-preserved châteaux. Only **Château de Thoury**, with ancient hunting memorabilia and *objets d'art* on display, is open to the public.

♣ Château de Thoury
Dompierre. ☎ 04 70 42 00 41. **Open** Apr–Oct: daily. 🖼️ 🚫 restricted.

Gilded ceiling, Château de Lapalisse

Vichy ❻

Allier. 🏙️ 26,000. 🚆 🚌 🛈 19 rue du Parc (04 70 98 71 94). 🛒 Wed.

THIS SMALL CITY on the Allier River has been known since the Roman era for its hot and cold springs, and reputed cures for rheumatism, arthritis and digestive complaints. The celebrated letter-writer Madame de Sévigné and the daughters of Louis XV came here in the late 17th and 18th centuries – the former compared the showers to "a rehearsal for Purgatory." The

Interior of the original Thermal Establishment building in Vichy

visits of Napoleon III in the 1860s put Vichy on the map and made taking the waters fashionable. The small town was spruced up and became a favorite among the French nobility and the world's wealthy middle classes. These days, the grand old Thermal Establishment, built in 1900, has been turned into a shopping center The modern baths are state-of-the-art and

Vichy poster (about 1930–50) by Badia-Vilato

strictly for medical purposes. A doctor's prescription and a reservation 30 days in advance are required for all aquatic treatments.

Vichy's fortunes changed for the better once again in the 1960s with the damming of the Allier, creating a huge lake in the town center. Vichy soon became a thriving center for watersports and international events. For a small fee, you can have a taste of sports from aikido to water-skiing or learn canoeing on the 3-km-long (2-mile) artificial river.

The focal point of life in Vichy is the **Parc des Sources** in the center of town, with its turn-of-the-century bandstand (afternoon concerts in season), Belle Epoque glass-roofed shopping centers, and the Grand Casino and Opera House. Here there is gambling every afternoon and musical performances in the evenings, and an atmosphere of gaiety pervades. Also open to the public are the beautiful bronze taps of the **Source**

Celestin, in a riverside park containing vestiges of a convent bearing the same name. Only by making an effort to imagine the city in grainy black-and-white newsreel style is there the slightest reminder of the wartime Vichy government which was based in the town from 1940–44 *(see p61)*.

🌿 **Source Celestin**
Boulevard Kennedy.
Open daily. ♿

Thiers ❼

Puy de Dôme. 🏠 *15,000.* 🚉 🚌
ℹ️ *Maison de Pirou (04 73 80 65 65).*
🛒 *Thu & Sat.*

ACCORDING TO the writer La Bruyère, Thiers "seems painted on the slope of the hill," hanging dramatically as it does on a ravine over a sharp bend in the Durolle River. The city has been renowned for cutlery since the Middle Ages, when legend has it that Crusaders brought back techniques of metalwork from the Middle East. With grindstones powered by dozens of waterfalls on the opposite bank of the river, Thiers produced everything from table knives to guillotine blades, and cutlery remains its major industry today, much of it on display in the Cutlery Museum, the **Musée de la Coutellerie**.

The Old Town is filled with mysterious quarters like "the Corner of Chance" and "Hell's Hollow," honeycombed with tortuous streets and well-restored 15th–17th-century houses. Many have elaborately-carved wooden façades, like the Maison du Pirou in place

PILGRIMAGES AND OSTENSIONS

Parishes in the Auvergne and the Limousin are renowned for honoring their saints in outdoor processions. Ascension Day sees the Virgin of Orcival carried above the village by night, accompanied by gypsies and their children for baptism. Every seven years a score of villages in the Limousin hold *Ostensions*, when the saints' relics are paraded through the streets into the surrounding woods. The *Ostension* season begins the Sunday after Easter and runs until June. The next event in the seven-year cycle will be held in 2002.

The Virgin of Orcival, carried in procession above the village (1903)

Pirou. The view to the west from the rampart terrace, toward the Monts Dômes and the Monts Dore, is often splendid at sunset.

🏛️ **Musée de la Coutellerie**
Maison des Coutelliers, 21–23 & 58 rue de la Coutellerie. 📞 *04 73 80 58 86.* **Open** *Jun–Sep: daily; Oct–May: Tue–Sun.* **Closed** *Jan 1, May 1, Sep 14, Nov 1, Dec 25.* 📷

Issoire ❽

Puy de Dôme. 🏠 *15,000.* 🚉
ℹ️ *place du Général de Gaulle (04 73 89 15 90).* 🛒 *Sat.*

MOST OF OLD ISSOIRE was destroyed in the 17th-century Wars of Religion. The present-day town has been an important industrial center

since the end of World War II. Not only does Issoire have a thriving aeronautical tradition, it is also a mecca for glider pilots, who come from miles around to take advantage of the strong local air currents.

One of the few relics of old Issoire, the colorful 12th-century abbey church of **St-Austremoine** is one of the great Romanesque churches of the region. The capitals depict scenes from the *Life of Christ* (one of the Apostles at the Last Supper has fallen asleep at the table), or imaginary demons and beasts. The 15th-century fresco of the *Last Judgment* shows Bosch-like figures of sinners being cast into the mouth of a dragon, with one damsel being carted off to hell in a handbasket.

Thiers from the south, spreading over the slopes above the Durolle River

St-Nectaire ⑨

Puys de Dôme. 🏠 650. 🔄 ℹ️ *Les Grandes Thermes (04 73 88 50 86).*

THE AUVERGNE is noted for Romanesque churches. The **Eglise St-Nectaire** in the upper village of St-Nectaire-le Haut, with its soaring, elegant proportions, is one of the most beautiful. The 103 stone capitals, 22 of them poly-chrome, are vividly carved, and the treasury includes a gold bust of St. Baudime and a wooden Notre-Dame-de-Mont-Cornadore, both marvels of 12th-century work-manship. The lower village, St-Nectaire-le-Bas, is a spa with more than 40 hot and cold springs, used in the treatment of kidney and meta-bolic problems.

Environs
The 12th-century citadel of **Château de Murol**, partially in ruins, offers costumed guides demonstrating medieval life and knightly pursuits. It is wonderful for children.

🏰 Château de Murol
Murol. 🅲 *04 73 88 67 11.* **Open** *Apr–Sep: daily; Oct–Mar: Sat, Sun & school hols.* 🈺

Fontaine d'Amboise (1515) in Clermont-Ferrand

Clermont-Ferrand ⑩

Puy de Dôme. 🏠 140,000. ✈️ 🔄 🔄 ℹ️ *place de la Victoire (04 73 98 65 00).* 🔄 *Mon–Sat.*

CLERMONT-FERRAND began as two distinct – and rival – cities, united only in 1630. Clermont is a lively and bust-ling commercial center and student town, with thriving cafés and restaurants. It was a Celtic settlement before the Roman era, had a cathedral as early as the 5th century, and by 1095 was significant enough for the pope to announce the First Crusade there. The Counts of Auvergne, challenging the episcopal power of Clermont, established their base in what is now old Montferrand, a short drive from Clermont city center. Built on a bastide pattern *(see p435)*, this is a time warp of quiet streets and Renaissance houses.

Place St-Pierre is Clermont's principal marketplace, with a daily food market that is especially good on Saturdays. Nearby, the **Fontaine d'Amboise** (1515), a tiered fantasy in black lava, looks out to the Puy de Dôme peak. The pedestrianized rue du Port, lined with small shops, leads steeply downhill from the fountain to the **Basilique Notre-Dame-du-Port**. This is one of the most important Romanesque churches in the region. The stone interior is beautifully proportioned, with a magnifi-cent raised choir and vivid carved capitals – look for Largesse battling Avarice, in the form of two knights with chain mail and pikes.

The contrast with the black lava **Cathédrale de Notre-Dame-de-l'Assomption** is startling, from austere 12th-century Romanesque to high-flying 13th-century Gothic.

Raised choir in the Basilique Notre-Dame-du-Port

CLERMONT CITY CENTER

Basilique Notre-
 Dame-du-Port ③
Cathédrale de Notre-
 Dame-de-
 l'Assomption ④
Fontaine
 d'Amboise ②
Place St-Pierre ①

KEY

🅿 Parking

ℹ Tourist information

✛ Church

0 meters   250

0 yards   250

The graceful lines of the interior are due to the strong local stone used for construction, allowing pillars to be thinner and the whole structure lighter. The dark volcanic rock provides a foil for the jewel-like 12th–15th-century stained-glass windows, believed to be from the same workshop as Sainte-Chapelle's in Paris (see pp80–81).

The old section of Montferrand thrived from the 13th to the 17th centuries, and many fine houses – known as *hôtels particuliers* – built by prosperous merchants have survived. Some of the best of

Michelin Man, c.1910

these, with Italianate loggias, mullioned windows and intriguing courtyards, line ancient **rue Kléber**. Between Clermont and old Montferrand lies a third mini-city, the headquarters and factories of the Michelin rubber and tire company, founded here in 1830, which dominates the town.

Environs
Once the rival of Clermont-Ferrand for supremacy in Auvergne, **Riom** is a somber provincial town of black stone houses and lava fountains. The 14th-century château of Duke Jean de Berry was razed in the 19th century to build the Palais de Justice; all that remains is the delicate Sainte-Chapelle, with its lovely 15th-century stained-glass windows.

Riom's greatest treasure is a graceful Madonna holding an infant with a small bird in his hand. The statue is housed in the Eglise de Notre-Dame-du-Marthuret, originally built in the 14th century, but much changed since then.

Choir inside the Cathédrale de Notre-Dame-de-l'Assomption

Orcival ⑪

Puy de Dôme. 🏠 *300.*
ℹ *04 73 65 82 55.*

CRAMMED WITH HOTELS and crowded in summer, Orcival is nevertheless well worth visiting for its Romanesque church, the **Basilique d'Orcival**, which many would say is the best in the region. Completed at the beginning of the 12th century, and typically Auvergne Romanesque in style, the apse is multi-tiered and the side walls are supported by powerful buttresses and strong arches. Inside, the ornate silver and vermilion *Virgin and Child* (in the formal, forward-facing position known as "in majesty") is enigmatic in its rigid, square chair. With an interior lit by 14 windows, and a spacious crypt, the proportions of the building itself are the most graceful aspect.

Virgin and Child in the **Basilique d'Orcival**

Aerial view of Puy de Dôme in the Monts Dômes range

Monts Dômes ⑫

Puy de Dôme. 🚄 🚌 🚆 Clermont-
Ferrand. 🚶 Puy de Dôme summit
(04 73 62 21 45: Apr–Oct).
Montlosier (04 73 65 64 00).

T HE YOUNGEST RANGE of the
Auvergne volcanoes at
4,000 years old, the Monts
Dômes, or Chaîne des Puys,
encompasses 112 extinct
volcanoes aligned over a 30-
km (19-mile) stretch just
west of Clermont-Ferrand.
At the center, the **Puy de
Dôme** towers above a high
plateau. A concentric road
off the N922 spirals up the
peak at a steady 12 percent
gradient, while the steeper,
original switchback Roman
path is still used by hikers.
At the summit – a half-hour
walk farther – are the vestiges of the Roman temple of
Mercury and a telecommunications tower. And on a rare
clear day, there is another
very special reward – the
breathtaking view right across
the volcano.

The volcanic Roche Tuilière below
Col de Guéry in the Monts Dore

In the southwest corner of the
Monts Dômes region is the
Château de Cordès, a small,
privately-owned 15th-century
manor house. The formal gardens were laid out by Le Nôtre
(see p169) who also designed
the gardens at Versailles.

♠ **Château de Cordès**
Orcival. ⓒ 04 73 65 81 34.
Open Easter–Oct: daily call for
appointments out of season). 🎫

Monts Dore ⑬

Puy de Dôme. 🚄 Clermont-Ferrand.
🚌 🚆 Le Mont-Dore. 🚶 Montlosier
(04 73 65 64 00).

T HREE GIANT VOLCANOES – the
Puy de Sancy, the Banne
d'Ordanche and the Puy de
l'Aiguiller – and their secondary cones make up the Monts
Dore: dark green, heavily
wooded mountains laced with
rivers and lakes and dotted
with summer and winter
resorts for skiing, hiking, paragliding, canoeing and sailing.
The 1,885-m (6,185-ft) **Puy
de Sancy** is the highest point
in Central France. Its peak
can be reached by taking the
cable car from the town of Le
Mont-Dore, followed by a long
hike across open terrain. From
Le Mont-Dore, there is an
exhilarating scenic drive on
the D36 which leads to the
Couze de Chambon Valley, a
beautiful stretch of high moorland threaded with waterfalls.
The area has two very popular spa towns: **La Bourboule**
is a sunny resort mainly
devoted to children's ailments,
and it even has a Children's

Casino attached to the **Grand
Casino**. At Le Mont-Dore, the
Etablissement Therma, for
asthma and respiratory ailments, has a grandiose turn-
of-the-century interior.
Below the Col de Guéry on
the D983, the eroded volcanic
Roche Sanadoire and **Roche
Tuilière** stand up like two
gigantic gateposts; from their
peaks there are far-reaching
views over the wooded
Cirque de Chausse and the
valley beyond.

♨ **Etablissement Thermal**
1 place du Panthéon, Le Mont-Dore.
ⓒ 04 73 65 05 10. **Open** mid-May–
Oct 9: Mon–Sat. 🎫 ♿

Church at La Bourboule in the
Monts Dore

Uzerche ⑭

Corrèze. 🏘 3,500. 🚆 🚌 🚶 place
de la Lunade (05 55 73 15 71).

U ZERCHE is an impressive
sight: gray slate roofs,
turrets and bell towers rising
from a hill above the Vézère
River. This prosperous town
never capitulated during the
conflicts of the Middle Ages,
and earlier withstood a seven-
year siege by Moorish forces
in 732. On the point of surrender, the townspeople sent a
feast out to their enemy – in
fact, the last of their supplies.
The Moors, thinking such
lavish offerings meant the city
had stores to spare, gave up.
The Romanesque **Église St-
Pierre** crests the hill above
the town. Beyond Uzerche,
the Vézère cuts through the
green gorges of the Saillant.

CANTAL CHEESE

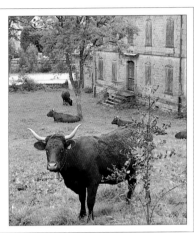

Transhumance is still practiced in the Auvergne, with the local Salers cattle kept in barns in the valleys during winter and led up to mountain pastures for the summer. The robust grasses and flowers – gentian, myrtle, anemone – on which the cows graze produce a flavorful milk that is the basis for the region's great cheese, Cantal. Curds were once pressed through cheesecloth by hand, but now modern methods prevail. Cantal is the key ingredient in *aligot* – the potato-and-cheese purée flavored with garlic that is one of the region's most famous dishes.

Salers cattle enjoying rich pastures

Turenne ⓯

Corrèze. 🐾 *750.* 🚉 🚍
ℹ️ *Ancienne Mairie (summer: 05 55 85 94 38; winter: 05 55 85 91 15).*

Turenne is one of the most appealing medieval towns in the Corrèze. Crescent-shaped and clustered on the cliffside, the town was the last independent feudal fiefdom in France, under the absolute rule of the La Tour d'Auvergne family until 1738. Henri de la Tour d'Auvergne, their most illustrious member, was a marshal of France under Louis XIV, and one of the greatest soldiers of modern times.

Now the sole remains of the **Château du Turenne** are the 13th-century Clock Tower and 11th-century Tower of Caesar, from which there is an amazing 360-degree view of the Cantal Mountains across to the Dordogne Valley. Not far away is the 16th-century collegiate chuch and the **Chapelle des Capucins** dating from the 18th century.

⚜️ **Château du Turenne**
🎫 *05 55 85 91 87.* **Open** *Easter–Oct: daily; Nov–Feb: Sun am.* 🗓️

Collonges-la-Rouge ⓰

Corrèze. 🐾 *400.* 🚍

There's something a little unsettling about Collonges' unique carmine sandstone architecture, quite beautiful in individual houses but somewhat sinister *en masse*, especially in those buildings with bands of white mortar outlining the red stone blocks. Founded in the 8th century, Collonges came under the rule of Turenne, whose burghers built the sturdy turreted houses in the surrounding vineyards. Be sure to see the communal bread oven in the marketplace, and the 11th-century church, which was later fortified with a tower keep. The unusual carved white limestone tympanum shows a man driving a bear, among several other lively figures.

Salers ⓱

Cantal. 🐾 *450.* 🚉 ℹ️ *place Tyssandier d'Escous (04 71 40 70 68).* 🛒 *Wed.*

A solid, handsome town of gray lava houses and 15th-century ramparts, Salers sits atop a steep escarpment at the edge of the Cantal Mountains. It is one of few virtually intact Renaissance villages in the region. The church has an admirable polychrome *mise en tombeau* (entombment), dated 1495, and five elaborate 17th-century Aubusson tapestries.

From the fountain, streets lead up to the cliff edge, and allow views of the surrounding valleys, with the ever-present sound of cowbells in the distance. The town is very crowded in the summer, but it makes a good starting point for excursions to the Puy Mary (*see p354*), the huge barrage in Bort-les-Orgues, the nearby Château de Val and the Cère Valley to the south.

Medieval Château de Val in Bort-les-Orgues near Salers

Puy Mary Peak in the volcanic Monts du Cantal

Monts du Cantal ⑱

Cantal. ✕ Aurillac. 🚌 🚋 Lioran.
🛈 Aurillac (04 71 48 46 58).

THE CANTAL MOUNTAINS were originally one enormous volcano – the oldest and the largest in Europe, dating from the Tertiary period. The highest peaks, the **Plomb du Cantal** at 1,855 m (6,086 ft) and the **Puy Mary** at 1,787 m (5,863 ft), are surrounded by ranges of smaller crests and deep river valleys. Driving the narrow, precipitous roads is a giddy experience, compounded by the grand vistas at every hairpin turn. Between peaks and gorges, rich mountain pastures provide summer grazing for red-gold Salers cows *(see p353)*. From the **Pas de Peyrol**, the highest road pass in the country at 1,582 m (5,191 ft), it's about a 45-minute journey on foot to the summit of the Puy Mary.

Environs
One of the finest of the Auvergne châteaux, **Château d'Anjony** was built by Louis II d'Anjony, a supporter of Joan of Arc *(see pp290–91)*. Highlights are the 16th-century frescoes: in the chapel, scenes from the Life and Passion of Christ, and upstairs in the *Salle des Preux* (Room of the Knights), a dazzling series of the nine heroes of chivalry. To the southwest lies the small market town of **Aurillac**, a good base from which to explore the Cantal region.

♙ Château d'Anjony
Tournemire. 📞 04 71 47 61 67.
Open mid-Jan–mid-Nov: daily. 🖼

La Chaise-Dieu ⑲

Haute-Loire. 🏠 965. 🚌 🛈 place de la Mairie (04 71 00 01 16). 🕰 Thu.

SOMBER AND MASSIVE, midway between Romanesque and Gothic, the abbey church of **St-Robert** is the prime reason to visit the small village of La Chaise-Dieu. The building dates from the 14th century and is an amalgam of styles and tastes. The choir, however, is sensational: 144 oak stalls carved with figures of Vice and Virtue. Above them, entirely covering the walls, are some of the loveliest tapestries in France. Made in Brussels and Arras in the early 16th century and depicting scenes from the Old and New Testaments, they are rich in color and detail.

On the outer walls of the choir, the 15th-century wall painting of the *Danse Macabre* shows Death in the form of skeletons leading rich and poor alike to their inevitable end. Beyond the cloister is the Echo room, in which two people whispering in opposite corners can hear one another perfectly – this was a clever medieval solution for hearing the confessions of lepers.

Le Puy-en-Velay ⑳

Haute-Loire. 🏠 23,000. ✕ 🚌 🚋
🛈 place du Breuil (04 71 09 38 41).
🕰 Wed & Sat. 🎏 Sep.

LOCATED IN THE BOWL of a volcanic cone, the extraordinary town of Le Puy teeters on a stunning series of rock outcrops and giant basalt pillars. The town appears to have three peaks, each topped with a landmark church or statue. Seen from afar, the ensemble is one of the most dramatic sights in France.

Statue of Notre-Dame-de-France at Le Puy

Now a commercial and tourist-oriented town, Le Puy's star attraction is its medieval **Holy City**. This became a pilgrimage center after the Bishop of Le Puy, Gotescalk, made one of the first pilgrimages to Santiago de Compostela in 962, and built the **Chapelle St-Michel d'Aiguilhe** upon his return.

Detail of *Danse Macabre* at St-Robert, in La Chaise-Dieu

THE AUVERGNE'S BLACK MADONNAS

The cult of the Virgin Mary has always been strong in the Auvergne and this is reflected in the concentration of her statues in the region. Carved in dark walnut or cedar, now blackened with age, the Madonnas are believed to originate from the Byzantine influence of the Crusaders. Perhaps the most famous Madonna is the one in Le-Puy-en-Velay, a 17th-century copy of one which belonged to Louis IX in the Middle Ages.

Louis IX's Black Virgin

Pilgrims from eastern France and Germany assembled at the **Cathédrale de Notre-Dame**, with its famous Black Madonna and "fever stone" – a Druid ceremonial stone with healing powers embedded in one of its walls – before setting off for Compostela.

Built on an early pagan site, the Cathédrale de Notre-Dame is a huge Romanesque structure. Multiform arches, carved palm and leaf designs and a checkerboard façade show the influences of Moorish Spain, and indicate the considerable cultural exchange that took place with southern France in the 11th and 12th centuries. In the transept are Romanesque frescoes, notably an 11th–12th-century St. Michael; in the sacristy, the treasury includes the Bible of Theodolphus, a handwritten document from the era of Charlemagne. The cathedral is the center of the Holy City complex that dominates the upper town, encompassing a baptistry, cloister, Prior's house and Penitents' chapel.

The colossal red statue of **Notre-Dame-de-France**, on the pinnacle of the Rocher Corneille, was erected in 1860, cast from 213 cannons captured at Sebastopol during the Crimean War. The statue is reached by a steep pathway, and can be climbed by an iron ladder on the inside.

The Chapelle St-Michel, like the cathedral, shows Moorish influences in the trefoil decoration and colored mosaics on the rounded arch over the main entrance. It seems to grow out of a giant finger of lava rock and is reached by a steep climb. The church is thought to be located on the site of a Roman temple to Mercury, and its center dates from the 10th century, although most of the building was constructed a century later. The floor has been constructed to follow the contours of the rock in places,

and the interior is ornamented with faded 10th-century murals and 20th-century stained glass.

In the lower city, narrow streets of 15th- and 16th-century houses lead to the Vinay Garden and the **Musée Crozatier**, which has a collection of handmade lace from the 16th century to the present – a craft that is now enjoying a revival. The museum also has a surprisingly good collection of medieval *objets d'art* and 15th-century paintings, with works attributed to Rubens, de Heem and Salomon Ruysdael.

In mid-September, Le Puy transforms itself into a masked and costumed Renaissance carnival for the Bird King Festival, an ancient tradition celebrating the skill of the city's best archers *(see p34)*.

⛪ Chapelle St-Michel d'Aiguilhe
Aiguilhe. **[** *04 71 09 50 03.*
Open *Feb–mid-Nov & Dec 21–Jan 5: daily.* ***Closed*** *Jan 1, Dec 25.*

⛪ Notre-Dame-de-France
Rocher Corneille. **[** *04 71 04 11 33.*
Open *Feb–Nov: daily; Dec, Jan & school vacs: pm only.* ***Closed*** *Dec 25, Jan 1.*

🏛 Musée Crozatier
Jardin Henri Vinay. **[** *04 71 09 38 90.*
Open *Wed–Mon.* ***Closed*** *Oct–Apr: Sun am; Jan 1, Nov 1, Dec 25.*

Chapelle St-Michel d'Aiguilhe, standing on a finger of lava rock

Ruins of the Castle of Calmont d'Olt in Espalion in the Lot Valley

Vallée du Lot ㉑

Aveyron. ✈ *Aurillac, Rodez.* 🚉 *Rodez, Séverac-le-Château.* 🚌 *St-Geniez, Conques.* 🛈 *Espalion (05 65 44 10 63).*

FROM MENDE and the old river port of La Canourgue all the way to Conques, the Lot River (or Olt in old usage) courses through its fertile valley past orchards, vineyards and pine forests. **St. Côme d'Olt**, near the Aubrac mountains, is an unspoiled, fortified village whose 15th-century church is surrounded by Medieval and Renaissance houses. At **Espalion**, the pastel stone houses and a turreted 16th-century castle are reflected in the river, which runs beneath a 13th-century arched stone bridge. The town has one of the best markets in the region on Friday mornings. Just outside town is the 11th-century Perse Church, whose carved capitals portray battling knights and imaginary birds sipping from a chalice.

Estaing was once the fiefdom of one of the greatest families of the Rouergue, dating back to the 13th century. The village nestles beneath its massive château (now a convent) on the river bank. The road passes through the Lot Gorge on the way to **Entraygues** ("between waters"), where the old quarter and 13th-century Gothic bridge are worth a visit. Beyond Entraygues, the river widens to join the Garonne.

Conques ㉒

See pp358–9.

Rodez ㉓

Aveyron. 👥 *25,000.* ✈ 🚉 🚌 🛈 *place Foch (05 65 68 02 27).* 🛒 *Wed & Sat.*

LIKE MANY medieval French cities, Rodez was politically divided: the shop-lined **place du Bourg** on one side of town and **place de la Cité**, near the cathedral, on the

***Entombment* in Rodez Cathedral**

other, reflect conflicting secular and ecclesiastical interests. Rodez's commercial center, the largest in the region, is probably the main attraction now, though if you find yourself here for a morning, the **Cathédrale Notre-Dame** makes a worthwhile diversion. This huge, pink stone building was constructed in 1277 and has a fortress-like west façade which once played a part in defending the town. The surrounding narrow streets only permit a view skyward to its magnificent, ornate belltower. The Gothic interior is dominated by a series of giant pillars and a soaring silver-piped organ topped by carved wooden angels. The 15th-century choir stalls show a magnificent panoply of creatures, including a winged lion, some fair demoiselles and one naughty fellow who is exposing his derrière.

ROBERT LOUIS STEVENSON

Robert Louis Stevenson (1850–94), best known for his novels *Treasure Island, Kidnapped* and *Dr. Jekyll and Mr. Hyde*, was also an accomplished travel writer. In 1878, he set off across the remote Cévennes mountain range with only a small donkey, Modestine, for company. His classic account of this eventful journey, *Travels with a Donkey in the Cévennes,* was published in the following year.

Robert Louis Stevenson

Dramatic scenery in Corniche des Cévennes national park

Corniche des Cévennes ㉔

Lozère, Gard. ✈ Rodez-Marcillac.
🚌 Alès. 🚌 St-Jean-du-Gard.
🛈 St-Jean-du-Gard (04 66 85 32 11).

THE DRAMATIC corniche road from Florac on the Tarn to St-Jean-du-Gard was cut in the early 18th century by the army of Louis XIV in pursuit of the Camisards, Protestant rebels who had no uniforms but fought in their ordinary shirts (*camiso* in the *langue d'oc*). The route of the D983 makes a spectacular drive. Fascination with the history of the Camisards was one of the reasons that the famous Scots writer Robert Louis Stevenson undertook his fabled trek in the Cévennes with Modestine, recounted in his *Travels with a Donkey*.

In St-Laurent-de-Treves, where fossil remains suggest dinosaurs once roamed the lagoon, there is a sweeping view of the Grands Causses and the peaks of Lozère and Aigoual. The Corniche finishes in St-Jean-du-Gard, where the **Musée des Vallées Cévenoles**, depicting typical peasant life, is located in a former 17th-century inn.

🏛 Musée des Vallées Cévenoles
95 Grand' rue, St-Jean-du-Gard.
📞 04 66 85 10 48. **Open** Jul–Aug: daily; Apr–Jun, Sep–Oct: 10am–noon, 2–7pm daily; Nov–Mar: Tue, Thu, Sun. **Closed** Jan 1, Dec 25. 📷 ♿

Grands Causses ㉕

Aveyron. ✈ Rodez-Marcillac. 🚌
🚌 Millau. 🛈 Millau (05 65 60 02 42).

THE CAUSSES are vast, arid limestone plateaus, alternating with surprisingly green, fertile canyon valleys. The only sign of life at times is a bird of prey wheeling in the sky, or an isolated stone farm or shepherd's hut. The whole area makes for some desolate hiking for those who like solitude.

The four Grands Causses – Sauveterre, Méjean, Noir and Larzac – stretch out east of the city of Millau, from Mende in the north to the valley of the Vis River in the south.

Among the sights in the Causses are the *chaos* – bizarre rock formations reputed to resemble ruined cities, and named accordingly: there's the *chaos* of **Montpellier-le-Vieux**, **Nîmes-le-Vieux** and **Roquesaltes**. **Aven Armand** and the **Dargilan Grotto** are vast and deep natural underground grottoes with equally astonishing formations.

A good place to head in the windy reaches of the Larzac Causse is the strange, rough-hewn stone village of **La Couvertoirade**, a fully enclosed citadel of the Knights Templar in the 12th century. The unpaved streets and medieval houses are an austere reminder of the dark side of the Middle Ages. There is an entrance fee to the village, payable at a tollbooth.

The Cause du Larzac's best-known village is probably **Roquefort-sur-Soulzon**, a small gray town terraced on the side of a crumbled limestone outcrop. It has one main street and one major product, Roquefort cheese. This is made from unpasteurized sheep's milk, seeded with a distinctive blue mold grown on loaves of bread, and aged in the warren of damp caves above the town.

View over Méjean, one of the four plateaus of the Grands Causses

Conques ❷

Tʜᴇ ᴠɪʟʟᴀɢᴇ of Conques clusters around the splendid Abbaye de Ste-Foy, hemmed into a rugged site against the hillside. Sainte Foy was a young girl who became an early Christian martyr; her relics were first kept at a rival monastery in Agen. In the 9th century a monk from Conques stole the relics, thereby attracting pilgrims to this remote spot and firmly establishing Conques as a stop on the route to Santiago de Compostela *(see pp390–91)*.

The treasury holds the most important collection of medieval and Renaissance gold work in western Europe. Some of it was made in the abbey's own workshops as early as the 9th century. The Romanesque abbey church has beautiful stained-glass windows and its tympanum is a triumph of medieval sculpture.

12th-century reliquary

View of the church from the village

The broad transepts were able to accommodate crowds of pilgrims.

Nave Interior
Pure and elegantly austere, the Romanesque interior dates from 1050–1135. The short nave soars to a height of 22 m (72 ft), with three tiers of arches topped by 250 decorative carved capitals.

Tympanum
This sculpture of 1135 depicts the Last Judgment, with the Devil in Hell (shown here) in the lower part of the sculpture and Christ in Heaven in the tympanum's central position.

CONQUES' TREASURES

The treasures date from the 9th to the 16th century, and are prized for both their beauty and their rarity. The gold-plated wood and silver reliquary of Ste. Foy is studded with gems, rock crystal and even an *intaglio* of Roman Emperor Caracalla. The body is 9th century, but the face may be older, possibly 5th century. Other magnificent pieces include an "A"-shaped reliquary said to be a gift from Charlemagne; the small but exquisite Pepin's shrine from AD 1000; and a late 15th-century processional cross.

The precious reliquary of Ste-Foy

VISITORS' CHECKLIST

Abbaye de Sainte-Foy, Conques.
🚍 05 65 69 85 12. 🚌 🚆
from Rodez. **Treasuries I and II open** Jul–Aug: 9am–7pm daily; Sep–Jun: 9am–noon (11am: Sun) & 2–6pm. 🎫 ✝ 8:15am & 11:30am Mon–Sat, 7:45am & 11am Sun. 📷 ♿ restricted. 🎦

Romanesque Chapels
The east end is three-tiered, topped by the blind arcades of the choir and a central bell tower. Three chapels surround the eastern apse, built to accommodate extra altars for the celebration of mass.

Treasury I
The precious contents of the treasury were hidden by the townspeople to prevent their destruction during the French Revolution. Perhaps surprisingly, all were returned.

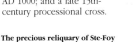

Entrance to Treasury I

The Cloister consists of a reconstructed square: only two sections of the original early 12th-century arcades remain. However, 30 of the original carved capitals are displayed in the refectory and in the Treasury II above the tourist office.

Gorges du Tarn 🔢

NEAR THE BEGINNING of its journey to meet the Garonne River, the Tarn flows through some of Europe's most spectacular gorges. For millions of years, the Tarn and its tributary, the Jonte, have eaten their way down through the limestone plateaus of the Cévennes, creating a sinuous forked canyon some 25 km (15 miles) long and nearly 400 m (1,300 ft) deep. The gorges are flanked by rocky bluffs and scaled by roads with dizzying bends and panoramic views, which are incredibly popular in the high season. The surrounding plateaus, or *causses*, are eerily different, forming an open, austere landscape, dry in summer and snow-clad in winter, where wandering sheep and isolated farms are sometimes the only signs of life.

Point Sublime
From 800 m (2,600 ft) up, there are stunning views of a major bend in the Tarn Gorge, with the Causse Méjean visible in the distance.

Outdoor Activities
The Tarn and Jonte gorges are popular for canoeing and rafting. Although relatively placid in summer, melting snow can make the rivers hazardous in spring.

Pas de Souci
Just upriver from Les Vignes, Pas de Souci flanks a narrow point in the gorge as the Tarn makes its way northward.

0 kilometers 5

0 miles 3

le Rozier

Millau

GORGES DU TARN

GORGES DE LA JON

CAUSSE NOI

D46

D995

D907

D907

D996

D110

N9

Tarn

Chaos de Montpellier-le-Vieux
Situated on the flank of the Causse Noir off the D110 is a remarkable geological site – bizarre rock formations created by limestone erosion.

La Malène
An old crossing-point between the Causse de Sauveterre and the Causse Méjean, this village, with its 14th-century fortified manor, is a good starting point for boat trips.

VISITORS' CHECKLIST

Lozère. 🛬 *Rodez-Marcillac.*
🚌 *Mende, Banassac, Séverac-le-Château.* 🚌 *Florac, Le Rozier.*
ℹ️ *Le Rozier (summer: 05 65 62 60 89). St-Enimie (04 66 48 53 44).*

CAUSSE DE SAUVETERRE

Ste-Enimie

Ispagnac

D907

Tarn

la Malène

CAUSSE MEJEAN

D986

Aven Armand

Jonte

D996

otte de argilan

D39

Meyrueis

Aven Armand Caves
On the Causse Méjean, many stalactites in the caves are tinted by minerals that are deposited by the slowly trickling water.

Causse Méjean
The high plateaus or causses *are a botanist's paradise in spring and summer, with over 900 species of wildflowers, including orchids.*

THE WILD CÉVENNES

One of the least populated parts of France, this area is well known for its wildflowers and birds of prey, and griffon vultures were once common here. These giant but harmless scavengers nearly died out earlier this century through being hunted, but now a reintroduction program has led to growing numbers breeding in the Gorges de la Jonte.

Yellow wort

Kidney vetch

Green-winged orchid

Wildflowers *found in this thinly populated area include unusual alpine plants.*

The griffon vulture, *which now breeds in the region, has a wingspan of over 2.5 m (8 ft).*

THE RHÔNE VALLEY AND FRENCH ALPS

LOIRE · RHÔNE · AIN · ISÈRE · DRÔME
ARDÈCHE · HAUTE-SAVOIE · SAVOIE · HAUTES-ALPES

I TS TWO MOST IMPORTANT *geographical features, the Alps and the Rhône River, give this region both its name and its dramatic character. The east is dominated by majestic snowcapped peaks, while the Rhône provides a vital conduit between north and south.*

The Romans recognized this strategic route when they founded Lyon over 2,000 years ago. Today Lyon, with its great museums and fine Renaissance buildings, is the second city of France. It is one of the country's most vital commercial and cultural centers as well as the undisputed capital of French gastronomy. To the north lie the flat marshlands of the Dombes and the rich agricultural Bresse plain. Here, too, are the famous Beaujolais vineyards which, along with the Côtes du Rhône, make the region such an important wine producer.

The French Alps have some of the world's most popular year-round resort areas: internationally renowned ski resorts such as Chamonix, Mégève and Courchevel, and historic cities like Chambéry, capital of Savoy before it joined France. Elegant spa towns line the shores of Lac Léman (Lake Geneva). Grenoble, a bustling university city and high-tech center, is flanked by two of the most spectacular nature reserves in France, the Chartreuse and the Vercors.

To the south, orchards and fields of sunflowers give way to brilliant rows of lavender interspersed with vineyards and olive groves. Châteaux and ancient towns dot the landscape. Mountains and pretty, old-fashioned spa towns characterize the rugged Ardèche, and the deeply scoured gorges along the Ardèche River offer some of the wildest scenery in France.

The restored Ferme de la Forêt at St-Trivier-de-Courtes, north of Bourg-en-Bresse

◁ Annecy's medieval quarter

Exploring the Rhône Valley and French Alps

Lyon is the region's largest city, famed for its historic buildings and gastronomic tradition. Wine lovers can choose between the vineyards of the Beaujolais, Rhône Valley and Drôme region to the south. To the west, the Ardèche offers rugged wilderness, canoeing and climbing. Spa devotees from around the world flock to Évian-les-Bains and Aix-les-Bains, while the Alps are a favorite destination for sports enthusiasts *(see pp312–13)*.

SIGHTS AT A GLANCE

The Pont des Amours in Annecy

Pont-en-Royans in the Vercors

GETTING AROUND

Lyon and Geneva are the main transit hubs of the region, both easily reached from Paris by TGV (2 hr and 3 hr respectively). Aside from the Alpine regions, local train and bus services tend to be slow and inconvenient. A car is essential if you wish to get off the most heavily traveled autoroutes – the most important ones being the A7, linking Lyon with Valence and the south; and the A40 and A43/A41, which run east to the Alps. The two international airports nearest the Alps are the Geneva-Cointrin airport in Switzerland and the Satolas airport near Lyon. Note that high Alpine passes can be closed between November and June.

KEY

	Highway
	Major road
	Minor road
	Scenic route
	River
☆	Viewing point

Farms around Le Poët Laval, near Montélimar

Bourg-en-Bresse ❶

Ain. 🏛 *43,000.* 🚃 🚌 **ℹ** *Centre Culturel Albert Camus, 6 av Alsace-Lorraine (04 74 22 49 40).* 🛒 *Wed & Sat.*

BOURG-EN-BRESSE is a busy market town, with some beautifully restored half-timbered buildings. It is best known for its tasty *poulet de Bresse* (chickens raised in the flat agricultural region of Bresse and designated *appellation contrôlée, see p309*); and its abbey church of **Brou** on the southeast edge of town.

The latter (no longer a place of worship) has become one of the most visited sites in France. Flamboyant Gothic in style, it was built between 1505 and 1536 by Margaret of Austria after the death of her husband Philibert, Duke of Savoy, in 1504.

The couple's finely sculpted Carrara marble tombs can be seen in the choir, along with the tomb of Margaret of Bourbon, Philibert's mother, who died in 1483. Notice also the beautifully carved choir stalls, stained-glass windows, and rood screen with its elegant basket-handle arching.

The adjacent cloisters house a small museum with a good collection of 16th- and 17th-century Dutch and Flemish masters, as well as contemporary works by local artists.

Tomb of Margaret of Austria in the abbey church of Brou at Bourg-en-Bresse

Environs
About 24 km (15 miles) north of Bourg-en-Bresse at St-Trivier-de-Courtes, the restored **Ferme-Musée de la Forêt** offers a look at farm life in the region during the 17th century. The ancient house has what is known locally as a Saracen chimney, with a brick hood in the center of the room, similar to constructions in Sicily and Portugal, and a collection of antique farm implements.

Bresse chickens

🏛 **Ferme-Musée de la Forêt**
📞 *04 74 30 71 89.*
Open *Apr–Nov 11: Wed–Mon.*
🔲

The Dombes ❷

Ain. 🚠 *Lyon.* 🚃 *Lyon, Villars les Dombes, Bourg-en-Bresse.* 🚌 *Villars-les-Dombes (from Bourg-en-Bresse).* **ℹ** *3 pl de Hôtel de Ville, Villars-Dombes (04 74 98 06 29).*

THIS FLAT, glacier-gouged plateau south of Bourg-en-Bresse is dotted with small hills, ponds and marshes, making it popular with anglers and bird-watchers.

In the middle of the area at **Villars-les-Dombes** is an ornithological park, the **Parc des Oiseaux**. Over 400 species of native and exotic birds live here, including tufted herons, vultures, pink flamingos, emus, and ostriches.

🦅 **Parc des Oiseaux**
Route Nationale 83, Villars-les-Dombes. 📞 *04 74 98 05 54.* **Open** *daily.* 📷 🔲

Pérouges ❸

Ain. 🏛 *900.* 🚃 *Meximieux-Pérouges.* 🚌 **ℹ** *04 74 61 01 14.*

ORIGINALLY the home of a colony of immigrants from Perugia, Pérouges is a fortified hilltop village of medieval houses and cobblestone streets. In its heyday in the 13th century it was a thriving center of linen weaving, but with the mechanization of the industry in the 19th century, the local population dwindled from 1,500 to 90.

Restoration of its historic buildings and a new influx of craftsmen have breathed new life into Pérouges. Not surprisingly, the village has often been used as the setting for historical dramas such as *The Three Musketeers* and *Monsieur Vincent*. The village's main square, place de la Halle, is shaded by a huge lime tree planted in 1792 to honor the Revolution.

A Tour of Beaujolais

BEAUJOLAIS is an ideal area for wine tasting, offering delicious, affordable wine and glorious countryside. The south of the region produces most of the Beaujolais Nouveau, released fresh from the cellars on the third Thursday of November each year. In the north are the ten superior quality *cru* wines – St-Amour, Juliénas, Moulin-à-Vent, Chénas, Fleurie, Chiroubles,

Morgon, Brouilly, Côte de Brouilly and Regnié – most of which can be visited in a day's drive. The distinctive *maisons du pays* have living quarters built over the wine cellar. Almost every village has its *cave* (wine cellar), offering tastings and a glimpse of the wine culture that dominates local life.

Côte de Brouilly

Juliénas ①
Famous for *coq au vin*, this village stores and sells wine in its church, and château, and in the Maison de la Dime, a 16th-century tithe house.

Moulin-à-Vent ②
This 17th-century windmill has lovely views of the Saône Valley. Tastings of the oldest *cru* in the region are held in the *caves* next door.

MACON →

Chénas

Vineyard of Gamay grapes

Chiroubles ⑦
A bust in the village square honors Victor Pulliat, who saved the vines from the phylloxera blight in the 1880s by using American vine stocks.

Romanèche-Thorins

Fleurie ③
The chapel of the Madonna (1875) stands guard over the vineyards, and village restaurants serve local *andouillettes au Fleurie*.

Villié-Morgon ④
Wine tasting is in the cellars of the 18th-century château in the village center. The Château de Corcelles has a Renaissance courtyard.

KEY

▬▬	Tour route
══	Other roads
ᙏ	Viewing point

0 kilometers 2

0 miles 1

Beaujeu ⑥
Once the ancient capital of the region, Beaujeu offers tastings in this Renaissance wooden house, and in the 17th-century Hospices de Beaujeu.

Régnié-Durette

Cercié

Brouilly ⑤
The hill, with its tiny 19th-century chapel of Notre-Dame du Raisin, offers fine views and an annual Beaujolais wine festival.

VILLEFRANCHE-SUR-SAONE

Street-by-Street: Lyon ❹

O N THE WEST BANK of the Saône River, the restored old
quarter of Vieux Lyon is an atmospheric warren of
cobbled streets, *traboules* (covered passageways),
Renaissance palaces, first-class restaurants, lively
bouchons (bistros) and chic designer shops. It is
also the site of the Roman city of Lugdunum, the
commercial and military capital of Gaul
founded by Julius Caesar in 44 BC.
Vestiges of this prosperous city can be
seen in the superb Gallo-Roman
museum at the top of Fourvière Hill.
Two excavated Roman theaters still stage
performances from opera to rock concerts.
At the foot of the hill is the finest collection
of Renaissance mansions in France – a
testimony to the enormous wealth brought to
the city by banking, printing and the silk trade.

★ Théâtres Romains
*There are two Roman
amphitheaters here: the
Grand Théâtre, the oldest
theater in France, built in
15 BC to seat 30,000
spectators and still used for
modern performances; and
the smaller Odéon, with its
geometric tiled flooring.*

**★ Musée de la Civilisation
Gallo-Romaine**
*This underground museum
contains a rich collection of
statues, mosaics, coins and
inscriptions evoking Lyon's
Roman past.*

Entrance
to funicular

Cathédrale St-Jean
*Begun in the late 12th century,
cathedral has a 14th-century ast
nomical clock that shows religi
feast days till the year 2019.*

STAR SIGHTS

★ **Théâtres Romains**

★ **Musée de la
Civilisation
Gallo-Romaine**

★ **Basilique Notre-Dame
de Fourvière**

★ Basilique Notre-Dame de Fourvière
This gaudy mock-Byzantine creation – a riot of turrets and crenelations, marble and mosaic – was built in the late 19th century and has become one of the symbols of Lyon.

Entrance to funicular

The Chemin du Rosaire is a beautiful path leading down from Notre-Dame de Fourvière, with spectacular views of the sprawling metropolis below.

The Tour Métallique was erected in 1893 and is now used as a television transmitter.

VISITORS' CHECKLIST

Rhône. 420,000. 25 km (16 miles) E Lyon. Perrache, Part-Dieu (08 36 35 35 35). Perrache (04 78 71 70 00). place Bellecour (04 72 77 69 69). Tue–Sun. Biennale Internationale d'Art Contemporain & Biennale Internationale de la Danse (Sep). **Hôtel Gudagne** 04 78 42 03 61. **Open** Wed–Mon. **Closed** public hols. **Musée de la Civilisation Gallo-Romaine** 04 72 38 81 90. **Open** Wed–Sun. **Closed** public hols.

Rue Juiverie boasts a number of splendid Renaissance mansions – watch for the Hôtel Paterin at No. 4 and the Hôtel Bullioud at No. 8.

| 0 meters | 100 |
| 0 yards | 100 |

Rue St-Jean and rue du Boeuf are lined with Renaissance mansions, the former homes of bankers and silk merchants.

The 15th-century Hôtel Gadagne houses two museums: the **Musée Historique de Lyon** and the charming **Musée de la Marionnette**, which exhibits the famous Lyonnais puppets.

KEY

– – – Suggested route

Exploring Lyon

FRANCE'S SECOND CITY, dramatically sited on the banks of the Rhône and Saône rivers, has been a vital gateway between north and south since ancient times. Upon arriving you immediately feel a *brin du sud*, or touch of the south. The crowds are not as quick-stepping as they are in Paris, and the sun is often shining here when it's rainy and cold in the north. Despite its importance as a banking, textile and pharmaceutical center, most of the French immediately associate Lyon with their palates. The city is packed with restaurants, ranging from simple *bouchons* (bistros) to some of the most opulent tables in France.

The rue St-Jean in Vieux Lyon

The Presqu'île
The heart of Lyon is the Presqu'île, the narrow peninsula of land between the Saône and Rhône rivers, just north of their confluence. A pedestrianized shopping street, the rue de la République, links the twin poles of civic life: the vast **place Bellecour**, with its equestrian statue of Louis XIV in the middle, and the **place des Terreaux**. The latter is overlooked by Lyon's ornate 17th-century Hôtel de Ville (town hall) and the Palais St-Pierre, a former Benedictine convent and now the home of the **Musée des Beaux Arts**. In the middle of the square is a monumental 19th-century fountain by Bartholdi, sculptor of the Statue of Liberty.

Behind the town hall, architect Jean Nouvel's futuristic **Opéra de Lyon** – a black barrel vault of steel and glass encased in a Neo-Classical shell – reopened its doors in 1993 to a storm of public criticism.

A few blocks to the south, the **Musée de l'Imprimerie** illustrates Lyon's contribution to the early days of printing in the late 15th century.

Two other museums worth visiting in the Presqu'île are the **Musée Historique des Tissus**, which houses an extraordinary collection of silks and tapestries dating from early Christian times to the present day, and the **Musée des Arts Décoratifs**, which displays a range of tapestries, furniture, porcelain and *objets d'art*.

Nearby, the **Abbaye St-Martin d'Ainay** is an impressively restored Carolingian church dating from 1107.

LYON CITY CENTER

Abbaye St-Martin d'Ainay ⑬
Amphithéâtre des Trois Gaulles ①
Basilique Notre-Dame
    de Fourvière ⑨
Cathédrale St-Jean ⑫
Eglise St-Polycarpe ②
Hôtel Gadagne ⑦
Hôtel de Ville ④
Musée de la Civilisation
    Gallo-Romaine ⑩
Musée de l'Imprimerie
    et de la Banque ⑥
Musée des Arts Décoratifs ⑭
Musée des Beaux Arts ⑤
Musée Historique des Tissus ⑮
Opéra de Lyon ③
Théâtres Romains ⑪
Tour Métallique ⑧

KEY

See pp368–9
Ⓜ Metro station
Ⓟ Parking
Tourist information
Church

0 meters   250
0 yards   250

Food market on quai St-Antoine

La Croix-Rousse

This industrial area north of the Presqu'île became the center of the city's silk-weaving industry in the 15th century. It still has covered passages known as *traboules*, used by the weavers to transport their finished fabrics. To get a sense of them, enter at No. 6 place des Terreaux and continue along till you reach the **Eglise St-Polycarpe**. From here, it is a short walk to the ruins of the **Amphithéâtre des Trois Gaulles**, built in AD 19, and the **Maison des Canuts**, where you can see a traditional silk loom in operation.

La Part-Dieu

This modern business area on the east bank of the Rhône River is the site of the TGV railroad station, a new, mammoth shopping complex and a public library. The **Auditorium Maurice-Ravel**, a venue for important cultural events, is also found nearby.

🏛 Musée de l'Imprimerie
13 rue de la Poulaillerie.
📞 04 78 37 65 98.
Open Wed–Sun. **Closed** public hols. 📷

🏛 Musée Historique des Tissus
34 rue de la Charité. **📞** 04 78 37 15 05.
Open Tue–Sun. **Closed** public hols. 📷

🏛 Musée des Arts Décoratifs
30 rue de la Charité. **📞** 04 78 37 15 05. **Open** Tue–Sun. **Closed** public hols. 📷

🏛 Maison des Canuts
10–12 rue d'Ivry. **📞** 04 78 28 62 04.
Open Mon–Sat. **Closed** public hols. 📷 ♿

Musée des Beaux Arts

LYON'S RECENTLY RENOVATED musee des beaux arts showcases the country's largest and most important collection of art after the Louvre. The museum is housed in the 17th-century Palais St-Pierre, a former Benedictine convent for the daughters of the nobility. The Musée d'Art Contemporain, formerly located in the Palais St-Pierre, is now at 81 Cité Internationale, north of the Jardin Tête d'Or. Housed in a building designed by Renzo Piano, it specializes in works dating from after the mid-1900s.

ANTIQUITIES

INCLUDED in this wide-ranging collection are Egyptian archaeological finds, Etruscan statuettes and 4,000-year-old Cypriot ceramics. The antiquities department occupies the ground floor of the museum, the rest of which is devoted to temporary exhibits.

SCULPTURE AND OBJETS D'ART

OCCUPYING the old chapel on the ground floor, the sculpture department includes works from the French Romanesque period and Italian Renaissance, as well as late 19th- and early 20th-century pieces. Represented are Rodin and Bourdelle (whose statues also appear in the courtyard), Maillol, Despiau and Pompon among others. The huge *objets d'art* collection on the first floor, comprises medieval ivories, bronzes and ceramics, coins, medals, weapons, jewelry, furniture and tapestries.

Fleurs des Champs (1845) by Louis Janmot of the Lyon School

Odalisque (1841) by James Pradier

PAINTINGS AND DRAWINGS

THE MUSEUM'S superb collection of paintings occupies the first and second floors. It covers all periods and includes works by Spanish and Dutch masters; the French schools of the 17th, 18th and 19th centuries; Impressionist and modern paintings; and works by the Lyon School, whose exquisite flower paintings were used as sources of inspiration by the designers of silk fabrics through the ages. On the first floor, the Cabinet d'Arts Graphiques has over 4,000 drawings and etchings by such artists as Delacroix, Poussin, Géricault, Degas and Rodin (by appointment only).

🏛 Musée des Beaux Arts
Palais St-Pierre, 20 place des Terreaux.
📞 04 72 10 17 40. **Open**
Wed–Sun. **Closed** public hols. 📷

La Méduse (1923) by Alexeï von Jawlensky

Châtiment de Lycurgue in the Musée Archéologique, St-Romain-en-Gal

Vienne **⑤**

Isère. 🏛 29,000. 🚊 🚍 🚹 cours
Brillier (04 74 53 80 30). 🛒 Sat.

No OTHER CITY in the Rhône
Valley offers such a
concentration of architectural
history as Vienne. Located in a
natural basin of land between
the river and the hills, this site
was recognized for both its
strategic and aesthetic advan-
tages by the Romans, who
vastly expanded an existing
village when they invaded the
area in the 1st century BC.

The center of the Roman
town was the **Temple
d'Auguste et Livie** (25 BC)
on place du Palais, a handsome structure supported by
Corinthian columns. Not far
away off place de Miremont

**Vienne's Temple d'Auguste et Livie
(1st century BC)**

are the remains of the **Théâtre
de Cybèle**, a temple dedicated
to the goddess Cybele, whose
worship involved orgiastic rites.

The **Théâtre Romain**, at
the foot of Mont Pipet off
rue du Cirque, was one of the
largest amphitheaters in Roman
France, capable of seating
over 13,000 spectators. It was
restored in 1938, and is now
used for a variety of events,
including an international jazz
festival in the first two weeks
of July each year. From the
very top seats the view of the
town and river is spectacular.

Other interesting Roman
vestiges include a fragment of
Roman road in the public
gardens and, on the southern
edge of town, the **Pyramide
du Cirque**, a curious structure about 20 m (65 feet) high
that was once the centerpiece
of the chariot racetrack. The
**Musée des Beaux Arts et
d'Archéologie** also has a good
collection of Gallo-Roman
artifacts, as well as 18th-century
French faïence and 17th-
century paintings by lesser-
known artists from the region.

The **Cathédrale de St-
Maurice** is the city's most
important medieval monu-
ment. It was built between
the 12th and 16th centuries
and represents an unusual
hybrid of Romanesque and
Gothic styles. The interior has
three aisles but no transept,
and contains many fine
Romanesque sculptures.

Two of Vienne's earliest
Christian churches are the
12th-century **Eglise St-André-
le-Bas**, with richly carved
capitals in its nave and cloister, and the **Eglise St-Pierre**,
parts of which date from the
5th and 6th centuries. The
latter houses the **Musée
Lapidaire**, a museum of
stone carving with a collection
of bas-reliefs and statues of
Gallo-Roman buildings.

🏛 **Musée des Beaux
Arts et d'Archéologie**
Place de Miremont
📞 04 74 85 50 42. **Open** Apr–Oct:
Tue–Sun; Nov–Mar: Tue–Sat, Sun am.
Closed Jan 1, May 1, Nov 1 & 11,
Dec 25. 🚫
🏛 **Musée Lapidaire**
Place St-Pierre. 📞 04 74 85 20 35.
Open Tue–Sun. **Closed** Jan 1, May 1,
Nov 1 & 11, Dec 25. 🚫 ♿

Vienne's Cathédrale de St-Maurice

St-Romain-en-Gal **⑥**

Rhône. 🏛 1,300. 🚊 Vienne.

IN 1967, BUILDING WORK in this
commercial town directly
across the Rhône from Vienne
revealed extensive remains of
a significant Roman community
dating from 100 BC to AD 300.
It comprises the remnants of
villas, public baths, shops and
warehouses. Of particular
interest is the House of the
Ocean Gods, with a magnificent mosaic floor depicting
the bearded Neptune and
other ocean images.

Much of what has been
unearthed during the ongoing
excavations is housed in the
Musée Archéologique

adjoining the ruins. The impressive collection includes household objects, murals and mosaics. The star exhibit is the *Châtiment de Lycurgue (Chastisement of Lycurgus)*, a mosaic discovered in 1907.

🏛 Musée Archéologique
📞 04 74 53 74 01. **Open** Tue–Sun.
Closed public hols. 🖼 ⚙

St-Étienne ❼

Loire. 🏘 *200,000.* ✈ 🚊 🚌
ℹ av de la Libération (04 77 49 39 00).
🎡 *daily.*

THE DOUR industrial renown brought to this city by coal mining and armaments is no longer really deserved. The downtown area around place des Peuple is lively and animated, and, nearby, the **Musée d'Art et d'Industrie** will fascinate anyone with a mechanical bent. Its covers St-Étienne's industrial background, including the development of the revolutionary Jacquard loom.

The city's main attraction, however, is its **Musée d'Art Moderne**, a sprawling contemporary building on the northern edge of the city just off the N82. The museum houses changing exhibitions and also a growing collection of 20th-century art, including works by Andy Warhol and wFrank Stella.

Detail of the bizarre Palais Idéal du Facteur Cheval at Hauterives

🏛 Musée d'Art et d'Industrie
Place Louis Comte. **📞** 04 77 33 04 85. **Closed** for renovation until early 2001. 🖼 ⚙
🏛 Musée d'Art Moderne
La Terrasse. **📞** 04 77 79 52 52.
Open daily. **Closed** Jan 1, May 1, Jul 14, Aug 15, Nov 1, Dec 25. 🖼 ⚙

Palais Idéal du Facteur Cheval ❽

Hauterives, Drôme. 🚌 *Romans-sur-Isère.* **📞** 04 75 68 81 19. **Open** daily.
Closed Jan 1, Dec 25. 🖼 ⚙

AT HAUTERIVES, 25 km (15 miles) north of Romans-sur-Isère on the D538, is one of the greatest follies of France, an eccentric "palace" constructed entirely of stones and evoking Egyptian, Roman, Aztec and Siamese styles of architecture. It was built single-handedly by a local postman, Ferdinand Cheval, who collected the stones during his daily rounds on horseback. His neighbors thought he was crazy, but the project attracted the admiring attention of surrealist André Breton and other artists.

The interior of the palace is inscribed with numerous mottos and exortations by Cheval, the most poignant of which refers to his assiduous efforts to realize his lifelong fantasy: "1879–1912: 10,000 days, 93,000 hours, 33 years of toil."

THE RHÔNE'S BRIDGES

The Rhône has played a crucial role in French history, transporting armies and commercial traffic between the north and south. It has always been dangerous, a challenge to boatmen and builders for centuries. In 1825 the brilliant engineer Marc Seguin built the first suspension bridge using steel wire cables. This was followed by another 20 along the length of the Rhône, forever transforming communications between east and west.

Suspension bridge over the Rhône at Tournon-sur-Rhône

The town of Tournon-sur-Rhône

Tournon-sur-Rhône ❾

Ardèche. 🏘 10,000. 🚌 ℹ️ Hôtel de la Tourette (04 75 08 10 23). 🛒 Wed & Sat.

SITUATED AT THE FOOT of impressive granite hills, Tournon is a lovely town with gracious tree-lined promenades and an imposing 11th–16th-century **château**. The latter houses a museum of local history, and has fine views of the town and river from its terraces.

The adjacent **Collégiale St-Julien**, with its square bell tower and elaborate façade, is an interesting example of the Italian influence on architecture in the region during the 14th century. Inside is the powerful *Resurrection*, painted in 1576 by Capassin, a pupil of Raphael.

On quai Charles de Gaulle, the **Lycée Gabriel-Faure** is the oldest secondary school in France, dating from 1536.

Directly across the Rhône from Tournon, the village of **Tain l'Hermitage** is famous for its steep-climbing vineyards that produce both red and white Hermitage, the finest (and most expensive) of all Côtes du Rhône wines.

Environs
From Tournon's main square, the place Jean Jaurès, a narrow, twisting road marked the **Route Panoramique** leads via the villages of Plats and St-Romain-de-Lerps to St-Péray. This route offers breathtaking views at every turn, and, at St-Romain, you are rewarded with a superb panorama extending over 13 *départements*.

Valence ❿

Drôme. 🏘 65,000. 🚌 🚐 ℹ️ parvis de la Gare (04 75 44 90 40). 🛒 Wed & Sat.

VALENCE is a large, thriving market town set on the east bank of the Rhône and looking across to the cliffs of the Ardèche. Its principal sight is the Romanesque **Cathédrale St-Apollinaire** on place des Clercs, founded in 1095 and rebuilt in the 17th century.

Alongside the cathedral in the former bishop's palace, the small **Musée des Beaux Arts** contains a collection of late 18th-century chalk drawings of Rome by Hubert Robert.

A short walk from here are two Renaissance mansions. The **Maison des Têtes** at No. 57 Grande Rue was built in 1532 and is embellished

with the sculpted heads of various ancient Greeks including Aristotle, Homer and Hippocrates. On rue Pérollerie, the **Maison Dupré-Latour** has a finely sculptured porch and staircase.

The **Parc Jouvet**, south of avenue Gambetta, offers 14 acres (6 hectares) of pools and gardens, with fine views across the river to the ruined **Château de Crussol**.

🏛 **Musée des Beaux Arts**
4 place des Ormeaux. 📞 04 75 79 20 80. **Open** daily. **Closed** Mon, Tue, Thu & Fri am, public hols. 📷 except Sun.

The limestone Pont d'Arc

The Ardèche ⓫

Ardèche. ✈️ Avignon. 🚌 Montélimar, Pont St-Esprit. 🚐 Montélimar, Vallon Pont d'Arc. ℹ️ Vallon Pont d'Arc (04 75 88 04 01).

OVER THE COURSE OF thousands of years, wind and water have endowed this south-central region of France

---

CÔTES DU RHÔNE

Rising in the Swiss Alps and traveling south to the Mediterranean, the mighty Rhône is the common thread that links the many vineyards of the Rhône Valley. A hierarchy of *appellations* is divided into three levels of quality: at the base, the regional Côtes du Rhône provides the bulk of the Rhône's wines; next, Côtes du Rhône-Villages comprises a plethora of picturesque villages; and, at the top, there are 13 individual *appellations*. The most famous are the steep slopes of Hermitage and Côte Rôtie in the northern Rhône, and historic Châteauneuf-du-Pape *(see p493)* in the south. The lion's share of production is of red wine based on the syrah grape, which is often spicy, full-bodied and robust.

Harvest in a Côtes du Rhône vineyard

with such a wild and rugged landscape that it is often more reminiscent of the American Southwest than the verdure commonly associated with the French countryside. This visible drama is repeated underground as well, since the Ardèche is honeycombed with enormous stalagmite- and stalactite-ornamented caves. The most impressive are the **Aven d'Orgnac** (*aven* meaning pothole) to the south of Vallon-Pont-d'Arc, and the **Grotte de la Madeleine**, reached via a marked path from the D290.

For those who prefer to stay above ground, the most arresting natural scenery in the region is the **Gorges de l'Ardèche**, best seen from the D290, a two-lane road with frequent viewing points that parallels the recessed river for 32 km (20 miles). Nearly at the head of the gorge, heading west, is the **Pont d'Arc**, a natural limestone "bridge" spanning the river, created by erosion and the elements.

Canoeing and white-water rafting are the two most popular sports here. All the equipment necessary can be rented locally; operators at Vallon-Pont-d'Arc (among many other places) rent out two-person canoes and arrange return transportation from St-Martin d'Ardèche, 32 km (20 miles) downstream. Note that the Ardèche River is one of France's fastest flowing rivers – it is safest in May and June; by fall its waters can be

The village of Vogüé on the banks of the Ardèche River

unpredictable and dangerous, especially for beginners.

The softer side of the region is found in its ancient and picturesque villages, gracious spa towns, vineyards and plantations of Spanish chestnuts (from which the delectable *marron glacé* is produced).

Some 13 km (8 miles) south of Aubenas, the 12th-century village of **Balazuc** is typical of the region, its stone houses built on a clifftop overlooking a secluded gorge of the Ardèche River. There are fine views as you approach and leave the village on the D294.

Neighboring **Vogüé** is nestled between the Ardèche River and a limestone cliff. A tiny but atmospheric village, its most commanding sight is the 12th-century **Château de Vogüé**, once the seat of the barons of Languedoc. Rebuilt in the 17th century, the building houses a museum featuring exhibitions about the region.

♣ **Château de Vogüé**
◗ 04 75 37 01 95. **Open** *Jul–Aug: daily; Easter–Jun, Oct–Nov: Sat, Sun & public hols.*

Vals-les-Bains ⑫

Ardèche. 🏘 *3,700.* 🚄 🛈 *Gare Routière (04 75 37 49 27).* 🛒 *Thu & Sun.*

THIS SMALL SPA TOWN retains a hint of its past elegance. It is situated in the valley of the Volane, where there are at least 150 springs, of which all but two are cold. The water, which contains bicarbonate of soda and other minerals, is said to help with digestive problems, rheumatism and diabetes.

Discovered around 1600, Vals-les-Bains is one of the few spas in southern France to have been overlooked by the Romans. The town reached the height of its popularity in the late 19th century, and most of its parks and architecture recall a little of the *Belle Epoque*. With its casino, landscaped parks, and a selection of hotels and restaurants, Vals is a convenient first stop for an exploration of the Ardèche.

Environs

About 15 km (9 miles) east of Vals is the superb Romanesque church of **St-Julien du Serre**.

The Gorges de l'Ardèche, between Vallon-Pont-d'Arc and Pont St-Esprit

A farm near Le Poët Laval, east of Montélimar

Montélimar ⓭

Drôme. 🏠 *31,000.* 🚊 🚌
ℹ️ *Allées Provençales (04 75 01
00 20).* 🚲 *Wed & Sat.*

WHETHER you choose to
make a detour to
Montélimar will largely depend
on how sweet a tooth you
might have. The main curiosity
of this market town is its medieval center, chock-full of shops
selling almond-studded nougat.
This splendid confection has
been made here since the start
of the 17th century, when the
almond tree was first introduced into France from Asia.
  The **Château des Adhémar**,
a mélange of 12th-, 14th- and
16th-century architecture,
surveys the town from a tall
hill to the east.

⛪ **Château des Adhémar**
📞 *04 75 01 07 85.* **Open** *Apr–Oct:
daily; Nov–Mar: Wed–Mon.* **Closed**
Jan 1, Dec 25. 📷 ♿

Environs

The countryside east of
Montélimar is full of picturesque medieval villages and
scenic routes. **La Bégude-de-
Mazenc** is a thriving little vacation center, with its fortified
Old Town perched on a hilltop.
Farther east is **Le Poët Laval**, a
tiny medieval village of honey-
colored stone houses set in
the Alpine foothills. **Dieulefit**,
the capital of this beautiful
region, has several small hotels
and restaurants, as well as
facilities for tennis, swimming
and fishing. To the south, the
fortified village of **Taulignan**
is known for its cuisine based
on truffles, the local delicacy.

Grignan ⓮

Drôme. 🏠 *1,300.* 🚊 ℹ️ *Grande
Rue (04 75 46 56 75).* 🚲 *Tue.*

ATTRACTIVELY SITUATED on a
rocky hill surrounded by
fields of lavender, this charming
little village owes its fame to
Madame de Sévigné, who
wrote many of her celebrated
letters when she was staying
at the **Château de Grignan**.
  Built during the 15th and
16th centuries, the château is
one of the finest Renaissance
structures in this part of France.
Its interior contains a good
collection of Louis XII furniture and Aubusson tapestries.
  From the château's terrace,
a panoramic view extends as
far as the Vivarais Mountains
in the Ardèche. Directly below
the terrace, the **Eglise de St-
Saveur** was built in the 1530s,
and contains the tomb of
Madame de Sévigné, who died
in the château in 1696 at the
age of 69.

⛪ **Château de Grignan**
📞 *04 75 46 51 56.* **Open** *Apr–Oct:
daily; Nov–Mar: Wed–Mon.* **Closed**
Jan 1, Dec 25. 📷

Nyons ⓯

Drôme. 🏠 *7,000.* 🚊 ℹ️ *place de
la Libération (04 75 26 10 35).* 🚲 *Thu.*

NYONS is synonymous with
olives in France, since
the region is a major center of
olive production. A variety of
olive products can be bought
here at the colorful Thursday
morning market, from soap to
tapenade, the olive paste so
popular in the south.
  The **quartier des Forts** is
Nyons' oldest quarter, a warren
of narrow streets and stepped
alleyways, the most rewarding
of which is the covered rue
des Grands Forts. Spanning the
Aygues River is a graceful 13th-
century bridge; on its town side
are several old mills turned
into shops where you can see
the enormous presses once
used to extract olive oil. The
Musée de l'Olivier further
explains the cultivation of the
olive tree and the myriad
local uses found for its fruit.
  There is a fine view of the
area from the belvedere overlooking the town. Sheltered
as it is by mountains, Nyons
enjoys an almost exotic climate,
with all the trees and plants of
the Riviera to be found here.

🏛 **Musée de l'Olivier**
Ave des Tilleuls. 📞 *04 75 26 12 12.*
Open *Mar–Oct: daily; Nov–Feb:
Tue–Sat.* 📷 ♿

Environs

From Nyons, the D94 leads
west to **Suze-la-Rousse**, a
pleasant wine-producing village that, during the Middle
Ages, was the most important
town in the area. Today, it is
best known for its "university
of wine," one of the most respected centers of enology in

The hilltop town of Grignan and its Renaissance château

Olive groves just outside Nyons

the world. It is housed in the 14th-century **Château de Suze-la-Rousse**, the hunting lodge of the princes of Orange. The interior courtyard is a masterpiece of Renaissance architecture and some rooms preserve original paint and stuccowork.

♣ **Château de Suze-la-Rousse**
🄲 04 75 04 81 44. **Open** Apr–Oct: daily; Nov–Mar: Wed–Mon. **Closed** Jan 1, Dec 25. 🖾

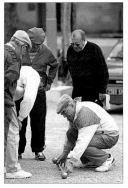

Playing *boules* in Nyons

Briançon ⑯

Hautes Alpes. 🏠 12,000. 🚊 🚌 🛈 place du Temple (04 92 21 08 50). 🖾 Wed.

BRIANÇON – the highest town in Europe at 1,320 m (4,330 feet) – has been an important stronghold since pre-Roman times, guarding as it does the road to the Col de Montgenèvre, one of the oldest and most important passes into Italy. At the beginning of the 18th century, the town was fortified with ramparts and gates – still splendidly intact – by Louis XIV's military architect, Vauban. If driving, park at the Champs de Mars, and enter the pedestrianized Old Town via the **Porte de Pignerol**.

This leads to the **Grande Rue**, a steep, narrow street with a stream running down the middle, bordered by lovely period houses. The nearby **Eglise de Notre-Dame** dates from 1718, and was also built by Vauban with an eye to defense. To visit Vauban's **citadel**, stop by the tourist office, which organizes guided tours.

Today, Briançon is a major sports center, offering skiing in winter, and rafting, cycling and *parapente* in summer.

Environs

Just west of Briançon, the **Parc National des Ecrins** is the largest of the French national parks, offering lofty peaks and glaciers, and a magnificent variety of Alpine flowers.

The **Parc Régional du Queyras** is reached from Briançon over the rugged Col de l'Izoard. A wall of 3,000-m (9,850-ft) peaks separates this wild and beautiful national park from neighboring Italy.

Le Bourg d'Oisans ⑰

Isère. 🏠 2,900. 🚊 🛈 quai Girard (04 76 80 03 25). 🖾 Sat.

LE BOURG D'OISANS is an ideal base from which to explore the Romanche Valley and other adjoining valleys. The area provides numerous opportunities for outdoor sports including cycling, rock-climbing, and skiing, in the nearby resort of **L'Alpe d'Huez**.

Silver and other minerals have been mined here since the Middle Ages, and today the town has a scientific reputation as a center for geology and mineralogy. Its **Musée des Mineraux et de la Faune des Alpes** is renowned for its collection of crystals and precious stones.

🏛 **Musée des Minéraux et de la Faune des Alpes**
🄲 04 76 80 27 54. **Open** 2–6pm; Jul–Aug: 11am–7pm. **Closed** Jan 1, Nov 15, Dec 25. 🖾 🖾

LIFE ON HIGH

The Alpine ibex is one of the rarest inhabitants of the French Alps, living high above the tree line in all but the coldest part of the year. Until the creation of the Parc National de la Vanoise, this sure-footed climber had become almost extinct in France, but as a result of rigorous conservation there are now over 500. Both males and females have horns; in the oldest males they can be almost 1 m (3 ft) long.

An ibex in the Parc National de la Vanoise

GRENOBLE TOWN CENTER

Eglise St-André ④
Fort de la Bastille ①
Musée Dauphinois ②
Musée de Grenoble ⑥
Musée Stendhal ⑤
Palais de Justice ③
Église Saint-Laurent
et Musée
Archéologique ⑦

KEY

🚋 Tramway
➤ Cable Car
🅿 Parking
ℹ Tourist information
✝ Church

0 meters   250
0 yards   250

Grenoble's former town hall, now the Musée Stendhal

Grenoble ⑱

Isère. 🏙 200,000. ✈ 🚉 🚌
ℹ 14 rue de la République
(04 76 42 41 41). 🗓 Tue–Sun.

ANCIENT CAPITAL of the
Dauphiné region and site
of the 1968 Winter Olympics,
Grenoble is a thriving city,
home to the science-oriented
University of Grenoble, and a
center of chemical and electronics industries and nuclear
research. It is attractively situated at the confluence of the
Drac and Isère rivers, with the
Vercors and Chartreuse mountains to the west and north.

A cable car starting at quai
Stéphane-Jay whisks you up
to the 16th-century **Fort de
la Bastille**, where you are
rewarded with superb views of
the city and surrounding mountains. From here, paths lead
down through the Parc Guy
Pape and Jardin des Dauphins
to the **Musée Dauphinois**, a
regional museum in a 17th-
century convent devoted to
local history, arts and crafts.

On the left bank of the
Isère, the focus of life is the
pedestrian area around place
Grenette, a lively square lined
with sidewalk cafés. Nearby,
the place St-André is the heart
of the medieval city, overlooked by Grenoble's oldest
buildings including the 13th-
century **Eglise St-André** and
15th-century **Palais de Justice**.

In the former town hall, the
Musée Stendhal houses an exhibition on the life of the 19th-
century novelist from Grenoble.
The **Musée de Grenoble**, on
the place de Lavalette, exhibits
art from every period, including a superb modern collection
with works by Chagall, Picasso
and Matisse, among others. On
rue Hébert, the **Musée de la
Résistance** contains a collection of documents relating to
the French Resistance.

Temporary displays of modern art can be seen at the
**Centre National d'Art Con-
temporain** (better known as
"Le Magasin"), a renovated
warehouse on the Cours Berriat. In the quartier Malherbe,
the **Maison de la Culture** ("Le
Cargo") hosts everything from
film festivals to orchestral
concerts. It is due to undergo
extensive renovation from
mid-1998, and events will be
moved to other venues.

🏛 **Musée Dauphinois**
30 rue Maurice Gignoux. 📞 04 76
85 19 01. **Open** Wed–Mon. **Closed**
Jan 1, May 1 Dec, 25. 🎟 ♿
🏛 **Musée Stendhal**
1 rue Hector Berlioz. 📞 04 76 54 44
14. Call for opening times. ♿

Grenoble's gondola cable car

🏛 **Musée de Grenoble**
5 place de Lavalette. **[** 04 76 63 44
44. **Open** Wed–Mon. **Closed** Jan 1,
May 1, Dec 25. 🎥 🔔

🏛 **Musée de la Résistance**
14 rue Hébert. **[** 04 76 42 38 53.
Open Wed–Mon. **Closed** Jan 1,
May 1, Dec 25. 🎥 🔔

🏛 **CNAC (Le Magasin)**
155 Cours Berriat. **[** 04 76 21 95 84.
Open Tue–Sun (during exhibitions).
Closed May 1, Dec 25. 🎥 🔔

🏛 **Maison de la Culture**
4 rue Paul Claudel. **[** 04 76 25 92
00. **Open** Sep–Jun: Tue–Sat pm. 🎥
obligatory. **Closed** Dec 24–Jan 4, some
school hols & all public hols. 🎥 🔔

The Vercors ⑲

Isère & Drôme. ✈ Grenoble. 🚉
Romans-sur-Isère, St-Marcellien,
Grenoble. 🚌 Pont-en-Royans,
Romans-sur-Isère. 🛈 Pont-en-Royans
(04 76 36 09 10).

To THE SOUTH and west of
Grenoble, the Vercors is
one of the most magnificent
regional parks in France – a
wilderness of pine forests,
mountains, waterfalls, caves
and deep, narrow gorges.

The D531 out of Grenoble
passes through **Villard-de-
Lans** – a good base for
excursions in the area – and
continues west to the dark
Gorges de la Bournes. About
8 km (5 miles) farther west,
the hamlet of **Pont-en-Royans**
is situated on a very narrow
limestone gorge, its stone
houses built into the rocks
overlooking the Bourne River.

South of Pont-en-Royans
along the D76, the **Route de
Combe-Laval** snakes along a
sheer cliff above the roaring
river below. The **Grands
Goulets**, 6.5 km (4 miles) to
the east, is a spectacularly
deep, narrow gorge overlooked
by sheer cliffs that virtually
shut out the sky above. The
best-known mountain in the
park is the **Mont Aiguille**, a
soaring outcrop of rock rising
2,086 m (6,844 ft).

The Vercors was a key base
for the French Resistance
during World War II. In July
1944 the Germans launched
an aerial attack on the region,
flattening several of its villages.
There are Resistance museums
at Vassieux and Grenoble.

Cows grazing in the Chartreuse

The Chartreuse ⑳

Isère & Savoie. ✈ Grenoble,
Chambéry. 🚉 Grenoble, Voiron.
🚌 St-Pierre-de-Chartreuse. 🛈 St-
Pierre-de-Chartreuse (04 76 88 62 08).

From GRENOBLE, the D512
leads north toward
Chambéry into the Chartreuse,
a majestic region of mountains
and forests where hydroelec-
tricity was invented in the late
19th century. The **Monastère
de la Grande Chartreuse** is
the main local landmark, situated just west of St-Pierre-de-
Chartreuse off the D520-B.

Founded by St. Bruno in
1084, the monastery owes its
fame to the sticky green and
yellow Chartreuse liqueurs first
produced by the monks in
1605. The recipe, based on
a secret herbal elixir of 130
ingredients, is now produced
in the nearby town of Voiron.

The monastery itself is
inhabited by about 40 monks
who live in silence and seclusion. It is not open to visitors,
but there is a museum at the
entrance, the **Musée de la
Correrie**, which faithfully
depicts the daily routine of
the Carthusian monks.

🏛 **Musée de la Correrie**
St-Pierre-de-Chartreuse. **[** 04 76 88
60 45. **Open** Easter–Oct: daily. 🎥

A farm in the pine-clad mountains of the Chartreuse

Chambéry ㉑

Savoie. 🏛 56,000. ✕ 🚊 🚌
ℹ 24 boulevard de la Colonne
(04 79 33 42 47). 🕑 Tue, Sat.

O NCE THE CAPITAL of Savoy,
this dignified city has
aristocratic airs and a distinctly
Italianate feel. Its best-loved
monument is the splendidly
extravagant **Fontaine des
Eléphants** on rue de Boigne.
It was erected in 1838 to
honor the Comte de Boigne,
a native son who left to his
hometown some of the
fortune he amassed in India.

The **Château des Ducs de
Savoie**, at the opposite end of
rue de Boigne, was built in the
14th century and is now mostly
occupied by the Préfecture
(police). Only parts of the
building can be visited, such
as the late Gothic Ste-Chapelle.

On the southeast edge of
town is the 17th-century country house, **Les Charmettes**,
where the Romantic philosopher Rousseau lived
with his mistress
Madame de Warens
from 1732–42. It is
worth a visit for its
vine-covered gardens
and small museum of
Rousseau memorabilia.

🏛 **Les Charmettes**
892 chemin des Charmettes.
📞 04 79 33 39 44.
Open Wed–Mon. **Closed**
public hols. 🔲

The Lac du Bourget at Aix-les-Bains

Aix-les-Bains ㉒

Savoie. 🏛 25,000. ✕ 🚊 🚌
ℹ pl Jean Mollard (04 79 35 05 92).
🕑 Wed & Sat.

T HE GREAT Romantic poet
Lamartine rhapsodized over
the beauty of Lac du Bourget,
site of the gracious spa town of
Aix-les-Bains. The heart of the
town is the 19th-century
Thermes Nationaux,
thermal baths which
were first enjoyed by
the Romans over
2,000 years ago – in the
basement the remains
of the original Roman
baths can still be seen.
Today, this huge es-
tablishment receives
more *curistes* than
any other spa in
France. Opposite

**Roman statue in
the Temple of Diana**

the baths, the 2nd-century AD
Temple of Diana contains a
collection of Gallo-Roman artifacts. The nearby **Musée Faure**
is an art-lover's paradise, with
its collection of Impressionist
paintings, including Degas
and Sisley, Rodin sculptures
and Lamartine memorabilia.

🏛 **Thermes Nationaux**
Pl Maurice Mollard. 📞 04 79 35 38 50.
Open Tue–Sat. 🔲 obligatory.
Closed mid-Dec–mid-Jan, May 1,
Jul 14, Aug 15. 🔲
🏛 **Musée Faure**
Villa des Chimères, 10 bd des Côtes.
📞 04 79 61 06 57. **Open** Wed–Mon.
Closed Dec 18–Jan 2, public hols.
🔲 ♿

Environs
Boats leave from Aix's Grand
Port and sail across Lac du
Bourget to the **Abbaye
d'Hautecombe**, a Benedictine
abbey containing the mausoleum of the Savoyard dynasty.

The small town of **Le
Revard**, just east of Aix on
the D913, has spectacular
views of the lake on one side
and Mont Blanc on the other.

Annecy ㉓

Haute Savoie. 🏛 50,000. ✕ 🚊 🚌
ℹ 1 rue Jean Jaurès (04 50 45 00 33).
🕑 Tue, Fri & Sun am.

A NNECY IS ONE of the most
charming and attractive
towns in the Alps, set at the

Annecy's 12th-century Palais de l'Isle, with the Thiou Canal in the foreground

Cycling along the shores of Lac Léman (Lake Geneva)

northern tip of Lac d'Annecy and surrounded by snow-capped mountains. Its small medieval quarter is laced with canals, flower-covered bridges and arcaded streets. Strolling around is the main attraction, particularly on market day, though there are also specific sights well worth a visit: the formidable **Palais de l'Isle**, a 12th-century prison in the middle of the Thiou Canal; and the turreted **Château d'Annecy**, set high on a hill above the town, with fine views of Vieil Annecy and the crystal-clear lake beyond.

The best spot for swimming and water sports is at the eastern end of the avenue d'Albigny near the Imperial Palace hotel, while boat trips leave from the quai Thiou.

Environs

One of the best ways to enjoy the area's spectacular scenery is to take a boat from Annecy to **Talloires**, a tiny lakeside village celebrated for its prestigious hotels and restaurants. Facing Talloires across the narrowest part of the lake is the 15th-century **Château de Duingt** (not open to visitors).

On the west bank of the lake, Semnoz Mountain and its summit, the **Crêt de Châtillon**, offer superb views of Mont Blanc and the Alps.

Lac Léman ㉔

Haute Savoie & Switzerland. 🚣
Geneva. 🚉 🚌 Geneva, Thonon-les-Bains, Évian-les-Bains. 🛈 Thonon-les-Bains (04 50 71 55 55).

THE STIRRING SCENERY and gentle climate of the French shore of Lake Geneva (Lac Léman to the French) has made it a popular and fashionable resort area since the first spa buildings were erected at Évian-les-Bains in 1839.

Yvoire is a fine place to begin a visit to the area. This medieval walled fishing port is guarded by a massive 14th-century castle, and its tightly-packed houses are bedecked with colorful flower boxes.

Farther east along Lac Léman is **Thonon-les-Bains**, a prosperous, well-manicured little spa town perched on a cliff overlooking the lake. A funicular takes you down to Rives, the small harbor at the foot of the cliffs, where you can rent a sailboat or take an excursion boat to the Swiss cities of Geneva and Lausanne. Just outside the town is the 15th-century **Château de Ripaille**, made famous by its onetime resident, Duke Amadeus VIII, who later became antipope (Felix V).

Though it has been modernized and acquired an international reputation for its eponymous spring water, **Évian-les-Bains** still exudes a polite *vie en rose* charm. The tree-lined lakefront promenade teems with leisurely strollers, while more energetic types can avail themselves of all kinds of sports activities including tennis, golf, riding, sailing and skiing in the winter. State-of-the-art spa treatments are available, and the exotic domed casino is busy at night, offering blackjack, roulette and baccarat as well as other games.

From Évian there are daily ferries across Lake Geneva to Lausanne in Switzerland, as well as bus excursions into the surrounding mountains.

Évian-les-Bains' Hôtel Royal
(see p563)

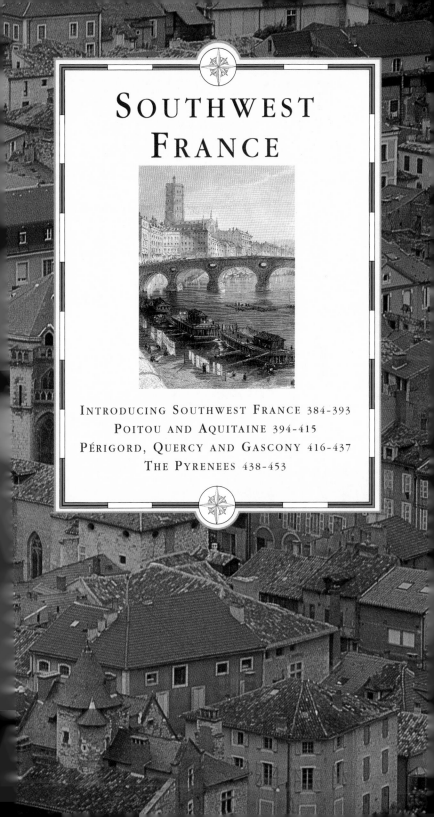

SOUTHWEST
FRANCE

Introducing Southwest France

THE SOUTHWEST IS FARMING FRANCE, a green and peaceful land nurturing crops from sunflowers to *foie gras*. Other key country products include Landes forest timber, Bordeaux wines and Cognac. Major modern industries, including aerospace, are focused on the two chief cities, Bordeaux and Toulouse. Visitors are mainly drawn to the wide Atlantic beaches, the ski slopes of the Pyrenees and the rural calm of the Dordogne. The major sights of this popular region are shown here and include some of France's most celebrated Romanesque buildings.

La Rochelle

Roman Ruins, Saintes

La Rochelle's harbor *is today a haven for pleasure yachts as well as an important commercial port (see p406). Tour de la Chaîne and Tour St-Nicolas protect the entrance of the old port. The town's historic center is filled with cobbled streets lined by merchants' houses.*

Grand Théâtre, Bordeaux

Bordeaux *is a town of grand buildings and monuments, including its theater. The Monument aux Girondins, with its magnificent bronze statues and fountains, stands at the 18th-century Esplanade des Quinconces (see pp410–12).*

POITOU AND AQUITAINE
(See pp394–415)

THE PYRENEES
(See pp438–53)

| 0 kilometers | 50 |
| 0 miles | 50 |

Notre-Dame-la-Grande, Poitiers

Notre-Dame-la-Grande *is the queen among Poitiers' churches (see pp402–3). It has fine stained-glass windows and a splendid Romanesque façade, richly decorated in the Poitevin style.*

PERIGORD, QUERCY
AND GASCONY
(See pp416–37)

Rocamadour *is both a place of pilgrimage and a tourist spot, its chapels and shrines clinging to the edge of the rocky hillside (see pp426–7). Among its many venerated features is the statue of the Black Virgin and Child.*

Lascaux

Rocamadour

Moissac

St-Sernin, Toulouse

Albi Cathedral

Cirque de Gavarnie

Moissac Abbey *is the pre-eminent medieval monastery in southwest France (see pp432–3). Its tympanum, representing the Apocalypse, and the cloister capitals are outstanding examples of Romanesque sculpture.*

Regional Food: Southwest France

THE RENAISSANCE KING HENRI IV'S declaration, "Great cooking and great wines make a paradise on earth," sums up the wonderful and varied cuisine of southwest France. Oysters and mussels proliferate along the Arcachon and Marennes coastline, and in the countryside around Bordeaux, the vine dominates to such an extent that wines are used in the cooking of practically every regional dish – *à la bordelaise* generally translates as "with a wine sauce."

Garlic

In Périgord, Quercy and Gascony, geese, ducks and goats are raised for *foie gras, confit* and cheese. Truffles found in the forests are highly prized and costly and are used sparingly in soups, sauces, *pâté* and stuffings. Goose fat is used for cooking dishes such as *cassoulet* and *daube de boeuf*.

In Basque country, the local chili pepper, the *piment d'Espelette*, spices everything from Bayonne's famous ham and *piperade*, to fish and stews.

Piperade *is a popular Basque country dish of a fluffy omelette or scrambled eggs mixed with garlic, peppers and ham.*

Foie gras *is the enlarged liver of a goose or duck that has been force-fed on maize. It may be cooked in port or brandy.*

Pain de campagne, *the traditional round, rustic country loaf, is quite hard to find today, but a few dedicated bakers still make it. The sour dough is baked in a traditional wood-fired oven, with the smoke from the fire helping to flavor the bread.*

Toulouse sausage

Duck

Haricot beans

Garlic sausage

Cassoulet *is a dish that arouses fierce competition among the dedicated cooks of the southwest. It is a thick stew of white haricot beans, cooked with a variety of sausages and cuts of meat. There are several versions of cassoulet, which can include duck, fresh or salt pork, or mutton.*

Homard persillé *is a lobster terrine cooked in a flavored stock with parsley and herbs.*

Chèvre tiede sur un lit de salade *is grilled goat's cheese, served on a bed of green salad, usually with croutons.*

Duck with cèpes is made from confit of duck (meat cooked and preserved in its own fat) with wild mushrooms and garlic.

Fresh truffles are often cooked in an omelette to bring out their earthy flavor. Périgord truffles are considered the best.

Rabbit with prunes is a classic casserole combination, using the celebrated local Agen prunes for a sweet-sour flavor.

Saucisson sec

Saucisson au poivre

Saucissons are fresh or dried (sec) sausages available all over France. They can include a variety of meat, herbs and spices.

Goat's cheese is often preserved in olive oil, with bay leaves, black peppercorns and thyme added for flavor.

Marzipan loaf, a Basque specialty known as touron, is made of almond paste with pistachios, hazelnuts and fruit.

WILD MUSHROOMS

Mushroom hunting is a favorite pastime for the French. Varieties include the big and fleshy *cèpes (Boletus edulis)*, the egg-yolk colored *chanterelles (Cantharellus cibarius)*, and the brown *morilles* (morels). Fresh wild mushrooms make a less expensive but equally delicious substitute for truffles.

Chanterelles

Morille

Cèpe

Walnut oil is a popular dressing for salads in the southwest. Walnut trees grow in the valleys here, thriving even in the thin soil of the uplands. The Dordogne produces more walnuts than any other French region.

Armagnac   Cognac   Quercy Noix

DRINKS

Besides fine wines, the region's most famous drink is brandy, a spirit made from white grapes. Brandies are distilled in both Cognac and Armagnac, and are best drunk following a meal. In Quercy, there is an aperitif called Quercy Noix, which is made from walnuts.

France's Wine Regions: Bordeaux

Barrel-making

BORDEAUX IS THE WORLD'S largest fine wine region, and, for red wines, certainly the most familiar outside France. Following Henry II's marriage to Eleanor of Aquitaine, three centuries of courtly commerce with Great Britain ensured that claret was served at the finest foreign tables. In the 19th century, canny merchants capitalized on this fame and brought fantastic financial prosperity to the region, and with it, the famous 1855 Classification of the Médoc, a rating system for châteaux that is still used today.

LOCATOR MAP

Bordeaux wine region

Picking red Merlot grapes at Château Palmer

Cos d'Estournel, like all the châteaux included in the 1855 league of crus classés ("classed growths"), proudly proclaims the fact on its label.

WINE REGIONS

The great wine-producing areas of Bordeaux straddle two great rivers; the land between the rivers ("Entre-Deux-Mers") produces lesser, mainly white wines. The rivers, and the river port of Bordeaux itself, have been crucial to the trade in Bordeaux wines; some of the prettiest châteaux line the river banks, enabling easy transportation.

KEY FACTS ABOUT BORDEAUX WINES

Location and Climate
Climatic conditions may vary not only from one year to another, but also within the region itself. The soils tend to be gravelly in the Médoc and Graves, and clayey on the right bank.

Grape Varieties
The five main red grape varieties are the *Cabernet Sauvignon, Cabernet Franc, Merlot, Petit Verdot* and *Malbec*, with Cabernet the dominant grape on the west side of the Gironde, Merlot to the east. Most Bordeaux reds are, however, a blend of grapes. *Sauvignon Blanc* and *Sémillon* are grown and often blended for both dry and sweet whites.

Good Producers
(reds) Latour, Margaux, Haut-Brion, Cos d'Estournel, Montrose, Léoville Lascases, Léoville Barton, Lascombes, Pichon Longueville, Pichon Lalande, Lynch-Bages, Palmer, Rausan-Ségla, Duhart Milon, Clerc Milon, Grand Puy Lacoste, Sociando-Mallet, d'Angludet, Monbrison, Les Ormes de Pez, de Pez, Phélan-Segur, Chasse-Spleen, Poujeaux, Domaine de Chevalier, Pape Clément, Cheval Blanc, Canon, Pavie, l'Angelus, Le Tertre Rôteboeuf, Larmande, Troplong Mondot, La Conseillante.

Good Vintages
(reds) 1990, 1989, 1988, 1986, 1985.

Haut-Brion, in the top division of Bordeaux's Classification, was and still is the single Graves château in this league of Médoc properties.

The famous legend that guarantees château-bottling originated in Bordeaux, as a check to unscrupulous merchants.

Lac d'Ho
Ca

L
Lac

Arcacho

Cap
Ferret

Lac de C
et de Sanc

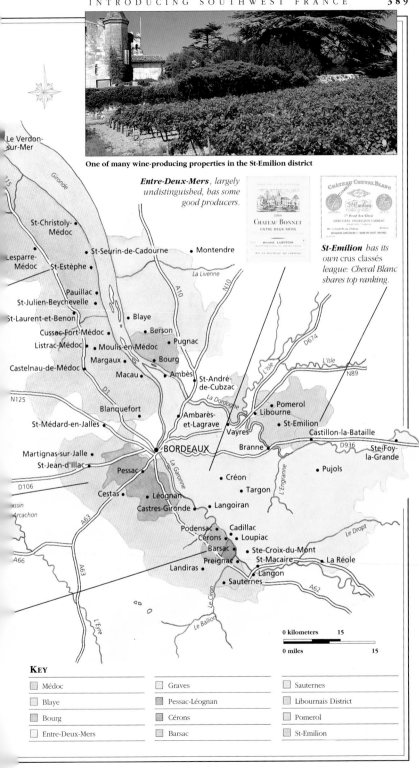

One of many wine-producing properties in the St-Emilion district

Entre-Deux-Mers, largely undistinguished, has some good producers.

St-Emilion has its own crus classés league: Cheval Blanc shares top ranking.

Le Verdon-sur-Mer

Gironde

St-Christoly-Médoc

Lesparre-Médoc

St-Estèphe

St-Seurin-de-Cadourne

Montendre

La Livenne

A10

N10

Pauillac

St-Julien-Beychevelle

St-Laurent-et-Benon

Cussac-Fort-Médoc

Listrac-Médoc

Moulis-en-Médoc

Margaux

Castelnau-de-Médoc

Macau

Blaye

Berson

Pugnac

Bourg

Ambès

St-André-de-Cubzac

La Dordogne

D674

L'Isle

N89

Pomerol

Libourne

St-Emilion

D1

N125

Blanquefort

Ambarès-et-Lagrave

Vayres

St-Médard-en-Jalles

Castillon-la-Bataille

Martignas-sur-Jalle

St-Jean-d'Illac

BORDEAUX

Branne

D936

Ste-Foy-la-Grande

Pessac

Créon

La Garonne

L'Engranne

Pujols

D106

Cestas

Léognan

Targon

Bassin Arcachon

A63

Castres-Gironde

Langoiran

A66

A63

Podensac

Cérons

Cadillac

Loupiac

Le Dropt

Barsac

Preignac

Ste-Croix-du-Mont

St-Macaire

La Réole

Landiras

Langon

Le Ciron

Sauternes

A62

L'Eyre

Le Ballion

0 kilometers 15

0 miles 15

KEY

☐ Médoc

☐ Blaye

☐ Bourg

☐ Entre-Deux-Mers

☐ Graves

☐ Pessac-Léognan

☐ Cérons

☐ Barsac

☐ Sauternes

☐ Libournais District

☐ Pomerol

☐ St-Emilion

The Road to Compostela

Scallop symbol

THROUGHOUT THE MIDDLE AGES millions of Christians visited Santiago de Compostela in Spain to pay homage at the shrine of St. James (Santiago). They traveled across France staying in monasteries or simple shelters and would return with a scallop shell, the symbol of St. James, as a souvenir. Most pilgrims went in hope of redemption and were often on the road for years. In 1140, a monk named Picaud wrote one of the world's first travel guides about the pilgrimage. Today, travelers can follow the same routes, passing through ancient towns and villages with their magnificent shrines and churches.

Foreign pilgrims joined at ports such as St-Malo.

The original cathedral of Santiago de Compostela was built in 813 by Alfonso II over the tomb of St. James. In 1075 construction started on the grandiose Romanesque church seen today which has, among other later additions, a resplendent 17th–18th-century Baroque façade.

The routes converged on Santiago de Compostela.

Most pilgrims crossed the Pyrenees at Roncesvalles.

James the Greater, an apostle, came to Spain to spread the Gospel, according to legend. On his return to Judea, he was martyred by Herod. His remains were taken to Spain by boat and lay hidden for 800 years.

The powerful Cluny Monastery in Burgundy (see pp44–5), and its affiliated monasteries, played an important role in promoting the pilgrimage. They built shelters and set up churches and shrines housing precious relics, to encourage the pilgrims on their way.

THE PILGRIMS' WAY

Paris, Vézelay *(see pp326–7)*, Le Puy *(see p354)* and Arles are the rallying points for the four "official" routes across France. They cross the Pyrenees at Roncesvalles and Somport, and merge at Puente la Reina to form one route, culminating at the shrine on the Galician coast.

Conques purloined relics to boost its prestige.

Le Puy was a main rallying point for pilgrims.

WHAT TO SEE TODAY

Huge Romanesque churches, including Ste-Madeleine at Vézelay *(see p326)*, Ste-Foy at Conques *(pp358–9)* and St-Sernin at Toulouse *(p437)*, along with many small chapels, were built to accommodate large numbers of pilgrims.

Basilique Ste-Madeleine, Vézelay

The first recorded pilgrim was the bishop of Le Puy in 951. But pilgrims have probably been coming to Santiago since 814, soon after the saint's tomb was found.

The reliquary of Ste-Foy, at Conques, is in one of many elaborate shrines on the way that drew crowds of pilgrims. A saint's relics were thought to have miraculous powers.

The name Santiago de Compostela is believed to originate from the Latin Campus stellae *(field of stars). Legend has it that strange stars were seen hovering over a field in 814, and on July 25, now the feast of Santiago, the saint's remains were found.*

Caves of the Southwest

SOUTHWEST FRANCE is well known for its spectacular rock formations, created by the slow accumulation of dissolved mineral deposits. Caves and rock shelters exist throughout limestone country in France. But in the foothills of the Pyrenees and the Dordogne they also have something else to offer the visitor: a collection of extraordinary rock paintings, some dating back to the last Ice Age. These art forms were created when prehistoric peoples evolved and began engraving, painting and carving. This unique artistic tradition lasted for more than 25,000 years, reaching its zenith around 17,000 years ago. Some very fine examples of cave painting are still visible today.

Ancient cave paintings at Lascaux

CAVES OF THE DORDOGNE

There are many different cave systems to visit in or near the Dordogne Valley. The entire Périgord region contains one of the densest concentrations of prehistoric sites anywhere in the world. In an uncertain climate, its rivers flanked by caves and rock shelters proved very attractive to prehistoric man.

CAVE FORMATION

Limestone is laid down in layers containing fissures that allow water to penetrate beneath the surface. Over thousands of years, the water slowly dissolves the rock, first forming potholes and then larger caverns. Stalactites develop where water drips from the cave roof; stalagmites grow upward from the floor.

Grotte du Grand Roc in the Vézère Valley, Limousin

Fissure | Limestone layers
Impermeable rock

Pothole
Fallen rocks | Chamber

Cavern formed by rockfall
Stalactites | Stalagmites

1 *Water percolates through fissures, slowly dissolving the surrounding rock.*

2 *The water produces potholes and loosens surrounding rocks, which gradually fall away.*

3 *Dripping water containing dissolved limestone forms stalactites and stalagmites.*

GOUFFRE DE PADIRAC

Chasm entrance · Elevators · Permeable limestone · Galerie de la Fontaine · Le Grand Cristal · Salle du Grand Dôme

Impermeable rock · Salle de la Fontaine · Rivière Plane (Smooth River) · Lac de la Pluie (Rain Lake) · Pas du Crocodile (Crocodile Track) · Lac des Grands Gours (Great Barrier Lake)

Underground river and chambers of the Gouffre de Padirac

Prehistoric caves at Les Eyzies

VISITING THE CAVES

Cougnac contains chasms ("gouffres") and galleries and its prehistoric paintings include human figures. Around **Les Eyzies** (see pp424–5) are the major caves of **Font de Gaume, Les Combarelles** and **La Mouthe**, which have some beautiful prehistoric paintings and drawings, as does **Rouffignac** in its extensive network of caves. **Grand Roc** has chambers containing a profusion of stalactites and stalagmites. For more unusual rock formations, the chasm at **La Fage**, northeast of Les Eyzies, leads to chambers and galleries with magnificent examples.

On the south bank of the Dordogne, an underground river and lake with extraordinary rock formations can be seen at **Lacave**. The gigantic chasm and caverns at **Padirac** (p428) are even more spectacular. The caves at **Lascaux** with the finest prehistoric paintings have been closed, but the exceptional replica at **Lascaux II** (p424) is well worth seeing. Farther south, **Pech-Merle's** caverns (p428) have impressive rock formations.

THE STORY OF CAVE ART

The first prehistoric cave paintings in Europe were discovered in northwest Spain in 1879. Since then, over 200 decorated caves and rock shelters have been found in Spain and France, mainly in the Dordogne region. A wide range of clues, from stone lamps to miraculously preserved footprints, has helped prehistorians work out the techniques the cave artists used. But their motives remain mysterious. Nearly all the paintings are of animals, with few humans, and many of them are in inaccessible underground chambers. The paintings undoubtedly had a symbolic or magical significance; a new theory suggests they were the work of shamens.

The techniques used by Ice Age artists, who worked by lamplight, included cutting outlines into soft rock, using natural contours as part of the design. Black lines and shading were produced by charcoal, while color washes were applied with mineral pigments such as kaolin and hematite. Hand silhouettes were made by sucking up diluted pigment and blowing it through a plant stem to form a fine spray. When the hand was removed from the rock, its eerie shape was left behind.

Decorated stone lamp discovered in Lascaux cave

Kaolin

Charcoal

Hematite

The Great Bull from the Hall of Bulls frieze at Lascaux

POITOU AND AQUITAINE

DEUX-SÈVRES · VIENNE · CHARENTE-MARITIME
CHARENTE · GIRONDE · LANDES

T HIS VAST AREA *of southwest France spans a quarter of the country's windswept Atlantic coastline, a great expanse of fine sandy beaches. The region stretches from the marshes of the Marais Poitevin to the great pine forests of the Landes. Central to it is the celebrated wine region of Bordeaux and its great châteaux.*

The turbulent history of Poitou and Aquitaine, fought over for centuries, has left a rich architectural and cultural heritage. The great arch and amphitheater at Saintes bear witness to Roman influence in the area. In the Middle Ages, the pilgrimage route to Santiago de Compostela *(see pp390–91)* created an impressive legacy of Romanesque churches, such as those at Poitiers and Parthenay, as well as tiny chapels and glowing frescoes. The Hundred Years' War *(see pp48–9)* caused great upheaval but also resulted in the construction of mighty defense keeps by the English Plantagenet kings. As a result of the Wars of Religion *(see pp50–51)*, many towns, churches and châteaux were destroyed and had to be rebuilt.

Present-day Poitiers is a big, thriving commercial center. To the west are the historic ports of La Rochelle and Rochefort. Farther south, the wine-producing district of Bordeaux combines with Cognac, famous for its brandy, to supply an important part of the region's income. The city of Bordeaux is as prosperous today as in Roman times, combining a lively cultural scene with elegant 18th-century architecture. Its wines complement the region's cuisine: eels, mussels and oysters from the coast; and salty lamb and goat's cheeses from the inland pastures.

Shuttered houses in St-Martin-de-Ré, on Ile de Ré, off the coast of La Rochelle

◁ **The seaside resort of Arcachon by the sandy dunes of the Bassin d'Arcachon**

Exploring Poitou and Aquitaine

BLESSED WITH a seemingly endless Atlantic coastline, abundant navigable waterways, excellent ports and the finest wine and brandy in the world, the region is ideal for a relaxing vacation. Today most summer visitors head straight for the beaches with their thundering waves, but there is also lush countryside inland with a lot to offer. Fine medieval architecture can be seen along the pilgrim's route to Santiago de Compostela *(see pp390–91)*, and châteaux of all shapes and sizes characterize the wine districts around Bordeaux. The only modern city of major importance in the region, Bordeaux is worth a visit for its elegant 18th-century architecture as well as for its rich cultural life. The vast man-made forest of Les Landes also adds to this greatly undervalued corner of France.

Beach life in Bassin d'Arcachon on the Côte d'Argent

GETTING AROUND

The region's main highway is the A10 autoroute connecting Paris and Poitiers with Bordeaux and points east, such as Toulouse, west to Rochefort and south (Bayonne and Spain). This road carries most of the heavy traffic in the area, relieving the excellent smaller roads, which are largely a joy to drive along. The Paris-Poitiers-Angoulême-Bordeaux TGV line has halved rail travel times (Paris–Bordeaux 3 3/4 hr). Bordeaux operates an international airport, as well as bus services to most European capitals. From Poitiers there are buses to several nearby towns, including Parthenay, Chauvigny and St-Savin.

The harbor at Île de Ré

SIGHTS AT A GLANCE

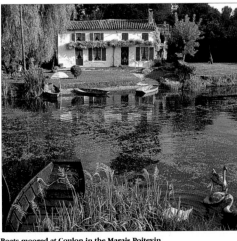

Boats moored at Coulon in the Marais Poitevin

KEY

- Highway
- Major road
- Minor road
- Scenic route
- River
- Viewing point

0 kilometers 25

0 miles 25

Rose window of St-Médard, Thouars

Thouars ❶

Deux-Sèvres. 🏛 12,600. 🚊 🚌 🚶
3 bis Bd Pierre Curie (05 49 66 17 65).
🚌 Tue & Fri.

Thouars, on a rocky outcrop surrounded by the Thouet River, is on the border between Anjou and Poitou. There are as many roofs of northern slate as of southern red tiles.

In the center lies **Eglise St-Médard**. Its Romanesque façade is a perfect example of the Poitevin style that is typical of the region *(see p402)*, although a splendid Gothic rose window has been added. Lined with half-timbered medieval houses, the rue du Château leads up to the 17th-century château that dominates the town. It now houses a lycée and is open to the public during the summer.

East of Thouars lies the moated **Château d'Oiron**, which now hosts contemporary art exhibitions. A masterpiece of Renaissance architecture, it was built in 1518–49.

⚜ Château d'Oiron
79100 Oiron. 📞 05 49 96 51 25.
Open daily. **Closed** public hols. 🎫

Parthenay ❷

Deux-Sèvres. 🏛 11,000. 🚊 🚌
🚶 8 rue de la Vaux-St-Jacques (05 49 64 24 24). 🚌 Wed.

Parthenay is a classic, sleepy provincial town, typical of western France – except on Wednesday mornings, when France's second biggest livestock market is held here. In the Middle Ages, the town was an important stop on the route to Santiago de Compostela *(see pp390–91)*, and it is easy to imagine the processions of pilgrims in the medieval quarter. Steep and cobbled, rue de la Vaux-St-Jacques winds up to the 13th-century ramparts, leading on from the fortified Porte St-Jacques, which guards a 13th-century bridge over the Thouet River.

West of Parthenay, the 12th-century church of **St-Pierre de Parthenay-le-Vieux** has a splendid Poitevin façade, featuring Samson and the Lion and a cavalier with a falcon.

Marais Poitevin ❸

Charente-Maritime, Deux-Sèvres, Vendée. ✈ La Rochelle. 🚊 Niort, Coulon, Marans. 🚌 Coulon, Arçais. 🚶 Coulon (05 49 35 99 29).

The Poitevin marshes, which have been slowly drained with canals, dikes and sluices for a thousand years, cover about 90,000 hectares (222,000 acres) between Niort and the sea. The area is now a national park, divided into two parts. To the north and south of the Sèvre estuary is the fertile Marais Désséché (dry marsh), where cereal crops are grown. The huge swath of the Marais Mouillé (wet marsh) is upstream toward Niort.

The wet marshes, known as Venise Verte (Green Venice), are the most interesting. They are crisscrossed by a labyrinth of weed-choked canals, adorned with orchids and waterlilies, shaded by poplars and beeches, and supporting a rich variety of birds and other wildlife. The *maraîchins* who live here stoutly maintain that much of the huge, water-logged forest is unexplored. The picturesque whitewashed villages hereabouts are all built on high ground, and the customary means of transportation is a flat-bottomed boat, known as a *platte*.

Coulon, St-Hilaire-la-Palud, La Garette, and Arçais, as well as Damvix and Maillezais in the Vendée, are all convenient starting points for boat trips around the marshes (allow at least three hours). Boats can

Medieval houses lining the cobbled rue de la Vaux-St-Jacques in Parthenay

Flat-bottomed boats moored at Coulon in the Marais Poitevin

be rented with or without a guide. Make sure you bring plenty of insect repellent.

Coulon is the largest and best equipped village, and the district's capital. In the aquarium here lurks the largest and ugliest freshwater fish in captivity in France, a 20-kilo (45-lb) *silure*, or sheatfish. From here there are also river cruises departing along the main channel of the Sèvre.

The Plantagenet donjon in Niort, now housing a local museum

Niort ❹

Deux-Sèvres. 🚶 58,000. 🚉 🚌
ℹ️ rue Ernest Perochon (05 49 24 18 79). 🗓️ Thu & Sat.

ONCE A MEDIEVAL PORT by the green waters of the Sèvre, Niort is now a prosperous industrial town specializing in machine tools, electronics, chemicals and insurance.

Its closeness to the marshes is evident in local specialties – eels, snails and angelica. This herb has been cultivated in the wetlands for centuries and is used for anything from liqueur to ice cream.

The town's immediate attraction is the huge 12th-century donjon overlooking the Vieux Ponts. Built by Henry II and Richard the Lion-Heart, it played an important role during the Hundred Years' War and was later used as a prison. One prisoner was the father of Madame de Maintenon *(see p52),* who was born in Niort and spent

her childhood there. The donjon is now a museum concentrating on local arts and crafts, and archaeology.

Environs
Halfway to Poitiers is the small town of **St-Maixent-L'Ecole**. A marvel of light and space, its abbey church is a Flamboyant Gothic reconstruction by François Le Duc (1670) of a building destroyed during the Wars of Religion. Farther west, the **Tumulus de Bougon** consists of five tumuli (burial mounds), the oldest dating from 4500 BC.

Melle ❺

Deux-Sèvres. 🚶 4,000. 🚌 ℹ️ rue E Travers (05 49 29 15 10). 🗓️ Fri.

A ROMAN SILVER MINE was the origin of Melle, which in the 9th century had the only mint in Aquitaine. Later, its fame derived from the *baudet de Poitou,* an especially sturdy mule bred in the area. Now Melle is better known for its churches, of which the finest is **St-Hilaire**. Built in a delightful riverside setting, it has a 12th-century Poitevin façade with an equestrian statue, thought to be of the Emperor Constantine, above the north door. The capitals in the nave have elaborate motifs ranging from angels to bizarre beasts.

Environs
To the northwest, the abbey in **Celles-sur-Belle** has a great Moorish doorway that contrasts strongly with the rest of the church, a 17th-century restoration in Gothic style.

Equestrian statue of Constantine on the façade of St-Hilaire, Melle

Canal in the Venise Verte region of the Marais Poitevin ▷

Poitiers ❻

THREE OF THE GREATEST BATTLES in French history were fought around Poitiers, the most famous in 732 when Charles Martel halted the Arab invasion. After two periods of English rule *(see p47)*, the town thrived during the reign of Jean de Berry (1369–1416), the great sponsor of the arts. Its university, founded in 1431, made Poitiers a major intellectual center and boasted Rabelais among its students. The Wars of Religion left Poitiers in chaos, and not until the late 19th century did any major development take place. Today, however, the town is a modern and dynamic regional capital, with a rich architectural heritage in its historic center.

Fresco in Eglise St-Hilaire-le-Grand

🔒 Notre-Dame-la-Grande
Despite its name, Notre-Dame-la-Grande is not a large church. One of Poitiers' great pilgrim churches, it is most celebrated for its 12th-century masterpiece of lively Poitevin sculpture. In the choir is a Romanesque fresco of Christ and the Virgin. Most of the chapels were added during the Renaissance.

♛ Palais de Justice
Pl Alphonse-le-Petit. 📞 *05 49 50 22 00.* **Open** *Mon–Fri.*
Behind the bland Renaissance façade is the 12th-century great hall of the palace of the Angevin kings, Henry II and Richard the Lion-Heart. This is thought to be the scene of Joan of Arc's examination by a council of theologians in 1429.

🔒 Cathédrale St-Pierre
The 13th-century carved choir stalls in St-Pierre are by far the oldest in France. Note the huge 12th-century east window showing the Crucifixion. The tiny figures of the cathedral's

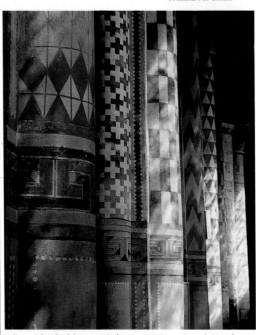

Pillars with colorful geometrical patterns in Notre-Dame-la-Grande

NOTRE-DAME-LA-GRANDE

Triangular gable

Cone-shaped pinnacles

Christ in Majesty is shown in the center of the gable, surrounded by symbols of the evangelists.

Blind arcading is a distinctive feature of the Poitevin façade.

The portals on the Poitevin façade are deep and richly sculpted, often showing a pronounced Moorish influence.

The 12 apostles are represented by statues in the arcatures, together with the first bishop St. Hilaire and his disciple St. Martin.

FUTUROSCOPE

Futuroscope is a fantastic theme park exploring state-of-the-art visual technology in a futuristic architectural environment. Attractions include the "magic carpet" cinema, with one of its two screens placed on the floor, creating the sensation of "flying" over land. The crystal-like Kinemax has the biggest screen in Europe.

Futuroscope's Kinemax

VISITORS' CHECKLIST

Vienne. 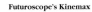 84,000. ✈ 5 km (3 miles) W Poitiers. 🚌 🚌 ℹ 8 rue des Grandes Ecoles (05 49 41 21 24). 🚌 Tue–Sun. 🎭 Printemps Musical (1st two weeks Apr).

⛪ Eglise St-Hilaire-le-Grand

Fires and reconstructions have made St-Hilaire a mosaic of different styles. With its origins in the 6th century, the church still displays an 11th-century bell tower and a 12th-century nave.

patrons (Henry II and Eleanor of Aquitaine) are crouched at the foot of the window.

⛪ Eglise Ste-Radegonde

Housed in this church is the 6th-century tomb of Radegonde, who founded the Abbaye de Ste-Croix – the first nunnery in France – on this site. In the choir are 13th-century windows recounting the life of the saint.

⛪ Baptistère St-Jean

Rue Jean Jaurès. **Open** Jul–Aug: daily; Sep–Jun: Wed–Mon. 🎫 The polygonal 4th-century Baptistère St-Jean is one of the oldest Christian buildings

in France. Many of the earliest converts were baptized here. Now a museum, it contains Romanesque frescoes of Christ and Emperor Constantine, and some Merovingian sarcophagi.

🏛 Musée Sainte-Croix

3 bis rue Jean Jaurès. 📞 05 49 41 07 53. **Open** daily. **Closed** public hols. 🎫 Musée Sainte-Croix exhibits an eclectic mixture of Classical and medieval archaeology, and a wide range of paintings and sculpture. Three bronzes by Camille Claudel are on display, including *La Valse*. There is also a gallery of local artifacts and paintings.

🏛 Médiathèque François Mitterrand

4 rue de l'Université. 📞 05 49 52 31 51. **Open** Tue–Sat. 🎫 This modern building, in the historic quarter, is renowned for its communications technology. Inside, the **Musée du Moyen Age** displays medieval manuscripts and engravings.

Environs

The **Futuroscope**, 7 km (4.5 miles) north of Poitiers, is a museum of developments in visual communications.

🏛 Futuroscope

Jaunay-Clan. 📞 05 49 49 30 00. **Open** daily. 🎫

POITIERS CITY CENTER

Baptistère St-Jean ⑤
Cathédrale St-Pierre ③
Eglise St-Hilaire-le-Grand ⑦
Eglise Ste-Radegonde ④
Musée Sainte-Croix ⑥
Notre-Dame-la-Grande ①
Palais de Justice ②

KEY

🚉 Railroad station
🚌 Bus station
P Parking
ℹ Tourist information
✝ Church

0 meters   250
0 yards   250

The castle ruins of Angles-sur-Anglin with the old watermill in the foreground

Abbaye de Nouaillé-Maupertuis ❼

Nouaillé-Maupertuis. 📞 05 49 55 35 69. **Church open** 9am–6pm. ♿ restricted.

ON THE BANKS of the Miosson River lies the Abbaye de Nouaillé-Maupertuis. First mentioned in 780, the abbey became independent in 808 and followed the Benedictine rule. Apart from the beauty of the site, it is also worth a visit for its church, built in the 11th–12th centuries and reconstructed several times. Behind the altar is the 10th-century sarcophagus of St. Junien, with three great heraldic carved eagles.

More interesting is the nearby battlefield, scene of the great English victory at Poitiers by the Black Prince in 1356. The view has changed little in 600 years. Drive down the small road to La Cardinerie (to the right off the D142), which leads to the river crossing at Gue de L'Omme, the epicenter of the battle. There is a monument halfway up the hill where the heaviest fighting took place, and where the French king Jean le Bon was isolated and captured. He had put up a heroic single-handed resistance with nothing but his battle-ax and his small son Philippe to tell him where the next English knight was coming from.

Chauvigny ❽

Vienne. 👥 7,000. 🚉 🚌 *5 rue St-Pierre (05 49 46 39 01).* 🛒 Sat.

CHAUVIGNY, on its steep promontory overlooking the broad Vienne River, has the distinction of being able to display the ruins of no fewer than four fortified medieval castles. Stone from the local quarry was so plentiful that nobody ever bothered to demolish earlier castles for building material.

Nevertheless, the best thing in this town is the 11th–12th-century **Eglise St-Pierre**, whose decorated capitals are a real treasure – particularly those in the choir. The carvings represent biblical scenes, along with monsters,

Monster capitals in Eglise St-Pierre in Chauvigny

sphinxes and sirens. Look for the one that says *Gofridus me fecit* (Gofridus made me), with wonderfully natural scenes of the Epiphany.

Environs
Nearby is the lovely **Château de Touffou**, a Renaissance dream on the banks of the Vienne, with terraces and hanging flowers. Just to the north of it is the sleepy village of **Bonneuil-Matours**. Its Romanesque church has richly ornate choir stalls.

🏰 **Château de Touffou**
Bonnes. 📞 05 49 56 08 48. **Open** mid-Jun–mid-Sep: Wed–Mon; Oct–May: Sat, Sun & public hols. 🚫

Angles-sur-Anglin ❾

Vienne. 👥 420. 🛈 *14 La Place (05 49 48 86 87 or 05 49 48 61 20).* 🛒 Sun.

THE VILLAGE OF ANGLES lies in an extremely beautiful riverside setting, dominated by its castle ruins. Adding to the charm is an old watermill by the slow-running Anglin River, graced by waterlilies and swaying reeds.

Angles is also famous for its tradition of fine needlework, the *jours d'Angles*, which is determinedly maintained by the local women today.

The village is delightful to visit off season, but in summer the narrow streets become too crowded for comfort.

St-Savin ⑩

Vienne. 🏛 *1,100.* 🚇
ℹ️ *20 pl de la Libération (05 49 48 11 00).* 🚌 *Fri.*

THE GLORY of St-Savin is its 11th-century abbey church with its slender Gothic spire and huge nave.

The abbey had enormous influence until the Hundred Years' War, when it was burned down. It was later pillaged several times during the Wars of Religion. Despite restoration work by monks in the 17th century and again in the 19th century, the church seems untouched.

Its interior contains the most magnificent series of 12th-century Romanesque frescoes in Europe. These wallpaintings were among the very first in France to be classified *Monument Historique* in 1836, by Prosper Merimée, author of *Carmen,* and Inspector of Historical Monuments. Some of the frescoes were restored between 1967–74 and the collection is now protected by UNESCO. A full-scale replica of the St-Savin murals can be seen at the Palais de Chaillot in Paris *(see pp106–7).*

Bell tower of St-Savin

Montmorillon ⑪

Vienne. 🏛 *7,200.* 🚇 ℹ️ *2 pl du Marechal Leclerc (05 49 91 11 96).* 🚌 *Wed & Sat.*

MONTMORILLON, built on both banks of the calm Gartempe River, has its origins in the 11th century. Like most towns in the region, it had a difficult time during the Hundred Years' War and the Wars of Religion. Some buildings survived, such as **Eglise Notre-Dame**, which has beautiful frescoes in its 12th-century crypt. They include scenes from the life of St. Catherine of Alexandria.

Environs
Half an hour's walk from the Pont de Chez Ragon, south of Montmorillon, is the **Portes d'Enfer**, a dramatically shaped rock above the sudden rapids of the Gartempe.

Confolens ⑫

Charente. 🏛 *3,150.* 🚇 ℹ️ *place des Marronniers (05 45 84 22 22).* 🚌 *Wed & Sat.*

ON THE BORDER with Limousin, Confolens was once an important frontier town with eight churches, but now suffers from rural exodus. Efforts to prevent the town's isolation include the annual international folklore festival. Every August, the town is transformed into a tumultuous mix of music, costumes and crafts from all over the world.

Of historical interest is the medieval bridge across the Vienne, heavily restored in the early 19th century.

Charroux ⑬

Vienne. 🏛 *1,400.* ℹ️ *2 route de Chatain (05 49 87 60 12).* 🚌 *Thu.*

THE 8TH-CENTURY **Abbaye du St-Sauveur** in Charroux was once one of the richest abbeys in the region. Today, it has become no more than a ruin open to the sky.

Its chief contribution to history was made in the 10th century, when the Council of Charroux declared the "Truce of God," the earliest-known attempt to regulate war in the manner of the Geneva convention. Rules included: "Christian soldiers may not plunder churches, strike priests or steal peasants' livestock while campaigning."

The huge tower marking the center of the church, and some superb sculpture from the original abbey portal in the small museum here, give an idea of what Charroux must have been like in its heyday.

ST-SAVIN WALL PAINTINGS

The frescoes of St-Savin represent Old Testament history from the Creation to the Ten Commandments. The sequence starts to the left of the entrance with the Creation of the stars and of Eve. It continues with scenes from Noah's Ark to the Tower of Babel, the story of Joseph and the parting of the Red Sea. It is believed that all the frescoes were created by the same group of artists, due to the similarity in style. Their harmonious colors – red and yellow ocher, green, black and white – have been softened by time.

Noah's Ark, from a 12th-century wall painting in St-Savin

Aulnay ⑭

Charente-Maritime. 🏠 1,400.
🛈 290 avenue de l'Eglise (05 46 33 14 44). 🛋 Sun.

PERHAPS the most unusual fact about the lovely 12th-century **Eglise St-Pierre** in Aulnay is that it was all built at once; there is no ill-fitting apse or transept added to an original nave. Surrounded by nothing but cypresses, it has remained the same since the time of the great pilgrimages.

The church is covered in glorious sculpture, particularly the outside of the south transept. It is a rare example of a complete Romanesque façade, with rank on rank of raucous monsters and graceful human figures. Look for the donkey with a harp. Inside the church there is a pillar decorated with elephants, inscribed "Here be Elephants."

Façade of Eglise St-Pierre at Aulnay

La Rochelle ⑮

Charente-Maritime. 🏠 71,000. ✈
🚉 🚌 🛈 place de la Petite Sirène, Le Gabut (05 46 41 14 68). 🛋 daily.

LA ROCHELLE, a commercial center and busy port since the 11th century, has suffered much from a distressing tendency to back the wrong side – the English and the Calvinists, for example. This led to a ruthless siege of the city by Cardinal Richelieu in 1628, during which 23,000 people starved to death. The walls were destroyed and the city's

Tour St-Nicolas in La Rochelle

privileges withdrawn. The glory of La Rochelle is the old harbor surrounded by stately buildings. The harbor is now the biggest yachting center on France's Atlantic coast. On either side of its entrance are **Tour de la Chaîne** and **Tour St-Nicolas**. A huge chain used to be strung between them to ward off attack from the sea.

La Rochelle is easy to explore on foot, though its cobbled streets and many arcades can be impossibly congested in high summer. To get an overview, climb the 15th-century **Tour de la Lanterne**. Its inner walls were covered in graffiti by prisoners, mostly foreign mariners, in the 17th–19th centuries. Ships are the most common motif.

The study of the 18th-century scientist Clément Lafaille is preserved in the **Muséum d'Histoire Naturelle**, complete with shell collection and display cabinets. There are also stuffed animals and African masks. The town's relation to the New World is treated in the **Musée du Nouveau Monde**. Emigration as well as commerce and the slave trade are explained through old maps, paintings and artifacts.

The richly decorated 16th-century courtyard façade of the **Hôtel de Ville** is worth a visit, as is the delightful collection of perfume bottles in the **Musée du Flacon à Parfum** in the parfumerie at No. 33 rue du Temple.

Outside the old center is the huge **Aquarium**. Glass tunnels lead through tanks with different marine biotopes, including sharks and turtles.

🏰 **Tour de la Lanterne**
Le Port. 🕿 05 46 41 56 04. **Open** Apr–Sep: daily; Oct–Mar: Wed–Mon. **Closed** Jan 1, May 1, Nov 1 & 11, Dec 25. 🗢

🏛 **Muséum d'Histoire Naturelle**
28 rue Albert Premier. 🕿 05 46 41 18 25. **Open** Tue–Sat & Sun pm. **Closed** public hols. 🗢

🏛 **Musée du Nouveau Monde**
10 rue Fleuriau. 🕿 05 46 41 46 50. **Open** Wed–Mon. **Closed** Jan 1, May 1, Jul 14, Nov 1 & Dec 25. 🗢

🐠 **Aquarium**
Port des Minimes. 🕿 05 46 34 00 00. **Open** daily. 🗢 ♿

Environs
Ile de Ré, also known as the white island, is a long stretch of chalky cliffs and dunes, with a rich birdlife. Since 1988 it has been connected to the mainland by a 3-km-long (2-mile) bridge.

Head for **St-Martin-de-Ré**, the island's main village. Apart from its 17th-century ramparts, there are plenty of seafood restaurants serving oysters from the island's oyster beds.

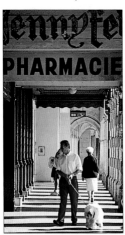

Arcade in rue du Palais, La Rochelle

Rochefort ⑯

Charente-Maritime. 🏠 28,000. 🚉
🚌 🛈 av Sadi-Carnot (05 46 99 08 60). 🛋 Tue, Thu & Sat.

THE HISTORIC RIVAL of La Rochelle, Rochefort was built by Colbert (see pp52–3) in the 17th century to be the

Phare des Baleines on the eastern point of Ile de Ré, just outside La Rochelle

greatest shipyard in France, producing over 300 sailing vessels per year.

Today, this maritime heritage can be traced in the **Corderie Royale** (royal ropeworks) from 1670. Beautifully restored, the building now houses an exhibition on ropemaking. The **Musée de la Marine** displays splendid models of all ships built in the arsenal.

The noble and somewhat austere town is now more famous as the birthplace of the flamboyant writer Pierre Loti (1850–1923). The author's extravagant **Maison de Pierre Loti** is filled with lush souvenirs in an oriental decor.

The **Musée d'Art et d'Histoire** has an interesting ethnographic collection and a relief map of the old shipyard.

🚢 **La Corderie Royale**
Centre International de la Mer, rue Audebert. [05 46 87 01 90. **Open** daily. **Closed** Jan 1, Dec 25. 📷 ♿
🏛 **Musée de la Marine**
Place de la Galissonnière. [05 46 99 86 57. **Open** Wed–Mon. **Closed** public hols (except Easter & Pentecost). 📷
🏛 **Maison de Pierre Loti**
141 rue Pierre Loti. [05 46 99 16 88. **Open** Wed–Mon; Jul–mid-Sep: daily. **Closed** Dec 20–Jan 20, public hols. 📷
🏛 **Musée d'Art et d'Histoire**
63 avenue Charles de Gaulle. [05 46 99 83 99. **Open** Tue–Sat: pm only. **Closed** public hols. 📷

Environs
Ile d'Aix is served by a ferry from Fouras on the mainland. Napoleon was briefly kept here before being exiled to St.

Helena. There are Napoleonic mementos in the **Musée Napoléonien**. The camel he rode in the Egyptian campaign is in the **Musée Africain**.

🏛 **Musée Napoléonien**
30 rue Napoléon. [05 46 84 66 40. **Open** Wed–Mon. **Closed** May 1. 📷
🏛 **Musée Africain**
Rue Napoléon. [05 46 84 66 40. **Open** Thu–Tue. **Closed** May 1. 📷 ♿

Napoleon, who was detained on Ile d'Aix in 1814

Île d'Oléron ⑰

Charente-Maritime. ✈ La Rochelle. 🚉 Rochefort, Marennes (summer), then bus. ⛴ from La Rochelle. 🛈 Bourcefranc (05 46 85 65 23).

OLERON is the second largest French island after Corsica, and a very popular holiday resort. Its south coast, the **Côte Sauvage**, is all dunes and pine forest, with excellent beaches at Vert Bois and Grande Plage, near the fishing

port of La Cotinière. The north is more prosaic, largely given over to farming and fishing.

The miniature train from **St-Trojan** makes an interesting excursion through dunes and woodlands to the Pointe de Maumusson (summer only).

Brouage ⑱

Charente-Maritime. 🏠 180. 🛈 2 rue de Québec, Hiers-Brouage (05 46 85 19 16).

CARDINAL Richelieu's fortress in Brouage, his base during the Siege of La Rochelle (1627–8), once overlooked a thriving harbor, but its wealth and population declined in the 18th century as the ocean receded. In 1659, Marie Mancini was sent into exile here by her uncle, Cardinal Mazarin, who did not approve of her liaison with Louis XIV. The king never forgot the beautiful Marie. Even on his way back from his wedding, he stayed alone at Brouage in the room once occupied by his first great love. Today, the **ramparts** form a peaceful backdrop for the villagers working in the oyster beds below.

Environs
There are two reasons to go to **Marennes**, southwest of Brouage: the famous greentinged oysters and the view from the steeple of Eglise St-Pierre-de-Sales. Nearby is the 18th-century **Château de la Gataudière**, with an exhibition of horsedrawn vehicles.

One of Royan's five popular beaches

Royan ⑲

Charente-Maritime. 🏠 17,500. 🚊
🚌 ⛴ to Verdon only. ℹ️ Rond-
Point de la Poste (05 46 05 04 71).
🏛 daily.

BADLY DAMAGED by Allied
carpet-bombing at the end
of World War II, Royan is
now thoroughly modern and
completely different in tone
from the rest of the towns
on this weather-beaten coast.
With five beaches of fine
sand, here called *conches*, it
becomes a heavily populated
resort in the summer months.

Built between 1955 and
1958, **Eglise Notre-Dame** is a
remarkable early example of
reinforced concrete architecture. Its interior is flooded
with color and light through
the stained-glass windows.

A change from all the
modern architecture is offered
by the outstanding Renaissance
Phare de Cordouan. Various
lighthouses have been erected
on the site since the 11th
century. The present one was
finished in 1611, with a chapel

inside. The construction was
later reinforced and 40 m
(130 ft) added to its height.
Since 1789, the only thing that
has changed is the lighting
method. Boat trips that
include Phare de Cordouan
leave from Royan harbor.

Talmont-sur-
Gironde ⑳

Charente-Maritime. 🏠 83.
ℹ️ rue de L'Église (05 46 90 16 25).

THE TINY Romanesque
Eglise Ste-Radegonde is
perched on a spit of land overlooking the Gironde. Built in
1094, the church's apse was
designed to resemble the bow
of a ship – which is apt, since
the nave has already fallen
into the sea. A 15th-century
façade closes off what's left.
Inside are richly decorated
capitals, including a tableau
of St. George and the Dragon.

Talmont is a jewel of a
village, packed full of little
white houses covered with
climbing roses in summer.

Saintes ㉑

Charente-Maritime. 🏠 27,000. 🚊
🚌 ℹ️ Villa Musso, 62 cours National
(05 46 74 23 82). 🏛 Tue–Sun.

SAINTES, capital of the
Saintonge region, has an
extraordinarily rich architectural heritage. For centuries, it
possessed the only bridge over
the lower Charente, well used
by pilgrims heading for
Santiago de Compostela. The
Roman bridge no longer
exists, but you can still admire
the magnificent **Arch of
Germanicus** (AD 19) that
used to mark its entrance.

On the same side of the
river is the simple and beautiful **Abbaye aux Dames**. Consecrated in 1047, the church
was modernized in the 12th
century. During the 17th–18th
centuries, many young noble
ladies were educated here.
Look for the decorated portal
and the vigorous 12th-century
head of Christ in the apse.

On the left bank is the 1st-
century Roman **amphitheater**.
Farther away lies the more
unknown gem, **Eglise St-
Eutrope**. In the 15th century,
this church had the misfortune
to effect a miraculous cure of
the dropsy on Louis XI. In a
paroxysm of gratitude, he did
his best to wreck it with
unsightly Gothic additions.
Luckily, its rare Romanesque
capitals have survived.

Arch of Germanicus in Saintes

Cognac ㉒

Charente. 🏠 20,000. 🚊 🚌
ℹ️ 16 rue du 14 Juillet (05 45 82 10
71). 🏛 daily.

WHEREVER YOU SPOT the
telltale black lichen stains
from alcohol evaporation on
the exterior of the buildings

Necropolis in the monolithic Eglise St-Jean in Aubeterre-sur-Dronne

here, you may be sure that you are looking at yet another storehouse of cognac.

Head for the best distillery, **Cognac Otard**, situated in the 15th–16th-century château where François I was born. The distillery was established in 1795 by a Scot named Otard, who ruthlessly demolished an old chapel in the process. However, a great part of the Renaissance architecture has been saved and can be enjoyed during the tour, which includes a cognac-tasting.

Cognac in traditional snifter

The basic material for cognac is local white wine low in alcohol, which is then distilled. The resultant pale spirit is aged in oak barrels for 5–40 years before being bottled. The skill lies in the blending – therefore, the only guide to quality is the name and the duration of aging.

🍷 Cognac Otard
Château de Cognac, bd Denfert-Rochereau. [05 45 36 88 86.
Open Apr–Oct: daily; Nov–Dec: Mon–Fri. **Closed** public hols.

Angoulême ㉓

Charente. 🏠 46,000. 🚆 🚌
🛈 7 bis, rue du Chat (05 45 95 16 84). 🚩 Wed & Sat.

THE CELEBRATED 12th-century **Cathédrale St-Pierre**, which dominates this thriving industrial center, is the fourth to be built on the site. One of its most interesting features is the Romanesque frieze on the façade, wonderfully rich in detail. Some exaggerated restoration work was carried out by the 19th-century architect Abadie. In his eagerness to wipe out all details added after the 12th century, he even managed to destroy a 6th-century crypt.

Unfortunately, he was also let loose on the old château, transforming it into a Neo-Gothic **Hôtel de Ville** (town hall). However, the 15th-century tower where Marguerite d'Angoulême was born in 1492 still stands. A statue of her can be seen in the garden. Sister of François I, she spoke six languages, had an important role in foreign politics and wrote the very popular novel *Heptameon*.

The ramparts offer a long bracing walk with views over the Charente Valley.

The **Centre National de la Bande Dessinée et de l'Image** has a reference collection of French print and film cartoons since 1946. Its museum presents cartoon personalities such as Tintin, Asterix, and Snoopy.

🏛 Centre National de la Bande Dessinée et de l'Image
121 rue de Bordeaux. [05 45 38 65 65. **Open** Tue–Sun (daily during school hols). **Closed** Jan 1, May 1, Dec 25. 🖼 ♿

Environs
Angoulême used to be famous for its papermills. The **Moulin de Fleurac** in Nersac has a museum and still produces rag paper in the traditional 18th-century manner.

🍷 Moulin du Verger Puymoyen
[05 45 61 10 38. **Open** daily. 🖼

Aubeterre-sur-Dronne ㉔

Charente. 🏠 390. 🚆 🛈 Rue St Jean (05 45 98 57 18). 🚩 Thu & Sun.

THE CHIEF ORNAMENT of this pretty white village is the weird monolithic **Eglise St-Jean**. Dug out of the white chalky cliff that gave the village its name (Alba Terra – White Earth), some parts of it date back to the 6th century. Between the Revolution and 1860, it served as the village's cemetery. It contains an early Christian baptismal font and an octagonal reliquary.

Detail from the Romanesque façade of Cathédrale St-Pierre in Angoulême

Street-by-Street: Bordeaux ㉕

BUILT ON A CURVE of the Garonne River, Bordeaux has been a major port since pre-Roman times and for centuries a focus and crossroads of European trade. Today Bordeaux shows little visible evidence of the Romans, Franks and English or the Wars of Religion that have marked its past. This forward-looking town, the fifth-largest in France, is an industrial and maritime sprawl surrounding a noble 18th-century center.

Along the waterfront of this wealthy wine metropolis is a long sweep of elegant Classical façades, first built to mask the medieval slums behind. Adding to the magnificence is the Esplanade des Quinconces, the Grand Théâtre and the Place de la Bourse.

Eglise Notre-Dame, built 1684–1707

The Maison du Vin gives information on wine tours.

★ **Grand Théâtre**
Built in 1773–80, the theater is a masterpiece of the Classical style, crowned by 12 statues of the muses.

STAR SIGHTS

★ **Grand Théâtre**

★ **Esplanade des Quinconces**

★ **Place de la Bourse**

KEY

– – – Suggested route

| 0 meters | 100 |
| 0 yards | 100 |

RUE CONDILLAC

COURS DE L'INTENDANCE

RUE MAUTREC

ALLEES DE TOURN

PL DE LA COMEDIE

COURS DU 30 JUILL

RUE STE CATHERINE

RUE ST REMI

COURS DU CHAPEAU ROUGE

RUE ESPRIT DES LOIS

ALLEES D'ORLEANS

PL DE LA BOURSE

LA GARONNE

The quais, lined with graceful façades, make a beautiful walk along the Garonne.

★ **Place de la Bourse**
This elegant and harmonious square is flanked by two majestic 18th-century buildings, Palais de la Bourse and Hôtel des Douanes.

★ Esplanade des Quinconces

Replacing the 15th-century Château de Trompette, this vast space of tree-lined esplanades with statues and fountains was created in 1827–58.

VISITORS' CHECKLIST

Gironde. 🚶 214,000. ✈ 10 km (6 miles) W Bordeaux. 🚉 Gare St-Jean, rue Charles Domerq. 🚌 Place des Quinconces. ℹ 12 cours du 30 Juillet (05 56 00 66 00). 🚌 daily. 🎷 L'Eté Girondin (jazz: Jul–Aug); Fête du Vin Nouveau (end Oct).

Quartier des Chartrons, the old merchants' quarter, has fine 18th-century buildings.

The Monument aux Girondins is a richly adorned monument (1804–1902). It commemorates the Girondists sent to the guillotine by Robespierre during the Terror (1793–5).

Le CAPC

This museum of contemporary art and cultural center opened in 1990 in an early 19th-century warehouse.

Terraces provide good views over the river.

Loading wine barrels in 19th-century Bordeaux

THE BORDEAUX WINE TRADE

After Marseille, Bordeaux is the oldest trading port in France. From Roman times the export of wine was the basis for a modest prosperity, but under English rule (1154–1453, *see pp46–9*), the merchants began making immense fortunes from their monopoly of wine sales to England. After the discovery of the New World, Bordeaux took advantage of its Atlantic position to diversify and extend its wine market. Today the Bordeaux region produces over 44 million cases of wine per year.

GRAND THÉÂTRE DE BORDEAUX

Statues of the muses   Grand staircase

Concert hall

The façade's 12 Corinthian columns

Auditorium with paneling and gilded columns

Stage

Exploring Bordeaux

The liveliest part of Bordeaux is the triangle formed by Cours de l'Intendance, Cours Clemenceau and Allées de Tourny, where the fashionable boutiques and famous cafés are. Department stores line the pedestrianized rue Ste-Catherine and Porte-Dijeaux.

♛ Grand Théâtre

Place de la Comédie. **(** 05 56 48 58 54.
Built by the architect Victor Louis, the 18th-century Grand Théâtre is one of the finest Classical constructions of its type in France. The auditorium is renowned for its extraordinary acoustics. The spectacular main staircase was later imitated by Garnier for the Paris Opéra *(see p93)*.

⛪ Eglise St-Seurin

This church is somewhat chaotic, with a patchwork of styles ranging from the 11th to the 18th century. Most interesting are the 6th-century Gallo-Roman sarcophagi in the crypt, and a fine bishop's throne of sculpted stone, dating from the 14th century.

⛪ Basilique St-Michel

It took 200 years to build the massive Basilique St-Michel, begun in 1350. Cleaned and restored in the 1990s, this triple-naved edifice prides itself on the remarkable statue of St. Ursula with her flock of penitents, in one of the side-chapels. Its freestanding belfry, built in 1472–92, is the tallest in southern France at 114 m (374 ft).

⌂ Musée des Beaux Arts

20 cours d'Albret. **(** 05 56 10 16 93. **Open** Wed–Mon. **Closed** public hols. 🖼 ⛝
Housed in the northern and southern wings of the Hôtel de Ville, this museum houses an excellent collection of paintings, ranging from the Renaissance to our time. Special masterpieces include works by Titian, Veronese, Rubens, Delacroix, Corot, Renoir, Matisse and Boudin.

⌂ Musée d'Aquitaine

20 cours Pasteur. **(** 05 56 01 51 00. **Open** Tue–Sun. **Closed** public hols. 🖼 ⛝
This important museum traces life in the region from prehistoric times to the present, through artifacts, furniture and viticulture tools. Among its more spectacular exhibits are the Tayac treasure from the 2nd century BC, including a magnificent gold torque, and the Garonne treasure, a hoard of over 4,000 Roman coins.

Calm street in Bordeaux by the Porte de la Grosse Cloche

⛪ Cathédrale St-André

The nave of this gigantic church was begun in the 11th century and modified 200 years later. The Gothic choir and transepts were added in the 14th and 15th centuries. The excellent medieval sculptures on the Porte Royale include scenes from the Last Judgment.

⌂ Le CAPC

Entrepôt Lainé, 7 rue Ferrère. **(** 05 56 00 81 50. **Open** Tue–Sun pm. **Closed** Jan 1, May 1, Dec 25. 🖼 ⛝
The CAPC (Centre d'Arts Plastiques Contemporains) is housed in a superbly converted 19th-century warehouse and opened as a museum in 1990. There are regular themed exhibitions from the permanent collection of contemporary art. The museum also functions as a cultural center, with special film screenings, lectures and debates.

St-Émilion ㉖

Gironde. 🚏 *2,800.* 🚉 ⓘ *place de Créneaux (05 57 55 28 28).* 🛒 *Sun.*

TO MOST PEOPLE, St-Émilion is the *appellation* of a fine red wine *(see pp388–9)*. It is, however, also the name of a charming village in the middle of the wine-growing district. Its origins go back to the 8th century when the hermit Émilion dug out a cave for himself in the rock. A monastery followed, and by the Middle Ages St-Émilion had become a small town. Today medieval houses still line the narrow streets, and parts of the 13th-century ramparts remain. There is also an interesting monolithic church, dug out of the chalky cliff by followers of Saint Émilion after his death.

Famous châteaux in the district include the elegant **Figeac**, **Cheval Blanc** and **Ausone**, all of them St-Émilion Premier Crus Classés.

Vineyard close to Margaux in the Médoc region west of Bordeaux

Pauillac ㉗

Gironde. 🏠 5,700. 🚉 🚌 **i** quai de Pauillac, la Verrerie (05 56 59 03 08). 🛒 Tue & Sat.

ONE OF THE MOST famous areas in the Médoc wine region (see pp388–9) is the commune of Pauillac. Three of its châteaux are Médoc Premier Crus Classés. The **Château Mouton-Rothschild** uses leading artists to create its wine labels and houses a small museum of paintings on wine themes from all over the world. The **Château Lafite-Rothschild** is of medieval origin and the **Château Latour** is recognizable by its distinctive stone turret. They can be visited by appointment (contact the tourist office). The town of Pauillac is on the west bank of the Gironde. In the 19th century it was the bustling arrival point for transatlantic steamships, but now the sleepy port is mostly used by pleasure boats. There are picturesque river views from the quais and plenty of cafés serving the local wine.

BORDEAUX WINE CHÂTEAUX

The château is at the heart of the quality system in Bordeaux, the world's largest fine wine region. A château includes a vineyard and a building, which can range from the most basic to the grandest, from historic to modern. But the château is also the symbol of a tradition and of the philosophy that a wine's quality and character spring from the soil. Some châteaux welcome visitors for wine tasting as well as buying. The Maison du Vin and the tourist office in Bordeaux (see p411) offer information and tours.

Latour in Pauillac is famous for its powerful wines and the medieval stone turret which appears on its label.

Cheval Blanc, *a great château in the St-Émilion area, boasts a rich, spicy Premier Grand Cru.*

Margaux, *built in 1802, produces a classic Margaux Premier Cru of the same elegant proportions as its Palladian façade.*

Palmer, *dating from 1856, is Neo-Renaissance in style and produces a very fine Margaux Troisième Cru.*

Gruaud-Larose *is a cream-colored château with a Classical façade, distinguished by its full-bodied St-Julien Deuxième Cru Classé.*

Vieux Château Certan *is Belgian-owned and one of the great historic properties of Pomerol. Its wines are consistently in the first rank in the district, challenged only by Pétrus.*

The immense Dune du Pilat, stretching almost 3 km (2 miles) south of the inlet to Bassin d'Arcachon

La Côte d'Argent ㉘

Gironde, Landes. 🚶 Bordeaux, Biarritz.
🚃 Soulac-sur-Mer, Arcachon, Labenne,
Dax. 🚌 Lacanau, Arcachon, Mimizan.
🛈 Lacanau (05 56 03 21 01),
Mimizan-Plage (05 58 09 11 20),
Capbreton (05 58 72 12 11).

THE LONG STRETCH of coast
between Pointe de Grave
on the Gironde estuary and
Bayonne *(see p442)* is called
La Côte d'Argent – the "Silver
Coast." It is virtually one vast
beach of shifting sand dunes.
Treeplanting has now slowed
down their progress.

The coast is dotted with seaside resorts like **Soulac-sur-
Mer** in the north, followed by
the big **Lacanau-Océan** and
Mimizan-Plage. Down in the
south is **Hossegor** with its
salty lake, and **Capbreton**.
Modern vacation resorts have
been integrated with the old.

Inland is a string of lakes
popular for fishing and boating. They are connected to
each other and the ocean by
courants, lively water currents,
such as the **Courant d'Huchet**
from Etang de Léon. Boat trips
are available.

Bassin d'Arcachon ㉙

Gironde. 🏛 12,000. 🚃 🚌
🛈 esplanade Georges Pompidou
(05 57 52 97 77). 🛥 daily.

IN THE MIDDLE of the Côte
d'Argent the straight coastline suddenly forms a lagoon.
Famous for its natural beauty,
fine beaches and oysters, the
Bassin d'Arcachon is a
protected area, perfect for
vacationers, sailing enthusiasts and seafood lovers.

The basin is dotted with
smaller amorphous resorts,
beaches and fishing/oyster
villages, all worth exploring.

Cap Ferret, the northern
headland that protects the
basin from stiff Atlantic
winds, is a preserve of the
wealthy, whose luxurious
villas stand among the pines.
Look for the small road under
the trees from Lège, which
leads to the wild, magnificent
beach of Grand-Crohot.

Between Cap Ferret and
Arcachon, near Gujan-
Mestras, the **Parc Ornithologique du Teich** provides
care and shelter for damaged
birds and endangered species.
For the bird-watcher, there
are two fascinating walks,
each carefully marked: an
introductory one, and another
of greater length. Both

provide concealed observation
points from which people can
watch the wildfowl without
disturbing them.

Arcachon was created as
a seaside resort in 1845. Its
popularity grew, and in the
late 19th and early 20th
centuries, the elegant villas in
the calm Ville d'Hiver were
built. The livelier Ville d'Eté,
facing the lagoon, has a
casino and sports facilities.

The immense **Dune du
Pilat** is the largest sand dune
in Europe. It is nearly 3 km
(2 miles) long, 115 m (375 ft)
high and 500 m (1,625 ft)
wide. Aside from its panoramic view, the dune is a
magnificent vantage point in
autumn for viewing flocks of
migratory birds as they pass
overhead on their way to the
sanctuary at Le Teich.

🦅 Parc Ornithologique du Teich
Le Teich. 📞 05 56 22 80 93. **Open**
daily. 🌐 ♿

Parc Ornithologique du Teich, a bird sanctuary in Bassin d'Arcachon

LANDES FOREST

The vast, totally artificial 19th-century forest of Les Landes was an ambitious project to make use of an area of sand and marshes. Pines and grasses were planted to anchor the coastal dunes, and inland dunes were stabilized with a mixture of pines, reeds and broom. In 1855 the land was drained, and is now covered with pine groves and undergrowth, preserving a delicate ecological balance.

Pine trees in the Landes forest

Les Landes 🖦

Gironde, Landes. 🛧 *Bordeaux.* 🚊 *Morcenx, Dax, Mont de Marsan.* 🚌 *Mont de Marsan.* 🛈 *Mont de Marsan (05 58 05 87 37).*

ALMOST ENTIRELY covered by an immense pine forest, the Landes area extends over the two *départements* of Gironde and Landes. The soil here is uniformly sandy. Until a century ago, the whole region became a swamp in winter, because of a layer of tufa (porous rock) just under the surface that retained water from the brackish lakes. Any settlement or agriculture close to the sea was impossible due to the constantly shifting dunes. Furthermore, the mouth of the Adour River kept moving from Capbreton to Vieux-Boucau and back, a distance of 32 km (20 miles).

The Adour was stabilized near Bayonne by a canal in the 16th century. This was the start of the slow conquest of the Landes. The planting of pine trees ultimately wiped out the migrant shepherds and their flocks. Today, the inner Landes is still very under-populated,

but wealthy from its pinewood and pine derivatives. The coastal strip has a large influx of vacationers.

In 1970, part of the forest was made into a nature park. Here, a small steam train takes visitors to **Marqueze**, where a typical 19th-century *airial* (clearing) has been restored. It commemorates the vanished world of Les Landes before the draining of the marshes, when shepherds still used stilts to get about. There are traditional *auberges landaises*, wooden houses with sloping roofs, as well as henhouses built on stilts because of the foxes. In **Luxey**, a museum recalls old techniques of tapping and distilling of resin.

Lévignacq, near the coast, is a perfect Landais village with a remarkable 14th-century fortified church full of charming naive frescoes.

Mont-de-Marsan 🖷

Landes. 🖦 *32,000.* 🚊 🚌 🛈 *6 place du Général Leclerc (05 58 05 87 37).* 🗓 *Tue–Sat.*

A BULLFIGHTING MECCA, Mont-de-Marsan attracts all the great bullfighters of France and Spain during the summer season. A less bloodthirsty local variant of the sport, very popular here, is the *course landaise*, in which the object is to vault over the horns and back of a charging cow.

The administrative capital of the Landes is also known for its hippodrome and the production of poultry and *foie gras*.

Sculpture from the first half of the 20th century can be seen at **Musée Despiau-Wlérick**.

Dax 🖸

Landes. 🖦 *20,000.* 🚊 🚌 🛈 *place Thiers (05 58 56 86 86).* 🗓 *Sat, Sun am.*

THE THERMAL SPA of Dax is second only to Aix-les-Bains *(see p380)* in importance. Its hot springs, with a constant temperature of 64° C (147° F) and tonic mud from the Adour, have been soothing aches and pains and promoting tranquillity since the time of Emperor Augustus.

Apart from the 13th-century doorway of the otherwise 17th-century **Cathédrale Notre-Dame**, there isn't much of architectural interest in this warm, peaceful town. But the promenade along the Adour River is charming, and the bullring is world-renowned.

La Force (1937) by Raoul Lamourdieu, in the bullfighting capital of Mont-de-Marsan

PÉRIGORD, QUERCY AND GASCONY

DORDOGNE · LOT · TARN · HAUTE GARONNE · LOT-ET-GARONNE
TARN-ET-GARONNE · GERS · CORRÈZE

I F ARCHAEOLOGY IS ANY GUIDE, *the southwest of France has been continuously inhabited by mankind for tens of thousands of years, longer than any other area in Europe. The landscape of these historic regions seems to have an ancient familiarity, derived from centuries of people living in harmony with the land.*

The great cave sites around Les Eyzies and Lascaux harbor the earliest evidence known of primitive art. The castles, bastides *(see p435)* and churches that grace the countryside from Périgueux to the Pyrenees, and from the Bay of Biscay to Toulouse and to the Mediterranean, belong to a far more recent past. From the coming of Christianity until the late 18th century, this region was the battlefield for a string of conflicts. The English fought and lost the Hundred Years' War for Aquitaine (1345–1453); this was followed by intermittent Wars of Religion, in which Catholics fought Huguenots (French Protestants) in a series of massacres and guerilla wars *(see pp48–49).*

Today nothing is left of these old struggles but crumbling ramparts, keeps and bastides, which are part of the region's cultural and artistic heritage, attracting thousands of visitors every year. Yet it is as well to remember that all the great sights here, from the impressive abbey church at Moissac, whose 12th-century portal is a masterpiece of Romanesque art, to the awesome clifftop site of Rocamadour; these, too, have suffered badly at one time or another from the attacks of marauding soldiers.

This region may seem incomparably rich in all the ingredients for a good vacation – uncluttered landscapes, empty roads, clean rivers and good regional cuisine – but the economy is rather fragile. Over the last century, the southwest has suffered from a decline in the old peasant way of life, resulting in a population migration away from the countryside to the surrounding towns.

Périgord geese, raised for the area's celebrated *foie gras*

◁ **La Roque-Gageac in the Dordogne Valley**

Exploring Périgord, Quercy and Gascony

THE MARKET TOWNS of Périgueux, Cahors and Albi make good bases for exploring the region, and are quieter alternatives to Toulouse – the only major urban center. Elsewhere, the green hills and sleepy villages of Gascony and Périgord are mainly for those who appreciate the slow pace of life in the countryside. But if you want more than peace and good food, this region offers some of the finest medieval architecture in France, along with Europe's most important prehistoric caves, notably Lascaux.

The medieval hilltop town of Cordes

GETTING AROUND

The west–east Autoroute des Deux Mers (A62) is the main road route through the region, linking Bordeaux, the Atlantic coast and the Mediterranean. The N20 from Limoges provides alternative access to the Dordogne and Quercy. Buses and mainline railroads, including a Bordeaux–Marseille TGV, pass along the same two axes. They meet at Toulouse, where an international airport has daily flights to and from most European destinations.

KEY

▬▬	Highway
▭▭	Major road
▭▭	Minor road
▬▬	Scenic route
〰	River
☆	Viewing point

0 kilometers   25

0 miles   25

To Limoges
Poitiers

ST-ROBERT

To Clermont-
Ferrand

SCAUX II ⑥ ST-AMAND-DE-COLY
⑦

ARLAT ⑪

DOMME
⑫

AUTOIRE
⑮

GOUFFRE
DE PADIRAC ⑭

⑬
ROCAMADOUR

FIGEAC

To Rodez
Montpellier

⑯ CAHORS

Bourdeilles on the Dronne River

㉒ MOISSAC

GORGES DE
AVEYRON ㉔

CORDES
㉕

㉓
MONTAUBAN

N88

Tarn

ALBI
㉖

D99

TOULOUSE

㉗ CASTRES

㉘

To Carcassonne

St-Jean-de-Côle ❶

Dordogne. 🚶 *350.*
ℹ️ *05 53 62 14 15*

S T-JEAN-DE-COLE's medieval, humpbacked bridge gives the best view of this lovely Dordogne village set in hilly countryside. Stone and half-timbered houses, roofed with the distinctive red-brown tiles of the region, cram the narrow streets around the main square. Here stand a covered marketplace, château, and 12th-century church.

The cupola of the church used to be the largest in the region, bigger even than those of the cathedrals. Too large, it seems, for it fell down twice in the 18th and 19th centuries. The second time it happened the builders gave up, and there has been a plank ceiling ever since.

Main square in the lovely village of St-Jean-de-Côle

St-Robert ❷

Corrèze. 🚶 *350.* ℹ️ *Le Mairie (05 55 25 11 12).*

S T-ROBERT IS a substantial hilltop village with wide views over the meadows, poplars and walnut trees of the Dordogne countryside. There is also an early 12th-century priory filled with appealing details, many in a tongue-in-cheek Romanesque style. Look for the capital attached to the ambulatory wall with the carving of two old men pulling each others' beards; and the 13th-century wooden Christ figure from the Spanish School. Classical music concerts take place in the central square in summer, during the last week of July and the first week of August.

Brantôme Abbey, with belfry

Brantôme ❸

Dordogne. 🚶 *2,100.* 🚌 ℹ️ *Pavillon Renaissance (05 53 05 80 52).* 🛒 *Fri.*

S URROUNDED on all sides by the brisk Dronne River, and bisected by heavy traffic, Brantôme boasts a solid reputation for good restaurants, ancient riverside gardens, and a medieval abbey now used as the town hall.

'The massive abbey, topped by an ornate 11th-century belfry, overshadows the village. Its most unlikely abbot, appointed at the age of 15, was the poet Pierre de Bourdeille (1540–1614), whose lovers were rumored to have included Mary, Queen of Scots. After a crippling fall, Bourdeille retired here in 1569 to write his racy memoirs. You can wander the stone staircases and cloisters, and pass through the main courtyard to a series of caves hollowed out of the cliffs. In one is a huge crucifixion scene cut into the

stone during the 16th century. Across the river is the **Musée Rêve et Miniatures**, a private collection of doll houses in a variety of period styles. Each one is authentically furnished, down to the smallest detail such as textiles and crockery.

Outside Brantôme stands the fine Renaissance **Château de Puyguilhem**.

🏛 **Musée Rêve et Miniatures**
8 rue Puyjoli. 📞 *05 53 35 29 00.*
Open *Apr–Nov: Tue–Sun (Jul–Sep: daily).* 🖼

♣ **Château de Puyguilhem**
Villars. 📞 *05 53 54 82 18.* **Open** *Feb–Dec: Tue–Sun (Jul–Aug: daily).* 🖼 ♿

Bourdeilles ❹

Dordogne. 🚶 *800.* ℹ️ *Le Mairie (05 53 03 42 96).*

T HIS SMALL TOWN has everything – a narrow Gothic bridge with cutwater piers spanning the Dronne, a mill upstream and a medieval **château**. The 16th-century additions to the castle were designed in a hurry by the châtelaine Jacquette de Montbron, who was expecting a visit from Queen Catherine de' Medici. When the royal visit was called off, so were the building works. The highlight of the château is the gilded salon on the first floor, decorated in the 1560s by Ambroise le Noble, an artist of the Fontainebleau School.

♣ **Château de Bourdeilles**
📞 *05 53 03 73 36.* **Open** *Feb–Dec: Wed–Mon (Jul–Aug: daily).* 🖼

The impressive Château de Bourdeilles towering above the town

Cathédrale St-Front in Périgueux, restored in the 19th century

Périgueux ❺

Dordogne. 🏠 32,000. ✕ 🚊 🚌
🛈 26 place Francheville (05 53
10 63). 🕭 daily.

THE ANCIENT and truly gastronomic city of Périgueux,
like its neighbors Bergerac
and Riberac, should be
visited on market day, when
stalls in the lively medieval
core offer the pick of local
specialties, including
truffles, *charcuterie*
(prepared meats) and the
succulent pies called
pâtés de Périgord.

Périgueux, now the
busy regional capital,
has long been the
crossroads of Péri-
gord. The earliest
part remaining today
is the quarter known
as **La Cité**, once the
important Gallo-Roman
settlement of Vesunna.
Those interested in
archaeology should
begin here. From Roman
times to the Middle
Ages, this was the focus
of Périgueux. Most of
the fabric of Vesunna

was torn down in the 3rd
century, but some vestiges of
a temple, a sumptuous villa,
and a huge arena remain. The
Eglise St-Etienne, with
origins dating to the 12th
century, is also in this area.

Walking up the hill from La
Cité to the city's dazzling white
cathedral, you pass through
bustling streets and squares,
each with its market activity.
This is the medieval quarter
of **Le Puy St-Front**, which
began to flourish as
pilgrims on their way
to Santiago de Com-
postela *(see pp390–91)*
visited the cathedral.
They brought wealth
and prestige to
the quarter and it
gradually eclipsed
La Cité in political
importance.
At the top stands the
imposing **Cathédrale
St-Front**, the largest in
southwestern France.
The Romanesque con-
struction was heavily
restored (some say to

**19th-century stained glass
in Cathédrale St-Front**

death) in the 19th century,
when architect Paul Abadie
added the fanciful domes and
cones. He later used St-Front
as inspiration for the Sacré-
Coeur in Paris *(see p130)*.

Other gems of medieval and
Renaissance architecture in this
newly cleaned-up area include
Maison Estignard, at No. 3
rue Limogeanne, with its unusual corkscrew staircase, and
houses along rue Aubergerie
and rue de la Constitution.

Also in the cathedral
quarter is the **Musée du
Périgord**, one of the most
comprehensive prehistory
museums in France. High-
lights are remnants of burials
dating back 70,000 years, and
beautiful Roman mosaics,
glass, earthenware and other
artifacts from Vesunna.

🏛 **Musée du Périgord**
22 cours Tourny. 📞 05 53 06 40 70.
Open Wed–Mon. **Closed** public
hols. 🔖

St-Amand-de-Coly ❻

Dordogne. 📞 05 53 51 67 50.
Open daily. 🚻

THIS abbey church is an
outstanding example of
fortress architecture, built in
the 12th–13th century by
Augustinian monks to protect
their monastery. There are
two lines of defense: a high
stone rampart and, behind it,
the arched tower of the
church itself. The tower looks
more like a castle keep, and
slits show where it was once
pierced by a score of arrows.

Inside, the church is beautifully simple, with pure lines,
a flat ribbed vault, a 12th-cen-
tury cupola, a soaring nave,
and a stone floor sloping
upward to the altar. Yet even
this interior was arranged for
defense, with a gallery from
which enemies within the
building could be attacked.

St-Amand was heavily dam-
aged during the Hundred
Years' War. In 1575, it survived
a siege by 2,000 Huguenot
cavalry-men and a six-day
bombardment by cannon.
Religious life here came to
an end after the Revolution.

Sarlat

Sculptures of geese in Sarlat

Sᴀʀʟᴀᴛ-ʟᴀ-Cᴀɴᴇᴅᴀ features the highest concentration of medieval, Renaissance and 17th-century façades of any town in France. Its prosperity was a reflection of the privileged status it was granted in return for loyalty to the French crown during the Hundred Years' War. Behind the nondescript rue de la République are narrow lanes and archways, and ancient, ocher-colored stone town houses rich in ornamental detail. Protected by law since 1962, Sarlat's buildings now form an outdoor museum. The town is also famous for one of the best markets in France.

Place de la Liberté
The Renaissance heart of Sarlat is now lined with luxury shops and cafés.

Rue des Consuls contains 16th- and 17th-century mansions, built for the town's middle-class merchants, magistrates and church officials.

Rue Jean-Jacques Rousseau was the main street until rue de la République (known as "La Traverse") was built in the 19th century.

Walnuts, a key Périgord crop

Sᴀʀʟᴀᴛ Mᴀʀᴋᴇᴛ

Every Saturday, the great Sarlat market is held in place de la Liberté, along with a full-scale fair that attracts locals from all around the surrounding countryside. Sarlat lies at the heart of the nation's *foie gras* and walnut trades. These typical Périgord products absorb much of the town's attention and supply a good proportion of its revenue, as they did during Sarlat's heyday in the 13th and 14th centuries. Other local specialties are black truffles dug up in the woods in January, and wild mushrooms.

Seek out, too, the cheeses of every shape, age and hue, and the huge range of pork delicacies available – choose from canned, fresh, smoked, dried, salted, fried, baked or boiled.

Bulbs of pink garlic

Town walls

Kᴇʏ

– – – Suggested route

0 meters   50

0 yards   50

Rue de la Salamandre
This lane was named after the salamander emblem of King François I, seen on many of the town's 16th-century houses.

VISITORS' CHECKLIST

Dordogne. 🏠 10,500. 🚆 av de la Gare (05 53 59 00 21). 🚌 31 rue de Cahors (05 53 59 01 48). 🛈 pl de la Liberté (05 53 31 45 45). 🛒 Wed & Sat. 🎭 Theater (Jul–Aug); Film (Nov).

Lanterne des Morts (Lantern of the Dead)
The conical tower in the cemetery was built to commemorate St. Bernard's sermons in Sarlat in August 1147.

Cathédrale St-Sacerdos
Built largely in the 16th and 17th centuries, the cathedral is remarkable for its magnificent 18th-century organ.

The Chapelle des Pénitents Bleus, built in pure Romanesque style, is the last vestige of the 12th-century abbey.

The former Bishop's Palace, with remains of a 16th-century loggia and a Renaissance interior, is now the municipal theater.

Cour des Fontaines
A pure spring here attracted the monks who founded Sarlat's first abbey in the 9th century.

Painting of a bull from the original cave at Lascaux

Lascaux II ➐

Montignac. ☎ *05 53 51 95 03.*
Open *Feb–Jun & Sep–Dec: Tue–Sun;*
Jul–Aug: daily. **Closed** *Jan 1, Dec 25.* 🖼

Lascaux is the most famous of the prehistoric sites clustered around the junction of the Vézère and Beune rivers *(see pp392–3).* Two young boys and their dog, Robot, came across the caves and their astonishing palaeolithic paintings in 1940, and the importance of their discovery was swiftly recognized.

Lascaux has been closed to the public since 1963 because of deterioration, but an exact copy, known as Lascaux II, has been created a few minutes' walk down the hillside, using the same materials. The replica is beautiful and is well worth seeing: high-antlered elk, bison and plump horses cover the walls, moving in herds or files, surrounded by arrows and geometric symbols thought to have had ritual significance.

Bergerac ➑

Dordogne. 🚶 *28,000.* ✈ 🚌 🚉
🛈 *rue Neuve d'Argenson (05 53 57 03 11).* 🛒 *Wed & Sat.*

This small port, a tobacco farming and commercial center, spreads itself over both sides of the Dordogne. Chief attractions are its extraordinary **Musée du Tabac** (tobacco museum), and its food and wine, which are invariably excellent. Bergerac's

most celebrated wine is Monbazillac, a sweet white wine, often drunk on ceremonial occasions. On display in the small, lively museum are some American Indian pipes and ivory tobacco graters.

🏛 **Musée du Tabac**
Maison Peyrarède, place du Feu.
☎ *05 53 63 04 13.* **Open** *Tue–Sun.*
Closed *public hols.* 🖼 ♿

Les Eyzies ➒

Dordogne. 🚶 *900.* 🚉 🛈 *place de la Mairie (05 53 06 97 05).* 🛒 *Mon.*

Four major prehistoric sites and a group of smaller caves cluster around the unassuming village of Les Eyzies. Head first for the **Musée National de Préhistoire**, in a 16th-century castle overlooking the village. The timelines and other exhibits are useful for putting the vast area of prehistoric painting and sculpture into context.

The **Grotte de Font de Gaume**, a good 20-minute walk from the road, is the logical first stop after the museum in Les Eyzies. This cave, discovered in 1901, contains the finest ensemble of prehistoric paintings still open to the public in France. Close by is the **Grotte des Combarelles**, with paintings of bison, reindeer, magic symbols and human figures, and a major series of

Les Eyzies, a center for the area's concentration of prehistoric caves

carvings. Farther on, you reach the rock shelter of **Abri du Cap Blanc**, discovered in 1911, with a rare, life-size frieze of horses and bison sculpted in the rock.

On the other side of Les Eyzies is the cave system in **Rouffignac**, a favorite place for excursions since the 15th century. There are 8 km (5 miles) of caves here, 2.5 km (1.5 miles) of which are served by electric train. The paintings include drawings of mammoths, and a frieze of two bison challenging each other to combat.

Tickets for all the caves sell out fast, especially in the summer months, so arrive early to be sure of getting in.

Musée National de Préhistoire

🏛 **Musée National de Préhistoire**
📞 05 53 06 45 45. **Open** Wed–Mon. **Closed** Dec 25, Jan 1. 📷
📷 **Grotte de Font de Gaume**
📞 05 53 06 90 80. **Open** Thu–Tue by appt. **Closed** Jan 1, May 1, Nov 1, Nov 11, Dec 25. 📷
📷 **Grotte des Combarelles**
📞 05 53 06 90 80. **Open** Thu–Tue. **Closed** Jan 1, May 1, Nov 1, Nov 11, Dec 25. 📷
📷 **Abri du Cap Blanc**
Marquay, Les Eyzies. 📞 05 53 59 21 74. **Open** Apr–Oct: daily. 📷 ♿
📷 **Grotte de Rouffignac**
📞 05 53 05 41 71. **Open** Apr–Oct: daily. 📷 ♿

Dordogne Valley ⑩

Dordogne. ✈ Bergerac. 🚌 Beynac, Bergerac, Le Buisson de Cadouin. ℹ Le Buisson de Cadouin (05 53 22 06 09).

P ROBABLY no river in France crosses so varied a landscape and such different geological formations as the

View of Domme from the medieval gateway of Porte de la Combe

Dordogne. Starting in deep granite gorges in the Massif Central, it continues through fertile lowlands, then enters the limestone Causse country around Souillac. By the time the Dordogne has wound down to the Garonne, it is almost 3 km (2 miles) wide.

Don't be put off by the touristy image of this famous valley. Despite being a popular vacation spot, it is a beautiful area for wandering. Several villages make good stopping-off points, including Limeuil, Beynac, and La Roque-Gageac from where flat-bottomed *gabarres* (riverboats) ferry visitors in summer.

Perched high above the river, southwest of Sarlat, is the 17th-century **Château de Marqueyssac**. Its topiary park offers panoramic views from Domme to Beynac, and of the Château de Castelnaud on the opposite river bank.

Sarlat ⑪

See pp422–3.

Domme ⑫

Dordogne. 👥 1,000. ℹ place de la Halle (05 53 31 71 00). 🛒 Thu.

H ENRY MILLER wrote: "Just to glimpse the black, mysterious river at Domme from the beautiful bluff . . . is something to be grateful for all one's life." Domme itself is a neat bastide (*see p435*) of golden stone, with medieval gateways still standing. People come here to admire the view, which takes in the Dordogne Valley from Beynac in the west to Montfort in the east, and wander the maze of old streets inside the walls. There is also a large cavern under the 19th-century covered market (access by elevator from April to December) where the inhabitants hid at tense moments during the Hundred Years' War and the 16th-century Wars of Religion. Despite a seemingly impregnable position, 30 Huguenots captured Domme by scaling the cliffs at night and opening the gates.

A *cingle* (loop) of the Dordogne River, seen from the town of Domme

Rocamadour ⑬

Black Virgin and Child

ROCAMADOUR BECAME one of the most famous centers of pilgrimage following the discovery in 1166 of an ancient grave and sepulcher containing an undecayed body, said to be that of the early Christian hermit St. Amadour. The discovery unleashed a spate of miracles heralded, it is claimed, by the bell above the Black Virgin and Child in the Chapel of Notre-Dame. Although the town suffered with the decline of pilgrimages in the 17th and 18th centuries, it was heavily restored in the 19th century. Still a holy shrine, as well as a popular tourist destination, Rocamadour's site on a rocky peak above the Alzou Valley is phenomenal. The best views are to be had from the village of L'Hospitalet.

The château stands on the site of a fort which protected the sanctuary from the west.

St. Michael's Chapel contains well-preserved 12th-century frescoes.

General View
Rocamadour is at its most breathtaking in the sunlight of early morning: the cluster of medieval houses, towers and battlements seems to sprout from the base of the cliff.

The Tomb of St. Amadour once held the body of the hermit called *roc amator* (lover of rock), from whom the town took its name.

Museum of Sacred Art

Grand Stairway
Pilgrims would climb this broad flight of steps on their knees as they said their rosaries. The stairway leads to a square on the next level, around which the main pilgrim chapels are grouped.

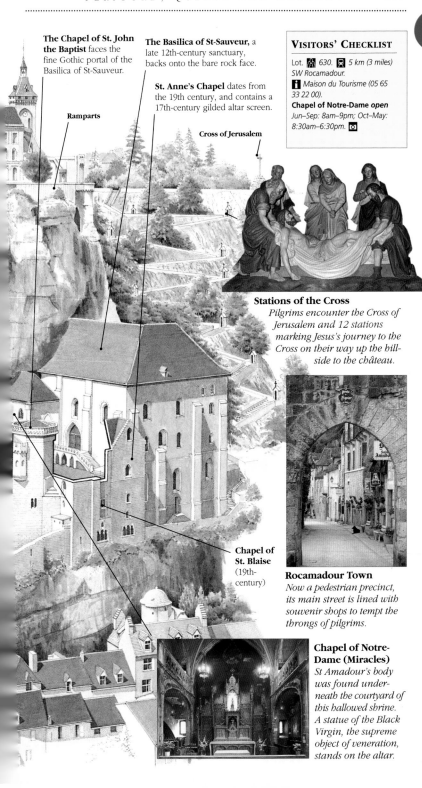

The Chapel of St. John the Baptist faces the fine Gothic portal of the Basilica of St-Sauveur.

Ramparts

The Basilica of St-Sauveur, a late 12th-century sanctuary, backs onto the bare rock face.

St. Anne's Chapel dates from the 19th century, and contains a 17th-century gilded altar screen.

Cross of Jerusalem

VISITORS' CHECKLIST

Lot. 🚂 630. 🚉 5 km (3 miles) SW Rocamadour. ℹ Maison du Tourisme (05 65 33 22 00). **Chapel of Notre-Dame open** Jun–Sep: 8am–9pm; Oct–May: 8:30am–6:30pm. 📷

Stations of the Cross
Pilgrims encounter the Cross of Jerusalem and 12 stations marking Jesus's journey to the Cross on their way up the hillside to the château.

Chapel of St. Blaise (19th-century)

Rocamadour Town
Now a pedestrian precinct, its main street is lined with souvenir shops to tempt the throngs of pilgrims.

Chapel of Notre-Dame (Miracles)
St Amadour's body was found underneath the courtyard of this hallowed shrine. A statue of the Black Virgin, the supreme object of veneration, stands on the altar.

Gouffre de Padirac ⑭

Lot. ☎ 05 65 33 64 56. **Open** Apr–mid-Oct: daily. ♿

FORMED BY THE COLLAPSE of a cave, this huge crater measures 35 m (115 ft) wide and 75 m (245 ft) deep. The stunning succession of galleries at the bottom *(see p393)* has been a great tourist attraction since its discovery in the late 19th century. The immense chamber known as the Salle du Grand Dôme dwarfs the tallest of cathedrals.

Autoire ⑮

Lot. 🏠 250.

THIS IS ONE of the loveliest places in Quercy, the fertile area east of Périgord. There are no grand monuments or dramatic history, just a beau-

tifully unspoiled site at the mouth of the Autoire gorge. The **Château de Limarque** on the main square, and the **Château de Busqueille** overlooking it, are both built in characteristic Quercy style, with turrets and small towers. Elsewhere, elaborate, raised dovecotes typical of the region stand in the middle of fields or are attached to houses.

Outside Autoire, past a 30-m (100-ft) waterfall, a path leads to a rock amphitheater giving panoramic views of the region.

The picturesque village of Autoire, seen from across the gorge

Cahors ⑯

Lot. 🏠 20,000. 🚌 🚆 ℹ place François Mitterrand (05 65 53 20 65). 🛒 Wed & Sat.

THE CHIEF TOWN of rural Quercy, 2,000-year-old Cahors, is encircled by the natural defenses of the Lot River. This small commercial center is famous for truffles, a Saturday morning market, and the dark, heady Cahors wine that was produced as far back as Roman times. Cahors' main street is boulevard Gambetta, a typical southern thoroughfare lined with plane trees, cafés, and shops. This street, like many others in France, was named after the dashing radical Léon Gambetta (1838–82), who was born in Cahors and led France to recovery after the war with Prussia in 1870.

Cathédrale de St-Etienne, entrenched behind the narrow streets of Cahors' Old Town,

A Tour of Two Rivers

FLANKED BY SPECTACULAR LIMESTONE CLIFFS, the beautiful Lot and Célé valleys feature ancient medieval villages and castles, narrow gorges, and rushing waterfalls along lazy stretches of river. An unhurried tour of both valleys, around 160 km (100 miles), is best spread over two days, so that some gastronomic delights can be enjoyed as well as the superb views. The slow, winding road from Cahors, well-known for the 14th-century Pont Valentré, meanders beside the wide river Lot. This is the home of truffles, *confit* (conserve) of duck and goose, delicious goat's cheese, and the almost black Cahors wine. The town of Figeac, with its old quarter and choice of hotels and restaurants, offers an ideal overnight stop.

Grotte du Pech-Merle ①
This 25,000-year-old prehistoric site outside Cabrerets has huge chambers painted with mammoths, horses, bison, and human figures.

St.-Cirq-Lapopie ⑥
Perched high above the Lot, one of France's prettiest villages has a 15th-century church and wood-framed houses built into the cliffs.

dates back to 1119. It has some fine medieval details: don't miss the lively figures of the Romanesque north door and tympanum, depicting the Ascension, or the huge cupola above the nave (said to be the largest in France). They are covered in 14th-century frescoes depicting the stoning of St. Stephen (St. Étienne). The Renaissance cloisters are decorated with some intricate, though damaged, carvings.

Also worth seeking out in the cathedral quarter is the ornate 16th-century **Maison de Roaldès**, its north facade decorated with the tree, sun, and rose of Quercy motifs. It was here that Henri of Navarre (who later became King Henri IV) stayed for one night in 1580 after surrounding and capturing Cahors.

The town's landmark monument is the **Pont Valentré**, a fortified bridge with seven pointed arches and

The fortified Pont Valentré spanning the Lot River at Cahors

three towers that spans the river. It was built between 1308 and 1360 and has withstood many attacks since then. A breathtaking sight, it is claimed that the bridge is one of the most photographed monuments in all of France. Inside the middle tower, the Tour du Diable (Devil's Tower), is a small museum

with displays relating to the history of the bridge and the town.

Environs
Situated about 60 km (37 miles) to the west of Cahors is the **Château de Bonaguil**, a superb example of military architecture dating from the Middle Ages.

Marcilhac-sur-Célé ②
This ancient village has a ruined 10th-century Benedictine abbey. Just outside is the Grotte de Bellevue, with its stalagmites and other strange underground rock formations.

Espagnac-Ste-Eulalie ③
The 12th-century Priory of Notre-Dame-Ste-Eulalie has an elaborate bell tower.

St Pierre-Toirac

Figeac ④
Excellent hotels and restaurants are located here as well as the Musée Champollion, with its mold of the Rosetta stone.

Cajarc ⑤
Medieval houses still survive in this tiny village. A short drive away is the Renaissance Château de Cénevières.

KEY

▬▬	Tour route
═ ═	Other roads

kilometers 5

miles 5

Orchards and vineyards outside Agen

Agen ^⑰

Lot-et-Garonne. 🚶 30,500. ✈ 🚉
🚌 🚹 107 boulevard Carnot
(05 53 47 36 09). 🛍 Wed, Sat & Sun.

IN A RECENT nationwide poll, the inhabitants of Agen – an attractive, unhurried provincial capital on the Garonne – were shown to be easily the most contented people in the country. The town is the mecca of French rugby (its team has won three championship titles in recent years), and the prune production center of France.

But the town has other treasures in addition to happy citizens and succulent plums. The **Musée Municipal des Beaux Arts** contains fine paintings by Goya, including his *Ascent in a Hot-Air Balloon;* Sisley's *September Morning;* and one of Corot's best landscapes, *L'étang de Ville Avray*. The undisputed jewel of the collection is the Greek marble *Vénus du Mas,* a beautifully proportioned statue dating from the 1st century BC, discovered nearby in 1876.

Around the town, vast orchards of regimented plum trees are a prominent feature of the landscape. Crusaders returning from the Middle East brought the fruit to France in the 11th century, and monks in the nearby Lot Valley were the first to dry plums for prunes in commercial quantities. Agen's factories now produce approximately 35,500 tons of prunes each year.

🏛 Musée Municipal des Beaux Arts
Place du Docteur Esquirol. 📞 05 53 69 47 23. **Open** Wed–Mon. **Closed** Jan 1, May 1, Nov 1, Dec 25. 🌐

Environs
The fortified village of Moirax has a 12th-century Romanesque church of great beauty and symmetry, formerly part of a Cluniac priory. Two of the appealingly sculpted capitals depict biblical accounts of Daniel in the lions' den, and Original Sin.

Larressingle ^⑱

Gers. 🚶 150. 🚌 to Condom. 🚹
Larressingle (05 62 28 00 80).

WITH ITS RAMPARTS, ruined donjon (defense tower) and fortress gate, Larressingle is a tiny fortified village in the middle of the Gascon countryside. It dates from the 13th century, and is one of the last remaining Gascon villages with its walls still intact. The state of preservation is unique, and gives an idea of what life must have been like for the small, embattled local communities, which had to live for decades under conditions of perpetual warfare.

Condom ^⑲

Gers. 🚶 8,000. 🚌 🚹 place
Bossuet (05 62 28 00 80). 🛍 Wed.

LONG A CENTER for the Armagnac trade, Condom is a market town built around the late-Gothic **Cathédrale St-Pierre**. In 1569 during the Wars of Religion, the Huguenot (French Protestant) army threatened to demolish the cathedral, but Condom's citizens averted this by paying a ransom of F30,000.

The Baïse River skirts the town center. Notable among Condom's fine 17th–18th-century mansions is the **Hôtel de Cugnac** on avenue Général de Gaulle, with its ancient *chai* (wine storehouse) and distillery. On the other side of the town center, the **Musée de l'Armagnac** is the place to find out, finally, what the difference between the brandy of Armagnac and Cognac really is.

🏛 Musée de l'Armagnac
2 rue Jules Ferry.
📞 05 62 28 31 41.
Open Wed–Mon. **Closed** public hols.
🌐 ♿

ARMAGNAC

Armagnac is one of the world's most expensive brandies. It is also one of the most jealously guarded: about 40 percent of it never leaves Gascony, and 4/5 of the remainder never leaves France. The vineyards of Armagnac roughly straddle the border between the Gers and the Lot-et-Garonne regions and the Landes. Similar in style to Cognac, its more famous neighbor, Armagnac's single distillation leaves more individual flavors in the spirit. The majority of small, independent producers offer direct sale to the public: watch for the battered, often half-hidden farm signs advertising *Vente Directe*.

A Tenarèze Armagnac

D'ARTAGNAN

Gascons call their domain the "Pays d'Artagnan" after Alexandre Dumas' rollicking hero from *The Three Musketeers* (1844). The character of d'Artagnan was based on Charles de Batz, a typical Gascon whose chivalry, passion and impetuousness made him ideal as a musketeer, or royal bodyguard. De Batz's life was as fast and furious as that of the fictional hero, and he performed a feat of courtliness by arresting Louis XIV's most formidable minister without causing the slightest offense. The French have other opinions of the Gascon nature too: a *promesse de Gascon*, for example, means an empty promise.

Statue of Dumas' musketeer d'Artagnan in Auch

a mix of prophets, patriarchs and apostles, with 360 individually characterized figures and exceptional colors. Three depict the key biblical events of the Creation, the Crucifixion and the Resurrection.

Auch went through an urbanization program in the 18th century, when the Allées d'Etigny, flanked by the grand Hôtel de Ville and Palais de Justice, were built. Some fine houses from this period line the pedestrianized rue Dessoles. Auch's restaurants are known for their hearty dishes, including *foie gras de canard* (fattened duck liver).

Auch ❷⓿

Gers. ⬛ *25,000.* ▢ ▢ ℹ *1 rue Dessoles (05 62 05 22 89).* ♻ *Thu & Sat.*

THE ANCIENT capital of the Gers department, Auch (pronounced "Ohsh") has long been a sleepy place that comes alive on market days. The new town by the station is not a place that encourages you to linger. Head instead for the Old Town on the out-

Medallion from Cathédrale de Ste-Marie

crop overlooking the Gers River. If you climb the 232 stone steps from the river, you arrive directly in front of the late-Gothic **Cathédrale de Ste-Marie**, begun in 1489. The furnishings of the cathedral are remarkable: highlights are the carved wooden choir stalls depicting more than 1,500 biblical, historical and mythological characters, and the equally magnificent 15th-century stained glass, attributed to Arnaud de Moles. The windows show

Auvillar ❷①

Tarn-et-Garonne. ⬛ *1,000.* ℹ *Le Mairie (05 63 39 57 33).*

A PERFECT complement to the high emotion of Moissac *(see pp432–3)*, Auvillar is one of the loveliest hilltop villages in France. It has a triangular marketplace lined with half-timbered arcades at its center, and extensive views from the promenade overlooking the Garonne River. There are picnic spots along this panoramic path plus an orientation map. This includes all but the chimneys visible in the distance, belonging to the nuclear plant at Golfech.

Sunflowers, a popular crop in southwest France, grown for their seeds and oil

Moissac ㉒

Abbot Durand

THE VILLAGE OF MOISSAC nestles among vineyards of sweet Chasselas grapes, with the abbey of St-Pierre its undisputed highlight. Founded in the 7th century by a Benedictine monk, the abbey was subsequently ransacked by Arabs, Normans and Hungarians. In 1047, the Moissac Abbey was united with the rich foundation at Cluny and prospered under the direction of Abbot Durand de Bredon. By the 12th century it had become the preeminent monastery in southwest France. The south portal created during this period is a masterpiece of Romanesque sculpture.

Abbey of St-Pierre
The church's exterior belongs to two periods: one part, in stone, is Romanesque, the other, in brick, is Gothic.

Christ in Majesty
The figure of Christ sits in judgment at the center of the scene. He holds the Book of Life in His left hand and raises His right in benediction.

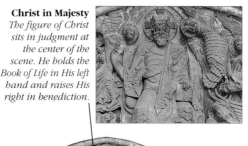

Tympanum
The lower register of the balanced, compact tympanum shows the expressive "24 Elders with crowns of gold" from St. John's vision.

★ South Portal
The carved south portal (1100–1130) is a masterful translation into stone of St. John's dramatic vision of the Apocalypse (Book of Revelation, Chapters 4 and 5). The Evangelists Matthew, Mark, Luke and John appear as "four beasts full of eyes." Moorish details on the door jambs reflect the contemporary cultural exchange between France and Spain..

VISITORS' CHECKLIST

Tarn-et-Garonne. 🏠 🚌 ℹ️
6 place Durand de Bredon (05 63
04 01 85). **Abbey open** 8am–
6pm daily. **Closed** Jan 1, Dec 25.
📷 ✝ 6:30pm Mon–Fri, 7:30pm
Sat, 10:30am Sun. 📷 ✔

★ **Cloister**
*The late 11th-century
cloister is lined with
alternate double and single
columns in white, pink,
green and gray marble. In
all, there are 76 richly
decorated arches.*

FLOORPLAN: CHURCH AND CLOISTER

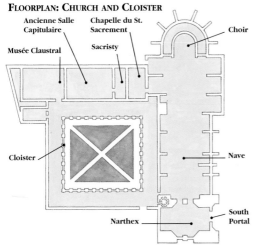

Ancienne Salle
Capitulaire

Chapelle du St.
Sacrement

Musée Claustral

Sacristy

Choir

Cloister

Nave

South
Portal

Narthex

Cloister Capitals
*Flowers, beasts and scenes
from both the Old and New
Testaments are featured in
these superbly sculptured
11th-century Romanesque
capitals.*

STAR FEATURES

★ **South Portal**

★ **Cloister**

Montauban ㉓

Tarn-et-Garonne. 🏠 *54,000.* 🚌 🚉
ℹ️ *place Prax-Paris (05 63 63 60 60).*
🛒 *Sat.*

MONTAUBAN deserves more
attention than it usually
gets, as Toulouse's little pink-
brick sister and the capital of
the 17th-century "Protestant
Republic" of southern France.
The painter Ingres was born
in Montauban in 1780, and
the town's great treasure is the
Musée Ingres, an exceptional
bequest of several paintings
and 4,000 drawings. Part of
the museum's collection
includes works by sculptor
Emile Bourdelle, an associate
of Rodin, also from the town.
  Above all, Montauban is a
civilized shopping center,
with a double-arcaded main
square (place Nationale) built
in the 17th and 18th centuries.
A few streets away lies the
stark white **Cathédrale Notre-
Dame**, built on the orders of
Louis XIV in 1685, in the back-
lash against Protestant heresy.

🏛 **Musée Ingres**
Palais Episcopal. ☎ *05 63 22 12 91.*
Open Tue–Sun (Jul–Aug: daily).
Closed Jan 1, Jul 14, Nov 1, Nov 11,
Dec 25. 📷

Gorges
de l'Aveyron ㉔

Tarn-et-Garonne. ✈ *Toulouse.* 🚉
Montauban, Lexos. 🚌 *Montauban.*
ℹ️ *Montauban (05 63 63 31 40).*

AT THE Gorges de l'Aveyron,
the sweltering plains of
Montauban change abruptly
to cool, chestnut-wooded hills.
Unlike the other villages
of Périgord and Quercy, these
precariously perched villages
were obsessed with defense.
  The château in Bruniquel,
founded in the 6th century, is
built over the lip of a preci-
pice, reached by a steep walk
through the village. Farther
along the D115, the village of
Penne's position on the tip of
a giant rock fang is even more
extreme. The gorge narrows
and darkens; from St-Antonin-
Noble-Val, fixed firmly to its
rock face, the valley turns
toward Cordes.

Cordes **⑳**

Tarn. 🏛 *970.* 🚉 🚌 **ℹ** *place Bouteillerie (05 63 56 00 52).* ⛴ *Sat.*

GLORIOUSLY SITED Cordes, lining a ridge above the Cerou River, is sometimes known as Cordes-sur-Ciel: a fitting description, as the town seems suspended against the skyline. During the 13th-century Cathar wars the entire town was excommunicated. Devastating epidemics of plague later sent it into decline, and the town was in an advanced state of decay at the beginning of this century.

Restoration work under the care of the artist Yves Brayer began in the 1940s. The ramparts and many of the gates built in 1222 by the town's founder, Albigensian Count Raymond VII of Toulouse, have been well-preserved. Also intact are Gothic houses such as the 14th-century **Maison du Grand Fauconnier**, with falcons carved on its façade, and the **Maison du Grand Veneur** (Great Huntsman's House), which line the unbelievably steep cobbled streets.

Today, lovely as it is from a distance, Cordes on its hilltop still exudes a sense of loss. The town of which Albert Camus once wrote, "Everything is beautiful there, even regret," is now dependent on tourism. "Medieval" crafts for visitors abound, but nothing remains of the weaving, *pastel* (blue pigment) and leather industries that paid for so many of Cordes' ancient buildings.

Cathédrale de Ste-Cécile perched above the town of Albi

Albi **㉖**

Tarn. 🏛 *47,000.* 🚉 🚌 **ℹ** *Palais de la Berbie, place Ste-Cécile (05 63 49 48 80).* ⛴ *Sat.*

LIKE MANY other large towns in this part of the world, Albi is not only red, but also red-hot, and definitely not for brief afternoon visits. You need to get up in the cool early morning to walk the streets around the market and the **Cathédrale de Ste-Cécile**.

Then head for the **Musée Henri de Toulouse-Lautrec** in the Palais de la Berbie, ahead of the crowds. The museum contains the most complete permanent collection of the artist's work in existence, including paintings, drawings, and his famous posters for the Moulin-Rouge. There are also canvases by Matisse, Dufy, and Yves Brayer.

After a stroll around the beautiful terraced gardens of the Palais de la Berbie overlooking the Tarn River, head for the vast red-brick cathedral, built in the aftermath of the Albigensian crusade in 1265.

It was intended as a reminder to potential heretics that the Church meant business. From a distance, its semicircular towers and narrow windows give it the appearance more of a fortress than a place of worship. Every feature, from the huge bell tower to the apocalyptic fresco of the *Last Judgment*, is on a giant scale built deliberately to dwarf the average human being.

🏛 **Musée Toulouse-Lautrec**
Palais de la Berbie.
📞 *05 63 49 48 70.* **Open** *Apr–Sep: daily; Oct–Mar: Wed–Mon.* **Closed** *Jan 1, May 1, Nov 1, Dec 25.*
🎫 ♿

Castres **㉗**

Tarn. 🏛 *47,000.* ✈ 🚉 🚌 **ℹ** *3 rue Milhau-Ducommun (05 63 62 63 62).* ⛴ *Tue, Thu–Sat.*

CASTRES HAS BEEN a center for the fabric industry since the 14th century. Today it is also the headquarters of one of France's biggest pharmaceutical companies and a busy, relaxed, southern town. In the large collection of Spanish art in the **Musée Goya**, the artist himself is well represented by a large, misty council scene and by a series of powerful prints, *Los Caprichos*. Outside, the formal gardens between the town hall and the Agout River were designed in the 17th century by Le Nôtre (*see p169*), the landscape architect of Vaux-le-Vicomte and Versailles.

🏛 **Musée Goya**
Hôtel de Ville. 📞 *05 63 71 59 30 or 05 63 71 59 27.* **Open** *Jul–Aug: daily; Sep– Jun: Tue–Sun.* **Closed** *Jan 1, May 1, Nov 1, Dec 25.* 🎫

TOULOUSE-LAUTREC

Comte Henri de Toulouse-Lautrec was born in Albi in 1864. Crippled at 15 as a result of two falls, he moved to Paris in 1882, recording the life of the city's cabarets, brothels, racecourses and circuses. A dedicated craftsman, his bold, vivid posters did much to establish lithography as a major art form. Alcoholism and syphilis led to his early death at the age of 36.

Lautrec's *La Modiste* (1900)

Bastide Towns

BASTIDE TOWNS were hurriedly built in the 13th century by both the English and the French, to encourage settlement of empty areas before the Hundred Years' War. They are the medieval equivalent of "new towns," with their planned grid of streets and fortified perimeters. Over 300 bastide towns and villages still survive between Périgord and the Pyrenees.

A broad arcaded marketplace is the central feature of most bastides. Montauban's arcades still shelter a variety of shops.

Lauzerte, founded in 1241 by the Count of Toulouse, is a typical bastide town of gray stone houses. The town, long an English outpost, is perched for security on the brow of a hill.

The church could be used as a keep when the bastide's outer fortifications had been breached.

The central square is surrounded by a grid of interconnecting streets and alleys. This differs markedly from the usual jumble of medieval houses and lanes.

Stone houses protected the perimeter.

MONFLANQUIN
This military bastide town was built by the French in 1256 on a strategic north–south route. It changed hands several times during the Hundred Years' War.

Today, the bastides form a convenient network of market towns, known as the route des bastides. The best time to visit them is on market day, when the central squares are crammed with stalls.

Porte de la Jane in Cordes is a typical bastide feature. These narrow gateways were easily barred by portcullises.

Toulouse

TOULOUSE, THE MOST IMPORTANT TOWN in southwest France, is the country's fourth largest metropolis, and a major industrial and university city. The area is also famous for its aerospace industry (Concorde, Airbus, the Ariane space rocket all originated here), as shown by the new Cité de l'Espace just outside the city.

Best seen on foot, Toulouse has fine regional cuisine, two striking cathedrals, lively street life and a rose-brick Old Town which, as the French say, is "Pink at dawn, red at noon and mauve at dusk."

The Garonne River, crossed by the Pont Neuf, and bordered by tree-lined quays

Houseboats at their moorings on the Canal du Midi

Exploring Toulouse

This warm southern city has steadily expanded, crescent-like, from its original Roman site on the Garonne's. First it was a flourishing Visigoth city, then a Renaissance town of towered brick palaces built with the wealth generated by the *pastel* (blue pigment) and grain trades. The grandest of these palaces still survive in the Old Town, which has place du Capitole and the huge 18th-century **Hôtel de Ville** at its heart. Here, and in place St-Georges and rue Alsace Lorraine, is the main concentration of shops, bars and cafés.

The University of Toulouse, founded in 1229, has always supplied the city with an intellectual weight to match its wealth. Today the vocal, student population keeps prices down in the city's many cafés, oyster bars and bookstores, and in the fleamarket held on Sunday on place St-Sernin.

A ring of 18th- and 19th-century boulevards encircles the city, surrounded in turn by a tangle of highways. Today, the ultra-modern driverless metro system connects the center with the suburbs.

⛪ Les Jacobins

The church was begun in 1229 and completed over the next two centuries. The first Dominican convent, founded to combat dissent in the region, Les Jacobins became the founding institution of Toulouse University. Its church is a masterpiece of Gothic building, features a soaring, 22-branched palm tree vault in the apse. The bell tower (1294) with no spire is much imitated in southwest France. The delicate Gothic Chapelle St-Antonin (1337) contains frescoes of the Apocalypse dating from 1341.

🏛 Musée des Augustins

21 rue de Metz. 🄲 *05 61 22 21 82.* **Open** *Wed–Mon.* **Closed** *Jan 1, May 1, Dec 25.* 🈺 🅰

Toulouse became a center of Romanesque art in Europe due to its position on the route to Santiago de Compostela *(see*

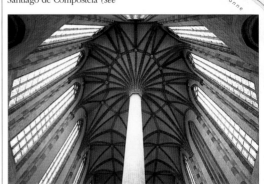

Palm vaulting in the apse of Les Jacobins

pp390–91). This museum has sculptures from the period, and incorporates cloisters from a 14th-century Augustinian priory, and 12th-century Romanesque capitals, many from the **Basilique de Notre-Dame-de-la-Daurade**. Also featured are 16th–19th-century French, Italian, and Flemish paintings.

Façade of Musée des Augustins

♣ **Hôtel d'Assézat**

Place d'Assézat. ▯ *05 61 12 06 89.* **Open** *Tue–Sun.* **Closed** *Jan 1, Dec 25.* 🖼 ♿

This 16th-century palace now houses the Fondation Bemberg, which is named after local art lover

Georges Bemberg. His fine collection covers Renaissance paintings, *objets d'art* and bronzes, as well as 19th- and 20th-century French paintings.

🔒 **Basilique de St-Sernin**

This is the largest Romanesque basilica in Europe, built in the 11th–12th centuries to accommodate pilgrims on their way to Santiago de Compostela. Highlights are the octagonal brick belfry, with rows of decorative brick arches topped by pepper pot turrets and a spire. Beautiful 11th-century marble bas-reliefs of Christ and the symbols of the Evangelists by Bernard Gilduin are in the ambulatory.

🏛 **Cité de l'Espace**

Avenue Jean Gonord. ▯ *05 62 71 64 80.* **Open** *Tue–Sun.* 🖼 ♿
To the southeast of Toulouse, this "Space park" features a planetarium and interactive exhibits related to the exploration of space. One of these is a replica of the Ariane 5 rocket. In the control room visitiors can learn how to launch rockets and satellites.

The tiered, 12th-century tower of Basilique de St-Sernin

SIGHTS AT A GLANCE

Basilique de Notre-Dame-de-la Daurade ④
Basilique de St-Sernin ①
Hôtel d'Assézat ⑤
Hôtel de Ville ②
Les Jacobins ③
Musée des Augustins ⑥

KEY

🅿 Parking

ℹ Tourist information

✝ Church

0 meters	250
0 yards	250

THE PYRENEES

PYRÉNÉES-ATLANTIQUES · HAUTES-PYRÉNÉES · ARIÈGE
HAUTE-GARONNE

T HE MOUNTAINS *dominate life in the French Pyrenees. A region in many ways closer to Spain than France, for centuries its remote terrain and tenacious people have given heretics a hiding place and refugees an escape route. Today it is the last remaining wilderness in southern Europe and a habitat for rare animal species.*

Heading east from the Atlantic coast, the hills are wonderfully lush after the plains of Aquitaine. The deeper the Pyrenees are penetrated, the steeper the valley sides and the more gigantic the snow-clad peaks become. This is magnificent, empty, dangerous country, to be approached with caution and respect. In summer the region offers over 1,600 km (1,000 miles) of walking trails, as well as camping, fishing and climbing. In winter there is both cross-country and alpine skiing at the busy resorts along the border, which are much livelier than their Spanish counterparts.

Historically, the Pyrenees are known as the birthplace of Henri IV, who put an end to the Wars of Religion in 1593 and united France, though the region has been characterized more often by independent fiefdoms. The region's oldest inhabitants, the Basque people *(see p445)* have maintained their own language and culture, and their resorts of Bayonne, Biarritz and St-Jean-de-Luz reflect this, looking to the sea and to summer visitors for their livelihood.

Inland, Pau, Tarbes and Foix rely on tourism and medium-scale industry, while Lourdes receives four million pilgrims every year. For the rest, life has been regulated by agriculture, though economic restraints today are causing an exodus from the land.

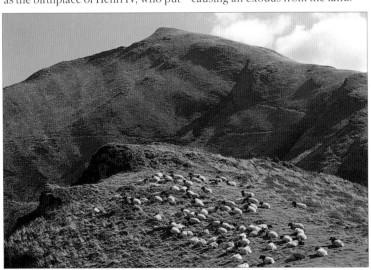

Countryside around St-Lizier, in the heart of the Pyrenean countryside

◁ **Barèges, a ski resort and spa town in the Hautes-Pyrénées**

Exploring the Pyrenees

THE TOWERING PYRENEES cut across southwest France from the Mediterranean to the Atlantic coast, encompassing the craggy citadel of Montségur, the pilgrimage center of Lourdes, Pau in the hilly Béarn country, and the Basque port of Bayonne. This formidable range, an unspoiled paradise for hikers, anglers and skiers, is as lush on its French side as it is arid in Spain, and contains the wild and beautiful Parc National des Pyrénées. Throughout the region, visitors can expect cool temperatures and grandiose scenery. Lovers of art and architecture will be richly rewarded by St-Bertrand-de-Comminges and St-Jean-de-Luz, among the region's important sights.

Marzipan sweets, a specialty of southwest France *(see p387)*

The galleried church in the Basque village of Espelette

GETTING AROUND

Access to the Basque coast in the western Pyrenees is via the A63 from Bordeaux. The length of the Pyrenees, including the mountain valleys, is served by the A64 that runs between Lannemesan, near Tarbes, and Bayonne. Once you are high up, expect narrow, twisting roads and slow driving. The scenic but demanding D918/118 corniche road crosses 18 high passes between the Atlantic and the Mediterranean.

There are airports in Biarritz, Pau and Lourdes. These three towns, along with Orthez and Tarbes, are on the train route that loops south between Bordeaux and Toulouse.

Sights at a Glance

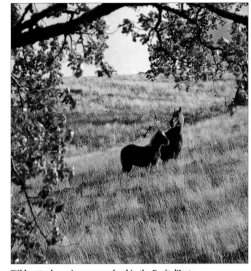

Wild pottock ponies on moorland in the Forêt d'Iraty

To Toulouse ↗

St-Jean-de-Luz seen from Ciboure, across the Nivelle estuary

Key

▬▬	Highway
▬▬	Major road
▬▬	Minor road
▬▬	Scenic route
∿	River
☼	Viewing point

0 kilometers   25

0 miles   25

Bayonne ❶

Pyrénées-Atlantiques. 🏠 40,000. 🚉
🚌 🛈 place des Basques (05 59 46
01 46). 🛒 Mon–Sat (am only).

Bayonne, capital of the
French Basque country,
lies between two rivers – the
turbulent Nive, which arrives
straight from the mountains,
and the wide, languid Adour.
An important town since
Roman times because of its
command of one of the few
easily passable roads to
Spain, Bayonne prospered as
a free port under English rule
from 1154 to 1451. Since then,
it has successfully withstood
14 sieges, including a particularly bloody one directed by
Wellington in 1813.
   Grand Bayonne, the district
around the cathedral, can be
easily explored on foot. The
13th-century **Cathédrale de
Sainte-Marie** was begun
under English rule and is
northern Gothic in style rather
than Pyrenean Romanesque.
Look for the handsome
cloister and the 15th-century
knocker on the north door –
if a fugitive could manage to
put a hand to this, he was
entitled to sanctuary. The
surrounding pedestrian streets
combine to form a lively
shopping area, especially the
arcaded rue du Pont Neuf,
with cafés serving a Bayonne
specialty – wickedly luxurious
hot chocolate – and shops
selling Bayonne ham and the
spicy local *Loukinkos* sausage.

**Grand Bayonne, clustered around
the twin-spired cathedral**

Lighthouse at Biarritz

Petit Bayonne lies on the
opposite side of the quay-
lined Nive River. The **Musée
Basque** gives an excellent
introduction to the customs
of the Basque nation, with
reconstructed home interiors
and exhibits on seafaring.
Nearby, the **Musée Bonnat**
houses a superb art gallery.
The first floor here is a must
for art lovers, with sketches
by Leonardo, Van Dyck,
Rembrandt and Rubens, and
paintings by Goya, Constable,
Poussin and Ingres.

🏛 **Musée Basque**
1 rue Marengo. 📞 05 59 59 08 98.
Closed until 2001.
🏛 **Musée Bonnat**
5 rue Jacques Lafitte. 📞 05 59 59 08
52. *Open* Wed–Mon.
Closed public hols. 🖼 ⚿

Biarritz ❷

Pyrénées-Atlantiques. 🏠 29,000. ✈
🚉 🚌 🛈 Javalquinto, square
d'Ixelles (05 59 22 37 10). 🛒 daily.

Biarritz, west of Bayonne,
has a grandiose center, but
has developed along the
coast by residential suburbs.
The resort began as a whaling
port but was transformed into
a playground for the European
rich in the 19th century. Its
popularity was assured when
Empress Eugénie discovered
its mild winter climate during
the reign of her husband,
Napoleon III.
   Nowadays, about a quarter
of Biarritz's population are
retired people. The town has
three good beaches, with the
best surfing in Europe, two

casinos, and one of the last
great luxury hotels in France,
the Palais *(see p569),* formerly the residence of Eugénie.
   In the port des Pêcheurs, the
Musée de la Mer aquarium is
home to specimens of some
of the marine life found in
the Bay of Biscay. Next to it,
the Atalaye watchtower was
used until the 16th-century to
send out smoke signals
whenever a school of whales
was seen approaching the
port. Below both, a narrow
causeway leads across to the
Rocher de la Vierge, offering
far-reaching views along the
whole of the Basque coast.

🏛 **Musée de la Mer**
Esplanade du Rocher-de-la-Vièrge,
14 plateau Atalaye. 📞 05 59 24 02
59. *Open* daily. 🖼 ⚿

Altar in Eglise St-Jean-Baptiste

St-Jean-de-Luz ❸

Pyrénées-Atlantiques. 🏠 13,000.
🚉 🚌 🛈 place Maréchal Foch
(05 59 26 03 16). 🛒 Tue & Fri.

St-Jean is a sleepy fishing
village out of season and
a scorching tourist town in
August, with shops to rival
the chic rue du Faubourg St-
Honoré in Paris. In the 11th
century, whale carcasses
were towed into St-Jean to be
divided up by the whole
village. The natural harbor
protects the shoreline,
making it one of the few
beaches safe for swimming
along this stretch of coast.
   One of the most important
historical events in St-Jean was
the wedding of Louis XIV
and the Infanta Maria Teresa

St-Jean-de-Luz, a fishing village that explodes into life in summer

of Spain in 1660, a union that had the effect of sealing the long-awaited alliance between France and Spain, only to embroil the two countries ultimately in the War of the Spanish Succession. This wedding took place at the **Eglise St-Jean-Baptiste**, still the biggest and best of the great Basque churches, a triple-galleried marvel with a glittering 17th-century altarpiece and an atmosphere of gaiety and fervor. The gate through which the Sun King led his bride was immediately walled up by masons: look for the plaque on the street marking the place.

Other sights that should not be missed in St-Jean include the **Maison Louis XIV**, with its contemporary furnishings, where the king stayed in 1660. The port is busy in the summer, while the restaurants behind the covered markets serve sizzling bowls full of *chipirons* – squid cooked in their own ink – a local specialty.

🏛 **Maison Louis XIV**
Place Louis XIV. 📞 05 59 26 01 56.
Open Sat am. 📷

Environs
On the other side of the Nivelle River, **Ciboure** was the birthplace of composer Maurice Ravel. It is characterized by 18th-century merchants' houses, steep narrow

streets and seafood restaurants. A two-hour coastal walk leads to the neighboring village of **Socoa**, where the lighthouse on the clifftop offers a fine view of the coast all the way to Biarritz.

Basque men in traditional berets

Ainhoa ❹

Pyrénées-Atlantiques. 🏠 550. 🚌

A TINY TOWNSHIP on the road to the Spanish border, Ainhoa was founded in the 12th century as a waystation on the road to Santiago de Compostela *(see pp390–91)*.

The main street of 17th-century whitewashed Basque houses and a galleried church from the same period survive.

Environs
There is a similar church in the village of **Espelette** nearby. Typically Basque in style, the galleries boosted the seating capacity and had the added effect of separating the men from the women and children in the main part of the church. Espelette is the trading center for *pottocks*, an ancient local breed of pony, auctioned here at the end of January. It is also the shrine of the local crop, the red pimento pepper, especially in October when a pepper festival is held here.

In the opposite direction from Ainhoa, at the foot of the St-Ignace Pass, lies the pretty mountain village of **Sare**. From here you can reach the summit of la Rhune by cog railroad. This provides the best vantage point in the entire Pays Basque.

Basque farmhouse near Espelette

Sauveterre-de-Béarn and the remains of the fortified bridge over the Gave d'Oloron

Orthez **❺**

Pyrénées-Atlantiques. 🚶 *10,700.* 🚉
🚌 ⓘ *Maison de Jeanne d'Albret,
rue du Bourg Vieux (05 59 69 02 75,
05 59 69 37 50).* ▲ *Tue.*

ORTHEZ is an important
Béarn market town, its
13th–14th-century bridge a
vital river-crossing point over
the Gave de Pau in the Middle
Ages. It has a Tuesday
morning market held from
November to February, selling
foie gras, smoked and air-
cured Bayonne hams, and all
kinds of poultry and fresh
produce. Fine buildings line
the rue du Bourg Vieux,
especially the house of Jeanne
d'Albret, mother of Henry IV,
on the corner of rue Roarie.
Jeanne's enthusiasm for the
Protestant faith alienated both
her own subjects and Charles
X, and ultimately caused the
Béarn region to be drawn into
the Wars of Religion (1562–93).

Sauveterre-de-Béarn **❻**

Pyrénées-Atlantiques. 🚶 *1,500.*
🚌 ⓘ *Parc de la Mairie, (05 59 38
50 17).* ▲ *Wed & Sat.*

AN ATTRACTIVE market town,
Sauveterre is worth an
overnight stay. It has breathtaking views southward over
the Gave d'Oloron, the single

arch of the river's fortified
bridge, and the 16th-century
Château de Nays. Fishermen
gather here for the annual
world salmon-fishing championships, held in the Oloron
between March and July.

Be sure, also, to visit the
Château de Laàs, located
9 km (5.5 miles) along the
D27 from Sauveterre, which
has an excellent collection of
18th-century decorative art
and furniture – notably the
bed that Napoleon slept in (if
the bitter taste of failure
allowed him to enjoy any
repose) on the night after his
defeat at Waterloo.

♣ **Château de Laàs**
📞 *05 59 38 91 53.* **Open** *Apr–Oct:
Wed–Mon.* 📷 ♿

**The Château de Nays at Sauveterre
in the Béarn region**

St-Jean-Pied-de-Port **❼**

Pyrénées-Atlantiques. 🚶 *1,500.* 🚉
🚌 ⓘ *14 place Charles de Gaulle
(05 59 37 03 57).* ▲ *Mon.*

ST-JEAN-PIED-DE-PORT is the
old capital of Basse-
Navarre and lies at the foot of
the Roncesvalles Pass. Here
the Basques crushed the rear-
guard of Charlemagne's army
in 778 and killed its commander, Roland, later glorified
in the *Chanson de Roland.*

Throughout the Middle Ages
this red sandstone fortress
town was famous as the last
rallying point before entering
Spain on the pilgrim road to
Santiago de Compostela *(see
pp390–91).* As soon as a
group of pilgrims was
spotted, the townsfolk would
ring the church bells to show
them the way, and the pilgrims
would sing in response.

Visitors and pilgrims in all
seasons still provide St-Jean
with its fame. They enter
the narrow streets of the upper
town on foot from the Porte
d'Espagne, and pass cafés,
hotels and restaurants on the
way up. The ramparts are
worth the steep climb, as is the
citadel with panoramic view.

On Mondays the town hosts
a livestock market, Basque
pelote matches and, in summer, running of the bulls.

Forêt d'Iraty ❽

Pyrénées-Aquitaine. 🚉 🚌 St-Jean-Pied-de-Port. 🅸 Larrau (05 59 28 51 29).

A WILD PLATEAU of beech woods and moorland, the Forêt d'Iraty is famous for its cross-country skiing and walking. Here the ancient breed of Basque ponies, the *pottocks*, run half-wild. These creatures have not changed at all since the prehistoric inhabitants of the region traced their silhouettes on the walls of local caves.

The visitors' center at Larrau publishes maps of local walks. The best begins at the Chalet Pedro parking lot, south of the lake on the Iraty Plateau, and follows the GR10 to 3,000-year-old standing stones on the western side of the Sommet d'Occabé.

Oloron-Ste-Marie ❾

Pyrénées-Atlantiques. 🚶 11,000. 🚉 🚌 🅸 place de la Résistance (05 59 39 98 00). 🛍 Fri.

OLORON, A SMALL TOWN at the junction of the Aspe and Ossau valleys, has grown from a Celtiberian settlement. There are huge agricultural fairs here in May and September, and the town is famed for producing the famous classic French berets.

BASQUE CULTURE

Most of Basque country is in Spain, but around 10 percent lies within France. The Basque people have their own complex language, isolated from other European tongues, and their music, games and folklore are equally distinct. French Basques are less fiercely separatist than their Spanish counterparts, but both are still deeply attached to their unique way of life.

Pelota, the traditional Basque game

Marble doorway of Eglise Ste-Marie

The town's great glory is the doorway of the Romanesque **Eglise Ste-Marie**, with its biblical and Pyrenean scenes. Spain lies just on the other side of the Somport Pass, at the head of the mountainous Aspe Valley, and the influence of Spanish stonemasons is evident in Oloron's **Eglise Sainte-Croix** with its Moorish-style vaulting. These two churches are Oloron's only sights, leaving time to head up the Aspe Valley to try one of the area's famous sheep's cheeses, or mixed cow and goat's cheeses.

A side road leads to Lescun, huddled around its church, beyond which is a spectacular range of saw-toothed peaks topped by the **Pic d'Anie** at 2,504 m (8,215 ft), one of the most beautiful spots in the Pyrenees. Sadly, at nearby Somport, a controversial highway and tunnel project was permitted, despite it posing a threat to the traditional mountain agricultural economy, and the last habitat of the Pyrenean brown bear.

High moorland above the Forêt d'Iraty, long stripped of timber for use by the French and Spanish navies

Gobelin tapestry in the Château de Pau

Pau ⑩

Pyrénées-Atlantiques. 🏛 *87,000.* ✈
🚃 🚌 ℹ *place Royale (05 59 27 27
08).* 🖐 *Mon–Sat.*

A LIVELY university town,
with elegant Belle Epoque
architecture and shady parks,
Pau is the capital of the Béarn
region, and the most interesting big town in the central
Pyrenees. The weather in
autumn and winter is mild,
so this has been a favourite
resort of affluent foreigners,
especially the English, since
the early 19th century.

Pau is chiefly famous as the
birthplace of King Henry IV.
His mother, Jeanne d'Albret,
travelled for 19 days by carriage from Picardy, in the
eighth month of her preg-
nancy, just to have her baby
here. She sang during her
labour, convinced that if she
did so, Henry would grow up
as tough and resilient as she
was. As soon as the infant
was born, his lips were
smeared with garlic and local
Jurançon wine, in keeping
with the traditional custom.

The town's principal sight is
the **Château de Pau**, first remodelled in the 14th century
for the ruler of Béarn, Gaston
Phoebus *(see p453).* It was
heavily restored 400 years
later. Marguerite d'Angoulême,
sister of the King of France,
resided here in the late 16th
century, and transformed the
town into a centre for the arts
and free thinking.

◁ **Foothills of the Pyrenees**

The château's 16th-century
Gobelin tapestries, made by
Flemish weavers working in
Paris, are fabulous, and the
Musée Béarnais on the third
floor is a veritable treasure
house of information about
the history, traditions and
culture of the Béarn.

Outside, the boulevard des
Pyrénées affords both glorious
views of the gardens below
and a glimpse of the highest
Pyrenean peaks, which are
often snow-capped all year
round. Continue from here to
the eclectic **Musée des
Beaux Arts**, where there is a
splendid Degas, the *Cotton
Exchange, New Orleans*;
Rubens' *Last Judgment;* and
works by El Greco.

♣ Château de Pau
Rue du Château. 📞 *05 59 82 38 00.*
Open *daily.* **Closed** *Jan 1, May 1,
Dec 25.* 🎫 🖐 **Musée Béarnais** *open
daily.* **Closed** *Jan 1, May 1, Dec 25.* 🖐

🏛 Musée des Beaux Arts
Rue Mathieu-Lalanne. 📞 *05 59 27 33
02.* **Open** *Wed–Mon.* **Closed** *public
hols.* 🖐

Tarbes ⑪

Hautes-Pyrénées. 🏛 *48,000.* 🚊
🚃 🚌 ℹ *3 cours Gambetta
(05 62 51 30 31).* 🖐 *Thu, Sat & Sun.*

T ARBES is the most pros-
perous town in the Bigorre
region, a center for chemical
and engineering industries
with good shops and a major
agricultural market. The
Jardin Massey in the middle
of town was designed at the
turn of the 19th century and is
one of the loveliest parks in
the southwest. It has many
rare plants, including the North
American sassafras. The cavalry
museum in the **Musée Massey**
is a must, with its dashing
uniforms from 19th- and 20th-
century regiments; nor are the
thoroughbred stallions at the
French National Stud.

🏛 Musée Massey
Jardin Massey. 📞 *05 62 36 31 49.*
Open *Jul–Aug: daily; Sep–Jun:
Wed–Sun.* **Closed** *public hols.* 🖐

Lourdes ⑫

Hautes-Pyrénées. 🏛 *16,500.* 🚊 🚃
🚌 ℹ *place Peyramale (05 62 42 77
40).* 🖐 *alternate Thu.*

L OURDES, one of the great
modern shrines of Europe,
owes its celebrity to visions
of the Virgin experienced by
a 14-year-old girl, Bernadette
Soubirous, in 1858.

Château de Pau, birthplace of Henry IV in 1553

Four million people annually visit the **Grotte Massabielle**, the cave where the visions occurred, and the one room on rue des Petits-Fossés where Bernadette's family lived, in search of a miracle cure for disability or disease.

If one is not led there by faith, Lourdes is best avoided, or left to those who really need it. Visit the **Grottes de Bétharram** for underground rides by boat and train through its vast caverns, or the **Musée Pyrénéen**, with fascinating exhibits on the first pioneering climbers who opened up these ranges.

Grottes de Bétharram

St-Pé-de-Bigorre. 05 62 41 80 04. **Open** mid-Apr–mid-Oct: daily.

Spectacular limestone formations at the Grottes de Bétharram

Pilgrims participating in open-air mass at Lourdes

Musée Pyrénéen

Château Fort, rue du Fort. 05 62 42 37 37. **Open** Apr–Oct: daily; Nov–Mar: Wed–Mon. **Closed** public hols (winter only).

Parc National des Pyrénées ⑬

See pp450–51.

Luz-St-Sauveur ⑭

Hautes-Pyrénées. 1,200. Lourdes. place du 8 mai (05 62 92 81 60). Mon.

Luz-St-Sauveur is an attractive spa town, with an unusual church built in the 14th century by the Hospitaliers de Saint Jean de Jérusalem (later the Knights of Malta), an order established to protect pilgrims. The church is fortified with gun slits that look out over the town and valley. These provided protection for pilgrims on the way to Santiago de Compostela.

Environs
The elegant spa town of **Cauterets** makes a good base for climbing, skiing and walking in the rugged mountains of the Bigorre region.

Gavarnie is a former way-station on the Santiago de Compostela pilgrim route. A good track, accessible on foot or by donkey, leads from the village to the spectacular natural rock amphitheater known as the **Cirque de Gavarnie**, one of the most popular tourist sights in the Pyrenean mountain range. Here the longest waterfall in Europe, at 240 m (787 ft), cascades off the mountain into space, encircled by eleven 3,000-m (9,800-ft) peaks.

The **Observatoire Pic du Midi de Bigorre** can be reached via Barèges, the Col de Tourmalet and then a 30-minute walk. The French are proud of the observatory, high in the Pyrenees. It has supplied the clearest images of Venus and other planets in the solar system so far obtained from the Earth's surface. The vast 2-m (6.5-ft) telescope mapped out the moon in preparation for NASA's Apollo missions.

Observatoire Pic du Midi de Bigorre

Le Sommet des Loisirs, Pic du Midi, Bagnères de Bigorre. 05 62 95 82 00. **Closed** until 2004.

THE MIRACLE OF LOURDES

In 1858 a young girl named Bernadette Soubirous experienced 18 visions of the Virgin at the Grotte Massabielle near the town. Despite being told to keep away from the cave by her mother – and the local magistrate – she was guided to a spring with miraculous healing powers. The church endorsed the miracles in the 1860s, and since then, many people claim to have been cured by the holy water. A huge Religious City of shrines, churches and hospices has since grown up around the spring, with a dynamic tourist industry to match.

Bernadette's vision

Parc National des Pyrénées ⓭

Pyrenean ibex

THE PYRENEES National Park, designated in 1967, extends 100 km (62 miles) along the French and Spanish frontier. It boasts some of the most spectacular scenery in Europe, ranging from meadows glimmering with butterflies to high peaks, snowcapped even in summer. Variations in altitude and climate make the park rich in flora and fauna. One of the most enjoyable ways to see it is on foot: within the park are 350 km (217 miles) of well-marked footpaths.

Vallée d'Aspe
Jagged peaks tower above the Vallée d'Aspe and the Cirque de Lescun. This area is now threatened by a new highway (see p445).

PIC D'ANIE
▲
2,504 m
(8,215 ft)

VALLÉE D'ASPE

N134

VALLÉE D'OSSAU

↑ PAU

Laruns

D934

PIC DE LA SAGETTE
▲
2,301 m
(7,550 ft)

PIC DU MIDI D'OSSAU
▲
2,884 m
(9,462 ft)

Col du Somport, the Somport pass (1,632 m/5,354 ft), is a rugged route into Spain, snow-bound December–April.

Pic d'Anie
The limestone-flanked 2,504-m (8,215-ft) Pic d'Anie overlooks rich upland pastures watered by melting snow. In spring, the ground is ablaze with Pyrenean varieties of gentian and columbine, found nowhere else.

Pic du Midi d'Ossau
A tough trail leads from the Bious-Artigues Lake at the base of the Pic du Midi d'Ossau and encircles the formidable, tooth-shaped summit (2,884 m/9,462 ft).

PYRENEAN WILDLIFE

The Pyrenees are home to a rich variety of wild creatures, many of them unique to the range. The ibex, a member of the antelope family, is still numerous in the valleys of Ossau and Cauterets. Birds of prey include the Egyptian, griffon and bearded vultures. Ground predators range from the rare Pyrenean lynx to civet, pine marten and stoat. The desman, a tiny aquatic mammal related to the mole, is found in many of the mountain streams.

Pyrenean fritillary *flowers through late spring and early summer in mountain pastures.*

The Turk's Cap Lily *flowers June–August on rocky slopes up to 2,200 m (7,218 ft).*

Brèche de Roland
The famous breach in the sheer crest of the Cirque de Gavarnie forms a gateway between France and Spain.

TIPS FOR WALKERS

The park is crossed by a network of numbered trails. Each is well marked and shows the length of time needed. En route are mountain huts offering a meal and a bed for the night. For maps and information visit the Park Office at Cauterets or the tourist office at Luz-St-Sauveur *(see p449)*, both open year-round.

Walking the trail in high summer

The GR10 long-distance trail is one of the great walks of France, linking the Atlantic with the Mediterranean.

Argelès-Gazost

D918

Arrens

D105

D918

D921

Cauterets

PIC DU MIDI DE BIGORRE
2,865 m
(9,400 ft)

TOULOUSE →

Luz-St-Sauveur

D918

M A S S I F   D E
N E O U V I E L L E

BALAITOUS
3,146 m
(10,322 ft)

PIC DE
NEOUVIELLE
3,094 m
(10,151 ft)

VIGNEMALE
3,296 m
(10,814 ft)

D921

D922

kilometers 5

miles 5

Gavarnie

KEY

— National Park boundary

---- French/Spanish border

- - GR10 walking route

Brèche de Roland

e Egyptian vulture *is seen over the Pyrenees, especially rocky cliff faces.*

Pyrenean bears *are close to extinction but a few still live in the Ossau and Aspe valleys.*

Cleopatra

Scarce Swallowtail

These butterflies *are among several colorful species found at high altitudes.*

Arreau

Hautes-Pyrénées. 860.
Château des Nestes (05 62 98
63 15). Thu.

ARREAU STANDS at the junction of the Aure and Louron rivers. A small, bustling half-timbered town with good shops and restaurants, this is the place to buy the basics (maps, walking boots, spiked walking sticks) for hiking or fishing in the mountains.

Environs

St-Lary Soulan is a ski resort up the valley, a base for exploring the entire Massif du Néouvielle in summer; the roads leading from the town will get you up to very high altitudes by car, and then you need to walk. Head for the village of Fabian and the smattering of lakes above it, where the GR10 (see p451) and other well-marked trails crisscross the peaks. Here you may see golden eagles or an enormous lammergeier (vulture) soaring overhead.

St-Bertrand-de-Comminges

Haute-Garonne. 220.
Montregeau, then taxi. Les
Oliveitains, parvis de la Cathédrale
(05 61 95 44 44).

THE PRETTY hilltop town of St-Bertrand is the most remarkable artistic and historic site in the Central Pyrenees and the site of an acclaimed summer music festival (see p33). Some of

Cloisters in the Cathédrale Ste-Marie, St-Bertrand-de-Comminges

the best sculpture in the region adorns the portal of the **Cathédrale Ste-Marie**. The adjoining Romanesque and Gothic cloisters contain sarcophagi, carved capitals and statues of the four Evangelists.

St-Bertrand's origins lie on the plain below, in the city founded by the great Roman statesman Pompey in 72 BC. At that time it consisted of two thermal baths, a theater, a temple, a market and a Christian basilica. All were destroyed by Gontran, the grandson of Clovis (see p202), in 585, and six centuries were to pass before the Bishop of Comminges, Bertrand de l'Isle, saw the site as a potential location for a new cathedral and monastery. The town, which was relatively unimportant in political terms, became reestablished as a major religious center.

Inside the cathedral, look out for the 66 magnificently carved choirstalls and the 16th-century organ case. The tomb of Bertrand de l'Isle is situated at the far end of the choir, with

an altar beside it; the beautiful marble tomb in the Virgin's chapel just off the nave is that of Hugues de Châtillon, a bishop who provided funds for the completion of the cathedral in the 14th century.

Cathédrale Ste-Marie
05 61 89 04 91. **Open** daily.
Closed Sun am.

Fresco in the Cathédrale St-Lizier

St-Lizier

Ariège. 1,600. place de
l'Eglise (05 61 96 77 77).

ST-LIZIER is located in the Ariège, a region famous for its steep-sided valleys and wild mountain scenery. The village dates back to Roman times, and by the Middle Ages was an important religious center, only to be superseded in the 12th century by St-Girons nearby. St-Lizier has the distinction of possessing two cathedrals; the finest is the 12th–14th-century **Cathédrale St-Lizier** in the lower town. It boasts Romanesque frescoes and a cloister with carved columns,

The imposing 12th-century Cathédrale Ste-Marie above St-Bertrand

St-Lizier, with snow-capped mountains in the distance

but the **Cathédrale de la Sède** in the upper town, reached on foot through narrow streets, has the better view.

Foix ⑱

Ariège. 🏘 10,500. 🚌 🚉 ℹ️ 45 cours Gabriel Fauré (05 61 65 12 12). 🛒 1st, 3rd & 5th Mon of each month.

WITH ITS BATTLEMENTS and towers, Foix stands directly above the junction of the Arget and Ariège rivers. In the Middle Ages, Foix's dynasty of counts ruled the whole of the Béarn area. Count Gaston Phoebus (1331–91) was the most flamboyant, a poet who surrounded himself with troubadours and wrote a famous treatise on hunting. He was a ruthless politician, who also had his own brother and his only son put to death.

Some of the pleasures of the medieval court are recreated in the local summer fair, the largest in France. The 15th-century keep of the **Château de Foix** is always worth climbing just for the view. The small and much-restored 14th-century **Eglise de St-Volusien**, on the banks of the Ariège River, is delightful in its simplicity and grace.

♣ Château de Foix
📞 05 61 65 56 05. **Open** daily. **Closed** Oct–Apr: Mon, Wed. 🅿️

Montségur ⑲

Ariège. 🏘 100. ℹ️ La Mairie (05 61 03 03 03 or 05 61 01 10 27). 🅿️ 🅿️

THE TOWN of Montségur is famous as the last stronghold of the Cathars (see p481). From the parking area at the foot of the mount, a path leads up to the small fortress town, occupied in the 13th century by faydits (dispossessed aristocrats) and the Cathar garrison. The Cathars lived outside the fortress, in houses clinging to the rock. Staunchly opposed to Catholic authority, the Cathar troops unwisely marched on Avignonnet in 1243 and massacred members of the Inquisitional tribunal. In retaliation, an army of 10,000 laid siege to Montségur for ten months. When captured, 225 Cathars burnt themselves to death rather than convert.

Mirepoix ⑳

Ariège. 🏘 3,000. 🚌 ℹ️ place du Maréchal Leclerc (05 61 68 83 76). 🛒 Mon & Thu.

MIREPOIX IS A TRADITIONAL bastide town (see p435) with a huge main square – one of the loveliest in the southwest – surrounded by beamed 13th–15th-century arcades and half-timbered houses.

The **cathedral**, begun in 1343 with the last additions made in 1867, boasts the widest Gothic nave (22 m/72 ft) in France.

The best times to visit the town are on market days, when the square is covered with vendors selling a mass of local produce.

The arcaded main square at Mirepoix

THE SOUTH OF FRANCE

Introducing the South of France

THE SOUTH is France's most popular vacation region, drawing millions of visitors each year to the Riviera resorts and modern beach cities to the west. Agriculture is a mainstay of the economy, producing early fruits and an abundance of affordable wine. The new high-tech industries of Nice and Montpellier reflect the region's key role in the developing south coast sunbelt, while Corsica still preserves much of its natural beauty. The map shows the major sights of this sun-blessed region.

Pont du Gard, *a 2,000-year-old bridge (see p485), is a major feat of Roman engineering. It was a key link in the 17-km (10.5-mile) aqueduct, parts of which were underground, carrying fresh water from a spring at Uzes to Nîmes.*

Pont du Gard

St-Guilhem-le-Désert

LANGUEDOC-ROUSSILLON
(See pp466–87)

Carcassonne

Peyrepertuse

St-Martin-de-Canigou

0 kilometers 50

0 miles 50

The Camargue *lies at the mouth of the Rhône delta, where marshland and inland seas support a rich selection of wildlife. Three visitors' centers give a good introduction to this fragile area with its population of pink flamingos and white horses (see pp500–1).*

Avignon, *enclosed by massive ramparts, became papal territory when popes decamped from Rome (see p493) in the 14th century, taking up residence in the Palais des Papes that towers over the town. In summer the town is the scene of the popular Avignon Festival.*

Palais des Papes, Avignon

Musée Matisse, Nice

PROVENCE AND THE COTE D'AZUR
(See pp488–521)

**Giacometti statue,
St-Paul-de-Vence**

Camargue

CORSICA
(See pp522–33)

**Statue of Napoleon,
Ajaccio**

0 kilometers   50

0 miles   50

The Côte d'Azur *has attracted sun worshipers and celebrities since the 1920s (see pp464–5). The coast also offers some prize collections of 20th-century art (pp462–3) and such famous yearly events as the Cannes Film Festival and Antibes Jazz Festival.*

Regional Food: the South

I T'S A HEADY EXPERIENCE just to stand, look and sniff in a Provençal market. Tables sag under piles of braided pink garlic, fresh and colorful peppers, tomatoes, eggplant, zucchini and asparagus. The Cavaillon melons are so ripe they've split, leaking sweet perfume. In the fall and winter an earthy, fragrant scent fills the air; wild mushrooms, Swiss chards, cardoons, walnuts, quinces, pumpkins, fennel and wrinkled black olives all crowd the stalls.

Coastal Provence is famous for fish soups, including *bouillabaisse* and *bourride*, a garlic fish stew. Lamb is the most common meat in Provence; the best comes from the Camargue and the Crau where lambs graze on herbs and salt-marsh grass. Languedoc-Roussillon

Rosemary supplies France with the first of the season's peaches, cherries and apricots. Its coastal waters provide a bountiful sea harvest of plump mussels, oysters and *tellines* (tiny clams). Farther south, the island of Corsica has a robust cuisine with a strong Italian influence, with chestnuts as an important staple.

Salade Niçoise *comes in many versions but always includes lettuce, green beans, tomatoes, black olives, eggs and anchovies.*

Pistou soup *is a rich vegetable and bean soup flavored with pistou, a sauce of basil, garlic and olive oil.*

Fish broth

Croutons

Red snapper

Conger eel

Monkfish

Red mullet

Rouille (meaning "rust"), a mayonnaise of chilies and garlic

Bouillabaisse, *a fish soup originating in Marseille, is a luxury today. It consists of an assortment of local seafood including monkfish, mullet, snapper, scorpion fish and conger eel, flavored with tomatoes, saffron and olive oil. Traditionally, the fish broth is served first with croutons spread with* rouille, *a spicy mayonnaise. The fish is eaten afterward.*

Ratatouille *is a stew of onions, eggplant, zucchini, tomatoes and peppers, cooked in olive oil and garlic.*

Pissaladière *is similar to pizza, garnished with onions, olives and anchovies. Every* boulangerie *in Provence sells it.*

Aïoli *is a sauce made of egg yolks, garlic and olive oil. It is served with salt cod, boiled eggs, snails or raw vegetables.*

Daube de boeuf *is a stew of beef, lamb or mutton with red wine, cooked in a pot-bellied casserole called a "daubière."*

Brandade de morue, *a specialty of Nîmes, is a purée of salt cod with cream, olive oil, garlic and potatoes.*

Tarte au citron *is a sweet- pastry pie filled with a creamy lemon mixture. Menton is well known for its lemon crop.*

Fougasse *is a flattish, lattice-like bread variously studded with black olives, anchovies, onions and spices. The sweet version is flavored with almonds.*

Olives and Olive Oil

Most of the olive crop is crushed for oil. Ripe olives are black and the unripe ones are green; both can be preserved in brine or oil. At the end of the olive harvest it is customary to eat bread with *tapenade*, a paste of black olives, capers, anchovies and olive oil.

Tapenade

Black olives

Honey *comes in many flavors, depending on the diet of the bees, which can include a wide variety of flowers and herbs such as lavender, orange blossom, rosemary or thyme.*

Pitted olives

Olive oil

Tisanes

In the south of France, tisanes (flower and herb infusions or teas) are popular drinks, especially after meals. Lime flower *(tilleul)* is the most popular, considered good for the digestion and for sleep. Camomile tea stimulates the kidneys, and lemon verbena *(verveine)* soothes the liver.

Lemon verbena   **Camomile**   **Lime flower**

France's Wine Regions: the South

Cellar sign,
Banyuls

A MASSIVE ARC stretching from Banyuls, in the extreme southwest corner of France, to Nice, close to the Italian border, encompasses the Mediterranean vineyards of Languedoc-Roussillon and Provence. This was for a century an area of mass-produced wine, and much is still of *vin de table* quality. Today, however, the more dynamic producers are applying new technology to traditional and classic grape varieties to revive southern France's nobler heritage of generous, warm, aromatic wines, evocative of sun-baked stone, the scent of wild herbs, and the shimmering waters of the Mediterranean.

LOCATOR MAP

▨ *Languedoc-Roussillon & Provence*

Coteaux du Languedoc is one of the more recently designated appellations *for the new generation of good southern wines.*

This full, red Fitou bears a name that reflects the importance of the terroir, or native soil, to many southern French winemakers.

Stop here to try the wines of Rivesaltes – idiosyncratic yet distinctive, exotic sweet white Muscats and rich, portlike reds.

0 kilometers   25

0 miles   25

KEY

▨ Collioure & Banyuls	▨ Costières du Gard
▨ Côtes de Roussillon	▨ Coteaux d'Aix en Provence
▨ Côtes de Roussillon Villages	▨ Côtes de Provence
▨ Fitou	▨ Cassis
▨ Corbières	▨ Bandol & Côtes de Provence
▨ Minervois	▨ Coteaux Varois
▨ Coteaux du Languedoc	▨ Bellet

Rugged valley slopes in Corbières

Hand-picking grapes for Côtes de Provence red wine

WINE REGIONS

Both in the Provence wine region, east of Aix and
Marseille, and in the larger Languedoc-Roussillon
area to the west, new, quality wine *appellations*
are joining the more familiar names.

*Spicy Provençal rosés, long
famous, have improved beyond
recognition in the last decade,
thanks to new technology.*

Bandol *is a small* appellation
*that, unusually, bases its well-
deserved reputation for quality
entirely on a traditional southern
French red grape, the Mourvèdre.*

KEY FACTS ABOUT WINES OF THE SOUTH

Location and Climate
A warm and sunny climate helps
to create generously alcoholic
wines. The flat coastal plains
support acres of vines, but generally the best
sites are on the schist and limestone hillsides.

Grape Varieties
Mass-produced grapes such as
Carignan and **Aramon** are giving
way to quality varieties such as
Syrah, Mourvèdre and **Grenache**.
Cabernet Sauvignon, **Merlot** and **Syrah**,
and the whites **Chardonnay**, **Sauvignon
Blanc** and **Viognier**, are increasingly used
for *vins de pays*. Rich, sweet whites are made
from the aromatic, honeyed **Muscat** grape.

Good Producers
Corbières & Minervois: La Voulte
Gasparets, Saint Auriol, Lastours,
Villerambert-Julien, Daniel
Domergue. *Faugères*: Château des
Estanilles, Gilbert Alquier, Château de la
Liquiere. *St. Chinian*: Château Cazals-Viel,
Domaine des Jougla, Cave de Roquebrun.
Coteaux du Languedoc and vins de pays:
Mas Jullien, Prieuré de St. Jean de Bebian,
Mas de Daumas Gassac, Pech-Celeyran.
Roussillon: Domaine Gauby, Domaine de la
Rectorie. *Provence*: Domaine Tempier, Dom-
aine de Pibarnon, Domaine de Trevallon,
Mas de la Dame, Mas de Gourgonnier, Dom-
aine Richeaume, Domaine de la Bernarde,
Commanderie de Peyrassol, La Courtade.

Artists and Writers in the South of France

ARTISTS AND WRITERS have helped create our image of the South of France – the poet Stephen Liégeard even gave the Côte d'Azur its name in 1887. Many writers, French and foreign, found a haven in the warmth of the south. From Cézanne to Van Gogh, Monet to Picasso, artists have been inspired by the luminous light and brilliant colors of this seductive region. Today it is rich in art museums, some devoted to single artists like Matisse, Picasso and Chagall, others with varied collections such as those in Céret, Nîmes, Montpellier, St-Tropez, St-Paul-de-Vence and Nice *(see pp472–517)*.

Monet's palette

Picasso and Françoise Gilot on the Golfe Juan, 1948

Paul Cézanne's studio in Aix-en-Provence *(see p501)*

FESTIVE LIGHT

THE IMPRESSIONISTS were fascinated by the effects of light, and Monet was entranced by "the glaring festive light" of the south that made colors so intense he said no one would believe they were real if painted accurately. In 1883 Renoir came with him to the south, returning often to paint his voluptuous nudes in the filtered golden light. Bonnard, too, settled here, painting endless views of the red tiled roofs and palm trees.

Post-Impressionists Van Gogh and Gauguin arrived in 1888, attracted by the region's rich colors. Cézanne, who was born in Aix in 1839, analyzed and painted the structure of nature, above all the landscape of Provence and his beloved Mont-Ste-Victoire. Pointillist Paul Signac came to St-Tropez to paint sea and sky in a rainbow palette of dots.

THE WILD BEASTS

THE FAUVES, DUBBED "Wild Beasts" for their unnaturally bright and wild colors, led one of the first 20th-century avant-garde movements, founded by Matisse in Collioure in 1905 *(see p25)*. Other Fauves included Derain, Vlaminck, Marquet, Van Dongen and Dufy. Matisse visited Corsica in 1898, and then St-Tropez, and was inspired by the lushness of Provence to paint the celebrated *Luxe, Calme et Volupté*. Eventually he settled in Nice, where he painted his great series of Odalisques. He wrote, "What made me stay are the great colored reflections of January, the luminosity of daylight." The exquisite blue-and-white chapel he designed in Vence is one of the most moving of his later works *(see p513)*.

Vincent Van Gogh's *Sunflowers* (1888)

PICASSO COUNTRY

THE SOUTH of France is, without question, Picasso country. His nymphs and sea urchins, his monumental women running on the beach, his shapes and colors, ceramics and sculpture are all derived from the hard shadows and bright colors of the south.

Pablo Picasso was born in Malaga in Spain in 1881 but spent much of his life on the French Mediterranean, developing Cubism with Braque in Céret in 1911, and arriving in Juan-les-Pins in 1920. He was in Antibes when war broke out in 1939, where he painted *Night Fishing at Antibes*, a luminous nocturnal seascape. He returned in 1946 and was given the Grimaldi Palace to use as a studio. It is now a Picasso Museum *(see p511)*. He also worked in Vallauris, producing ceramics and sculptures *(see p512)*.

Deux Femmes Courant sur la Plage (1933) by Pablo Picasso

LOST CAVIAR DAYS

JUST AS F. Scott Fitzgerald wrote the Jazz Age into existence, so he captured the glittering life on the Riviera with *Tender is the Night*. He and Zelda arrived in 1924 attracted, like many expatriate writers, by the warm climate and the cheap, easy living. "One could get away with more on the summer Riviera, and whatever happened seemed to have something to do with art," he wrote. They passed their villa on to another American, Ernest Hemingway. Many other writers flocked there including Katherine Mansfield, D.H. Lawrence, Aldous Huxley, Friedrich Nietzsche, Lawrence Durrell and Graham Greene. Some, like Somerset Maugham, led a glamorous lifestyle surrounded by exotic guests. Colette was an early visitor to St-Tropez, and in 1954, Françoise Sagan captured the youthful hedonism of the time in her novel, *Bonjour Tristesse*.

Scott and Zelda Fitzgerald with daughter Scottie

NEW REALISM

IN THE 1950s Nice produced its own school of artists, the *Nouveaux Réalistes*, including Yves Klein, Arman, Martial Raysse, Tinguely, César, Niki de Saint Phalle and Daniel Spoerri *(see pp516–17)*. They explored the possibilities of everyday objects – Arman sliced violins, packaged and displayed trash; Tinguely exploded TV sets and cars. They had a light-hearted approach: "We live in a land of vacations, which gives us the spirit of nonsense," said Klein. He painted solid blue canvases of his personal color, International Klein Blue, taking the inspiration of the Mediterranean to its limit.

PROVENÇAL WRITERS

The regions of Provence and Languedoc have always had a distinct literary identity, ever since the troubadours in the 12th–13th centuries composed their love poetry in the *langue d'oc* Provençal, a Latin-based language. In the last century, many regional writers have been inspired by the landscape and local traditions. They were influenced by the 19th-century Felibrige movement to revive the language, led by Nobel prize-winning poet Frédéric Mistral. Some, like Daudet and filmmaker-turned-writer Marcel Pagnol, celebrate the Provençal character. Others, such as Jean Giono, explore the connection between nature and humanity.

Frédéric Mistral in the Petit Journal

Beaches in the South of France

A train poster by Domengue
advertising the Côte d'Azur

The Carlton Hotel logo

THE GLAMOROUS Mediterranean coast is France's foremost vacation playground. To the east lie the Riviera's big, traditional resorts such as Menton, Nice, Cannes and Monte-Carlo. To the west are smaller resorts in coves and bays like St-Tropez and Cassis. Farther on is the long, sandy shore of Languedoc-Roussillon, where government investment since the 1960s has transformed mosquito-infested swamp into miles of clean, sandy beaches. New vacation resorts range from modern beach cities to replicas of fishing villages.

The beaches are sandy west of Antibes; eastward, they are naturally rocky, so any sand is imported. Antipollution drives mean that most beaches are now clean, except in a few spots west of Marseille and around Nice. Beaches around towns often charge fees but are usually well equipped.

Sète *(p482)* is a seaport with a network of canals. Stretching southward are 15 km (9.5 miles) of unspoiled, sandy beaches with lots of room, even in high season.

Stes-Maries-de-la-Mer *(p500)*, set among the sand dunes of the Camargue, offers white sandy beaches and a naturist beach 6 km (4 miles) to the east. Horse riding is offered.

La Grande-Motte (p485) *is a huge vacation beach resort with excellent sports facilities, famous for its bizarre ziggurat architecture.*

Cap d'Agde (p477) *is a vast modern resort with long, white sandy beaches and sports facilities of all kinds. It has Europe's largest naturist colony, accommodating 20,000 visitors.*

0 kilometers   25

0 miles   25

In Victorian times *the Côte d'Azur, or Riviera,
was the fashionable vacation spot for Europe's
royalty and rich. They came to gamble and
escape northern winters. Summer bathing did not
come into vogue until the 1920s. Today the
Riviera is busy all year-round, with the glamorous
beaches and nightlife still a major attraction.*

Menton *(p519)*
has a warm climate
in winter, and year-
round beach
weather. Its
sheltered, rocky
beaches are backed
by beautiful villas.

Cannes *(p510),* famous
for its film festival, takes
great pride in its golden
beaches, keeping them
scrupulously clean.

Cassis *(p503)* is a charming fishing
village with a popular casino, white
cliffs and some lovely hidden
creeks nearby.

Cap Ferrat (p518) *is
a wooded peninsula
that has a 10-km (6-
mile) craggy cliff walk
offering glimpses of
grand villas and
private beaches.*

St-Tropez *(p506) is flanked by golden
beaches mostly occupied by stylish
"clubs," offering amenities at a price.*

Nice (p516), *Côte d'Azur's capital, has 5 km (3 miles) of beaches
along its seafront. Although pebbly,
they are clean, and the private
ones are cheaper than in Cannes.*

LANGUEDOC-ROUSSILLON

AUDE · GARD · HÉRAULT · PYRÉNÉES-ORIENTALES

THE TWO DISTINCT PROVINCES *of Languedoc and Roussillon stretch from the foothills of the Pyrenees on the Spanish border to the mouth of the Rhône. The flat beaches and lagoons of the coast form a perfect sunbelt accommodating millions of vacationers every year. In between is a dry, sunburned land producing half of France's table wine and the season's first peaches and cherries.*

Beyond such sensuous pleasures are many layers of history, including the unification of the two provinces. The formerly independent Languedoc once spoke Occitan, the tongue of the troubadours, and still cherishes its separate identity. Roussillon was a Spanish possession until the treaty of the Pyrenees in 1659. Its Catalan heritage is displayed everywhere from the road signs to the Sardana dance, and the flavor of Spain is evident in the popularity of bullfights, paella and gaudily painted façades.

This stretch of coastline was the first place in Gaul to be settled by the Romans, their enduring legacy evident in the great amphitheater at Nîmes and the magnificent engineering of the Pont du Gard. The abbeys of St-Martin-du-Canigou, St-Michel-de-Cuxa and St-Guilhem-le-Désert are superb examples of early Romanesque architecture, unaffected by Northern Gothic. The great craggy Cathar castles and the perfectly restored medieval Cité of Carcassonne bear witness to the bloody battles of the Middle Ages.

In parts, the region remains wild and untamed: from the high plateaus of the Cerdagne, to the wild hills of the Corbières or the remote uplands of Haut Languedoc. But it also has the most youthful and progressive cities in France: Montpellier, the ancient university city and capital of the region, and Nîmes, with its exuberant *feria* and bullfights. The whole area is typified by an insouciant mixture of ancient and modern, from Roman temples and postmodern architecture in its cities to solar power and ancient abbeys in the mountains.

A sunny stretch of coastline at Cap d'Agde

◁ **The abbey of Saint-Martin-du-Canigou perched on Mount Canigou**

Exploring Languedoc-Roussillon

LANGUEDOC-ROUSSILLON combines miles of gentle coastline with a rugged hinterland. Its clean, sandy beaches are perfect for family vacations, with places ranging from traditional fishing villages to new tourist resorts. Inland is quieter, with acres of vineyards in the Corbières and Minervois and mountain walks in the Haut Languedoc and Cerdagne. A rich architectural heritage ranges from Roman to Romanesque, contrasting with the modern, vibrant atmosphere of the main cities.

Jousting on the canal, a regular summer event in Sète

SIGHTS AT A GLANCE

MONTS DE
L'ESPINOUSE

PARC RÉGIONAL DU
HAUT LANGUEDOC
⑳

To Castres
Albi

N112

To Toulouse

MONTAGNE NOIRE

⑯ MINERVE

BÉZIERS

N113

Canal du Midi

CARCASSONNE
⑮

D119

NARBONNE
⑬

MONTAGNE
LA CLAPE

LIMOUX

A61

D613

CORBIÈRES ⑫

To Foix

D117

SALSES
⑪

CERDAGNE
①

PERPIGNAN
⑩

PRIEURÉ DE
SERRABONE

PRADES
②   ③
VILLEFRANCHE-
DE-CONFLENT
⑤

ST-MICHEL-
DE-CUXA

ELNE ⑨

COLLIOURE
⑧

④
ST-MARTIN-
DU-CANIGOU

⑥ CÉRET

To Andorra

To Barcelona

GETTING AROUND

Montpellier's international airport serves the region, with
smaller airports at Perpignan
and Nîmes. The TGV stops in
Montpellier and a good rail network connects the main towns.
The main highways are the
Autoroute des Deux Mers,
giving access from the west,
and the A9, following the coast.
Smaller roads, even in the
mountains, are well maintained.
Barges along the Canal du
Midi are a leisurely alternative.

KEY

▨	Highway
▭	Major road
▭	Minor road
▬	Scenic route
⌇	River
⁂	Viewing point

0 kilometers 25

0 miles 25

The ruined Barbarossa tower at Gruissan on the Golfe du Lion

Cerdagne ❶

Pyrénées-Orientales. 🚉 Perpignan.
🚌 🚍 Mont Louis, Bourg Madame.
ℹ️ Mont Louis (04 68 04 21 97 or 04 68 04 21 18).

THE REMOTE CERDAGNE, an independent state in the Middle Ages, is today divided between Spain and France. Its high plateaus offer skiing and walking along clear mountain lakes in pine and chestnut forests. The Little Yellow Train is an excellent way to sample the area in a day. Stops include **Mont Louis**, a town fortified by Vauban, Louis XIV's military architect, which still accommodates French troops; the ski resort of **Font-Romeu**; and **Latour-de-Carol**, along with the tiny village of **Yravals** below it. Nearby **Odeillo** is the site of a huge solar furnace, 45 m (150 ft) tall and 50 m (165 ft) wide. Established in 1969, its giant curved mirrors are a remarkable sight in the valley.

Villefranche-de-Conflent ❷

Pyrénées-Orientales. 👥 260. 🚌 🚍
ℹ️ 1 place de l'Eglise (04 68 96 22 96).

IN MEDIEVAL TIMES Villefranche's position at the narrowest point of the Têt Valley made it an eminently defensible fortress against Moorish invasion. Today, fragments of 11th-century walls remain, along with massive ramparts, gates and Fort Liberia, high above the gorge, all built by

Abbey cloisters of St-Michel-de-Cuxa

Vauban in the 17th century. The 12th-century **Eglise de St-Jacques** has fine carved capitals from the workshops of St-Michel-de-Cuxa, and Catalan painted wooden statues, including a 14th-century *Virgin and Child*. The 13th-century oak door is embellished with intricate local wrought ironwork, a craft still apparent on many of the shop signs in town. From the streets of lo-

Statue in St-Jacques, Villefranche

cally quarried pink marble you can make the climb up to the **Grottes des Canalettes**, a superb underground setting for concerts. Alternatively, climb aboard the Little Yellow Train up onto the magnificent mountain plain of the Cerdagne.

St-Michel-de-Cuxa ❸

Prades, Pyrénées-Orientales.
☎ 04 68 96 15 35. **Open** daily.
Closed Sun am, religious hols. 🎫 ♿

PRADES, a small, pink marble town in the Têt Valley, is typical of the local style. The **Eglise St-Pierre** has a southern Gothic wrought-iron belfry and a Baroque Catalan interior. But the town is distinguished by the beautiful pre-Romanesque abbey of St-Michel-de-Cuxa, which lies 3 km (2 miles) farther up the valley, and by the legacy of the Spanish cellist Pablo Casals. Casals spent many years here in exile from Franco's Spain; every August the abbey provides the setting for the Prades music festival held in his memory.

An early example of monastic architecture, St-Michel-de-Cuxa Abbey was founded by Benedictine monks in 878 and rapidly became renowned throughout France and Spain. Distinctive keyhole arches showing Moorish influence pierce the massive walls of the abbey church, which was consecrated in 974. The mottled pink marble cloisters, with their superbly carved capitals, were added later, in the 12th century.

After the Revolution the building was abandoned, and

THE LITTLE YELLOW TRAIN

Arrive early for the best seats in the carriages of *Le Petit Train Jaune*, which winds its way on narrow-gauge tracks through gorges and across towering viaducts up into the Cerdagne, stopping at small mountain stations along the way. Built in 1910 to improve access to the mountains, it now operates mainly for tourists, beginning at Villefranche-de-Conflent and terminating at Latour-de-Carol.

The Little Yellow Train, with open carriages for summer visitors

its famous carvings looted. From 1913, George Grey Bernard, a visiting American artist, began to discover some of the capitals incorporated in local buildings. He sold the carvings to the Metropolitan Museum of Art in New York in 1925, where they formed the basis of the Cloisters Museum – a faithful re-creation of a Romanesque abbey in the unlikely setting of Manhattan.

St-Martin-du-Canigou **❹**

Casteil. **📞** 04 68 05 50 03.
Open (guided tours) mid-Jun–mid-Sep: daily (10am, noon, 2pm, 3pm, 4pm, 5pm); mid-Sep–mid-Jun: Wed–Mon (2:30pm, 3:30pm, 4:30pm). 🏛️

SAINT-MARTIN-DU-CANIGOU is situated in a spectacularly remote site a third of the way up Pic du Canigou, on a jagged spur of rock approached only by jeep or a 40-minute climb on foot from Casteil or by hiring a jeep from Vernet-les-Bains. The abbey was built between 1001 and 1026, and financed by Guifred, Count of Cerdagne, who abandoned his family and entered the monastery in 1035. He was buried there 14 years later in a tomb he carved from the rock himself, and which can still be seen. The church is early

Nun at St-Martin

Romanesque, based on a simple basilican plan. Two churches are built, quite literally, one on top of the other, making the lower church the crypt for the upper building.

The abbey complex is best viewed from above by continuing up the path. From there, its irregular design clinging to the rock is framed by the dramatic mountain setting – the ensemble a tribute to the ingenuity and vitality of its early builders.

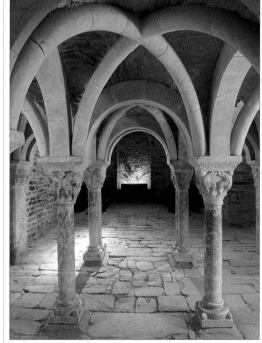

Serrabone Priory's chapel tribune, with columns of local marble

Prieuré de Serrabone **❺**

Serrabone. **📞** 04 68 84 09 30.
Open daily. **Closed** Jan 1, May 1, Nov 1, Dec 25. 🏛️

PERCHED HIGH UP on the northern flanks of Pic du Canigou, the sacred mountain of the Catalans, is the priory of Serrabone. A final lap of hairpin turns on the approach road (the D618) reveals the simple square tower and round apse of this remote Romanesque abbey, surrounded by a botanical garden of local herbs and woodland plants clinging to the mountain side.

Inside the cool, austere 12th-century building is a surprisingly elaborate chapel tribune, its columns and arches glowing from the local red-veined marble, carved by the anonymous Master of Cuxa, whose work appears throughout the region. Note the strange beasts and verdant flora featured in the capital carvings, especially the rose of Roussillon.

The 11th-century cloister of St-Martin-du-Canigou

Céret ❻

Pyrénées-Orientales. 🏠 8,000. 🚌
ℹ av Clémenceau (04 68 87 00 53).
🏠 Sat.

CÉRET IS A CHERRY TREE TOWN, surrounded by a glorious cloud of pink blossoms in the early spring, and producing the very first fruits of the year. The tiled and painted façades and loggias of the buildings have a Spanish feel, and the town was popular with Picasso, Braque and Matisse. Today, as a result, Céret is distinguished by the recently extended **Musée d'Art Moderne**, its sophisticated modern architecture housing a remarkable collection that includes Catalan artists Tapiès and Capdeville, a series of bowls by Picasso painted with bullfighting scenes, and works by Matisse, Chagall, Juan Gris and Salvador Dalí.

The town's Catalan heritage is evident in regular bullfights held in the arena, and in its Sardana dance festival at the end of August.

🏛 Musée d'Art Moderne

Bd Maréchal Joffre. 📞 04 68 87 27 76.
Open May–Sep: daily; Oct–Apr:
Wed–Mon. **Closed** Jan 1, May 1,
Nov 1, Dec 25. 🅿 ♿

Environs

From Céret the D115 follows the Tech Valley to the spa

Statue by Aristide Maillol, Banyuls

town of **Amélie-les-Bains**, where fragments of Roman baths have been discovered. Beyond, in **Arles-sur-Tech**, the Eglise de Ste-Marie contains 12th-century frescoes, and a sarcophagus beside the church door which, according to local legend, produces drops of unaccountably pure water every year.

Catalan flag

Côte Vermeille ❼

Pyrénées-Orientales. ✈ Perpignan.
🚊 Collioure, Cerbère. 🚌 Collioure,
Banyuls-sur-Mer. 🚢 Port Vendres.
ℹ Collioure (04 68 82 15 47),
Cerbère (04 68 88 42 36).

HERE THE PYRENEES meet the Mediterranean, the coast road twisting and turning around secluded pebbly coves

and rocky outcrops. The *vermeille* (vermilion-tinted) rock of the headlands gives this stretch of coast, the loveliest to be found in Languedoc-Roussillon, its name.

The Côte Vermeille extends all the way to the Costa Brava in northern Spain. With its Catalan character, it is as redolent of Spain as of France. **Argelès-Plage** has three sandy beaches and a palm-fringed promenade, and is the largest camping center in Europe. The small resort of **Cerbère** is the last French town before the border, flying the red and gold Catalan flag to signal its true allegiance. All along the coast, terraced vineyards cling to the rocky hillsides, producing strong, sweet wines like Banyuls and Muscat. The difficult terrain makes harvesting a laborious process. Vines were first planted here by Greek settlers in the 7th century BC, and Banyuls itself has wine cellars dating back to the Middle Ages.

Banyuls is also famous as the birthplace of Aristide Maillol, the 19th-century sculptor, whose work can be seen all over the region. **Port Vendres**, with fortifications built by the indefatigable Vauban (architect to Louis XIV), is a fishing port, with anchovies its main catch.

The spectacular Côte Vermeille, seen from the coast road south of Banyuls

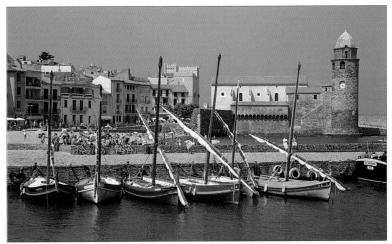

Collioure Harbor, with one of its beaches and the Eglise Notre-Dame-des-Anges

Collioure ❽

Pyrénées-Orientales. 🏠 2,700. 🚊
🚌 ℹ️ place du 18 juin (04 68 82 15
47). 🛍️ Wed & Sun.

THE COLORS of Collioure first
attracted Matisse here in
1905: brightly stuccoed houses
sheltered by cypresses and
gaily painted fishing boats, all
bathed in the famous luminous
light, and washed by a gentle
sea. Other artists including
André Derain worked here
under Matisse's influence and
were dubbed *fauves* (wild
beasts) for their wild experiments with color. Art galleries
and souvenir shops now fill
the cobbled streets, but this
small fishing port has changed
surprisingly little since then,
with anchovies still its main
business. Three salting houses
are evidence of this tradition.

Three sheltered beaches,
both pebble and sand, nestle
around the harbor, dominated
by the bulk of the **Château
Royal**, which forms part of the
harbor wall. It was first built
by the Knights Templar in
the 13th century, and
Collioure became the main
port of entry for Perpignan,
remaining under the rule of
Spanish Aragon until France
took over in 1659. The outer
fortifications were reinforced
ten years later by Vauban,
who demolished much of the
original town in the process.
Today the château can be
toured, or visited for its
exhibitions of modern art.

The **Eglise Notre-Dame-
des-Anges** on Collioure's
quayside was rebuilt in the
17th century to replace the
church that was destroyed by
Vauban. A former lighthouse
was incorporated into the
fabric of the new church as a
bell tower. Inside the church
are no fewer than five
Baroque altarpieces by
Joseph Sunyer and other
Catalan masters of the genre.

Be warned that Collioure
is extremely popular in July
and August, with visitors cram-
ming the tiny streets. Long
lines of traffic are possible,
too, though the building of
another route, the D86, has
helped to ease congestion.

⚓ Château Royal
📞 04 68 82 06 43. **Open** daily. **Closed**
Jan 1, May 1, Dec 25. 📷

Elne ❾

Pyrénées-Orientales. 🏠 6,500. 🚊
🚌 ℹ️ rue de Dr Bolte (04 68 22 05
07). 🛍️ Mon, Wed & Fri.

THE ANCIENT TOWN of Elne
accommodated Hannibal
and his elephants in 218 BC
on his epic journey to Rome,
and was one of the most important towns in Roussillon
until the 16th century. Today
it is famed for the 11th-century
**Cathédrale de Ste-Eulalie et
Ste-Julie**, with its superb
cloister. Milky blue-veined
marble has been carved into
exquisite capitals, embellished
with a riot of flowers, figures
and arabesques. The side nearest the cathedral dates from the
1100s; the remaining three are
13th- to 14th-century. From the
front of the cathedral are views
of the vines and orchards of
the surrounding plain.

Carved capital at Elne, showing "The Dream of the Magi"

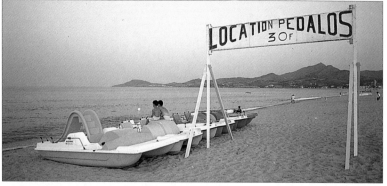

A wide, sandy beach near Perpignan, ideally suited to family vacations

Perpignan ⑩

Pyrénées-Orientales. 🚶 108,000. 🚹 🚇 🚉 🛈 *place Armand Lanoux (04 68 66 30 30).* 🛒 *daily.*

CATALAN PERPIGNAN has a distinctly southern feel, with palm trees lining the Têt River promenade, house and shop façades painted vibrant turquoise and pink, and the streets of the Arab quarter selling aromatic spices, couscous and paella.

Today Perpignan is the vibrant capital of Roussillon, and has an important position on the developing Mediterranean sunbelt. But it reached its zenith in the 13th and 14th centuries under the kings of Majorca and the kings of Aragon, who controlled great swathes of northern Spain and southern France. Their vast **Palais des Rois de Majorque** still straddles a substantial area in the southern part of

the city. Perpignan's strong Catalan identity is evident during the twice-weekly summer celebrations when the Sardana is danced in the place de la Loge. It is a key Catalan symbol, danced proudly by young and old. Arms raised, concentric circles of dancers keep step to the heady accompaniment of a Catalan woodwind band.

One of Perpignan's finest buildings, the **Loge de Mer**, lies at the head of the square. Built in 1397 to house the Maritime Exchange, only the eastern section retains the original Gothic design. The rest of the building was rebuilt in Renaissance style in 1540 with sumptuous carved wooden ceilings and sculpted window frames. While visitors

Devout Christ in St-Jean

are sometimes offended by the sight of a fast-food restaurant inside, the result is that the Loge de Mer has avoided becoming a hushed museum piece. Instead, it remains the center of Perpignan life – elegant cafés cluster around it, producing a constant buzz of activity.

Next door is the **Hôtel de Ville** with its stone façade and wrought-iron gates. Inside, parts of the arcaded courtyard date back to 1315; at the center is Aristide Maillol's allegorical sculpture, *The Mediterranean* (1950).

To the east is the labyrinthine cathedral quarter of St-Jean, made up of small streets and squares containing some fine 14th- and 15th-century buildings.

🔒 Cathédrale St-Jean

Place de Gambetta.
Topped by a stunning wrought-iron belfry, construction of this cathedral was begun in 1324 and was finally completed in 1509. It is made up almost entirely from river pebbles layered with red brick, a style common throughout the region due to the relative scarcity of other building materials.

Inside the gloomy interior, the nave is flanked by gilded altarpieces and painted wooden statues, with a massive pre-Romanesque marble font. A cloistered cemetery adjoins the

---

THE ANNUAL PROCESSION DE LA SANCH

There is a very Catalan atmosphere in Perpignan during the annual Good Friday procession of the Confraternity of La Sanch (Brotherhood of the Holy Blood). Originally dedicated to the comfort of condemned prisoners in the 15th century, members of the brotherhood still wear macabre red or black robes as they carry sacred relics and the crucifix from the Chapel of the Devout Christ to the cathedral.

Church and the Chapel of the Devout Christ with its precious, poignantly realistic medieval wooden Crucifixion. The cathedral replaced the 11th-century church of St-Jean-le-Vieux, whose superb Romanesque doorway can be glimpsed through the gates to the left of the main entrance.

Palais des Rois de Majorque

2 Rue des Archers. (04 68 34 48 29. **Open** daily. **Closed** Jan 1, May 1, Nov 1, Dec 25.

Access to the vast 13th-century fortified palace of the Kings of Majorca is as circuitous today as it was intended to be for invading soldiers. Flights of steps zigzag within the sheer red-brick ramparts, begun in the 15th century and added to successively over the next two centuries. Eventually, the elegant gardens and substantial castle within are revealed, entered by way of the Tour de l'Hommage, from the top of which is a panoramic view of the city, mountains and sea.

The palace itself is built around a central arcaded courtyard, flanked on one side by the Salle de Majorque, a great hall with a triple fire-place and giant Gothic arched windows. Adjacent, two royal chapels built one above the other show southern Gothic style at its best: pointed arches, patterned frescoes and elaborate tilework demonstrating a distinct Moorish influence. The fine rose marble doorway of the upper King's Chapel is a typical example of the

Courtyard in the Hôtel de Ville

Roussillon Romanesque style, although the sculpted capitals are Gothic. Today the great courtyard is sometimes used for concerts.

Musée Catalan

Le Castillet. (04 68 35 42 05. **Open** Wed–Mon. **Closed** public hols.

The red-brick tower and pink belfry of the Castillet, built as the town gate in 1368, was at one time a prison and is all that remains of the town walls. It now houses a collection of Catalan craft objects, including agricultural implements, kitchen furniture, looms, and glazed terra-cotta pots used for storing water and oil.

Musée Hyacinthe-Rigaud

16 rue de l'Ange. (04 68 35 43 40. **Open** Wed–Mon. **Closed** public hols. This magnificent 17th-century mansion has an art collection dominated by Hyacinthe Rigaud (1659–1743), who was born in Perpignan and was court painter to both Louis

XIV and Louis XV. Other works range from the 13th century to the present day and include a large number of 14th- to 16th-century Catalan and Spanish paintings, among them the *Retable de la Trinité* (1489) by the Master of Canapost.

There are sculptures by Aristide Maillol, born in nearby Banyuls, and works by Raoul Dufy, Picasso, Jean-Baptiste Greuze, Jean-Auguste Ingres and Théodore Géricault. On the ground floor is a collection of Hispano-Moorish ceramics.

Fort tower and ramparts, Salses

Salses ⓫

Pyrénées-Orientales. 2,500. place de la République (04 68 38 66 13). Wed.

LOOKING LIKE a giant sand-castle against the ocher earth of the Corbières vineyards, the **Fort de Salses** stands at the old frontier of Spain and France. It guards the narrow passage between the mountains and the Mediterranean lagoons, and was built by King Ferdinand of Aragon between 1497 and 1506 to defend Spain's possession of Roussillon. Its massive walls and rounded towers are a classic example of Spanish military architecture, designed to deflect the new threat posed by gunpowder.

Inside were underground stabling for 300 horses and a subterranean passageway around the inner courtyard.

There is a wonderful view from the keep over the lagoons and surrounding coastline.

The pebble and red-brick Cathédrale de St-Jean in Perpignan

Vineyards covering the hilly terrain of the Corbières

Corbières ⑫

Aude. ✈ Perpignan. 🚉 Salses-le-Château, Lézignan-Corbières.
🚌 Lézignan-Corbières, Salses-le-Château, St Paul-de-Fenouillet. 🛈
Lézignan-Corbières (04 68 27 05 42).

STILL ONE of the wildest parts of France, with few roads, let alone villages, the Corbières is best known for its wine and the great craggy hulks of the Cathar castles (see p481). Much of the land is untamed *garrigue* (scrubland), fragrant with honeysuckle and broom; promising south-facing slopes have been cleared and are planted with vines.

To the south are the spectacular medieval castles of **Peyrepertuse** and **Quéribus**, the latter one of the last Cathar strongholds. **Villerouge-Termenes** celebrates its turbulent past with an annual medieval banquet. To the west is the barren, uninhabited Razès area in the upper Aude Valley. Its best-kept secret is the village of **Alet-les-Bains**, with beautifully preserved half-timbered houses and the remains of a Benedictine abbey, battle-scarred from the Wars of Religion.

Narbonne ⑬

Aude. 🏛 46,000. 🚉 🚌 🛈 place Roger Salengro (04 68 65 15 60).
🛒 Thu & Sun.

NARBONNE is a medium-sized, cheerful town profiting from the booming wine region that surrounds it. The town is bisected by the tree-shaded Canal de la Robine; to the north is the restored medieval quarter with many elegant shops and good restaurants. Located here is one of Narbonne's most intriguing tourist attractions, the **Horreum**. These underground granaries and grain chutes date from the 1st century BC, when Narbonne was a major port and capital of the largest Roman province in Gaul.

The town prospered through the Middle Ages until the 15th century, when the harbor silted up and the course of the Aude River changed, taking Narbonne's fortunes with it. By then, an important bishopric had been established and an ambitious cathedral project, modeled on the great Gothic cathedrals of the North, was underway. However, the full grandiose design was abandoned and just the chancel, begun in 1272, became the **Cathédrale St-Just et St-Pasteur** we see today.

It is still enormous, enhanced by 14th-century sculptures, fine stained-glass windows and an 18th-century carved organ. Aubusson and Gobelin tapestries adorn the walls, and the Chapel of the Anonciade houses a treasury of manuscripts, jeweled reliquaries and tapestries.

The unfinished transept now forms a courtyard, and between the cathedral and the adjacent **Palais des Archevêques** (Archbishops' Palace) lie cloisters with four magnificent galleries of 14th-century vaulting.

This huge palace and cathedral complex dominates the center of Narbonne. Between the Palais des Archevêques' massive 14th-century towers is the town hall, with a 19th-century Neo-Gothic façade by Viollet le Duc (see p190), the architect who so determinedly

The vaulted chancel of Cathédrale St-Just et St-Pasteur in Narbonne

CANAL DU MIDI

From Sète to Toulouse the 240-km (149-mile) Canal du Midi winds its way between plane trees, vineyards and sleepy villages. The complex system of locks, aqueducts and bridges is a remarkable feat of engineering, built by the Béziers salt-tax baron Paul Riquet. Completed in 1681, it encouraged Languedoc trade and established a vital link, via the Garonne River, between the Atlantic and the Mediterranean. Today it is used by tourist barges.

Tranquil waterway of the Canal du Midi

The Cistercian Abbaye de Fontfroide (1093), southwest of Narbonne

restored medieval France. The palace itself is divided into the Palais Vieux (Old Palace) and the Palais Neuf (New Palace). Narbonne's most important museums are in the Palais Neuf, on the left as you enter through the low medieval arches of the passage de l'Ancre. The **Musée d'Archéologie et de Préhistoire** collection includes fragments of Narbonne's Roman heritage, from milestones and parts of the original walls to an assemblage of domestic objects, coins, tools and glassware. The **Chapelle de la Madeleine** is decorated with a 14th-century wall painting and houses a collection of Greek vases, sarcophagi and mosaics.

In the archbishops' former apartments is the **Musée d'Art et d'Histoire**, which is as interesting for its luxurious furnishings and richly decorated ceilings as for its art collection. This includes some fine paintings by Canaletto, Brueghel, Boucher and Veronese as well as a large selection of local earthenware.

South of the Canal de la Robine are a number of fine mansions, including the Renaissance **Maison des Trois Nourrices** on the corner of rue des Trois-Nourrices and rue Edgard-Quinet. Nearby is the **Musée Lapidaire**, with architectural fragments from Gallo-Roman Narbonne, and the 13th-century Gothic **Basilique St-Paul-Serge**. The present building retains the crypt and some sarcophagi of an earlier church on this site.

Horreum
Rue Rouget-de-l'Isle. **(** 04 68 32 45 30. **Open** May–Sep: daily; Oct–Apr: Tue–Sun. **Closed** Jan 1, May 1, Jul 14, Dec 25.

Musée d'Archéologie et de Préhistoire/Musée d'Art et d'Histoire
Palais des Archevêques. **(** 04 68 90 30 54. **Open** May–Sep: daily; Oct–Apr: Tue–Sun. **Closed** Jan 1, May 1, Jul 14, Dec 25.

Musée Lapidaire
Eglise Notre-Dame de Lamourguié. **(** 04 68 65 53 58. **Open** Jul–Aug: daily. **Closed** Jul 14.

Environs
Thirteen kilometers (8 miles) southwest of Narbonne, the Cistercian **Abbaye de Fontfroide** is worth visiting for its elegant cloister. The abbey is tucked away in a quiet valley, surrounded by cypress trees.

Golfe du Lion ⑭

Aude, Hérault. ✈ ⊡ ⊞ Montpellier. ⌂ Sète. **i** Grande Motte (04 67 29 03 37).

UNTIL THE 1960s most of this coast was a mosquito-infested swamp, interspersed with tiny fishing villages. Vestiges of the past are found in small towns like **Gruissan** with its medieval Barbarossa tower, but government investment has transformed most of this 100-km (65-mile), sandy coastline into a series of vacation resorts. Modern architecture predominates, but the developments have been environmentally sensitive, and long coastal stretches have not been built up.

Port Leucate and **Port Bacarès** are both ideal for watersports. The huge beach development at **Cap d'Agde** accommodates thousands of people every year, and is the largest naturist resort in Europe. Inland, the old town of **Agde** is noted for its black basalt buildings, particularly the 12th-century, fortresslike **Cathédrale St-Etienne**.

A wide, sandy beach on the Cap d'Agde

Carcassonne ⓯

THE CITADEL OF CARCASSONNE is a perfectly restored medieval town. It crowns a steep bank above the Aude River, a fairy-tale sight of turrets and ramparts overlooking the Basse Ville below. The strategic position of the citadel, between the Atlantic and the Mediterranean and on the corridor between the Iberian Peninsula and the rest of Europe, led to its original settlement, consolidated by the Romans in the 2nd century BC. It became a key element in medieval military conflicts. At its zenith in the 12th century, it was ruled by the Trencavels, who built the château and cathedral. Military advances and the Treaty of the Pyrenees in 1659, which relocated the French-Spanish border, left its superb fortifications obsolete, and it fell into decline. The attentions of architectural historian Viollet-le-Duc *(see p190)* led to its restoration in the 19th century.

The Restored Citadel
Restoration of La Cité has always been controversial. Critics complain it looks too new, favoring a more romantic ruin.

★ Château Comtal
A fortress within a fortress, the château has a moat, five towers and defensive wooden galleries on the walls.

Bishop's Tower

Porte d'Aude

The ramparts
were built by King Louis VIII, Louis IX, and Philip the Bold, in the 13th century.

RUE ST LOUIS
R DAME CARCAS
RUE TRENCAVEL
RUE DU ...
LICES HAUTES
R PORTE D'AUD

STAR SIGHTS

★ **Château Comtal**

★ **Basilique St-Nazaire**

★ Basilique St-Nazaire
Within the Romanesque and Gothic cathedral is the famous Siege Stone, said to depict the 1209 Siege of Carcassonne by crusaders.

0 meters   50

0 yards   50

KEY

– – – Suggested route

RELIGIOUS PERSECUTION

Carcassonne's strategic position meant it was often at the center of religious conflict. The Cathars *(see p481)* were given sanctuary here in 1209 by Raymond-Roger Trencavel when besieged by Simon de Montfort in his crusade against heresy. In the 14th century the Inquisition continued to root out the Cathars. This painting depicts intended victims.

***Les Emmurés de Carcassonne,*
J.P. Laurens**

Gallo-Roman walls

PL ST JEAN

R DU MOULIN D'AVAR

R ST JEAN

R VIOLLET LE DUC

R NOTRE DAME

R CROS MAYREVIEILLE

R DU TRESAU

R DU GRAND PUITS

LICES BASSES

PL MARCOU

The Great Well

Main entrance to La Cité

Musée Lapidaire
The collection includes Roman amphorae and terra-cotta, Romanesque murals and fragments from the cathedral, a set of Gothic windows and these medieval stone missiles.

Porte Narbonnaise
Flanked by two sandstone towers, built in 1280, the defenses included two portcullises, two iron doors, a moat and a drawbridge.

Old City Entrance
Entering La Cité is still a step back in time, although it is one of France's top tourist destinations, filled with souvenir shops.

The *lices*, the easily defended spaces between the inner and outer ramparts, were also used for jousting, crossbow practice and for storage of timber and other materials.

Béziers with its medieval cathedral, seen from Pont Vieux in the southwest

Minerve 🔞

Hérault. 🏛 100. 🛈 La Mairie (04 68 91 81 43).

IN THE PARCHED, arid hills of the Minervois, surrounded by grapevines and not much else, Minerve appears defiant on its rocky outcropping at the confluence of the Cesse and Briant rivers. It is defended by what the Minervois call the "Candela" (Candle), an octagonal tower, which is all that remains of the medieval château. In 1210, the small town resisted the vengeful Simon de Montfort, scourge of the Cathars, in a siege lasting seven weeks. This culminated in the execution of 140 Cathars, who were burned at the stake after refusing to renounce their faith.

Today visitors enter Minerve by a high bridge spanning the gorge. Turn right and follow the route of the Cathars past the Romanesque arch of the Porte des Templiers to the 12th-century **Eglise St-Etienne**. Outside the church is a crudely carved dove, symbol of the Cathars, and within is a 5th-century white marble altar table, one of the oldest artifacts in the region.

A rocky path follows the riverbed below the town, where the water has cut out caves and two bridges – the Grand Pont and the Petit Pont – from the soft limestone.

Béziers 🔞

Hérault. 🏛 76,000. ✈ 🚃 🚌 🛈 Palais des Congrès, 29 av Saint Saëns (04 67 76 47 00). 📅 Fri.

FAMOUS FOR its bullfights and rugby, and the wine of the surrounding region, Béziers has several other points of interest. It seems turned in on itself, its roads leading up to the massive 14th-century **Cathédrale St-Nazaire**, with its fine sculpture, stained glass and frescoes. In 1209, several thousand citizens were massacred in the crusade against the Cathars. The papal legate's troops were ordered not to discriminate between Catholics and Cathars, but to "Kill them all. God will recognize his own!"

Statue of the engineer Paul Riquet in the allées Paul Riquet, Béziers

The **Musée du Biterrois** holds exhibitions on local history, wine and the Canal du Midi, engineered in the late 17th century by Paul Riquet, Béziers' most famous son (see p476). His statue presides over the allées Paul Riquet, the broad esplanade at the foot of the hill. This is lined by two double rows of plane trees and large canopied restaurants, a civilized focus to this otherwise businesslike town.

🏛 **Musée du Biterrois**
Caserne St-Jacques. 📞 04 67 36 71 01.
Open Tue–Sun. **Closed** Jan 1, May 1, Dec 25. 🚫 ♿

Environs
Oppidum d'Ensérune is a superb Roman site, on a hill overlooking the Béziers plain and the mountains to the north. The original pre-Roman settlement is revealed in the substantial foundations of houses, some with huge terra-cotta storage jars buried in the floor. The **Musée de l'Oppidum d'Ensérune** has a good archaeological collection, from Celtic, Greek and Roman vases to jewelry, funeral fragments and weapons.

🏛 **Musée de l'Oppidum d'Ensérune**
Nissan lez Ensérune. 📞 04 67 37 01 23. **Open** daily. **Closed** Jan 1, May 1, Nov 1 & 11, Dec 25. 🚫 ♿ ground floor only.

The Cathars

THE CATHARS (from Greek *katharos*, meaning pure) were a 13th-century Christian sect critical of corruption in the established church. Cathar dissent flourished in independent Languedoc as an expression of separatism, but the rebellion was rapidly exploited for political purposes. Peter II of Aragon was eager to annex Languedoc, and Philippe II of France joined forces with the pope to crush the Cathar heretics in a crusade led by Simon de Montfort in 1209. This heralded the start of over a century of ruthless killing and torture.

CATHAR CASTLES

The Cathars took refuge in the defensive castles of the Corbières and Ariège. Peyrepertuse is one of the most remote, difficult to get to even today: a long, narrow stone citadel hacked from a high, craggy peak over 609 m (2,000 ft) high.

Cathars (also known as Albigensians) believed in the duality of good and evil. They considered the material world entirely evil. To be truly pure they had to renounce the world and be nonviolent, vegetarian and sexually abstinent.

The crusade against the Cathars was vicious. Heretics' land was promised to the crusaders by the pope, who assured forgiveness in advance of their crimes. In 1209, 20,000 citizens were massacred in Béziers and, the following year, 140 were burned to death in Minerve. In 1244, 225 Cathars died defending one of their last fortresses at Montségur.

CATHAR COUNTRY

Castles and towns with a Cathar association, some of them spectacular sites, are concentrated in Languedoc-Roussillon, the center of Catharism in the Middle Ages.

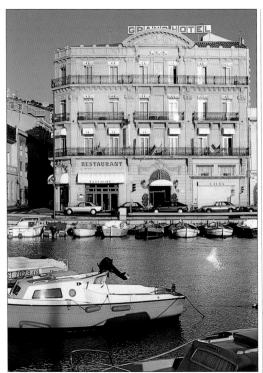

The impressive Grand Hotel *(see p571)* on quai de la Résistance, Sète

Sète ⑱

Hérault. 🏠 *42,000.* 🚉 🚌 ⛴
ℹ *60 Grand' Rue Mario Roustan
(04 67 74 71 71).* ⛴ *Wed & Fri.*

SÈTE IS A MAJOR FISHING and
industrial port. It has a
gutsier, more raffish air than
much of the leisure-oriented
Mediterranean, with its shops
selling ships' lamps and

**Cimetière Marin in Sète, burial
place of the poet Paul Valéry**

propellers, and its quayside
restaurants full of hungry
sailors demolishing vast
platters of mussels, oysters
and sea snails straight off the
boat. Most of Sète's restaurants can be found in a stroll
along the Grand Canal, with
its Italianate houses painted
in pastel colors and with
wrought-iron balconies overlooking Sète's network of
canals and bridges. Boisterous
water-jousting tournaments,
which date back to 1666, form
part of the two-week festival
held in summer *(see p33)*.

Above the town is the
Cimetière Marin on Mont St-
Clair, where Sète's most
famous son, poet Paul Valéry
(1871-1945), is buried, and
where there is a small museum
to his memory. From an observation platform, there are
breathtaking views of the
coast and the mountains of
the Cévennes. Beyond is the
Bassin de Thau, a major oyster production center, and to
the south are windswept,
sandy beaches.

Pézenas ⑲

Hérault. 🏠 *8,000.* 🚉 **ℹ** *place
Gambetta (04 67 98 36 40).* ⛴ *Sat.*

PÉZENAS IS A COMPACT and
charming little town easily
appreciated in a gentle stroll
of its main sights, well-
marked, and abounding in
revealing small details. Here
an exquisitely carved Renaissance window, there a fine
old doorway, in a niche a
lovely Madonna, all frag-
mentary evidence of Pézenas'
past glory as the seat of local
government in the 16th–17th
centuries. Then the town also
played artistic host to many
glittering troupes of musicians
and actors, most notably the
dramatist Molière in the 1650s.

Best of all are the glimpses
of fine houses through courtyard doorways. Examples
include the **Hôtel des Barons
de Lacoste**, at 8 rue François-
Oustrin, with its beautiful
stone staircase, and the
Maison des Pauvres at 12
rue Alfred Sabatier, with its
three galleries and a staircase.

Look for the medieval shop
window on rue Triperie-
Vieille, and just within the
14th-century **Porte Faugères**
(Faugères Gate) the narrow
streets of the Jewish ghetto,
which has a chilling feeling of
enclosure. Shops selling
antiques, secondhand goods
and books add to the pleasures of Pézenas. All around
the town, vines stretch as far
as the eye can see, covering
the prosperous plain.

**The stone foyer of the Hôtel des
Barons de Lacoste in Pézenas**

Parc Régional du Haut Languedoc ⑳

Hérault, Tarn. ✈ Béziers.
🚉 Bédarieux, Bézier. 🚌 St-Pons-de-Thomières, Mazamet, Lamalou-les-Bains. ℹ St-Pons-de-Thomières (04 67 97 06 65).

THE HIGH LIMESTONE plateaus and wooded slopes of upper Languedoc are a world away from the coast. From the Montagne Noire, a mountainous region between Béziers and Castres, up into the Cévennes is a landscape of remote sheep farms, eroded rock formations and deep river gorges. Much of this area has been designated the Parc Régional du Haut Languedoc, the second largest of the French national parks after Ecrins.

St-Pons-de-Thomières is the entrance, with access to forest and mountain trails for walking and riding, plus a wildlife research center, where one can glimpse the mouflons (wild mountain sheep), eagles and wild boar, which were once a common sight in the region.

If you take the D908 from St-Pons through the park you pass the village of **Olargues** with its 12th-century bridge over the Jaur River. **Lamalou-les-Bains**, on the park's eastern edge, is a small spa town with a restored Belle Epoque spa building and a theater and a soporifically slow pace.

Outside the park boundaries to the northeast there are spectacular natural phenomena. At the **Cirque de Navacelles**, the Vis River has joined up with itself, cutting out an entire island. On it sits the peaceful village of Navacelles, visible from the road higher up. The **Grotte des Demoiselles** is one of the most magnificent in an area full of caves, where you walk through a calcified world. A funicular train takes visitors from the foot of the mountain to the top.

The **Grotte de Clamouse** is also an extraordinary experience, the reflections from underground rivers and pools flickering on the cavern roofs, with stalagmites resembling dripping candles and stalactites soaring Gothic columns.

🎏 **Grotte des Demoiselles**
St-Bauzille-de-Putois. 📞 04 67 73 70 02. **Open** daily. **Closed** Jan 1, Dec 25.
♿ 🔲
🎏 **Grotte de Clamouse**
Rte de St-Guilhem-le-Désert, St-Jean-de-Fos. 📞 04 67 57 71 05. **Open** Mar–Oct: daily; Nov–Feb: Sun–Fri. 🔲

Apse of St-Guilhem-le-Désert

St-Guilhem-le-Désert ㉑

Hérault. 🏘 200. 🚌 ℹ Maison Communale (04 67 57 44 33).

TUCKED AWAY in the Celette Mountains, St-Guilhem-le-Désert is no longer as remote as when Guillaume of Aquitaine retired here as a hermit in the 9th century. After a lifetime as a soldier, Guillaume received a fragment of the True Cross from Emperor Charlemagne and established a monastery in this ravine above the Hérault River.

Vestiges of the first 10th-century church have been discovered but most of the building is a superb example of 11th–12th-century Romanesque architecture. Its lovely apsidal chapels dominate the heights of the village, behind which the carved doorway opens onto a central square.

Within the church is a somber barrel-vaulted central aisle leading to the sunlit central apse. Only two galleries of the cloisters remain: the rest are in New York's Cloisters Museum, along with carvings from St-Michel-de-Cuxa (see p471).

Extraordinary limestone formations at the Grotte de Clamouse

MONTPELLIER CITY CENTER

Cathédrale de St-Pierre ⑤
Château d'Eau ①
CORUM ⑫
Hôtel de Manse ⑧
Hôtel de Mirman ⑨
Hôtel des Trésoriers
   de la Bourse ⑥
Jardin des Plantes ③
Musée Fabre ⑩
Musée
   Languedocien ⑦
Notre-Dame
   des Tables ⑪
Place de
   la Comédie ⑬
Promenade de Peyrou ②
Tour de la Babote ⑭
Tours des Pins ④

KEY

🅿 Parking

✝ Church

0 meters 250

0 yards 250

**Outdoor café in the place de la
Comédie, Montpellier**

Montpellier ㉒

Hérault. 🏛 *211,000.* ✈ 🚌 🚆
ℹ *allée de Tourisme, Le Triangle Bas
(04 67 58 67 58).* 🛍 *daily.*

MONTPELLIER is one of the
liveliest and most progressive cities in the south, with a
quarter of its population
under 25. On a summer evening when its university is in
session, it may seem more like
a rock festival than the capital
of Languedoc-Roussillon. The
center of the action is the egg-
shaped **place de la**
Comédie, known as "l'Oeuf,"
("the egg") with its 19th-cen-
tury opera house fronted by
the Fontaine des Trois Graces
and surrounded by buzzing
cafés. An esplanade of plane
trees and fountains leads to the
CORUM, an opera and conference center typical of the
city's brave new architectural
projects. The best of these is
Ricardo Bofill's postmodern
housing complex known as
Antigone, which is modeled on
St. Peter's in Rome.

Montpellier was founded
relatively late for this region
of ancient Roman towns, developing in the 10th century
as a result of the spice trade
with the Middle East. The city's
medical school was founded
in 1220, partly as a result of
this cross-fertilization of
knowledge between the two
cultures, and remains one of
the most respected in France.

Most of Montpellier was
ravaged by the Wars of Religion in the 16th century.
Only the **Tour de la Babote**
and the **Tours des Pins**
remain of the 12th-century
fortifications. There are few
fine churches, with the excep-
tion of the **Cathédrale de St-**
Pierre and the 18th-century
Notre-Dame des Tables.

Reconstruction in the 17th
century included the building
of mansions with elegant courtyards, stone staircases and
balconies. Examples open to
the public include **Hôtel de
Manse** on rue Embouque-
d'Or, **Hôtel de Mirman** near
place des Martyrs de la
Resistance and **Hôtel des
Trésoriers de la Bourse**.
The Hôtel des Lunaret houses
the **Musée Languedocien**
which exhibits Romanesque
and prehistoric artifacts.

Another 17th-century building houses the **Musée Fabre,**
with its collection of mainly
French paintings. Highlights
include Courbet's famous

PONT DU GARD   ← To Uzès

Left bank

The bridge comprises
three tiers of
continuous arches.

Bonjour M. Courbet, Berthe Morisot's *L'Eté*, Robert Delaunay's *Nature Morte Portugaise*, and some evocative paintings of the region by Raoul Dufy and François Desnoyer.

A good place to view the city's position between mountains and sea is from the **Promenade de Peyrou**, a grand 18th-century square dominated by the **Château d'Eau** and the aqueduct that used to serve the city. Just to the north is the **Jardin des Plantes**. France's oldest botanical gardens, they were created in 1953.

🏛 **Musée Languedocien**
7 rue Jacques Coeur. 📞 *04 67 52 93 03. Open Mon–Sat. Closed public hols.* 🚫

🏛 **Musée Fabre**
39 bd Bonne Nouvelle. 📞 *04 67 14 83 00. Open Tue–Sun. Closed Jan 1, May 1, Jul 14, Nov 1 & 11, Dec 25.* 🚫♿

Château d'Eau, Montpellier

La Grande-Motte ❷❸

Hérault. 🏘 *7,000.* 🚆 🛈 *place de la Mairie (04 67 29 03 37).* 🚌 *Sun (& Thu: mid-Jun–mid-Sep).*

THE BIZARRE white towers of this modern beach resort exemplify the development of the Languedoc-Roussillon coast. One of a number of

La Grande-Motte

beach cities on the lakes south of Montpellier, there are marinas and facilities for every kind of sport from tennis and golf to water sports, all flanked by golden beaches and pine forests. To the east are Le Grau-du-Roi, once a tiny fishing village, and Port-Camargue, with its big marina.

Aigues-Mortes ❷❹

Gard. 🏘 *5,000.* 🚆 🚌 🛈 *Porte de la Gardette (04 66 53 73 00).* 🚌 *Wed & Sun.*

THE BEST APPROACH to this perfectly preserved walled town is across the salt marshes of the Petite Camargue. Now marooned 5 km (3 miles) from the sea, the defenses of this once-important port have become a tourist experience, worth visiting more for the effect of the ensemble than for the tacky shops within. Aigues-Mortes ("Place of Dead Waters") was established by Louis XI in the 13th century to consolidate his power, and built according to a strict grid pattern. By climbing up the

Tour de Constance you can walk out onto the rectangular walls, that afford a superb view over the Camargue.

Environs

Across the salt lagoons to the northeast is **St-Gilles-du-Gard**, also once an important medieval port. Today it is worth a detour to see the superbly sculpted 12th-century façade of its abbey church. This was originally established by the monks of Cluny Abbey as a shrine to St. Gilles, and a resting place on the famous pilgrimage route to Santiago de Compostela (*see pp390–91*).

Pont du Gard ❷❺

Gard. 🚌 *from Nîmes.*

No AMOUNT OF FAME can diminish the first sight of the 2,000-year-old Pont du Gard. The Romans themselves considered it the best testimony to the greatness of the Roman Empire, and at 49 m (160 ft) it was the highest bridge they ever built. It is made from enormous blocks of stone, hauled into place with an ingenious system of pulleys and a vast phalanx of slave labor. The huge build-up of calcium in the water channels suggests that the aqueduct was in continuous use for 400–500 years.

A dizzying view can be had by walking along the very top of the aqueduct, which originally carried water to Nîmes along a 50-km (31-mile) route from the springs at Uzès. This charming town has an arcaded marketplace and several fine medieval towers including the lovely 12th-century Tour Fenestrelle.

Water channel

To Nîmes →

Right bank

Roman inscriptions include a damaged phallus carving as a good luck symbol.

Some stones weighed about 6 tons.

Nîmes ㉖

LISTED NUMBER ONE on the tourist map of Nîmes is the bus stop designed by Philippe Starck, who is also credited with reworking the city's pedestrian zone. Such innovations are part of the city's current design renaissance. Architectural projects range from imaginative housing to a glittering new arts complex, under the guidance of a dynamic mayor. An important crossroads in the ancient world, Nîmes is equally well-known for its Roman antiquities such as the amphitheater, the best preserved of its kind. The city is also famous for its festivals and bullfights. These are good times to see the rest of Nîmes with its museums, archaeological collections and Old Town of narrow streets and intimate squares.

Arches of the Roman amphitheater

Historic Nîmes

Nîmes has always had a turbulent history, and suffered particularly during the 16th-century Wars of Religion when the Romanesque **Cathédrale Notre-Dame et St-Castor** was badly damaged. During the 17th and 18th centuries the town prospered from textile manufacturing, one of the most enduring products being denim, or "de Nîmes." Many of the fine houses of this period have been restored, and elegant examples can be seen on rue de l'Aspic, rue des Marchands and rue de Chapitre in the Old Town. Just outside the town center is the futuristic apartment building, **Nemausus I**.

The Roman gate, the **Porte Auguste**, built 20 years before the temple of **Maison Carrée**, was once part of one

of the longest city walls in Gaul. Of the original arches still standing, two (large) were for carts and chariots and two (smaller) ones for pedestrians. The other major Roman remnant is the **Castellum**, where water used to arrive from the Pont du Gard (*see p485*). From the Castellum it was distributed around the city through thick pipes.

Jug from Musée Archéologique

🌿 Jardin de la Fontaine

Quai de la Fontaine. **Open** daily. ♿
When the Romans arrived in Nîmes, they found a town established by the Gauls, centered on source of a spring. They named the town Nemausus, after their river god. In the 18th century, formal gardens were constructed,

Jardin de la Fontaine, with a view over the city

and a network of limpid pools
and cool stone terraces remains. High above the garden
on Mont Cavalier is
the octagonal Tour
Magne, once a key
part of the Roman walls.

**Arms of the city in a sculpture
by Martial Raysse**

♌ Les Arènes

Bd des Arènes. 📞 *04 66 76 72 77.*
Open *daily.* **Closed** *Jan 1, May 1, Dec
25 & on performance days.* 🏛 ♿

All roads lead to the amphitheater, Les Arènes. Built at
the end of the 1st century AD,

the design of the oval arena
and tiers of stone seats accommodated huge crowds of up
to 25,000 spectators. Today it
is in use again, a perfect spot
for concerts, sporting events
and bullfights.

♟ Maison Carrée

Place de la Maison Carrée. 📞 *04
66 67 29 11.* **Open** *daily.*
Square House is a very
prosaic name for this
elegant Roman temple,
the pride of Nîmes.
Built between 2-3 AD,
it is one of the best
preserved in the
world, with finely
fluted Corinthian
columns and
a sculpted
frieze.

🏛 Musée
des Beaux
Arts

Rue Cité Foulc. 📞
04 66 67 38 21. **Open**
Tue–Sun. **Closed** *Jan 1, May
1, Nov 11, Dec 25.* 🏛 ♿
This fine arts museum
houses an eclectic col-
lection of Dutch, French,
Italian and Flemish works,
most notably Jacopo
Bassano's *Susanna and the
Elders,* and the *Mystic
Marriage of St. Catherine*
by Michele Giambono.
The Gallo-Roman
mosaic of *The Marriage
of Admetus,* discovered in
1882, is featured on the
main floor.

🏛 Musée Archéologique

Musée d'Histoire Naturelle, 13 bis bd
Amiral Courbet. 📞 *04 66 67 25 57.*
Open *Tue–Sun.* **Closed** *Jan 1, May 1,
Nov 11, Dec 25.* 🏛
The museum's collection of
Roman statues, ceramics,
glass, coins and mosaics is
housed in Nîmes' natural
history museum. The exhibits

The Maison Carrée, now a museum

include important Iron Age
menhir statues.

🏛 Carré d'Art

Place de la Maison Carrée. 📞 *04 66
76 35 35.* **Open** *Tue–Sun.* 🏛 ♿
Nîmes' controversial arts complex, by the British architect
Sir Norman Foster, opened in
1993. Five floors of this glass
and steel temple, that was
built in tribute to the Maison
Carrée opposite, lie underground. The complex incorporates a library, a roof-terrace
restaurant around a huge
glass atrium, and the Musée
d'Art Contemporain. The
latter's French collection
includes works by Raysse,
Boltanski and Lavier.

**Bullfight at
Les Arènes in Nîmes**

KEY

🅿 Parking

ℹ Tourist information

✝ Church

0 meters	250
0 yards	250

PROVENCE AND THE CÔTE D'AZUR

BOUCHES-DU-RHÔNE · VAUCLUSE · VAR
ALPES-DE-HAUTE-PROVENCE · ALPES-MARITIMES

FROM ITS HERB-SCENTED HILLS *to its yacht-filled harbors, no other region of France fires the imagination as strongly as Provence. The vivid landscape and luminous light have inspired artists and writers from Van Gogh to Picasso, F. Scott Fitzgerald to Pagnol.*

The borders of Provence are defined by nature: to the west, the Rhône; south, the Mediterranean; and north, where the olive trees end. To the east are the Alps and a border which has shifted over the centuries between France and Italy. Within is a contrasting terrain of plummeting gorges, Camargue saltflats, lavender fields and sun-drenched beaches.

Past visitors have left their mark. In Orange and Arles, the buildings of Roman *Provincia* are still in use. Fortified villages like Èze were built to withstand the Saracen pirates who plagued the coast in the 6th century.

In the 19th century, rich Europeans sought winter warmth on the Riviera; by the 1920s, high society was in residence all year, and their elegant villas remain.

The warm sunlight nurtures intense flavors and colors. Peppers, garlic and olives transform a netful of Mediterranean fish into that vibrant epitome of Provençal cuisine, *bouillabaisse.*

The image of Provence bathed in sunshine is marred only when the bitter Mistral wind scours the land. It has shaped a people as hardy as the olive tree, yet quick to embrace life to the full the moment the sun returns.

Cap Martin, seen from the village of Roquebrune

◁ **Lavender fields near the Gorges du Verdon**

Exploring Provence

THIS SUN-DRENCHED southeastern region is France's most popular vacation destination. Sun worshipers cram the beaches in the summer months, and entertainment includes jazz festivals, bullfights, car races, casinos and *boules* games. Inland is a paradise for walkers and nature lovers, with remote mountain plateaus, perched villages and dramatic river gorges.

Promenade des Anglais, Nice

SIGHTS AT A GLANCE

To Briançon

BARCELONNETTE

DIGNE-LES-BAINS
23

MERCANTOUR

Verdon

Var

ALPES-MARITIMES **41**

GORGES DU VERDON

D2211

GORGES DU LOUP

33

VENCE
34
35 ST-PAUL-DE-VENCE
36

GRASSE
26

BIOT **31**
VALLAURIS
30
27
CANNES

DRAGUIGNAN

32 CAGNES-SUR-MER
29 ANTIBES
28 CAP D'ANTIBES

ÉZE
39 **43**
37 VILLEFRANCHE-SUR-MER
38 CAP FERRAT

40 ROQUEBRUNE-CAP-MARTIN
MONACO

MENTON
42

FRÉJUS **24**
25
ST-RAPHAËL

STE-MAXIME

22 ST-TROPEZ

MASSIF DES MAURES

21

PROVENÇALE

Argens

HYÈRES
19

LE LAVANDOU

20
ÎLES D'HYÈRES

GETTING AROUND

The largest airport in the region, and second busiest in France, is Nice. Fly-drive packages are popular, but are mainly recommended for touring inland. Traffic jams on coastal roads in high season can be avoided by using the autoroutes. Main coastal towns have good bus and train links, and bikes can be rented at most train stations. The Chemin de Fer de Provence railroad runs from Nice to Digne-les-Bains through spectacular mountain scenery. Mountain roads, though tortuous, are good.

KEY

	Highway
	Major road
	Minor road
	Scenic route
	River
	Viewing point

0 kilometers   25

0 miles   25

Spectacular scenery near the quiet market town of Forcalquier

Mont Ventoux ❶

Vaucluse. ⊠ *Avignon.* 🚌 *Orange.*
🚌 *Bédoin.* 🛈 *Bédoin (04 90 65 63 95).*

THE NAME means "Windy Mountain" in Provençal, and deservedly so. A variety of flora and fauna may be found on the lower slopes, but moss is the only plant life to survive at the peak, where the winter temperature can drop to –27° C (–17° F). The bare white scree at the summit makes it look snowcapped even during summer.

In 1336, the poet Petrarch made the first recorded ascent of the 1,909-m (6,261-ft) peak. Today, a road leads to the radio beacon pinnacle, but the trip should not be attempted in bad weather. At other times, spectacular views from the top make the effort worthwhile.

Roman mosaic from the Villa du Paon in Vaison-la-Romaine

Vaison-la-Romaine ❷

Vaucluse. 🚶 *5,600.* 🚌 🛈 *place du Chanoine Sautel (04 90 36 51 30).* 🚲 *Tue.*

THIS SITE on the banks of the Ouvèze has been settled since the Bronze Age, but its name stems from five centuries as a prosperous Roman town.

Although the upper town, dominated by the ruins of a 12th-century castle, has some charming narrow streets, stone houses and fountains, Vaison's main attractions lie on the opposite side of the river.

Today, the **Roman City** is split into two districts: Puymin and La Villasse. At Puymin, an opulent mansion, the Villa du Paon, and a Roman theater have been uncovered. In 1992, the Ouvèze River burst its banks, taking many lives in

Vaison and the nearby area. Damage to some ruins, such as the Roman bridge, has since been repaired. Also at Vaison is the fine, Romanesque **Cathédrale Notre-Dame-de-Nazareth** with medieval cloisters.

🏛 Roman City

Fouilles de Puymin, place du Chanoine Sautel. 🕻 *04 90 36 51 30.* **Open** *Wed–Mon.* **Closed** *Jan 1, May 1, Dec 25.* 🅿

Orange ❸

Vaucluse. 🚶 *29,000.* 🚌 🚌 🛈 *cours Aristide Briand (04 90 34 70 88).* 🚲 *Thu.*

ORANGE IS A thriving regional center. The fields and orchards and, in particular, the great vineyards of the Côtes du Rhône, make it an important marketplace for produce such as grapes, olives, honey and truffles. In contrast, visitors should explore the area around the 17th-century Hôtel de Ville, where attractive streets open onto quiet, shady squares. Orange has two of the greatest Roman monuments in Europe.

🏛 Roman Theater

Place de Frères-Mounet. 🕻 *04 90 51 17 60.* **Open** *daily.* **Closed** *Jan 1, Dec 25.* 🅿 ♿
Dating from the 1st-century AD reign of Augustus, the well-preserved theater has perfect acoustics. Still in use, it is a spectacular setting for world-famous concerts. The back wall ("the finest wall in my kingdom," said Louis XIV) rises to a height of 38 m (125 ft) and is 103 m (338 ft) wide.

🏛 Triumphal Arch

Avenue de l'Arc de Triomphe.
The triple-arched monument was built about AD 20. It is

Statue of Augustus Caesar in the Roman Theater at Orange

elaborately decorated: battle scenes and military trophies are mingled with flowers and fruits. Inscriptions to the glory of Tiberius were added later.

🏛 Musée de la Ville

Rue Nadeleine-Rock. 🕻 *04 90 51 18 24.* **Open** *daily.* **Closed** *Jan 1, Dec 25.* 🅿
Relics here reflect the history of Orange, including 400 marble fragments which proved to be plans of the area based on three surveys. The earliest dates to the reign of the Emperor Vespasian in the 1st century BC.

Châteauneuf-du-Pape ❹

Vaucluse. 🚶 *2,100.* 🚌 *Sorgues, then bus.* 🛈 *place du Portail (04 90 83 71 08).* 🚲 *Fri.*

HERE, IN THE 14TH CENTURY, the popes of Avignon chose to build a new castle (*château neuf*) and plant the vineyards from which one of

View across the vineyards of Châteauneuf-du-Pape

the finest wines of the Côtes du Rhône is produced. Now, almost every doorway in this attractive little town seems to open into a *vigneron's* cellar.

After the Wars of Religion *(see pp50–51)*, all that remained of the papal fortress were a few fragments of walls and tower, but the ruins look spectacular and offer magnificent views across to Avignon and the Vaucluse uplands beyond.

Wine festivals punctuate the year, including the Fête de la Véraison in August *(see p34)*, when the grapes start to ripen, and the Ban des Vendages in September, when the grapes are ready to be harvested.

Avignon ❺

Vaucluse. 🏘 *87,000.* ✈ 🚊 🚍
🛈 *41 cours Jean Jaurès (04 90 82 65 11).* 🛒 *Tue–Sun.*

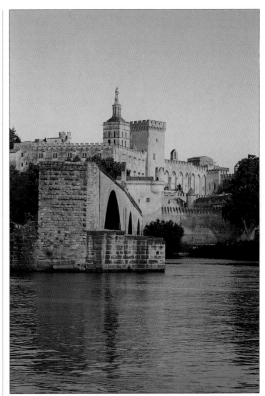
Pont St-Bénézet and the Palais des Papes in Avignon

MASSIVE RAMPARTS enclose one of the most fascinating towns in southern France. The huge **Palais des Papes** *(see pp494–5)* is the dominant feature, but the town contains other riches. To the north of the Palais is the 13th-century **Petit Palais**, once the Archbishop of Avignon's residence. It has received such notorious guests as Cesare Borgia and Louis XIV. Now a museum, it displays Romanesque and Gothic sculpture and medieval paintings of the Avignon and Italian Schools, with works by Botticelli and Carpaccio.

The rue Joseph-Vernet and rue du Roi-René are lined with many splendid 17th- and 18th-century houses. There are also some notable churches, such as the **Cathédrale de Notre-Dame-des-Doms**, with its Romanesque cupola, and the 14th-century **Eglise St-Didier**. The **Musée Lapidaire** contains statues, mosaics and carvings from pre-Roman Provence. The **Musée Calvet** features a superb array of exhibits, such as wrought-iron works and Roman finds. It also gives an overview of French art during the past 500 years, with works by Rodin, Utrillo and Dufy.

The place de l'Horloge is the center of Avignon's social life. Under the town hall's Gothic clock tower are sidewalk cafés and a merry-go-round from 1900. One of the prettiest streets is the rue des Teinturiers. Until the 19th century, brightly patterned calico called *indiennes* was printed here, and it inspired today's Provençal patterns.

From mid-July until mid-August, Avignon's Festival takes place at the Palais des Papes *(see p33)*. France's

Outdoor performance at the Avignon Festival

largest festival, it includes ballet, drama and classical concerts. The "Off" festival has street theater and music from folk to jazz. Most commonly associated with Avignon is the song about dancing *Sur le Pont d'Avignon.* Built from 1171–1185, the **Pont St-Bénézet** had 22 arches, until most were destroyed by floods in 1668. One of the remaining arches bears the tiny Chapelle St-Nicolas. People danced on an island below the bridge but over the years, *sous* (under) has become *sur* (on).

🏛 **Petit Palais**
Place du Palais. 📞 *04 90 86 44 58.*
Open *Wed–Mon.* **Closed** *Jan 1, May 1, Jul 14, Nov 1, Dec 25.* 🏷

🏛 **Musée Lapidaire**
27 rue de la République. 📞 *04 90 85 75 38.* **Open** *Wed–Mon.* **Closed** *some public hols.* 🏷 ♿

🏛 **Musée Calvet**
65 rue Joseph Vernet. 📞 *04 90 86 33 84.* **Open** *Wed–Mon.* **Closed** *some public hols.* ♿ 🏷 📷

Palais des Papes

Confronted with factional strife in Rome and encouraged by the scheming of Philippe IV of France, Pope Clement V moved the papal court to Avignon in 1309. Here it remained until 1376, during which time his successors transformed the modest episcopal building into the present magnificent palace. Its heavy fortification was vital to defend against rogue bands of mercenaries. Today it is empty of the luxurious trappings of 14th-century court life – virtually all the furnishings and works of art were destroyed or looted in the course of the centuries.

Pope Clement VI (1342–52)

Benedict XII's cloister incorporates the guest and staff wings, and the Benedictine chapel.

Trouillas tower

Bell tower

Military Architecture
The palace and its ten towers were designed as an impregnable fortress. It eventually covered an area of 15,000 sq m (148,000 sq ft).

La Gache tower

Corner tower

Champeaux gate

The Avignon Popes

Seven "official" popes reigned in Avignon until 1376. They were followed by two "anti-popes," the last of whom, Benedict XIII, fled in 1403. Popes or anti-popes, few were known for their sanctity. Clement V died eating powdered emeralds, prescribed as an indigestion cure; Clement VI (1342–52) thought that the best way to honor God was through luxury. Petrarch was shocked by "the filth of the universe" at court. In 1367, Urban V tried to return the Curia (papal court) to Rome, a move that became permanent in 1376.

Benedict XII (1334–42)

Consistory Hall
Simone Martini's frescoes (1340) were taken from the cathedral to replace works destroyed by fire in the papal reception hall in 1413.

Papal Power
More like a war-lord's citadel than a papal palace, the building's heavy fortification reflects the insecure climate of 14th-century religious life.

VISITORS' CHECKLIST

Place du Palais, Avignon. **04 90 25 50 00. Open** Nov–Mar: 9:30am–5:45pm; Apr–Oct: 9am–7pm daily (Jul: 9am–9pm; Aug–Sep 15: 9am– 8pm). Last adm: 45 mins before closing. **Closed** Jan 1, Dec 25. in the gardens in summer.

★ **Grand Tinel**
A series of fine 17th- and 19th century Gobelin tapestries now hang in the vast banquet hall, where cardinals gathered to elect a new pope.

Angels' tower

★ **Stag Room**
Fourteenth-century hunting frescoes and ceramic tiles make Clement VI's study the palace's most lovely room.

Pope's chamber

Great courtyard

BUILDING THE PALACE

The palace comprises Pope Benedict XII's simple Palais Vieux (1334–42) and Clement VI's flamboyant Palais Neuf (1342–52). Ten towers, some of which are more than 50 m (164 ft) high, are set in the walls to protect its four wings.

The Great Chapel is 20 m (66 ft) high and covers an area of 780 sq m (8,400 sq ft).

The Great Audience Hall is divided into two naves by five columns with bestiary sculpture on their capitals.

STAR FEATURES

★ **Grand Tinel**

★ **Stag Room**

KEY

☐ By Benedict XII (1334–42)

☐ By Clement VI (1342–52)

Carpentras

Vauclause. 🏛 *25,500.* 🚆 ℹ️ *170 allée Jaurès (04 90 63 57 88).* 🛒 *Fri.*

IN 1320, CARPENTRAS became capital of the papal county of Venaissin, and remained so until 1791. Modern boulevards trace the former ramparts, with only one original gate, the Porte d'Orange, surviving.

In the Middle Ages, the town was home to a large Jewish community, and it remains a Jewish center. The 1367 **Synagogue** is the oldest in France. The Sanctuary has been restored but the baths and bakery are unchanged.

While not openly persecuted under papal rule, many Jews changed faith, entering **Cathédrale St-Siffrein** by the Porte Juive (Jews' Door).

The Law Courts were built in 1640 as the episcopal palace. Its Criminal Court has 17th-century carved tablets of the local towns. In the pharmacy of the Hôtel-Dieu, the 18th-century cupboards are painted with quaint figures of monkey "doctors." More regional art and history is on display at the **Musée Sobirats**.

🃏 **Synagogue**
Place Maurice Charretier.
📞 *04 90 63 39 97.* **Open** *Mon–Fri.*
Closed *Jewish feast days.*
🏛 **Musée Sobirats**
Rue du Collège. 📞 *04 90 63 04 92.*
Open *Wed–Mon.* 📷 ♿ *restricted.*

Riverfront and watermill at Fontaine-de-Vaucluse

Fontaine-de-Vaucluse

Vauclause. 🏛 *500.* 🚆 ℹ️ *chemin de la Fontaine (04 90 20 32 22).*

THE MAIN ATTRACTION here is the source of the Sorgue River. It is the most powerful spring in France, gushing at up to 90,000 liters (19,800 gallons) per second from an underground river at the foot of a cliff. It powers a paper mill that still employs 15th-century techniques. There are also several museums. One is devoted to the poet Petrarch, who lived and wrote here, and another to the French Resistance of World War II. More bizarre is the macabre **Musée Historique de la Justice et de l'Injustice**, where the exhibits include a guillotine.

Perched village of Gordes

Gordes

Vauclause. 🏛 *2,000.* ℹ️ *Le Château (04 90 72 02 75).* 🛒 *Tue.*

PERCHED VILLAGES abound in Provence, but Gordes is said to attract the most visitors, and it is easy to understand why. Dominated by a 16th-century château, the town forms such a harmonious whole that it might have been designed by an architect. The arcaded medieval lanes add to the attractive hilltop position.

Just south lies the **Village des Bories**, a bizarre, primitive habitat. Bories are tiny beehive-shaped huts built of overlapping dry stones. The construction techniques are thought to date back to Neolithic times. This group was inhabited from the 16th to the early 20th centuries.

The **Abbaye de Sénanque**, north of Gourdes, is one of the finest Romanesque Cistercian monasteries in France.

♠ **Château de Gordes**
📞 *04 90 72 02 75.* **Open** *Mon–Fri.*
Closed *Jan 1, May 1, Dec 25.* 📷
⋔ **Village des Bories**
Les Savourins, Route de Cavaillon. 📞
04 90 72 03 48. **Open** *daily.* 📷 ♿

Luberon

Vauclause. ✈ *Avignon.* 🚆 *Cavaillon, Avignon.* 🚌 *Apt.* ℹ️ *Apt (04 90 74 03 18).*

A HUGE LIMESTONE range, the Montagne du Luberon is one of the most appealing areas of Provence. Rising to 1,125 m (3,690 ft), it combines wild areas with picturesque villages. Almost the entire area is designated a regional nature park. Within it are more than 1,000 plant species and cedar and oak forests. The wildlife is varied, with eagles, vultures, snakes, beavers, wild boar and the largest European lizards. The park headquarters are in **Apt**, the capital of the Luberon.

Once notorious as the haunt of highwaymen, the Luberon hills now hide sumptuous vacation homes. The major village is **Bonnieux**, with its 12th-century church and 13th-century walls. Also popular are **Roussillon**, with red ocher buildings; **Lacoste**, the site of the ruins of the Marquis de Sade's castle; and **Ansouis**, with its 14th-century Eglise St-Martin and 17th-century castle. **Ménerbes**, drew to it the writer Peter Mayle, whose tales of life here brought this quiet region a worldwide audience.

Herb stall at St-Rémy-de-Provence

St-Rémy-de-Provence ❿

Bouches-du-Rhône. 🏠 9,500. 🚌
🛈 place Jean Jaurès (04 90 92 05 22). 🔄 Wed & Sat.

FOR CENTURIES St-Rémy, with its tree-lined boulevards, fountains and narrow streets, had two claims to fame. One was that Vincent Van Gogh spent a year here, in 1889–90, at the St-Paul-de-Mausole hospital. *Wheat Field with Cypress* and *Ravine* are among the 150 works he produced here. St-Rémy-de-Provence was also the birthplace in 1503 of

Nostradamus, known for his cryptic prophecies. But, in 1921, St-Rémy found new fame when archaeologists unearthed the fascinating Roman ruins at **Glanum**. Little remains of the ancient city, sacked in AD 480 by the Goths, but the site is very impressive. Around the ruins of an arch from the first century BC are the foundations of buildings, fragments of walls and a vast mausoleum, decorated with such scenes as the death of Adonis.

🏛 Glanum
🛈 04 90 92 23 79. **Open** daily. **Closed** Jan 1, May 1, Nov 1 & 11, Dec 25. 🕸

Les Baux-de-Provence ⓫

Bouches-du-Rhône. 🏠 460. 🚌
Arles. 🛈 ilôt "Post Tenebras Lux" (04 90 54 34 39).

ONE OF THE STRANGEST places in Provence, the deserted citadel of Les Baux stands like a natural extension of a huge rocky plateau. The ruined castle and old houses overlook the Val d'Enfer (Infernal Valley), with its weird rocks, once the haunt of witches and goblins according to legend.

In the Middle Ages, Les Baux was home to powerful feudal lords, who claimed descent from the Magus Balthazar. It was the most famous of the Provençal Cours d'Amour, at which troubadours sang the praises of high-born ladies. The ideal of everlasting but unrequited courtly love contrasts with the war-like nature of the citadel's lords.

The glory of Les Baux ended in 1632. It had become a Protestant stronghold and Louis XIII ordered its destruction.

Deserted medieval citadel of Les Baux-de-Provence

The living village below has a pleasant little square, the 12th-century **Eglise St-Vincent** and the **Musée Yves Brayer**. In 1821, bauxite was discovered (and named) here, and the closed quarries now form the backdrop for audio-visual theme programs, the **Cathédrale d'Images**.

To the southwest are the ruins of the **Abbaye de Montmajour**. Its 12th-century Romanesque Eglise de Notre-Dame, is noted for its circular crypt.

🏛 Musée Yves Brayer
Hôtel des Porcelet. 🛈 04 90 54 36 99. **Open** daily. **Closed** Jan–mid-Feb. 🕸

Parading the Tarasque, 1850

Tarascon ⓬

Bouches-du-Rhône. 🏠 11,000. 🚌
🛈 59 rue des Halles (04 90 91 03 52). 🔄 Tue.

ACCORDING TO LEGEND, the town takes its name from the Tarasque, a monster, half-animal and half-fish, which terrorized the countryside. It was tamed by Sainte Marthe, who is buried in the church here. An effigy of the Tarasque is still paraded through the streets each June *(see p33)*.

The striking 15th-century **château** on the banks of the Rhône is one of the finest examples of Gothic military architecture in Provence. Its somber exterior gives no hint of the beauties within: the Flemish-Gothic courtyard; the spiral staircase; and the painted ceilings of the banqueting hall.

On the opposite bank is Beaucaire, its own ruined castle surrounded by gardens.

♣ Château
Bd du Roi René. 🛈 04 90 91 01 93. **Open** Apr–Sep: daily; Oct–May: Wed–Mon. **Closed** Jan 1, May 1, Nov 1 & 11, Dec 25. 🕸

Arles ⓭

FEW OTHER TOWNS IN PROVENCE combine all the region's charms as well as Arles. Its position on the Rhône makes it a natural, historic gateway to the Camargue *(see pp500–1)*. Its Roman remains, such as the arena and Constantine's baths, are complemented by the ocher walls and Roman-tiled roofs of later buildings. A bastion of Provençal tradition and culture, its museums are among the best in the region. Van Gogh spent time here in 1888–9, but Arles is no longer the industrial town he painted. Visitors are now its main business, and entertainment ranges from the Arles Festival to bullfights.

Emperor Constantine

Palais Constantine was once a grand imperial palace. Now only its vast Roman baths remain, dating from the 4th century AD. They are remarkably well preserved and give an idea of the luxury that bathers enjoyed.

Musée Réattu
This museum, in the old Commandery of the Knights of Malta, houses witty Picasso sketches, paintings by the local artist Jacques Réattu (1760–1833) and sculptures by Ossip Zadkine, including La Grande Odalisque *(1932), above.*

Museon Arlaten
In 1904 the poet Frédéric Mistral used his Nobel Prize money to establish this museum devoted to his beloved native Provence. Parts of the collection are arranged in room settings, and even the museum guides wear traditional Arles costume.

Espace Van Gogh, in a former hospital where the artist was treated in 1889, is a cultural center devoted to his life and work.

★ **Eglise St-Trophime**
This church combines a noble 12th-century Romanesque exterior with superb Romanesque and Gothic cloisters. The ornate main portal is carved with saints and apostles.

Tourist information

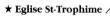

0 meters	100
0 yards	100

LES ALYSCAMPS

A tree-lined avenue of broken medieval tombs is the focal point of these "Elysian Fields" to the southeast of Arles. It became Christian in the 4th century and was a prestigious burial ground until the 12th century. Some sarcophagi were sold and are in museums; others have been neglected. Mentioned in Dante's *Inferno*, painted by Van Gogh and Gauguin, it is a place for thought and inspiration.

Les Alyscamps by **Paul Gauguin**

VISITORS' CHECKLIST

Bouches-du-Rhône. 🚶 *52,600.*
✈ *25 km (15 miles) NW Arles.* 🚃
🚌 *av Paulin Talbot.* 🛈 *pl de la République (04 90 18 41 20).*
🛒 *Wed & Sat.* 🎭 *Arles Festival (Jul); Premices du Riz (Sep).*
Museon Arlaten *open Jul–Sep: daily; Oct–Jun: Tue–Sun.* **Closed** *public hols.* 🖼 **Musée Réattu** *open daily.* **Closed** *public hols.* 🖼

To train and bus stations

★ Roman Amphitheater

This is one of the best-preserved monuments of Roman Provence. Each arch is supported by Doric and Corinthian columns. In summer there are bull contests in the 20,000-seat arena. The top tier provides a panoramic view of Arles.

Notre-Dame-de-la-Major is the church in which the *gardiens* (cowboys) of the Camargue celebrate the feast day of their patron saint, St. George. Although the building dates from the 12th to 17th centuries, a Roman temple existed on this spot hundreds of years earlier.

★ Roman Theater

Once a fortress, its stones were later used for other buildings. Today, the theater stages the Arles Festival. Its remaining columns are called the "two widows."

STAR SIGHTS

★ **Roman Amphitheater**

★ **Roman Theater**

★ **Eglise St-Trophime**

KEY

– – – Suggested route

The Camargue ⑭

Camargue gardian

THE RHONE DELTA was responsible for the formation of the 140,000 ha (346,000 acres) of wetlands, pastures, dunes and salt flats that make up the Camargue, but human efforts are needed to preserve it. The region now maintains a fragile eco-logical balance, in which a unique collection of flora flourishes, including tamarisk and narcissi, and fauna such as egrets and ibises. The pastures provide grazing for sheep, cattle and small white Arabian-type horses, ridden by the *gardians* or cowboys, a hardy community who traditionally lived in thatched huts *(cabanes)* and still play their part in keeping Camargue traditions alive.

Sunset over the Camargue

Black Bulls
In a Provençal bull contest (known as a course*), the animals are not killed. Instead, red rosettes are plucked from between their horns with a small hook.*

N572

D570

Mas du Pont de Rousty

Le Petit Rhône

D37

Méjanes •

P

PLAINE DE LA CAMARGUE

Etang de Vaccarès

D570

PARC REGIONAL DE CAMA

P

i Centre de Ginès

PETITE CAMARGUE

0 kilometers 5

0 miles 5

• Stes-Maries-de-la-Mer

MEDITERRANEE

Les Stes-Maries-de-la-Mer
The May gypsy pilgrimage to this fortified church marks the legendary arrival by boat in AD 18 of Mary Magdalene, St. Martha and the sister of the Virgin Mary. Statues in the church depict the event.

Flamingoes
These striking birds are always associated with the Camargue, but the region supports many other breeds, including herons, kingfishers, owls and birds of prey. The area around Ginès is the best place to see them.

KEY

— Nature preserve boundary

– – Walking routes

- - Walking and cycling routes

White Horses
*These small, sturdy horses, which are
never stabled, were once used to thresh
grain. The foal's dark coat turns the
familiar white after about five years.*

Gardians' Cabin
*Traditionally, gardians lived in
thatched cabins. Today,
members of the gardian
brotherhood show off
their horsemanship
in the Arles arena
each April.*

Mountains of Salt
*Sea salt is the Camargue's
main "harvest." Through-
out the summer, sea water
evaporates from huge brine
pans and the crystals are
heaped into camelles up to
8 m (26 ft) high.*

Aix-en-Provence ⓯

Bouches du Rhône. 👥 126,000. 🚉
🚌 🛈 2 place du Général de Gaulle
(04 42 16 11 61). 🛒 daily.

FOUNDED BY the Romans in
103 BC, Aix was frequently
attacked, first by the Visigoths
in AD 477, later by Lombards,
Franks and Saracens. Despite
this, the city prospered. By the
end of the 12th century it was
capital of Provence. A center
of art and learning, it reached
its peak in the 15th century
during the reign of "Good
King" René. He is shown in
Nicolas Froment's *Triptych of
the Burning Bush* in the 13th-
century Gothic **Cathédrale de
St-Sauveur**, also noted for its
16th-century walnut doors,
Merovingian baptistry and
Romanesque cloisters. Aix's
many museums include the
Musée Granet of fine arts and
archaeology, and the **Musée
des Tapisseries** (tapestries),
in the Palais de l'Archevêché.

Aix has been called "the
city of a thousand fountains."
Three of the best are situated
along cours Mirabeau. On one
side of this elegant, tree-lined
avenue are 17th- and 18th-
century buildings with sculpted
doorways and wrought-iron
balconies. On the other are
the cafés that are so much a
part of the city's social life.

The Old Town is centered on
place de l'Hôtel de Ville, with
its colorful flower market.

In the northwest of the town
is the **Pavillon de Vendôme**,
housing furniture and works
of art by Van Loo.

Aix's most famous son is
Paul Cézanne. His studio, the
Atelier de Cézanne, is kept as
it was when he died in 1906.
Montagne Ste-Victoire, which
inspired many of his paintings,
lies 15 km (9 miles) east of Aix.

🏛 **Musée Granet**
13 rue Cardinale. 📞 04 42 38 14
70. **Open** Wed–Mon. **Closed** some
public hols.
🏛 **Musée des Tapisseries**
28 pl des Martyrs de la Résistance.
📞 04 42 23 09 91. **Open** Wed–
Mon. **Closed** some public hols.
🏠 **Atelier de Cézanne**
9 av Paul Cézanne. 📞 04 42 21 06
53. **Open** daily. **Closed** some public
hols.

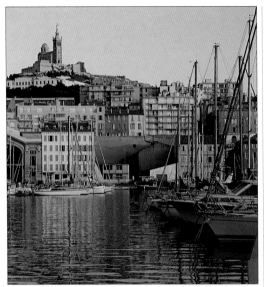

Old harbor of Marseille, looking toward the quai de Rive Neuve

Marseille ⑯

Bouches-du-Rhône. 🏠 800,000.
🚶 🚃 🚌 🚢 🛈 4 La Canebière
(04 91 13 89 00). 🛒 daily.

A GREEK SETTLEMENT founded in the 7th century BC, then called Massilia, Marseille was seized by the Romans in 49 BC. It became the "Gateway to the West" for most Oriental trade. France's largest port and second-largest city has close links with the Middle East and North Africa. It is exotic, cosmopolitan and lively, with a reputation for corruption and drug trafficking. The Vieux Port was the setting for Marcel Pagnol's comic trilogy, *Marius, Fanny* and *César*, satirizing the Marseillais character.

In Marseille, narrow stepped streets, quiet squares and fine 18th-century façades contrast with the bustle of boulevard Canebière and the Cité Radieuse, Le Corbusier's post-war radical housing complex. A striking new landmark is L'Hôtel du Département, the local government headquarters, a bright blue structure on stilts, designed by the British architect Will Alsop.

The old harbor now only handles small boats, but its daily fish market is renowned. Gourmets agree that the *bouillabaisse (see p458)* is very authentic here.

Several museums in the old harbor area include the **Musée des Docks Romains.** The wreck of a Roman ship found in 1974 is exhibited at the **Musée d'Histoire de Marseille,** and there are paintings of old Marseille at the **Musée de Vieux Marseille**.

⚓ Château d'If
📞 04 91 59 02 30. **Open** daily. 📷
The Château d'If (Castle of Yew) stands on a tiny island 2 km (1 mile) southwest of the port. A formidable fortress, it was built in 1524 to house artillery, but was never put to military use and later became a prison. Alexandre Dumas' fictional "Count of Monte Cristo" was supposed to have been imprisoned here, and visitors can see a special cell, complete with escape hole.

Most real-life inmates were either common criminals or political prisoners.

🔒 Notre-Dame-de-la-Garde
Built between 1853 and 1864, this Neo-Byzantine basilica dominates the city. Its belfry, 46 m (151 ft) high, is capped by a huge gilded statue of the Virgin. The lavishly decorated interior has colored marble and mosaic facings.

🔒 Abbaye St-Victor
Similar to a fortress in appearance, the abbey was rebuilt in the 11th century after destruction by the Saracens. In the French Revolution, the rebels used it as a barracks and prison. There is an intriguing crypt in the abbey's church, with an original catacomb chapel and a number of pagan and Christian sarcophagi.

On February 2 each year, St-Victor becomes a place of pilgrimage. Boat-shaped cakes are sold to commemorate the legendary arrival of St. Mary Magdalene, Lazarus and St. Martha nearly 2,000 years ago.

🔒 Cathédrale de la Major
Built in Neo-Byzantine style, this is the largest 19th-century church in France, 70 m (230 ft) high and 141 m (463 ft) long. In the crypt are the tombs of the bishops of Marseille. By it is the small and beautiful Ancienne Cathédrale de la Major.

🏛 Vieille Charité
2 rue de la Charité.
📞 04 91 14 58 80. **Open** Tue–Sun.
Closed public hols. 📷 ♿
In 1640, the construction of a shelter "for the poor and beggars" of Marseille was begun by royal decree. One hundred years later, Pierre Puget's hospital and domed

Le Corbusier's innovative Cité Radieuse in Marseille

Fish market at Marseille

church were finally opened. Now, the restored building houses the Musée d'Archéologie Egyptienne, with its fine collection of Egyptian artifacts.

🏛 Musée des Beaux Arts
Palais Longchamp, place Henri Dunan. 📞 04 91 62 21 17. **Open** Tue–Sun. **Closed** Jan 1, May 1, Dec 25. 📷
This museum is housed in the handsome 19th-century Palais Longchamp. Works include Michel Serre's graphic views of Marseille's plague of 1721, Pierre Puget's town plans for the city, and murals depicting it in Greek and Roman times.

Cassis ⑰
Bouches-du-Rhône. 🏠 8,000. 🚌 🚪 ℹ place Baragnon (04 42 01 71 17). 🗓 Wed & Fri.

MANY OF THE VILLAGES along this coast have been built up to the point where they have all but lost their original charm, but Cassis is still much the same little fishing port that attracted such artists as Dufy, Signac and Derain. This is a place in which to relax at a waterside café, watching the fishermen or street performers, while enjoying a plate of seafood and a bottle of the local dry white wine for which Cassis is famous.

From Marseille to Cassis, the coastline forms narrow inlets, called **Calanques**, their jagged white cliffs (some as much as 400 m/1,312 ft high) reflected in dazzling turquoise water. Wildlife abounds here, with countless seabirds, foxes, stone martens, bats, large snakes and lizards. The flora is no less impressive, with more than 900 plant species, of which 50 are classified as rare. The En-Vau and Sormiou Calanques are especially lovely.

Toulon ⑱
Var. 🏠 170,000. ✈ 🚌 🚪 🚢 ℹ Place Raimu (04 94 18 53 00). 🗓 Tue–Sun.

THIS NAVAL BASE has a long maritime history. In 1793 it was captured by an Anglo-Spanish fleet, but was boldly retaken by the then-unknown young commander Napoleon Bonaparte. Nearly 150 years later, Nazi troops took Toulon. The French fleet, trapped in the harbor, sank its own ships to keep them from the enemy.

The **Musée de la Marine** is a focus for this history, with such artifacts as finely crafted figureheads and model ships.

The tower of the former town hall is virtually all that remains of the prewar quai Cronstadt. Rebuilt and renamed quai Stalingrad, its many cafés and shops make it a favorite meeting place for Toulonnais. The war-damaged Old Town has a few original buildings, and the market is well worth a visit.

🏛 Musée de la Marine
Place Monsenergue. 📞 04 94 02 02 01. **Open** Apr–Sep: daily; Oct, Dec–Mar: Wed–Mon. **Closed** public hols. 📷 ♿

Paul Signac's *Cap Canaille*, painted at Cassis in 1889

Tour of the Gorges du Verdon

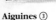

THE VERDON GORGES constitute one of the most dramatic natural sights in Europe. The dark green Verdon River flows through a deeply cut valley with twisted rocks and cone-shaped peaks. In places, the Gorges reach depths of 700 m (2,297 ft), passing through largely uninhabited country between the vast natural amphitheater of Moustiers-Ste-Marie and the narrow streets of Castellane. Dramatic viewpoints on the suggested circular route include the Balcons de la Mescla, just beyond the Pont de l'Artuby, where the Verdon and Artuby Gorges meet, and the Point Sublime.

Lac de Ste-Croix

D957   D952

③

D71   CORNICH

Aiguines ③
This village has an atttractive 17th-century château with four pepper-mill-shaped towers. There is a fine view of the artificial Lac de Sainte-Croix.

Verdon Gorges from the Castellane road

Hyères ⑲

Var. 52,000.

Rotonde Jean Salusse (04 94 65 18 55). Tue, Sat & 3rd Thu of month.

TOWARD THE END of the 18th century, Hyères became one of the first health resorts of the Côte d'Azur. Among its many distinguished visitors during the next century were Queen Victoria, Robert Louis Stevenson and Edith Wharton.

The main sights are found in the medieval streets of the Vieille Ville that lead past the spacious, flagstoned place Massillon (scene of a colorful daily market) to a ruined castle and panoramic views over the coast.

Modern Hyères is imbued with a lingering Belle Epoque charm that has become popular with experimental filmmakers. It continues to attract a health-conscious crowd and is a major center for aquatic sports.

Fishing off Porquerolles, the largest of the Iles d'Hyères

Moustiers-Ste-Marie ④
Set in a deep ravine, this village is famous for pottery. Suspended across the twin peaks above it is an iron chain with a star, first placed there after the Crusades.

La Palud sur-Verdon ⑤
This village is on the Route des Crêtes, one of the most wild and beautiful walks.

Point Sublime ⑥
From this superb viewpoint 180 m (591 ft) high, two walking routes lead to the bottom.

Castellane ①
This town has a 14th-century clock tower and a lion fountain. On a cliff high above it, once used as a lookout, is the tiny chapel of Notre-Dame du Roc.

KEY

▬▬▬	Tour route
═══	Other roads
☆	Viewing point

0 kilometers 2

0 miles 2

Pont de l'Artuby ②
From this boldly curved bridge there is a breathtaking view of the gorge 250 m (820 ft) below.

Îles d'Hyères ⑳

Var. ✈ Toulon-Hyères. 🚍 🚌 🚤 Hyères. ℹ Hyères (04 94 65 18 55).

THIS GLAMOROUS TRIO of islands, sometimes referred to as the Iles d'Or, after the gold color of their cliffs, can be easily reached by boat from mainland Hyères.

Porquerolles, the largest of the three, measures 7 km (4.5 miles) by 3 km (2 miles). It is covered in rich vegetation, much of which, for instance the Mexican bellombra tree, was introduced via a variety of exotic foreign climes.

The island's main town, also known as Porquerolles, looks more like a North African colonial settlement than any Provençal village. It was established in 1820 as a retirement town for Napoleon's most honored troops.

All the island's beaches lie along the northern coastline. The long, sandy Plage Notre-Dame, one of the finest beaches in Provence, sits in a sheltered bay about an hour's walk from Porquerolles.

A stroll around lush, hilly **Port-Cros**, covering just 2.5 sq km (1 sq mile), takes the best part of a day. It rises to 195 m (640 ft), the highest point on any of the islands.

Port-Cros has been a national park since 1963. A unique reserve of Mediterranean flora and fauna, its surrounding waters are also protected. There is even a 300 m (984 ft) scenic swimming route. You can buy a waterproof guide to the underwater life, which includes rare rock fish.

The wild, virtually treeless **Île de Levant** is reached by boat from Port-Cros. Its main draw is the oldest naturist colony in France, Héliopolis, founded in 1931. The eastern half of the island, controlled by the French navy, is permanently closed to the public.

Massif des Maures ㉑

Var. ✈ Toulon-Hyères. 🚍 Fréjus, Hyères, or Toulon. 🚌 Bormes-les-Mimosas. 🚤 Toulon. ℹ Bormes-les-Mimosas (04 94 01 38 38).

THE DENSE WILDERNESS of pine, oak and sweet chestnut covering the Maures mountain range probably gave rise to its name, meaning dark or gloomy. It extends nearly 65 km (40 miles) between Hyères and Fréjus.

The D558 north of Cogolin offers a route to the heart of the Maures. Along the way is Garde-Freinet, well known for its bottle cork industry.

Northwest of Cannet-des-Maures, in splendid isolation, lies the Romanesque Abbaye de Thoronet. With the abbeys at Sénanque, in Vaucluse, and Silvacane, in the Bouches-du-Rhône, it is known as one of the "Three Sisters" of Provence.

Harborside at St-Tropez

St-Tropez ㉒

Var. 🏛 6,000. 🚌 ℹ️ quai Jean
Jaurès (04 94 97 45 21). 🚤 Tue & Sat.

THE GEOGRAPHY of St-Tropez
kept it untouched by the
earliest development of the
Côte d'Azur. Tucked away at
the tip of a peninsula, it is the
only north-facing town on the
coast and so did not appeal
to those seeking a warm and
sheltered winter resort. In
1892, the painter Paul Signac
was among the first outsiders
to respond to its unspoiled
charm, encouraging friends,
such as the painters Van
Dongen, Matisse and Bonnard,
to join him. In the 1920s, the
chic Parisian writer Colette
also made her home here. St-
Tropez also began to attract
star-spotters, hoping for a
glimpse of celebrities such
as the Prince of Wales.

During World War II, the
beaches around St-Tropez
were the scene of Allied
landings, and the town was
heavily bombed. Then, in the
1950s, young Parisians began
to arrive, and the Bardot-
Vadim film helped to create
the reputation of modern St-
Tropez as a playground for
gilded youth. The wild public
behavior and turbulent love
affairs of Roger Vadim, Brigitte
Bardot, Sacha Distel and
others left fiction far behind.
Mass tourism followed, with
visitors once again more interested in spotting a celebrity
than in visiting the **Musée de
la Marine** in the 16th-century
citadel above the town, or the
Musée de l'Annonciade with
its outstanding collection of

works by Signac, Derain,
Rouault, Bonnard and others.
Bardot had a villa at La
Madrague, but tourists invaded
her privacy, so she left.

Today, there are far more
luxury yachts than fishing
boats moored in St-Tropez
harbor. Its cafés make ideal
bases for people- and yacht-
watching. Another center of
the action is place des Lices,
both for the Harley-Davidson
set and the morning market.

St-Tropez has its own small
beaches but the best are to be
found just outside the town,
including the golden curve of
Pampelonne, jammed with
beach clubs and fashionable
restaurants. This is the beach
on which to see and be seen.
St-Tropez has no train station,
so driving and parking can be
a nightmare in summer.

It is said that St-Tropez
takes its name from a Roman
soldier martyred as a Christian
by the Emperor Nero. Each
year in May, a *bravade* in his

honor takes place, when an
effigy of the saint is carried
through the town to the accompaniment of musket fire.

Nearby are two small towns
of differing character but equal
charm. **Port-Grimaud** was
only built in 1966 but the
sensitive use of traditional
architecture and materials
makes it seem older. Most
of its "streets" are canals and
many homes have their own
mooring. Up in the hills, the
winding streets of **Ramatuelle**
have been restored to bijou
perfection by the largely
celebrity population.

🏛 **Musée de la Marine**
Montée de la Citadelle. ☎ 04 94 97
49 53. **Open** mid-Dec–mid-Nov: Wed–
Mon. **Closed** Jan 1, May 1, Dec 25. 🖼️
🏛 **Musée de l'Annonciade**
Place Grammont. ☎ 04 94 97 04 01.
Open Dec–Oct: Wed–Mon. **Closed**
Jan 1, Ascension, May 1, Dec 25. 🖼️

**Stylish solution to the traffic
problems in St-Tropez**

BRIGITTE BARDOT

Brigitte Bardot in 1956

In 1956, Brigitte Bardot's film,
And God Created Woman,
was shot in St-Tropez by her
new husband, Roger Vadim.
By settling in St-Tropez, "BB"
the sex goddess changed the
fortunes of the sleepy little
fishing village and ultimately
the Côte d'Azur, making it
the center of her hedonistic
lifestyle. In 1974, on her 40th
birthday, she celebrated her
retirement from films at Club
55 on Pampelonne Beach, and
now devotes her time to her
animal sanctuary.

Digne-les-Bains ㉓

Alpes-de-Haute-Provence. 👥 16,000.
🚉 🚌 ℹ *Rond point du 11 Novembre*
(04 92 31 42 73). 🛒 *Wed & Sat.*

THIS CHARMING town in the foothills of the Alps appears in Victor Hugo's *Les Miserables*: the hero stole a bishop's candlesticks. A trip on the *Train des Pignes* from Nice offers superb views. Digne's attractions include a spa, the lavender festival *(see p34)* and the **Fondation Alexandra David-Néel**, a Tibetan center.

🏛 **Fondation Alexandra David-Néel**,
27 av du Juin. 📞 *04 92 31 32 38.*
Open daily. ♿

Fréjus ㉔

Var. 👥 53,000. 🚉 🚌 ℹ *325 rue Jean Jaurès (04 94 17 19 19).*
🛒 *Tue, Fri.*

THE MODERN TOWN of Fréjus is dwarfed in importance by two impressive historic sites. The remains of the Roman port of **Amphithéâtre** (founded by Julius Caesar in 49 BC) may not be as complete as those at Orange or Arles, but they are of exceptional variety. A great amphitheater, fragments of an aqueduct, a theater and part of a rampart gateway remain. The sea has receded over the centuries and there are few traces of the original harbor.

The cathedral on place Formigé marks the entrance to the **Cité Episcopale**. The fortified enclave includes the 5th-century baptistry, one of the oldest in France, and the cathedral cloister, its coffered medieval roof decorated with scenes from the Apocalypse.

In 1959, Fréjus was hit by a wall of water as the Malpasset Barrage burst. To the north, the ruined dam can still be seen.

🏛 **Amphithéâtre**
Rue Henri Vadon. 📞 *04 94 17 19 19.*
Open *Wed–Mon.* **Closed** *Jan 1, May 1, Dec 25.* ♿
🏛 **Cité Episcopale**
58 rue de Fleury. 📞 *04 94 51 26 30.*
Open *Apr–Sep: daily; Oct–Mar: Tue–Sun.* **Closed** *Jan 1, May 1, Nov 1 & 11, Dec 25.* 📷

THE CREATION OF A PERFUME

The best perfumes begin as a formula of essential oils extracted from natural sources. The blend of aromas is created by a perfumer called a "nose" because of his or her exceptional sense of smell. A perfume may use as many as 300 essences, all painstakingly extracted from plants by various methods: steam distillation, extraction by volatile solvents, and *enfleurage à froid* (for costly or potent essences). With this process, pungent blossoms are placed onto layers of fats for several days until the fats are saturated. The oils are then "washed" out with alcohol, and when this evaporates, it leaves the pure perfume essence behind.

Lavender water

Grasse flowers

St-Raphaël ㉕

Var. 👥 28,000. 🚉 🚌 ℹ *Rue Waldeck Rousseau (04 94 19 52 52).*
🛒 *daily.*

DELIGHTFULLY SITUATED, St-Raphaël is a charming, old-style Côte d'Azur resort with Art Nouveau architecture and a palm-fronded promenade. Aside from its beaches, it offers a marina, a casino, Roman ruins, a 12th-century church and a museum that displays treasures salvaged from a Roman wreck.

It was here that Napoleon Bonaparte landed in 1799 upon his return from Egypt.

Grasse ㉖

Alpes-Maritimes. 👥 44,000. 🚌 *Palais des Congrès.* ℹ *(04 93 36 03 56).* 🛒 *Tue–Sun.*

CRADLED BY HILLS, with views out to sea, Grasse is surrounded by fields of flowers: lavender, mimosa, jasmine and roses. Grasse has been the center of the world's perfume industry since the 16th century, when Catherine de' Médici set the fashion for scented leather gloves. At that time, Grasse was also known as the center for leather tanning. The

tanneries have gone, but the perfume houses founded in the 18th and 19th centuries are still in business; however today Grasse perfumes are mostly made from imported flowers or chemical essences. Fragonard and Molinard have their own museums, but the best place to learn more is at the **Musée Internationale de la Parfumerie**, which has a garden of fragrant plants.

Grasse was the birthplace of Jean-Honoré Fragonard, the artist. The **Villa-Musée Fragonard** is decorated with murals by his son. Fragonard's only known religious work is in the **Cathédrale de Nôtre-Dame-du-Puy** in the Old Town, with two paintings by Rubens. The place aux Aires and the place du Cours typify the unspoiled charm of Grasse, surrounded by narrow arcaded streets with Renaissance staircases and balconies.

🏛 **Musée International de la Parfumerie**
8 place du Cours. 📞 *04 93 36 80 20.* **Open** *Jun–Sep: daily; Oct–May: Wed–Sun.* **Closed** *public hols.* 📷 ♿
🏛 **Villa-Musée Fragonard**
23 bd Fragonard. 📞 *04 93 36 01 61.* **Open** *Jun–Sep: daily; Oct–May: Wed–Sun.* **Closed** *public hols.* 📷 *(free Wed & Sun).*

Statue honoring Jean-Honoré Fragonard in Grasse

Lavender fields near Puimoisson, Alpes-de-Haute-Provence ▷

High summer on the beach at Cannes, overlooked by the Carlton Hotel

Cannes ㉗

Alpes-Maritimes. 🏠 70,000. 🚊 🚌
🛥️ 🛈 Palais des Festivals, 1 La
Croisette (04 93 39 24 53). 🎪 Tue–Sun.

JUST AS GRASSE is synonymous with the perfume industry, the first thing that most people associate with Cannes is its many festivals, especially the International Film Festival held each May. There is, however, much more to the city than these glittering events. It was Lord Brougham, the British Lord Chancellor, who put Cannes on the map, although Prosper Mérimée, Inspector of Historic Monuments, allegedly visited Cannes two months before him. Lord Brougham stopped here in 1834, unable to reach Nice due to a cholera outbreak there. Struck by the beauty and mild climate of what was then just a small fishing port, he built a villa here. Other foreigners followed, and Cannes became established as a top Mediterranean resort.

The Old Town that Lord Brougham knew is centered in the Le Suquet district, on the slopes of Mont Chevalier. Part of the old city wall can still be seen on place de la Castre, which is dominated by the **Notre-Dame de l'Espérance**, built in the 16th and 17th centuries in the Provençal Gothic style. An 11th-century watchtower is another attraction, and the castle keep houses the **Musée de la Castre**, the eclectic finds of a 19th-century Dutch explorer, Baron Lycklama.

The famed **boulevard de la Croisette** is lined with gardens and palm trees. One side is occupied by luxury boutiques and hotels such as the Carlton, built in Belle Epoque style, whose twin cupolas were modeled on the breasts of La Belle Otero, a famous member of the 19th-century *demi-monde*. Opposite are some of the finest sandy beaches on this coast. Once one of the world's grandest thoroughfares, the faded glamour of the Croisette revives at festival time.

🛥️ Iles de Lérins

🚢 depart from: Gare Maritime, Vieux Port. 🛈 Esterel Chanteclair (04 93 38 66 33), Compagnie Maritime Cannoise (04 93 38 66 33), Horizon IV (04 92 98 71 36).
Just off the coast from Cannes are the Iles de Lérins. The fort on **Ile Sainte-Marguerite** is where the mysterious Man in the Iron Mask was imprisoned

CANNES FILM FESTIVAL

The first Cannes Film Festival took place in 1946 and, for almost 20 years, it remained a small and exclusive affair, attended by the artists and celebrities who lived or were staying on the coast. The arrival of the "starlet," especially Brigitte Bardot, in the mid-1950s marked the change from artistic event to media circus, but Cannes remains the international marketplace for filmmakers and distributors, with the *Palme d'Or* prize conferring high status on its winner. The annual film festival is held in the huge Palais des Festivals, opened in 1982. It has three auditoriums, two exhibition halls, conference rooms, a casino, a nightclub and a restaurant.

Gérard Depardieu and family arriving at the festival

in the late 17th century. A popular theory is that his face had to be hidden because he resembled some one very important indeed – possibly even Louis XIV. Visitors can see the tiny cell that held him for over ten years. **Ile Saint-Honorat** has an 11th-century tower in which the resident monks took refuge during raids by Saracens. There are also five ancient chapels. Both islands offer peaceful woodland walks, fine views and quiet coves for swimming.

Beside the boulevard de la Croisette

Cap d'Antibes ❷

Alpes-Maritimes. ✈ Nice. 🚇 Antibes. 🚢 Nice. ℹ Antibes (04 92 90 53 00).

WITH ITS SUMPTUOUS villas in their lush grounds, this rocky, wooded peninsula, known as "the Cap" to its regular visitors, has been a symbol of luxury life on the Riviera since it was frequented by F. Scott Fitzgerald and the rich American set in the 1920s. One of the wealthiest of all, magnate Frank Jay Gould, invested in the resort of Juan-les-Pins, and it became the focus of high life on the Cap. Today, memories of the Jazz Age live on at the Jazz Festival, when international stars perform under the pines *(see p33).*

At the highest point of the peninsula, the sailors' chapel of **La Garoupe** has a collection of votive offerings and a 14th-century Russian icon. Nearby is the **Jardin Thuret**, created in 1856 to acclimatize

tropical plants. Much of the exotic flora of the region began its naturalization here.

🌿 **Jardin Thuret**
41 bd du Cap. 📞 04 93 67 88 00. **Open** Mon–Fri. **Closed** public hols.

Antibes ❷

Alpes-Maritimes. 🏠 70,000. 🚇 🚌 🚢 ℹ 11 place du Gal de Gaulle (04 92 90 53 00). 🚢 Tue–Sun.

THE LIVELY TOWN of Antibes was founded by the Greeks as Antipolis and settled by the Romans. In the 14th century, Savoy's possession of the town was contended by France until it fell to them in 1481, after which **Fort Carré** was built and the port, now a center of Mediterranean yachting, was remodelled by Vauban.

The Château Grimaldi, formerly a residence of Monaco's ruling family, was built in the 12th century and retains its Romanesque tower. It now houses the **Musée Picasso**. In 1946, the artist used part of the castle as a studio and, in gratitude, donated all 150 works completed during his

The Goat (1946) by Pablo Picasso

stay, including *The Goat*. Most are inspired by his love of the sea, including *La Joie de Vivre*.

The pottery in the **Musée d'Archéologie** includes objects salvaged from shipwrecks from the Middle Ages to the 18th century.

🏛 **Musée Picasso**
Château Grimaldi. 📞 04 92 90 54 20. **Open** Tue–Sun. **Closed** public hols. ♿ 🚫

🏛 **Musée d'Archéologie**
1 av Meziere. 📞 04 92 90 54 35. **Open** Dec–Oct: Tue–Sun. **Closed** public hols. ♿ 🚫

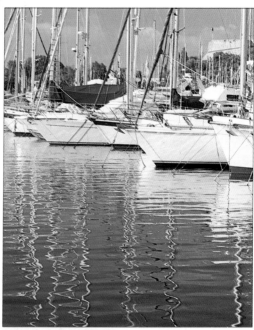

Sailboats in the harbor at Antibes

Vallauris ③⓪

Alpes-Maritimes. 👥 24,000. 🚊 🚌
🛈 square 8 mai 1945 (04 93 63 82 58).
🚢 Tue–Sun.

VALLAURIS OWES its fame to
the influence of Pablo
Picasso, who rescued the
town's dying pottery industry
and stimulated a revival of
the craft. In 1951, the village
commissioned Picasso to
paint a mural in the deconsecrated chapel next to the
castle, and his *War and
Peace* (1952) is the chief exhibit of the **Musée Picasso**. In
the main square is a bronze
statue, *Man with a Sheep*, which
Picasso donated to the town.

🏛 **Musée Picasso**
Place de la Libération. 📞 04 93 64
16 05. **Open** Wed–Mon. **Closed**
public hols. 📷 ♿ ground floor only.

Biot ③①

Alpes-Maritimes. 👥 8,000. 🚊 🚌
🛈 place de la Chapelle (04 93 65 05
85). 🚢 Tue & Fri.

A TYPICAL LITTLE hill village,
Biot has retained its charm
and has always attracted artists
and artisans. The best known
is Fernand Léger, who made
his first ceramics here in 1949.
Examples of these, and other
works by him, are shown in the
Musée Fernand Léger outside
town. Its external wall boasts
a huge mosaic by the artist.
The town is also famous for
its bubble-flecked glassware.
The craft of the glassblowers
can be seen (and purchased)
at the **Verrerie de Biot**.

🏛 **Musée Fernand Léger**
Chemin Val-de-Pôme. 📞 04 92 91 50
30. **Open** Wed–Mon. **Closed** Jan 1,
May 1, Dec 25. 📷 ♿
🏠 **La Verrerie de Biot**
Chemin des Combes. 📞 04 93 65 03
00. **Open** daily. **Closed** Dec 25. ♿

Renoir's studio at the Maison Les Collettes in Cagnes-sur-Mer

Cagnes-sur-Mer ③②

Alpes-Maritimes. 👥 43,000. 🚊 🚌
🛈 6 bd Maréchal Juin (04 93 20 61 64).
🚢 Tue–Fri.

CAGNES-SUR-MER is divided
into three districts. The
oldest and most interesting is
Haut-de-Cagnes, with its steep
streets, covered passageways
and ancient buildings, including a number of Renaissance
arcaded houses. The other
districts are Cagnes-Ville, the
modern town where hotels
and shops are concentrated,
and Cros-de-Cagnes, a sea-side
fishing resort and yachting

harbor. The **Château** in Haut-
de-Cagnes was built in the
14th century and reworked in
the 17th by Henri Grimaldi.
Behind the fortress walls is a
shady courtyard with a 200-
year-old pepper tree. The
surrounding marble columns
conceal a museum devoted to
the olive tree, and a small
collection of modern Mediterranean art. There is also a
group of paintings bequeathed
by *chanteuse* Suzy Solidor.
The 40 works, all portraits of
her, are by such artists as Marie
Laurencin and Cocteau. On
the ceiling of the banquet hall
is a vast illusionistic fresco of
the *Fall of Phaeton* painted
by Carlone in 1621–4.
The last 12 years of Pierre
Auguste Renoir's life were
spent in Cagnes, at the **Maison
Les Collettes**, where the
warm, dry climate helped to
ease his arthritis. The house
has been kept almost exactly
as it was when he died in

Exterior of the Musée Fernand Léger in Biot, with a mural by the artist

1919 and contains ten of his paintings. It is set in a magnificent olive grove, in which can be seen his great bronze *Venus Victrix*.

⚓ **Château de Cagnes**
📞 04 93 20 85 57. **Open** *Jul–Sep: daily; Oct–Jun: Wed–Mon.* **Closed** *mid-Nov–mid-Dec.* 📷
🏛 **Maison Les Collettes**
📞 04 93 20 61 07. **Open** *Wed–Mon.* **Closed** *Oct 20–Nov 9 & public hols.* 📷

La Ferme des Colettes (1915) by Renoir, in Cagnes-sur-Mer

Gorges du Loup 🟒

Alpes-Maritimes. 🚌 *Nice.*
🚆 *Cagnes-sur-Mer.* 🚌 *Grasse.*
🚌 *Nice.* 🛈 *Grasse (04 93 36 66 66).*

THE LOUP RIVER rises in the Pre-Alps behind Grasse and cuts a deep path down to the Mediterranean. Along its route are dramatic cascades and spectacular views. The superb countryside is crowned by the perched villages for which the region is famous.

Gourdon owes much of its appeal to its ancient houses, grouped around a 13th-century **Château** built on the site of a Saracen stronghold and perched dizzyingly on the cliffside. Its terraced gardens were laid out by Le Nôtre *(see p169)*, who landscaped the gardens of Versailles. The museum houses a collection of naive art, including a work by Henri Rousseau.

Tourrette-sur-Loup is a fortified village in which the ramparts are formed by the outer houses. It is surrounded by fields of violets, for which it is famous, grown for use in perfume and candied sweets.

⚓ **Château Gourdon**
📞 04 93 09 68 02. **Open** *Jun–Sep: daily; Oct–May: Wed–Mon.* 📷 ♿

Vence 🟤

Alpes-Maritimes. 🚌 *15,000.* 🚆 🛈 *place du Grand Jardin (04 93 58 06 38).* 🛒 *Tue, Thu & Fri.*

VENCE'S GENTLE CLIMATE has always been its main attraction; today it is surrounded by vacation villas. It was an important religious center in the Middle Ages. The **Cathédrale**, built on the site of a temple of Mars, was restored by Vence's most famous bishop, Antoine Godeau. A 5th-century Roman sarcophagus serves as its altar. Also noteworthy are the Carolingian wall carvings, the 15th-century carved choir stalls and Godeau's tomb.

Just within the ramparts of the Old Town, which retains its 13th–14th-century town gates, is place du Peyra, once a Roman forum. Its urn-shaped fountain, built in 1822, still provides fresh water. On the edge of town, the **Chapelle du Rosaire** was built from 1946–51 and decorated by Henri Matisse,

Domed roof in Vence

in gratitude to the nuns who nursed him during an illness. On its white walls, biblical scenes are reduced to simple black lines tinted by splashes of light from the blue and yellow stained-glass windows.

🔒 **Chapelle du Rosaire**
Av Henri Matisse. 📞 04 93 58 03 26. **Open** *Tue & Thu (Fri–Mon & Wed by appt only, 48 hrs notice reqd); school hols: Tue–Sat pm.* **Closed** *Nov.* 📷 📹

Market day in the Old Town of Vence

Street-by-Street: St-Paul-de-Vence ⑤

Restaurant sign, St-Paul-de-Vence

O NE OF THE MOST famous and tourist-thronged hill villages of the Nice hinterland, St-Paul-de-Vence was once a French frontier post facing Savoy. Its 16th-century ramparts offer views over a landscape of cypress trees, and red-roofed villas with palm trees and swimming pools. The village has been heavily restored but its winding streets and medieval buildings are authentic. It has proved a magnet for artists, both established and aspiring, throughout the 20th century. Today galleries and studios dominate the village.

View of St-Paul-de-Vence
The local landscape is a favorite subject for artists. Neo-Impressionist Paul Signac (1863–1935) painted this view of St. Paul.

Ramparts provide a walk that encircles the village.

The Chapelle des Penitents Blancs is 16th century.

To Fondation Maeght

Auberge de la Colombe d'Or

The Boules court and adjacent café are the village social center.

PLACE DE GAULLE

R DE L'ETOURNE

RUE DES DORIERS

RUE DES BAUQUES

R DE LA CA

RUE GRANDE

COURTINE ST PAUL

BASTION ST REMY

FONDATION MAEGHT

Built in 1964 by Paris art dealers Aimé and Marguerite Maeght, this is one of Europe's finest museums of modern art. The striking pink and white building, set outside St-Paul, was designed by Catalan architect José-Luis Sert, who worked on it directly with artists such as Miró and Chagall. Inside are paintings by Bonnard, Braque, Kandinsky, Chagall and others. There are also summer concerts, a library and screenings of art films. In the terraced gardens, sculptures, mobiles and mosaics by Arp, Calder, Miró, Giacometti and Hepworth are set amid the pine trees.

L'homme qui Marche by Giacometti

The Colombe d'Or
This famous auberge includes a Léger mural (above) on the terrace; a Braque dove by the pool; a Picasso and a Matisse in the dining room.

Eglise Collégiale
Begun in the 12th century, the church's treasures include a painting of St. Catherine, attributed to Tintoretto.

The Musée d'Histoire de Saint-Paul, contains tableaux of scenes from the town's past.

Le Donjon, a grim medieval building, was used as a prison until the 19th century.

Grand Fountain
This charming cobble-stoned place has a pretty urn-shaped fountain.

VISITORS' CHECKLIST

Alpes-Maritimes. 2,900. 12 place du Grand Jardin, Vence (04 93 58 37 60). Maison de la Tour, 2 rue Grande (04 93 32 86 95). **Fondation Maeght** open daily.

Rue Grande
The doors of the 16th- and 17th-century houses bear coats-of-arms.

RUE DU HAUT FOUR
LE PONTIS
R DU PLUS BAS FOUR
RUE GRANDE
RUE GRANDE
PLACE DE L'HOSPICE
REMPARTS OUEST

CELEBRITY VILLAGE

The Colombe d'Or (Golden Dove) auberge *(see p574)* was popular with many of the artists and writers who flocked to the Riviera in the 1920s. Early patrons included Picasso, Soutine, Modigliani, Signac, Colette and Cocteau. They often paid for their rooms and meals with paintings, resulting in the priceless collection that can be seen by diners today. The rich and famous have continued to come to St-Paul: Zelda and F. Scott Fitzgerald had a dramatic fight over Isadora Duncan at dinner here one night, and Yves Montand married Simone Signoret on the terrace. A photo display of celebrity visitors in the St-Paul museum features Sartre and de Beauvoir, Greta Garbo, Sophia Loren, Burt Lancaster and Catherine Deneuve.

Artist Marc Chagall (1887–1985), who moved to St-Paul-de-Vence in 1950

Nice ❸❻

Nice's Old Quarter

T HE LARGEST RESORT on the Mediterranean coast and the fifth biggest city in France, with its second busiest airport, Nice was founded by the Greeks and colonized by the Romans. Its temperate winter climate and verdant subtropical vegetation have long attracted visitors. Until World War II, it was popular with aristocrats, including Tsar Nicholas I's widow who visited in 1856, and Queen Victoria who stayed in 1895. This glittering past has contributed to Nice becoming capital of the Côte d'Azur, and today it is also a center for business conferences and package vacations. Nice has good museums, good beaches and an atmospheric street life. Best of all is Carnival: 18 days of celebrations finishing on Shrove Tuesday in a fireworks display and the Battle of the Flowers *(see p35).*

Yachts at anchor in Nice harbor

Exploring Nice

The promenade des Anglais, running right along the seafront, was built in the 1830s with funds raised by the English colony. Today, it is an 8-lane, 5-km (3-mile) highway, with galleries, shops and grand hotels like the **Negresco**, reflecting Nice's prosperity.

Nice also has a dark side, recorded in 1982 by English author, Graham Greene. He wrote a controversial attack on Jacques Médécin, the city's right-wing mayor, who fled to Paraguay to avoid standing trial in France.

Nice was Italian until 1860, and the pastel façades and balconies of the Old Town have a distinctly Italianate feel. It lies at the foot of a hill still known as the Château, for the castle that once stood there. The district is fast being restored, and its tall, narrow buildings now house artists and galleries, boutiques and restaurants. The daily flower and vegetable market in the

cours Saleya is a visual treat and a delight for shoppers.

The Cimiez district, on the hills overlooking the town, is the fashionable quarter of Nice. The old monastery of Notre-Dame-de-Cimiez is well worth a visit. Lower down on the hillside are the remains of an extensive Roman settlement, with vestiges of the great baths and an amphitheater. Artifacts from the excavations are on display at the archaeological museum, next door to the Musée Matisse.

🏛 Musée Matisse

164 av des Arènes de Cimiez.
【 04 93 81 08 08. **Open** Wed–Mon.
Closed some public hols. 📷 ♿
Inspired by the Mediterranean light, Matisse spent many years in Nice. The museum, housed in and below the 17th-century Arena Villa, displays drawings, paintings, bronzes, fabrics and artifacts. Highlights include *Still Life With Pomegranates* and his last completed work, *Flowers and Fruits.*

🏛 Palais Lascaris

15 rue Droite. 【 04 93 62 05 54.
Open Tue–Sun. **Closed** some public hols.
This 17th-century stucco palace is decorated with ornate woodwork, Flemish tapestries and illusionistic ceilings thought to be by Carlone. Its small but delightful collection includes a reconstruction of an 18th-century apothecary's shop.

🏛 Musée d'Art Contemporain

Promenade des Arts. 【 04 93 62 61 62. **Open** Wed–Mon. **Closed** Jan 1, Easter, May 1, Dec 25. 📷 ♿
The museum occupies a strikingly original complex of four marble-faced towers linked by glass passageways. The collection is particularly strong in Neo-Realism and Pop Art, with works by Andy Warhol, Jean Tinguely and Niki de Saint-Phalle. Also well represented are such Ecole de Nice artists as César, Arman and Yves Klein.

Blue Nude IV (1952) by Henri Matisse

An azure view – relaxing on the promenade des Anglais

✚ Cathédrale Ste-Réparate

This 17th-century Baroque building is surmounted by a handsome tiled dome. Its interior is lavishly decorated with plasterwork, marble and original paneling.

🏛 Musée Chagall

Avenue du Docteur Ménard. **℃** 04 93 53 87 20. **Open** Wed–Mon. **Closed** various public hols. 🖼 🕭 This is the largest collection of works by Marc Chagall, with paintings, drawings, sculpture, stained glass and mosaics. Best of all are the 17 canvases of the artist's *Biblical Message*.

🏛 Musée des Beaux Arts

33 avenue des Baumettes. **℃** 04 93 44 50 72. **Open** Tue–Sun. **Closed** Jan 1, Easter, May 1, Dec 25. 🕭 The 19th-century home of a Ukrainian princess displays works sent to Nice by Napoleon III after Italy ceded the city to France in 1860. Works by Dufy, Monet, Renoir and Sisley add to its appeal.

🏛 Palais Masséna

65 rue du France. **℃** 04 93 88 11 34. **Open** Dec–Oct: Tue–Sun. **Closed** Jan 1, Dec 25. 🖼 This 19th-century palace is filled with paintings of the

Nice school, local folk art and ephemera such as Carnival posters, and a gold cloak once worn by Napoleon's beloved Josephine. It also contains works by the Impressionists and Provençal ceramics. The Italianate building belonged to the great-grandson of Napoleon's Nice-born Marshal.

✚ Cathédrale Orthodoxe Russe St-Nicolas

Completed in 1912, the cathedral was built in memory of a young Tsarevitch who died of consumption here in 1865. The exterior is of pink brick and gray marble, with elaborate mosaics. The interior is resplendent with icons and fine woodwork. The onion domes make this Nice's most exotic landmark.

NICE

KEY

🚌 Bus station

🅿 Parking

🛈 Tourist information

✚ Church

0 meters 250
0 yards 250

Chapelle St-Pierre, Villefranche

Villefranche-sur-Mer **37**

Alpes-Maritimes. 🏘 *8,000.* 🚌 🚗
ℹ *Jardin François Binon (04 93 01 73 68).* 🛒 *Tue, Sat, Sun & public hols.*

ONE OF THE MOST perfectly situated towns on the coast, Villefranche lies at the foot of hills forming a sheltered amphitheater. The town overlooks a beautiful natural harbor that is deep enough to be a naval port of call.

The bright and animated waterfront is lined by Italianate façades with cafés and bars from which to watch the fishermen. Here, too, is the medieval **Chapelle St-Pierre**, which, after years of service storing fishing nets, was restored in 1957 and decorated by Jean Cocteau. His frescoes depict non-religious images as well as the life of St. Peter.

Also worth a visit is the 16th-century **Citadelle St-Elme**, incorporating the town hall and two art galleries.

Behind the harbor, the streets are narrow, winding, and often stepped or enclosed by overhanging buildings. Walking through them, you get the odd glimpse of the harbor. The vaulted 13th-century rue Obscure has always provided shelter from bombardment, right up to World War II.

🏠 **Chapelle St-Pierre**
Port de Villefranche. 📞 *04 93 76 90 70.* **Open** *mid-Dec–mid-Nov: Tue–Sun.* **Closed** *Dec 25.* 🚫

Cap Ferrat **38**

Alpes-Maritimes. ✈ *Nice.* 🚍 *Nice.* 🚉 *Beaulieu-sur-Mer.* 🚌 ℹ *St-Jean-Cap-Ferrat (04 93 76 08 90).*

THE PENINSULA of Cap Ferrat boasts some of the most sumptuous villas found on the Riviera. From 1926 until the author's death, the best-known was Somerset Maugham's Villa Mauresque, where Maugham received celebrities from Noël Coward and Winston Churchill to the Duke of Windsor.

High walls guard most of the exclusive villas, but possibly the finest of all is open to the public. The **Fondation Ephrussi de Rothschild** is a terra-cotta and marble mansion set in themed gardens on the crest of the cape. It belonged to the Baroness Ephrussi de Rothschild, who bequeathed it to the Institut de France in 1934. It is furnished as she left it, with her collections of priceless porcelain, items that belonged to Marie Antoinette, tapestries and paintings, and a unique collection of working drawings by Fragonard.

The town of **Beaulieu** lies where the cape joins the mainland, overlooking the Baie des Fourmis. A pleasant marina with an exceptionally mild climate and very fine hotels, it is the site of another unique house, the extraordinary **Villa Kerylos**. Built between 1902 and 1908 for archaeologist Theodore Reinach in imitation of an ancient Greek residence, it contains lovingly reproduced mosaics, frescoes and furniture.

🏛 **Fondation Ephrussi de Rothschild**
Cap Ferrat. 📞 *04 93 01 33 09.* **Open** *daily.* **Closed** *Dec 25.* 🚫 ♿ ✦
🏛 **Villa Kerylos**
Impasse Gustave Eiffel, Beaulieu. 📞 *04 93 01 01 44.* **Open** *daily.* **Closed** *mid-Nov–mid-Dec; Jan 1; Dec 25.* 🚫 ♿ ✦

Greek-style Villa Kerylos at Beaulieu on Cap Ferrat

Louis XV salon at the Fondation Ephrussi de Rothschild, Cap Ferrat

Èze ❸

Alpes-Maritimes. 🏘 *2,600.* 🚃 🚌
ℹ *place de Gaulle (04 93 41 26 00).*

FOR MANY, ÈZE is the ultimate perched village, balancing on a rocky pinnacle high above the Mediterranean. Every summer, thousands of visitors stream through the 14th-century fortified gate and throng the narrow streets. The carefully restored, flower-decked buildings mainly house shops, galleries and craft workshops. At the top of the village, the ruined château is surrounded by the lush tropical plants of the **Jardin Exotique**. The view from here is superb.

Farther along the Upper Corniche is the Roman Alpine Trophy of **La Turbie** *(see pp42–3).* Built in 6 BC, the vast structure dominates the surrounding village and has magnificent views overlooking Monaco.

❧ **Jardin Exotique**
Rue du Château. 📞 *04 93 41 10 11.*
Open *daily.* 🏷
🔺 **La Turbie**
Open *daily.* 🏷 🏷

Roquebrune-Cap-Martin ❹

Alpes-Maritimes. 🚊 *Nice.* 🚃 🚌
ℹ *20 av Paul Doumer (04 93 35 62 87).*
🗓 *daily.*

THE MEDIEVAL VILLAGE of Roquebrune overlooks the wooded cape where the villas of the rich and famous still abound. Visitors here have included Coco Chanel and Greta Garbo. The cape has not always been kind to its guests. Poet W.B. Yeats died here in 1939, and the architect Le Corbusier was drowned off the coast in 1965.

In 1467, Roquebrune believed that by acting scenes from the Passion it escaped the plague, and every August it continues this tradition.

View from Roquebrune

Alpes-Maritimes ❹

Alpes-Maritimes. 🛫 *Nice.* 🚃 *Nice.*
🚌 *Peille.* 🚢 *Nice.* ℹ *Peille (04 93 91 71 71).*

IN THE HINTERLAND of the Côte d'Azur, it is still possible to find quiet, unspoiled villages off the tourist track. The tiny twin villages of **Peille** and **Peillon** are typical. Both have changed little since the Middle Ages, perched on outcrops over the Paillon River, their streets a mass of steps and arches. Peille, the more remote, even has its own dialect. The Alpes-Maritimes countryside is also unspoiled, its craggy gorges, tumbling rivers and wind-swept plateaus just a few hours from the coast. Of note are the ancient rock carvings of the **Vallée des Merveilles** and rare wildlife in the **Parc National du Mercantour**.

Menton ❷

Alpes-Maritimes. 🏘 *30,000.* 🚃 🚌
ℹ *Palais de l'Europe, avenue Boyer (04 92 41 76 76).* 🗓 *daily.*

MENTON'S BEACHES, with the Alps and the golden buildings and Belle Epoque villas of the Old Town as a backdrop, would be enough to lure most visitors. In the 19th century, Queen Victoria and famous writers and poets often vacationed here. Tropical gardens and citrus fruits thrive in its perfect climate, mild even in February for the famous lemon festival *(see p35).*

Among Menton's sights is the **Eglise St-Michel**, a superb example of Baroque architecture in yellow and pink stone. The square before it is paved with a mosaic of the Grimaldi coat of arms. The **Hôtel de Ville**, in the center of town, was decorated in 1957 by Jean Cocteau. Drawings, paintings, ceramics and stage designs by the renowned artist are displayed in the **Musée Cocteau**, housed in a 17th-century fort.

Inside the Palais Carnolès, the **Musée des Beaux Arts** features works from the Middle ages to the 20th century.

🏛 **Hôtel de Ville**
Place Ardoiono. 📞 *04 92 10 50 00.*
Open *Mon–Fri.* **Closed** *public hols.* 🏷
🏛 **Musée Cocteau**
Bastion du Port. 📞 *04 93 57 72 30.*
Open *Wed–Mon.* **Closed** *public hols.*
🏛 **Musée des Beaux Arts**
3 avenue de la Madone. 📞 *04 93 35 49 71.* **Open** *Wed–Sun.* **Closed** *public hols.*

Mosaic at the Musée Cocteau in Menton

Monaco ⑬

TRAVELERS TO MONACO by car would do well to take the Moyenne Corniche, one of the most beautiful highways in the world, with incomparable views of the Mediterranean coastline. Arriving among the skyscrapers of Monaco today, it is hard to imagine the turbulence of its history. At first a Greek settlement, later taken by the Romans, it was bought from the Genoese in 1297 by the Grimaldis who, in spite of bitter family feuds and at least one political assassination, still rule as the world's oldest monarchy. Monaco covers 1.9 sq km (0.74 sq miles) and, although its size has increased by one-third in the form of landfills, it still occupies an area smaller than that of New York City's Central Park.

Aerial view of Monaco

Grand Casino

Exploring Monaco

Monaco owes its renown principally to its Grand Casino. Source of countless legends, it was instituted in 1856 by Charles III to save himself from bankruptcy. The first casino was opened in 1865 on a barren promontory (later named Monte-Carlo in his honor) across the harbor from ancient Monaco-Ville. So successful was Charles's money-making venture that, by 1870, he was able to abolish taxation for his people. Today, Monaco is a tax haven for thousands, and its residents have the highest per capita income in the world.

Visitors come from all over the world for the Grand Prix de Monaco in May and the Monte Carlo Rally in January (see p35). Many of the greatest singers perform in the opera season. There is a fireworks festival (July–August), and an international circus festival at the end of January as well as world-class ballet and concerts. Facilities exist for every sort of leisure activity, and there is plenty else to enjoy without going broke, including **Fort Antoine** and the Neo-Romanesque **Cathédrale**.

🎰 Grand Casino

Place du Casino. 📞 00 377 92 16 23 00. **Open** daily. ♿
Designed in 1878 by Charles Garnier, architect of the Paris Opéra (see p93), and set in formal gardens, the Casino gives a splendid view over Monaco. The lavish interior is still decorated in Belle Epoque style, recalling an era when this was the rendezvous of Russian Grand Dukes, English lords and other adventurers. Anyone can play the odds on the one-armed bandits of the Salle Blanche or the roulette wheels of the Salle Europe. Even the most exclusive of the gaming rooms can be visited at a price, but their tables are for the big spenders only.

♠ Palais du Prince

Place du Palais. 📞 00 377 93 25 18 31. **Open** Jun–Oct: daily. 📷
Monaco-Ville, the seat of government, is the site of the 13th-century Palais du Prince. The interior, with its priceless furniture and carpets and its

Skyscrapers and apartment blocks of modern Monte-Carlo

MONACO'S ROYAL FAMILY

Since 1949, Monaco has been in the charge of its most effective ruler ever. Businesslike Prince Rainier III is descended from a Grimaldi who entered the Monaco fortress in 1297 disguised as a monk. Rainier's wife, former film star Grace Kelly, died tragically in 1982. Their son, Albert, is heir to the throne but his sisters, Caroline and Stephanie, are the main focus of media attention.

Prince Rainier III, Princess Grace and Princess Caroline

VISITORS' CHECKLIST

Monaco. 🚶 30,000. ✈ 7 km (4.5 miles) SW Nice. 🚉 av Prince Pierre (00 377 93 10 60 15). 🛈 2a bd des Moulins (00 377 92 16 61 16). 🚢 daily. 🎪 Festival du Cirque (Jan–Feb); International Fireworks Festival (Jul–Aug); Fête Nationale Monégasque (Nov).

ships. Marine explorer Jacques Cousteau established his research center here.

🌸 Jardin Exotique

62 bd du Jardin Exotique. 🕻 00 377 93 15 29 80. **Open** daily. **Closed** Nov 19, Dec 25. ⬛ ⬛ to part of garden only. These gardens are considered to be the finest in Europe, with a huge range of tropical and subtropical plants. In the park, a museum of anthropology offers evidence that bears, mammoths and hippopotami once lived on the coast here.

magnificent frescoes, is open to the public only during the prince's absence. The changing of the guard takes place daily at 11:55am.

🏛 Musée des Souvenirs Napoléoniens

Place du Palais. 🕻 00 377 93 25 18 31. **Open** Jun–mid-Nov: daily; mid-Dec–May: Tue–Sun. ⬛ ⬛ A genealogical tree on the wall traces the family links between the Grimaldis and Bonapartes. Also on display are Napoleon's personal effects and

clothing, and portraits of Napoleon and Josephine.

✖ Musée Océanographique

Av Saint-Martin. 🕻 00 377 93 15 36 00. **Open** daily. ⬛ ⬛ This museum was founded in 1910 by Prince Albert I, using his casino profits. Its aquarium, fed with sea water, holds rare species of marine plants and animals. The museum houses an important scientific collection, diving equipment and model

Guard outside the Palais du Prince

🏛 Musée des Automates et Poupées d'Autrefois

17 av Princesse Grace. 🕻 00 377 93 30 91 26. **Open** daily. **Closed** Jan 1, May 1, Nov 19, Dec 25. ⬛ This museum houses over 400 dolls from the 18th century to the present. The delightful automata are set in motion several times each day.

MONACO

Cathédrale ④
Grand Casino ⑥
Jardin Exotique ①
Musée Océanographique ⑤
Musée des Souvenirs Napoléoniens ②
Palais du Prince ③

KEY

━ Grand Prix circuit
🚉 Railroad station
🅿 Parking
🛈 Tourist information
✝ Church

0 meters   250
0 yards   250

CORSICA

··

HAUTE-CORSE · CORSE-DU-SUD

*C*ORSICA, *where the people speak their own Italian dialect, has all the attributes of a mini-continent. There are tropical palm trees, vineyards, olive and orange groves, forests of chestnut and indigenous pine, alpine lakes and cool mountain torrents filled with trout. Most distinctive of all is the parched maquis (scrub), heavy with the scent of myrtle, which Napoleon swore he could smell from the sea.*

The third-largest island in the Mediterranean after Sicily and Sardinia, Corsica has been a problem and a bafflement to mainland France ever since 1769, when it was "sold" to Louis XV by the Genoese for 40 million francs. Before that, following years of struggle, the Corsican people had enjoyed 15 years of independence under the leadership of Pasquale Paoli. They understandably felt cheated by the deal with the French, and have resented them ever since. To vacationers visiting the island – in July and August tourists outnumber the inhabitants six to one – the Corsican-French relationship may not appear to be an adverse one. However, there is a strong (and sometimes violent) separatist movement, which does deter some tourists. As a result, Corsica's wild beauty has been preserved to an extent not seen in the rest of the Mediterranean.

From the 11th to the 13th century, Corsica was a colony of the old Tuscan republic of Pisa, whose builders founded beautifully proportioned Romanesque churches. These buildings are, along with the megalithic stone warriors in Filitosa, the noblest monuments to be seen here. Otherwise, this birthplace of Napoleon remains a place of wild seacoasts and mountain peaks, one of the last unspoiled corners of the Mediterranean: poor, depopulated, beautiful, old-fashioned and doggedly aloof.

The village of Oletta in the Nebbio region around St-Florent

◁ **A fisherman with feline friends in Bastia**

Exploring Corsica

CORSICA'S MAIN APPEAL is its scenery: a wildly beautiful landscape of mountains, forests, myrtle-scented maquis and countless miles of sandy beaches. Late spring (when the wild flowers are in bloom) and early fall are the best times to visit – the temperature is moderate and there aren't too many visitors. The island is renowned for its superb hiking trails, some of which become cross-country skiing trails during the winter season. Downhill skiing is also possible in February and March.

Calvi's port and 15th-century citadel

KEY

▬▬	Major road
▭▭	Minor road
▬▬	Scenic route
⊥⊥⊥	Scenic railroad
◥	River
☀	Viewing point

WINDS OF CORSICA

The island is affected by winds from every direction. The two not shown here are the Mezzogiorno, which blows at noon, and the Terrana, strongest at midnight.

Tramontane (cold wind blowing from the north)

Maestrale (can be very strong)

Grecale (bringing rain in winter)

Ponente (milder west wind)

Levante (warm)

Libeccio (bringing rain in winter)

Sirocco (dusty wind from Africa)

L'ÎLE ROUSSE ❹
❺ CALVI
CALENZANA
BALAGNE
Tartagine
D51
MONTE CINTO
PARC NA...
GOLFE DE PORTO ❾
PORTO
LES CALANCHE
D70...
GR20
❿ CARGESE
D23
GOLFE DE SAGONE
D101
N193
D51
AJACCIO ❶❶
ÎLES SANGUINAIRES
GOLFE D'AJACCIO
N196
❶❷ FILITOS...
GOLFE DE VALINCO
PROPRIANO
SART...

SIGHTS AT A GLANCE

The Calanche cliffs in the Golfe de Porto

GETTING AROUND

Car ferries (which should be booked well in advance) depart from Marseille, Nice and Toulon, arriving at Bastia, L'Île Rousse, Calvi, Ajaccio and Propriano. There are also ferries from Sardinia and the Italian ports of Genoa, Livorno and La Spezia. Small airports are based at Ajaccio, Bastia, Calvi and Figari (near Bonifacio). Corsica's roads are narrow, twisting and often tortuously slow, though breathtaking views reward the effort. A car is almost a must for exploring the island, as public transportation is limited. Carry spare gas – gas stations are few and far between.

0 kilometers   20

0 miles   10

Corte's Old Town, with its citadel high up on a rocky outcrop

Cap Corse ❶

Haute-Corse. ✈ Bastia. 🚌 Bastia,
Macinaggio, Rogliano. 🚢 Bastia.
ℹ Bastia (04 95 55 96 85).

CAP CORSE is the northern
tip of Corsica, 40 km (25
miles) in length but seldom
more than 12 km (7.5 miles)
wide, pointing like an accusatory finger toward Genoa.

There are two roads out of
Bastia to the cape: the D81
leading west across the mountains and joining up with the
D80 after the wine village of
Patrimonio; and the D80 traveling north along the eastern
shore to **Erbalunga** and
Macinaggio. Either way the
road is narrow and twisting, a
foretaste of what awaits you
nearly everywhere in Corsica.

From the coastal village of
Lavasina, the D54 leads left
off the D80 to Pozzo; from
here it is a 5-hour round-trip
on foot to the 1,307-m (4,300-ft)
summit of **Monte Stello**, the
highest peak on the cape. The
360-degree view from the top
takes in St-Florent to the west,
the massif of central Corsica
to the south and the Italian
island of Elba to the east.

Farther up the coast, the
restored **Tour de Losse** is one
of many 16th-century Genoese
towers along the coast – part
of an elaborate system which
enabled all Corsican towns to
be warned within two hours
of impending barbarian raids.

The charming 18th-century
fishing port of **Centuri**, near
the tip of the peninsula on the
west coast, is an ideal spot
for a delicious seafood feast.
Pino, a pretty little village

straggling down the green
mountainside farther to the
south, has no hotel, only a
lovely little church dedicated
to the Virgin, full of model
ships placed there by mariners
grateful for her protection.

On the way south along the
vertiginous lower corniche,
be sure to turn left up the hill
to **Canari**. One of the larger
villages in this area, Canari has
a jewel of a 12th-century Pisan
church, Santa Maria Assunta,
a magnificent view across the
sea, and a thoroughly convivial
hotel-restaurant. All the byroads in this thickly wooded
area seem to lead somewhere
interesting. There are literally
dozens of picturesque hamlets
in the vicinity, and it should
be borne in mind that from
this point onward the landscape becomes steadily less
attractive as the road winds
on past the old asbestos
works and beaches of
black sand below **Nonza**.

The village of Erbalunga on the east coast of Cap Corse

Bastia ❷

Haute-Corse. 🏠 39,000. ✈ 🚌
🚢 🚆 ℹ place St-Nicolas (04 95 55
96 85). 🛒 Tue–Sun.

A THRIVING PORT and the
administrative capital of
Upper Corsica, Bastia is utterly
different in style from its sedate
west coast rival, Ajaccio. The
Genoese citadel and colorful
19th-century Italianate buildings around the old port are for
many people their first taste of
the authentic Mediterranean –
as it was half a century ago,
and as it stubbornly remains
in our imagination.

The center of Bastiais life is
the **place St-Nicolas**, facing
the wharf where ferries from
the mainland and Italy arrive.
Heading south along the
waterfront you come to the
place de l'Hôtel de Ville,
site of a bustling outdoor
food market each morning.
Bordering the square are the
early 17th-century **Chapelle
de l'Immaculée Conception**,
with its ornate 18th-century
interior, and the mid-17th-century **Eglise de St-Jean-Baptiste**, whose façade
dominates the Vieux Port.

From here it is a short walk
up to the 16th-century **citadel**,
where there are two more
churches worth seeing: the
Baroque **Chapelle Sainte-Croix**, with its striking *Black
Christ*, fished out of the sea by
Bastiais fishermen in 1428;
and the 15th-century **Sainte-Marie**, which has a *Virgin*
made of a ton of solid silver.

Bastia's Vieux Port seen from the Jetée du Dragon

St-Florent ❸

Haute-Corse. 🏔 *1,400.* 🅿 ℹ
Bâtiment Administratif (04 95 37 06 04).
🛒 *1st Wed of month.*

S T-FLORENT IS almost a
Corsican St-Tropez – chic,
affluent and packed with
yachts from all over the
Mediterranean. Its citadel
(closed to visitors) dates from
1439, and is a fine example of
Genoese military architecture.
The town itself is pleasant to
wander through; its main
attraction, the 12th-century
Pisan **Cathédrale de Santa
Maria Assunta**, lies just inland
on the road to Poggio-d'Oletta.

Environs
A leisurely 4-hour tour by car
of the **Nebbio** region, which
extends in an amphitheater
around St-Florent, might take
in the following: **Santo Pietro
di Tenda**; **Murato**, famous for
its magnificent **Eglise de San
Michele de Murato**, a 12th-
century Pisan Romanesque
construction built of white and
green stone; the **San Stefano**
pass, with the sea on either
side; **Oletta**, which produces a
special blue cheese made from
ewes' milk; the **Teghime** pass;
and finally, the wine village of
Patrimonio, where there is
a strange, big-eared menhir
dating from 900–800 BC.
  Along the coast to the west
of St-Florent lies the barren, uninhabited **Désert des Agriates**.
If you can face the 10-km
(6-mile) trip to the sea – on
foot, by bike or by motorcycle
– the Saleccia beach here is
by far the most beautiful and
solitary beach on the island.

San Michele de Murato

L'Île Rousse ❹

Haute-Corse. 🏔 *2,300.* 🚉 🚌 ⛴
ℹ *place Paoli (04 95 60 04 35).*
🛒 *daily.*

F OUNDED IN 1758 by
Pasquale Paoli, leader of
independent Corsica, L'Île
Rousse is today a major
vacation resort and
ferry terminal. The
center of town is the
plane-shaded place
Paoli, dominated by
a marble statue of
Corsica's national hero.
On the north side of the
square is the covered
market, with the Old
Town just beyond.
  In the summer, L'Île
Rousse becomes hid-
eously crowded, its
beaches a mass of
bodies. It is worth
traveling 10 km (6 miles) up
the coast to **Lozari**, which
offers a magnificent, virtually
unspoiled stretch of sand.

**French foreign
legionnaire**

Environs
One very pleasant way to
discover the **Balagne** region
is to take the tram from L'Île
Rousse to Calvi and back.
This odd little service runs
from June to September each
year, more or less keeping to
the coastline and stopping at
Algajola, Lumio and various
vacation villages along the way.

Calvi ❺

Haute-Corse. 🏔 *5,000.* 🚉 🚌 ⛴
ℹ *Port de Plaisance (04 95 65 16 67).*
🛒 *daily.*

C ALVI, where Nelson lost his
eye in an "explosion of
stones" in 1794, is today half
military town, half cheap vacation resort. Its 15th-century
citadel is garrisoned by a
crack French regiment of the
foreign legion; while beyond
the ferry port is a seedy,
apparently endless camp-
site and trailer park.
  The town makes a
halfhearted case for
being the birthplace of
Christopher Columbus,
but there is no real evi-
dence to support this.
A much better claim to
fame is the food, which is
very good and reasonably
priced by Corsican stan-
dards. There is also a very
respectable jazz festival
held at Calvi in the
third week of June.
  Outside of town, the
19th-century **Chapelle
de Notre-Dame de la Serra**
is gloriously situated on a hilltop commanding extensive
views in all directions.

The Chapelle de Notre-Dame de la Serra, 6 km (3.5 miles) southwest of Calvi

Corte's 15th-century citadel at dawn

The Niolo ❻

Haute-Corse. 🚌 Bastia.
🛈 Calacuccia (04 95 48 05 22).

THE NIOLO, west of Corte,
extends westward to the
Vergio pass and the upper
Golo basin, and to the east as
far as the Scala di Santa Regina.
It includes Corsica's highest
mountain, the 2,700-m (8,859-
ft) **Monte Cinto**, and its biggest river, the **Golo**, which
meets the sea south of Bastia.

Unique among the regions
of Corsica, the Niolo persists
in the cultivation of livestock
as its economic mainstay.

The main town, **Calacuccia**,
is convenient for excursions
to Monte Cinto. The nearby ski
resort of **Haut Asco** is best
reached by the D147 from
Asco, but enthusiasts can
walk from Calacuccia (8–9
hours). To the south is the
huge forest of **Valdu Niello**.

Corte ❼

Haute-Corse. 🏠 6,000. 🚉 🚌
🛈 15 quartier Quatre Fontaines (04
95 46 26 70). 🚂 Fri.

IN THE geographical center of
Corsica, Corte was the
chosen capital of the independence leader Pasquale Paoli
from 1755–69, and today is the
seat of the island's university.
In the Old Town is the 15th-
century citadel, housing the
Musée de la Corse. Its exhibits
relate to traditional Corsican
life and anthropology.

Corte is the best base for
exploring nearby mountain
areas, because it stands exactly
halfway along the GR20, the
legendary 220-km (137-mile)
trail from Calenzana to Conca.

🏛 **Musée de la Corse**
La Citadelle. 📞 04 95 45 25 45.
Open mid-Jun–mid-Sep: 10am–
7:30pm daily; mid-Sep–mid-Jun:
10am–12:30pm, 2–5:45pm Tue–Sat.
Closed public hols. 🏛 ♿ ✔

Environs
Don't miss the wildly beautiful
Gorges de la Restonica,
about 12 km (7.5 miles) out
of town via the D623. Above
these gorges adventurous
walkers may wish to make the
well-marked climb to the
snow-fed **Lac de Melo** (allow
60–90 minutes); or the **Lac de
Capitello**, 30 minutes farther
on, where the snow stays as
late as early June. The path –
in winter a cross-country ski
trail – follows the river.

South of Corte, the **Forêt de
Vizzavona** features beech and
pine woodland crisscrossed by
trout-filled streams and walking trails (notably the GR20). It
is a perfect refuge from the
summer heat and is also an
excuse to take the small train
up from Ajaccio or Bastia,
which stops at Vizzavona.

The Castagniccia ❽

Haute-Corse. 🚠 Bastia. 🚉 Corte,
Ponte Leccia. 🚌 Piedicroce, La Porta,
Valle-d'Alesani. 🛈 Piedicroce
(04 95 35 82 54).

EAST OF CORTE is the hilly,
chestnut-covered region of
Castagniccia (literally "small
chestnut grove"), which most
Corsicans agree is the very
heart and kernel of the island.
It was here that independence
leader Pasquale Paoli was
born in 1725, and that the re-
volts against Genoa and later
France began in earnest in
1729. Alas, many of the villages
in this beautiful, remote area
are nearly empty, their inhabitants having joined the 800,000
or so Corsicans (almost three
times the present population)
who live and work in mainland France or Italy. It seems
hard to believe that in the 17th
century, when the great chestnut forests introduced here
by the Genoese were at the
height of their production, this
was the most prosperous and
populated region in Corsica.

The D71 from Ponte Leccia
(north of Corte) to the east
coast winds through the center
of the Castagniccia region,
and to see it at a leisurely
pace will take the best part
of a day. Arm yourself with a
picnic before you start, because there are few supplies
available to buy en route.

◁ **Limestone cliffs of Bonifacio** (see p533)

Golfe de Porto ⑨

Corse-du-Sud. ✈ 🚌 ⛴ *Ajaccio.*
📍 *Porto.* ℹ *Porto (04 95 26 10 55).*

Porto is sited at the head of the Golfe de Porto, one of the most beautiful bays in the Mediterranean, which for the sake of its fauna and flora has been included in UNESCO's list of the world's common cultural heritage sites. So far, the only effect of this on Porto town has been to send hotel and restaurant prices through the roof. The best things here are the sunset from the magnificent Genoese watchtower, and the boat heading out to the Calanche, Scandola and Girolata.

The **Calanche** begin 2 km (1.2 miles) out of Porto, on the road to Piana. These 300-m (1,000-ft) red granite cliffs plunge truly to the sea, and are breathtaking. They are accessible only by boat or on foot: well-defined trails start from the Tête du Chien and the Pont de Mezanu, while boat tickets are available at Porto's Hôtel Le Cyrnée.

Otherwise the pretty village of **Piana**, just south of Porto, is a good starting point and a much more pleasant place to stay than Porto.

Detailed information about walking in this area can be obtained on the spot; one very worthwhile destination is the cove at **Ficajola** just below Piana, which has a delightful beach.

Porto's marina and Genoese watchtower

Environs

The road over the mountains from Porto to Calvi offers no more than a taste of this grandiose corner of Corsica – you have to take to the sea to view it properly (ferries from Porto and Galéria). **Girolata**, a tiny hamlet north of Porto, can be reached only by sea or by walking a mule path (4 hours round-trip) from a clearly marked point 23 km (14 miles) north of Porto on the D81.

At the mouth of the Golfe de Girolata, the **Réserve Naturelle de Scandola**, instituted in 1975, is the first land-and-sea reserve in France, covering over 1,000 hectares (2,500 acres) of sea, and a similar area of cliffs, caves and maquis (shrubbery). Marine life is abundant in these protected waters; there are ospreys, puffins and falcons.

CORSICAN FLOWERS

For lovers of wild-flowers, Corsica is a Mediterranean jewel. Much of the island is covered with maquis, a tangle of aromatic shrubs and low trees that flowers from late winter onward. Among its dense variety are the showy **Rock-rose** rockroses, which shower the ground with short-lived pink or white petals, and brilliant yellow broom. Grassy and rocky slopes are good places to spot the widespread tassel hyacinth and the Illyrian sea lily, which grows only in Corsica and Sardinia.

Spanish broom

Illyrian sea lily

Tassel hyacinth

The town of Piana with the Calanche in the background

Cargèse's Greek rite church

Cargèse ⑩

Corse-du-Sud. 🚶 *900.* 🚌 ℹ️ *rue du Docteur Dragacci (04 95 26 41 31).*

Cargèse overlooks the sea from a promontory between the bays of Sagone and Pero. It is a small town with an odd history: many of the people who live here are the descendants of 17th-century Greek refugees from Turkish rule, given asylum in Corsica.

A few Cargèsiens still speak Greek, and their icon-filled Eastern (Greek) rite church still faces its Catholic counterpart in an attitude that must once have seemed deliberately confrontational. Nowadays the old rivalries have long since vanished, and the Orthodox priest and Catholic *curé* often stand in for one another.

There are many splendid beaches in the vicinity, notably at **Pero** and **Chiuni** just to the north, and at **Ménasina** and **Stagnoli** to the south.

Ajaccio ⑪

Corse-du-Sud. 🚶 *59,000.* ✈️ 🚌 🚢 🚌 ℹ️ *place Foch (04 95 51 53 03).* 🗓️ *Tue–Sun.*

Ajaccio, a noisy, busy town by Corsican standards, was the birthplace of Napoleon Bonaparte in 1769. Napoleon never returned to Corsica after crowning himself emperor of the French in 1804, but the town – the modern capital of nationalist Corsica – celebrates his birthday every August 15.

The **Cathédrale Notre-Dame de la Miséricorde**, where Napoleon was baptized on July 21, 1771, was built in the late 1500s. It houses Eugène Delacroix's famous painting *Vierge du Sacré-Coeur.*

A few streets away, the **Maison Bonaparte**, where Napoleon was born and spent his childhood, contains family portraits, period furniture and assorted memorabilia. The building was occupied for a brief spell by Hudson Lowe, Napoleon's future jailer on St-Helena, after the Bonaparte family was ejected by the citizens of Ajaccio in 1793.

More interesting is the superb collection of artworks assembled on the coattails of Napoleon by his uncle, Cardinal Fesch, who looted numerous churches, palaces and museums during the Italian campaign and brought the priceless swag home to Ajaccio. Housed in the 19th-century Palais Fesch, the **Musée Fesch** contains the finest collection of Italian primitive art in France after the Louvre. Among its masterpieces are

works by Botticelli, Titian and Veronese. Next to the Palais Fesch stands the **Chapelle Impériale**, built in 1855 by Napoleon III to accommodate the tombs of the Bonapartes.

From here, walk back along the quay to the Jetée de la Citadelle, which offers superb views of the town, the marina and the Golfe d'Ajaccio. The adjacent 16th-century **citadel** is occupied by the army.

🏛️ **Maison Bonaparte**
Rue St-Charles. 📞 *04 95 21 43 89.* **Open** *Mon am, Sun am.* 🚫
🏛️ **Musée Fesch**
50 rue Fesch. 📞 *04 95 21 48 17.* **Open** *summer: Wed–Mon; winter: Tue–Sat.* **Closed** *public hols.* 🚫 ♿

Environs
From the quai de la Citadelle there are daily excursions to the **Îles Sanguinaires** at the mouth of the Golfe d'Ajaccio.

A statue-menhir at Filitosa

Filitosa ⑫

Centre Préhistorique de Filitosa, Corse-du-Sud. 📞 *04 95 74 00 91.* **Open** *Apr–Oct: daily.* 🚫 ♿ *museum only.*

The 4,000-year-old, life-size stone warriors of Filitosa are the most spectacular relics of megalithic man in Corsica. Discovered in 1946, these phallic granite menhirs represent an interesting progression from mere silhouettes to more detailed sculpture, etched with human features and even weapons.

The five most recent and most sophisticated figures (about 1500 BC) stand around a thousand-year-old olive

Statue of Napoleon by Laboureur in place Maréchal Foch, Ajaccio

The fortified Old Town of Bonifacio, with the harbor in the foreground

tree, in the field below a tumulus. Other finds, which include a heavily armed warrior with shield, helmet and sword, can be seen in the site's archaeological museum.

Sartène ⓭

Corse-du-Sud. 🏛 3,600. 🚌 🚉 ℹ 6 rue Borgo (04 95 77 15 40). 🛒 winter: Tue & Sat; summer: Wed–Mon.

SARTÈNE is a medieval fortified town of narrow cobbled streets and gray granite houses rising above the Rizzanese Valley. Founded by the Genoese in the early 16th century, it has survived attacks by Barbary pirates and centuries of bloody feuding among the town's leading families.

Despite all this, Sartène has a reputation for deep piety, reinforced each year by the oldest and most intense Christian ceremony in Corsica, the Good Friday *Catenacciu* – literally, the "chained one." A red-hooded penitent, barefoot and in chains, drags a wooden cross through the Old Town in a reenactment of Christ's ascent to Golgotha.

Environs
Just outside of town in Sartène's former prison, the **Musée de Préhistoire Corse** contains fascinating artifacts from the Neolithic period, the Bronze Age and Iron Age.

🏛 Musée de Préhistoire Corse
Rue Croce. 📞 04 95 77 01 09. **Open** mid-Jun–mid-Sep: Mon–Sat; mid-Sep–mid-Jun: Mon–Fri. **Closed** public hols. 🈺

Bonifacio ⓮

Corse-du-Sud. 🏛 2,700. 🚌 🚉 ℹ place de l'Europe (04 95 73 11 88). 🛒 Wed.

BONIFACIO is the southernmost town in Corsica, dramatically sited on a limestone cliff peninsula with some of the most stunning views in the Mediterranean *(see pp528–9).* Its handsome harbor at the foot of the cliffs is the focus of life: cafés, restaurants and boutiques abound and boats depart regularly for neighboring Sardinia and the uninhabited islands of Lavezzi and Cavallo.

From the harbor, steps lead up to Bonifacio's fortified Old Town. The citadel, built by the conquering Genoese at the end of the 12th century, has long been the town's main defensive post, and from 1963–83 was the headquarters of the French foreign legion. From here, wander down to the tip of the promontory to see the two old windmills and the ruins of a Franciscan monastery.

Côte Orientale ⓯

Haute-Corse & Corse-du-Sud. 🛬 Bastia. 🚌 Porto-Vecchio, Aléria, Salenzara. 🚉 Bastia, Porto-Vecchio. ℹ Aléria (04 95 57 06 26), Porto-Vecchio (04 95 70 09 58).

THE FLAT and dreary alluvial plain stretching from Bastia to Solenzara has been rich farmland since 1945, the year it was finally drained and rid of malaria. More recently, vacation resorts and even high-rise hotels have mushroomed along the coast, cashing in on its long, sandy beaches.

The best sight in **Mariana**, which is otherwise uncomfortably close to the Bastia-Poretta airport, is the early 12th-century cathedral of Mariana known as **La Canonica**. A short distance away is the slightly older **Eglise de San Perteo**, surrounded by meadows.

About halfway down the coast, the port of **Aléria**, originally a Greek colony and the base for Rome's conquest of Corsica in 259 BC, is interesting for its rich archaeological heritage. Just outside town, a museum housed in the 16th-century Fort de Matra chronicles daily life in Roman Aléria.

Toward the southern tip of the island, the fortified town of **Porto-Vecchio**, built by Corsica's Genoese conquerors, is now an extremely popular seaside resort. The setting is perfect for the conventional seaside vacation, with umbrella pines, cork oak forests and glorious white sandy beaches within easy reach of the town, especially at **Palombaggia** and **Pinarello**.

The Golfe de Porto-Vecchio

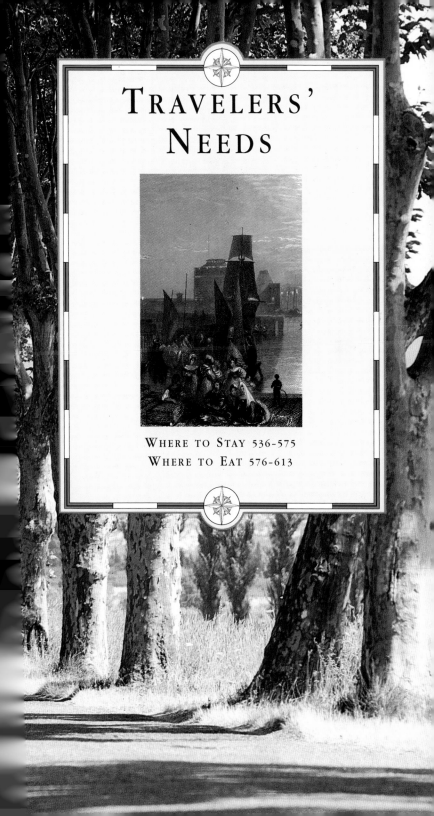

TRAVELERS'
NEEDS

WHERE TO STAY

MANY OF FRANCE'S 22,000 registered hotels are charming, unique and well priced. These four pages describe the types of hotels we have reviewed and provide tips on what to expect from French hotels. The hotel listings pages *(see pp540–75)* describe some of the best hotels around the country in every price category and style, from slick, modern chain hotels to small, classic, family-run establishments. Also included are *chambres d'hôte* (a sort of French bed-and-breakfast), which range from simple farms to grand châteaux, as well as the best hostels. France is full of furnished vacation apartments and houses, and information is given on renting a rural home, or *gîte*, and on how to get the most out of a camping vacation.

The Hôtel Euzkadi at Espelette in the Pyrenees *(see p569)*

THE CLASSIC FAMILY HOTEL

IF YOU'RE TOURING on a budget, the small, family-run, family-oriented hotel lurking in virtually every village and town is for you. It's likely to be the focal point of the village, with the bar and dining room (if the food is fairly good) full of locals. The atmosphere is entirely informal, with children, cats and dogs happily at home. In the hotel's dozen or so bedrooms, old-fashioned charm will make up for a lack of up-to-date decor and for the mere trickle of hot water in the shower.

The annual *Logis de France* guide details over 4,000 of these family-run, mainly one- and two-star hotel-restaurants. They tend to be located in small towns or rural locations; there are none in Paris. Most are no more than roadside inns, but off the beaten track you will discover many converted farmhouses and inexpensive seaside hotels. The *Logis* is a useful reference, but the quality of places listed can be uneven.

THE CHÂTEAU HOTEL

MANY OF FRANCE's châteaux and mansions have been converted into luxury hotels. They include everything from Renaissance buildings with sweeping lawns to medieval castles with battlements and keeps. Grand hotels are found all over France, with rich pickings in the Loire, the Savoie, the Haute-Savoie and the Rhône Delta. Properties included in the **Relais et Châteaux** brochure are recommended.

Typically, rooms are beautifully designed and the food is *haute cuisine*. Bedrooms range from grand suites to more simple abodes, often in converted farm buildings, making it possible, if you're willing to forgo four-poster beds and antiques, to live in luxury without going broke.

THE CITY HOTEL

EVERY BIG CITY has a group of hotels close to the train station or port. They range from cheap accommodations to a grand hotel or two. The most famous city hotels are the palace hotels in Paris and the Riviera resorts such as Nice and Cannes. Note that many city hotels do not have a restaurant. It is always worth checking the quality of the bedroom before you officially check in.

THE MODERN CHAIN HOTEL

BRANCHES OF MODERN hotel chains are useful for inexpensive pitstops if you're traveling through France. Many are situated on the outskirts of towns, near highways or main roads. The cheapest are the one-star, no-frills **Formula 1** motels, offering bedrooms with a double and single bed and no private bathroom.

Two-star chains include **Ibis/ Arcade**, **Campanile**, **Climat de France** and **Inter Hôtel**. Three-star chains include **Novotel** and **Mercure/Altéa**; both offer private bathrooms and allow one child to stay at no charge, provided the whole

Le Négresco in Nice on the Côte d'Azur *(see p573)*

The Meurice Hotel in the Tuileries Quarter of Paris *(see p541)*

family sleeps in one room
(Novotel has free accom-
modations for two under-16s).

THE RESTAURANT-WITH-ROOMS

THROUGHOUT FRANCE, many
of the better restaurants
offer accommodations.
Usually, the bedrooms match
the restaurant's quality and are
priced accordingly. Sometimes,
though, gourmet restaurants
have simple bedrooms hidden
away upstairs – great finds for
those who like to splurge on
food while saving on lodging.
Refer to the restaurant listings
on pages 580–613.

MEALS AND FACILITIES

IN HIGH SEASON, many resort
hotels insist on half board,
or *demi-pension* (a per-person
rate for the room, dinner and
breakfast). There is also full
board, or *pension*, which covers
lunch too. While it is cheaper
to opt for inclusive rates, meals
come from set or limited-choice
menus, which often omit the
more interesting dishes.
Many smaller family-run
hotels do not provide meals
on Sunday evenings and often
stop serving dinner as early
as 9pm on other days.

Rooms usually have double
beds; twin or single beds must
be requested when booking.
All mid-range hotels have a
choice of bathroom facilities.
A walk down the corridor to a
separate bathroom can reduce
the room rate considerably. A
bathroom with a bath *(un
bain)* usually costs more than
one with a shower *(une
douche); un cabinet de toilette*
has a sink and bidet, without
a bath, shower or toilet. If
you do not have *pension* or
demi-pension accommodations,
breakfast is often an added
charge. Go instead to the local
café, which may be cheaper
and more filling.

**Hôtel de l'Abbaye at Talloires in
the French Alps** *(see p564)*

GRADINGS

FRENCH HOTELS ARE GRADED
from zero stars to four stars
(plus "four star luxury"). Stars
indicate the hotel's facilities.
Hotels with two or more stars
must have an elevator where
appropriate and a phone in
every bedroom and at least 40
percent of their rooms must
have bathrooms. Three-star
hotels must provide room
service breakfast and have 80
percent of rooms with baths.
Only four-star hotels must
have a restaurant and all of
their rooms with baths.

PRICES

RATES, inclusive of tax and
service, are quoted per
room (apart from *pension* and
demi-pension arrangements).
There is usually a small supple-
ment for a third person in a
room for two, and little re-
duction for single travelers.
As a rule, the higher the star
rating, the more you pay. Rates
for a double room start from
about F130 per night for a one-
star hotel and go up to F500
or more for a four-star hotel.
Costs also vary geographically,
with remote rural areas like
Brittany being the cheapest.
In fashionable areas like the
Dordogne and Provence,
expect to pay 20 percent
more, and another 20 percent
again for Paris and the Côte
d'Azur. Prices vary seasonally
too, with coastal and alpine
areas raising rates by up to 50
percent in peak periods.

BOOKING

ALWAYS BOOK well in ad-
vance for Paris, and for
hotels in popular tourist areas
in July and August.
In resort areas, most hotels
close from October to March,
so it is wise to phone ahead
when traveling out of season to
make sure the place is open.
Reservations can normally be
held with a credit card at all
but the humblest hotels. If
you want to make a booking
while you are in France, there
are tourist offices in all main
cities that provide a hotel
reservation service up to eight
days in advance.

The dining room of the Grand Hôtel, Sète *(see p571)*

BED-AND-BREAKFASTS

FRENCH bed-and-breakfasts, called *chambres d'hôte,* come in all shapes and sizes, from tiny cottages to elaborate châteaux full of family portraits and antiques, plus some *ferme-auberges (see p577).* In all cases you will stay in a private home, and should not expect hotel services or amenities. Many offer dinner – *table d'hôte* – on request, where you usually dine *en famille.* Over 5,000 rural *chambres d'hôte* are registered and inspected by **Gîtes de France**. Watch for the green *chambres d'hôte* signs at the side of the road.

Roadside signs also lead to many B&Bs that are not registered. Information on these is available from local tourist offices.

The Gîtes de France logo

HOUSE RENTALS

THE FABLED *gîte* is a rural vacation home often converted from a farmhouse or its out-buildings. A *gîte* vacation is a popular and cheap way to see France, particularly out of season, but you must book many months in advance for the best *gîtes*. **Gîtes de France** registers some 40,000 *gîtes,* all inspected and graded to indicate the level of facilities. You can choose from a selection of 2,500 in the company's main brochure (available from the French Government Tourist Office), or book direct. Each of its 95 regional offices produces a booklet with all the *gîtes* in its *département,* which comes with a booking form. These are also available through the head office in Paris, **Maison des Gîtes de France**, which itself publishes a series of listings catering for those with more specialised requirements. These include *gîtes* for skiing, *gîtes* with horses, rural *gîtes,* and serious luxury *gîtes*.

France has many other kinds of furnished home rentals: expensive south-coast villas; ski resort chalets; city and coastal apartments. The *Allo Vacances* brochure, from the **French Government Tourist Office,** lists real estate agents offering vacation rentals.

CAMPING

ELEVEN THOUSAND official sites are spread around France's diverse countryside. The **Fédération Française de Camping et de Caravaning** publishes a comprehensive list, updated every year. Gîtes de France's *Camping à la Ferme* guide covers some simpler sites on farm land.

Campsites are graded from one to four stars. Three- and four-star sites are usually impressively spacious with many amenities and electricity connections for most tents and campers. One- and two-star sites always have toilets, a public phone and running water (though one-star sites sometimes have only cold water). What they lack in facilities they often make up for in peacefulness and rural charm.

Note that some sites accept only visitors with a **camping carnet** (pass). *Carnets* are available from the organizations listed opposite.

HOSTELS

HOSTELS are a money-saving option for single travelers, though for those traveling with a partner, cheap hotels are often no more expensive.

The IYHF's hosteling guide details the **FUAJ's** (Fédération Unie des Auberges de Jeunesse) 220 hostels around France, open to all ages and offering dormitory accommodations. If you are not a member of the **YHA** (Youth Hostel Association) in your home

A Bordeaux campsite in high season

country, you have to pay a small surcharge each time you stay in a French youth hostel.

UCRIF (Union des Centres de Rencontres Internationales de France) has 63 centers with a cultural bias throughout France. All have single, shared and dormitory accommodations and a restaurant.

In the summer, it is possible to stay in university rooms. Contact **CROUS** (Centre Régional des Oeuvres Universitaires et Scolaires) for details.

Gîtes d'étapes are usually large farmhouses with dormitories close to walking, bicycling and horse riding trails. Gîtes de France's *Gîtes d'Etapes* guide lists 1,000 of these sites throughout the country.

DISABLED TRAVELERS

G ET IN TOUCH with **Mobility International USA** for details on wheelchair access to hotels, youth hostel and house rental chains in France. They may also provide information about access to privately owned hotels.

The Carlton International Continental in Cannes *(see p572)*

CNRH (Comité National pour la Réadaptation des Handicapés) offers information on accessible hotels. The **Association des Paralysés de France** also publishes a guide to accessible accommodations called *Où Ferons Nous Etape.*

Gîtes de France produces *Gîtes Accessibles aux Handicapés*, a guide to *gîtes* suitable for disabled people.

FURTHER INFORMATION

T HE INVALUABLE *Traveler in France Reference Guide,* listing hotel chains, reservation agencies and companies for every type of package vacation, is published by the French Government Tourist Office. It also distributes *Logis de France* guides, and all the booklets for château-hotels, château-B&Bs and Café-Couette. However, it only distributes the *Relais et Châteaux* guide to those in person.

The first port of call for all non-hotel accommodations in the French countryside should be Gîtes de France.

When in France, local tourist offices are the best source of information for B&Bs and furnished rentals.

Loisirs Acceuil are special booking agencies that offer information on hotels, campsites, *gîtes* and B&Bs in their areas. There are 53 *Loisirs Acceuil* throughout France; the French Government Tourist Office provides contact numbers.

DIRECTORY

CHAIN HOTELS

Campanile
[020 8569 6969 *in UK.*
[01 64 62 46 46 *in France.*

Climat de France and Inter Hôtel
[(1) (800) 332 5332 *in US.* [0800 1122 *for Climat de France in France.*
[01 42 06 46 46 *for Inter Hôtel in France.*

Formula 1
No central reservation number.
[020 8741 1001 *in UK for brochure.*

Ibis/Novotel, Mercure
[(1) (800) 221 4542 *in US.* [01 60 77 27 27 *in France.*

Relais et Châteaux in the UK
[(212) 856 0115 *for a brochure.*
www.relaischateaux.fr

HOUSE RENTALS

Gîtes de France
178 Piccadilly, London W1V 9DB. [020 7493 3480.

Gîtes de France
59 St-Lazare, 75009 Paris.
[01 49 70 75 75.
www.gites-de-France.fr

HOSTELS

CROUS
39 av G-Bernanos, 75231 Paris Cedex 05.
[01 40 51 36 00.

FUAJ (Fédération Unie des Auberges de Jeunesse)
9 rue Brantome, 75003 Paris.
[01 48 04 70 40.

UCRIF
27, rue de Turbigo, 75002 Paris. [01 40 26 57 64.

American Youth Hostel Association
1108 K Street NW, Washington, DC 20005.
[(202) 783 0717.

BED-AND-BREAKFASTS

Café-Couette
8 rue de l'Isly, 75008 Paris.
[01 42 94 92 00.

CAMPING

Fédération Française de Camping et de Caravaning
78 rue de Rivoli, 75004 Paris. [01 42 72 84 08.

CAMPING ASSOCIATIONS IN THE US AND UK

American Automobile Association
[(407) 444 7000.

American Automobile Touring Alliance
[(617) 237 2600.

Camping and Caravaning Club
[(024 76) 422 024 (UK).

DISABLED TRAVELERS

Association des Paralysés de France
17 bd August Blanqui 75013 Paris.
[01 40 78 69 00.

CNRH (Comité National pour la Réadaptation des Handicapés)
236 bis, rue de Tolbiac, 75013 Paris.
[01 53 80 66 66.

Mobility International USA
PO Box 3551, Eugene, Oregon 97403.
[(541) 343 1284.

ADDITIONAL INFORMATION

French Government Tourist Office
444 Madison Avenue, New York, NY 10022.
[(212) 838 7800.

Choosing a Hotel

The hotels in this guide have been selected across a wide price range for their excellent facilities and location. Many also have a highly recommended restaurant. The chart lists the hotels by region, starting with Paris; color-coded thumb tabs indicate the regions covered on each page. For more details on restaurants, see pp580–613.

	Price	Credit Cards	Children's Facilities	Parking Facilities	Swimming Pool	Garden
PARIS						
ILE ST-LOUIS: *Hôtel des Deux Iles.* Map 9 C4. 59 rue St-Louis-en-l'Ile, 75004. ☎ 01 43 26 13 35. FAX 01 43 29 60 25. *Rooms: 17.* It's a privilege to stay on the Ile St-Louis. The prices here are reasonable, although the bedrooms are quite small. 🛏 📺	(F)(F)(F)(F)	AE V	●	■		■
ILE ST-LOUIS: *Hôtel du Jeu de Paume.* Map 9 C4. 54 rue St-Louis-en-l'Ile, 75004. ☎ 01 43 26 14 18. FAX 01 40 46 02 76. *Rooms: 32.* A welcoming, exemplary family hotel. Features include a glass-walled elevator, wooden beams, old terra-cotta paving and a sauna. 🛏 📺	(F)(F)(F)(F)	AE DC JCB MC V	●			■
THE MARAIS: *Hôtel de la Place des Vosges.* Map 10 D4. 12 rue de Birague, 75004. ☎ 01 42 72 60 46. FAX 01 42 72 02 64. *Rooms: 16.* A charming old building close to one of the prettiest squares in Paris. The largest rooms, on the top floor, have good views. 🛏 📺	(F)(F)(F)	DC JCB MC V				
THE MARAIS: *Hôtel de la Bretonnerie.* Map 9 C3. 22 rue Ste-Croix de la Bretonnerie, 75004. ☎ 01 48 87 77 63. FAX 01 42 77 26 78. *Rooms: 30.* Situated on a charming street, this is one of the most comfortable hotels in the Marais. Spacious bedrooms with antique furniture. 🛏 📺	(F)(F)(F)(F)	MC V	●			
THE MARAIS: *St-Paul-le-Marais.* Map 10 D3. 8 rue de Sévigné, 75004 . ☎ 01 48 04 97 27 FAX 01 48 87 37 04. *Rooms: 27.* Old timber and stone create a rustic environment. If you want to be away from the traffic noise, ask for a room facing the courtyard. 🛏 📺	(F)(F)(F)(F)	AE DC MC V	●			■
THE MARAIS: *Pavillion de la Reine.* Map 10 D3. 28 place des Vosges, 75003. ☎ 01 40 29 19 19. FAX 01 40 29 19 20. *Rooms: 55.* This is the luxury hotel of the Marais. The bedrooms have been sumptuously renovated. The courtyard is a haven of peace. 🛏 📺	(F)(F)(F)(F)(F)	AE DC MC V	●	■		■
BEAUBOURG: *Hôtel Beaubourg.* Map 9 B2. 11 rue Simon Lefranc, 75004. ☎ 01 42 74 34 24. FAX 01 42 78 68 11. *Rooms: 28.* An extremely comfortable and well-equipped hotel, tastefully restored and decorated, with a pretty courtyard garden. 🛏 📺	(F)(F)(F)	AE DC MC V				■
BEAUBOURG: *Hôtel Britannique.* Map 9 A3. 20 avenue Victoria, 75001. ☎ 01 42 33 74 59. FAX 01 42 33 82 65. *Rooms: 40.* A reasonably priced, friendly, family-run hotel in a renovated 19th-century building. 🛏 📺	(F)(F)(F)	AE DC MC V	●			
LES HALLES: *Hôtel Agora.* Map 9 A2. 7 rue de la Cossonerie, 75001. ☎ 01 42 33 46 02. FAX 01 42 33 80 99. *Rooms: 29.* A quirkily renovated hotel in a relatively quiet street. The cozy rooms are decorated with polished chests and old paintings. 🛏 📺	(F)(F)(F)	AE DC MC V	●			
LES HALLES: *Hôtel St-Merry.* Map 9 B3. 78 rue de la Verrerie, 75004. ☎ 01 42 78 14 15. FAX 01 40 29 06 82. *Rooms: 11.* The building incorporates the austere St-Merry church and is decorated in 17th-century style with canopied beds and period rugs. 🛏	(F)(F)(F)(F)	V				
TUILERIES QUARTER: *Hôtel Brighton.* Map 8 D1. 218 rue de Rivoli, 75001. ☎ 01 47 03 61 61. FAX 01 42 60 41 78. *Rooms: 70.* The bedrooms have large windows looking onto the courtyard or the Jardin des Tuileries. Courtyard rooms are quieter but less attractive. 🛏 📺	(F)(F)(F)(F)	AE DC MC V	●			
TUILERIES QUARTER: *Hôtel de Crillon.* Map 7 C1. 10 pl de la Concorde, 75008. ☎ 01 44 71 15 00. FAX 01 44 71 15 02. *Rooms: 160.* Occupying an unrivaled position in the heart of the city, this hotel offers luxurious yet restrained elegance. Magnificent terrace. 🛏 📺	(F)(F)(F)(F)(F)	AE DC MC V	●			■

	Price categories	Facilities description	Credit Cards	Children's Facilities	Parking Facilities	Swimming Pool	Garden

Price categories for a standard double room (not per person) for one night, including tax and service charges, but not including breakfast.
Ⓕ under F200
ⒻⒻ F200–400
ⒻⒻⒻ F400–600
ⒻⒻⒻⒻ F600–1,000
ⒻⒻⒻⒻⒻ over F1,000

CHILDREN'S FACILITIES
Cribs and baby-sitting available. Some hotels provide children's portions and high chairs in the restaurant.

PARKING FACILITIES
Parking provided by the hotel in either a private lot or a private garage very close by.

SWIMMING POOL
Hotel pools are often quite small and are outdoors unless otherwise stated.

GARDEN
Hotel with garden, courtyard or terrace, often providing tables for eating outside.

Hotel	Price	Credit Cards	Children's Facilities	Parking Facilities	Swimming Pool	Garden
TUILERIES QUARTER: *Hôtel du Louvre.* **Map 8** E1. Place André Malraux, 75001. ☎ 01 44 58 38 38. FAX 01 44 58 38 01. *Rooms: 197.* If you stay in this hotel, book the Pissarro suite, where the artist painted *Place du Théâtre Français.* Very good brasserie. 🖼 ▤ TV	ⒻⒻⒻⒻ	AE DC MC V	●			■
TUILERIES QUARTER: *Intercontinental.* **Map 8** D1. 3 rue de Castiglione, 75001. ☎ 01 44 77 11 11. FAX 01 44 77 14 60. *Rooms: 450.* This elegant late 19th-century hotel was designed by Charles Garnier, architect of the Paris Opéra, and is used for fashion shows. 🖼 ▤ TV	ⒻⒻⒻⒻ	AE DC MC V	●			■
TUILERIES QUARTER: *Meurice.* **Map 8** D1. 228 rue de Rivoli, 75001. ☎ 01 44 58 10 10. FAX 01 44 58 10 15. *Rooms: 180.* A perfect example of successful restoration, with excellent replicas of the original plasterwork and furnishings. 🖼 ▤ TV	ⒻⒻⒻⒻ	AE DC MC V	●			
TUILERIES QUARTER: *Ritz.* **Map 4** D5. 15 place Vendôme, 75001. ☎ 01 43 16 30 30. FAX 01 43 16 31 78. *Rooms: 170.* After a century, this hotel still lives up to its discreet, great reputation. Original Louis XVI furniture, fireplaces and chandeliers. 🖼 ▤ TV	ⒻⒻⒻⒻ	AE DC MC V	●	■	●	■
OPÉRA QUARTER: *Ambassador.* **Map 4** E4. 16 bd Haussmann, 75009. ☎ 01 42 46 92 63. FAX 01 40 22 08 74. *Rooms: 289.* One of the best examples of Paris's Art Deco hotels, restored to its former glory with deep carpeting and antique furniture. The ground floor has crystal chandeliers, and the food is outstanding. 🖼 ▤ TV	ⒻⒻⒻⒻ	AE DC MC V	●			
OPÉRA QUARTER: *Grand Hôtel.* **Map 4** D5. 2 rue Scribe, 75009. ☎ 01 40 07 32 32. FAX 01 42 66 12 51. *Rooms: 514.* Millions have been invested in this hotel – bedrooms are equipped with the utmost in comfort and there is a health club. 🖼 ▤ TV	ⒻⒻⒻⒻ	AE DC MC V	●			
OPÉRA QUARTER: *Westminster.* **Map 4** D5. 13 rue de la Paix, 75002. ☎ 01 42 61 57 46. FAX 01 42 60 30 66. *Rooms: 102.* The bedrooms are pleasantly furnished, some in period style with marble mantelpieces, chandeliers and 18th-century clocks. 🖼 ▤ TV	ⒻⒻⒻⒻ	AE DC MC V	●	■		
INVALIDES QUARTER: *Pavillon.* **Map 7** A2. 54 rue Saint Dominique, 75007. ☎ 01 45 51 42 87. FAX 01 45 51 32 79. *Rooms: 18.* A small, family-run hotel that guarantees peace and quiet. Although the rooms are small, they are pleasantly decorated. Breakfast is served in the courtyard in summer. 🖼 TV	ⒻⒻⒻ	AE DC MC V	●			■
INVALIDES QUARTER: *Hôtel de Varenne.* **Map 7** B2. 44 rue de Bourgogne, 75007. ☎ 01 45 51 45 55. FAX 01 45 51 86 63. *Rooms: 24.* A severe façade conceals a narrow courtyard where guests breakfast in the summer. Double-glazed windows in the bedrooms minimizes street noise. Rooms overlooking the courtyard are quiet and cheerful. 🖼 TV	ⒻⒻⒻ	AE MC V	●			■
INVALIDES QUARTER: *Hôtel de Suède.* **Map 7** B4. 31 rue Vaneau, 75007. ☎ 01 47 05 00 08. FAX 01 47 05 69 27. *Rooms: 39.* This elegant, late 18th-century style hotel overlooks the park of the Hôtel Matignon, home of the prime minister. 🖼 TV	ⒻⒻⒻ	AE MC V	●			■
INVALIDES QUARTER: *Hôtel de Bourgogne et Montana.* **Map 7** B2. 3 rue de Bourgogne, 75007. ☎ 01 45 51 20 22. FAX 01 45 56 11 98. *Rooms: 33.* Features include a mahogany bar, old elevator and circular hall with pink marble columns. The bedrooms are more ordinary, except for those on the fourth floor, which have fantastic views. 🖼 ▤ TV	ⒻⒻⒻⒻ	AE DC MC V	●			
EIFFEL TOWER QUARTER: *Grand Hôtel Lévêque.* **Map 6** F3. 29 rue Cler, 75007. ☎ 01 47 05 49 15. FAX 01 45 50 49 36. *Rooms: 50.* Very reasonable hotel with a superb location and friendly owners. Rooms vary in price and size but are all bright and airy. 🖼 ▤ TV	ⒻⒻ	AE DC MC V	●	■	●	

For key to symbols see back flap

Price categories for a standard double room (not per person) for one night, including tax and service charges, but not including breakfast.	**CHILDREN'S FACILITIES** Cribs and baby-sitting available. Some hotels provide children's portions and high chairs in the restaurant.			

Price categories for a standard double room (not per person) for one night, including tax and service charges, but not including breakfast.
Ⓕ under F200
ⒻⒻ F200–400
ⒻⒻⒻ F400–600
ⒻⒻⒻⒻ F600–1,000
ⒻⒻⒻⒻⒻ over F1,000

CHILDREN'S FACILITIES
Cribs and baby-sitting available. Some hotels provide children's portions and high chairs in the restaurant.
PARKING FACILITIES
Parking provided by the hotel in either a private lot or a private garage very close by.
SWIMMING POOL
Hotel pools are often quite small and are outdoors unless otherwise stated.
GARDEN
Hotel with garden, courtyard or terrace, often providing tables for eating outside.

	CREDIT CARDS	CHILDREN'S FACILITIES	PARKING FACILITIES	SWIMMING POOL	GARDEN
CHAILLOT QUARTER: *Alexander.* **Map 1 B5.** ⒻⒻⒻⒻ 102 av Victor Hugo, 75116. 📞 01 45 53 64 65. FAX 01 45 53 12 51. *Rooms: 62.* This comfortable, traditional hotel reflects the bourgeois self-confidence of avenue Victor Hugo. The small, quiet public rooms convey a sense of warmth and intimacy. 🛏 ▤ TV	AE DC MC V				▦
CHAILLOT QUARTER: *Hôtel Paris Kléber Palace.* **Map 5 C1.** ⒻⒻⒻⒻ 81 avenue Kléber, 75116. 📞 01 44 05 75 75. FAX 01 44 05 74 74. *Rooms: 83.* Rooms in this hotel by Spanish architect Ricardo Bofill are elegant and luxurious. The lobby is planted with bamboo trees. 🛏 ▤ TV	AE DC MC V	●	▦	●	
CHAILLOT QUARTER: *Raphaël.* **Map 2 D4.** ⒻⒻⒻⒻ 17 avenue Kléber, 75116. 📞 01 44 28 00 28. FAX 01 45 01 21 50. *Rooms: 90.* Many films are shot in the Neo-Gothic bar of this timeless hotel, where stars shelter from the paparazzi. A Turner hangs in the hall. 🛏 ▤ TV	AE DC MC V	●			
CHAILLOT QUARTER: *Villa Maillot.* **Map 1 C4.** ⒻⒻⒻⒻ 143 avenue de Malakoff, 75116. 📞 01 53 64 52 52. FAX 01 45 00 60 61. *Rooms: 42.* A modern hotel with furnishings inspired by Art Deco. The rooms have large beds, jewelry safes and marble bathrooms. 🛏 ▤ TV &	AE DC MC V	●	▦		
CHAMPS-ELYSÉES: *Résidence Lord Byron.* **Map 2 E4.** ⒻⒻⒻ 5 rue Chateaubriand, 75008. 📞 01 43 59 89 98. FAX 01 42 89 46 04. *Rooms: 31.* This small, discreet hotel has a courtyard garden for summer breakfasts. The bedrooms are relatively quiet but not large. 🛏 TV	AE DC JCB MC V	●			▦
CHAMPS-ELYSÉES: *Atala.* **Map 2 E4.** ⒻⒻⒻⒻⒻ 10 rue Chateaubriand, 75008. 📞 01 45 62 01 62. FAX 01 42 25 66 38. *Rooms: 48.* Situated in a quiet street close to the busy Champs-Elysées, the Atala's rooms overlook a tranquil garden with tall trees. The eighth-floor bedrooms have spectacular views of the Eiffel Tower. 🛏 ▤ TV	AE DC JCB MC V	●	▦		▦
CHAMPS-ELYSÉES: *Bristol.* **Map 3 A4.** ⒻⒻⒻⒻⒻ 112 rue du Faubourg St-Honoré, 75008. 📞 01 53 43 43 00. FAX 01 53 43 43 01. *Rooms: 180.* One of the city's finest hotels. The large rooms are sumptuously decorated with antiques and have magnificent bathrooms. 🛏 ▤ TV	AE DC JCB MC V	●	▦	●	▦
CHAMPS-ELYSÉES: *Concorde La Fayette.* **Map 1 C2.** ⒻⒻⒻⒻⒻ 3 pl du Général Koenig, 75017. 📞 01 40 68 50 68. FAX 01 40 68 50 38. *Rooms: 970.* A high-tech tower bristling with facilities including a fitness club, a shopping gallery and an amazing bar on the 33rd floor. 🛏 ▤ TV	AE DC MC V	●			
CHAMPS-ELYSÉES: *Four Seasons.* **Map 2 E5.** ⒻⒻⒻⒻⒻ 31 avenue George V, 75008. 📞 01 53 53 28 05. FAX 01 53 53 28 15. *Rooms: 245.* A legendary hotel dotted with secret salons, old furniture and paintings. It also has a wide range of facilities. 🛏 ▤ TV	AE DC MC V	●	▦		▦
CHAMPS-ELYSÉES: *Plaza Athénée.* **Map 6 F1.** ⒻⒻⒻⒻⒻ 25 avenue Montaigne, 75008. 📞 01 53 67 66 65. FAX 01 53 67 66 66. *Rooms: 185.* A hotel for honeymooners and old aristocracy, which conforms to the highest contemporary standards of luxury. 🛏 ▤ TV	AE DC MC V	●	▦		▦
CHAMPS-ELYSÉES: *Royal Monceau.* **Map 2 F3.** ⒻⒻⒻⒻⒻ 37 avenue Hoche, 75008. 📞 01 42 99 88 00. FAX 01 42 99 89 90. *Rooms: 219.* The elegant Royal Monceau features one of Paris's most luxurious health clubs and one of the city's best Italian restaurants. 🛏 ▤ TV	AE DC MC V	●	▦	●	
ST-GERMAIN-DES-PRÉS: *Hôtel Solférino.* **Map 7 C2.** ⒻⒻⒻ 91 rue de Lille, 75007. 📞 01 47 05 85 54. FAX 01 45 55 51 16. *Rooms: 33.* A small bed and breakfast hotel close to the Musée d'Orsay with simply furnished rooms and a splendid rooftop view. An excellent value. 🛏 TV	AE MC V	●			

St-Germain-des-Prés: *Buci Latin.* **Map 8** E4. ⓕⓕⓕ
34 rue du Buci, 75006. **C** 01 43 29 07 20. **FAX** 01 43 29 67 44. *Rooms: 27.*
A trendy hotel with a minimalist decor; attracts a young crowd.
Several suites have balconies and big whirlpool baths. 🛏 ▤ TV
AE DC MC V

St-Germain-des-Prés: *Hôtel St-Germain-des-Prés.* **Map 8** E4. ⓕⓕⓕ
36 rue Bonaparte, 75006. **C** 01 43 26 00 19. **FAX** 01 40 46 83 63. *Rooms: 30.*
Although this charming and unusual Left Bank hotel is on a busy
street, the noise rarely intrudes. The bedrooms vary in size. 🛏 ▤ TV
AE MC V

St-Germain-des-Prés: *Hôtel de l'Université.* **Map 8** D3. ⓕⓕⓕⓕ
22 rue de l'Université, 75007. **C** 01 42 61 09 39. **FAX** 01 42 60 40 84. *Rooms: 27.*
A converted 17th-century town house with antiques and tapestries
in its public rooms. The basement is a 14th-century crypt. 🛏 ▤ TV
AE MC V

Latin Quarter: *Esmeralda.* **Map 9** A4. ⓕⓕⓕ
4 rue St-Julien-le Pauvre, 75005. **C** 01 43 54 19 20. **FAX** 01 40 51 00 68. *Rooms: 19.*
The decor reflects contrasting ages and styles behind old stone walls
and under beamed ceilings. The best rooms overlook Notre-Dame. 🛏

Latin Quarter: *Hôtel des Grandes Ecoles.* **Map 9** B5. ⓕⓕⓕ
75 rue Cardinal Lemoine, 75005. **C** 01 43 26 79 23. **FAX** 01 43 25 28 15. *Rooms: 51.*
An astonishing cluster of three small houses with a garden. Two of
the buildings have retained their old-fashioned charm. 🛏
MC V

Latin Quarter: *Hôtel des Grands Hommes.* **Map 13** A1. ⓕⓕⓕ
17 place du Panthéon, 75005. **C** 01 46 34 19 60. **FAX** 01 43 26 67 32. *Rooms: 32.*
Sorbonne teachers frequent this quiet family hotel close to the Jardin
du Luxembourg. The attic rooms have views of the Panthéon. 🛏 ▤ TV
AE DC MC V

Latin Quarter: *Hôtel de Notre-Dame.* **Map 9** B5. ⓕⓕⓕⓕ
19 rue Maître Albert, 75005. **C** 01 43 26 79 00. **FAX** 01 46 33 50 11. *Rooms: 34.*
Situated in a quiet street, this small hotel makes an ideal base
for exploring old Paris. 🛏 TV
AE MC V

Latin Quarter: *Hôtel du Panthéon.* **Map 13** A1. ⓕⓕⓕⓕ
19 place du Panthéon, 75005. **C** 01 43 54 32 95. **FAX** 01 43 26 64 65. *Rooms: 34.*
This hotel is managed by the same family as the Hôtel des Grands
Hommes, and the welcome is equally warm. 🛏 TV
AE DC MC V

Latin Quarter: *Hôtel les Degrés de Notre-Dame.* **Map 9** B4. ⓕⓕⓕⓕ
10 rue des Grands-Degrés, 75005. **C** 01 43 25 88 38. **FAX** 01 40 46 95 34. *Rooms: 10.*
Choose between a quiet bedroom or one with a wonderful view
of Notre-Dame from the window. Conveniently located. 🛏 TV
MC V

Luxembourg Quarter: *Perreyve.* **Map 8** E5. ⓕⓕⓕ
63 rue Madame, 75006. **C** 01 45 48 35 01. **FAX** 01 42 84 03 30. *Rooms: 30.*
The bedrooms here are sober, simple and clean. The corner ones and
those in the attic on the sixth floor are the best. 🛏 TV
AE DC MC V

Luxembourg Quarter: *Récamier.* **Map 8** E4. ⓕⓕⓕ
3 bis place St-Sulpice, 75006. **C** 01 43 26 04 89. **FAX** 01 46 33 27 73. *Rooms: 30.*
A family hotel with no television sets or restaurant. Try to get a room
that looks onto both the courtyard and the square. 🛏
MC V

Luxembourg Quarter: *Hôtel de l'Abbaye St-Germain.* ⓕⓕⓕⓕ
Map 8 D5. 10 rue Cassette, 75006. **C** 01 45 44 38 11. **FAX** 01 45 48 07 86. *Rooms: 46.*
Once an abbey, this elegant hotel still basks in a tranquil atmosphere.
There is a pretty courtyard and a real fire in the lounge. 🛏 ▤ TV
AE MC V

Jardin des Plantes Quarter: *Le Jardin des Plantes.* **Map 13** B1. ⓕⓕⓕ
5 rue Linné, 75005. **C** 01 47 07 06 20. **FAX** 01 47 07 62 74. *Rooms: 33.*
This cheerfully decorated hotel in a residential area near the gardens
has a rooftop terrace and a sauna in the vaulted cellar. 🛏 TV
DC MC V

Montparnasse: *Ferrandi.* **Map 11** C1. ⓕⓕⓕ
92 rue du Cherche-Midi, 75006. **C** 01 42 22 97 40. **FAX** 01 45 44 89 97. *Rooms: 42.*
A quiet hotel with a fireplace in the lounge and comfortable
bedrooms, many with four-poster or canopied beds. 🛏 ▤ TV
AE DC MC V

Montparnasse: *L'Atelier Montparnasse.* **Map 12** D1. ⓕⓕⓕ
49 rue Vavin, 75006. **C** 01 46 33 60 00. **FAX** 01 40 51 04 21. *Rooms: 17.*
Visitors receive a gracious family welcome at this original hotel. The
bathrooms have mosaic reproductions of famous paintings. 🛏 ▤ TV
AE DC MC V

Price categories for a standard double room (not per person) for one night, including tax and service charges, but not including breakfast.
- (F) under F200
- (F)(F) F200–400
- (F)(F)(F) F400–600
- (F)(F)(F)(F) F600–1,000
- (F)(F)(F)(F)(F) over F1,000

CHILDREN'S FACILITIES
Cribs and baby-sitting available. Some hotels provide children's portions and high chairs in the restaurant.

PARKING FACILITIES
Parking provided by the hotel in either a private lot or a private garage very close by.

SWIMMING POOL
Hotel pools are often quite small and are outdoors unless otherwise stated.

GARDEN
Hotel with garden, courtyard or terrace, often providing tables for eating outside.

	Price	Credit Cards	Children's Facilities	Parking Facilities	Swimming Pool	Garden
MONTPARNASSE: *Hôtel la Ste-Beuve.* Map 12 D1. 9 rue Ste Beuve, 75006. 01 45 48 20 07. FAX 01 45 48 67 52. *Rooms: 22.* There is a warm and cozy atmosphere in this carefully restored hotel. Breakfast is served at bridge tables or on sofas in the salon.	(F)(F)(F)	AE MC V	●			
MONTPARNASSE: *Lenox Montparnasse.* Map 12 D2. 15 rue Delambre, 75014. 01 43 35 34 50. FAX 01 43 20 46 64. *Rooms: 52.* The overall atmosphere is one of restrained elegance. Each of the six large suites on the upper floor has a fireplace.	(F)(F)(F)(F)	AE DC MC V	●			
MONTPARNASSE: *Villa des Artistes.* Map 12 D2. 9 rue de la Grande Chaumière, 75006. 01 43 26 60 86. FAX 01 43 54 73 70. *Rooms: 60.* The main charm of this hotel, which aims to evoke the Belle Epoque, is the large patio garden where you can breakfast in peace.	(F)(F)(F)	AE DC MC V	●			■
MONTMARTRE: *Timhôtel.* Map 4 E1. 11 rue Ravignan, 75018. 01 42 55 74 79. FAX 01 42 55 71 01. *Rooms: 60.* This is one of Montmartre's most delightful hotels. It borders a quiet, charming square, and there are good views from the top floors.	(F)(F)(F)	AE DC MC V	●			
MONTMARTRE: *Terrass.* Map 4 E1. 12 rue Joseph-de-Maistre, 75018. 01 46 06 72 85. FAX 01 42 52 29 11. *Rooms: 101.* There are panoramic views over the rooftops of Paris from the upper floors. A few bedrooms retain original Art Deco woodwork.	(F)(F)(F)(F)(F)	AE DC MC V	●	■		

ILE DE FRANCE

	Price	Credit Cards	Children's Facilities	Parking Facilities	Swimming Pool	Garden
BARBIZON: *Hostellerie la Dague* 5 Grand rue, 77630. 01 60 66 40 49. FAX 01 60 69 24 59. *Rooms: 25.* This rustic yet chic ivy-hung hotel is popular with Parisians, so book well in advance. The traditional French restaurant is charming.	(F)(F)	DC MC V	●	■		■
FONTAINEBLEAU: *Hôtel de l'Aigle Noir* 27 pl Napoléon, 77300. 01 60 74 60 00. FAX 01 60 74 00 01. *Rooms: 56.* This prestigious mansion overlooks Fontainebleau château and its vast park. Gourmet cuisine and impeccable service.	(F)(F)(F)(F)	AE DC MC V	●	■	●	■
FONTENAY-TRÉSIGNY: *Le Manoir* Départementale 402, 77610. 01 64 25 91 17. FAX 01 64 25 95 49. *Rooms: 20.* This dreamy manor house set in vast grounds must be most visitors' idea of rural bliss. Distinguished guests arrive by helicopter.	(F)(F)(F)(F)	AE DC MC V	●	■	●	■
HERBEVILLE: *Le Mont au Vent* 2 rue de Maule, 78580. 01 30 90 65 22. FAX 01 34 75 12 54. *Rooms: 6.* Set in appealing countryside, this small village hotel makes a good base for visiting Versailles. Price includes breakfast. Cash only.	(F)(F)(F)		●	■		■
ROISSY-CHARLES-DE-GAULLE: *Novotel Paris Roissy* Charles de Gaulle Airport, 95705. 01 49 19 27 27. FAX 01 49 19 27 99. *Rooms: 201.* This standard chain hotel is one of the best emergency or en route stopovers. Convenience and efficiency are its hallmarks.	(F)(F)(F)	AE DC MC V	●	■		
ST-GERMAIN-EN-LAYE: *La Forestière* 1 av du Président Kennedy, 78100. 01 39 10 38 38. FAX 01 39 73 73 88. *Rooms: 30.* Exuding an air of rural sophistication, this secluded hotel is set in woodland. Enjoy the gastronomic delights in the restaurant.	(F)(F)(F)(F)	AE MC V	●	■		
ST-GERMAIN-EN-LAYE: *Pavillon Henri IV* 19–21 rue Thiers, 78100. 01 39 10 15 15. FAX 01 39 73 93 73. *Rooms: 42.* This sumptuous hotel-restaurant occupies an elegant lodge built by Henri IV where Louis XIV was born and Alexandre Dumas wrote *The Three Musketeers.* Panoramic views over the Seine Valley.	(F)(F)(F)(F)(F)	AE DC MC V	●	■		■

VERSAILLES: *Hôtel de Clagny* (F)(F)
6 impasse de Clagny, 78000. ☎ 01 39 50 18 09. FAX 01 39 50 85 17. *Rooms: 21.*
Conveniently close to the station and in a quiet location. The rooms are simply furnished and unremarkable, but the hospitality is genuine. 🖼 TV
Cards: DC, MC, V

VERSAILLES: *Trianon Palace* (F)(F)(F)(F)(F)
1 bd de la Reine, 78000. ☎ 01 30 84 38 00. FAX 01 39 49 00 77. *Rooms: 192.*
Undoubtedly the most spendid hotel in the region, deserving the accolade "palace," blending in with the Classical lines of the Versailles park. The gourmet restaurant is the jewel in the crown. 🖼 ▤ TV
Cards: AE, DC, MC, V

VILLEPREUX: *Château de Villepreux* (F)(F)(F)(F)
Chemin de Grand-Maison, 78450. ☎ 01 30 81 78 00.
FAX 01 30 56 12 12. *Rooms: 10.*
This grand, privately owned chambres d'hôte has been in the Saint-Seine family for 200 years. Close to the St-Nom-la-Bretèche golf course. 🖼
Cards: MC, V

LE NORD AND PICARDY

AMIENS: *Hôtel de Normandie* (F)(F)
1 bis rue Lamartine, 80000. ☎ 03 22 91 74 99. FAX 03 22 92 06 56. *Rooms: 28.*
Five minutes' walk from the station and near the cathedral, this turn-of-the-century hotel represents quiet and simplicity in a busy city. TV
Cards: AE, DC, MC, V

AMIENS: *La Résidence* (F)(F)
17 rue Porion, 80000. ☎ 03 22 92 27 67. FAX 03 22 92 46 16. *Rooms: 21.*
An exceptionally comfortable hotel with tastefully decorated rooms and antique furniture. Only a few steps from the cathedral. 🖼 TV
Cards: DC, MC, V

ARMBOUTS-CAPPEL: *Hôtel du Lac* (F)(F)(F)
2 bordure du lac, 59380. ☎ 03 28 60 70 60. FAX 03 28 61 06 39. *Rooms: 66.*
South of Dunkerque, set beside a lake known for its abundant bird life, this is an exceptionally comfortable and modern hotel. 🖼 TV
Cards: AE, DC, MC, V

BERCK-SUR-MER: *Hôtel Neptune* (F)(F)
Esplanade Parmentier, 62600. ☎ 03 21 09 21 21. FAX 03 21 09 29 29. *Rooms: 63.*
An airy and elegant hotel on the seafront. Rooms are simple but stylish with white and blue decor. The restaurant has great sea views. 🖼 TV
Cards: AE, DC, MC, V

BOULOGNE-SUR-MER: *Hôtel Métropole* (F)(F)(F)
51 rue Thiers, 62200. ☎ 03 21 31 54 30. FAX 03 21 30 45 72. *Rooms: 25.*
Boulogne is notoriously short of hotels with character, but this one is exceptionally comfortable and convenient for shopping. 🖼 TV
Cards: AE, DC, MC, V

CALAIS: *Le Climat de France* (F)(F)
Digue G Berthe, 62100. ☎ 03 21 34 64 64. FAX 03 21 34 35 39. *Rooms: 45.*
Overlooking the beach is this comfortable and convenient hotel, a welcoming establishment with an inexpensive restaurant. 🖼 TV
Cards: AE, DC, MC, V

CAMBRAI: *Le Mouton Blanc* (F)(F)
33 rue Alsace Lorraine, 59400. ☎ 03 27 81 30 16. FAX 03 27 81 83 54. *Rooms: 32.*
Situated between the beautiful old church of St-Géry and the center of the historic town, this hotel offers convenience and comfort. 🖼 TV
Cards: AE, MC, V

DUNKERQUE: *Trianon Hôtel* (F)(F)
20 rue de la Colline, 59240. ☎ 03 28 63 39 15. FAX 03 28 63 34 57. *Rooms: 12.*
Peacefully situated, this charming hotel offers good value for money.
🖼 TV
Cards: V

FREVENT: *Le Vert Bocage* (F)(F)
Monchel-sur-Canche, 62270. ☎ 03 21 47 96 75. FAX 03 21 03 24 17. *Rooms: 10.*
Set in its own large and well-laid-out garden with a small lake, this modern hotel is a haven of calm and comfort. 🖼 TV
Cards: MC, V

GOSNAY: *La Chartreuse de Val St-Esprit* (F)(F)(F)
1 rue de Fouquières, 62199. ☎ 03 21 62 80 00. FAX 03 21 62 42 50. *Rooms: 56.*
A sumptuous, peaceful château with much of its original furniture. Its *restaurant gastronomique* specializes in fresh seafood, and the dining room is a setting in which to enjoy dining in style. 🖼 ▤ TV
Cards: AE, DC, MC, V

GUISE: *Hôtel Champagne Picardie* (F)(F)
41 rue A Godin, 02120. ☎ 03 23 61 37 85. *Rooms: 12.*
A mansion in the historic town of Guise, the hotel backs onto its own substantial garden, which is overlooked by half the bedrooms. 🖼 TV
Cards: MC, V

<table>
<tr><td>Price categories for a standard double room (not per person) for one night, including tax and service charges, but not including breakfast.
Ⓕ under F200
ⒻⒻ F200–400
ⒻⒻⒻ F400–600
ⒻⒻⒻⒻ F600–1,000
ⒻⒻⒻⒻⒻ over F1,000</td>
<td>CHILDREN'S FACILITIES
Cribs and baby-sitting available. Some hotels provide children's portions and high chairs in the restaurant.
PARKING FACILITIES
Parking provided by the hotel in either a private lot or a private garage very close by.
SWIMMING POOL
Hotel pools are often quite small and are outdoors unless otherwise stated.
GARDEN
Hotel with garden, courtyard or terrace, often providing tables for eating outside.</td></tr>
</table>

Hotel		CREDIT CARDS	CHILDREN'S FACILITIES	PARKING FACILITIES	SWIMMING POOL	GARDEN
LAON: *Hôtel de la Bannière de France* ⒻⒻ 11 rue Franklin Roosevelt, 02000. 📞 03 23 23 21 44. FAX 03 23 23 31 56. **Rooms:** 18. Charming coaching inn within the ancient walled town of Laon. Good views and a convenient stop to and from the Channel ports. 🛏 TV		AE DC MC V	●	▪		
LAON: *Hostellerie St-Vincent* ⒻⒻ 29 avenue Charles de Gaulle, 02000. 📞 03 23 23 42 43. FAX 03 23 79 22 55. **Rooms:** 47. A comfortable and modern establishment, easy to find on the east side of this ancient town. Both hotel and restaurant are good value. 🛏 TV		AE MC V		▪		▪
LE TOUQUET: *Hôtel Moderne* ⒻⒻ 41 re Jean-Monnet, 62520. 📞 03 21 05 15 33. FAX 03 21 05 41 60. **Rooms:** 26. Not far from the market place, this is an accessible hotel offering both half and full board. 🛏 TV		MC DC V		▪		
LE TOUQUET: *Novotel-Thalamer* ⒻⒻⒻⒻ Front de Mer, 62520. 📞 03 21 09 85 00. FAX 03 21 09 85 10. **Rooms:** 149. Large hotel on the seafront offering bright, functional rooms with superb views. Relax in the saltwater spa and sauna. 🛏 TV		AE MC V	●	▪	●	▪
LONGPONT: *Hôtel de l'Abbaye* ⒻⒻ 8 rue des Tourelles, 02600. 📞 03 23 96 02 44. FAX 03 23 96 02 44. **Rooms:** 11. The name is taken from a 12th-century ruined abbey nearby and the hotel is almost as old. Good restaurant serving local cuisine. 🛏		MC V	●			▪
MAUBEUGE: *Hôtel Shakespeare* ⒻⒻ 3 rue du Commerce, 59600. 📞 03 27 65 14 14. FAX 03 27 64 04 66. **Rooms:** 35. Modern, functional and efficiently run hotel with a friendly atmosphere. There is a restaurant and a comfortable bar. 🛏 TV		AE DC MC V		▪		▪
MONTREUIL: *Le Darnetal* ⒻⒻ Place Darnetal, 62170. 📞 03 21 06 04 87. FAX 03 21 86 64 67. **Rooms:** 4. Booking is essential at this hotel-restaurant in the old fortified town of Montreuil. Old-style rooms all with en-suite bathrooms. The dinner menu is excellent, especially the oyster dishes. 🛏		AE DC MC V				
PÉRONNE: *Hostellerie des Remparts* ⒻⒻ 21 rue Beaubois, 80200. 📞 03 22 84 01 22. FAX 03 22 84 31 96. **Rooms:** 16. Some rooms overlook the old fortifications of the town and their ornamental gardens. Substantial refurbishment has lessened its old-fashioned character. 🛏 TV		AE DC MC V	●	▪		▪
REUILLY-SAUVIGNY: *L'Auberge le Relais* ⒻⒻⒻ 2 rue de Paris, 02850. 📞 03 23 70 35 36. FAX 03 23 70 27 76. **Rooms:** 7. An old *ferme-auberge* with modern additions, a delight in this village. It has a glass conservatory overlooking a lovely garden. 🛏 🍽 TV		AE DC MC V		▪		▪
ST-OMER: *Hôtel St-Louis* ⒻⒻ 25 rue d'Arras, 62500. 📞 03 21 38 35 21. FAX 03 21 38 57 26. **Rooms:** 30. Right in the center of town, this 18th-century coaching inn has modernized bedrooms but its restaurant retains the flavor of the old days. 🛏 TV		AE MC V	●	▪		▪
ST-QUENTIN: *Grand Hôtel* ⒻⒻⒻ 6–8 rue Dachery, 02100. 📞 03 23 62 69 77. FAX 03 23 62 53 52. **Rooms:** 24. Well-designed and tastefully decorated rooms. The restaurant, *Le Président*, is a must for dinner and breakfast as well. 🛏 TV		AE DC JCB MC V	●	▪		
SARS-POTERIES: *Hôtel Fleuri* ⒻⒻ 65 rue du Général de Gaulle, 59216. 📞 03 27 61 62 72. **Rooms:** 11. Simple but charming bed-and-breakfast accommodation with an excellent restaurant next door. 🛏		MC V		▪		▪

	Price	Cards				

VERVINS: *La Tour de Roy* ⒻⒻⒻ — AE MC V
45 rue du Général Leclerc, 02140. **〖** 03 23 98 00 11. **FAX** 03 23 98 00 72. *Rooms: 18.*
An exceptionally comfortable and quiet hotel, with outdoor
tables and a splendid garden. 🔲 ▤ TV

WIMEREUX: *Hôtel Paul et Virginie* ⒻⒻ — MC V
19 rue Général de Gaulle, 62930. **〖** 03 21 32 42 12. **FAX** 03 21 87 65 85. *Rooms: 15.*
This attractive 19th-century building stands neatly between the beach
and shops, in a delightful seaside town. Caters to families. 🔲 TV

CHAMPAGNE

ANDELOT: *Le Cantarel* ⒻⒻ — DC MC V
Place Cantarel, 52700. **〖** 03 25 01 31 13. **FAX** 03 25 03 15 41. *Rooms: 8.*
Andelot lies northeast of Chaumont on the road to Neufchâteau. This
hotel in the village square has a good, inexpensive restaurant. 🔲 TV

BOURBONNE-LES-BAINS: *Hôtel Jeanne d'Arc* ⒻⒻ — AE MC V
Rue Amiral-Pierre, 52400. **〖** 03 25 90 46 00. **FAX** 03 25 90 46 00. *Rooms: 32.*
The town is a thermal spa and this well-equipped hotel is right beside
the pump room. The surrounding countryside is magnificent. 🔲 TV

CHÂLONS-EN-CHAMPAGNE: *Hôtel du Pot d'Etain* ⒻⒻ — AE DC MC V
18 place de la République, 51000. **〖** 03 26 68 09 09. **FAX** 03 26 68 58 18. *Rooms: 27*
This 15th-century private hotel in the center of town is run by a family
of bakers – and there are freshly baked croissants for breakfast. 🔲 TV

CHAMPILLON: *Royal Champagne* ⒻⒻⒻⒻⒻ — AE DC MC V
Bellevue, 51160. **〖** 03 26 52 87 11. **FAX** 03 26 52 89 69. *Rooms: 29.*
Situated on the summit of the wooded Montagne de Reims, this
16th-century staging-post houses a charming hotel-restaurant. 🔲 TV

CHARLEVILLE-MÉZIÈRES: *Le Clèves* ⒻⒻ — AE DC MC V
43 rue de l'Arquebuse, 08000. **〖** 03 24 33 10 75. **FAX** 03 24 59 01 25. *Rooms: 46.*
This hotel is on a quiet street next door to the house where the
poet Rimbaud was born. Elegant and comfortable dining room. 🔲 TV

CHARLEVILLE-MÉZIÈRES: *Le Relais du Square* ⒻⒻ — AE DC MC V
3 place de la Gare, 08000. **〖** 03 24 33 38 76. **FAX** 03 24 33 56 66. *Rooms: 49.*
Despite the address, the hotel is out of earshot of the trains. There is a
cozy bar, and the hotel is connected to a good restaurant. 🔲 TV

CHAUMONT: *Le Grand Val* ⒻⒻ — AE DC MC V
Route de Langres, 52000. **〖** 03 25 03 90 35. **FAX** 03 25 32 11 80. *Rooms: 52.*
On the road to Langres and Dijon stands this hotel built out of stone
with wood paneling and fine views across the Marne Valley. 🔲

EPERNAY: *Hôtel de la Cloche* Ⓕ — AE MC V
3 place Mendès-France, 51200. **〖** 03 26 55 15 15. **FAX** 03 26 55 64 88. *Rooms: 19.*
This is the best hotel-restaurant in its category in Epernay, the capital
of Champagne. *La Cloche* offers modest but sunny rooms and a good
restaurant serving a choice of regional specialties. 🔲 TV

EPERNAY: *Micheline & Jean-Marie Tarlant* ⒻⒻ — MC V
Oeuilly, RN3, 51480. **〖** 03 26 58 30 60. **FAX** 03 26 58 37 31. *Rooms: 4.*
Grapepickers' cottages have been converted into guest rooms on
this family-run wine estate. Breakfast is in a charming conservatory
and can be followed by a visit to the champagne cellars below. 🔲

ETOGES: *Château d'Etoges* ⒻⒻⒻⒻ — AE DC MC V
4 rue Richebourg, 51270. **〖** 03 26 59 30 08. **FAX** 03 26 59 35 57. *Rooms: 21.*
This impressive 17th-century château, with moat and decorative towers,
is still inhabited and presented very much as a grand private home. 🔲 TV

HAYBES-SUR-MEUSE: *L'Ermitage Moulin Labotte* ⒻⒻ — MC V
08170 Haybes-sur-Meuse. **〖** 03 24 41 13 44. **FAX** 03 24 40 46 72. *Rooms: 10.*
A remote 18th-century converted mill set in woodland. There is
an atmospheric dining room with a slate floor and mill wheel. 🔲 TV

LANGRES: *Grand Hôtel de l'Europe* ⒻⒻ — MC V
23–25 rue Diderot, 52200. **〖** 03 25 87 10 88. **FAX** 03 25 87 60 65. *Rooms: 27.*
The hotel is easy to find, in the main street of this market town. It is a
listed 17th-century building, with a beautifully preserved dining room
of the period, but with modernized bedrooms. 🔲 TV

For key to symbols see back flap

Price categories for a standard double room (not per person) for one night, including tax and service charges, but not including breakfast.
Ⓕ under F200
ⒻⒻ F200–400
ⒻⒻⒻ F400–600
ⒻⒻⒻⒻ F600–1,000
ⒻⒻⒻⒻⒻ over F1,000

CHILDREN'S FACILITIES
Cribs and baby-sitting available. Some hotels provide children's portions and high chairs in the restaurant.
PARKING FACILITIES
Parking provided by the hotel in either a private car lot or a private garage very close by.
SWIMMING POOL
Hotel pools are often quite small and are outdoors unless otherwise stated.
GARDEN
Hotel with garden, courtyard or terrace, often providing tables for eating outside.

	CREDIT CARDS	CHILDREN'S FACILITIES	PARKING FACILITIES	SWIMMING POOL	GARDEN
MAGNANT: *Le Val Moret* — ⒻⒻ 10110 Magnant. (03 25 29 85 12. FAX 03 25 29 70 81. **Rooms:** 30. A single-story modern motel on the highway from Calais to Dijon. Comfortable, with a good, reasonably priced restaurant. 🚐 📺	AE MC V	●	■		■
MESNIL-ST-PÉRE: *L'Auberge du Lac* — ⒻⒻⒻ 10140 Mesnil-St-Pére. (03 25 41 27 16. FAX 03 25 41 57 59. **Rooms:** 21. This old-fashioned inn takes its name from the nearby lake in the Forêt d'Orient, where fishing, bathing and tennis are all available. 🚐 📺	MC V	●	■		■
MONTHERMÉ: *Le Franco-Belge* — ⒻⒻ 2 rue Pasteur, 08800. (03 24 53 01 20. FAX 03 24 53 54 49. **Rooms:** 15. A family-run hotel overlooking the village square. The cuisine is prepared using fresh garden produce. 🚐 📺	MC V		■		■
REIMS: *Hôtel Crystal* — ⒻⒻ 86 place Drouet d'Erlon, 51100. (03 26 88 44 44. FAX 03 26 47 49 28. **Rooms:** 31. This old-fashioned hotel borders the liveliest square in Reims, yet is surprisingly quiet. In summer, breakfast is served on the terrace. 🚐 📺	AE MC V				■
REIMS: *Boyer les Crayères* — ⒻⒻⒻⒻⒻ 64 bd Henri Vasnier, 51100. (03 26 82 80 80. FAX 03 26 82 65 52. **Rooms:** 19. This is a renowned hotel on the gastronomic and champagne-tasting trail. Discreetly sumptuous, it occupies a Belle Epoque mansion set in attractive grounds on the outskirts of Reims. 🚐 📋 📺	AE DC MC V	●	■		■
RETHEL: *Le Moderne* — ⒻⒻ Place de la Gare, 08300. (03 24 38 44 54. FAX 03 24 38 37 84. **Rooms:** 22. A thoroughly modernized establishment that guarantees peace and comfort. Excellent local cuisine is served in the restaurant. 🚐 📺	AE DC MC V		■		■
ST-DIZIER: *Hôtel Gambetta* — ⒻⒻ 62 rue Gambetta, 52100. (03 25 56 52 10. FAX 03 25 56 39 47. **Rooms:** 63. A modern establishment with conference facilities and an inexpensive restaurant. Many tourists come to St-Dizier to see the birdlife at the famous Lac du Der-Chantecoq nearby. 🚐 📺	AE DC MC V	●	■		
SEDAN: *L'Auberge du Port* — ⒻⒻ Bazeilles, 08140. (03 24 27 13 89. FAX 03 24 29 35 58. **Rooms:** 20. Exceptionally comfortable hotel on the banks of the Meuse River, ideal for visitors in search of peace and quiet. Meals on the terrace. 🚐 📺	AE DC MC V		■		■
SEPT-SAULX: *Le Cheval Blanc* — ⒻⒻⒻⒻ Rue du Moulin, 51400. (03 26 03 90 27. FAX 03 26 03 97 09. **Rooms:** 25. Set among champagne vineyards, this hotel-restaurant makes a convenient stopover for visitors to Alsace and Burgundy. The gourmet restaurant is well worth a visit. 🚐 📺	AE DC MC V	●	■		■
TROYES: *Grand Hôtel* — ⒻⒻ 4 av Maréchal-Joffre, 10000. (03 25 79 90 90. FAX 03 25 78 48 93. **Rooms:** 100. A large, modern establishment incorporating no less than eight restaurants, including a brasserie, pizzeria and *gastronomique*. 🚐 📺	AE MC V	●	■	●	■
TROYES: *Hôtel des Comtes de Champagne* — ⒻⒻ 54–56 rue de la Monnaie, 10000. (03 25 73 11 70. FAX 03 25 73 06 02. **Rooms:** 27. This sturdy private mansion, located on a quiet street, was once the medieval bank of the Counts of Champagne. Unique rooms with period furniture. Perfect for exploring the city center. 🚐 📺	MC V	●	■		■
VIGNORY: *Le Relais Verdoyant* — ⒻⒻ Quartier de la Gare, 52320. (03 25 02 44 49. FAX 03 25 01 96 89. **Rooms:** 7. An old converted country farm in a peaceful hamlet. Halfway between Chaumont and Joinville. Friendly and totally relaxing. 🚐 📺	MC V	●	■		■

ALSACE AND LORRAINE

BAREMBACH: *Château de Barembach* ⓕⓕⓕ
5 rue du Mal de Lattre, 67130. 📞 03 88 97 97 50. FAX 03 88 47 17 19. **Rooms:** 15.
An exquisite Renaissance château, now a family-run hotel. An ideal
vacation center with outdoor facilities including a tennis court. 🚗 TV

| | AE DC MC V | ● | ▦ | | ▦ |

COLMAR: *Hôtel Beauséjour* ⓕⓕ
25 rue du Ladhof, 68000. 📞 08 03 80 30 68. FAX 08 03 80 38 68. **Rooms:** 44.
A family hotel – reasonably priced family rooms, some with kitchenette.
Facilities include children's play area, sauna and fitness room. 🚗 TV

| | AE MC V | ● | ▦ | | ▦ |

COLMAR: *Hôtel le Maréchal* ⓕⓕⓕⓕ
4–6 place des Six-Montagnes-Noires, 68000. 📞 03 89 41 60 32.
FAX 03 89 24 59 40. **Rooms:** 30.
A 16th-century timber-framed house, Colmar's premier city-center hotel
is on the waterfront in the atmospheric Petite Venise quarter. 🚗 ▤ TV

| | AE MC V | ● | ▦ | | ▦ |

EGUISHEIM: *Hostellerie du Pape* ⓕⓕⓕ
10 Grand rue, 68420. 📞 03 89 41 41 21. FAX 03 89 41 41 31. **Rooms:** 33.
An appealing hotel-restaurant set in the most perfectly preserved small
town, bordering the oldest quarter and well-situated for shopping. 🚗 TV

| | AE DC MC V | ● | ▦ | | ▦ |

EPINAL: *Hôtel de l'Europe* ⓕⓕ
16 rue Blaudez, 88000. 📞 03 29 82 21 04. FAX 03 29 64 23 47. **Rooms:** 36.
Across the river from the Musée des Vosges, the hotel is an old building
carefully modernized, some rooms in Louis XV style. Sauna. 🚗 TV

| | DC MC V | ● | ▦ | | ▦ |

GÉRARDMER: *M Paul Gegout* ⓕ
Le Phény, 123 Chemin des Rochottes, 88400. 📞 03 29 63 03 39. **Rooms:** 3.
Farmhouse overlooking the Vosges mountains, with simple, rustic
rooms and wonderful views. Excellent local cuisine.

| | | | ▦ | | ▦ |

METZ: *Grand Hôtel de Metz* ⓕⓕ
3 rue des Clercs, 57000. 📞 03 87 36 16 33. FAX 03 87 74 17 04. **Rooms:** 62.
Close to the cathedral, market and restaurants, this established hotel
combines a Neo-Baroque lobby with countrified rooms. 🚗 TV

| | AE DC MC V | ● | ▦ | | ▦ |

MOLSHEIM: *Hôtel Bugatti* ⓕⓕ
Rue de la Commanderie, 67120. 📞 03 88 49 89 00. FAX 03 88 38 36 00. **Rooms:** 45.
Molsheim is where the great motor manufacturer Bugatti lived, and the
factory still stands across from the hotel. Guests can use the pool at the
Hôtel Diana, and there are riding stables nearby. 🚗 TV

| | AE MC V | ● | ▦ | | ▦ |

MULHOUSE: *Novotel Mulhouse–Sausheim* ⓕⓕⓕ
Rue de L'Ile-Napoléon, 68390. 📞 03 89 61 84 84. FAX 03 89 61 77 99. **Rooms:** 77.
The Novotel chain offers great family bargains and caters to
children – there is a toddlers' play area. 🚗 ▤ TV

| | AE DC MC V | ● | ▦ | ● | ▦ |

NANCY: *Hôtel Albert 1er et Astoria* ⓕⓕ
3 rue Armée-Patton, 54000. 📞 03 33 40 31 24. FAX 03 33 28 47 78. **Rooms:** 85.
This welcoming hotel is just a few minutes' walk from place Stanislas. The
decor is modern and the rooms well-equipped, comfortable and quiet. 🚗 TV

| | AE DC MC V | | ▦ | | |

NANCY: *Grand Hôtel de la Reine* ⓕⓕⓕⓕ
2 place Stanislas, 54000. 📞 03 83 35 03 01. FAX 03 83 32 86 04. **Rooms:** 48.
An elegant, luxurious stately home in the town's main square.
The restaurant offers an excellent fixed-price menu. 🚗 TV

| | AE DC MC V | ● | | | ▦ |

OBERNAI: *Hôtel des Vosges* ⓕⓕ
5 place de la Gare, 67210. 📞 03 88 95 53 78. FAX 03 88 49 92 65. **Rooms:** 20.
There is nothing pretentious about this functional, modern hotel.
Standards are high and the restaurant is reasonably priced. 🚗 TV

| | MC V | | ▦ | | ▦ |

REMIREMONT: *Hôtel du Cheval de Bronze* ⓕⓕ
59 rue Charles de Gaulle, 88200. 📞 03 29 62 52 24. FAX 03 29 62 34 90. **Rooms:** 35.
An old-fashioned hotel that is a useful stopover for travelers crossing
Alsace or Lorraine and a good base for exploring the Vosges. There is
no restaurant, but the owner is happy to make recommendations. 🚗 TV

| | AE MC V | ● | ▦ | | ▦ |

RIBEAUVILLE: *Hôtel de Mouton* ⓕⓕ
5 place de la Sinne, 68150. 📞 03 89 73 60 11. FAX 03 89 73 74 62. **Rooms:** 14
A delightful 14th-century wine-grower's house in the old quarter.
Spacious, charming rooms and inexpensive restaurant. 🚗 TV

| | MC V | | | | ▦ |

Price categories for a standard double room (not per person) for one night, including tax and service charges, but not including breakfast.
Ⓕ under F200
ⒻⒻ F200–400
ⒻⒻⒻ F400–600
ⒻⒻⒻⒻ F600–1,000
ⒻⒻⒻⒻⒻ over F1,000

CHILDREN'S FACILITIES
Cribs and baby-sitting available. Some hotels provide children's portions and high chairs in the restaurant.

PARKING FACILITIES
Parking provided by the hotel in either a private car lot or a private garage very close by.

SWIMMING POOL
Hotel pools are often quite small and are outdoors unless otherwise stated.

GARDEN
Hotel with garden, courtyard or terrace, often providing tables for eating outside.

	CREDIT CARDS	CHILDREN'S FACILITIES	PARKING FACILITIES	SWIMMING POOL	GARDEN
SAVERNE: *Chez Jean* ⒻⒻⒻ 3 rue de la Gare, 67700. 【 03 88 91 10 19. FAX 03 88 91 27 45. **Rooms:** 25. A four-story traditional Alsatian house with views of the hills behind the town. There is a delightful wine bar downstairs. 🔲 TV	AE DC MC V		■		■
SELESTAT: *Auberge des Alliés* ⒻⒻ 39 rue des Chevaliers, 67600. 【 03 88 92 09 34. FAX 03 88 92 12 88. **Rooms:** 19. The decor of this charming *logis de France* is one of exposed beams, polished wood and decorative knick-knacks. 🔲 TV	MC V				
STRASBOURG: *Au Cerf d'Or* ⒻⒻ 6 place de l'Hôpital, 67000. 【 03 88 36 20 05. FAX 03 88 36 68 67. **Rooms:** 37. The main hotel has more charming rooms, but the annex offers a small pool and sauna. Nearby are several waterfront restaurants. 🔲 TV	MC V	●		●	
STRASBOURG: *Relais Mercure* ⒻⒻ 3 rue Maire Kuss, 67000. 【 03 88 32 80 80. FAX 03 88 23 05 39. **Rooms:** 52. An old-fashioned red-brick hotel with very helpful management. 🔲 ▤ TV	AE MC V				■
STRASBOURG: *Régent Petite France* ⒻⒻⒻⒻⒻ 5 rue des Moulins, 67000. 【 03 88 76 43 43. FAX 03 88 76 43 76. **Rooms:** 72. The city's most prestigious and ideally located deluxe hotel. Set in a converted water mill, it overlooks the Petite France district. 🔲 ▤ TV	AE DC MC V	●	■		■
VERDUN: *Hostellerie du Coq Hardie* ⒻⒻⒻ 8 avenue de la Victoire, 55100. 【 03 29 86 36 36. FAX 03 29 86 09 21. **Rooms:** 35. This handsome Lorraine hotel offers traditional comfort and a friendly reception. Delicious traditional cooking, but somewhat expensive. 🔲 TV	AE DC MC V		■		
WANTZENAU: *Le Moulin de la Wantzenau* ⒻⒻⒻ 3 impasse de Moulin, 67610. 【 03 88 59 22 22. FAX 03 88 59 22 00. **Rooms:** 20. This imposing converted mill is actually a pleasant place to stop en route to Lorraine and Germany. Peaceful atmosphere. 🔲 TV	AE MC V	●	■		■

NORMANDY

	CREDIT CARDS	CHILDREN'S FACILITIES	PARKING FACILITIES	SWIMMING POOL	GARDEN
L'AIGLE: *Hôtel du Dauphin* ⒻⒻ Place de la Halle, 61300. 【 02 33 84 18 00. FAX 02 33 34 09 28. **Rooms:** 30. A fine inn built out of stone, close to the biggest market in Normandy. High-class rooms, traditional hospitality and business facilities. 🔲 TV	AE DC MC V	●	■		
ALENÇON: *Hôtel le Châpeau Rouge* ⒻⒻ 3 boulevard Duchamp, 61000. 【 02 33 26 20 23. FAX 02 33 26 54 05. **Rooms:** 14. A modern hotel ten minutes' walk from the town center. The restaurant (of the same name) next door is English-run. TV	AE MC V	●	■		
BAGNOLES DE L'ORNE: *Hôtel de Normandie* ⒻⒻ 2 av de la Ferté-Macé, 61140. 【 02 33 30 80 16. FAX 02 33 37 06 19. **Rooms:** 20. A handsome old inn with a highly recommended restaurant. In addition to the attractive garden there is a fine view from the front across wooded countryside and park. Reasonably priced. 🔲 TV	AE DC MC V	●	■		■
BALISNE: *Hôtel Moulin de Balisne* ⒻⒻ Le Moulin de Balisne, 27130. 【 02 32 32 03 48. FAX 02 32 60 11 22. **Rooms:** 12. Set in its own vast park, this country hotel is especially delightful. The conversion of the ancient mill has been tastefully done. 🔲 TV	AE DC MC V	●	■		■
BÉNOUVILLE: *Le Manoir d'Hastings* ⒻⒻⒻ 18 avenue de la Côte-de-Nacre, 14970. 【 02 31 44 62 43. FAX 02 31 44 76 18. **Rooms:** 15. A modern hotel built onto a 17th-century building, which is now the restaurant. Each bedroom has its own sitting room. Helpful staff. 🔲 TV	AE DC MC V	●	■		■

BRIONNE: *Auberge du Vieux Donjon* ⓕⓕ
Place Frémont-des-Essarts, 27800. 【 *02 32 44 80 62*. FAX *02 32 45 83 23*. **Rooms:** 8.
A perfect old-fashioned country inn on the edge of the market square.
For centuries farmers have come here to enjoy a hearty meal. 🛏 📺
MC V

CABOURG: *Grand Hôtel* ⓕⓕⓕⓕ
Promenade Marcel Proust, 14390. 【 *02 31 91 01 79*. FAX *02 31 24 03 20*. **Rooms:** 70.
A huge, white Belle Epoque hotel on the seafront, with vast
rooms and balconies. Marcel Proust often stayed here. 🛏 📺
AE DC MC V

CAEN: *Le Relais des Gourmets* ⓕⓕⓕ
15 rue de Geôle, 14000. 【 *02 31 86 06 01*. FAX *02 31 39 06 00*. **Rooms:** 28.
A modern hotel built and decorated in traditional style, with an elegant
dining room. Impressive views of Caen château. 🛏 📺
AE DC MC V

CAEN: *Hôtel Mercure* ⓕⓕⓕ
1 rue Courtonne, 14000. 【 *02 31 47 24 24*. FAX *02 31 47 43 88*. **Rooms:** 114.
Despite its central location, the atmosphere is quietly elegant,
with great attention paid to the comfort of the guests. 🛏 ▤ 📺
AE DC MC V

CEAUX: *Le Relais du Mont* ⓕⓕ
Labuvette, 50220. (Route N175.) 【 *02 33 70 92 55*. FAX *02 33 70 94 57*. **Rooms:** 28.
Facing west with splendid sunsets over Mont-St-Michel, this modern
hotel offers family rooms and an excellent restaurant. 🛏 📺
AE MC V

DEAUVILLE: *Hôtel Normandy* ⓕⓕⓕⓕ
38 rue J-Mermoz, 14800. 【 *02 31 98 66 22*. FAX *02 31 98 66 23*. **Rooms:** 308.
Despite its modernization, this friendly hotel has retained its original
charm. Meals are served in the courtyard under the apple trees. 🛏 📺
AE DC MC V

EVREUX: *Le Paris* ⓕ
32 rue de la Harpe, 27000. 【 *02 32 39 12 97*. **Rooms:** 6.
Quietly situated in a pedestrian street, close to the cathedral and the town
center. Clean, simple rooms are sensibly priced, and the welcome is warm.
AE DC MC V

FALAISE: *Hôtel de la Poste* ⓕⓕ
38 rue Georges-Clemenceau,14700. 【 *02 31 90 13 14*. FAX *02 31 90 01 81*. **Rooms:** 20.
The hotel offers comfortable rooms, and the restaurant is very
reasonably priced. The busy street quiets down at night. 🛏 📺
AE MC V

FÉCAMP: *Hôtel de l'Univers* ⓕⓕ
5 place St-Etienne, 76400. 【 *02 35 28 05 88*. FAX *02 35 27 82 58*. **Rooms:** 16.
An inexpensive and family-run hotel in the center of this attractive,
busy fishing port. Facilities are simple, but the staff is attentive. 🛏 📺
MC V

FONTENAI-SUR-ORNE: *Le Faisan Doré* ⓕⓕ
Route de Paris, 61200. 【 *02 33 67 18 11*. FAX *02 33 35 82 15*. **Rooms:** 14.
A large, moderately priced and impressively professional hotel. There
is a beautiful garden with a terrace for outdoor dining in summer. 🛏 📺
AE MC V

GACÉ: *Castel le Morphée* ⓕⓕ
2 route de Lisieux, 61230. 【 *02 33 35 51 01*. FAX *02 33 35 51 62*. **Rooms:** 11.
Large, turreted house set back from the road. Rooms in the main
building are elegant, those in the annex more cottagelike. 🛏 📺
AE DC MC V

GRANDCAMP-MAISY: *Hôtel Duguésclin* ⓕⓕ
4 quai Crampon, 14450. 【 *02 31 22 64 22*. FAX *02 31 22 34 79*. **Rooms:** 30.
Friendly and efficiently-run modern hotel on the seafront of this small
fishing port. Boasts an excellent restaurant. 🛏 📺
AE MC V

GRANVILLE: *Hôtel Normandy Chaumière* ⓕⓕ
20 rue Dr Paul Poirier, 50400. 【 *02 33 50 01 71*. FAX *02 33 50 15 34*. **Rooms:** 6.
The hotel is close to shops, restaurants and the casino in this charming
town. Highly recommended restaurant serving excellent seafood. 🛏 📺
MC V

HONFLEUR: *La Ferme St-Siméon* ⓕⓕⓕⓕ
Rue A Marais, 14600. 【 *02 31 89 23 61*. FAX *02 31 89 48 48*. **Rooms:** 34.
Ancient farmhouse on the Seine estuary, beautifully converted into guest
rooms. Renoir, Cézanne and other Impressionists used to meet here. 🛏 📺
AE MC V

ISIGNY-SUR-MER: *Hôtel de France* ⓕⓕ
17 rue Emile-Demagny, 14230. 【 *02 31 22 00 33*. FAX *02 31 22 79 19*. **Rooms:** 19.
A friendly and comfortable small hotel in this picturesque fishing port.
Local ingredients are featured in the excellent restaurant. 🛏 📺
AE DC V

Price categories for a standard double room (not per person) for one night, including tax and service charges, but not including breakfast.
(F) under F200
(F)(F) F200–400
(F)(F)(F) F400–600
(F)(F)(F)(F) F600–1,000
(F)(F)(F)(F)(F) over F1,000

CHILDREN'S FACILITIES
Cribs and baby-sitting available. Some hotels provide children's portions and high chairs in the restaurant.

PARKING FACILITIES
Parking provided by the hotel in either a private car lot or a private garage very close by.

SWIMMING POOL
Hotel pools are often quite small and are outdoors unless otherwise stated.

GARDEN
Hotel with garden, courtyard or terrace, often providing tables for eating outside.

Hotel		Credit Cards	Children's Facilities	Parking Facilities	Swimming Pool	Garden
LISIEUX: *Grand Hôtel de l'Espérance* 16 boulevard Ste-Anne, 14100. **(**02 31 62 17 53. **FAX** 02 31 62 34 00. ***Rooms:*** 100. This traditional half-timbered Norman building is on a busy street, but double-glazed windows ensure peace and quiet.	(F)(F)	AE DC MC V		■		
MESNIL-VAL: *Hostellerie de la Vieille Ferme* 23 rue de la Mer, 76910. **(**02 35 86 72 18. **FAX** 02 35 86 12 67. ***Rooms:*** 33. Set in its own park, this 18th-century farmhouse has several attractively converted outbuildings that are part of the hotel complex.	(F)(F)(F)	AE DC MC V	●			■
MORTAGNE-AU-PERCHE: *Hostellerie Genty-Home* 4 rue Notre-Dame, 61400. **(**02 33 25 11 53. **FAX** 02 33 25 41 38. ***Rooms:*** 8. A traditional inn built of stone in the center of this unspoiled market town. Inside, the decor varies from functional in the hotel to ornate in the reproduction Louis XV gastronomic restaurant.	(F)(F)	AE MC V	●			■
MORTAIN: *Hôtel de la Poste* Place des Arcades, 50140. **(**02 33 59 00 05. **FAX** 02 33 69 53 89. ***Rooms:*** 28. Situated on the spectacular Cherbourg peninsula, Mortain has a lovely river overlooked by this family-run hotel.	(F)(F)	MC V	●	■		■
PONT-AUDEMER: *Belle-Isle-sur-Risle* 112 Route de Rouen, 27500. **(**02 32 56 96 22. **FAX** 02 32 42 88 96. ***Rooms:*** 19. Set on an island in its own large garden of ancient trees and roses, the hotel boasts exceptionally comfortable bedrooms and superb cuisine in the arched basement.	(F)(F)(F)(F)	AE DC MC V	●	■	●	■
PONT DE L'ARCHE: *Hôtel de la Tour* 41 quai Foch, 27340. **(**02 35 23 00 99. **FAX** 02 35 23 46 22. ***Rooms:*** 16. A pretty 18th-century Norman house with comfortably renovated rooms, overlooking either the patio garden, the ramparts, or the river.	(F)(F)			■		■
ROUEN: *Hôtel de Bordeaux* 9 place de la République, 76000. **(**02 35 71 93 58. **FAX** 02 35 71 92 15. ***Rooms:*** 48. A functional, friendly and well-run hotel overlooking the Seine on one side and the cathedral towers on the other. English spoken.	(F)(F)	AE DC MC V	●	■		
ROUEN: *Hôtel de Lisieux* 4 rue de la Savonnerie, 76000. **(**02 35 71 87 73. **FAX** 02 35 89 31 52. ***Rooms:*** 30. The staff are friendly and helpful, the rooms are spacious, some of them with views of the river and cathedral. This establishment is an excellent value and the owner is gracious.	(F)(F)	AE DC MC V	●			
SAINT-LÔ: *Hôtel des Voyageurs* 5–7 avenue de Briovère, 50000. **(**02 33 05 08 63. **FAX** 02 33 05 14 34. ***Rooms:*** 31. A professional establishment where the rooms are comfortable and quiet. The restaurant specializes in seafood.	(F)(F)	AE DC MC V	●	■		■
ST-PATERNE: *Château de St-Paterne* 72610 St-Paterne. **(**02 33 27 54 71. **FAX** 02 33 29 16 71. ***Rooms:*** 8. This is not so much a hotel as a family château, with a fixed menu served *en famille*. The De Valbrays still live in this beautiful château, set in its own park just on the outskirts of Alençon.	(F)(F)(F)	AE MC	●	■		■
SÉES: *Hôtel du Cheval Blanc* 1 place St-Pierre, 61500. **(**02 33 27 80 48. **FAX** 02 33 28 58 05. ***Rooms:*** 9. A discreet and comfortable hotel on the route south from the Channel ports. It represents the best of French provincial hospitality.	(F)(F)	MC V	●	■		
VERNON: *Hôtel d'Evreux* 11 place d'Evreux, 27200. **(**02 32 21 16 12. **FAX** 02 32 21 32 73. ***Rooms:*** 18. An 18th-century coaching inn with a romantic courtyard where, on warm summer evenings, guests can enjoy fine cuisine outside.	(F)(F)	AE DC MC V	●	■		■

BRITTANY

AUDIERNE: *Le Goyen* ⓕⓕⓕ
Place Jean-Simon, 29770. 〖 02 98 70 08 88. 𝙵𝙰𝚇 02 98 70 18 77. **Rooms:** 27.
Most of the bedrooms in this restored old building overlook the fishing
port that supplies the hotel's superb restaurant. 🛏 📺
AE MC V

BREST: *Hôtel de la Corniche* ⓕⓕ
1 rue Amiral-Nicol, 29200. 〖 02 98 45 12 42. 𝙵𝙰𝚇 02 98 49 01 53. **Rooms:** 16.
This modern hotel, built of local stone in the Breton style, is on the west
side of the city near the naval base. It is convenient as a base for walks
along the scenic coastline. Facilities include a tennis court. 🛏 📺
AE MC V

CANCALE: *Hôtel Richeux* ⓕⓕⓕⓕⓕ
Le Point du Jour, 35260. 〖 02 99 89 64 76. 𝙵𝙰𝚇 02 99 89 88 47. **Rooms:** 13.
A charming Art-Deco villa with views of the bay of Mont-St-Michel.
The rooms are furnished with antiques. 🛏 📺
AE DC MC V

CARNAC: *Lann Roz* ⓕⓕⓕ
36 avenue de la Poste, 56340. 〖 02 97 52 10 48. 𝙵𝙰𝚇 02 97 52 24 36. **Rooms:** 13.
A friendly hotel with a pretty garden ten minutes' walk from the beach.
The restaurant has a fine wine list. 🛏 📺
AE MC V

CESSON-SÉVIGNÉ: *Hôtel Germinal* ⓕⓕ
9 cours de la Vilaine, 35510. 〖 02 99 83 11 01. 𝙵𝙰𝚇 02 99 83 45 16. **Rooms:** 20.
A river runs on both sides of this converted mill. The decor is rustic
with traditional wooden furniture. 🛏 📺
AE MC V

DINARD: *Le Prieuré* ⓕⓕ
1 place Général de Gaulle, 35800. 〖 02 99 46 13 74. 𝙵𝙰𝚇 02 99 46 81 90. **Rooms:** 4.
A reservation is essential at this hotel facing the western edge of
Prieuré beach. Its restaurant is an exceptionally good value. 🛏 📺
MC V

FOUGÈRES: *Balzac Hôtel* ⓕⓕ
15 rue Nationale, 35300. 〖 02 99 99 42 46. 𝙵𝙰𝚇 02 99 99 65 43. **Rooms:** 20.
In one of the prettiest towns in western France, this quiet hotel,
furnished in 18th-century style, offers a warm welcome. 🛏 📺
AE DC MC V

GROIX (ÎLE DE): *Hôtel de la Marine* ⓕⓕ
7 rue Général-de-Gaulle, 56590. 〖 02 97 86 80 05. 𝙵𝙰𝚇 02 97 86 56 37. **Rooms:** 22.
This old stone house on the island of Groix is filled with traditional
furniture. A relaxing hideaway. 🛏
MC V

LA FORÊT-FOUESNANT: *Le Manoir du Stang* ⓕⓕⓕⓕⓕ
29940 La Forêt-Fouesnant. 〖 & 𝙵𝙰𝚇 02 98 56 97 37. **Rooms:** 24.
A fabulous Renaissance manor house set in a large park with
woodland and a lake. The interior features ancient paneling and
antique furniture that has been in the family for generations. 🛏

LAMBALLE: *Hôtel de l'Angleterre* ⓕⓕ
29 boulevard Jobert, 22400. 〖 02 96 31 00 16. 𝙵𝙰𝚇 02 96 31 91 54. **Rooms:** 19.
A comfortable hotel opposite the railroad station, suitable for an
inexpensive overnight stop. Reasonable fixed-price menu. 🛏 📺
AE DC MC V

MORLAIX: *Hôtel de l'Europe* ⓕⓕ
1 rue d'Aiguillon, 29600. 〖 02 98 62 11 99. 𝙵𝙰𝚇 02 98 88 83 38. **Rooms:** 60.
This Second Empire hotel is filled with furniture from earlier periods.
The brasserie and grill offer excellent meals. Centrally located. 🛏 📺
AE DC MC V

PÉNESTIN: *Hôtel Loscolo* ⓕⓕⓕ
La Pointe de Loscolo, 56760. 〖 02 99 90 31 90. 𝙵𝙰𝚇 02 99 90 32 14. **Rooms:** 16.
A modern building on a cape with magnificent sea views to both sides
and good walking nearby. The restaurant serves rich cuisine. 🛏 📺
MC V

PLÉVEN: *Le Manoir de Vaumadeuc* ⓕⓕⓕⓕ
22130 Pléven. 〖 02 96 84 46 17. 𝙵𝙰𝚇 02 96 84 40 16. **Rooms:** 14.
This old manor house, with its graceful bay windows and fine
staircase, dates back to the 15th century. The park around it
includes a beautiful rose garden. 🛏
AE DC MC V

PLOUGASTEL-DAOULAS: *Hôtel Kastel Roc'h* ⓕⓕ
Roc'h Kérézen, 29470. 〖 02 98 40 32 00. 𝙵𝙰𝚇 02 98 04 25 40. **Rooms:** 45.
Near Océanopolis and the marina, this hotel has some family rooms
that make it a good base for a vacation with children. 🛏 📺
AE MC V

		Price categories for a standard double room (not per person) for one night, including tax and service charges, but not including breakfast. **F** under F200 **FF** F200–400 **FFF** F400–600 **FFFF** F600–1,000 **FFFFF** over F1,000	**CHILDREN'S FACILITIES** Cribs and baby-sitting available. Some hotels provide children's portions and high chairs in the restaurant. **PARKING FACILITIES** Parking provided by the hotel in either a private car lot or a private garage very close by. **SWIMMING POOL** Hotel pools are often quite small and are outdoors unless otherwise stated. **GARDEN** Hotel with garden, courtyard or terrace, often providing tables for eating outside.	CREDIT CARDS	CHILDREN'S FACILITIES	PARKING FACILITIES	SWIMMING POOL	GARDEN

PLUMAUDAN: *Le Plessis* **FF**
22350 Plumaudan. **C** 02 96 86 00 44. *Rooms: 3.*
A comfortable 18th-century farmhouse in the Breton countryside near Dinan. Friendly relaxed atmosphere. Serves only vegetarian meals.

| | | | ■ | |

QUIBERON: *Hôtel Bellevue* **FFF**
Rue Tiviec, 56170. **C** 02 97 50 16 28. **FAX** 02 97 30 44 34. *Rooms: 40.*
Forming an L-shape around its swimming pool, the Bellevue is near the seafront and casino. It has a comfortable lounge and bar. 🚗 📺

| AE MC V | ● | ■ | ● | ■ |

QUIMPER: *La Tour d'Auvergne* **FFF**
13 rue des Réguaires, 29000. **C** 02 98 95 08 70. **FAX** 02 98 95 17 31. *Rooms: 42.*
A recently refurbished hotel with a pretty courtyard and a friendly family atmosphere. The bedrooms are spacious and comfortable. 🚗 📺

| AE MC V | | ■ | | |

ROSCOFF: *Hôtel Bellevue* **FF**
Rue Jeanne-d'Arc, 29680. **C** 02 98 61 23 38. **FAX** 02 98 61 11 80. *Rooms: 18.*
An old Breton house enjoying fine views of the sea and the old port. To the rear is a pleasant garden with deckchairs where the drinks are served. The restaurant specializes in fish and Loire white wines. 🚗 📺

| MC V | ● | ■ | | ■ |

ST-MALO: *Hôtel Elisabeth* **FFFF**
2 rue des Cordiers, 35400. **C** 02 99 56 24 98. **FAX** 02 99 56 39 24. *Rooms: 17.*
Situated within the ramparts of the old town, the building has a 16th-century façade. English satellite TV is available. 🚗 📺

| AE DC MC V | ● | ■ | | |

VANNES: *La Marébaudière* **FFF**
4 rue Aristide-Briand, 56000. **C** 02 97 47 34 29. **FAX** 02 97 54 14 11. *Rooms: 41.*
A peaceful hotel decorated with flair. Some of the beds are antique. The beautifully-preserved old walled town is a short walk away. 🚗 📺

| AE MC V | | ■ | | |

THE LOIRE VALLEY

AMBOISE: *Le Choiseul* **FFFFF**
36 quai Charles-Guinot, 37400. **C** 02 47 30 45 45. **FAX** 02 47 30 46 10. *Rooms: 32.*
An ivy-covered manor set in elegant grounds. The famous cellars can be visited. A sophisticated restaurant serves fish cooked in wine. 🚗 📺

| AE DC MC V | ● | ■ | ● | ■ |

AZAY-LE-RIDEAU: *Le Clos Philippa* **FF**
10 rue Pineau, 37190. **C** 02 47 45 26 49. **FAX** 02 45 45 31 46. *Rooms: 4.*
Guests at this 18th-century house have the use of the owner's drawing room, sitting room, library and grounds. There is no restaurant. 🚗

| MC V | | ■ | | ■ |

AZAY-LE-RIDEAU: *Manoir de la Rémonière* **FFF**
La Chapelle St-Blaise, 37190. **C** 02 47 45 24 88. **FAX** 02 47 45 45 69. *Rooms: 6.*
A manor house on romantic grounds that are perfect for children to play in. Meals include homegrown vegetables. 🚗

| | | ■ | ● | ■ |

BEAUGENCY: *Hotel de la Sologne* **FF**
6 place St-Firmin, 45190. **C** 02 38 44 50 27. **FAX** 02 38 44 90 19. *Rooms: 16.*
This old-fashioned hotel is on the main square, overlooking the ruined castle keep. Breakfast is served in an attractive winter garden. 🚗 📺

| MC V | | | | |

BEAUGENCY: *Hotel de l'Abbaye* **FFF**
2 quai de l'Abbaye, 45190. **C** 02 38 44 67 35. **FAX** 02 38 44 87 92. *Rooms: 18.*
Ask for a room in one of the former monastic cells of this restored abbey beside the river. The restaurant is good but overpriced. 🚗 📺

| AE DC MC V | ● | ■ | | ■ |

LA BOHALLE: *L'Hermitage* **FF**
5 route de Brain, 49800. **C** 02 41 54 96 05. *Rooms: 2.*
Run by a Scottish-French couple, this *chambres d'hôtes* in a charming fishing village on the north bank of the Loire is a simple but friendly place to stay. The owners are happy to advise on local sights.

| | ● | ■ | | ■ |

BOURGUEIL: *Châteaux des Réaux* Ⓕ Ⓕ Ⓕ Ⓕ AE MC V
Le Port-Boulet, 37140. 📞 02 47 95 14 40. 🆕 FAX 02 47 95 18 34. *Rooms: 17.*
A lovingly restored brick and stone Renaissance château in a
wine-growing area. The owners enjoy showing visitors around. 🚗

BRÉHÉMONT: *Les Brunets* Ⓕ Ⓕ
37130 Bréhémont. 📞 02 47 96 55 81. *Rooms: 3.*
This charming country house in an unspoiled village on the Loire is
owned by a helpful English couple. 🚗 TV

BRÉHÉMONT: *Le Castel de Bray et Monts* Ⓕ Ⓕ Ⓕ MC V
Le Bourg, 37130. 📞 02 47 96 70 47. FAX 02 47 96 57 36. *Rooms: 8.*
An attractive 18th-century mansion that sits next to a stream in ample
grounds. The rooms are charming and breakfast is excellent. 🚗 TV

CHAMBORD: *Hôtel Saint-Michel* Ⓕ Ⓕ MC V
41250 Chambord. 📞 02 54 20 31 31. FAX 02 54 20 36 40. *Rooms: 38.*
Book ahead at this old-fashioned hotel and ask for a room with a view
of the château. The restaurant is stuffy but the cuisine good. 🚗 TV

CHAMPIGNÉ: *Château des Briottières* Ⓕ Ⓕ Ⓕ Ⓕ AE MC V
49330 Champigné. 📞 02 41 42 00 02. FAX 02 41 42 01 55. *Rooms: 14.*
Classical, family-run white château once used as a film set. Romantic
dinners are on offer as well as food and wine-tasting trips. 🚗

CHARTRES: *Grand Monarque* Ⓕ Ⓕ Ⓕ Ⓕ AE DC MC V
22 place des Epars, 28005. 📞 02 37 21 00 72. FAX 02 37 36 34 18. *Rooms: 53.*
An efficiently managed modern hotel on the edge of the old quarter.
It has a recommended gourmet restaurant. 🚗 TV

CHENONCEAUX: *Hostel du Roy* Ⓕ Ⓕ AE MC V
9 rue de Dr Bretonneau, 37150. 📞 02 47 23 90 17. FAX 02 47 23 89 81. *Rooms: 37.*
A sprawling hotel-restaurant with simple but appealing bedrooms and
a dining room hung with hunting trophies. Local wines served. 🚗 TV

CHINON: *Hôtel Diderot* Ⓕ Ⓕ AE DC MC V
4 rue Buffon, 37500. 📞 02 47 93 18 87. FAX 02 47 93 37 10. *Rooms: 27.*
An elegant, creeper-clad 18th-century house on a quiet street. The
bedrooms are simple but some have good views. 🚗

CHINON: *Hôtel de France* Ⓕ Ⓕ AE DC MC V
47 place de Gen-de-Gaulle, 37500. 📞 02 47 93 33 91. FAX 02 47 98 37 03. *Rooms: 30.*
This underrated hotel, comfortable and friendly but without frills, is
situated in the Old Quarter a short way from the scenic main street. 🚗 TV

CHINON: *Hostellerie Gargantua* Ⓕ Ⓕ AE MC V
73 rue Voltaire, 37500. 📞 02 47 93 04 71. *Rooms: 7.*
With its pointed roof and turret, this old building overlooking the river
is a local landmark. Its cuisine blends the traditional and modern. 🚗

FONDETTES: *Manoir du Grand Martigny* Ⓕ Ⓕ Ⓕ Ⓕ
37230 Fondettes. 📞 02 47 42 29 87. FAX 02 47 42 24 44. *Rooms: 7.*
Wild and wooded grounds surround this quirky manor house, which
is less formal than other Loire château hotels. There is no restaurant. 🚗

FONTEVRAUD-L'ABBAYE: *Hôtellerie Prieuré St-Lazare* Ⓕ Ⓕ Ⓕ AE MC V
49590 Fontevraud-L'Abbaye. 📞 02 41 51 73 16. FAX 02 41 51 75 50. *Rooms: 52.*
This atmospheric hotel is housed in the former St-Lazare priory, within
the famous abbey complex. 🚗 TV

GENNES: *Le Prieuré* Ⓕ Ⓕ Ⓕ Ⓕ Ⓕ AE DC MC V
Chênehutte-les-Tuffeaux, 49350. 📞 02 41 67 90 14. FAX 02 41 67 92 24. *Rooms: 35.*
Most of the rooms in this luxurious Renaissance manor look out onto
the Loire. A gourmet restaurant adds to the appeal. 🚗 TV

GIEN: *Hôtel du Rivage* Ⓕ Ⓕ Ⓕ AE DC V
1 quai de Nice, 45500. 📞 02 38 37 79 00. FAX 02 38 38 10 21. *Rooms: 19.*
This riverside hotel is renowned for its exquisite cuisine.
🚗 📋 TV

LA CHARTRE-SUR-LE-LOIR: *Hôtel de France* Ⓕ Ⓕ MC V
20 place de la République, 72340. 📞 02 43 44 40 16. FAX 02 43 79 62 20. *Rooms: 17.*
This hotel in the town center has a garden beside the river. Its
restaurant serves generous portions and has won awards. 🚗 TV

For key to symbols see back flap

Price categories for a standard double room (not per person) for one night, including tax and service charges, but not including breakfast.
Ⓕ under F200
ⒻⒻ F200–400
ⒻⒻⒻ F400–600
ⒻⒻⒻⒻ F600–1,000
ⒻⒻⒻⒻⒻ over F1,000

CHILDREN'S FACILITIES
Cribs and baby-sitting available. Some hotels provide children's portions and high chairs in the restaurant.

PARKING FACILITIES
Parking provided by the hotel in either a private lot or a private garage very close by.

SWIMMING POOL
Hotel pools are often quite small and are outdoors unless otherwise stated.

GARDEN
Hotel with garden, courtyard or terrace, often providing tables for eating outside.

	Credit Cards	Children's Facilities	Parking Facilities	Swimming Pool	Garden
LE MANS: *Ibis Centre* ⒻⒻ Quai Ledru-Rolin, 72000. ☎ 02 43 23 18 23. FAX 02 43 24 00 72. **Rooms:** 85. Overlooking the river and the Old Quarter, this is the best hotel in Le Mans for budget travelers. It serves a good buffet breakfast. 🖥 TV	AE DC JCB MC V	●			■
LOCHES: *Hôtel de France* ⒻⒻ 6 rue Picois, 37600. ☎ 02 47 59 00 32. FAX 02 47 59 28 66. **Rooms:** 19. This elegant hotel is situated near the medieval gate. Guests are expected to have dinner on the premises. The restaurant is excellent. 🖥 TV	DC MC V		■		■
LUYNES: *Domaine de Beauvois* ⒻⒻⒻⒻ Route de Cleré, 37230. ☎ 02 47 55 50 11. FAX 02 47 55 59 62. **Rooms:** 40. Built around a 15th-century tower and overlooking its own lake, the Domaine has large rooms and a celebrated restaurant. 🖥 TV	AE DC MC V	●	■		■
MARÇAY: *Château de Marçay* ⒻⒻⒻⒻⒻ 37500 Marçay. ☎ 02 47 93 03 47. FAX 02 47 93 45 33. **Rooms:** 34. Service and cuisine in this elegant château-hotel are impeccable. There are good views over the surrounding parkland and vineyards. 🖥 TV	AE DC MC V	●	■	●	■
MONTBAZON: *Château d'Artigny* ⒻⒻⒻⒻ Route de Monts, 37250. ☎ 02 47 34 30 30. FAX 02 47 34 30 39. **Rooms:** 43. The grandiose Classical exterior is matched by a formal Empire-style interior. A gourmet restaurant serves regional specialties. 🖥 TV	AE DC MC V	●	■	●	■
MONTLOUIS-SUR-LOIRE: *Château de la Bourdaisière* ⒻⒻⒻⒻ 25 rue de la Bourdaisière, 37270. ☎ 02 47 45 16 31. FAX 02 47 45 09 11. **Rooms:** 17. A magnificent château which has been refurbished as luxury accommodations. Gabrielle d'Estrées, Henri IV's mistress, was born here in 1565. Facilities include tennis courts and horseback riding. 🖥 TV	MC V	●	■	●	■
MONTREUIL-BELLAY: *Demeure des Petits Augustins* ⒻⒻ 49260 Montreuil-Bellay. ☎ 02 41 52 33 88. FAX 02 41 52 33 88. **Rooms:** 3. Guests are made welcome in this 17th-century town mansion. The spacious, individually styled bedrooms overlook a charming courtyard. The "white" suite is especially recommended. 🖥	MC V	●	■		■
MONTREUIL-BELLAY: *Splendid Hôtel* ⒻⒻ 139 rue Docteur-Gaudrez, 49260. ☎ 02 41 53 10 00. FAX 02 41 52 45 17. **Rooms:** 60. An old-fashioned hotel in the center of town with an excellent regional restaurant. The annex has quieter, more stylish rooms. 🖥 TV	MC V		■		■
MUIDES-SUR-LOIRE: *Château de Colliers* ⒻⒻⒻⒻ 41500 Muides-sur-Loire. ☎ 02 54 87 50 75. FAX 02 54 87 03 64. **Rooms:** 5. This château, set among woods a short drive east of Blois, combines grandeur with rusticity. 🖥	MC V	●	■		■
NANTES: *Jules Verne* ⒻⒻⒻ 3 rue du Couëdic, 44000. ☎ 02 40 35 74 50. FAX 02 40 20 09 35. **Rooms:** 65. A modern hotel on a pedestrian square, offering friendly service and comfortable rooms. Parking in the nearby place du Commerce. 🖥 ▤ TV	AE DC MC V	●	■		
NANTES: *Hôtel la Perouse* ⒻⒻⒻ 3 allée Duquesne, 44000. ☎ 02 40 89 75 00. FAX 02 40 89 76 00. **Rooms:** 46 This chic hotel, which opened in 1993, offers crisp, contemporary design and efficient service. It is reasonably quiet for a city hotel. 🖥 ▤ TV	AE DC MC V	●	■		
NOIZAY: *Château de Noizay* ⒻⒻⒻⒻ 37210 Noizay. ☎ 02 47 52 11 01. FAX 02 47 52 04 64. **Rooms:** 14. A compact Renaissance château set in Classical gardens on the right bank of the Loire. The rooms are discreetly and elegantly furnished. In good weather breakfast is served on the terrace. 🖥 TV	AE DC MC V	●	■	●	■

ONZAIN: *Domaine des Hauts de Loire* ⓕⓕⓕⓕ
Route d'Herbault, 41150. 📞 02 54 20 72 57. FAX 02 54 20 77 32. **Rooms:** 15.
A count's former hunting lodge with large grounds and a lake, this is an unashamedly expensive place to relax and enjoy good food.
Cards: AE DC MC V — ● ■ ● ■

ROCHECORBON: *Les Hautes Roches* ⓕⓕⓕⓕ
86 quai de la Loire, 37210. 📞 02 47 52 88 88. FAX 02 47 52 81 30. **Rooms:** 15.
The underground rooms hewn into the chalk in this "troglodyte" hotel are less spacious but more atmospheric than the rest.
Cards: AE DC V — ● ■

ROMORANTIN-LANTHENAY: *Grand Hôtel Lion d'Or* ⓕⓕⓕⓕ
69 rue Clémenceau, 41200. 📞 02 94 15 15. FAX 02 54 88 24 87. **Rooms:** 16.
This former 17th-century stopping point is now a gastronomic halt in a historic but untourist town in the watery Sologne landscape.
Cards: AE DC MC V — ●

ST-JULIEN-LE-PAUVRE: *Château de la Renaudière* ⓕⓕⓕ
72240 Saint-Julien-le-Pauvre. 📞 02 43 20 71 09. **Rooms:** 3.
A gracious château, owned by the Marquis de Mascureau, set among rolling meadows between Le Mans and Laval. The family enjoys introducing visitors to the lesser-known châteaux of the region.
— ● ■

ST-LAMBERT-DES-LEVÉES: *La Croix de la Voulte* ⓕⓕ
Route de Boumois, 49400. 📞 02 41 38 46 66. FAX 02 41 38 46 66. **Rooms:** 4.
The rooms in this old manor outside Saumur are all different and the furnishings stylish. Ask for directions when you book.
— ■ ■

SAUMUR: *Hôtel Anne d'Anjou* ⓕⓕⓕ
32–34 quai Mayaud, 49400. 📞 02 41 67 30 30. FAX 02 41 67 51 00. **Rooms:** 50.
The decor in this elegant mansion beside the Loire River is sophisticated and romantic. The courtyard and grand staircase are impressive.
Cards: AE DC MC V — ● ■

TOURS: *Hôtel Balzac* ⓕⓕ
47 rue de la Scellerie, 37000. 📞 02 47 05 40 87. FAX 02 47 05 67 93. **Rooms:** 18.
Cozy and inviting, this old-fashioned hotel is situated between the theater and the cathedral. Drinks are served in the courtyard.
Cards: AE DC MC V

TOURS: *Hôtel Moderne* ⓕⓕ
1–3 rue Victor Laloux, 37000. 📞 02 47 05 32 81. FAX 02 47 05 71 50. **Rooms:** 23.
A convenient location, a warm welcome and a good restaurant easily make up for the rooms, which are comfortable but a little shabby.
Cards: AE MC V

TOURS: *Hôtel de l'Univers* ⓕⓕⓕⓕ
5 boulevard Heurteloup, 37000. 📞 02 47 05 37 12. FAX 02 47 61 51 80. **Rooms:** 85.
Statesmen, including Winston Churchill, and royals have stayed at this luxurious Belle Epoque hotel. The rooms have antique furniture.
Cards: AE DC MC V — ● ■

VARADES: *Le Grand Patis* ⓕⓕ
44370 Varades. 📞 02 40 83 42 28. **Rooms:** 5.
Rooms in this restored château are simple, clean and spacious. Two have stone balconies overlooking the peaceful, leafy grounds.
— ■ ■

VOUVRAY: *Château de Jallanges* ⓕⓕⓕⓕ
Vallée de Vaugoudy, 37210. 📞 02 47 52 06 66. FAX 02 47 52 11 18. **Rooms:** 6.
An imposing Renaissance brick mansion, now a family home, with stylish and comfortable rooms. Guests are taken on a guided tour from chapel to turrets. A good base for exploring Touraine.
Cards: AE MC V — ■ ● ■

BURGUNDY AND FRANCHE-COMTÉ

ARBOIS: *Jean-Paul Jeunet* ⓕⓕⓕ
9 rue de l'Hôtel de Ville, 39600. 📞 03 84 66 05 67. FAX 03 84 66 24 20. **Rooms:** 18.
In the center of this picturesque town, Jeunet offers modern amenities and comfort. Good selection of Jura wines in the restaurant.
Cards: AE DC MC V — ● ■ ● ■

ARNAY-LE-DUC: *Chez Camille* ⓕⓕⓕ
1 place Edouard-Herriot, 21230. 📞 03 80 90 01 38. FAX 03 80 90 04 64. **Rooms:** 11.
An attractive and tastefully decorated hotel with spacious bedrooms and antique furniture. The hotel offers warmth and peace with its huge open fire in the lounge and double-glazed windows. Traditional cuisine.
Cards: AE DC MC V — ● ■

AUTUN: *Les Granges* ⓕⓕ
Monthélon, 71400. 📞 03 85 52 22 99. **Rooms:** 3.
This working farm is a good base to explore the Burgundian countryside and Autun. Friendly owners, but no restaurant. Cash only.
— ■ ■

Price categories for a standard double room (not per person) for one night, including tax and service charges, but not including breakfast.
Ⓕ under F200
ⒻⒻ F200–400
ⒻⒻⒻ F400–600
ⒻⒻⒻⒻ F600–1,000
ⒻⒻⒻⒻⒻ over F1,000

CHILDREN'S FACILITIES
Cribs and baby-sitting available. Some hotels provide children's portions and high chairs in the restaurant.

PARKING FACILITIES
Parking provided by the hotel in either a private lot or a private garage very close by.

SWIMMING POOL
Hotel pools are often quite small and are outdoors unless otherwise stated.

GARDEN
Hotel with garden, courtyard or terrace, often providing tables for eating outside.

	CREDIT CARDS	CHILDREN'S FACILITIES	PARKING FACILITIES	SWIMMING POOL	GARDEN
AUTUN: *Hôtel St-Louis* ⒻⒻⒻ 6 rue de l'Arbalète, 71400. **C** *03 85 52 21 03.* **FAX** *03 85 86 32 54.* **Rooms:** *39.* This quiet hotel was once a coach stop. Rooms vary in price, the most expensive being Napoleon's former bedchamber. 🚗 TV	AE MC V	●	▪		▪
BEAUNE: *Hôtel du Parc* ⒻⒻ Route Verdun, Levernois, 21200. **C** *03 80 24 63 00.* **FAX** *03 80 24 21 19.* **Rooms:** *25.* A quiet, quaint country hotel on the outskirts of Beaune, set in a beautiful park. A good base for visiting the nearby vineyards. 🚗 TV	MC V	●	▪		▪
BEAUNE: *Le Home* ⒻⒻ 138 route Dijon, 21200. **C** *03 80 22 16 43.* **FAX** *03 80 24 90 74.* **Rooms:** *20.* Set back from the main road in a charming courtyard is this simple, homey hotel just outside the town. Clean and comfortable. 🚗	MC V	●	▪		
BEAUNE: *Hôtel du Cep* ⒻⒻⒻⒻ 27 rue Maufoux, 21200. **C** *03 80 22 35 48.* **FAX** *03 80 22 76 80.* **Rooms:** *56.* In the heart of the Old Town is this subdued and elegant hotel, tastefully renovated in a Renaissance style. Each bedroom is named after a wine of the Côte d'Or vineyards. Restaurant and bar. 🚗 ▤ TV	AE DC MC V	●	▪		▪
BESANÇON: *Hôtel Mercure Parc Micaud* ⒻⒻⒻ 3 avenue E Droz, 25000. **C** *03 81 80 14 44.* **FAX** *03 81 53 29 83.* **Rooms:** *91.* A luxury modern hotel on the waterfront offering comfort, good breakfasts and an excellent restaurant called *Le Vesontio.* 🚗 TV	AE DC MC V	●			
BOUILLAND: *Le Vieux Moulin* ⒻⒻⒻⒻ 21420 Bouilland. **C** *03 80 21 51 16.* **FAX** *03 80 21 59 90.* **Rooms:** *26.* A recently renovated mill located in one of the most spectacular villages in Burgundy. The chef is renowned for his creativity. 🚗 TV	MC V	●	▪	●	▪
CHABLIS: *Hostellerie de Clos* ⒻⒻⒻ Rue Jules-Rathier, 89800. **C** *03 86 42 10 63.* **FAX** *03 86 42 17 11.* **Rooms:** *26.* The owner has renovated a medieval convent in the middle of this famed village. The rooms are modern and comfortable, the garden is delightful and the restaurant is one of the best in the region. 🚗 TV	AE MC V	●	▪		▪
CHAILLY-SUR-ARMANÇON: *Château de Chailly* ⒻⒻⒻⒻⒻ 21320 Chailly-sur-Armançon. **C** *03 80 90 30 30.* **FAX** *03 80 90 30 00.* **Rooms:** *45.* A Japanese industrialist has restored this magnificent château, installing every detail of luxury, including a golf course. 🚗 TV	AE DC MC V	●	▪	●	▪
CHÂTEAU CHINON: *Hôtel du Vieux Morvan* ⒻⒻ 8 place Gudin, 58120. **C** *03 86 85 05 01.* **FAX** *03 86 85 02 78.* **Rooms:** *24.* François Mitterrand learned he had become President here – for years he visited this hotel and always stayed in room 15. The manageress has since retired but the hotel retains its rustic, old-world style. 🚗 TV	MC V	●	▪		
CLUNY: *Hostellerie de Bourgogne* ⒻⒻⒻⒻ Place de l'Abbaye, 71250. **C** *03 85 59 00 58.* **FAX** *03 85 59 03 73.* **Rooms:** *15.* This old-fashioned auberge is located next door to the magnificent Cluny abbey. Excellent restaurant serving refined cuisine. 🚗 TV	AE DC MC V	●	▪		
DIJON: *Hostellerie le Sauvage* ⒻⒻ 64 rue Monge, 21000. **C** *03 80 41 31 21.* **FAX** *03 80 42 06 07.* **Rooms:** *21.* This city hotel is conveniently located near the main sights and the historic center. The restaurant specializes in steaks and grills. 🚗 TV	MC V		▪		▪
FLAVIGNY-SUR-OZERAIN: *Mme. Marc Brigand* Ⓕ 21150 Flavigny-sur-Ozerain. **C** *03 80 96 20 91.* **Rooms:** *3.* Simple accommodation in an old-fashioned house brought to life by its lively owners. Meals available and cash only.		●	▪		

FONTETTE: *Hôtel Crispol* ⒻⒻⒻ
St-Père-sous-Vezelay, 89450. **℄** *03 86 33 26 25.* **FAX** *03 86 33 33 10.* **Rooms:** *12.*
Well-planned and chic decor in this very luxurious and modern
hotel. Generous and imaginative local cooking.
AE MC V

GEVREY-CHAMBERTIN: *Hôtel des Grands Crus* ⒻⒻⒻ
Route des Grands Crus, 21220. **℄** *03 80 34 34 15.* **FAX** *03 80 51 89 07.* **Rooms:** *24.*
A light and airy, old-style hotel with wonderful views over the vine-
yards. No restaurant but several good restaurants in the village.
MC V

GEVREY-CHAMBERTIN: *Mme. Geneviève Sylvain* ⒻⒻ
14 rue de l'Eglise, 21220. **℄** *03 80 51 86 39.* **Rooms:** *3.*
Friendly owners run this spacious *chambres d'hôte.* Ideal location
for exploring the village restaurants and local wine tastings.

JOIGNY: *La Côte St-Jacques* ⒻⒻⒻⒻⒻ
14 Faubourg Paris, 89300. **℄** *03 86 62 09 70.* **FAX** *03 86 91 49 70.* **Rooms:** *29.*
Known as a mini-Versailles, this glamorous and lavish hotel
sits beside the Yonne River. The restaurant is outstanding.
AE DC MC V

LEVERNOIS: *Le Parc* ⒻⒻⒻ
21200 Levernois. **℄** *03 80 22 22 51.* **FAX** *03 80 24 21 19.* **Rooms:** *25.*
Set in the heart of beautiful park land, this hotel offers a relaxing retreat.
Hot-air ballooning is possible in the area.
AE MC V

LIGNY-LE-CHATEL: *Relais Saint-Vincent* ⒻⒻ
14 Grande-Rue, 89144. **℄** *03 86 47 53 38.* **FAX** *03 86 47 54 16.* **Rooms:** *15.*
An ancient half-timbered house, well equipped with modern comforts.
The restaurant serves regional specialties.
AE DC MC V

OYE-ET-PALLET: *Hôtel Parnet* ⒻⒻ
11 rue de la Fauconnière, 25160. **℄** *03 81 89 42 03.* **FAX** *03 81 89 41 47.* **Rooms:** *17.*
In the Jura Mountains, this is a great place to take a cross-country
skiing vacation. Clean, comfortable and calm. Good food.
MC V

POLIGNY: *Hostellerie des Monts de Vaux* ⒻⒻⒻⒻ
39800 Poligny. **℄** *03 84 37 12 50.* **FAX** *03 84 37 09 07.* **Rooms:** *10*
An elegant old coaching inn on the outskirts of Poligny. Friendly
owners, good Jura cuisine and wine, and tennis courts.
AE DC MC V

PULIGNY-MONTRACHET: *Le Montrachet* ⒻⒻⒻ
Place des Marroniers, 21190. **℄** *03 80 21 30 06.* **FAX** *03 80 21 39 06.* **Rooms:** *32.*
A quiet resting spot in the heart of Burgundy wine country. The
restaurant serves good food and has an excellent wine list.
AE DC MC V

ST-GERVAIS-EN-VALLIÈRE: *Moulin d'Hauterive* ⒻⒻⒻ
Chaublanc, 71350. **℄** *03 85 91 55 56.* **FAX** *03 85 91 89 65.* **Rooms:** *19.*
A converted watermill in a secluded setting with a tennis court and
sauna. The owner serves inventive home cooking.
AE DC MC V

ST-PÈRE-SOUS-VÉZELAY: *Mme. Demeure* ⒻⒻ
Le Petit Cléret, Fontette, 89450. **℄** *03 86 33 25 87.* **Rooms:** *2.*
This charming period house is run as a *chambres d'hôte* by two
animal lovers. Choose the upstairs room under the eaves.

SAULIEU: *La Côte d'Or* ⒻⒻⒻⒻⒻ
2 rue Argentine, 21210. **℄** *03 80 90 53 53.* **FAX** *03 80 64 08 92.* **Rooms:** *32.*
Regarded as one of the best and most innovative restaurants in France.
Some of the older rooms are relatively inexpensive.
AE DC MC V

TONNERRE: *L'Abbaye St-Michel* ⒻⒻⒻⒻ
Montée de St-Michel, 89700. **℄** *03 86 55 05 99.* **FAX** *03 86 55 00 10.* **Rooms:** *11.*
A renovated abbey that now houses a celebrated Burgundy
restaurant. The hotel blends old and modern styles.
AE DC MC V

TOURNUS: *Château de Beaufer* ⒻⒻⒻⒻ
71700 Tournus. **℄** *03 85 51 18 24.* **FAX** *03 85 51 25 04.* **Rooms:** *6.*
Choose between a room in the ivy-clad 16th-century château or one in the
annex. Restaurants are a short drive away.
MC V

VÉZELAY: *Cabalus* ⒻⒻ
Rue St-Pierre, 89450. **℄** *03 86 33 20 66.* **FAX** *03 86 33 38 03.* **Rooms:** *7.*
This 12th-century building, the abbey's former hostelry, is in the middle
of the Old Town. There are good views from some of the rooms.
AE MC V

For key to symbols see back flap

Price categories for a standard double room (not per person) for one night, including tax and service charges, but not including breakfast.
- Ⓕ under F200
- ⒻⒻ F200–400
- ⒻⒻⒻ F400–600
- ⒻⒻⒻⒻ F600–1,000
- ⒻⒻⒻⒻⒻ over F1,000

CHILDREN'S FACILITIES
Cribs and baby-sitting available. Some hotels provide children's portions and high chairs in the restaurant.

PARKING FACILITIES
Parking provided by the hotel in either a private lot or a private garage very close by.

SWIMMING POOL
Hotel pools are often quite small and are outdoors unless otherwise stated.

GARDEN
Hotel with garden, courtyard or terrace, often providing tables for eating outside.

	Credit Cards	Children's Facilities	Parking Facilities	Swimming Pool	Garden
VÉZELAY: *L'Espérance* ⒻⒻⒻ St-Père-sous-Vézelay, 89450. 〖 03 86 33 39 10. FAX 03 86 33 26 15. **Rooms:** 21. Some of the rooms overlook the garden; others are in a renovated mill. Above all, guests come for the famous restaurant. 🔙 TV	AE DC V	●	■	●	■
VONNAS: *Georges Blanc* ⒻⒻⒻⒻⒻ 01540 Vonnas. 〖 04 74 50 90 90. FAX 04 74 50 08 80. **Rooms:** 32. A sumptuous hotel-restaurant with luxurious rooms built and furnished in modern country style using stone, tiles, and tapestries. 🔙 ▤ TV	AE DC MC V	●	■		■
THE MASSIF CENTRAL					
AUBUSSON-D'AUVERGNE: *Au Bon Coin* Ⓕ 63120 Aubusson-d'Auvergne. 〖 04 73 53 55 78. FAX 04 73 53 56 29. **Rooms:** 6. The friendly owner of this rustic inn is also the mayor of the town, and the tasty cuisine reflects his pride in local culinary traditions.	MC V	●			
BEAULIEU-SUR-DORDOGNE: *Château d'Arnac* ⒻⒻⒻ Nonards, 19120. 〖 05 55 91 54 13. FAX 05 55 91 52 62. **Rooms:** 3. The hospitable English owners have restored this château, keeping some original details. The grounds include a small lake. Dinner available. 🔙			■		■
BELCASTEL: *Le Vieux Pont* ⒻⒻⒻ 12390 Belcastel. 〖 05 65 64 52 29. FAX 05 65 64 44 32. **Rooms:** 7. This annex to the Fagegaltier sisters' imaginative but affordable restaurant overlooks the medieval village and its castle. 🔙 TV	MC V		■		
CALVINET: *Hôtel Beauséjour* ⒻⒻ Route de Maurs, 15340. 〖 04 71 49 91 68. FAX 04 71 49 98 63. **Rooms:** 12. A recently renovated, bright and cheery hotel with a highly distinctive cuisine. The town is renowned for its schist roofs. 🔙 TV	MC V	●	■		
CHAMALIÈRES: *Hôtel Radio* ⒻⒻⒻ 43 avenue Pierre-Curie, 63400. 〖 04 73 30 87 83. FAX 04 73 36 42 44. **Rooms:** 26. Quiet Art Deco building decorated with vintage radios, perched on a hill overlooking Clermont-Ferrand. First-class cuisine. 🔙 TV	AE DC MC V	●	■		■
FLORAC: *Grand Hôtel du Parc* ⒻⒻ 47 avenue Jean-Monestier, 48400. 〖 04 66 45 03 05. FAX 04 66 45 11 81. **Rooms:** 60. There is an old-fashioned atmosphere to this cavernous hotel set in attractive grounds. The prices are quite reasonable. 🔙 TV	AE DC MC V		■	●	■
LAGUIOLE: *Michel Bras* ⒻⒻⒻⒻ Route de l'Aubrac, 12210. 〖 05 65 51 18 20. FAX 05 65 48 47 02. **Rooms:** 15. The Auvergne's most prestigious chef, whose cuisine is renowned for its use of wild plants, offers superb, ultramodern rooms overlooking the Aubrac Plateau. The atmosphere is surprisingly friendly. 🔙 TV	AE MC V	●	■		
LAQUEUILLE: *Les Clarines* ⒻⒻ Laqueuille-Gare, 63820. 〖 04 73 22 00 43. FAX 04 73 22 06 10. **Rooms:** 12. Simple rooms and dependable food are available at this converted farmhouse high up in the midst of rolling countryside. 🔙 TV	AE DC MC V	●	■		
MILLAU: *Château de Creissels* ⒻⒻ Route de Ste-Afrique, 12100. 〖 05 65 60 16 59. FAX 05 65 61 24 63. **Rooms:** 31. A converted 11th-century *bastide* with a vaulted dining room and modern bedrooms. Simple regional food is on the menu. There are stunning views over the Tarn Valley. 🔙	AE DC MC V	●	■	●	
MOULINS: *Hôtel de Paris-Jacquemart* ⒻⒻⒻ 21 rue de Paris, 03000. 〖 04 70 44 00 58. FAX 04 70 34 05 39. **Rooms:** 27. A stylish stopover at the gateway to the Massif Central. The rooms and the cuisine have recently been given a facelift. 🔙 TV	AE DC MC V	●	■		■

Mur-de-Barrez: *Auberge de Barrez* ⓕⓕ AE MC V
Avenue du Carladez, 12600. **(** 05 65 66 00 76. **FAX** 05 65 66 07 98. **Rooms:** 18.
A welcoming and comfortable modern hotel in the heart of hiking country. Christian Gaudel's excellent cooking is a bonus.

Najac: *Oustal del Barry* ⓕⓕ AE DC MC V
Place du Bourg, 12270. **(** 05 65 29 74 32. **FAX** 05 65 29 75 32. **Rooms:** 20.
This rustic inn overlooks the square of one of France's most picturesque villages. The cuisine is highly distinctive.

Neuvèglise: *Auberge du Pont Lanau* ⓕⓕ AE DC MC V
15260 Neuvèglise. **(** 04 71 23 57 76. **FAX** 04 71 23 53 84. **Rooms:** 8.
This inn in the Gorges de la Truyère has small but well-proportioned rooms and serves good food with a regional accent.

Plaisance: *Les Magnolias* ⓕⓕ AE MC V
Rue des Magnolias, 12550. **(** 05 65 99 77 34. **FAX** 05 65 99 70 57. **Rooms:** 6.
Giant magnolias several hundred years old surround this unspoiled 14th-century country mansion furnished with antiques.

Pontaumur: *Hôtel de la Poste* ⓕⓕ MC V
Avenue du Marronnier, 63380. **(** 04 73 79 90 15. **FAX** 04 73 79 73 17. **Rooms:** 15.
A pleasantly decorated modern hotel in a small country town. The owner-chef believes in promoting the finest local ingredients.

Pontempeyrat: *Hôtel Mistou* ⓕⓕⓕ AE MC V
Craponne-sur-Arzon, 43500. **(** 04 77 50 62 46. **FAX** 04 77 50 66 70. **Rooms:** 14.
A delightfully quiet and secluded hotel in a converted old mill. Fun-loving Bernard Roux offers consistently inventive cooking.

Roanne: *Troisgros* ⓕⓕⓕⓕⓕ AE DC MC V
Place Jean-Troisgros, 42300. **(** 04 77 71 66 97. **FAX** 04 77 70 39 77. **Rooms:** 19.
What was once a humble station hotel has become a luxurious place to stay and a world-famous culinary attraction.

St-Bonnet-le-Froid: *Auberge des Cimes* ⓕⓕⓕ MC V
St-Bonnet-le-Froid, 43290. **(** 04 71 59 93 72. **FAX** 04 71 59 93 40. **Rooms:** 12.
Gourmet pilgrims compete for rooms at this exceptional village inn run by an inspired chef whose reputation is growing.

St-Flour: *Le Bout du Monde* ⓕⓕ MC V
St-Georges, 15100. **(** 04 71 60 15 84. **FAX** 04 71 73 05 10. **Rooms:** 14.
You'll get an old-fashioned welcome at this hotel in a quiet river valley. The restaurant serves local dishes at unbeatable prices.

St-Hilaire-le-Château: *Hôtel du Thaurion* ⓕⓕ AE DC MC V
23250 St-Hilaire-le-Château. **(** 05 55 64 50 12. **FAX** 05 55 64 90 92. **Rooms:** 9.
This renovated coach stop has been in the owner's family for 200 years. His cuisine is based on old local recipes.

St-Jean-du-Bruel: *Hôtel du Midi Papillon* ⓕ MC V
12230 St-Jean-du-Bruel. **(** 05 65 62 26 04. **FAX** 05 65 62 12 97. **Rooms:** 19.
A quiet, friendly hotel overlooking a flower garden and a river. The food is good and breakfast is especially recommended.

St-Privat-d'Allier: *La Vieille Auberge* ⓕⓕ MC V
Route de Saugues, 43580. **(** 04 71 57 20 56. **FAX** 04 71 57 22 50. **Rooms:** 17.
A recently renovated, pleasantly rustic village inn. The rooms and the food (hearty and simple) are an excellent value.

Salers: *Hostellerie de la Maronne* ⓕⓕⓕ AE MC V
Le Theil, St-Martin Valmeroux 15140. **(** 04 71 69 20 33. **FAX** 04 71 69 28 22. **Rooms:** 21.
Built as a 19th-century mansion, this stylish hotel is a peaceful haven. Its restaurant is a treat for gourmets.

Vichy: *Le Pavillon d'Enghien* ⓕⓕⓕ AE DC MC V
32 rue Callou, 03200. **(** 04 70 98 33 30. **FAX** 04 70 31 67 82. **Rooms:** 22.
There's something of Vichy's prewar spa atmosphere to this small, reasonably priced hotel opposite the Callou Baths.

Villefort: *Hôtel Balme* ⓕⓕ AE DC MC V
Place du Portalet, 48800. **(** 04 66 46 80 14. **FAX** 04 66 46 85 26. **Rooms:** 18.
An unusual hotel that has a mini-museum devoted to the chestnut. The cuisine is influenced by the chef's travels in the Orient.

	CREDIT CARDS	CHILDREN'S FACILITIES	PARKING FACILITIES	SWIMMING POOL	GARDEN
Price categories for a standard double room (not per person) for one night, including tax and service charges, but not including breakfast.　**CHILDREN'S FACILITIES** Cribs and baby-sitting available. Some hotels provide children's portions and high chairs in the restaurant.					

Price categories for a standard double room (not per person) for one night, including tax and service charges, but not including breakfast.

Ⓕ under F200
ⒻⒻ F200–400
ⒻⒻⒻ F400–600
ⒻⒻⒻⒻ F600–1,000
ⒻⒻⒻⒻⒻ over F1,000

CHILDREN'S FACILITIES
Cribs and baby-sitting available. Some hotels provide children's portions and high chairs in the restaurant.
PARKING FACILITIES
Parking provided by the hotel in either a private lot or a private garage very close by.
SWIMMING POOL
Hotel pools are often quite small and are outdoors unless otherwise stated.
GARDEN
Hotel with garden, courtyard or terrace, often providing tables for eating outside.

Hotel	Price	Credit Cards	Children's Facilities	Parking Facilities	Swimming Pool	Garden
VITRAC: *Auberge de la Tommette* 15220 Vitrac. 📞 04 71 64 70 94. ℻ 04 71 64 77 11. *Rooms: 15.* The main hotel stands in a flowery park. Its handsome dining room is attractively paneled. 🛏 📺	ⒻⒻ	AE MC V	●	■	●	■
YDES: *Château de Trancis* 15210 Ydes. 📞 04 71 40 60 40. ℻ 04 71 40 62 13. *Rooms: 7.* On the fringes of the Auvergne Regional Park, this stylish château offers well-equipped rooms and an ornate Louis XIV salon. 🛏 📺	ⒻⒻⒻⒻ	AE MC V		■	●	■

THE RHÔNE VALLEY AND FRENCH ALPS

Hotel	Price	Credit Cards	Children's Facilities	Parking Facilities	Swimming Pool	Garden
AIX-LES-BAINS: *Hôtel Le Manoir* 37 rue Georges-1er, 73105. 📞 04 79 61 44 00. ℻ 04 79 35 67 67. *Rooms: 73.* A charming old hotel in the Parc du Splendide-Royal, within walking distance of the thermal baths. 🛏 📺	ⒻⒻ	AE DC MC V	●	■	●	■
ALBERTVILLE: *Hôtel Million* 8 place de la Liberté, 73200. 📞 04 79 32 25 15. ℻ 04 79 32 25 36. *Rooms: 26.* Established in 1770 by an ancestor of the present owner, this hotel is known for its restaurant, which serves superb *savoyard* cuisine. 🛏 📺	ⒻⒻ	AE DC MC V				■
ANNECY: *Hôtel de l'Abbaye* 15 chemin de l'Abbaye, 74940. 📞 04 50 23 61 08. ℻ 04 50 27 77 65. *Rooms: 18.* A charming hotel-restaurant occupying a former 15th-century Dominican convent surrounded by gardens. 🛏 📺	ⒻⒻⒻ	AE DC MC V	●	■		■
BAGNOLS: *Château de Bagnols* 69620 Bagnols. 📞 04 74 71 40 00. ℻ 04 74 71 40 49. *Rooms: 20.* This exquisite 13th-century château north of Lyon is set on a hilltop surrounded by Beaujolais vineyards. 🛏 ▤ 📺	ⒻⒻⒻⒻⒻ	AE DC MC V	●	■		■
BOURG-EN-BRESSE: *Hôtel du Prieuré* 49–51 boulevard de Brou, 01000. 📞 04 72 22 44 60. ℻ 04 74 22 71 07. *Rooms: 14.* A charming hotel surrounded by gardens and 16th-century stone walls, only a minute's walk from the famous Eglise de Brou. The large bedrooms are furnished in French country style. 🛏 📺	ⒻⒻⒻ	AE DC MC V	●	■		■
CHAMBÉRY: *Hôtel des Princes* 4 rue de Boigne, 73000. 📞 04 79 33 45 36. ℻ 04 79 70 31 47. *Rooms: 45.* Set in the grandest section of the Old Town, this pleasantly old-fashioned hotel offers comfortable rooms and a good restaurant. 🛏 📺	ⒻⒻ	AE DC MC V	●	■		
CHAMONIX-MONT-BLANC: *Le Hameau Albert 1er* 119 impasse du Montenvers, 74402. 📞 04 50 53 05 09. ℻ 04 50 55 95 48. *Rooms: 41.* This large but welcoming chalet-style hotel offers elegantly furnished rooms with stupendous views of Mont Blanc. Its restaurant has a reputation for serving the best food in town. 🛏 📺	ⒻⒻⒻⒻⒻ	AE DC MC V	●	■	●	■
COMBLOUX: *Aux Ducs de Savoie* 253 route du Bouchet, 74920. 📞 04 50 58 61 43. ℻ 04 50 58 67 43. *Rooms: 50.* The rooms in this modern hotel are well-equipped and some of them face Mont Blanc. A five-course meal is served every night. 🛏 📺	ⒻⒻⒻ	AE DC MC V	●	■	●	■
CORDON: *Le Cordonant* 74700 Cordon. 📞 04 50 58 34 56. ℻ 04 50 47 95 57. *Rooms: 16.* A friendly family-run hotel west of Chamonix offering comfortable rooms with views of Mont Blanc and an excellent *table d'hôte* menu. 🛏 📺	ⒻⒻ	MC V		■		■
COURCHEVEL: *La Sivolière* 1850 Route des Chenus, 73120. 📞 04 79 08 08 33. ℻ 04 79 08 15 73. *Rooms: 30.* Attracting such distinguished guests as the Spanish royal family, this tastefully decorated hotel lies at the foot of the ski-runs. 🛏 📺	ⒻⒻⒻⒻ	MC V	●	■		

EVIAN-LES-BAINS: *Hôtel Royal* ⒻⒻⒻⒻ
Rive Sud du Lac-de-Génève, 74500. █ 04 50 26 85 00. FAX 04 55 37 28 92. *Rooms: 154.*
This imposing turn-of-the-century hotel houses six restaurants and offers everything from jogging trails to children's activities. �It TV
AE DC MC V

EVIAN-LES-BAINS: *Hôtel de la Verniaz et ses Chalets* ⒻⒻⒻⒻ
Avenue d'Abondance, 74500. █ 04 50 75 04 90. FAX 04 50 70 78 92. *Rooms: 34.*
Set on a hill above Evian, this glamorous establishment consists of a central villa and five chalets, each with its own garden. 🚱 ▤ TV
AE DC MC V

GRENOBLE: *Parc Hôtel* ⒻⒻⒻⒻⒻ
10 place Paul-Mistral, 38027. █ 04 76 85 81 23. FAX 04 76 46 49 88. *Rooms: 52.*
Grenoble's leading modern hotel offers comfortably furnished rooms with many amenities. Staff are friendly and helpful. 🚱 ▤ TV
AE DC MC V

LA CHAPELLE-EN-VERCORS: *Hôtel Bellier* ⒻⒻ
26420 La Chapelle-en-Vercors. █ 04 75 48 20 03. FAX 04 75 48 25 31. *Rooms: 12.*
Set in the Vercors massif southwest of Grenoble, this family-run chalet-style hotel is friendly and unassuming. 🚱 TV
AE DC MC V

LAMASTRE: *Château d'Urbillac* ⒻⒻⒻⒻ
Route de Vernoux, 07270. █ 04 75 06 42 11. FAX 04 75 06 52 75. *Rooms: 12.*
A 16th-century château, restored with rooms in 19th-century style and set in a vast area of parkland in the beautiful Ardèche region. 🚱
AE DC MC V

LE POËT LAVAL: *Les Hospitaliers* ⒻⒻⒻⒻ
26160 Le Poët Laval. █ 04 75 46 22 32. FAX 04 75 46 49 99. *Rooms: 22.*
A beautifully restored hotel in the center of a tiny medieval hilltop village east of Montélimar. First-class service and cuisine. 🚱
AE DC MC V

LES ROCHES-DE-CONDRIEU: *Hôtel Bellevue* ⒻⒻ
Quai du Rhône, 38370. █ 04 74 56 41 42. FAX 04 74 56 47 56. *Rooms: 18.*
This friendly modern hotel southwest of Vienne has comfortable rooms with balconies and a pleasant restaurant overlooking the Rhône River.
AE MC V

LYON: *Hôtel des Artistes* ⒻⒻⒻ
8 rue Gaspard-André, 69002. █ 04 78 42 04 88. FAX 04 78 42 93 76. *Rooms: 45.*
Close to place Bellecour and next door to the Théâtre des Célestins, this delightful hotel is a favorite haunt of actors and revue artists. 🚱 TV
AE DC MC V

LYON: *Hôtel Carlton* ⒻⒻⒻ
4 rue Jussieu, 69002. █ 04 78 42 56 51. FAX 04 78 42 10 71. *Rooms: 83.*
In the heart of the Presqu'île near the Rhône, this recently renovated hotel still retains traces of its elegant Belle Epoque days. 🚱 ▤ TV
AE DC JCB MC V

LYON: *Cour des Loges* ⒻⒻⒻⒻⒻ
6 rue du Boeuf, 69005. █ 04 78 42 75 75. FAX 04 72 40 93 61. *Rooms: 73.*
A luxury hotel occupying four renovated Renaissance mansions in the heart of Vieux Lyon. Bedrooms are modern in style. 🚱 ▤ TV
AE DC MC V

MALATAVERNE: *Domaine du Colombier* ⒻⒻⒻⒻ
Route de Donzère, 26780. █ 04 75 90 86 86. FAX 04 75 90 79 40. *Rooms: 25.*
Occupying a 14th-century abbey south of Montélimar, this welcoming hotel has stylish rooms and a big garden with a swimming pool. 🚱 TV
AE DC MC V

MANIGOD: *Hôtel de la Croix-Fry* ⒻⒻⒻⒻ
Route du Col de la Croix-Fry, 74230. █ 04 50 44 90 16. FAX 04 50 44 94 87. *Rooms: 12.*
High on a mountain pass east of Annecy, this delightful chalet-style hotel combines Alpine rustic with comfort and fine facilities. 🚱 TV
AE MC V

MEGÈVE: *Le Fer à Cheval* ⒻⒻⒻⒻ
36 route du Crêt-d'Arbois, 74120. █ 04 50 21 30 39. FAX 04 50 93 07 60. *Rooms: 47.*
A charming hotel with an authentic Savoy atmosphere. 🚱 TV
AE MC V

MORZINE: *Les Prodains* ⒻⒻ
Village des Prodains, 74110. █ 04 50 79 25 26. FAX 04 50 75 76 17. *Rooms: 14.*
Situated at the foot of the slopes in the village, facilities at Les Prodains include an outdoor swimming pool for summer bathing. 🚱 TV
MC V

PÉROUGES: *Hostellerie du Vieux Pérouges* ⒻⒻⒻⒻ
Place du Tilleul, 01800. █ 04 74 61 00 88. FAX 04 74 34 77 90. *Rooms: 28.*
This historic Bresson inn is a filmmaker's dream, converted from 13th-century buildings and set in a medieval hilltop village. 🚱 TV
AE MC V

Price categories for a standard double room (not per person) for one night, including tax and service charges, but not including breakfast.

- (F) under F200
- (F)(F) F200–400
- (F)(F)(F) F400–600
- (F)(F)(F)(F) F600–1,000
- (F)(F)(F)(F)(F) over F1,000

CHILDREN'S FACILITIES
Cribs and baby-sitting available. Some hotels provide children's portions and high chairs in the restaurant.

PARKING FACILITIES
Parking provided by the hotel in either a private lot or a private garage very close by.

SWIMMING POOL
Hotel pools are often quite small and are outdoors unless otherwise stated.

GARDEN
Hotel with garden, courtyard or terrace, often providing tables for eating outside.

Hotel	Price	Credit Cards	Children's Facilities	Parking Facilities	Swimming Pool	Garden
SAINT-LATTIER: *Le Lièvre Amoureux* Quartier de la Gare, 38840. ☎ 04 76 64 50 67. FAX 04 76 64 31 21. *Rooms: 12.* Facing the foothills of the Vercors, just east of Valence, is this small, welcoming hotel with a charming old-fashioned atmosphere.	(F)(F)	AE DC MC V	●	▣	●	▣
TALLOIRES: *Hôtel de l'Abbaye* Route du Port, 74290. ☎ 04 50 60 77 33. FAX 04 50 60 78 81. *Rooms: 31.* An elegant hotel occupying a former 17th-century Benedictine abbey, beautifully situated on the shores of Lac d'Annecy.	(F)(F)(F)(F)(F)	AE DC MC V	●	▣		▣
TALLOIRES: *Hôtel Beau-Site* 74290 Talloires. ☎ 04 50 60 71 04. FAX 04 50 60 79 22. *Rooms: 29.* This elegant hotel is especially noted for its warm and friendly atmosphere. Boating and water sports on the nearby lake.	(F)(F)(F)(F)	AE DC MC	●	▣	●	

POITOU AND AQUITAINE

Hotel	Price	Credit Cards	Children's Facilities	Parking Facilities	Swimming Pool	Garden
ARCACHON: *Arc-Hôtel-sur-Mer* 89 boulevard de la Plage, 33120. ☎ 05 56 83 06 85. FAX 05 56 83 53 72. *Rooms: 30.* An outdoor pool, sandy beach nearby, sea views and pleasant location enhance the appeal of this comfortable resort hotel.	(F)(F)(F)(F)	AE DC MC V	●	▣	●	▣
BEQUEY-CADILLAC: *Hôtel du Château de la Tour* Route départementale 10, 33410. ☎ 05 56 76 92 00. FAX 05 56 62 11 59. *Rooms: 32.* An appealing hotel with good facilities in a historic village. A good base to explore surrounding wine country.	(F)(F)	AE DC MC V	●	▣		▣
BORDEAUX: *Grand Hôtel Français* 12 rue du Temple, 33000. ☎ 05 56 48 10 35. FAX 05 56 81 76 18. *Rooms: 35.* A good value hotel in the center of town with attractively decorated, comfortable and quiet rooms. No restaurant.	(F)(F)(F)	AE DC MC V	●			
CIERZAC: *Moulin de Cierzac* 17520 Cierzac. ☎ 05 45 83 01 32. FAX 05 45 83 03 59. *Rooms: 10.* South of Cognac is this small hotel-restaurant in a 17th-century country house with a vast collection of Cognac, "the water of life."	(F)(F)	AE DC MC V		▣		▣
COGNAC: *Les Pigeons Blancs* 110 rue Jules Brisson, 16100. ☎ 05 45 82 16 36. FAX 05 45 82 29 29. *Rooms: 7.* A small, excellent value hotel-restaurant that has been in the same family since the 18th century.	(F)(F)(F)	AE DC MC V		▣		▣
CONFOLENS: *Hôtel de Vienne* 4 rue de la Ferrandie, 16500. ☎ 05 45 84 09 24. FAX 05 45 84 11 60. *Rooms: 15.* A basic and reasonably priced hotel with a perfect setting beside the Vienne River, and a lovely flowered terrace used for meals. Traditional decor and food. Ask for a room with a view.	(F)(F)	MC V				▣
COULON: *Hôtel du Marais* 46-48 quai Louis Tardy, 79510. ☎ 05 49 35 90 43. FAX 05 49 35 81 98. *Rooms: 18.* Situated in the mysterious fens of the Marais Poitevin is this lovely little hotel. Boats can be rented in the town.	(F)(F)	MC V	●			
EUGÉNIE-LES-BAINS: *Les Prés d'Eugénie* 40320 Eugénie-les-Bains. ☎ 05 58 05 06 07. FAX 05 58 51 10 10. *Rooms: 40.* The illustrious chef Michel Guérard draws worshipers to his delightful hotel, cuisine and thermal spa. Less costly accommodation is available on the same grounds. Truly a treat to stay here.	(F)(F)(F)(F)(F)	AE DC MC V	●	▣	●	▣
GRADIGNAN: *Le Chalet Lyrique* 169 cours du Général-de-Gaulle, 33170. ☎ 05 56 89 11 59. FAX 05 56 89 53 37. *Rooms: 44.* Not too far away from the Bordeaux-Mérignac airport, this is a pleasant stop-over with a magnificent patio.	(F)(F)	AE DC MC V	●	▣		▣

GRENADE-SUR-L'ADOUR: *Pain Adour et Fantasie* ⒻⒻⒻ
14–16 place de Tilleuls, 40270. 〖 05 58 45 18 80. FAX 05 58 45 16 57. *Rooms: 11.*
Timber and stone adorn this graceful 18th-century hotel set beside the
Adour River. A memorable setting and acclaimed cuisine.

HIERSAC: *Hostellerie de Maine Brun* ⒻⒻⒻ
La Vigerie, 16290. 〖 05 45 90 83 00. FAX 05 45 96 91 14. *Rooms: 20.*
A mill on the pretty banks of the Nouère has become a supremely
relaxing hotel with much to enjoy – cuisine, wines and Cognac.

HOSSEGOR: *Hôtel de la Plage* ⒻⒻ
Place des Landais, 40150. 〖 05 58 41 76 41. FAX 05 58 41 76 54. *Rooms: 7.*
Situated in a very popular summer resort is this affordable, attractive
hotel on the beach. Ask for a room with a sea view.

LA ROCHELLE: *Les Brises* ⒻⒻⒻ
Chemin de la Digue de Richelieu, 17000. 〖 05 46 43 89 37. FAX 05 46 43 27 97.
Rooms: 50. A comfortable and well-liked hotel to the west of this
handsome city. Wonderful views out to sea.

MAGESCQ: *Relais de la Poste* ⒻⒻⒻⒻ
40140 Magescq. 〖 05 58 47 70 25. FAX 05 58 47 76 17. *Rooms: 13.*
A small hotel with gardens and pools perfectly combining comfort,
celebrated cuisine, fine wines and family tradition.

MARGAUX: *Relais de Margaux* ⒻⒻⒻⒻ
Chemin de l'Ile Vincent, 33460. 〖 05 57 88 38 30. FAX 05 57 88 31 73. *Rooms: 64.*
The high price at this luxurious hotel is money well spent. Peaceful
setting, handsome grounds, pool, tennis and exquisite food.

MIMIZAN: *Au Bon Coin du Lac* ⒻⒻⒻ
34 avenue du lac, 40200. 〖 05 58 09 01 55. FAX 05 58 09 40 84. *Rooms: 18.*
The cuisine at this small hotel is a prime draw, not to mention its very
agreeable setting among pine trees beside a lake.

NIEUIL: *Château de Nieuil* ⒻⒻⒻⒻ
16270 Nieuil. 〖 05 45 71 36 38. FAX 05 45 71 46 45. *Rooms: 14.*
King François I hunted in the extensive park embracing this spectacular
Renaissance château, transformed in the 1930s into a hotel.

POITIERS: *Château Clos de la Ribaudière* ⒻⒻⒻ
Chasseneuil-du-Poitou, 86360. 〖 05 49 52 86 66. FAX 05 49 52 86 32. *Rooms: 41.*
A restored 19th-century house in a riverside park near Poitiers – a
haven of peace and comfort away from the busy city.

RETJONS: *L'Hostellerie Landaise* Ⓕ
40120 Retjons. 〖 05 58 93 36 33. *Rooms: 6.*
Architecturally a true *auberge landaise*, set in its own park with a
lake with ducks. A delightful stop featuring a very talented chef.

ROYAN: *Family Golf Hôtel* ⒻⒻⒻ
28 boulevard Garnier, 17200. 〖 05 46 05 14 66. FAX 05 46 06 52 56. *Rooms: 33.*
An unpretentious hotel on the seafront in a large and lively resort just
north of the Gironde. Centrally located, but no restaurant.

SABRES: *Auberge des Pins* ⒻⒻ
Route de la Piscine, 40630. 〖 05 58 07 50 47. FAX 05 58 07 56 74. *Rooms: 25.*
Deep in the forests of the Landes Regional Park, this comfortable
auberge has been called the very model of a family hotel.

ST-CLAUD: *Le Bragier* ⒻⒻ
16450 Saint-Claud. 〖 05 45 71 47 49. *Rooms: 3.*
On the edge of open meadows and woods in a rural hamlet is this
vegetarian chambres d'hôte where guests are encouraged to feel at home.

ST-EMILION: *Château Meylet* ⒻⒻ
"La Gomerie", 33330. 〖 05 57 24 68 85. *Rooms: 4.*
A renovated, homey farmhouse surrounded by its own vineyards –
perfect for exploring the area. Price includes a good breakfast.

ST-EMILION: *Hostellerie Plaisance* ⒻⒻⒻⒻ
5 place du Clocher, 33330. 〖 05 57 55 07 55. FAX 05 57 74 41 11. *Rooms: 12.*
An excellent small hotel in a striking building in the upper part of this
town, famous for its wine. Delicious food is served.

For key to symbols see back flap

	CREDIT CARDS	CHILDREN'S FACILITIES	PARKING FACILITIES	SWIMMING POOL	GARDEN

Price categories for a standard double room (not per person) for one night, including tax and service charges, but not including breakfast.
- Ⓕ under F200
- ⒻⒻ F200–400
- ⒻⒻⒻ F400–600
- ⒻⒻⒻⒻ F600–1,000
- ⒻⒻⒻⒻⒻ over F1,000

CHILDREN'S FACILITIES
Cribs and baby-sitting available. Some hotels provide children's portions and high chairs in the restaurant.

PARKING FACILITIES
Parking provided by the hotel in either a lot or a private garage very close by.

SWIMMING POOL
Hotel pools are often quite small and are outdoors unless otherwise stated.

GARDEN
Hotel with garden, courtyard or terrace, often providing tables for eating outside.

VELLUIRE: *Auberge de la Rivière* ⒻⒻ Rue Fouarne, 85770. 📞 05 51 52 32 15. FAX 05 51 52 37 42. **Rooms:** 11. A secluded, ivy-covered inn on the banks of the Vendée River. Rooms are comfortable with river views. Worth a visit for the superb food. 🛏 TV	MC V		■		■
VILLENEUVE-DE-MARSAN: *Hélène Darroze* ⒻⒻⒻ 57 Grand rue, 40190. 📞 05 58 45 20 07. FAX 05 58 45 82 67. **Rooms:** 14. A country-house hotel set in pine-shaded grounds. Darroze is a distinguished family name with a long tradition of fine cuisine. 🛏 TV	AE DC MC V	●	■	●	■

PÉRIGORD, QUERCY AND GASCONY

ALBI: *Hostellerie du Vigan* ⒻⒻ 16 place du Vigan, 81000. 📞 05 63 54 01 23. FAX 05 63 47 05 42. **Rooms:** 40. A very good value hotel in the center of town that is unpretentious, comfortable and inexpensive. Excellent restaurant. 🛏 TV	AE DC MC V	●	■		■
ALBI: *Hôtel St-Clair* ⒻⒻ 8 rue St-Clair, 81000. 📞 05 63 54 25 66. **Rooms:** 11. An 18th-century hotel that has been in the same family for generations. Nicely converted and furnished with antiques. Centrally located. 🛏 TV	MC V		■		
AUVILLAR: *d'Astros* ⒻⒻ Le Pin, 82340. 📞 05 63 95 95 20. FAX 05 63 95 93 55. **Rooms:** 4. A small, friendly guest house set well off the tourist track in a large, secluded garden. Also caters to vegetarians and special diets. 🛏		●			■
BEYNAC: *Hôtel Bonnet* ⒻⒻ 24220 Beynac. 📞 05 53 29 50 01. FAX 05 53 29 83 74. **Rooms:** 21. This small village hotel is named after the family who have owned it for years. Simple, airy and traditional in style. 🛏	AE MC V		■		■
BRANTÔME: *Le Chatenet* ⒻⒻⒻ 24310 Brantôme. 📞 05 53 05 81 08. FAX 05 53 05 85 52. **Rooms:** 8. Off the busy riverside road lies this beautifully restored 17th-century manor house. Facilities include tennis courts and a clubhouse. 🛏 TV	MC V	●	■	●	■
BRANTÔME: *Le Moulin de l'Abbaye* ⒻⒻⒻⒻ 1 route de Bourdeilles, 24310. 📞 05 53 05 80 22. FAX 05 53 05 75 27. **Rooms:** 20. A handsome, old, creeper-covered mill standing next to the Dronne River. The dining room extends to a terrace over the river. 🛏 TV	AE DC MC V	●	■		■
CAHORS: *Terminus* ⒻⒻⒻ 5 avenue Charles-de-Freycinet, 46000. 📞 05 65 35 24 50. FAX 05 65 22 06 40. **Rooms:** 22 A good find in the heart of truffle country, only two minutes from the station. Elegant 1920s-style decor and stained-glass windows. 🛏 TV	AE MC V	●	■		
CARSAC-AILLAC: *Le Relais du Touron* ⒻⒻ 24200 Carsac-Aillac. 📞 05 53 28 16 70. FAX 05 53 28 52 51. **Rooms:** 12. Set in wooded countryside just east of Sarlat is this serene, 19th-century small mansion. Simple but exquisitely cooked food. 🛏 TV	MC V		■		■
CHAMPAGNAC-DE-BELAIR: *Hôtel Moulin du Roc* ⒻⒻⒻⒻ 24530 Champagnac-de-Belair. 📞 05 53 02 86 00. FAX 05 53 54 21 31. **Rooms:** 13. In a beautiful setting by a quiet stream just outside Brantôme is this converted walnut mill. Indoor pool and wonderful food. 🛏 TV	AE DC MC V	●	■	●	■
COLY: *Manoir d'Hautegente* ⒻⒻⒻⒻ Coly 24120. 📞 05 53 51 68 03. FAX 05 53 50 38 52. **Rooms:** 14. Just north of Sarlat is this picturesque mansion, once the mill and forge of an abbey. Family-run, friendly hotel with real fireplaces, private fishing, swimming pool and library. 🛏 TV	AE DC MC V	●	■	●	■

CONDOM: *Hôtel des Trois Lys* Ⓕ Ⓕ Ⓕ
38 rue Gambetta, 32100. 【 *05 62 28 33 33*. FAX *05 62 28 41 85*. **Rooms:** 10.
In the heart of Armagnac country is this well-run 17th-century hotel.
Breakfast is served on the patio. 🛏 ≣ TV

AE DC MC V

DOMME: *Hôtel de l'Esplanade* Ⓕ Ⓕ
24250 Domme. 【 *05 53 28 31 41*. FAX *05 53 28 49 92*. **Rooms:** 25.
Perched on the clifftop is this hotel with a panoramic dining terrace.
Rooms are tastefully decorated, some with fantastic views. 🛏 ≣ TV

AE DC MC V

DURAS: *Hostellerie des Ducs* Ⓕ Ⓕ
47120 Duras. 【 *05 53 83 74 58*. FAX *05 53 83 75 03*. **Rooms:** 15.
Situated between the Dordogne and Garonne rivers is this simple,
family-run hostelry overlooking a 14th-century fortress. 🛏 TV

AE DC MC V

FLORIMONT-GAUMIERS: *La Daille* Ⓕ Ⓕ
24250 Dordogne. 【 *05 53 28 40 71*. **Rooms:** 4.
A short drive from Gaumier's, this stone-built farmhouse
has marvellous views. Good food. 🛏

GARABIT: *Hôtel-restaurant Beau Site* Ⓕ Ⓕ
Garabit, Loubaresse, 15320. 【 *05 71 23 41 46*. FAX *05 71 23 46 34*. **Rooms:** 17.
Well named for its spectacular views of the lake and Eiffel's viaduct, this hotel
also offers large, comfortable rooms, good food, and a heated pool. 🛏 TV

DC MC V

LACAVE: *Le Pont de l'Ouysse* Ⓕ Ⓕ Ⓕ
46200 Lacave. 【 *05 65 37 87 04*. FAX *05 65 32 77 41*. **Rooms:** 14.
A chic restaurant-with-rooms not far from Rocamadour. Inventive
variations on local dishes are offered. 🛏 ≣ TV

AE DC MC V

LA COQUILLE: *Hôtel des Voyageurs* Ⓕ Ⓕ
Rue de la République, 24450. 【 *05 53 52 80 13*. FAX *05 60 18 29*. **Rooms:** 10.
This small village hotel is friendly and comfortable.
Enjoy delicious regional food in the tartan dining room. 🛏 TV

MC V

LES EYZIES-DE-TAYAC: *Le Moulin de la Beune* Ⓕ Ⓕ
24620 Les Eyzies-de-Tayac. 【 *05 53 06 94 33*. FAX *05 53 06 98 06*. **Rooms:** 20
Huge, comfortable rooms in a converted mill. Reasonably priced
and efficiently run. The restaurant has a very good reputation. 🛏

AE MC V

LES EYZIES-DE-TAYAC: *Le Centenaire* Ⓕ Ⓕ Ⓕ Ⓕ
24620 Les Eyzies-de-Tayac. 【 *05 53 06 68 68*. FAX *05 53 06 92 41*. **Rooms:** 20.
A luxurious, modern hotel just outside the town. Spacious bedrooms
with balconies overlooking the lawn and swimming pool. 🛏 ≣ TV

AE DC MC V

MARQUAY: *Hôtel des Bories* Ⓕ Ⓕ
24620 Marquay. 【 *05 53 29 67 02*. FAX *05 53 29 64 15*. **Rooms:** 30.
An unassuming hotel at an outstanding price. Family-run with basic
rooms and beamed ceilings. Lake with water sports nearby. 🛏 TV

MC V

MERCUÈS: *Château de Mercuès* Ⓕ Ⓕ Ⓕ Ⓕ Ⓕ
46090 Mercuès. 【 *05 65 20 00 01*. FAX *05 65 20 05 72*. **Rooms:** 31.
Situated beside the Lot River is this 12th-century turreted château that
has been tastefully modernized. Generous breakfasts. 🛏 TV

AE DC MC V

MEYRONNE: *La Terrasse* Ⓕ Ⓕ
46200 Meyronne. 【 *05 65 32 21 60*. FAX *05 65 32 26 93*. **Rooms:** 18.
This converted monastery has some of its bedrooms in the adjacent
9th-century château. Meals are eaten in the large dining room. 🛏 TV

AE DC MC V

NONTRON: *Le Grand Hôtel* Ⓕ Ⓕ
3 place A-Agard, 24300. 【 *05 53 56 11 22*. FAX *05 53 56 59 94*. **Rooms:** 25.
Very reasonably priced and well-run hotel in the center of this market
town. Swimming pool, pretty garden and good, simple food. 🛏

MC V

PÉRIGUEUX: *Hôtel Périgord* Ⓕ Ⓕ
74 rue Victor Hugo, 24000. 【 *05 53 53 33 63*. FAX *05 53 08 19 74*. **Rooms:** 20.
Close to the old center of the delightful town is this fabulous
little find. The restaurant offers affordable, traditional cuisine. 🛏 TV

MC V

RIBÉRAC: *Pauliac* Ⓕ Ⓕ
Celles, 24600. 【 *05 53 91 97 45*. FAX *05 53 90 43 46*. **Rooms:** 5.
A basic, well-restored farmhouse set in a tiny hamlet. There is a
terraced garden and tables outside. Good, wholesome food. 🛏

MC V

For key to symbols see back flap

		Price categories for a standard double room (not per person) for one night, including tax and service charges, but not including breakfast. Ⓕ under F200 ⒻⒻ F200–400 ⒻⒻⒻ F400–600 ⒻⒻⒻⒻ F600–1,000 ⒻⒻⒻⒻⒻ over F1,000	**CHILDREN'S FACILITIES** Cribs and baby-sitting available. Some hotels provide children's portions and high chairs in the restaurant. **PARKING FACILITIES** Parking provided by the hotel in either a lot or a private garage very close by. **SWIMMING POOL** Hotel pools are often quite small and are outdoors unless otherwise stated. **GARDEN** Hotel with garden, courtyard or terrace, often providing tables for eating outside.	CREDIT CARDS	CHILDREN'S FACILITIES	PARKING FACILITIES	SWIMMING POOL	GARDEN

ROCAMADOUR: *Domaine de la Rhue* ⒻⒻⒻ
46500 Rocamadour. ☎ 05 65 33 71 50. FAX 05 65 33 72 48. *Rooms:* 12.
Only a few minutes' drive from Rocamadour is this peaceful hotel – a 19th-century stone building, imaginatively converted. Spacious rooms. 🛏
Credit Cards: DC MC V — Children's Facilities ● — Swimming Pool ●

ST-CIRQ-LAPOPIE: *Hôtel de la Pélissaria* ⒻⒻⒻ
46330 St-Cirq-Lapopie. ☎ 05 65 31 25 14. FAX 05 65 30 25 52. *Rooms:* 10.
A tiny hotel in a clifftop village above the Lot River. The rooms have tiled floors, white walls, exposed beams and pine doors. 🛏 📺
Credit Cards: MC V — Swimming Pool ●

SARLAT-LA-CANÉDA: *Hostellerie de Meysset* ⒻⒻⒻ
Route des Eyzies, 24200. ☎ 05 53 59 08 29. FAX 05 53 28 47 61. *Rooms:* 26.
Built in local style and set in its own park is this pleasant rural hotel. French windows open onto the lawn. Excellent food. 🛏 📺
Credit Cards: AE DC MC V — Children's Facilities ● — Parking ■ — Garden ■

TAMNIÈS: *Hôtel Laborderie* ⒻⒻ
24620 Tamniès. ☎ 05 53 29 68 59. FAX 05 53 29 65 31. *Rooms:* 40.
Between Sarlat and Les Eyzies lies this family-run, modern hotel. Log fires in winter and swimming and outdoor meals in summer. 🛏 📺
Credit Cards: MC V — Children's Facilities ● — Parking ■ — Swimming Pool ● — Garden ■

TOULOUSE: *Hôtel Albert 1er* ⒻⒻ
8 rue Rivals, 31000. ☎ 05 61 21 17 91. FAX 05 61 21 09 64. *Rooms:* 50.
A well-priced hotel, centrally situated with cheerful rooms and modern bathrooms. Small lounge and breakfast room but no restaurant. 🛏 🍽 📺
Credit Cards: AE DC MC V — Children's Facilities ●

TOULOUSE: *Hôtel Jean-Mermoz* ⒻⒻⒻ
50 rue Matabiau, 31000. ☎ 05 61 63 04 04. FAX 05 61 63 15 64. *Rooms:* 53.
A modern hotel in the center of town that is comfortable, friendly and surprisingly quiet. Pleasant garden and restaurant. 🛏 🍽 📺
Credit Cards: AE DC MC V — Children's Facilities ● — Parking ■ — Garden ■

VIEUX MAREUIL: *Château de Vieux-Mareuil* ⒻⒻⒻ
Rte Angoulême-Périgueux, 24340. ☎ 05 53 60 77 15. FAX 05 53 56 49 33. *Rooms:* 14.
Spacious bedrooms and delicious cuisine can be found at this 15th-century fortified hotel. Acres of parkland to explore. 🛏 📺
Credit Cards: AE DC MC V — Children's Facilities ● — Parking ■ — Swimming Pool ● — Garden ■

THE PYRENEES

AÏNHOA: *Hôtel-Restaurant Ithurria* ⒻⒻⒻ
64250 Aïnhoa. ☎ 05 59 29 92 11. FAX 05 59 29 81 28. *Rooms:* 27.
With its cozy rooms, beamed dining room and gourmet cooking, this old coaching inn in one of the prettiest Basque villages is a satisfying place to stay. 🛏 📺
Credit Cards: AE MC V — Children's Facilities ● — Parking ■ — Swimming Pool ● — Garden ■

ANGLET: *Château de Brindos* ⒻⒻⒻⒻ
Allée du Château, 64600. ☎ 05 59 23 17 68. FAX 05 59 23 48 47. *Rooms:* 13.
Life is calm and gracious here beside the peaceful lake. The beach is only a short drive away, and there is also a golf course nearby. 🛏 📺
Credit Cards: AE DC V — Children's Facilities ● — Parking ■ — Swimming Pool ● — Garden ■

ARGELÈS-GAZOST: *Hôtel le Miramont* ⒻⒻ
44 avenue des Pyrénées, 65400. ☎ 05 62 97 01 26. FAX 05 62 97 56 67. *Rooms:* 28.
A stylish, comfortable hotel with a garden in a small spa town. The attractive restaurant serves delicious food. 🛏 📺
Credit Cards: MC V — Children's Facilities ● — Parking ■ — Garden ■

ARREAU: *Hôtel d'Angleterre* ⒻⒻ
Route de Luchon, 65240. ☎ 05 62 98 63 30. FAX 05 62 98 69 66. *Rooms:* 24.
Four rivers flow through little Arreau, past slate-roofed houses. This 17th-century inn serves savory mountain food at a good price. A suitable base for exploring the stunning countryside. 🛏 📺
Credit Cards: MC V — Children's Facilities ● — Parking ■ — Swimming Pool ● — Garden ■

BARBAZAN: *Hostellerie de L'Aristou* ⒻⒻ
Route Sauveterre, 31510. ☎ 05 61 88 30 67. FAX 05 61 95 55 66. *Rooms:* 7.
This pleasant country house has a fine restaurant and is ideal for exploring the nearby Roman ruins. 🛏 📺
Credit Cards: AE DC MC V — Children's Facilities ● — Parking ■

BIARRITZ: *Château du Claire de Lune* Ⓕ Ⓕ Ⓕ
48 avenue Alan-Seeger, 64200. 【 *05 59 41 53 20.* FAX *05 59 41 53 29.* **Rooms:** *16.*
This Belle-Époque mansion converted into a relaxing hotel is
set back from the crowded coast amid scented gardens. 🛏 TV

	AE	●	▪		▪
	DC				
	MC				
	V				

BIARRITZ: *Hôtel Windsor* Ⓕ Ⓕ Ⓕ
Avenue Edouard-VII, 64200. 【 *05 59 24 08 52.* FAX *05 59 24 98 90.* **Rooms:** *48.*
Standing above the famous Grande Plage, featuring recently decorated
family rooms, this is a great spot for a vacation with kids. 🛏 TV

	AE	●	▪		
	DC				
	MC				
	V				

BIARRITZ: *Hôtel du Palais* Ⓕ Ⓕ Ⓕ Ⓕ Ⓕ
1 avenue de l'Impératrice, 64200. 【 *05 59 41 64 00.* FAX *05 59 41 67 99.* **Rooms:** *156.*
A magnificent hotel of enduring grandeur and elegance. The service
and food are impeccable; the mood refreshingly unstuffy.
🛏 TV ▤

	AE	●	▪	●	▪
	DC				
	JCB				
	MC				
	V				

ESPELETTE: *Hôtel Euzkadi* Ⓕ Ⓕ
64250 Espelette. 【 *05 59 93 91 88.* FAX *05 59 93 90 19.* **Rooms:** *32.*
Delicious Basque cooking has made this charming hotel very popular. 🛏 TV

	MC		▪		▪
	V				

FOIX: *Hôtel Audoye-Lons* Ⓕ Ⓕ
6 place G-Duthil, 09000. 【 *05 61 65 52 44.* FAX *05 61 02 68 18.* **Rooms:** *39.*
The big, period bedrooms and glass-enclosed dining room of this half-
timbered house in the Old Town are right above the river. 🛏 TV

	AE	●			▪
	DC				
	MC				
	V				

GAVARNIE: *Hôtel Vignemale* Ⓕ Ⓕ Ⓕ Ⓕ
65120 Gavarnie. 【 *05 62 92 40 00.* FAX *05 62 92 40 08.* **Rooms:** *25.*
This recently modernized hotel makes a comfortable base for walking the
mountain trails or enjoying the Cirque de Gavarnie. 🛏 TV

	AE	●			
	DC				
	MC				
	V				

NUZENAC: *L'Oustal* Ⓕ Ⓕ
Unac, 09250. 【 *05 61 64 48 44.* **Rooms:** *5.*
High in the wild Arr64ge, not far from Ax-les-Thermes, is this appealing
rural hostelry with marvelous views and excellent cuisine. 🛏

	MC				▪
	V				

OLORON-STE-MARIE: *L'Alysson* Ⓕ Ⓕ Ⓕ
Boulevard des Pyrénées, 64400. 【 *05 59 39 70 70.* FAX *05 59 39 24 47.* **Rooms:** *34.*
The most comfortable hotel in the picturesque riverside town, with
good food served in a modern dining room. 🛏 TV

	AE	●	▪		▪
	DC				
	MC				
	V				

PAU: *Grand Hôtel du Commerce* Ⓕ Ⓕ
9 rue Maréchal-Joffre, 64000. 【 *05 59 27 24 40.* FAX *05 59 83 81 74.* **Rooms:** *51.*
Conveniently located near the royal château, this popular, traditional
hotel has comfortable rooms and a reasonably priced restaurant. 🛏 TV

	AE	●	▪		▪
	DC				
	MC				
	V				

ST-ETIENNE-DE-BAÏGORRY: *Hôtel Arcé* Ⓕ Ⓕ Ⓕ Ⓕ
64430 St-Etienne-de-Baïgorry. 【 *05 59 37 40 14.* FAX *05 59 37 40 27.* **Rooms:** *22.*
Deep in the Basque Country is this friendly family hotel in a
wonderful setting beside the fast-flowing Nive des Aldudes. 🛏 TV

	MC	●	▪		▪
	V				

ST-GIRONS: *Hôtel Eychenne* Ⓕ Ⓕ Ⓕ
8 avenue Paul-Laffont, 09200. 【 *05 61 04 04 50.* FAX *05 61 96 07 20.* **Rooms:** *60.*
The antique furnishings, garden, swimming pool and excellent
restaurant combine to make this hotel truly distinctive. 🛏 TV

	AE		▪	●	▪
	MC				
	V				

ST-JEAN-DE-LUZ: *La Devinière* Ⓕ Ⓕ Ⓕ Ⓕ
5 rue Loquin, 64500. 【 *05 59 26 05 51.* FAX *05 59 51 26 38.* **Rooms:** *9.*
Quiet and tiny, with snug rooms elegantly furnished and an intimate
garden, this gem of a hotel is in the heart of the old city. 🛏

	MC	●			▪
	V				

ST-JEAN-DE-LUZ: *Le Parc Victoria* Ⓕ Ⓕ Ⓕ Ⓕ Ⓕ
5 rue Cépé, 64500. 【 *05 59 26 78 78.* FAX *05 59 26 78 08.* **Rooms:** *12.*
A glorious garden and swimming pool set off this Victorian mansion,
furnished in the style of the 1930s, near the beach. 🛏 ▤ TV

	AE	●	▪	●	▪
	DC				
	MC				
	V				

ST-JEAN-PIED-DE-PORT: *Hôtel les Pyrénées* Ⓕ Ⓕ Ⓕ Ⓕ
19 pl du Gén-de-Gaulle, 64220. 【 *05 59 37 01 01.* FAX *05 59 37 18 97.* **Rooms:** *20.*
Casual yet expensive, this hotel with its renowned Basque-based cuisine
provides a refuge from the summer crowds. 🛏 TV ▤

	AE	●	▪	●	▪
	DC				
	MC				
	V				

ST-JEAN-PIED-DE-PORT: *Hôtel Larramendy Andreinia* Ⓕ
Esterençuby, 64220. 【 *05 59 37 09 70.* FAX *05 59 37 36 05.* **Rooms:** *26.*
Set in a tiny village on the rippling river Nive, this Basque
hotel is an ideal base for ramblers. 🛏 TV

	MC	●	▪		
	V				

Price categories for a standard double room (not per person) for one night, including tax and service charges, but not including breakfast.
F under F200
FF F200–400
FFF F400–600
FFFF F600–1,000
FFFFF over F1,000

CHILDREN'S FACILITIES
Cribs and baby-sitting available. Some hotels provide children's portions and high chairs in the restaurant.

PARKING FACILITIES
Parking provided by the hotel in either a lot or a private garage very close by.

SWIMMING POOL
Hotel pools are often quite small and are outdoors unless otherwise stated.

GARDEN
Hotel with garden, courtyard or terrace, often providing tables for eating outside.

	CREDIT CARDS	CHILDREN'S FACILITIES	PARKING FACILITIES	SWIMMING POOL	GARDEN
SARE: *Hôtel Arraya* **FFF** Place du village, 64310. ☎ 05 59 54 20 46. FAX 05 59 54 27 04. **Rooms:** 20. This centrally located, modern hotel guarantees peace and comfort. Every bedroom has an en suite bathroom. 🛏 TV	AE MC V	●	■		■
TARBES: *Hôtel de l'Avenue* **FF** 778–80 av Bertrand-Barère, 65000. ☎ 05 62 93 06 36. **Rooms:** 26. A small family-run hotel only a two-minute walk from the station. The quietest rooms overlook an interior courtyard. 🛏 TV	MC V	●			

LANGUEDOC-ROUSSILLON

	CREDIT CARDS	CHILDREN'S FACILITIES	PARKING FACILITIES	SWIMMING POOL	GARDEN
AIGUES-MORTES: *Hôtel des Croisades* **FF** 2 rue du Port, 30220. ☎ 04 66 53 67 85. FAX 04 66 53 72 95. **Rooms:** 14. With friendly staff and a delightful garden, this hotel is excellent value for money. 🛏 ▤ TV	MC V	●	■		■
AIGUES-MORTES: *Hôtel Saint-Louis* **FFF** 10 rue de l'Amiral-Courbet, 30220. ☎ 04 66 53 72 68. FAX 04 66 53 75 92. **Rooms:** 22. This charming hotel is tucked within the stout stone walls of a lively city built by the saint-king Louis IX. The Camargue is nearby. 🛏 TV	AE DC MC V	●	■		■
BARJAC: *Hôtel le Mas du Termes* **FFF** Route de Bagnol-sur-Cèze, 30430. ☎ 04 66 24 56 31. FAX 04 66 24 58 54. **Rooms:** 32. Situated in beautiful country near the Ardèche gorges is this distinctive old hotel. The restaurant serves homemade wine. 🛏 TV	MC V	●	■	●	■
BÉZIERS: *Le Champ-de-Mars* **FF** 17 rue de Metz, 34500. ☎ 04 67 28 35 53. FAX 04 67 28 61 42. **Rooms:** 10. Newly renovated, the rooms here overlook the garden and offer excellent value for money. 🛏 TV	AE DC MC V	●			■
BOUZIGUES: *La Côte Bleue* **FF** Avenue Louis-Tudesq, 34140. ☎ 04 67 78 31 42. FAX 04 67 78 35 49. **Rooms:** 32. With its comfortable rooms, swimming pool and famous terraced restaurant on the seashore, this hotel is justifiably popular. 🛏 TV	AE MC V	●	■	●	■
CARCASSONNE: *Hôtel du Donjon* **FFF** 2 rue du Comte-Roger, 11000. ☎ 04 68 71 08 80. FAX 04 68 25 06 60. **Rooms:** 37. Right in the heart of the medieval city, this superb 14th-century building is full of modern comforts. 🛏 ▤ TV	AE DC MC V	●	■		■
CARCASSONE: *Hôtel Mercure la Vicomté* **FFF** 18 rue C Saint-Saens, 11000. ☎ 04 68 71 45 45. FAX 04 68 71 11 45. **Rooms:** 61. At the eastern entrance to the medieval city, this is a comfortable place for a stopover away from the summer crowds. 🛏 ▤ TV	AE DC MC V	●	■		
CASTILLON-DU-GARD: *Le Vieux Castillon* **FFFFF** Rue Citernasse, 30210. ☎ 04 66 37 61 61. FAX 04 66 37 28 17. **Rooms:** 35. Restored buildings in a medieval village near the Pont du Gard have been made into a stylish and discreet hotel. Even the pool is artfully set beside a ruined wall. 🛏 ▤ TV	AE DC MC V	●	■	●	■
CÉRET: *La Terrasse au Soleil* **FFFFF** Route de Fontfrède, 66400. ☎ 04 68 87 01 94. FAX 04 68 87 39 24. **Rooms:** 27. A peaceful and comfortable hotel set between the mountains and the sea, giving splendid views. There is a good restaurant. 🛏 ▤ TV	AE DC MC V	●	■	●	■
COLLIOURE: *Relais de Trois Mas* **FFFFF** Route de Port-Vendres, 66190. ☎ 04 68 82 05 07. FAX 04 68 82 38 08. **Rooms:** 23. The hotel consists of several tastefully restored buildings amid pine-shaded gardens. Every room has a sea or harbor view, and some have terraces. The restaurant, La Balette, is renowned. 🛏 ▤ TV	MC V	●	■	●	■

FUILLA: *Rozinante* (F)(F)
7 Cami Ribere Enclose, 66820. **(** 04 68 96 34 50. **FAX** 04 68 96 34 50. **Rooms:** *3.*
Nestling under Mount Canigou, this delightful guesthouse
boasts its own pool and luxurious lawns.

MINERVE: *Relais Chantovent* (F)(F) MC V
34210 Minerve. **(** 04 68 91 14 18. **FAX** 04 68 91 81 99. **Rooms:** *10.*
The hotel buildings are spread out in the narrow streets. The rooms
in the annex, a converted village house, have great character.

MONTPELLIER: *Hôtel Guilhem* (F)(F)(F) AE DC MC V
18 rue JJ-Rousseau, 34000. **(** 04 67 52 90 90. **FAX** 04 67 60 67 67. **Rooms:** *33.*
An appealing bed-and-breakfast hotel, run by friendly owners, which
provides peace and seclusion in a busy city.

NARBONNE: *Grand Hôtel du Languedoc* (F)(F) AE DC V
22 boulevard Gambetta, 11100. **(** 04 68 65 14 74. **FAX** 04 68 65 81 48. **Rooms:** *40.*
A cheerful city hotel only a short walk from the cathedral, shops
and museums. Its Belle Epoque-style restaurant is popular.

NÎMES: *Hôtel Plazza* (F)(F) AE DC JCB MC V
10 rue Roussy, 30000. **(** 04 66 76 16 20. **FAX** 04 66 67 65 99. **Rooms:** *28.*
A peaceful location and well-equipped bathrooms and bedrooms
make this modernized hotel a good choice.

NÎMES: *Imperator Concorde* (F)(F)(F)(F) AE DC MC V
Quai de la Fontaine, 30000. **(** 04 66 21 90 30. **FAX** 04 66 67 70 25. **Rooms:** *61.*
Nîmes' grandest hotel stands close to 17th-century gardens and
fountains, and some remarkable Roman architecture.

PERPIGNAN: *Hôtel de la Loge* (F)(F) AE DC MC V
1 rue des Fabriques-Nabot, 66000. **(** 04 68 34 41 02. **FAX** 04 68 34 25 13. **Rooms:** *22. *
In the heart of the city, close to the sights, is this calm, 16th-century
Catalan mansion with a mosaic forecourt and fountain.

PEYRIAC-MINERVOIS: *Château de Violet* (F)(F)(F) AE DC MC V
Route de Pépieux, 11160. **(** 04 68 78 10 42. **FAX** 04 68 78 30 01. **Rooms:** *12.*
Timbered ceilings and huge fireplaces add atmosphere to this château,
which presides over its own domain of parks and vineyards.

PONT DE MONTVERT: *Hôtel des Cévennes* (F)(F)
48220 Pont de Montvert. **(** 04 66 45 80 01. **Rooms:** *10.*
This traditional granite auberge overlooks the rushing Tarn. Choose rooms
1, 2, or 3 for a river view. The dining room offers a panorama of the village.

PRADES: *Grand Hôtel Thermal* (F)(F)(F) AE MC V
Molitg-les-Bains, 66500. **(** 04 68 05 00 50. **FAX** 04 68 05 02 91. **Rooms:** *70.*
A lakeside spa hotel surrounded by palm trees; very good value.

QUILLAN: *Hôtel Cartier* (F)(F) AE MC V
31 bd Charles de Gaulle, 11500. **(** 04 68 20 05 14. **FAX** 04 68 20 02 57. **Rooms:** *28.*
A comfortable, modest hotel-restaurant in the center of town.

ST-CYPRIEN-PLAGE: *Le Mas d'Huston* (F)(F)(F)(F) AE DC MC V
66750 St-Cyprien-Plage. **(** 04 68 37 63 63. **FAX** 04 68 37 64 64. **Rooms:** *50.*
A relaxing hotel by the beach with all the pleasures of a bustling
resort to hand. The restaurant overlooks a golf course.

SÈTE: *Grand Hôtel* (F)(F)(F) AE DC MC V
17 quai du Mar-de-Lattre-de-Tassigny, 34200. **(** 04 67 74 71 77.
FAX 04 67 74 29 27. **Rooms:** *45.*
Built in Belle Epoque style, this hotel overlooking Sète's Grand Canal
has a splendid palm-filled atrium and rooms with balconies.

SOMMIÈRES: *Auberge du Pont-Romain* (F)(F) AE DC MC V
2 rue Emile-Jamais, 30250. **(** 04 66 80 00 58. **FAX** 04 66 80 31 52. **Rooms:** *18.*
Behind a forbidding façade is a wonderful garden leading down to a
riverbank. The bedrooms are large, some with garden views.

UZÈS: *Le Mas d'Oléandre* (F)(F)
Saint-Médiers, 30700. **(** 04 66 22 63 43. **Rooms:** *6.*
A carefully restored farmhouse set in a secluded village surrounded by
vineyards. A good base for exploring and close to local restaurants.

Price categories for a standard double room (not per person) for one night, including tax and service charges, but not including breakfast.

- Ⓕ under F200
- ⒻⒻ F200–400
- ⒻⒻⒻ F400–600
- ⒻⒻⒻⒻ F600–1,000
- ⒻⒻⒻⒻⒻ over F1,000

CHILDREN'S FACILITIES
Cribs and baby-sitting available. Some hotels provide children's portions and high chairs in the restaurant.

PARKING FACILITIES
Parking provided by the hotel in either a lot or a private garage very close by.

SWIMMING POOL
Hotel pools are often quite small and are outdoors unless otherwise stated.

GARDEN
Hotel with garden, courtyard or terrace, often providing tables for eating outside.

	Price	CREDIT CARDS	CHILDREN'S FACILITIES	PARKING FACILITIES	SWIMMING POOL	GARDEN
UZÈS: *Château d'Arpaillargues* 30700 Uzès. **(** 04 66 22 14 48. FAX 04 66 22 56 10. **Rooms:** 29. An 18th-century château with tastefully decorated bedrooms, varying in size. Enjoy the exquisite cuisine by the pool or on the terrace. 🖼 🗐 TV	ⒻⒻⒻⒻ	AE DC MC V	●	●	●	●
VILLENEUVE-LES-BÉZIERS: *Maison Viner* 7 rue de la Fontaine, 34420. **(** 04 67 39 87 15. FAX 04 67 39 87 15. **Rooms:** 4. Beautifully restored period bed-and-breakfast just 5 km (3 miles) from the Mediterranean. Evening meals and picnic lunches available. 🖼	ⒻⒻ		●			

PROVENCE AND THE CÔTE D'AZUR

	Price	CREDIT CARDS	CHILDREN'S FACILITIES	PARKING FACILITIES	SWIMMING POOL	GARDEN
AIX-EN-PROVENCE: *Hôtel des Augustins* 3 rue de la Masse, 13100. **(** 04 42 27 28 59. FAX 04 42 26 74 87. **Rooms:** 29. A converted 12th-century convent with large and comfortable rooms in traditional Provençale style. A haven of peace in the heart of Aix. 🖼 🗐 TV	ⒻⒻⒻⒻ	AE DC MC V	●			
AIX-EN-PROVENCE: *Mas d'Entremont* Montée d'Avignon, Célony, 13090. **(** 04 42 17 42 42. FAX 04 42 21 15 83. **Rooms:** 18. This old Provençal farmhouse is now a luxurious hotel set in terraced grounds just outside Aix. Spacious and tastefully decorated. 🖼 🗐 TV	ⒻⒻⒻⒻ	MC V	●		●	●
ANTIBES: *Mas Djoliba* 29 av de Provence, 06600. **(** 04 93 34 02 48. FAX 04 93 34 05 81. **Rooms:** 13. A traditional Provençale hotel just a short walk from the center and beach. Set in a pretty garden it offers comfortable rooms in a rustic style. 🖼	ⒻⒻⒻ	AE DC MC V		●		●
ARLES: *Hôtel d'Arlatan* 26 rue du Sauvage, 13631. **(** 04 90 93 56 66. FAX 04 90 49 68 45. **Rooms:** 48. Situated in the heart of Arles, this hotel dates from the 16th century. Stone walls and a cavernous fireplace decorate the lounge. 🖼 🗐 TV	ⒻⒻⒻⒻ	AE DC MC V	●	●		●
AVIGNON: *L'Europe* 12 place Crillon, 84000. **(** 04 90 14 76 76. FAX 04 90 14 76 71. **Rooms:** 47. This has been Avignon's most refined hotel since Napoleon's day. Bedrooms are vast and elegant; the lounge is splendidly bedecked with tapestries above marble floors. Superb restaurant. 🖼 🗐 TV	ⒻⒻⒻⒻ	AE DC MC V	●	●		●
AVIGNON: *Hôtel de la Mirande* 4 place de la Mirande, 84000. **(** 04 90 85 93 93. FAX 04 90 86 26 85. **Rooms:** 20. An exquisite establishment with richly decorated rooms in Provençal style and fine antiques. There is a relaxing inner courtyard. 🖼 🗐 TV	ⒻⒻⒻⒻⒻ	AE DC MC V	●	●		●
BEAULIEU-SUR-MER: *Le Métropole* 15 bd du Marechal Leclerc, 06310. **(** 04 93 01 00 08. FAX 04 93 01 18 51. **Rooms:** 46. An Italianate palace complete with Mediterranean terrace, offering luxurious rooms and views across to St-Jean-Cap-Ferrat. 🖼 🗐 TV	ⒻⒻⒻⒻⒻ	AE MC V		●	●	●
BEAURECUEIL: *Relais Sainte-Victoire* 13100 Beaurecueil. **(** 04 42 66 94 98. FAX 04 42 66 85 96. **Rooms:** 10. A small hotel in a beautiful pastoral setting next to open fields under Mont-Ste-Victoire. A good value with a highly regarded restaurant. 🖼 🗐 TV	ⒻⒻⒻ	AE MC V	●	●	●	●
BORMES-LES-MIMOSAS: *Le Bellevue* 14 place Gambetta, 83230. **(** 04 94 71 15 15. **Rooms:** 12. Small, simple family-run hotel with spacious bedrooms and balconies overlooking a nest of terra-cotta roofs to the sea. 🖼	Ⓕ	MC V				
CANNES: *Carlton International* 58 bd de la Croisette, 06400. **(** 04 93 06 40 06. FAX 04 93 06 40 25. **Rooms:** 354. Home to stars during the film festival and businesspeople the rest of the year, the Carlton rivals Le Négresco as the Riviera's glittering jewel. A private beach allows you direct access from your yacht. 🖼 🗐 TV	ⒻⒻⒻⒻⒻ	AE DC MC V	●	●		

DIGNE-LES-BAINS: *Hôtel du Grand-Paris* (F)(F)(F)
19 bd Thiers, 04000. **[** *04 92 31 11 15.* **FAX** *04 92 32 32 82.* **Rooms:** *29.*
Once a convent, this atmospheric hotel offers comfortable rooms and
medieval surroundings in the heart of the town. 🛏 📺
AE DC MC V

FONTVIEILLE: *La Régalido* (F)(F)(F)(F)
Rue Mistral, 13990. **[** *04 90 54 60 22.* **FAX** *04 90 54 64 29.* **Rooms:** *15.*
This peaceful converted olive mill is one of the most delightful and
luxurious hotels in the area – covered in ivy, with a flowery garden.
Rooms are tastefully decorated, some with terraces. 🛏 ≡ 📺
AE DC MC V

FOX AMPHOUX: *L'Auberge du Vieux Fox* (F)(F)(F)
Place de l'Eglise, 83670. **[** *04 94 80 71 69.* **FAX** *04 94 80 78 38.* **Rooms:** *8.*
Parts of this hotel date back to the 11th century, when it was a coach
stop. Rooms are small but the sweeping views are splendid. 🛏 📺
AE MC V

JUAN-LES-PINS: *La Jabotte* (F)(F)
13 av M-Mauray, Cap d'Antibes, 06160. **[** *04 93 61 45 89.* **FAX** *04 93 61 07 04.* **Rooms:** *13.*
Five minutes' walk from the centers of Juan-les-Pins and Antibes,
this friendly hotel has a lot to offer for its price. It is also possible
to stay in one of the bungalows on the terrace. 🛏 📺
AE MC V

LA CADIÈRE D'AZUR: *Hostellerie Bérand* (F)(F)(F)
Rue Gabriel-Peri, 83740. **[** *04 94 90 11 43.* **FAX** *04 94 90 01 94.* **Rooms:** *40.*
A friendly hotel and restaurant on the main street of this village. Four
converted buildings with individually styled bedrooms. 🛏 ≡ 📺
AE MC V

LES ARCS-SUR-ARGENS: *Logis du Guetteur* (F)(F)(F)
Place du Château, 83460. **[** *04 94 73 30 82.* **FAX** *04 94 73 39 95.* **Rooms:** *10.*
This 11th-century château sits on top of a hill overlooking the village.
Atmospheric vaulted dining room and spacious bedrooms. 🛏 📺
AE DC MC V

LES BAUX-DE-PROVENCE: *Le Mas d'Aigret* (F)(F)(F)(F)
13520 Les Baux-de-Provence. **[** *04 90 54 33 54.* **FAX** *04 90 54 41 37.* **Rooms:** *15.*
A handsome, personal hotel only a short walk from the medieval citadel.
The dining room and some of the bedrooms of this intriguing old
farmhouse have been cut out of rock. 🛏 📺
AE DC MC V

NICE: *Hôtel Windsor* (F)(F)(F)
11 rue Dalpozzo, 06000. **[** *04 93 88 59 35.* **FAX** *04 93 88 94 57.* **Rooms:** *57.*
A friendly, family-run hotel with a palmed garden. Simple bedrooms
with modern murals, French windows and balconies. 🛏 ≡ 📺
AE DC MC V

NICE: *Le Négresco* (F)(F)(F)(F)(F)
37 prom des Anglais, 06000. **[** *04 93 16 64 00.* **FAX** *04 93 88 35 08.* **Rooms:** *143.*
The most famous hotel on the Riviera, recently renovated to even
more lofty heights of Belle Epoque grandeur. 🛏 ≡ 📺
AE DC MC V

PEILLON: *Auberge de la Madone* (F)(F)(F)(F)
06440 Peillon. **[** *04 93 79 91 17.* **FAX** *04 93 79 99 36.* **Rooms:** *20.*
A family-run modern inn in the remarkable perched village of Peillon.
Imaginative regional menus and comfortable bedrooms. 🛏
MC V

REILLANNE: *Auberge de Reillanne* (F)(F)
Le Pigeonnier, 04110. **[** *04 92 76 45 95.* **Rooms:** *7.*
A beautiful old country house in east Lubéron, secluded and off
the tourist track. The hotel is simple yet alluring – books line the
ancient shelves and the 20th century seems to have barely begun. 🛏
MC V

ROUSSILLON: *Le Mas de Garrigon* (F)(F)(F)(F)
Route de St-Saturnin-d'Apt, 84220. **[** *04 90 05 63 22.* **FAX** *04 90 05 70 01.* **Rooms:** *9.*
Set in pines in a secluded corner of Haute Provence, this traditional
country house is a perfect retreat. Classical music plays in the comfort-
able salons and each room has a private terrace. 🛏 📺
AE DC MC V

SAIGNON: *Auberge du Presbytère* (F)(F)
Place de la Fontaine, 84400. **[** *04 90 74 11 50.* **FAX** *04 90 04 68 51.* **Rooms:** *10.*
A small auberge in the square of this unspoiled hilltop village. Simple,
atmospheric bedrooms, local cuisine and the village bar. 🛏
AE MC V

ST-JEAN-CAP-FERRAT: *Clair Logis* (F)(F)(F)
12 av Centrale, 06230. **[** *04 93 76 04 57.* **FAX** *04 93 76 11 85.* **Rooms:** *18.*
This seductively old-fashioned villa with its large, mature garden is
a very good value. The larger rooms are in the main building. 🛏 📺
AE DC MC V

For key to symbols see back flap

Price categories for a standard double room (not per person) for one night, including tax and service charges, but not including breakfast.
- Ⓕ under F200
- ⒻⒻ F200–400
- ⒻⒻⒻ F400–600
- ⒻⒻⒻⒻ F600–1,000
- ⒻⒻⒻⒻⒻ over F1,000

CHILDREN'S FACILITIES
Cribs and baby-sitting available. Some hotels provide children's portions and high chairs in the restaurant.

PARKING FACILITIES
Parking provided by the hotel in either a lot or a private garage very close by.

SWIMMING POOL
Hotel pools are often quite small and are outdoors unless otherwise stated.

GARDEN
Hotel with garden, courtyard or terrace, often providing tables for eating outside.

	CREDIT CARDS	CHILDREN'S FACILITIES	PARKING FACILITIES	SWIMMING POOL	GARDEN
LES SAINTES-MARIES-DE-LA-MER: *Hostellerie de Cacharel* ⒻⒻⒻⒻ Route de Cacharel, 13460. 【 04 90 97 95 44. FAX 04 90 97 87 97. **Rooms:** 15. *Gardiens* or Provençal cowboys used to inhabit this ancient ranch in the heart of the marshes. The hotel is surprisingly comfortable with large rooms and relaxing lounges. Horseback riding is available. 🔁	AE DC MC V		■	●	■
ST-PAUL-DE-VENCE: *La Colombe d'Or* ⒻⒻⒻⒻⒻ Place De-Gaulle, 06570. 【 04 93 32 80 02. FAX 04 93 32 77 78. **Rooms:** 25. An old farmhouse once populated by Impressionist painters is now home to film stars and models. The rooms are luxurious but the real stars are originals by Picasso and Matisse *(see p514)*. 🔁 ▤ TV	AE DC MC V	●	■	●	■
ST-RÉMY-DE-PROVENCE: *Le Château de Roussan* ⒻⒻⒻⒻ Route de Tarascon, 13210. 【 04 90 92 11 63. FAX 04 90 92 50 59. **Rooms:** 21. One of the most beautiful hotels in Provence – a converted 18th-century château set in extensive formal grounds. 🔁	AE MC V		■		■
ST-RÉMY-DE-PROVENCE: *Le Mas de Carassins* ⒻⒻⒻ 1 chemin Gaulois, 13210. 【 04 90 92 15 48. **Rooms:** 10. A 19th-century farmhouse on the outskirts of town, decorated in country style. Expect a friendly atmosphere and helpful staff. 🔁	MC V		■		■
ST-TROPEZ: *Lou Cagnard* ⒻⒻ Avenue P Roussel, 83990. 【 04 94 97 04 24. FAX 04 94 97 09 44. **Rooms:** 19. A very popular, good-value hotel in the newest part of town, a short walk from the port. Cheerful bedrooms and pleasant courtyard. 🔁	MC V		■		■
SALON-DE-PROVENCE: *L'Abbaye de Sainte-Croix* ⒻⒻⒻⒻⒻ Route du Val-de-Cuech, 13300. 【 04 90 56 24 55. FAX 04 90 56 31 12. **Rooms:** 24. This converted 12th-century abbey retains its medieval charm. The bed-rooms, originally the monks' cells, vary in size. 🔁 ▤ TV	AE DC MC V	●		●	■
SEILLANS: *Hôtel les Deux Rocs* ⒻⒻ Place Font-d'-Amont, 83440. 【 04 94 76 87 32. FAX 04 94 76 88 68. **Rooms:** 14. A captivating 18th-century mansion hotel in the peaceful village square. Warm family atmosphere and excellent traditional food. 🔁	MC V		■		■
TOURTOUR: *La Petite Auberge* ⒻⒻⒻ 83690 Tourtour. 【 04 94 70 57 16. FAX 04 94 70 54 52. **Rooms:** 11. For peace and quiet, beautiful views and a rustic setting, head to Tourtour and this small auberge. 🔁 TV	AE DC MC V	●	■	●	■
TRIGANCE: *Château de Trigance* ⒻⒻⒻⒻ 83840 Trigance. 【 04 94 76 91 18. FAX 04 94 85 68 99. **Rooms:** 10. A unique and romantic hideaway in the mountain valleys. Four-poster beds, tapestries and vaulted ceilings adorn this 11th-century château, carefully restored by the owner. Access by private road. 🔁 TV	AE DC MC V	●	■	·	
VAISON-LA-ROMAINE: *Le Beffroi* ⒻⒻⒻ Rue de L'Évêché, Haute Ville, 84110. 【 04 90 36 04 71. FAX 04 90 36 24 78. **Rooms:** 22. This 16th-century hotel seduces its guests with antiques, fireplaces, tiled floors and paintings. Each room is individually furnished. 🔁 TV	AE DC MC V	●	■	●	■
VENCE: *Auberge les Seigneurs* ⒻⒻ Place du Frêne, 06140. 【 04 93 58 04 24. FAX 04 93 24 08 01. **Rooms:** 6. This restaurant-with-rooms is a medieval time capsule. Bedrooms are spartan but cheap. Good choice of Provençal specialties. 🔁	AE DC MC V				
VILLEFRANCHE-SUR-MER: *Hôtel Welcome* ⒻⒻⒻⒻ 1 quai Courbet, 06230. 【 04 93 76 76 93. FAX 04 93 76 27 66. **Rooms:** 32. This tall, narrow building stands over a fish restaurant near the old port. Most of the small but comfortable bedrooms have seaside balconies. The same family has run this hotel for half a century. 🔁 ▤ TV	AE DC MC V	●	■		■

CORSICA

AJACCIO: *Hôtel Dolce Vita* ⓕⓕⓕ
Route des Sanguinaires, 20000. [04 95 52 00 93. FAX 04 95 52 07 15. *Rooms:* 32.
Functional, modern hotel overlooking the sea with direct access to the
beach. Flashy decor and a floodlit swimming pool. 🚗 ▤ TV

AE				
DC				
MC				
V				

BARCAGGIO: *La Giraglia* ⓕⓕⓕ
Ersa, 20275. [04 95 35 60 54. FAX 04 95 35 65 92. *Rooms:* 14.
Off the tourist track, this modest seaside hotel with rustic rooms is ideal
for a peaceful stay. There are good seafood restaurants next door. 🚗

BASTIA: *Hôtel de la Corniche* ⓕⓕⓕ
San-Martino-di-Lota, 20200. [04 95 31 40 98. FAX 04 95 32 37 69. *Rooms:* 19.
A simple but good-value hotel on a winding road 10 minutes' drive
from Bastia. Breathtaking views from the terrace. 🚗 TV

AE				
DC				
MC				
V				

BONIFACIO: *Résidence du Centre Nautique* ⓕⓕⓕⓕ
Quai Nord, 20169. [04 95 73 02 11. FAX 04 95 73 17 47. *Rooms:* 10.
A perfect stop by the harbor for sailing enthusiasts. The rooms have
been converted into small duplexes. 🚗 ▤ TV

AE				
DC				
MC				
V				

BONIFACIO: *Hôtel Genovese* ⓕⓕⓕⓕⓕ
Quartier de la Citadelle, 20169. [04 95 73 12 34. FAX 04 95 73 09 03. *Rooms:* 14.
A luxury hotel in the Old Town that was once the legionnaires' barracks.
Refined, modern decor with grand rooms and suites. 🚗 ▤ TV

AE				
DC				
MC				
V				

CALVI: *Auberge de la Signoria* ⓕⓕⓕⓕⓕ
Rte de la Forêt de Bonifato, 20260. [04 95 65 93 00. FAX 04 95 65 38 77. *Rooms:* 10.
The owners have renovated this large house, retaining its original
character. A haven of seclusion and peace – candlelit dinners
served on the terrace under the palm trees. 🚗 ▤ TV

AE				
MC				
V				

CALVI: *Hôtel Balanéa* ⓕⓕⓕⓕ
6 rue Clémenceau, 20260. [04 95 65 94 94. FAX 04 95 65 29 71. *Rooms:* 37.
Recently renovated hotel in the center of town beside the harbor.
Spacious and well-decorated rooms with large bathrooms. 🚗 ▤ TV

AE				
DC				
MC				
V				

FELICETO: *Hôtel Mare e Monti* ⓕⓕ
20225 Feliceto. [04 95 63 02 00. FAX 04 95 63 02 01. *Rooms:* 18.
Set at the foot of rocky cliffs overlooking the sea, the house has been
in the same family since 1870. Expect a warm welcome and delicious,
traditional food, including fresh fruit from the garden. 🚗 TV

AE				
DC				
MC				
V				

L'ILE ROUSSE: *A Pastorella* ⓕⓕ
Monticello, 20220. [04 95 60 05 65. FAX 04 95 60 21 78. *Rooms:* 12.
Just inland, this traditional hotel sits in the village square. Originally a
bar and restaurant, rooms of various sizes have been added. 🚗

AE				
DC				
MC				
V				

L'ILE ROUSSE: *Santa Maria* ⓕⓕⓕⓕ
Route du Port, 20220. [04 95 63 05 05. FAX 04 95 60 32 48. *Rooms:* 56.
A modern hotel situated between two beaches with small but light and
comfortable rooms with balconies. Meals are served on request. 🚗 ▤ TV

AE				
DC				
MC				
V				

PIANA: *Les Roches Rouges* ⓕⓕⓕ
20115 Piana. [04 95 27 81 81. FAX 04 95 27 81 76. *Rooms:* 30.
An old Corsican house that has been refurbished – the rooms are plain
but there is a lovely restaurant with terrace and superb views. 🚗 TV

AE				
DC				
MC				
V				

PORTICCIO: *Le Maquis* ⓕⓕⓕⓕⓕ
20166 Porticcio. [04 95 25 05 55. FAX 04 95 25 11 70. *Rooms:* 27.
A stylish hotel consisting of white-shuttered buildings centered
around a terrace and freshwater pool. Excellent cuisine. 🚗 ▤ TV

AE				
DC				
MC				
V				

SARTÈNE: *Villa Piana* ⓕⓕ
Route de Propriano, 20100. [04 95 77 07 04. FAX 04 95 73 45 65 *Rooms:* 32.
A large, friendly Provençal-style villa with a splendid view across the
town to the mountains. The rooms are bright and airy, decorated in a
rustic style. Floodlit tennis courts. 🚗

AE				
DC				
MC				
V				

SPELONCATO: *A Spelunca* ⓕⓕ
20226 Speloncato. [04 95 61 50 38. FAX 04 95 61 53 14. *Rooms:* 18.
A magnificent hotel in the former palace of a local cardinal. Huge grand
rooms and excellent value. No restaurant. 🚗

| MC | | | | |
| V | | | | |

WHERE TO EAT

THE FRENCH consider eating well an essential part of their national birthright. There are few other places where people are as passionately knowledgeable about their cuisine and their wine. Restaurant reviews, as well as cooking and food shows on television, are avidly followed, and the general quality of both fresh food and restaurant meals is vastly better in France than it is in most other European countries.

This section begins with an overview of the different types of restaurants in France, with tips on eating out, reading the menu, ordering and service. Following this is a list of restaurants we have sampled, arranged by region and town *(see pp580–613)*. At the front of the book *(see pp20–3)*, there is a guide to a typical menu and an introduction to French wine. And, at the start of each of the five regional sections can be found the food and wine features of that particular area.

FRENCH EATING HABITS

THE TRADITIONAL large meal at noon survives mainly in rural regions. Nowadays, lunch is increasingly likely to consist of a sandwich, a salad or a steak in a café, while dinner is the main meal of the day. Usually, lunch is from noon to 2pm and dinner is from 8 to 10pm, with last orders taken 30 minutes before closing time.

Some family-owned places are closed on weekends, so it may be difficult to find a meal anywhere outside your hotel on Sundays, except in large cities. Outside major cities and in resort towns, restaurants and hotels are often closed out of season, so it is advisable to phone ahead.

Over the past few decades, French eating habits have changed dramatically. The growing popularity of the cuisine of former French colonies means that North African and Vietnamese places are now easy to find, as are Chinese restaurants. Burger and Tex-Mex joints are also popular with young people. As city-dwellers and suburbanites in France have become almost as health-conscious as other Europeans, there has been an explosion of "light" foods; and the rise of the *hypermarchés* (hypermarkets) has resulted in less fresh produce on the menu, as more frozen and prepared food is eaten.

REGIONAL COOKING

ONE OF the great pleasures of traveling in France is sampling the country's regional

Taverne Magenageuse in Mougins, Provence (see p612)

cuisine. In every *département* of France, menus will nearly always include local specialties, which reflect predominant local products and agriculture. A good way to divide France gastronomically is the butter/olive oil divide. In the north, butter is generally used in cooking; in the south, olive oil; and in the southwest, goose and duck fat predominate.

Each region takes great pride in its own cuisine. Nationally, the best known dishes come from four regions: Alsace, a province with close German ties; the southwest, where cassoulet, a rich stew of white beans, tomatoes, sausage and duck is a well-loved dish; the Alps, which gave fondue to the nation; and Provence, famed for bouillabaisse, a rich fish soup from Marseille.

The gastronomic capital of France is, however, considered to be Lyon, which boasts a significant proportion of France's best restaurants and many superb no-nonsense bistros known as *buchons*.

La Cigale, a Belle Epoque brasserie in Nantes (see p595)

RESTAURANTS

ENCOMPASSING the whole alphabet of French cuisine, restaurants in France range from tiny white-washed places with rush-bottomed chairs to stately, wood-paneled château dining rooms and the top kitchens of famous chefs. Many hotels have fine restaurants open to non-residents, a selection of which can be found in the hotel listings (*see pp540–75*).

Prices for restaurants of the same rating are more-or-less consistent throughout France except in large cities, where they can be more expensive. The quality of the food and service, though, is the most significant price factor, and a meal can easily cost up to F1,000 a person at one of the leading restaurants.

There is a number of different kinds of French cuisine that you may come across. *Haute cuisine* is the traditional cooking method, where the flavor of the food is enhanced with rich sauces. *Nouvelle cuisine* challenged this method, especially for the diet-conscious, in using light rather than creamy sauces, which bring out the texture and color of the ingredients. *Cuisine bourgeoise* is French home cooking. *Cuisine des Provinces* uses high-quality ingredients to prepare traditional rural dishes. Many top chefs favor *cuisine moderne,* which releases the natural flavor of the food. There has also been a revival of traditional methods.

The restaurant L'Excelsior at Nancy in Lorraine (*see p589*)

Camembert

BISTROS

WHEN THE FRENCH go out to eat, they are most likely to visit the broadest class of restaurant, the bistro. Bistros vary enormously – some urban bistros are formally decorated, while those in smaller cities and in the country tend to be more casual. They offer a good, moderately priced meal from a traditional menu of an *entrée* or *hors d'oeuvre* (appetizer), *plats mijotés* (simmered dishes) and *grillades* (grilled fish and meats), followed by cheese and dessert.

BRASSERIES

BRASSERIES have their origin in Alsace and were originally attached to breweries; the name brasserie actually means brewery. Usually found in larger cities, they are big, bustling places, many with fresh shellfish stands outside. They serve beer on tap, as well as a *vin de la maison* (house wine) and a variety of regional wines. Menus include simple fish and grilled meat dishes along with Alsatian specialties like *choucroute garnie* (sauerkraut with sausage and pork). Prices are very much on a par with those you would pay at bistros. Like cafés, brasseries are usually open from morning until night and serve food all day long.

FERME-AUBERGES

IN THE COUNTRY you may eat at a simple "farm inn," where good, inexpensive meals, often made with fresh farm produce, are taken with your host's family as part of your room and board. For more details on *ferme-auberges,* see Bed-and-Breakfasts on page 538.

CAFÉS

CAFÉS REPRESENT the soul of France. Every place but the tiniest hamlet can be counted on to have a café, open as a rule from early in the morning until 10pm or so. They serve drinks, coffee, tea, simple meals, and snacks such as salads, omelettes and sandwiches throughout the day, and usually provide a cheaper breakfast than most hotels.

In addition to serving refreshments, cafés are a good source of information and offer the traveler opportunities to observe the French at their most relaxed.

In villages, almost the entire population might drift in and out of the single café during the course of a day, while large cities have cafés that cater to a specific clientele, such as workers or students. In Paris's most famous cafés, celebrated intellectuals and artists have gathered to discuss their ideas (*see p142*).

Auberge du XII Siécle at Saché in the Loire Valley (*see p595*)

Tables outside a café in the Old Town of Nice on the Côte d'Azur

BISTRO ANNEXES

WITHIN THE PAST few years, "baby" bistros, or bistro annexes, have appeared in large cities, especially Paris and Lyon, as a new category of restaurant. They are lower-priced sister eateries of the famous – and more expensive – restaurants run by well-known chefs. Many of them offer *prix-fixe* (fixed-price) menus and the chance to sample the cooking of a celebrated kitchen in relaxed surroundings.

FAST FOOD

IF YOU WANT to avoid the American fast-food chains, wine bars and *salons du thé* are also affordable for light meals. Cafeterias, found in some shopping centers, serve tasty food at reasonable prices.

RESERVATIONS

IN CITIES and larger towns it is always best to make a reservation, especially from May to September. This rarely applies to cafés or in the country, where you can walk into most places without a reservation. However, if you are traveling in remote rural and resort areas off season, it is worth finding out first if the restaurant is open year-round.

If you have a reservation and your plans change, then you should call and cancel. Smaller restaurants, in particular, must fill all their tables to make a profit, and no-shows threaten their livelihood.

READING THE MENU AND ORDERING

WHEN THE MENU is presented, you'll usually be asked if you'd like an aperitif. Since many French people do not drink spirits before a meal, this could be Kir (white wine mixed with a dash of black-currant liqueur), vermouth, light port (drunk in France as a cocktail) or a soft drink.

Opening the menu, *les entrées* or *hors d'oeuvre* are appetizers. *Les plats* are the main courses, and most restaurants will offer a *plat du jour*, or daily special; these are often seasonal or local dishes of particular interest. A selection of dishes from a classic French menu is given on pages 20–21.

Cheese is served as a separate course between the main course and dessert. Coffee is always served black, unless you specify *"crème."* Alternatively, you can ask for a *tisane*, or herbal tea.

WINE

RESTAURANTS mark wine up considerably, so it can be expensive to drink fine wine with your meal. Local wine, however, is often served in carafes and is a good value. Ordering a *demi* (50 cl) or *quart* (25cl) carafe is a cheap and enjoyable way to try out a region's wines.

French law divides the country's wines into the following four classes, in ascending order of quality: Vin de Table, Vin de Pays, Vin Délimité de Qualité Supérieure (VDQS)

and Appellation d'Origine Contrôlée (AOC). The blended Vin de Table wines are rarely found in restaurants, but to choose a regional wine (Vins de Pays upward), refer to the wine features in the regional sections of this book. For an introduction to French wine, see pages 22–3.

When in doubt, order the house wine. These are usually good and also affordable.

WATER

TAP WATER is supplied upon request free of charge and is perfectly safe to drink. The French also pride themselves on their wide range of mineral waters. Favorite mealtime brands include Evian and the slightly carbonated Badoit.

Le Moulin de Mougins *(see p612)*

HOW TO PAY

VISA/Carte Bleue (V) is the most widely accepted credit card in France. Master-card/Access (MC), American Express (AE) and Diners Club (DC) are also commonly used. The abbreviations shown in brackets are used in the restaurant listings to indicate which card(s) each restaurant accepts.

La Tour d'Argent in the Latin Quarter of Paris *(see p583)*

Always carry plenty of cash, especially when touring the countryside, because many smaller restaurants still do not take credit cards. If in doubt, ask when you telephone to book a table.

SERVICE AND TIPPING

THE PACE of a French meal is generally leisurely. People think nothing of spending four hours at the table, so if you are pressed for time, go to a café or brasserie. A service charge of 12.5 to 15 percent is almost always included in the price of your meal, but most French people leave a few additional francs behind in a café, and an additional 5 percent or so of the total bill in other restaurants, which pride themselves on their service, an additional tip of 5 to 10 percent is correct.

Two francs is sufficient for toilet attendants, and F5 an item is appropriate for the cloakroom attendant.

DRESS CODE

EVEN WHEN DRESSED casually, the French are generally well turned out; visitors should aim for the same level of presentable comfort. Running shoes, shorts, and athletic wear or beachwear are unacceptable everywhere except cafés or beachside places.

The restaurant listings indicate which restaurants require men to wear a jacket and tie *(see pp580-613)*.

CHILDREN

FRENCH CHILDREN are introduced early to restaurants and are well received almost everywhere. However, few restaurants provide special facilities like high chairs or baby seats, because children are expected to behave sensibly and also because there is often not much extra room at the table.

PETS

DOGS are usually accepted at all but the most elegant restaurants. The French are

The Eychenne hotel-restaurant at St-Girons in the Pyrenees *(see p607)*

great dog lovers, so do not be surprised to see your neighbor's dog sitting at the adjacent *banquette*.

SMOKING

IN SPITE OF recent strict legislation requiring restaurants to provide their clientele with smoking and nonsmoking sections, a laissez-faire attitude prevails in most places. The owner of one Paris bistro now carries a portable no-smoking sign that he hangs on the wall over the table of anyone who requests a nonsmoking table. If you are sensitive to smoke, ask for a window table.

The Hôtel Royal at Evian-les-Bains in the French Alps *(see p563)*

WHEELCHAIR ACCESS

THOUGH THE RESTAURANTS of newer hotels usually provide wheelchair access, it is often limited elsewhere. A word when you are booking your table should ensure that you are given a conveniently located table and assistance, if needed, when you arrive.

The listings show restaurants with special facilities.

Refer also to page 539 of this book, which gives the names and addresses of organizations that provide advice to disabled travelers in France.

VEGETARIAN FOOD

FRANCE REMAINS difficult for vegetarians, although some progress has been made in recent years. In most non-vegetarian restaurants the main courses are firmly oriented toward meat and fish. However, you can often do well by ordering from the *entrées* and should never be timid about asking for a dish to be served without its meat content. If you make an advance request, most of the better restaurants will prepare a special vegetarian dish.

Only larger cities and university towns are likely to have completely vegetarian restaurants. Otherwise cafés, pizzerias, crêperies and oriental restaurants are good places to find vegetarian meals.

PICNICS

PICNICKING is the best way to enjoy the wonderful fresh produce, local bread and cheeses from the markets and enticing shops to be found all over France. For more details about the shops and markets of France, see pages 62–3.

Picnics are also a good way to eat cheaply and enjoy the French countryside. Picnicking areas along major roads are well marked and have tables and chairs.

Choosing a Restaurant

THE RESTAURANTS in this guide have been selected across a wide range of price categories for their good value, exceptional food and interesting location. This chart lists the restaurants by region, starting with Paris. Use the color-coded thumb tabs, which indicate the regions covered on each page, to guide you to the relevant section of the chart. *Bon Appétit!*

	CREDIT CARDS	CHILDREN'S FACILITIES	FIXED-PRICE MENU	GOOD WINE LIST	OUTDOOR TABLES
PARIS					
ILE DE LA CITÉ: *Le Caveau du Palais.* **Map 8 F3.** ⒻⒻ 17–19 place Dauphine, 75001. 【 *01 43 26 04 28.* Enjoy a selection of superb fish and meat dishes smoke-grilled over wood in this ancient stone-walled cellar. Closed Saturdays and Sundays.	AE MC V		■	●	■
ILE DE LA CITÉ: *Le Vieux Bistrot.* **Map 9 B4.** ⒻⒻⒻ 14 rue du Cloître-Notre-Dame, 75004. 【 *01 43 54 18 95.* An authentic bistro, frequented by many Parisian restaurateurs and entertainment stars. The food here is unpretentious and very good.	V			●	■
ILE ST-LOUIS: *Au Franc Pinot.* **Map 9 C4.** Ⓕ 1 quai de Bourbon, 75004. 【 *01 46 33 60 64.* The wine bar is on the ground floor and the restaurant is in the cellar. Excellent food and atmosphere.	MC V		■		
ILE ST-LOUIS: *Le Monde des Chimères.* **Map 9 C4.** ⒻⒻⒻ 69 rue St-Louis-en-l'Île, 75004. 【 *01 43 54 45 27.* A bistro in a 300-year-old house serving traditional family cooking made only with fresh produce.	MC V		■		
THE MARAIS: *Baracane.* **Map 10 E4.** ⒻⒻ 38 rue des Tournelles, 75004. 【 *01 42 71 43 33.* In spite of its touristy location this tiny restaurant serving southwestern cuisine has very good quality food at reasonable prices.	MC V		■		
THE MARAIS: *Le Bar à Huîtres.* **Map 10 E3.** ⒻⒻ 33 bd Beaumarchais, 75003. 【 *01 48 87 98 92.* Oysters and other shellfish predominate here. You can compose your own appetizer platter, then follow with a choice of fish or meat dishes.	AE MC V	●	■		■
THE MARAIS: *Miravile.* **Map 9 B3.** ⒻⒻⒻ 72 quai de l'Hôtel Ville, 75004. 【 *01 42 74 72 22.* The menu here is inventive and exciting, featuring such dishes as rabbit with olives, and lobster with potatoes. Vegetarian dishes available.	AE MC V		■	●	
THE MARAIS: *L'Ambroisie.* **Map 10 D3.** ⒻⒻⒻⒻ 9 pl des Vosges, 75004. 【 *01 42 78 51 45.* This discreet, romantic spot is one of only five Michelin three-star restaurants in Paris. Reservations are accepted one month ahead. 【	AE MC V			●	
BEAUBOURG: *Benoît.* **Map 9 B2.** ⒻⒻⒻⒻ 20 rue St Martin, 75004. 【 *01 42 72 25 76.* This is the Rolls-Royce of Paris bistros. The excellent traditional cuisine includes assorted cold salads, house *foie gras* and *boeuf à la mode*.	AE		■	●	
LES HALLES: *Chez Elle.* **Map 9 A2.** ⒻⒻ 7 rue des Prouvaires, 75001. 【 *01 45 08 04 10.* The menu is classic bistro, changing with the seasons and always based on fresh, local produce. Desserts are traditional and delicious, including the crème caramel.	AE MC V		■		■
LES HALLES: *Le Grizzli.* **Map 9 B3.** ⒻⒻ 7 rue St-Martin, 75004. 【 *01 48 87 77 56.* The owner orders much of the produce from his native southwest, including cured ham, cheese and wines made by his family.	AE MC V		■		■
LES HALLES: *Au Pied de Cochon.* **Map 8 F1.** ⒻⒻⒻ 6 rue Coquillière, 75001. 【 *01 40 13 77 00.* This famous institution in the heart of Les Halles is open every day, all day and all night, serving copious amounts of grilled pigs' feet and shellfish. Hearty cuisine and atmosphere but be prepared for lines after 10pm.	AE DC MC V		■		

		Average prices info	CREDIT CARDS	CHILDREN'S FACILITIES	FIXED-PRICE MENU	GOOD WINE LIST	OUTDOOR TABLES

Average prices for a three-course meal for one, including a half-bottle of house wine, tax and service:
Ⓕ under F150
ⒻⒻ F150–F250
ⒻⒻⒻ F250–F350
ⒻⒻⒻⒻ F350–F500
ⒻⒻⒻⒻⒻ over F500

CHILDREN'S FACILITIES
Some restaurants have high chairs and offer smaller portions for children.

FIXED-PRICE MENU
A good-value fixed-price menu available at lunch, dinner or both, often with three or more courses.

GOOD WINE LIST
Denotes a wide range of good wines, or otherwise a more specialized selection of local wines.

OUTDOOR TABLES
Facilities for eating outdoors, on a terrace or in a garden or courtyard, often with a good view.

TUILERIES QUARTER: *Le Grand Louvre.* **Map 8** F2.   ⒻⒻ
Le Louvre, 75001. 【 01 40 20 53 41.
It is rare to find such a good restaurant in a museum. André Daguin, a gastronomic star from the southwest, developed the menu.

Credit cards: AE DC MC V · Children's Facilities ● · Fixed-price Menu ■

TUILERIES QUARTER: *Armand au Palais Royal.* **Map 8** F1.   ⒻⒻ
6 rue de Beaujolais, 75001. 【 01 42 60 05 11.
Situated behind the Palais Royal, this charming restaurant was once a stable, but this is no reflection on the food, which is very Parisian.

Credit cards: AE MC V · Fixed-price Menu ■

TUILERIES QUARTER: *L'Espadon.* **Map 4** D5.   ⒻⒻⒻⒻⒻ
15 pl Vendôme, 75001. 【 01 43 16 30 80.
Part of the Ritz, this is one of the Parisian restaurants most highly rated by Michelin. Modern classic cuisine from chef Guy Legay. 🖙 🍴

Credit cards: AE DC MC V · Children's Facilities ● · Fixed-price Menu ■ · Good Wine List ● · Outdoor Tables ■

TUILERIES QUARTER: *Le Grand Véfour.* **Map 8** F1.   ⒻⒻⒻⒻⒻ
17 rue de Beaujolais, 75001. 【 01 42 96 56 27.
An 18th-century two-star Michelin restaurant, considered by many to be the most attractive in the city. This is the place for special occasions. 🖙 🍴

Credit cards: AE DC MC V · Fixed-price Menu ■ · Good Wine List ●

OPÉRA QUARTER: *Chartier.* **Map 4** F4.   Ⓕ
7 rue du Faubourg Montmartre, 75009. 【 01 47 70 86 29.
This cavernous restaurant packs in the crowds with its quick service and basic French food at budget prices. Popular with students, travelers and local *habitués*, the place bustles with an infectious bonhomie.

Credit cards: AE MC V · Fixed-price Menu ■

OPÉRA QUARTER: *A G Le Poète.*   ⒻⒻ
27 rue Pasquier, 75008. 【 01 47 42 00 64.
Soft lighting and red velvet decor provide a romantic setting for inspired cooking, with dishes such as red mullet and baby scallops on creamed wild nettles.

Credit cards: AE MC V · Fixed-price Menu ■

OPÉRA QUARTER: *Café Runtz.* **Map 4** F5.   ⒻⒻ
16 rue Favart, 75002. 【 01 42 96 69 86.
This pleasant brasserie is one of the few genuine Alsatian places in Paris where you can get regional specialties in huge portions.

Credit cards: AE DC MC V · Fixed-price Menu ■

OPÉRA QUARTER: *Le Vaudeville.* **Map 4** F5.   ⒻⒻ
29 rue Vivienne, 75002. 【 01 40 20 04 62.
The attractive Art Deco interior provides an appealing backdrop to the food: good shellfish, the chef's famous smoked salmon, and classic standbys like pigs' feet and *andouillette* (tripe sausage).

Credit cards: AE DC MC V · Children's Facilities ● · Fixed-price Menu ■ · Outdoor Tables ■

OPÉRA QUARTER: *Lucas Carton.* **Map 3** C5.   ⒻⒻⒻⒻⒻ
9 pl de la Madeleine, 75008. 【 01 42 65 22 90.
Awarded three Michelin stars, the cuisine here is imaginative and exotic. The decor is stunning, the service crisp and the crowd very dressy. 🍴

Credit cards: AE DC MC V · Fixed-price Menu ■ · Good Wine List ●

INVALIDES QUARTER: *Thoumieux.* **Map 7** A2.   ⒻⒻ
79 rue St-Dominique, 75007. 【 01 47 05 49 75.
This well-run restaurant is excellent. Ingredients are fresh, and virtually everything is made on the premises, including *foie gras* and *rillettes* (similar to pâté). The *cassoulet* (stew of white beans and meat) is a specialty here.

Credit cards: AE MC V · Children's Facilities ● · Fixed-price Menu ■

INVALIDES QUARTER: *L'Arpège.* **Map 7** B3.   ⒻⒻⒻⒻⒻ
84 rue de Varenne, 75007. 【 01 45 51 47 33.
Chef owner Alain Passard's restaurant is near the Musée Rodin. His lobster and turnip vinaigrette, and the duck Louise Passard are classics.

Credit cards: AE DC MC V · Fixed-price Menu ■ · Good Wine List ●

EIFFEL TOWER QUARTER: *La Serre.*   ⒻⒻ
29 rue de l'Exposition, 75007. 【 01 45 55 20 96.
A small, cozy neighborhood restaurant of a type that is becoming increasingly rare. Rustic specialties include *pot au feu* and *cassoulet*.

Credit cards: MC V · Children's Facilities ● · Fixed-price Menu ■

Average prices for a three-course meal for one, including a half-bottle of house wine, tax and service:
Ⓕ under F150
ⒻⒻ F150–F250
ⒻⒻⒻ F250–F350
ⒻⒻⒻⒻ F350–F500
ⒻⒻⒻⒻⒻ over F500

CHILDREN'S FACILITIES
Some restaurants have high chairs and offer smaller portions for children.

FIXED-PRICE MENU
A good-value fixed-price menu available at lunch, dinner or both, often with three or more courses.

GOOD WINE LIST
Denotes a wide range of good wines, or otherwise a more specialized selection of local wines.

OUTDOOR TABLES
Facilities for eating outdoors, on a terrace or in a garden or courtyard, often with a good view.

	CREDIT CARDS	CHILDREN'S FACILITIES	FIXED-PRICE MENU	GOOD WINE LIST	OUTDOOR TABLES
CHAILLOT QUARTER: *La Butte Chaillot.* Map 2 D5. ⒻⒻⒻ 110 bis av Kléber, 75116. 【 01 47 27 88 88. This is one of chef Guy Savoy's most recent restaurants. The sophisticated cuisine and the modern decor attract a very stylish crowd. 🅖	AE DC MC V		▪		▪
CHAILLOT QUARTER: *Le Relais du Parc.* Map 5 C1. ⒻⒻⒻ 55–57 av Raymond Poincaré, 75116. 【 01 44 05 66 10. Master chef Joël Robuchon, of the Michelin three-star Jamin restaurant, set the menu for this chic bistro. It features simple but delicious dishes. 🅖	AE DC MC V		▪	●	▪
CHAILLOT QUARTER: *Le Port-Alma.* Map 6 E1. ⒻⒻⒻⒻ 10 av de New-York, 75116. 【 01 47 23 75 11. The dishes here are influenced by the chef's native southwest France. Try the *bourride* (fish soup with garlic) or the sea bass in salt crust. 🅖	AE DC MC V		▪		
CHAILLOT QUARTER: *Alain Ducasse.* Map 9 C1. ⒻⒻⒻⒻⒻ 59 av Raymond Poincaré, 75116. 【 01 47 27 12 27. In a dining room decorated with *trompe l'oeil* and sculptures, Alain Ducasse creates the great classic dishes from meticulously chosen ingredients. 🅖 🅣	AE DC MC V	●	▪	●	
CHAMPS-ELYSÉES: *Berry's.* Map 3 B3. ⒻⒻ 44–46 rue de Naples, 75008. 【 01 40 75 01 56. The bistro annex of the excellent Grenadin restaurant features the cuisine of Le Berry, a region in the heart of France. Berry does a delicious leek and goat's cheese tart, and the pork dishes are also very tasty.	MC V		▪		
CHAMPS-ELYSÉES: *La Fermette Marbeuf 1900.* Map 2 F5. ⒻⒻⒻ 5 rue Marbeuf, 75008. 【 01 53 23 08 00. Come here to dine amid the stunning Belle Epoque decor. La Fermette serves good brasserie-style food, including a commendable set menu with many wines of *appellation contrôlée* status.	AE DC MC V		▪	●	▪
CHAMPS-ELYSÉES: *Le Cercle Ledoyen* ⒻⒻⒻ 1 av Duti, 75001. 【 01 53 05 10 00. Walls and ceiling of the handsome dining room are decorated with Parisian scenes. Food is simple yet refined: grilled brill with wild mushrooms, pheasant with quince and a wonderful range of chocolate desserts.	AE DC MC V		▪		▪
CHAMPS-ELYSÉES: *Au Petit Colombier.* Map 2 D3. ⒻⒻⒻⒻ 42 rue des Acacias, 75017. 【 01 43 80 28 54. The slightly rustic ambience of this comfortable restaurant complements the traditional provincial cuisine. An excellent place for a relaxing evening. 🅖	AE MC V		▪	●	
CHAMPS-ELYSÉES: *Lasserre.* ⒻⒻⒻⒻⒻ 17 av Franklin D Roosevelt, 75008. 【 01 43 59 53 43. For over 50 years, charismatic owner René Lasserre has labored to maintain one of the finest menus in Paris. Main courses are classics, desserts sublime. 🅣	AE MC V		▪	●	
CHAMPS-ELYSÉES: *Taillevent.* Map 2 F4. ⒻⒻⒻⒻⒻ 15 rue Lamennais, 75008. 【 01 45 61 12 90. Taillevent is the most elegant of Paris's three-star restaurants. The impeccable service, extraordinary wine list, and tempered Neo-Classic cuisine of Phillippe Legendre make for a memorable meal. 🅖 🅣	AE DC MC V			●	
ST-GERMAIN-DES-PRÉS: *Le Petit St-Benoît.* Map 8 E3. Ⓕ 4 rue St-Benoît, 75006. 【 01 42 60 27 92. This is the place for anyone who's on a budget or who wants to mix with the locals. The food is simple and tasty, and a good value.					▪
ST-GERMAIN-DES-PRÉS: *Marie et Fils.* Map 8 F4. ⒻⒻ 34 rue Mazarine, 75006. 【 01 43 26 69 49. Situated in the heart of St-Germain, this trendy restaurant provides delicious food – rabbit *terrine*, tuna steaks, and excellent desserts.	AE MC V		▪	●	▪

ST-GERMAIN-DES-PRÉS: *Restaurant Jacques Cagna.* **Map 8 F4.** ⓕⓕ AE MC V
14 rue des Grands Augustins, 75006. 📞 *01 43 26 49 39.*
This elegant 17th-century town house is a showcase for the excellent
classic-cum-contemporary cuisine of the chef/owner Jacques Cagna. 🍴

ST-GERMAIN-DES-PRÉS: *La Vigneraie* ⓕⓕ MC V
16 rue du Dragon, 75006. 📞 *01 45 48 57 04.*
This bustling Art Deco brasserie attracts a glittering clientele including
politicians and actors. Traditional dishes are its forte.

LATIN QUARTER: *Le Michalain.* **Map 9 B5.** ⓕ AE MC V
18 rue du Cardinal Lemoine, 75005. 📞 *01 43 54 29 50.*
A cozy bistro, about 10 minutes' walk from the Odéon, this offers friendly
service and very good food at budget prices.

LATIN QUARTER: *Bouillon Racine.* **Map 8 F5.** ⓕⓕ AE MC V
3 rue Racine, 75006. 📞 *01 44 32 15 60.*
Housed in a listed Art Nouveau building, this restaurant is now
rediscovering its former glory.

LATIN QUARTER: *Loubnane.* **Map 9 A4.** ⓕⓕ AE DC MC V
29 rue Galande, 75005. 📞 *01 43 26 70 60.*
This Lebanese restaurant serves generous mezzes under the watchful eye
of a patron whose main aim in life is the happiness of his customers.

LATIN QUARTER: *Le Bistrot d'A Côté.* **Map 9 B5.** ⓕⓕⓕ AE MC V
16 bd Saint-Germain, 75005. 📞 *01 43 54 59 10.*
The latest of star chef Michel Rostang's bistros, the menu offers a superb
selection of seafood and meat dishes cooked in classic Lyonnais style.

LATIN QUARTER: *La Tour d'Argent.* **Map 9 B5.** ⓕⓕⓕⓕ AE DC MC V
15–17 quai de la Tournelle, 75005. 📞 *01 43 54 23 31.*
Established in 1582, La Tour d'Argent consistently maintains top-class
status. The wine cellar must be one of the best in the world. 🍴

LUXEMBOURG QUARTER: *Perraudin.* **Map 12 F1.** ⓕ
157 rue St-Jacques, 75005. 📞 *01 46 33 15 75.*
Generations of students have come here to dig into home-cooked meals
at this turn-of-the-century bistro. The fixed-priced menu is a bargain.

LUXEMBOURG QUARTER: *Polidor.* **Map 8 F5.** ⓕ
41 rue Monsieur-le-Prince, 75006. 📞 *01 43 26 95 34.*
Artists, poets and writers have been attracted to this homey bistro
for decades. James Joyce was once a regular customer.

LUXEMBOURG QUARTER: *La Petite Cour.* **Map 8 E4.** ⓕⓕ AE MC V
8 rue Mabillon, 75006. 📞 *01 43 26 52 26.*
An old restaurant with a Napoleon III interior and a courtyard.
The menu includes skate with cabbage and beef stew with carrots.

LUXEMBOURG QUARTER: *Au Petit Marquéry.* **Map 13 B3.** ⓕⓕⓕ AE DC MC V
9 bd de Port-Royal, 75013. 📞 *01 43 31 58 59.*
Cold lobster *consommé* with caviar, mushroom salad with *foie gras* and
cod with spices are some of the unusual dishes served here.

MONTPARNASSE: *La Coupole.* **Map 12 D2.** ⓕⓕ AE DC MC V
102 bd du Montparnasse, 75014. 📞 *01 43 20 14 20.*
This is a lively and boisterous place all through the day and night. It has
been popular with artists and thinkers since 1927. Serves vegetarian dishes.

MONTPARNASSE: *L'Ostréade.* **Map 11 B2.** ⓕⓕ AE MC V
11 bd Vaugirard, 75015. 📞 *01 43 21 87 41.*
Next to the Gare Montparnasse, this is an attractive seafood restaurant.
The roast lobster, roast sea bass and Brittany oysters are delicious.

MONTPARNASSE: *La Cagouille.* **Map 11 C3.** ⓕⓕ AE MC V
10–12 pl Constantin Brancusi, 75014. 📞 *01 43 22 09 01.*
This is considered one of the best fish restaurants in Paris. The shellfish
platter is recommended. Also look for seasonal items on the menu.

MONTPARNASSE: *Le Vin des Rues.* **Map 12 D4.** ⓕⓕ
21 rue Boulard, 75014. 📞 *01 43 22 19 78.*
This is a good place to enjoy delicious and authentic
Lyonnaise cooking.

For key to symbols see back flap

| | **Average prices** for a three-course meal for one, including a half-bottle of house wine, tax and service:
F under F150
FF F150–F250
FFF F250–F350
FFFF F350–F500
FFFFF over F500 | **CHILDREN'S FACILITIES**
Some restaurants have high chairs and offer smaller portions for children.
FIXED-PRICE MENU
A good-value fixed-price menu available at lunch, dinner or both, often with three or more courses.
GOOD WINE LIST
Denotes a wide range of good wines, or otherwise a more specialized selection of local wines.
OUTDOOR TABLES
Facilities for eating outdoors, on a terrace or in a garden or courtyard, often with a good view. |

	CREDIT CARDS	CHILDREN'S FACILITIES	FIXED-PRICE MENU	GOOD WINE LIST	OUTDOOR TABLES
MONTPARNASSE: *La Regalade.* **Map 12** D5. **FFF** 49 av Jean Moulin, 75014. [01 45 45 68 58. The food here is outstanding, at a remarkable price. Chef Yves Camdeborde reinvents bistro cooking in his own inimitable style. [	MC V		■	●	
MONTMARTRE: *Au Grain de Folie.* **Map 4** F1. **F** 24 rue La-Vieuville, 75018. [01 42 58 15 57. This is a good-value vegetarian restaurant, portions are generous and organic wine is available. The specialty is the mixed vegetarian platter.			■		
MONTMARTRE: *Le Maquis* **FF** 69 rue Caulaincourt, 75018. [01 42 59 76 07. A pleasant bistro where you can enjoy a simple but delicious meal on the tree-shaded terrace. A very good value.	MC V	●	■		■
MONTMARTRE: *La Pomponette.* **Map 4** E1. **FF** 42 rue Lepic, 75018. [01 46 06 08 36. This is a restaurant to remember Montmartre by – the yellowing walls are covered with engravings, etchings, paintings and old photos of Montmartre as it was. Even the food has its own bohemian flavor.	MC V		■	●	■
MONTMARTRE: *Charlot Roi des Coquillages.* **Map 4** E2. **FFF** 12 place de Clichy, 75009. [01 53 20 48 00. Specialties here include *bouillabaisse* and a generous shellfish platter. The decor has retained its original 1930s style.	AE DC MC V	●	■		
MONTMARTRE: *Beauvilliers* **FFFF** 52 rue Lamarck, 75018. [01 42 54 54 42. Stepping into this restaurant, you are imbued with a sense of *joie de vivre*. Chef Edouard Carlier's cuisine is always exciting. [	AE DC MC V		■	●	■

ILE DE FRANCE

	CREDIT CARDS	CHILDREN'S FACILITIES	FIXED-PRICE MENU	GOOD WINE LIST	OUTDOOR TABLES
BARBIZON: *La Clé d'Or* **FF** 73 rue Grand. [01 60 66 40 96. This recently restored inn retains its old-world charm. Its specialties are shellfish, seafood and game in season.	AE DC MC V	●	■	●	■
BARBIZON: *Hostellerie les Pléiades* **FFF** 21 rue Grand. [01 60 66 40 25. Once the artist Daubigny's studio, this restaurant offers traditional cuisine such as kidneys and sweetbreads with wild mushrooms.	AE DC MC V	●	■	●	■
DAMPIERRE: *Auberge Saint-Pierre* **FFF** 1 rue de Chevreuse. [01 30 52 53 53. This half-timbered inn faces the grand Château de Dampierre. The menu offers classics such as *magret de canard* and *tête de veau* (calf's head).	MC V	●	■	●	■
DAMPIERRE: *Les Ecuries du Château* **FFF** Château de Dampierre. [01 30 52 52 99. Situated within the château, Les Ecuries offers a classic menu of seafood and meat dishes in a sophisticated setting.	AE DC MC V		■	●	
FONTAINEBLEAU: *Le Caveau des Ducs* **FFF** 24 rue de Ferrare. [01 64 22 05 05. Offers standard classic French cuisine in intimate rustic surroundings near to the fabulous Château de Fontainebleau.	AE MC V	●	■	●	■
MAISONS-LAFFITTE: *Le Tastevin* **FFFF** 9 avenue Eglé. [01 39 62 11 67. Outstanding cooking and carefully selected wines served in delightful surroundings make Michel Blanchet's restaurant one of the best in the Paris suburbs. Specialties include fish, seafood and poultry.	AE DC MC V		■	●	■

RAMBOUILLET: *Auberge Villa Marinette* (F)(F) MC V
20 av Général de Gaulle, D 906, Gazeran. (01 34 83 19 01.
Diners come here to enjoy the blend of Alsatian and Ile de France
specialties that include homemade terrines and fish dishes.

RUEIL-MALMAISON: *Relais de St-Cucufa* (F)(F)(F) AE V
114 rue Général-de-Miribel. (01 47 49 79 05.
Whether lunching in the garden or dining by the fire, guests can
enjoy specialties such as the crayfish ravioli or steamed salmon.

VERSAILLES: *Restaurant Chez Lazare* (F) AE MC V
18 rue de Satory. (01 39 50 41 45.
This fun South American restaurant is a pleasant change from French
classic cuisine. Seated below tiers of copper pots, diners enjoy
grilled fish and steaks. The fixed-price menu is for lunch only.

VERSAILLES: *Brasserie La Fontaine (Trianon Palace)* (F)(F) AE DC MC V
1 bd de la Reine. (01 30 84 38 47.
The annex to Les Trois Marches is no gourmet paradise
but allows visitors to enjoy a meal at acceptable prices in a beautiful
place. Serves seafood, grilled meats and rich chocolate desserts.

VERSAILLES: *Les Trois Marches (Trianon Palace)* (F)(F)(F)(F) AE DC MC V
1 bd de la Reine. (01 39 50 13 21.
The restaurant is part of the sumptuous palace overlooking the formal
gardens. The *haute cuisine* matches the splendor of the place.

LE NORD AND PICARDY

ABBEVILLE: *Au Châteaubriant* (F)(F) AE MC V
1 place de l'Hôtel de Ville. (03 22 24 08 23.
The *Quiche Picarde* (with sweet onions, ham and sour cream) and
steak in mushroom and Calvados sauce are recommended.

AMIENS: *La Couronne* (F)(F) AE MC V
64 rue Saint-Leu. (03 22 91 88 57.
To start, try a portion of homemade spicy duck pâté, followed
by a local specialty of salt marsh lamb from the Somme Abbey
nearby, accompanied by a Chinon wine.

ARRAS: *La Rapière* (F) AE MC V
44 Grand'Place. (03 21 55 09 92.
There are several menus, but the *menu régional* is a good value and offers
a varied selection of dishes. The chicken cooked in beer is delicious.

ARRAS: *La Faisanderie* (F)(F)(F)(F) AE DC MC V
45 Grand'Place. (03 21 48 20 76.
La Faisanderie is a classified historic building with a splendid brick-
vaulted dining room. The menu changes according to season.

AVESNES-SUR-HELPE: *La Crémaillière* (F)(F) MC V
26 place Général-Leclerc. (03 27 61 02 30.
A great place, with a menu featuring stuffed quails
and other local dishes.

CALAIS: *Le Channel* (F)(F)(F) AE DC MC V
3 bd de la Résistance, 62100. (03 21 34 42 30.
Watch the ships come and go as you enjoy a menu based on fresh
ingredients from the North Sea.

CAMBRAI: *L'Escargot* (F)(F) AE DC MC V
10 rue Général de Gaulle. (03 27 81 24 54.
Mme. Maton, the owner, has a regular clientele for her *plat du jour*,
which changes regularly. She also makes her own terrines and *foie gras*.

DOUAI: *La Terrasse* (F)(F)(F) AE MC V
36 terrasse St-Pierre. (03 27 88 70 04.
Breast of duck with fresh figs, and fillet of *sandre* (perch) on a bed
of sweet onions give some idea of the splendid cuisine available here.

DUNKERQUE: *Estaminet Flamand* (F) MC V
6 rue des Fusiliérs-Marins, 59140. (03 28 66 98 35
Delicious and authentic Flemish cuisine including charcoal-grilled
meats and sweet tarts

For key to symbols see back flap

<table>
<tr><td colspan="2">

Average prices for a three-course meal for one, including a half-bottle of house wine, tax and service:
F under F150
F F F150–F250
F F F F250–F350
F F F F F350–F500
F F F F F over F500

</td><td>

CHILDREN'S FACILITIES
Some restaurants have high chairs and offer smaller portions for children.
FIXED-PRICE MENU
A good-value fixed-price menu available at lunch, dinner or both, often with three or more courses.
GOOD WINE LIST
Denotes a wide range of good wines, or otherwise a more specialized selection of local wines.
OUTDOOR TABLES
Facilities for eating outdoors, on a terrace or in a garden or courtyard, often with a good view.

</td></tr>
</table>

	CREDIT CARDS	CHILDREN'S FACILITIES	FIXED-PRICE MENU	GOOD WINE LIST	OUTDOOR TABLES
DURY-LES-AMIENS: *L'Aubergade* **F F F** 78 Route Nationale, Saleux. [03 22 89 51 41. Try the chef's prizewinning *Charlotte de pommes de terre au pain d'épice et foie gras* (potato and spiced bread baked with *foie gras*).	AE MC V	●	■	●	
HALLINES: *L'Hostellerie St-Hubert* **F F F** 1 rue du Moulin. [03 21 39 77 77. The restaurant is situated in its own park at the edge of the Aa River. Offers a classic French menu with an impressive selection of cheeses.	DC MC V	●	■	●	
LILLE: *La Pâte Brisée* **F** 65 rue de la Monnaie. [03 20 74 29 00. Set in the Old Town, this rustic bistro specializes in bountiful servings of quiches, tarts, gratins, and mixed salads. It's always packed at lunch, so arrive early.	MC V	●	■		
LILLE: *Restaurant aux Moules* **F F** 34 rue de Béthune. [03 20 57 12 46. As its name suggests, mussels are the order of the day here, with a wide selection of styles. Local dishes such as *carbonnade flamande* are also good. Wash down your choice with local beer and enjoy the bustling, 1930s brasserie atmosphere.	AE DC MC V	●	■		
LONGUEAU: *La Potinière* **F F** 2 av Henri Barbusse. [03 22 46 22 83. Popular with the locals, this cozy restaurant offers a daily menu based on freshly bought produce. Dishes are richer in winter.	MC V	●	■		
MONTREUIL-SUR-MER: *Auberge de la Grenouillère* **F F F F** Rue de la Grenouillère, La Madeleine-sous-Montreuil. [03 21 06 07 22. This is an excellent restaurant, only 3 km (2 miles) west of Montreuil, for sampling French provincial cooking: braised quails with langoustines and frogs' legs are just two of the specialties.	AE DC MC V	●	■	●	●
POIX-DE-PICARDIE: *L'Auberge de la Forge* **F F F** Route Nationale 29, Caulières. [03 22 38 00 91. A traditional Picardy inn that serves good, old-fashioned, hearty fare: try the salt-marsh lamb or the trout with *foie gras*.	MC V	●	■	●	
ROYE: *La Flamiche* **F F F F** 20 place de l'Hôtel de Ville. [03 22 87 00 56. Braised eel and local wild duck with forest mushrooms are two particular favorites with diners here. Start with a *flamiche* (covered tart) of leeks or baked shrimps with grapefruit.	DC MC V	●	■	●	
ST-QUENTIN: *Le Pot d'Etain* **F F** Route Nationale 29, Holnon. [03 23 09 34 35. This is a newly opened and newly built hotel-restaurant with an emphasis on practicality and good service. The food is unpretentiously wholesome. 🅗	AE DC MC V	●	■	●	■
SANGATTE: *Les Dunes* **F F** Blériot-Plage. [03 21 34 54 30. By the beach, a short drive from the Channel Tunnel, this restaurant serves great seafood, including a cassoulet of mussels and cockles flambéed in whisky. 🅗	AE DC MC V	●	■		■
SARS-POTERIES: *L'Auberge Fleurie* **F F F** 67 rue Général-de-Gaulle. [03 27 61 62 48. Situated in pretty countryside, L'Auberge is an ancient, somewhat grand converted farmhouse. Game, venison, wild boar and partridge are in abundance in winter. A variety of shellfish also appear on the menu.	AE DC MC V	■	●	■	
WIMEREUX: *La Liégeoise* **F F** La digue. [03 21 31 61 15. At this fish restaurant, a salad of red mullet with balsamic vinegar makes a good appetizer, followed by braised turbot with scallops. 🅗	AE DC MC V	●	■	●	

CHAMPAGNE

AIX-EN-OTHE: *Auberge de la Scierie* — ⒻⒻⒻ — AE DC MC V
La Vove. 【 03 25 46 71 26.
This creeper-clad inn stands in a lovely garden by the river. The superb menu includes veal kidneys with cranberries, and snails in puff pastry.

AMBONNAY: *Auberge Saint-Vincent* — ⒻⒻⒻ — AE DC MC V
1 rue St-Vincent. 【 03 26 57 01 98.
This elegant restaurant with Louis XIII ceilings is a pleasure to dine in. The menu changes according to the season.

AUBRIVES: *Debette* — ⒻⒻ — AE MC V
2 place Louis-Debette. 【 03 24 41 64 72.
Ardennes specialties here include smoked ham, trout and game *terrines*. Splendid desserts are made with fruit from the owner's garden. 🪑

BIÈVRES: *Relais de St-Walfroy* — Ⓕ — AE MC V
Bièvres. 【 03 24 22 61 62.
An unusual dish on the menu is the braised guinea fowl with tiny mirabelle plums. There is also the perennial classic, *canard à l'orange*.

CHÂLONS-EN-CHAMPAGNE: *Les Ardennes* — ⒻⒻ — AE MC V
34 place de la République. 【 03 26 68 21 42.
The patron, M. Bouffonais, worked at the Savoy in London in the 1950s. His restaurant is a fine 17th-century house in this picturesque town. The menu is exceptionally wide with an extravagant selection of desserts.

CHAUMONT: *Bleu Comme Orange* — Ⓕ — MC V
11 rue Saint-Louis. 【 03 25 01 26 87.
Situated in the Old Quarter of Chaumont, this lively restaurant is always packed with locals at midday. It is essentially a *crêperie*, providing imaginative combinations of fillings.

EPERNAY: *L'Auberge Champenoise* — Ⓕ — MC V
Moussy. 【 03 26 54 03 48.
After visiting some of the vast champagne cellars in Epernay, this friendly inn is an excellent place to stop for an inexpensive meal.

L'EPINE: *Aux Armes de Champagne* — ⒻⒻⒻ — AE DC MC V
31 avenue du Luxembourg. 【 03 26 69 30 30.
This gourmet restaurant, which is in a pretty village just north of Châlons-en-Champagne, serves delicious regional specialties.

FLORENT-EN-ARGONNE: *Auberge de la Menyère* — ⒻⒻ — MC V
Rue Basse. 【 03 26 60 93 70.
The restaurant is a well-preserved, 400-year-old house set in a magnificent forest. Come in the hunting season to sample game with wild mushrooms.

JOINVILLE: *Le Soleil d'Or* — ⒻⒻ — AE DC MC V
9 rue des Capucins. 【 03 25 94 15 66.
Its monastic interior belies the restaurant's elegant service and eclectic menu. Try the tart of scallops with sweet basil. 🪑

LANGRES: *Le Lion d'Or* — ⒻⒻ — MC V
Route de Vesoul. 【 03 25 87 03 30.
This charming restaurant offers not only good regional food but also a panoramic view of the stunningly beautiful Lake Liez.

LE MESNIL-SUR-OGER: *Le Mesnil* — ⒻⒻⒻ — MC V
2 rue Pasteur. 【 03 26 57 95 57.
Just south of Epernay, between Cramant and Verbis, this gourmet restaurant is situated amid vineyards in one of the prettiest villages in Champagne. The *patron* is happy to show diners around his cellars.

NOGENT-SUR-SEINE: *Au Beau Rivage* — ⒻⒻ — MC V
20 rue Villiers-aux-Choux. 【 03 25 39 84 22.
Situated at the water's edge, this restaurant has a terrace overlooking the river. The menu's forte is fish cooked with fresh herbs.

REIMS: *La Coupole* — ⒻⒻ — AE DC MC V
73 place Drouet d'Erlon. 【 03 26 47 86 28.
La Coupole caters to all tastes, including vegetarian. The menu includes a wide range of *hors d'oeuvres*, imaginative salads and good fruit sorbets.

For key to symbols see back flap

<table>
<tr><td>

Average prices for a three-course meal for one, including a half-bottle of house wine, tax and service:

Ⓕ under F150
ⒻⒻ F150–F250
ⒻⒻⒻ F250–F350
ⒻⒻⒻⒻ F350–F500
ⒻⒻⒻⒻⒻ over F500

</td><td>

CHILDREN'S FACILITIES
Some restaurants have high chairs and offer smaller portions for children.

FIXED-PRICE MENU
A good-value fixed-price menu is available at lunch, dinner or both, usually with three courses.

GOOD WINE LIST
Denotes a wide range of good wines, or a more specialized selection of local wines.

OUTDOOR TABLES
Facilities for eating outdoors, on a terrace, or in a garden or courtyard, often with a good view.

</td></tr>
</table>

Column headers: CREDIT CARDS · CHILDREN'S FACILITIES · FIXED-PRICE MENU · GOOD WINE LIST · OUTDOOR TABLES

Restaurant	Price	Credit Cards	Children's Facilities	Fixed-Price Menu	Good Wine List	Outdoor Tables
REIMS: *Le Vigneron* Place Paul-Jamot. ☎ 03 26 79 86 86. This popular restaurant is particularly recommended for those who wish to sample dishes with a strong local flavor. A reservation is essential.	ⒻⒻ	MC V		■	●	■
REIMS: *Les Crayères* 64 boulevard Vasnier. ☎ 03 26 82 80 80. Set in ample grounds, this celebrated restaurant runs tours of its wine cellar. Specialties include smoked salmon and cream of caviar.	ⒻⒻⒻⒻ	AE DC MC V		■	●	■
ST-DIZIER: *La Gentilhommière* 29 rue Jean Jaurès. ☎ 03 25 56 32 97. Caul-wrapped chopped lamb with tarragon, and pike perch with a rich sauce made of the local forest mushrooms, are two favorites here. ♿	ⒻⒻ	MC V		■		
ST-DIZIER: *Hôtellerie du Moulin* Eclaron (9 km from St-Dizier). ☎ 03 25 04 17 76. Estimable food cooked with a light touch across a wide range of dishes in this wood-frame logis. ♿	ⒻⒻ	MC V	●	■	●	
ST-IMOGES: *La Maison du Vigneron* 51 Route Nationale. ☎ 03 26 52 88 00. Both a champagne house and a chic restaurant. Regional dishes are served and diners can enjoy the owner's champagne with their meals. ♿	ⒻⒻ	AE DC MC V	●	■	●	■
TROYES: *Le Jardin Gourmand* 31 rue Paillot de Montabert. ☎ 03 25 73 08 30. Set in the heart of the historic quarter, the restaurant occupies a romantic courtyard. This is the place to try the town's specialty – *andouillettes*.	ⒻⒻ	MC V		■		
TROYES: *Le Bourgogne* 40 rue Général de Gaulle. ☎ 03 25 73 02 67. Le Bourgogne is considered Troyes's finest restaurant (unfortunately, it's closed in August). Try the mousseline of pike or the hearty lamb stew.	ⒻⒻⒻ	MC V		■	●	

ALSACE AND LORRAINE

Restaurant	Price	Credit Cards	Children's Facilities	Fixed-Price Menu	Good Wine List	Outdoor Tables
BORNY: *Le Jardin de Bellevue* 58 rue Claude Bernard. ☎ 03 87 37 10 27. The chef has written a popular book about traditional Lorraine cuisine updated, and uses his own garden produce when available. ♿	ⒻⒻ	MC V	●	■	●	■
COLMAR: *Le Caveau Saint-Pierre* 24 rue de la Herse. ☎ 03 89 41 99 33. Reached by a boardwalk running alongside a canal in Colmar's pretty "Little Venice." At weekends in winter, the specialty to choose is the classic *baeckoff* (stew).	ⒻⒻ	V	●	■		
COLMAR: *La Maison des Têtes* 19 rue des Têtes. ☎ 03 89 24 43 43. The façade of this unique 17th-century brasserie is a registered historic monument. Serves traditional Alsace fare such as *choucroute*. ♿	ⒻⒻⒻ	AE DC MC V	●	■	●	■
DOLE: *Les Templiers* 35 Grande rue. ☎ 03 84 82 78 78. Adventurous dishes served in a truly sumptuous Gothic setting, and all at reasonable prices.	ⒻⒻ	AE DC MC V		■		
HAGUENAU: *Restaurant Barberousse* 8 place Barberousse. ☎ 03 88 73 31 09. Astonishingly good value, the lunchtime menu particularly. The dishes are unpretentious local fare: homemade foie gras and terrines, *choucroute* with meat or fish, and good hot desserts. ♿	ⒻⒻ	MC V	●	■		■

MARLENHEIM: *Le Cerf* Ⓕ Ⓕ Ⓕ | AE DC MC V
30 rue du Général-de-Gaulle. 📞 *03 88 87 73 73.*
This fine restaurant likes customers to arrive hungry. Alsatian cuisine here is at its richest, and the portions are immense. Vegetarians are welcomed. ♿

METZ: *Restaurant des Roches* Ⓕ Ⓕ | AE DC MC V
29 rue des Roches. 📞 *03 87 74 06 51.*
Predominantly a fish restaurant – filet of turbot with basil is very good – but there are plenty of meat dishes. The *soufflé glacé* is recommended.

MULHOUSE: *Restaurant de la Poste* Ⓕ Ⓕ Ⓕ | AE MC V
7 rue Général-de-Gaulle, Riedisheim. 📞 *03 89 44 07 71.*
Six generations of chefs have worked here to establish the reputation of this excellent restaurant. The menu is imaginative and varied.

NANCY: *L'Excelsior* Ⓕ Ⓕ | AE DC MC V
50 rue Henri Poincaré. 📞 *03 83 35 24 57.*
Take a step back in time and enjoy a delightful meal in this magnificent listed historic monument. The cuisine, like everything else about this restaurant, is classic French.

RIQUEWIHR: *Au Péché Mignon* Ⓕ | MC V
5 rue de Dinzheim. 📞 *03 89 49 04 17.*
This rustic restaurant offers robust Alsatian specialties, in *cuisine grand-mère* style – homey, and old-fashioned, with generous portions.

SAVERNE: *Taverne Katz* Ⓕ Ⓕ | MC V
80 Grand-Rue. 📞 *03 88 71 16 56.*
The cozy, polished-wood interior provides a perfect setting for traditional foods such as spaetzle (Alsatian noodles) and *jambonneau braisé* (ham).

SÉLESTAT: *Restaurant Jean-Frédéric Edel* Ⓕ Ⓕ Ⓕ | AE DC MC V
7 rue des Serruriers. 📞 *03 88 92 86 55.*
Homemade foie gras and tender filets of chicken with an exceptionally fine *choucroute* are two of the specialties in this renowned restaurant.

STRASBOURG: *Zum Strissel* Ⓕ | MC V
5 place de la Grande Boucherie. 📞 *03 88 32 14 73.*
An old-fashioned wine cellar in a 14th-century building near the cathedral. It serves mixed-meat stew, onion tart and pitchers of Alsatian wines.

STRASBOURG: *Restaurant au Crocodile* Ⓕ Ⓕ Ⓕ Ⓕ | AE DC MC V
10 rue de l'Outre. 📞 *03 88 32 13 02.*
This is probably Strasbourg's most exclusive restaurant. Visitors dine in opulent surroundings and their every whim is attended to. One of the recommended dishes is baked perch with smoked eel and carp roe.

TURCKHEIM: *Auberge du Brand* Ⓕ Ⓕ | MC V
8 Grand rue. 📞 *03 89 27 06 10.*
The cuisine has a regional flavor, but it is not as resolutely Alsatian as in the neighboring *winstubs* (wine bars). The service is prompt and discreet, and individual requests for vegetarian dishes are catered to.

VERDUN: *Le Coq Hardi* Ⓕ Ⓕ Ⓕ | AE DC MC V
8 avenue de la Victoire. 📞 *03 29 86 36 36.*
This gourmet restaurant is the best in Verdun, a city that otherwise has few good-quality, moderately priced restaurants.

NORMANDY

ACHERIE: *Le Manoir de l'Acherie* Ⓕ Ⓕ | AE MC V
50800 St-Cécil. 📞 *02 33 51 13 87.*
Calvados (apple brandy) is the flavor here – ham and even whiting are cooked in it and, of course, the apple tart is flambéed with it. ♿

ARGENTAN: *Restaurant d'Argentan* Ⓕ | MC V
22 rue Beigle, 61200. 📞 *02 33 36 19 38.*
Traditional peasant dishes, including Camembert salad and casserole of calves' sweetbreads, are served up here in this friendly restaurant.

AUDRIEU: *Château d'Audrieu* Ⓕ Ⓕ Ⓕ Ⓕ | AE MC V
Audrieu. 📞 *02 31 80 21 52.*
This 18th-century château was transformed into a luxurious hotel and restaurant in 1976. This is the place for an elegant dinner.

For key to symbols see back flap

Average prices for a three-course meal for one, including a half-bottle of house wine, tax and service: ⓕ under F150 ⓕⓕ F150–F250 ⓕⓕⓕ F250–F350 ⓕⓕⓕⓕ F350–F500 ⓕⓕⓕⓕⓕ over F500	**CHILDREN'S FACILITIES** Some restaurants have high chairs and offer smaller portions for children. **FIXED-PRICE MENU** A good-value fixed-price menu is available at lunch, dinner or both, usually with three courses. **GOOD WINE LIST** Denotes a wide range of good wines, or a more specialized selection of local wines. **OUTDOOR TABLES** Facilities for eating outdoors, on a terrace, or in a garden or courtyard, often with a good view.	CREDIT CARDS	CHILDREN'S FACILITIES	FIXED-PRICE MENU	GOOD WINE LIST	OUTDOOR TABLES
BAYEUX: *Le Lion d'Or* ⓕⓕⓕ 71 rue St Jean. 【 02 31 92 06 90. This 17th-century inn has been run by the same family since 1929, and serves delicious food. Try the unusual *foie gras* of duck with honey, hot andouille (sausage) or the mouth-watering forest mushroom tart.		AE DC MC V	●	■	●	
LE BEC-HELLOUIN: *Restaurant de la Tour* ⓕⓕ Place Guillaume-le-Conquérant. 【 02 32 44 86 15. It's best to reserve in advance to sample the traditional Norman cuisine here. After your meal you can buy Calvados and cider to take home with you.		AE DC MC V	●	■		■
CHAMPEAUX: *Au Marquis de Tombelaine* ⓕⓕ Sartilly. 【 02 33 61 85 94. The dishes to go for here are homemade foie gras, oysters and lobster Thermidor, accompanied by a bottle of Burgundy and ending with cheese.		MC V	●	■	●	■
CHERBOURG: *La Cendrée* ⓕ 18–20 passage Digard. 【 02 33 93 67 04. This simple but friendly restaurant offers probably the best value in town. It is popular with the locals and reservations are advisable.		MC V	●	■		
COSQUEVILLE: *Au Bouquet de Cosqueville* ⓕⓕⓕ Hameau Remond. 【 02 33 54 32 81. The specialties include lobster cooked in whisky, and turbot baked with leeks and truffles. For dessert try a fresh crêpe or crème brûlée. 【		MC V	●	■	●	■
CRESSERONS: *La Valise Gourmande* ⓕⓕ 7 route de Lion-sur-Mer. 【 02 31 37 39 10. Traditional Normandy food is served here against a setting of old beams and oak furniture. Try the mussels in butter, and *tergoule* (rice pudding).		MC V		■	●	■
DEAUVILLE: *Le Dauphin* ⓕⓕⓕ Le Breuil-en-Auge, Pont l'Evêque. 【 02 31 65 08 11. A reservation is essential for this much sought-after restaurant in a small hamlet. The owners, M. and Mme. Lecomte, spare no effort in making your visit a memorable one, and they take great pride in their cooking.		AE MC V		■	●	
DEAUVILLE: *Le Spinnaker* ⓕⓕⓕ 52 rue Mirabeau. 【 02 31 88 24 40. A one-star Michelin fish restaurant, this is one of Normandy's finest. The baked lobster in cider vinegar or turbot with shallots must be sampled. 【		AE DC MC V		■	●	
DIEPPE: *La Marmite Dieppoise* ⓕⓕ 8 rue St Jean. 【 02 35 84 24 26. Dieppe is one of the best places in France for seafood. The chef's *Marmite Dieppoise* is a tasty combination of fish and shellfish in a cream sauce.		MC V		■		
DOZULÉ: *Le Pavé d'Auge* ⓕⓕ Beuvron-en-Auge. 【 02 31 79 26 71. The highly talented chef at Le Pavé d'Auge likes to serve food made from local ingredients. The menu is strong on fish, with an assortment of meat and poultry dishes. The cheese platter has a good selection.		MC V	●	■		
GISORS: *Hostellerie des Trois Poissons* ⓕⓕ 13 rue Cappeville. 【 02 32 55 01 09. This half-timbered house, with an attractive terrace for summer dining, offers rabbit cooked in cider as its specialty.		V		■		■
HONFLEUR: *Le Champlain* ⓕⓕ 6 place Hamelin. 【 02 31 89 14 91. This family-run business uses only fresh farm produce. Favorites are scallops in puff pastry with orange butter and sautéed veal kidneys.		AE MC V		■		

HONFLEUR: *La Ferme St-Siméon* ⓕⓕⓕⓕⓕ
Rue A-Marais. 〖 02 31 89 23 61.
It is a delight to enjoy a light lunch here on the terrace. The food is
exquisitely prepared, featuring local seafood, poultry, fruits and cheese.

AE MC V

LA FERTÉ MACÉ: *Auberge le Clouet* ⓕⓕ
Chemin le Clouet. 〖 02 33 37 18 22.
An hour or two spent exploring the delightful, historic market town
should end with a meal of local specialties on this floral terrrace.

MC V

LOUVIERS: *Le Clos Normand* ⓕⓕ
16 rue de la Gare. 〖 02 32 40 03 56.
Mme. Deniau, the owner, loves to prepare food for appreciative guests
in this attractive 1890s town house. Vegetarian dishes served on request.

MC V

LYONS-LA-FORÊT: *La Licorne* ⓕⓕⓕ
Place Benserade. 〖 02 32 49 62 02.
The high quality belies the price in this 17th-century inn, where diners
eat in front of a massive fireplace. Vegetarians are catered to. 🅶

AE DC MC V

MONT-ST-MICHEL: *Hôtel Saint-Pierre* ⓕ
Grand Rue. 〖 02 33 60 14 03.
Lamb grazed on the salt marshes, known as *agneau pré-salé*, is featured
on the menu. Crab and sole are other favorites in this 15th-century building.

AE MC V

MONT-ST-MICHEL: *La Mère Poulard* ⓕⓕⓕⓕ
Grande-Rue. 〖 02 33 60 14 01.
Visitors from all over Europe come here to sample the famous *omelette
Mère Poulard*, cooked in a long-handled pan over a wood fire.

AE DC MC V

NONANT-LE-PIN: *Hôtel Saint-Pierre* ⓕ
Nonant-le Pin. 〖 02 33 39 94 04.
Set in the middle of France's horse-breeding country, the restaurant is on
the road to the Dordogne and Spain. The menu is simple but imaginative.

MC V

PUTANGES-PONT-ECREPIN: *Hôtel du Lion Ver* ⓕⓕ
Place de l'Hôtel-de-Ville. 〖 02 33 35 01 86.
The owner is especially proud of her veal cooked in local cider. The
lunchtime menu is a very good deal. Vegetarian dishes are available. 🅶

MC V

ROUEN: *La Marmite* ⓕⓕ
3 rue Florence 〖 02 35 71 75 55.
This attractive restaurant is housed in an 18th-century building. It
stays open late for guests to enjoy the romantic candlelit atmosphere.

AE MC V

ROUEN: *Restaurant Gill* ⓕⓕⓕⓕ
9 quai de la Bourse. 〖 02 35 71 16 14.
The *panaché de poissons* is a colorful dish of succulent fish and
seafood. Another specialty is pigs' feet with lentils.

AE DC MC V

ST-GERMAIN DE TALLEVENDE: *Auberge Saint-Germain* ⓕⓕ
Place de l'Eglise. 〖 02 31 68 24 13.
This is an ideal restaurant for families, with a menu of good home
cooking that caters to all tastes, including vegetarian. 🅶

MC V

THIBERVILLE: *La Levrette* ⓕ
10 rue de Lieurey. 〖 02 32 46 80 22.
Plain home cooking at competitive prices is the attractive feature of
this friendly place. Try the local free-range poultry.

V

TROUVILLE-SUR-MER: *Brasserie les Vapeurs* ⓕⓕ
160 boulevard Fernard-Moureaux. 〖 02 31 88 15 24.
Situated opposite the fish market, the seafood served here is truly fresh
and flavorful. You will be tempted to come back for more.

AE MC V

VEULES-LES-ROSES: *Les Galets* ⓕⓕⓕⓕ
3 rue Victor Hugo. 〖 02 35 97 61 33.
If you wish to have a meal by the sea, Les Galets is just the place.
A reservation is necessary as it is very popular with the locals.

AE MC V

VILLERS-BOCAGE: *Les Trois Rois* ⓕⓕ
2 place Jeanne d'Arc. 〖 02 31 77 00 32.
The special menu here, known as *mon marché*, consists of dishes
created by the owner from the catch of the day, fresh every morning.

AE DC MC V

Average prices for a three-course meal for one, including a half-bottle of house wine, tax and service: **Ⓕ** under F150 **ⒻⒻ** F150–F250 **ⒻⒻⒻ** F250–F350 **ⒻⒻⒻⒻ** F350–F500 **ⒻⒻⒻⒻⒻ** over F500	**CHILDREN'S FACILITIES** Some restaurants have high chairs and offer smaller portions for children. **FIXED-PRICE MENU** A good-value fixed-price menu is available at lunch, dinner or both, usually with three courses. **GOOD WINE LIST** Denotes a wide range of good wines, or a more specialized selection of local wines. **OUTDOOR TABLES** Facilities for eating outdoors, on a terrace, or in a garden or courtyard, often with a good view.	CREDIT CARDS	CHILDREN'S FACILITIES	FIXED-PRICE MENU	GOOD WINE LIST	OUTDOOR TABLES
BRITTANY						
AURAY: *L'Églantine* **ⒻⒻ** 17 place Saint-Sauveur, Saint-Goustan 56400. 🕻 *02 97 56 46 55.* Right on the port of Saint-Goustan, the fish here are simply prepared and wonderfully fresh.		MC V		■		
AURAY: *La Closerie de Kerdrain* **ⒻⒻⒻⒻ** 20 rue Louis-Billet. 🕻 *02 97 56 61 27.* A manor house with an imposing stone staircase and First Empire tapestries in the dining room. Specialties include sea bass and clams.		AE DC MC V	●	■	●	■
BELLE-ISLE-EN-TERRE: *Le Relais de l'Argoat* **ⒻⒻ** 9 rue de Guic. 🕻 *02 96 43 00 34.* This old coaching inn on the edge of a pretty village has two dining rooms with a very friendly atmosphere. An excellent cheeseboard.		MC V	●	■		
CONCARNEAU: *Le Galion* **ⒻⒻ** 15 rue St-Guénolé. 🕻 *02 98 97 30 16.* Situated on the tip of a peninsula, the restaurant is almost surrounded by water. It serves a wide range of fish in a romantic setting.		MC V	●	■		
DINAN: *Chez la Mère Pourcel* **ⒻⒻⒻ** 3 place des Merciers. 🕻 *02 96 39 03 80.* This restaurant is in a stunning old Gothic building. The menu changes seasonally and the standard is consistent, with excellent Loire wines.		AE DC MC V	●	■	●	■
FOUGÈRES: *Restaurant des Voyageurs* **ⒻⒻ** 10 place Gambetta. 🕻 *02 99 99 14 17.* Located in the town center, this restaurant has a high ceiling and massive chandeliers. The cuisine is local, with hearty game dishes in winter.		AE MC V	●	■		
HÉDÉ: *L'Hostellerie du Vieux Moulin* **ⒻⒻⒻ** Ancienne route de St-Malo. 🕻 *02 99 45 45 70.* The old mill was part of a complex built in the 19th century to supply water power, and it has views of the ruins of Hédé Castle. There are particularly good lunches of scallops, grilled prawns and duck.		AE DC MC V	●	■		■
LE CONQUET: *Les Boucaniers* **Ⓕ** 3 rue Poncelin. 🕻 *02 98 89 06 25.* A *crêperie* in a granite building done up as a fisherman's cottage. Try the crêpes with goat's cheese, or with orange and chocolate.		MC V	●			■
LORIENT: *Le Neptune* **ⒻⒻ** 15 ave de la Perrière. 🕻 *02 97 37 04 56.* Ask for a table in the rear dining room with conservatory. A wide range of fish is served, but try the lobster flambé or fricassée of monkfish.		AE DC MC V	●	■		
MORLAIX: *La Marée Bleue* **ⒻⒻ** 3 rampe St-Melaine. 🕻 *02 98 63 24 21.* Standing in the shadow of the viaduct, this old town house has become a first-class restaurant. Customers return often for the flawless fish dishes.		MC V	●	■	●	
PAIMPOL: *La Vieille Tour* **ⒻⒻ** 13 rue de l'Eglise. 🕻 *02 96 20 83 18.* This is a friendly, old-fashioned restaurant with the dining room on the first floor. Some rare delicacies are served, including ravioli stuffed with crayfish tails or cherry-filled chocolate mousse in raspberry sauce.		MC V	●	■		
PLÉLAN-LE-GRAND: *L'Auberge du Presbytère* **ⒻⒻ** Treffendel. 🕻 *02 99 61 00 76.* In an old priest's house that has changed little over the centuries, the chef serves poultry and pigeon in a number of traditional dishes.		MC V	●	■		■

PLOMEUR: *Le Relais Bigouden*   ⒻⒻ
Rue Pen Allée. 【 02 98 82 04 79.
A cheerful and friendly restaurant full of fresh flowers, where the specialties include duck cooked in fresh lime and lobster in a ragoût.

MC
V

PLOUNÉRIN: *Restaurant Patrick Jeffroy*   ⒻⒻⒻ
Le Bourg. 【 02 96 38 61 80.
The restaurant has 45 seats in two dining rooms. The crayfish with artichokes are a must, complemented by cider from the local château.

MC
V

PONT L'ABBÉ: *Le Relais de Ty-Boutic*   ⒻⒻ
Route de Plomeur. 【 02 98 87 03 90.
A serious gourmet, the chef has won several prizes. His best dishes are monkfish with cider, and prawns with leeks.

MC
V

QUIBERON: *Le Relax*   ⒻⒻ
27 boulevard Castéro. 【 02 97 50 12 84.
With lovely views over the sea and a pretty garden, you will find a wide selection of superbly cooked fish here, changing seasonally.

AE
DC
MC
V

QUIMPER: *L'Ambroisie*   ⒻⒻ
49 rue Elie Fréron. 【 02 98 95 00 02.
A short walk from the cathedral, this newly decorated restaurant has Francis Bacon prints on the walls. The fish and desserts are excellent.

MC
V

RENNES: *Le Corsaire*   ⒻⒻ
52 rue d'Antrain. 【 02 99 36 33 69.
In a grand town house, Le Corsaire is renowned locally. The braised oxtail and the *abalones* are specialties. Good Muscadet wines.

AE
DC
MC
V

RENNES: *Le Piano Blanc*   ⒻⒻ
Route de Sainte-Foix, 35000. 【 02 99 31 20 21.
Just outside the town, fish dishes are served under the lime trees in summer, and in front of a roaring fire in winter.

AE
MC
V

ST-BRIEUC: *Amadeus*   ⒻⒻⒻ
22 rue de Gouët. 【 02 96 33 92 44.
One of the oldest buildings in this historic town, the oak beams and stone walls remain. Fish predominates – fillet of sole dished up with duck liver is exceptional – and there is a wide range of desserts.

AE
MC
V

ST-MALO: *Le Franklin*   Ⓕ
4 chaussée du Sillon. 【 02 99 40 50 93.
A restaurant overlooking the sea. Specialties include fish cooked with spices and *pré-salé* lamb which is raised on the salt marshes.

AE
DC
MC
V

VITRÉ: *La Taverne de l'Ecu*   ⒻⒻ
12 rue Baudrairie. 【 02 99 75 11 09.
A half-timbered Renaissance house with a courtyard and a 16th-century dining room. The fish is delicate and tasty.

AE
MC
V

THE LOIRE VALLEY

AMBOISE: *Le Manoir St. Thomas*   ⒻⒻⒻ
Place Richelieu. 【 02 47 57 22 52.
The elaborate, Renaissance-style decor, the ability of the chef, and a sensational wine cellar make this place irresistible.

AE
DC
MC
V

ANGERS: *Restaurant La Ferme*   Ⓕ
2 place Freppel. 【 02 41 87 09 90.
A hectic restaurant that spills outdoors in summer. Rustic dishes like *coq au vin* and snails are popular, as is the white Anjou wine.

AE
MC
V

ANGERS: *La Terrasse*   ⒻⒻ
La Pointe de Bouchemaine, Bouchemaine. 【 02 41 77 11 96.
Located in a hamlet on the confluence of the Loire and Maine rivers, this panoramic restaurant cooks freshly caught eels, pike, salmon and other freshwater fish over an open fire.

AE
MC
V

ANGERS: *La Salamandre*   ⒻⒻⒻ
1 boulevard du Maréchal-Foch. 【 02 41 88 99 55.
The slightly kitsch interior belies the strength of the food. Sample ravioli stuffed with lobster, and steaks, fish soups and rich cheeses.

AE
DC
MC
V

	CREDIT CARDS	CHILDREN'S FACILITIES	FIXED-PRICE MENU	GOOD WINE LIST	OUTDOOR TABLES

Average prices for a three-course meal for one, including a half-bottle of house wine, tax and service:
Ⓕ under F150
ⒻⒻ F150–F250
ⒻⒻⒻ F250–F350
ⒻⒻⒻⒻ F350–F500
ⒻⒻⒻⒻⒻ over F500

CHILDREN'S FACILITIES
Some restaurants have high chairs and offer smaller portions for children.
FIXED-PRICE MENU
A good-value fixed-price menu is available at lunch, dinner or both, usually with three courses.
GOOD WINE LIST
Denotes a wide range of good wines, or a more specialized selection of local wines.
OUTDOOR TABLES
Facilities for eating outdoors, on a terrace, or in a garden or courtyard, often with a good view.

Restaurant	Price	Credit Cards	Children's Facilities	Fixed-Price Menu	Good Wine List	Outdoor Tables
BEAUGENCY: *Le P'tit Bateau* 54 rue du Pont. 📞 02 38 44 56 38. Near the château, Le P'tit Bateau is the most appealing restaurant in town. It is popular with the locals and offers fresh fish, game and wild mushrooms, all washed down with regional wines.	ⒻⒻ	MC V		■		■
BLOIS: *La Mesa* 11 rue Vauvert. 📞 02 54 78 70 70. Eat outside in the pretty square in the summer, and sample unusual salads from the Loire region, fish, veal and a range of tasty *crudités*.	Ⓕ	AE MC V		■		
BLOIS: *Le Duc de Guise* 15 place Louis XII. 📞 02 54 78 22 39. A boisterous family-oriented Italian restaurant near the château. Pizzas are cooked in traditional fashion, in wood-fired ovens. 🔣	ⒻⒻ	AE MC V	●	■		■
BLOIS: *La Péniche* Promenade du Mail. 📞 02 54 74 37 23. Located on a beautifully restored barge on the river. Fresh fish is served amid tables adorned with linen and flowers.	ⒻⒻ	AE DC MC V		■	●	
BOURGES: *La Courcillière* Rue de Babylone. 📞 02 48 24 41 91. Near the marshes with a view of the Yèrrc River, this serves delicious freshwater fish and duck and is worth the 20-minute walk from town.	ⒻⒻ	AE MC V	●	■		■
BOURGES: *Le Jardin Gourmand* 15 bis, boulevard Ernest-Renan. 📞 02 48 21 35 91. A gourmet restaurant in an old town house decorated with elegance and style. Specialties include seafood, curried lamb and poultry.	ⒻⒻ	AE MC V	●	■	●	■
BOURGUEIL: *L'Auberge la Lande* Borgueuil. 📞 02 47 97 92 41. This auberge, set in an old town house, uses only local produce for its homely but delicious dishes. There is a good choice of local Borgueil wines.	Ⓕ	MC V		■	●	
CHARTRES: *Le Buisson Ardent* 10 rue au Lait. 📞 02 37 34 04 66. With a splendid view of the cathedral, this restaurant is in the oldest part of Chartres. The new chef's baked salmon in vinaigrette and cod in coriander are very tasty.	ⒻⒻ	MC V	●	■	●	
CHARTRES: *Le Grand Monarque* 22 place des Epars. 📞 02 37 21 00 72. Established in a large farmhouse dating from the 17th century, the interior was refurbished in 1987. The food is uneven but can be excellent, and there is a first-rate wine cellar.	ⒻⒻⒻ	AE DC MC V	●	■	●	■
CHEVERNY: *Le Pousse-Rapière* Rue Nationale. 📞 02 54 79 94 23. Facing the château, the restaurant serves dishes from the Loire and Gascony; the Gascon influence shows in the *foie gras* and *cassoulet*.	ⒻⒻ	AE MC V	●	■	●	
CHINON: *Les Années 30* 78 rue Voltaire. 📞 02 47 93 37 18. An elegant little eatery on the way up to the château. Pike, pork *rillons* (cooked in fat and served cold) and *coq au vin* are served in an airy dining room, or out on the terrace.	ⒻⒻ	MC V	●	■	●	■
FONTEVRAUD-L'ABBAYE: *La Licorne* Allée Sainte-Cathérine. 📞 02 41 51 72 49. The elegant setting and pretty courtyard, plus the oysters and asparagus, make this a popular place to dine. Reserve tables in summer.	ⒻⒻⒻ	AE DC MC V		■	●	■

GIEN: *Le Rivage* — ⓕⓕⓕ — AE DC MC V
1 quai de Nice. 📞 *02 38 37 79 00*.
Eat on the flower-lined terrace overlooking the Loire. Sample rich meat dishes, an interesting cheese board and unusual local wines.

LA BOHALLE: *Auberge de la Gare* — ⓕ — MC V
3 impasse de la Gare. 📞 *02 41 80 41 20*.
After a dinner of snails, seafood, steak and good local cheeses take a stroll down to the riverbank behind this friendly inn.

LAMOTTE-BEUVRON: *Hôtel Tatin* — ⓕⓕⓕ — AE MC V
5 avenue de Vierzon. 📞 *02 54 88 00 03*.
The menu of game, trout and local red wine is overshadowed by this restaurant's famous dessert, *tarte Tatin* (upside-down apple pie).

LE MANS: *La Cité d'Aleth* — ⓕ — MC V
7 & 9 rue de la Vieille Porte. 📞 *02 43 28 73 81*.
A family-run crêperie in Le Vieux Mans, this offers *crêpes* of all descriptions, complemented by salads and fruity desserts. ♿

LE MANS: *Le Grenier à Sel* — ⓕⓕ — AE MC V
26 place de L'Eperon. 📞 *02 43 23 26 30*.
Well-situated for exploring the Old Town, this restaurant specializes in fish served with light sauces. ♿

LE MANS: *La Vie en Rose* — ⓕ — AE DC MC V
55 Grand Rue. 📞 *02 43 23 27 37*.
Stone walls and rose-colored decor create a soft mood. The cuisine is essentially *nouvelle*. Seafood dishes are beautifully presented.

MONTBAZON: *La Chancelière* — ⓕⓕⓕⓕ — MC V
1 place des Marronniers. 📞 *02 47 26 00 67*.
A real favorite with the locals, this has a newly decorated dining room and offers delicious pigs' feet, sweetbreads and regional fare.

NANTES: *La Taverne de Maitre Kanter* — ⓕ — AE DC MC V
1 place Royale. 📞 *02 40 48 55 28*.
Part of a reliable chain, this Alsatian tavern excels in its offerings of *choucroute* (sauerkraut) and cold meats. Try the beers, too.

NANTES: *La Cigale* — ⓕⓕ — MC V
4 place Graslin. 📞 *02 51 84 94 94*.
The interior of this Belle Epoque brasserie is decorated with tiles and gilding; the quality and choice of cuisine are also exceptional.

NANTES: *L'Atlantic* — ⓕⓕ — AE MC V
26 bd Stalingrad, 44000. 📞 *02 40 74 00 72*.
Good home cooking is on offer at this simple restaurant not far from the train station.

ORLÉANS: *Auberge de la Croix Blanche* — ⓕⓕ — MC V
Marcilly-en-Villette. 📞 *02 38 76 10 14*.
Twenty km (12 miles) south of Orléans, this auberge offers delicate fish, satisfying cheeses, dessert trolley and good Sauvignon wine.

ORLÉANS: *La Chancellerie* — ⓕⓕ — AE MC V
27 place du Martroi. 📞 *02 38 53 57 54*.
This brasserie on the town's main square draws people in with its liveliness. Staple brasserie fare is enlivened by the wines.

ORLÉANS: *La Tête de l'Art* — ⓕ — MC V
Cloître St-Pierre-Empont. 📞 *02 38 54 14 39*.
An enthusiastic young clientele give this a spirited atmosphere. The *tête de veau*, *coq au vin* and vast salads are very good choices. ♿

SACHÉ: *Auberge du XII Siécle* — ⓕⓕⓕ — MC V
Rue Principal. 📞 *02 47 26 88 77*.
In an old, historic building in the center of town, this auberge offers regional specialties such as *sandre* (a local fish) and *escargots*.

SAUMUR: *Auberge St-Pierre* — ⓕ — AE DC MC V
6 place St-Pierre. 📞 *02 41 51 26 25*.
This auberge is hidden in an old-fashioned square near the château. Its regional specialties include pike in butter and *coq au vin*. ♿

For key to symbols see back flap

	CREDIT CARDS	CHILDREN'S FACILITIES	FIXED-PRICE MENU	GOOD WINE LIST	OUTDOOR TABLES

Average prices for a three-course meal for one, including a half-bottle of house wine, tax and service:
Ⓕ under F150
ⒻⒻ F150–F250
ⒻⒻⒻ F250–F350
ⒻⒻⒻⒻ F350–F500
ⒻⒻⒻⒻⒻ over F500

CHILDREN'S FACILITIES
Some restaurants have high chairs and offer smaller portions for children.

FIXED-PRICE MENU
A good-value fixed-price menu is available at lunch, dinner or both, usually with three courses.

GOOD WINE LIST
Denotes a wide range of good wines, or a more specialized selection of local wines.

OUTDOOR TABLES
Facilities for eating outdoors, on a terrace, or in a garden or courtyard, often with a good view.

		Credit Cards	Children's Facilities	Fixed-Price Menu	Good Wine List	Outdoor Tables
SAUMUR: *Les Caves de Marson* Rou-Marson. 〖 02 41 50 50 05. Booking is essential at this troglodyte restaurant, with a fixed-price menu including pancakes with beans and goat's cheese.	Ⓕ	MC V	●			
TOURS: *L'Atelier Gourmand* 37 rue Etienne-Marcel, 37000. 〖 02 47 38 59 87. The chef here extends a warm welcome to his regulars, producing specialties that include ling in a tarragon cream sauce, and rabbit braised with spices.	ⒻⒻ	AE DC MC V		■	●	■
TOURS: *Les Naiades* 63 rue Blaise Pascal. 〖 02 47 05 27 92. The dining room has recently been renovated in Louis XV style. The pan-roasted prawns and pigeon in couscous should not be missed.	ⒻⒻ	MC V	●	■	●	
TOURS: *L'Arche de Meslay* Zone Industrielle, 37000. 〖 02 47 29 00 07. Well worth a detour despite the unpromising address. Try the turbot in Vouvray with *andouillettes* (tripe sausages) and the spiced ice cream.	ⒻⒻⒻ	AE MC V		■	●	
TOURS: *La Roche Le Roy* 55 rue de St-Avertin. 〖 02 47 27 22 00. Another Michelin-starred establishment, somewhat formal but in a romantic manor house. The emphasis is on seasonal fish and game. 〣	ⒻⒻⒻⒻ	AE DC MC V	●	■	●	■
TOURS: *Jean Bardet* 57 rue Groisson. 〖 02 47 41 41 11. The gastronomic temple of the Loire. With two Michelin stars and a dazzling wine list, diners revel in oysters, lobster, scallops and truffles of all kinds. Prices are better not taken into consideration!	ⒻⒻⒻⒻⒻ	AE DC MC V	●	■	●	
VENDOME: *Le Vieux Moulin* 21–23 rue du Change. 〖 02 54 72 29 10. Set in a well-converted mill, the brasserie is better known for its ambience than the strength of its pleasant, but unexceptional, food.	Ⓕ	MC V	●			■
VILLANDRY: *Domaine de la Giraudière* Route de Druye. 〖 02 47 50 08 60. A roadside working farm ideal for a country lunch. The produce is homegrown, the meals homemade: pâtés, stuffed tomatoes and quiches. 〣	Ⓕ	AE MC V	●	■		■
VOUVRAY: *La Cave Martin* 66 vallée Coquette. 〖 02 47 52 62 18. Carved into the rocks around wine caves, this restaurant has a typical rustic menu of *andouillettes* (sausages), duck and salads.	Ⓕ	MC V	●	■		■

BURGUNDY AND FRANCHE-COMTÉ

BEAUNE: *La Bouzerotte* Bouze les Beaune. 〖 03 80 26 01 37. In winter, a roaring fire makes this the coziest place in Burgundy. In summer, enjoy the warm evenings and the cuisine on the terrace. The hearty regional dishes are all cooked to order.	ⒻⒻ	MC V	●			■
BEAUNE: *La Ciboullette* 69 rue Lorraine. 〖 03 80 24 70 72. The decor is simple, but the bistro cooking is excellent, and the best value in Beaune. Solid, simple dishes include steak and pork.	ⒻⒻ	AE MC V	●	■		
BEAUNE: *Le Gourmandin* 8 place Carnot. 〖 03 80 24 07 88. A stainless steel modern interior is warmed by buzzing crowds. The chef provides good, satisfying bistro cooking including *boeuf bourguignon*.	ⒻⒻ	MC V		■		■

BEAUNE: *Les Coquines* ⓕⓕ — AE DC MC V
Ladoix Serrigny. 〖 03 80 26 43 58.
Feast on solid Burgundy cooking, with the emphasis on quantity. The restaurant is located in a vineyard and the wines are exceptional.

BEAUNE: *Jean-Crotet* ⓕⓕⓕⓕ — AE DC MC V
Route de Combertault, Levernois. 〖 03 80 24 73 58.
"Serious" cuisine is served up in a beautiful old mansion. The Bresse chicken and braised spiced sweetbreads are carefully cooked. 丞

CHAGNY: *Château de Bellecroix* ⓕⓕⓕⓕ — AE DC MC V
Route Nationale 6. 〖 03 85 87 13 86.
This charming mansion was once the property of the Order of the Knights of Malta and boasts a Neo-Gothic dining room. Local dishes are a specialty and the desserts are mouth-watering. 丞

CHAGNY: *Lameloise* ⓕⓕⓕⓕ — AE DC MC V
36 place d'Armes. 〖 03 85 87 65 65.
The cheapest Michelin three-star restaurant in France, this family-run restaurant is not the slightest bit pretentious. It exudes warmth and offers classic Burgundy cooking, done to perfection.

CHATEAUNEUF: *La Fontaine* ⓕⓕ — AE MC V
Chateauneuf. 〖 03 85 26 26 87.
An extravagant pink and pistachio mosaic interior sets the scene for inventive and delicious interpretations of traditional dishes.

CHATEAUNEUF: *Hostellerie du Château* ⓕⓕⓕ — AE DC MC V
Chateauneuf. 〖 03 80 49 22 00.
Set in a picturesque medieval village, this modestly priced inn is simple and friendly. The straightforward food is good value for money.

DIJON: *Le Bistrot des Halles* ⓕⓕ — MC V
10 rue Bannelier. 〖 03 80 49 94 15.
At lunchtime, this bistro is roaring. Next to the market, it attracts all sorts of food merchants and local business people, who come here to enjoy fish pâté, steak tartare and grilled lamb chops.

DIJON: *Breuil La Chouette* ⓕⓕ — AE DC MC V
1 rue de la Chouette. 〖 03 80 30 18 10.
An exponent of "old school" cuisine, the chef has injected new life into classics such as frogs' legs and salmon. The huge cellar boasts a fine slection of Burgundy wines. 丞

DIJON: *Le Chabrot* ⓕⓕ — V
36 rue Monge. 〖 03 80 30 69 61.
The cozy interior and chatty owner make this restaurant as popular as the good fixed-price menu. Burgundy wine is served by the glass.

DIJON: *Jean-Pierre Billoux* ⓕⓕⓕⓕ — AE DC MC V
13 place de la Libération. 〖 03 80 38 05 05.
Run by the most renowned chef in Dijon, its cooking effectively combines rustic traditional ingredients with novel flavors.

FONTANGY: *Ferme Auberge de la Morvandelle* ⓕ
Précy sous Thil. 〖 03 80 84 33 32.
This is a working farm, open to guests only on weekends. Book in advance to experience rabbit, guinea fowl and homemade tarts. 丞

GEVREY-CHAMBERTIN: *Le Bon Bistrot* ⓕ — MC V
Rue de Chambertin. 〖 03 80 34 33 20.
Mouthwatering Burgundian delicacies are served at very reasonable prices for this region. On fine days you can dine on the terrace.

GEVREY-CHAMBERTIN: *La Sommellerie* ⓕⓕⓕ — MC V
7 rue Souvert. 〖 03 80 34 31 48.
Stylish service and regional cuisine meet in a wine-colored dining room. Salmon ravioli with caviar and the Côtes de Nuit wine are a must.

GEVREY-CHAMBERTIN: *Les Millésimes* ⓕⓕⓕⓕ — MC V
25 rue de l'Eglise. 〖 03 80 51 84 24.
This family concern, in a wine-making cellar, provides friendly service, exotic cuisine and wonderful wines. Veal, sweetbreads, truffles and a superb cheese board make it a firm favorite with all who visit.

<table>
<tr><td>

Average prices for a three-course meal for one, including a half-bottle of house wine, tax and service:
Ⓕ under F150
ⒻⒻ F150–F250
ⒻⒻⒻ F250–F350
ⒻⒻⒻⒻ F350–F500
ⒻⒻⒻⒻⒻ over F500

</td><td>

CHILDREN'S FACILITIES
Some restaurants have high chairs and offer smaller portions for children.
FIXED-PRICE MENU
A good-value fixed-price menu at lunch, dinner or both, usually with three courses.
GOOD WINE LIST
Denotes a wide range of good wines, or a more specialized selection of local wines.
OUTDOOR TABLES
Facilities for eating outdoors, on a terrace or in a garden or courtyard, often with a good view.

</td></tr>
</table>

	CREDIT CARDS	CHILDREN'S FACILITIES	FIXED-PRICE MENU	GOOD WINE LIST	OUTDOOR TABLES
LA CROIX-BLANCHE: *Le Relais Mâconnais* ⒻⒻ Berze la Ville. 03 85 36 60 72. Burgundy beef cooked with red Mâcon wine, and slices of duck liver in strawberry vinegar are on the menu of this acclaimed restaurant.	AE DC MC V	●	■		■
MARCIGNY SOUS THIL: *L'Auberge Pénélopé* Ⓕ Marcigny. 03 80 64 52 34. A country inn on a quiet backroad. The unassuming exterior hides culinary invention at very reasonable prices. Worth a detour.	MC V		■		■
MEURSAULT: *Relais de la Diligence* ⒻⒻ 23 rue de la Gare. 03 80 21 21 32. In a drab location by an old station, the Relais bulges with locals on Sunday at lunchtime. The quantity and quality of dishes such as *coq au vin* and *boeuf bourguignon* is superb.	AE DC MC V	●	■	●	■
NITRY: *La Beursaudière* ⒻⒻ Chemin de Ronde. 03 86 33 69 69. The staff wear peasant costume. A full four-course meal – plainly presented but very appetizing – is served at a reasonable price.	AE DC MC V	●	■		■
QUARRÉ LES TOMBES: *Auberge de l'Atre* ⒻⒻⒻⒻ Les Lavaults. 03 86 32 20 79. The decorative interior of this restaurant in the Morvan region contrasts with the rustic simplicity of the building. It is known locally to offer the best value in its price range.	AE DC MC V	●	■		
RABOLIOT: *Le Raboliot* Ⓕ Place Marché. 02 38 97 44 52. In a village just off the A6, the style here is an eclectic mixture of Corsican and French cooking, with hefty portions of game in season.	MC V	●	■		
SAINTE-MAGNANCE: *La Chenevotte* ⒻⒻ Route Nationale 6. 03 86 33 14 79. A simple country inn with no pretensions. The decor is wooden and rustic, and the food is heartwarming. Go for Burgundy specialties like *coq au vin*.	MC V				
ST-LAURENT-SUR-SAÔNE: *Le St-Laurent* ⒻⒻ 1 quai Bouchacourt. 03 85 39 29 19. 1900s kitsch fills George Blanc's city bistro, which serves adventurous versions of local specialties. The white Mâcon wine is a good buy.	AE DC MC V	●	■		■
ST-PÈRE-SOUS-VÉZELAY: *Le Pré des Marguerites* ⒻⒻ St-Père-sous-Vézelay. 03 86 33 20 45. Somewhat antiseptic inside, this annex to *L'Espérance* offers a rustic menu of traditional Burgundian dishes in a cold environment.	AE MC V				
ST-PÈRE-SOUS-VÉZELAY: *L'Espérance* ⒻⒻⒻⒻⒻ St-Père-sous-Vézelay. 03 86 33 39 10. Arguably the greatest eating experience in Burgundy. An airy dining room leads onto a terrace with expansive views. Marc Meneau, one of France's finest chefs, turns traditional dishes into modern classics.	AE DC MC V	●	■	●	
SAULIEU: *La Poste* ⒻⒻ 1 rue Grillot. 03 80 64 05 67. This is a former coaching inn with well-preserved charm. Try sole and turbot *terrine* or pigeon in truffle juice, along with good local wines.	AE DC MC V	●	■	●	
SAULIEU: *La Côte d'Or* ⒻⒻⒻⒻⒻ 2 rue d'Argentine. 03 80 90 53 53. Old-fashioned decor misleads here. The chef serves up an imaginative *cuisine moderne*, including rabbit livers, snail and nettle soup and perch in wine. Very sumptuous with an extensive wine list.	AE DC MC V	●	■	●	

SENS: *Hôtel de Paris et de la Poste* ⒻⒻⒻ
97 rue de la République, 89100. 🕻 03 86 65 17 43.
This establishment has been run by the same family for three generations.
Diners watch as roasts are carved, and desserts are flambéed at the table.

TOURNUS: *Restaurant Greuze* ⒻⒻⒻⒻⒻ | AE MC V
1 rue A Thibaudet. 🕻 03 85 51 09 11.
Here's the place to enjoy some of the best classic cooking in France.
The restaurant is a monument to a bygone age, serving cognac-infused
quenelles, buttery frogs' legs and creamy choux pastry appetizers. ⓖ

VILLARS-FONTAINE: *Auberge du Coteau* Ⓕ | V
Villars-Fontaine, D35 W of Nuits St-Georges. 🕻 03 80 61 10 50.
Set among the vineyards of the Haute-Côtes de Nuits, this cosy inn
serves hearty Burgundy fare at great prices.

VILLENEUVE-SUR-YONNE: *Auberge la Lucarne aux Chouettes* ⒻⒻ | AE MC V
Quai Bretoche. 🕻 03 86 87 18 26.
Renovated by actress Leslie Caron, this restaurant has a lovely setting
by the Yonne River. The staff try very hard to please. ⓖ

VONNAS: *L'Ancienne Auberge* ⒻⒻ | AE DC MC V
Place de Marché. 🕻 04 74 50 90 50.
The clientele is often wealthy Parisians rather than locals. Fancier and
more expensive than most bistros, it is still well worth a visit. ⓖ

VONNAS: *Georges Blanc* ⒻⒻⒻⒻⒻ | AE DC MC V
Vonnas. 🕻 04 70 50 90 90.
A popular shrine of cooking, with smooth service in a dining room
crammed with antiques. The inventive menu includes fish and game. ⓖ

THE MASSIF CENTRAL

AUMONT-AUBRAC: *Prouhèze* ⒻⒻⒻ | AE V
2 route du Languedoc. 🕻 04 66 42 80 07.
The award-winning chef uses only the freshest ingredients to create
elegant and unusual flavors. The presentation is often a little basic. ⓖ

AURILLAC: *A la Reine Margot* ⒻⒻ | MC V
19 rue Guy-de-Veyre. 🕻 04 71 48 26 46.
The place to sample the rustic dishes of the Auvergne. The high
quality hams, pork and beef are the pride of the region.

BESSE-EN-CHANDESSE: *Les Mouflons* ⒻⒻ | MC V
Route de Super Besse. 🕻 04 73 79 56 93.
The fish is locally caught and delicious; try the salmon trout or the
turbot with *cèpes*, washed down with lively local Chanturgue red wine.

BOURGES: *Jacques-Coeur* ⒻⒻ | AE DC MC V
3 place Jacques-Coeur. 🕻 02 48 70 12 72.
Diners enjoy local specialties against a medieval backdrop. The cooking
can be bland; the best bet is the scallops, kidneys or Loire salmon. ⓖ

BOUSSAC: *Le Relais Creusois* ⒻⒻⒻ | MC V
Route de la Châtre. 🕻 05 55 65 02 20.
Expect the luxury here to come from the high standard of cuisine, not
the surroundings. The desserts are exquisite, as are the Bordeaux wines.

CLERMONT-FERRAND: *Le Chardonnay* Ⓕ | V
1 place Philipe-Marcombes. 🕻 04 73 90 18 28.
As well as enjoying hearty Auvergne cuisine, wine-lovers can consult
the *patron-sommelier* for his selection from the wide range of superb
wines, many of which can be sampled by the glass.

CLERMONT-FERRAND: *Le Charade* ⒻⒻ | AE DC MC V
51 rue Bonnabaud. 🕻 04 73 93 59 69.
The new chef is gaining confidence and making tasty salads,
duck and a range of delicious desserts. The fixed-price menu
includes wine. ⓖ

ESPALION: *Le Méjane* ⒻⒻⒻ | AE DC MC V
8 rue Méjane. 🕻 05 65 48 22 37.
Exceptionally good prices for a menu offering dishes such as
confit of rabbit with *foie gras* and snails with garlic cream.

For key to symbols see back flap

Average prices for a three-course meal for one, including a half-bottle of house wine, tax and service:
- Ⓕ under F150
- ⒻⒻ F150–F250
- ⒻⒻⒻ F250–F350
- ⒻⒻⒻⒻ F350–F500
- ⒻⒻⒻⒻⒻ over F500

CHILDREN'S FACILITIES
Some restaurants have high chairs and offer smaller portions for children.

FIXED-PRICE MENU
A good-value fixed-price menu available at lunch, dinner or both, usually with three courses.

GOOD WINE LIST
Denotes a wide range of good wines, or a more specialized selection of local wines.

OUTDOOR TABLES
Facilities for eating outdoors, on a terrace, or in a garden or courtyard, often with a good view.

	Credit Cards	Children's Facilities	Fixed-Price Menu	Good Wine List	Outdoor Tables
LAGUIOLE: *Michel Bras* ⒻⒻⒻⒻ Route de L'Aubrac. ☎ 05 65 51 18 20. A wall of glass gives views over the Aubrac countryside from Michel Bras' hilltop restaurant. The goat's and sheep's cheeses are recommended.	AE DC MC V	●	■		
LIMOGES: *Philippe Redon* ⒻⒻ 3 rue d'Aguesseau. ☎ 05 55 34 66 22. Philippe Redon offers first-class local ingredients, particularly fish. The dishes are conventional but well cooked, and the wines are good.	AE DC MC V	●	■	●	
MONTSALVY: *Auberge Fleurie* Ⓕ Place du Barry. ☎ 04 71 49 20 02. A friendly village inn with a cheery atmosphere and a motherly chef who prepares wonderful mushroom omelettes and green salads. ☒	MC V	●	■	●	■
MURAT: *Le Jarrousset* ⒻⒻⒻ Route Nationale 122. ☎ 04 71 20 10 69. This is a discreet, simple restaurant. The chef uses local ingredients like green lentils and "free-range" veal, cooked to perfection. ☒	MC V	●	■	●	■
RODEZ: *Le St-Amans* ⒻⒻ 12 rue de la Madeleine. ☎ 05 65 68 03 18. Traditional cooking with sophistication – the *cassoulet des fruits de mer* is flavored with aniseed, the pigeon with a touch of cocoa. ☒	MC V		■		
ROYAT: *La Belle Meunière* ⒻⒻ 25 avenue de la Vallée. ☎ 04 73 35 80 17. The chef, Jean-Claude Bon, won a Gault Millau award for his repertoire of regional dishes. The menu is regularly updated, but the classics include cabbage stuffed with pigs' feet and *crêpes* with Bleu d'Auvergne cheese. ☒	AE DC MC V	●	■		■
ST-ETIENNE: *Nouvelle* ⒻⒻ 30 rue St-Jean. ☎ 04 77 32 32 60. An elegant setting and attentive staff as well as the culinary treats make this a very popular restaurant. Advance booking is advised to ensure a chance to sample the inventive cuisine.	AE MC V		■		
ST-JEANNE-EN-VAL: *La Bergerie* ⒻⒻⒻ Sarpoil. ☎ 04 73 71 02 54. This restaurant has become a local favorite, so reservations are essential in the evening. Choose from an ever-changing, inventive menu. ☒	AE DC MC V	●	■		
ST-JULIEN-CHAPTEUIL: *Vidal* ⒻⒻⒻ Place du Marché. ☎ 04 71 08 70 50. The best quality local produce is served here, and the menus change according to the season. ☒	AE MC V	●	■	●	
VICHY: *La Veranda* ⒻⒻ 3 place Joseph-Aletti. ☎ 04 70 31 78 77. Part of the Aletti Palace Hotel, La Veranda serves rock lobster, beef and regional cheeses in modern surroundings.	AE DC MC V	●	■		■
THE RHÔNE VALLEY AND FRENCH ALPS					
AIX-LES-BAINS: *Lille* ⒻⒻ Grand Port. ☎ 04 79 63 40 00. One of the best restaurants in Aix, especially for the elaborate fish dishes. It is close to the landing docks for the lake steamers. ☒	AE DC MC V	●	■		■
BOURG-EN-BRESSE: *Jacques Guy* ⒻⒻⒻ 19 place Bernard. ☎ 04 74 45 29 11. The local specialty, *Bresse* chicken, is perfection, as are the *terrines* and *hors d'oeuvres*. Desserts and wines are also superb. ☒	AE DC MC V	●	■	●	■

CHAMBÉRY: *La Chaumière* (F)
14 rue Denfert-Rochereau. (04 79 33 16 26.
A cozy dining room that serves good quality traditional dishes. The fish, duck and *foie gras* are particular bargains. &
Credit cards: AE, MC, V

CHAMBÉRY: *L'Essentiel* (F)(F)(F)
183 place de la Gave. (04 79 96 97 27.
Talented young chef Jean-Michel Bouvier creates generous specialties including his winter salad with freshwater fish.
Credit cards: AE, MC, V

CHAMONIX: *Albert 1er* (F)(F)(F)(F)
119 impasse du Montenvers. (04 50 53 05 09.
The superb cooking of chef Pierre Carrier at this one-Michelin-star restaurant is matched by the wonderful views over Mont Blanc. The *foie gras* is especially recommended.
Credit cards: AE, DC, MC, V

CHAMONIX: *L'Impossible* (F)(F)
Route des Pélerins. (04 50 53 20 36.
Originally a farmhouse, the rustic dining room is warmed by a huge fire. There is an emphasis on cheese dishes such as traditional *raclette* and fondue. Entrecôte and tournedos steaks can be ordered too.
Credit cards: MC, V

COLLONGES-AU-MONT-D'OR: *Paul Bocuse* (F)(F)(F)(F)(F)
50 quai de la Plage. (04 72 42 90 90.
Try specialties like black truffle soup with pastry and fillet of sole with coriander and vanilla butter. The wines are also high quality. &
Credit cards: AE, DC, MC, V

COURCHEVEL: *La Bergerie* (F)(F)(F)
Route de Nogentil. (04 79 08 24 70.
Popular with the rich and famous, this is a two-tiered restaurant with dancing on the ground floor. Lunches and drinks are served upstairs.
Credit cards: AE, MC, V

COURCHEVEL: *Le Chabichou* (F)(F)(F)(F)
Quartier des Chenus. (04 79 08 00 55.
Reserve seats by the huge windows to enjoy views of the mountains. The cuisine is creative and exotic here, one of the most popular (but expensive) restaurants in this extensive resort. &
Credit cards: AE, DC, MC, V

EVIAN-LES-BAINS: *Savoy* (F)(F)
17 quai Charles Besson. (04 50 83 15 00.
The restaurant offers views of the lake and across into Switzerland. The Savoyard specialties include *fondue* and *gratin dauphinois*. &
Credit cards: AE, DC, MC, V

GRENOBLE: *Amerindia* (F)
4 place des Gordes. (04 76 51 58 39.
A bright and cheerful restaurant on a South American theme, with an enjoyable choice of vegetarian options on the menu.
Credit cards: MC, V

GRENOBLE: *Le Berlioz* (F)(F)(F)
4 rue de Strasbourg. (04 76 56 22 39.
Housed in an 18th-century mansion, this restaurant features a different seasonal menu with regional specialties each month. &
Credit cards: AE, DC, MC, V

LYON: *Le Bouchon aux Vins* (F)(F)
62 rue Mercière. (04 78 42 88 90.
A very popular restaurant serving regional cuisine. Try the *charcuterie*, rabbit and *pot-au-feu*, with praline tarts for dessert. &
Credit cards: AE, MC, V

LYON: *Le Mercière* (F)(F)
56 rue Mercière. (04 78 37 67 35.
A busy, first-class restaurant where reservations are essential. The fixed-price menu provides very substantial dishes, and the *à la carte* is a rare treat. Its offerings include snails, monkfish and mussels. &
Credit cards: AE, DC, MC, V

LYON: *Léon de Lyon* (F)(F)(F)(F)(F)
1 rue Pléney. (04 72 10 11 12.
The expert chef and owner serves local food with a modern twist, in a two-story building set on the Presqu'Île in the heart of the city. The menu changes ten times a year. &
Credit cards: AE, MC, V

LYON: *La Tour Rose* (F)(F)(F)(F)(F)
22 rue du Boeuf. (04 78 37 25 90.
In a Renaissance convent, the chef concentrates on flavorful fish and vegetables, also providing a huge cheeseboard and good wines.
Credit cards: AE, DC, MC, V

Average prices for a three-course meal for one, including a half-bottle of house wine, tax and service:
F under F150
FF F150–F250
FFF F250–F350
FFFF F350–F500
FFFFF over F500

CHILDREN'S FACILITIES
Some restaurants have high chairs and offer smaller portions for children.
FIXED-PRICE MENU
A good-value fixed-price menu available at lunch, dinner or both, usually with three courses.
GOOD WINE LIST
Denotes a wide range of good wines, or a more specialized selection of local wines.
OUTDOOR TABLES
Facilities for eating outdoors, on a terrace, or in a garden or courtyard, often with a good view.

	CREDIT CARDS	CHILDREN'S FACILITIES	FIXED-PRICE MENU	GOOD WINE LIST	OUTDOOR TABLES
MEGÈVE: *Le Chamoix* F Place de l'Eglise. 04 50 21 25 01. A popular restaurant in the center of town, serving such regional specialties as smoked ham.	MC V		■		
MEGÈVE: *Les Enfants Terribles* FF Place de l'Eglise. 04 50 58 76 69. A refined menu on which expensive ingredients like truffles and *foie gras* are used to brighten up locally inspired dishes. ⅄	AE MC V	●	■		■
MORZINE: *La Chamade* FF Morzine. 04 50 79 13 91. The extravagant draped décor of the dining room is complemented by beautifully presented main courses and delicate, exotic desserts. ⅄	DC MC V	●		●	■
PÉROUGES: *Hostellerie du Vieux Pérouges* FFF Place du Tilleul. 04 74 61 00 88. In a 13th-century timbered building, this restaurant is exceptionally good. Try *Ypocras*, a liqueur made to a recipe from medieval times.	AE MC V	●	■		
ROANNE: *Chez Troisgros* FFFFF Place de la Gare. 04 77 71 66 97. One of the most prestigious restaurants in France, with elegant contemporary decor. Dishes include salmon with sorrel. ⅄	AE DC MC V	●	■	●	
TALLOIRES: *Villa des Fleurs* FFF Route du Port. 04 50 60 71 14. The lake in the grounds here is picturesque, and it also provides the restaurant's main attraction – a rare, succulent fish called *féra*.	MC V	●	■		■
TALLOIRES: *Le Père Bise* FFFFF Route du Port. 04 50 60 72 01. A mixture of locals and wealthy tourists gathers to worship at one of France's gastronomic shrines. The faultless food and panoramic views of the garden and lake somewhat offset the very high prices! ⅄	AE DC MC V	●	■	●	■
THONON-LES-BAINS: *Le Belvédère* F 3 rue des Ursules. 04 50 71 75 64. Close to the shores of Lac Léman, Le Belvédère mainly serves *feuilletés*; light, assorted flaky pastries filled with meat and vegetables.	MC V	●			
VALENCE: *Restaurant Pic* FFFFF 285 avenue Victor-Hugo. 04 75 44 15 32. Fillet of sea bass in caviar, *charolais* beef and intricate desserts have helped the reputation of this establishment grow. ⅄	AE DC MC V		■	●	
VIENNE: *Magnard* FF 45 cours Brillier. 04 74 85 10 43. Traditional cuisine includes fillet of turbot with mussels, tournedos in a morel-flavored sauce and chicken with shrimp. ⅄	MC V	●	■		■

POITOU AND AQUITAINE

	CREDIT CARDS	CHILDREN'S FACILITIES	FIXED-PRICE MENU	GOOD WINE LIST	OUTDOOR TABLES
ANGOULÊME: *Auberge du Pont de la Meure* FF Nersac. 05 45 90 60 48. A combined café-restaurant beside the Charente River. Salads of chicken livers, stewed eel and goat in garlic are worth a special trip.	AE DC MC V		■	●	
BORDEAUX: *La Mamounia* F 51 rue Lafourie-Monbadon. 05 56 81 21 84. A draped ceiling lends a tentlike atmosphere to this smart Moroccan restaurant, which is a haven for vegetarians. Couscous is the main item on the menu. Sweet mint tea is served with your meal. ⅄	AE DC MC V		■	●	

BORDEAUX: *Chez Philippe* (F)(F) AE DC MC V
1 place du Parlement. 05 56 81 83 15.
A casual, lively spot specializing in fresh fish and shellfish, with the deserved reputation of being the best fish restaurant in Bordeaux.

BORDEAUX: *La Tupina* (F)(F) AE DC MC V
6 rue Porte de la Monnaie. 05 56 91 56 37.
Dishes are cooked over an open fire in a friendly atmosphere. Bistro food predominates, such as charcoal-grilled poultry and *pétoucles* (scallops).

BORDEAUX: *Le Clavel St-Jean* (F)(F) MC V
44 rue Charles-Domercq. 05 56 92 63 07.
This modern bistro is one of the few places where Bordeaux wine can be sampled by the glass. The menus are good and varied.

BORDEAUX: *Le Chapon Fin* (F)(F)(F)(F) AE DC MC V
5 rue de Montesquieu. 05 56 79 10 10.
Thick, meaty soup with chunks of pigeon and chestnuts, rich eel and red wine stew and local oysters are some of the treats here.

BOULIAC: *Le Bistroy* (F)(F) AE DC MC V
3 place Camille-Hostein. 04 57 97 06 06.
This buzzing place gets its food from the neighbouring top restaurant St-James, meaning the same sensational cuisine at a lower price.

COGNAC: *Les Pigeons Blancs* (F)(F) AE DC MC V
110 rue Jules Brisson. 05 45 82 16 36.
Owned by the same family since the 17th century, this old post house is an attractive place to eat. The service, wine and food are excellent.

CROUTELLE: *La Chenaie* (F)(F) AE MC V
Ligugé. 05 49 57 11 52.
Deep in the Poitevin hills, this cheery farmhouse offers tasty *salade de langouste*, rabbit with artichokes and rich local goat's cheese.

ILE DE RÉ: *Café du Phare* (F) MC V
St-Clément-des-Baleines. 05 46 29 46 66.
A café beneath the lighthouse serves the local specialty, *poutargue* (cod's roe, shallots and sour cream), in Art Deco surroundings.

JARNAC: *Restaurant du Château* (F)(F) AE MC V
15 place du Château. 05 45 81 07 17.
A traditional establishment, immensely popular with the locals, that produces prawn salads, sea bass and cabbage stuffed with rabbit.

LANGON: *Claude Darroze* (F)(F)(F)(F) AE DC MC V
95 cours du Général Leclerc. 05 56 63 00 48.
Gaudy *trompe l'oeil* decor should not detract from the generosity and quality of the food, best washed down with a premium local claret.

LA ROCHELLE: *Yachtman* (F)(F) MC V
23 quai Valin. 05 46 50 63 14.
Diners enjoy fresh seafood in comfortable portside surroundings. The cellar has a small but choice range of local wines.

LA ROCHELLE: *Richard Coutanceau* (F)(F)(F)(F) AE DC MC V
Plage de la Concurrence. 05 46 41 48 19.
Overlooking the beach, this is a big, bright restaurant run by a trendy young chef. Simple, authentic dishes combine with exotic desserts.

MARGAUX: *Le Savoie* (F)(F)
Rue de la Poste. 05 57 88 31 76.
This little town house, next to a *maison du vin*, offers good-value menus made up of simple yet original dishes, with fish as a specialty.

MIMIZAN: *Au Bon Coin du Lac* (F)(F)(F)(F) AE DC MC V
34 avenue du Lac. 05 58 09 01 55.
Plushness and luxury abound at this lakeside eatery. There are views of the lake from both the dining room and pretty terrace.

NIORT: *Les Mangeux du Lumas* (F)(F) AE MC V
La Garette. 05 49 35 93 42.
Sample a favorite local treat, *lumas* – tiny snails – bathed in butter, cream or a regional aperitif known as *pineau des Charentes*.

Average prices for a three-course meal for one, including a half-bottle of house wine, tax and service: Ⓕ under F150 ⒻⒻ F150–F250 ⒻⒻⒻ F250–F350 ⒻⒻⒻⒻ F350–F500 ⒻⒻⒻⒻⒻ over F500	**CHILDREN'S FACILITIES** Some restaurants have high chairs and offer smaller portions for children. **FIXED-PRICE MENU** A good-value fixed-price menu available at lunch, dinner or both, usually with three courses. **GOOD WINE LIST** Denotes a wide range of good wines, or a more specialized selection of local wines. **OUTDOOR TABLES** Facilities for eating outdoors, on a terrace, or in a garden or courtyard, often with a good view.	**CREDIT CARDS**	**CHILDREN'S FACILITIES**	**FIXED-PRICE MENU**	**GOOD WINE LIST**	**OUTDOOR TABLES**
PAUILLAC: *Château Cordeillan-Bages* ⒻⒻⒻⒻ Route des Châteaux. 【 05 56 59 24 24. The award winning wine waiter at this establishment, right in the heart of Bordeaux country, will guide you through the extensive wine list to find the perfect accompaniment to a splendid meal. 🔥	AE DC MC V	●	■	●	■
POITIERS: *Maxime* ⒻⒻ 4 rue St-Nicholas. 【 05 49 41 09 55. A chic restaurant for sophisticated palates. Dishes include tender duck in delicious Hungarian Tokay wine, monkfish and ravioli of hot oysters.	AE DC MC V	●	■		
ROYAN: *La Jabotière* ⒻⒻⒻ Pontaillac. 【 05 46 39 91 29. Modern cuisine is offered in a renovated beachfront restaurant. Choose the ravioli of rabbit in pistachio oil, fresh sole and apple gratin. 🔥	AE MC V	●	■		■
ST-EMILION: *Hostellerie de Plaisance* ⒻⒻⒻ Place du Clocher. 【 05 57 55 07 55. Enjoy the view over the roofs of the medieval town and sample good regional cuisine along with superb wines from across the country. 🔥	AE DC MC V	●	■	●	
SAINTES: *Brasserie Louis* ⒻⒻ 116 avenue Gambetta. 【 05 46 74 16 85. A local favorite, this is a crowded brasserie serving wonderful seafood – the *fruits de mer* are a must. A very good value.	MC V	●	■		■
PÉRIGORD, QUERCY AND GASCONY					
ALBI: *Hostellerie du Vigan* ⒻⒻ 16 place Vigan. 【 05 63 54 01 23. An unpretentious and inexpensive, somewhat businesslike place to eat, which produces good local dishes at a remarkable price. 🔥	AE DC MC V	●	■		
ALBI: *Le Moulin de la Mothe* ⒻⒻ Rue de la Mothe. 【 05 63 60 38 15. The restaurant is close to the cathedral in pretty grounds. Its typical Tarn dishes include perch fillets and roast pigeon. 🔥	AE DC MC V	●	■	●	■
AUCH: *L'Auberge de Lartigue* Ⓕ Saramon. 【 05 62 65 41 22. Don't be put off by appearances – this is wonderful, off-the-beaten-track Gascony. The *foie gras* comes in a variety of forms, all superb. 🔥		●	■		
AUCH: *Restaurant Roland Garreau* ⒻⒻⒻⒻⒻ 2 place de la Libération. 【 05 62 61 71 71. Avoid the experimental nature of some of the dishes and stay with the classics – *assiette des trois foie gras*, fresh goose and sweet wines.	AE DC MC V	●	■	●	
BARBOTAN-LES-THERMES: *La Bastide Gasconne* ⒻⒻ Barbotan-les-Thermes. 【 05 62 08 31 00. This restaurant is increasingly popular with the locals, always a good sign. Flawless dishes such as "pizza" of asparagus tips and mushrooms, sweetbreads and tuna marinated with green olives are served impeccably.	AE MC V	●	■		
BERGERAC: *Le Cyrano* ⒻⒻ 2 boulevard Montaigne. 【 05 53 57 02 76. Generous portions of regional food at a premium – a fixed-price menu of astonishing value. Wash it all down with local Bergerac wines.	MC V	●	■	●	
BRANTÔME: *Les Frères Charbonnel* ⒻⒻⒻ 57 rue Gambetta. 【 05 53 05 70 15. Bargain-priced wines, hearty salad, red mullet in lobster sauce and *foie gras* can be enjoyed while watching ducks on the Dronne River. 🔥	AE DC MC V	●	■	●	■

BRANTÔME: *Moulin de L'Abbaye* Ⓕ Ⓕ Ⓕ — AE DC MC V
1 route de Bourdeilles. ▐ 05 53 05 80 22.
Dine in luxury on traditional Perigord cooking complemented
by dishes such as *terrine* of brill. 🛇 🛏

BRANTÔME: *Le Moulin du Roc* Ⓕ Ⓕ Ⓕ Ⓕ — AE DC MC V
Champagnac-de-Belair. ▐ 05 53 02 86 00.
A converted oil mill in a romantic spot overlooking the Dronne River.
The cooking is inconsistent, but the fish is recommended. 🛇

CAHORS: *Le Troquet des Halles* Ⓕ — MC V
55 rue St-Maurice. ▐ 05 65 22 15 81.
This is a locals' restaurant right beside the market. The food is robust
and good – with a very cheap fixed-price menu. 🛇

CAHORS: *Claude Marco* Ⓕ Ⓕ — AE DC V
Lamagdelaine. ▐ 05 65 35 30 64.
A rustic restaurant with a cosy oak-beamed dining room and a delightful
terrace. An abundance of regional specialties are on offer, such as *foie gras*.

CAHORS: *Le Balandre* Ⓕ Ⓕ Ⓕ — AE DC MC V
5 avenue Charles-de-Freycinet. ▐ 05 65 30 01 97.
An immaculate dining room where you can enjoy generous helpings
of typical southwestern fare and a good selection of Cahors wines. 🛇

CASTELJALOUX: *La Vieille Auberge* Ⓕ Ⓕ
11 rue Posterne, 47700. ▐ 05 53 93 01 36.
Situated in the Old Town, this restaurant offers delicious Gasconne
specialties and excellent value for money.

DOMME: *L'Esplanade* Ⓕ Ⓕ Ⓕ Ⓕ — AE DC MC V
Place de la Barre. ▐ 05 53 28 31 41.
Avoid high prices here by sticking to trout, salmon or rack of lamb.
There are panoramic views from the huge yellow-and-blue restaurant. 🛇

LES-EYZIES-DE-TAYAC: *Cro-Magnon* Ⓕ Ⓕ Ⓕ — AE DC MC V
Les Eyzies-de-Tayac. ▐ 05 53 06 97 06.
An old-fashioned, vine-covered restaurant with beams and a giant fire-
place. *Foie gras*, pigeon and goose are featured on its regional menu. 🛇

MARMANDE: *Restaurant Trianon* Ⓕ Ⓕ — MC V
Route d'Agen. ▐ 05 53 20 80 94.
Fresh catch such as monkfish, pigeon and the house specialty of
lamprey eel from the Garonne River are on the menu here. 🛇

MONTAUBAN: *Le Ventadour* Ⓕ Ⓕ — AE MC V
23 quai Villebourbon. ▐ 05 63 63 34 58.
A popular place with the local townspeople, who appreciate the plain
cooking and reasonable prices at this centrally located restaurant.

MONTFORT-CAUDON: *La Ferme* Ⓕ Ⓕ — MC V
Caudon-de-Vitrac. ▐ 05 53 28 33 35.
It is worth a detour to sample the rustic charm of this restored farmhouse.
Rye bread soup, thick ham and lamb chops come in huge portions.

MONTRÉAL-DU-GERS: *Chez Simone* Ⓕ Ⓕ Ⓕ — AE MC V
Montréal-du-Gers. ▐ 05 62 29 44 40.
Another restaurant very much admired by people in the know, due to
the generous helpings of excellent locally produced *foie gras*.

PERIGUEUX: *Au Petit Chef* Ⓕ — DC MC V
5 place du Coderc. ▐ 05 53 53 16 03.
Choose the lowest price menu, comprising soup, a buffet of *hors d'oeuvres*,
main course, and pâtisserie – all homemade. Shut on Saturday evenings.

PÉRIGUEUX: *Hôtel-Restaurant Périgord* Ⓕ Ⓕ — V
74 rue Victor-Hugo. ▐ 05 53 53 33 63.
A delightful hotel, set in a leafy garden, serving highly regarded cuisine,
in its charmingly old-fashioned dining room. 🛇

PUYMIROL: *Les Loges de l'Aubergade* Ⓕ Ⓕ Ⓕ Ⓕ Ⓕ — AE DC MC V
52 rue Royale. ▐ 05 53 95 31 46.
One of the great restaurants of the southwest, this is not to be missed.
The beautiful medieval building on a hilltop adds to the delight. 🛇

For key to symbols see back flap

....

	CREDIT CARDS	CHILDREN'S FACILITIES	FIXED-PRICE MENU	GOOD WINE LIST	OUTDOOR TABLES

Average prices for a three-course meal for one, including a half-bottle of house wine, tax and service:
Ⓕ under F150
ⒻⒻ F150–F250
ⒻⒻⒻ F250–F350
ⒻⒻⒻⒻ F350–F500
ⒻⒻⒻⒻⒻ over F500

CHILDREN'S FACILITIES
Some restaurants have high chairs and offer smaller portions for children.
FIXED-PRICE MENU
A good-value fixed-price menu available at lunch, dinner or both, usually with three courses.
GOOD WINE LIST
Denotes a wide range of good wines, or a more specialized selection of local wines.
OUTDOOR TABLES
Facilities for eating outdoors, on a terrace, or in a garden or courtyard, often with a good view.

ROCAMADOUR: *Jehan de Valon*   ⒻⒻⒻ   AE DC MC V
Cité Médiévale. (05 65 33 63 08.
There are great views from this restaurant in the pedestrianized medieval town center. Lamb and duck liver are specialties. ⓗ

CREDIT CARDS	CHILDREN'S FACILITIES	FIXED-PRICE MENU	GOOD WINE LIST	OUTDOOR TABLES
AE DC MC V	■	■	●	■

TOULOUSE: *A la Truffe de Quercy*   Ⓕ   AE MC V
17 rue Croix-Baragnon. (05 61 53 34 24.
Traditional receipes have been handed down from father to son for 70 years in this rustic family restaurant. Try the *cassoulet*. ⓗ

AE MC V		■		

TOULOUSE: *La Côte de Bœuf*   ⒻⒻ   MC V
12 rue des Gestes. (05 61 21 19 61.
Small, efficient and supremely friendly restaurant offering huge steaks and known for its generous portions. The best value in town. ⓗ

MC V		■		■

TOULOUSE: *Brasserie des Beaux-Arts*   ⒻⒻⒻ   AE DC MC V
1 quai de la Daurade. (05 61 21 12 12.
An authentic brasserie serving local dishes. There is always a line. Try the oysters with house Riesling wine. ⓗ

AE DC MC V	●	■	●	■

TOULOUSE: *Les Jardins de l'Opéra (D. Toulousy)*   ⒻⒻⒻⒻ   AE DC MC V
1 place du Capitole. (05 61 23 07 76.
Without question one of the best places to eat in Toulouse. Found in a pretty courtyard in the middle of town, it produces great local cuisine.

AE DC MC V		■	●	

VILLEFRANCHE-DE-LAURAGAIS: *Hôtel de France*   Ⓕ   AE DC MC V
106 rue de la République. (05 61 81 62 17.
You are in *cassoulet* country here, and this 19th-century auberge prides itself on its reputation for making one of the best and most authentic in the region.

AE DC MC V	●	■		

THE PYRENEES

AINHOA: *Itburria*   ⒻⒻⒻ   AE MC V
Ainhoa. (05 59 29 92 11.
In the prettiest village of the Basque region, this restaurant serves delicious local fare such as lamb and purée of salt cod, with rosé Rioja wines.

AE MC V	●	■	●	

ARCANGUES: *Moulin d'Alotz*   ⒻⒻⒻ   MC V
Arcangues. (05 59 43 04 54.
A well-converted mill where the chef offers light country cooking such as pan-fried langoustines and turbot roasted with ceps. ⓗ

MC V	●	■		■

ARGELÈS-GAZOST: *Hostellerie le Relais*   ⒻⒻ   MC V
25 rue du Maréchal-Foch. (05 62 97 01 27.
The excellent value of the fixed-price menu makes this worth a detour; wide views of the mountains and reasonable wines add to the charm.

MC V	●	■		

AUDRESSEIN: *l'Auberge d'Audressein*   ⒻⒻ   AE DC MC V
Route de Luchon. (05 61 96 11 80.
This family-run logis is in a converted 19th-century forge and serves some of the best local cuisine, with game and *foie gras* strongly featured.

AE DC MC V	●	■	●	■

BAYONNE: *Euzkalduna*   Ⓕ
61 rue Pannecau. (05 59 59 28 02.
This is the place to try the aromatic, spicy, often peppery dishes that characterize Basque cuisine. The fish soup is excellent. Also recommended are the fried squid and mussels in vinaigrette. Open for lunch only.

			●	

BIARRITZ: *Les Platanes*   ⒻⒻ   AE MC V
32 avenue Beausoleil. (05 59 23 13 68.
Top-flight cooking, using only fresh products, in a friendly setting. The dining room will only seat 20 and it is advisable to book ahead. ⓗ

AE MC V	●	■		

BIARRITZ: *Ramona* Ⓕ Ⓕ | MC V
5 rue Centre. 📞 05 59 24 34 66.
Enjoy the reasonably priced, wide-ranging fixed-price menus in a Belle
Epoque brasserie. The local wines are of a high caliber. 🔥

CIBOURE: *Arrantzaleak* Ⓕ Ⓕ | AE DC MC V
Avenue Jean-Poulou. 📞 05 59 47 10 75.
An unassuming seafront building hides a real treat. Wonderfully fresh fish
is grilled on the open fire dominating the no-frills dining room. 🔥

ESPELETTE: *Euzkadi* Ⓕ Ⓕ | MC V
Espelette. 📞 05 59 93 91 88.
The locals gather here on Sundays for their favorite seasonal game,
salmon, peppers, omelette, blood sausage and substantial Rioja wines.

EUGÉNIE-LES-BAINS: *Les Prés d'Eugénie-Michel Guérard* Ⓕ Ⓕ Ⓕ Ⓕ | AE DC MC V
Eugénie-les-Bains. 📞 05 58 05 06 07.
The creator of *cuisine minceur* is chef here. Choose from a low-calorie
menu or a truly gourmet, richer one. All desserts are made to order. 🔥

GUÉTHARY-BIDART: *Les Frères Ibarboure* Ⓕ Ⓕ Ⓕ Ⓕ | AE DC MC V
Chemin de Talienia. 📞 05 59 54 81 64.
In an 18th-century manor amid woods, this is a rare treat – the regional
fare is full-flavored and faultless. The bill is surprisingly light. 🔥

JURANÇON: *Ruffet* Ⓕ Ⓕ Ⓕ | MC V
3 avenue Chateau-Touzet. 📞 05 59 06 25 13.
Good, traditional cuisine, a warm welcome and amiable service entice
diners to return. The duck comes in a number of guises, all delicious. 🔥

PAU: *La Gousse d'Ail* Ⓕ Ⓕ | MC V
12 rue du Hédas. 📞 05 59 27 31 55.
A pleasant, brick and stucco restaurant with beams and a big fireplace.
Its excellently priced menu makes it stand out in an area full of bistros. 🔥

PAU: *Chez Pierre* Ⓕ Ⓕ Ⓕ | AE DC MC V
16 rue Louis-Barthou. 📞 05 59 27 76 86.
A fine chef, an elegant setting in a 19th-century town house and a series
of creative dishes have ensured the reputation of this restaurant. 🔥

ST-GIRONS: *Eychenne* Ⓕ Ⓕ | DC MC V
8 avenue Paul Laffont. 📞 05 61 04 04 50.
A pretty restaurant in an old seminary, with period furniture. It has two
gardens where diners can enjoy pigeon, duck and fish specialties.

ST-JEAN-DE-LUZ: *Auberge Kaïku* Ⓕ Ⓕ | AE MC V
17 rue de la République. 📞 05 59 26 13 20.
Regional Basque dishes such as cuttlefish and pasta, shrimp, or beef
with truffles are served in the oldest house in town. 🔥

ST-JEAN-DE-LUZ: *Petit Grill Basque* Ⓕ | AE DC MC V
2 rue St Jacques. 📞 05 59 26 80 76.
Simple, good Basque home cooking (fish soup, squid, chicken
croquettes) served by jolly waitresses. Very good value. 🔥

ST-JEAN-PIED-DE-PORT: *Chalet Pedro* Ⓕ
Forêt d'Iraty. 📞 05 59 28 55 98.
A chalet in the mountains that caters to skiers and locals alike. Slow
service can't spoil the fresh trout or mushroom and garlic omelette. 🔥

ST-JEAN-PIED-DE-PORT: *Pyrénées* Ⓕ Ⓕ Ⓕ Ⓕ | AE DC MC V
19 place Charles de Gaulle. 📞 05 59 37 01 01.
A renowned restaurant serving the best local produce: Pyrenean
suckling lamb, salmon and, in season, wild morel mushrooms. 🔥

ST-SAVIN: *Le Viscos* Ⓕ Ⓕ Ⓕ | AE DC MC V
St-Savin. 📞 05 62 97 02 28.
In summer, eat outside on the flower-filled terrace overlooking the
Lavedan River. Specialties are monkfish and *foie gras*. 🔥

URT: *Auberge de la Galupe* Ⓕ Ⓕ Ⓕ Ⓕ | AE DC MC V
Place du Port. 📞 05 59 56 21 84.
A fishermans' inn making use of fine local produce – Montauzer ham,
salmon and eels from the Adour River, and sweet Jurançon wine. 🔥

Average prices for a three-course meal for one, including a half-bottle of house wine, tax and service:
Ⓕ under F150
ⒻⒻ F150–F250
ⒻⒻⒻ F250–F350
ⒻⒻⒻⒻ F350–F500
ⒻⒻⒻⒻⒻ over F500

CHILDREN'S FACILITIES
Some restaurants have high chairs and offer smaller portions for children.

FIXED-PRICE MENU
A good-value fixed-price menu available at lunch, dinner or both, usually with three courses.

GOOD WINE LIST
Denotes a wide range of good wines, or a more specialized selection of local wines.

OUTDOOR TABLES
Facilities for eating outdoors, on a terrace, or in a garden or courtyard, often with a good view.

LANGUEDOC-ROUSSILLON

	Credit Cards	Children's Facilities	Fixed-Price Menu	Good Wine List	Outdoor Tables
AIGUES-MORTES: *Café de Bontignes* ⒻⒻ 7 rue Pasteur. ☏ 04 66 53 93 95. Staff are friendly and specialties include free-range chicken, timbale of aubergines, and peach salad.	AE MC V		■		
AIGUES-MORTES: *Restaurant les Enganettes* Ⓕ 12 rue Morceau. ☏ 04 66 53 69 11. Excellent regional specialties are served in a rustic setting. Portions are very generous and all the food is freshly prepared.	DC MC V	●	■		■
ANDUZE: *Auberge des Trois Barbus* ⒻⒻⒻ Générargues. ☏ 04 66 61 72 12. Imaginative cooking with *foie gras* and truffles is presented in a rustic auberge. Lunch by the pool and soak up the views across the valley.	AE MC V	●			■
ANDUZE: *Les Demeures du Ranquet* ⒻⒻⒻ Le Ranquet, route de Saint-Hippolyte-du-Fort. ☏ 04 66 77 51 63. Located 6 km (4 miles) from Anduze, the owners of this lovingly restored building set in a forest of oak trees offer well-cooked traditional dishes.	DC MC V	●	■		
ARLES-SUR-TECH: *Hôtel les Glycines* ⒻⒻ Rue du Jeu-de-Paume. ☏ 04 68 39 10 09. Tasty food based on local produce, and many regional wines. There is a pretty walled garden that is ideal for summer dining. ⅃	AE MC V	●	■	●	■
BÉZIERS: *Le Framboisier* ⒻⒻⒻ 12 rue Boeildieu. ☏ 04 67 49 90 00. A gastronome's delight, this is an elegant establishment with a classic menu and long list of fine Languedoc-Roussillon wines. ⅃	AE DC MC V		■	●	
BOUZIGUES: *La Côte Bleue* ⒻⒻ Avenue Louis Tudesq. ☏ 04 67 78 30 87. Overlooking the saltwater lagoon of the Bassin de Thau, this is a large and open restaurant that offers fresher-than-fresh seafood and fish. ⅃	AE MC V		■		■
CARCASSONNE: *Brasserie Le Donjon* ⒻⒻ 4 rue Porte d'Aude. ☏ 04 68 25 95 72. An elegant, refreshingly modern brasserie in an otherwise completely medieval town. Regional specialties of *foie gras* and *cassoulet.* ⅃	AE DC MC V	●	■		■
CARCASSONNE: *Le Languedoc* ⒻⒻ 32 allée d'Iéna. ☏ 04 68 25 22 17. This pleasant restaurant is below the walled city in the less crowded town. *Cassoulet*, the filling bean stew that is the regional specialty, is a must, and there is a range of salads, savory dishes and desserts.	AE DC MC V	●	■		
CASTELNAUDARY: *Grand Hôtel Fourcade* ⒻⒻ 14 rue des Carmes. ☏ 04 68 23 02 08. In an Old Town bordering the Canal du Midi, this is an old-fashioned place to eat, with *cassoulet* the highlight of an interesting menu.	AE DC MC V	●	■		·
CASTELNOU: *L'Hostal* ⒻⒻ Carrer de la Patore. ☏ 04 68 53 45 42. In an artists' village, this restaurant fills up on the weekends, when locals flock in for *cargolade*, the Catalan feast of grilled meat and snails.	MC V	●	■		■
COLLIOURE: *La Frégate* ⒻⒻ Quai de l'Amirauté. ☏ 04 68 82 06 05. Wonderful fish soups, local anchovies and *bouillinades* (fish platters) are among the favorites in this jolly, quayside restaurant.	MC V	●	■		■

COLLIOURE: *La Balette*
Route de Port-Vendres. [04 68 82 05 07.
Beautifully set above the bay, this is a very popular place in summer –
a reservation is essential. Seafood stars in a wide range of Catalan dishes.

| | FFF | MC V | ● | ■ | ● | ■ |

CUCUGNAN: *Auberge du Vigneron*
2 rue Achille-Mir. [04 68 45 03 00.
Atmospheric restaurant in the former wine cellar of a charming inn,
serving dishes featuring duck and fruit in tasty combinations. &

| | FF | MC V | ● | ■ | ● | ■ |

FLORENSAC: *Léonce*
8 place de la République. [04 67 77 03 05.
It is well worth seeking out this restaurant, where the cooking is
inspired by local dishes. The fish dishes and desserts are heavenly.

| | FFF | AE DC MC V | ● | ■ | ● | |

LE VIGAN: *Le Mas Quayrol*
Aulas. [04 67 81 12 38.
A warm welcome and quality food are to be found here. The menu is
inventive, tasty and versatile, with fresh fish featured. &

| | FF | MC V | ● | ■ | | ■ |

MINERVE: *Relais Chantovent*
Minerve. [04 68 91 14 18.
The pretty medieval town, with its deep ravine, should not be missed,
neither should the regional cooking and good wines at the Relais. &

| | FF | MC V | ● | ■ | ● | ■ |

MONTPELLIER: *Chandelier*
La Coupole, 227 rue Léon Blum. [04 67 15 34 38.
Inventive seafood and fish dishes such as crayfish fritters and sea bass
with crushed olives are the stock-in-trade here.

| | FFFF | AE MC V | | ■ | ● | ■ |

MONTPELLIER: *La Réserve Rimbaud*
820 avenue de St-Maur. [04 67 72 52 53.
Sophisticated food at affordable prices in a relaxed riverside setting.
Grilled clams, and monkfish in cream and wine, are savory treats. &

| | FFF | AE DC MC V | | ■ | | ■ |

NARBONNE: *L'Auberge des Vignes*
Domaine de l'Hospitalet, route de Narbonne Plage. [04 68 45 28 50.
In the middle of a vineyard, this restaurant serves Mediterranean
cuisine, such as fish of the day with *tapenade* and saffron juice. &

| | FF | AE MC V | ● | | | ■ |

NARBONNE: *La Table St-Créscent*
Domaine St-Créscent le Viel. [04 68 41 37 37.
In an 8th-century oratory, this delightful restaurant serves elegant food
including a superb aubergine canelloni. Well chosen selection of local wines.

| | FF | AE DC MC V | | | ● | ■ |

NÎMES: *Nicolas*
1 rue Poise. [04 66 67 50 47.
Regional fare at good-value prices in a packed but friendly and
unpretentious atmosphere.

| | F | MC V | | ■ | | |

PERPIGNAN: *Casa Sansa*
3 rue Fabriques-Couvertes. [04 68 34 21 84.
A 14th-century wine cellar decorated with Catalan artifacts provides
the setting for true Catalan food: spicy meatballs, shrimp and anchovies.

| | F | AE MC V | | ■ | ● | ■ |

PERPIGNAN: *Le Chapon Fin*
18 boulevard Jean-Bourrat. [04 68 35 14 14.
This restaurant serves fine Catalan food, such as partridge stew with
peppers and oranges, as well as seafood and truffles. &

| | FFF | AE DC MC V | ● | ■ | ● | |

PERPIGNAN: *Le Mas Vermeil*
Traverse de Cabestany. [04 68 66 95 96.
The menu is unpretentious and simple, leaning toward the rich Catalan
style. Dine in the garden restaurant, complete with fountains. &

| | FFF | AE V | ● | ■ | | ■ |

PORT-VENDRES: *La Côte Vermeille*
Quai du Fanal. [04 68 82 05 71.
At a quayside restaurant, the culinary arts are concentrated on
delicate seafood and fish, but other dishes can be ordered. &

| | FFF | AE MC V | ● | ■ | | |

SAILLAGOUSE: *L'Atalaya*
L10, Saillagouse. [04 68 04 70 04.
A pretty auberge perched above the village. The original cuisine offers
pigeon in cranberry sauce, salmon mousse with dill and *foie gras*. A find!

| | FF | DC MC V | | ■ | ● | ■ |

Average prices for a three-course meal for one, including a half-bottle of house wine, tax and service: F under F150 $F$$F$ F150–F250 $F$$F$$F$ F250–F350 $F$$F$$F$$F$ F350–F500 $F$$F$$F$$F$$F$ over F500	**CHILDREN'S FACILITIES** Some restaurants have high chairs and offer smaller portions for children. **FIXED-PRICE MENU** A good-value fixed-price menu available at lunch, dinner or both, usually with three courses. **GOOD WINE LIST** Denotes a wide range of good wines, or a more specialized selection of local wines. **OUTDOOR TABLES** Facilities for eating outdoors, on a terrace, or in a garden or courtyard, often with a good view.

	CREDIT CARDS	CHILDREN'S FACILITIES	FIXED-PRICE MENU	GOOD WINE LIST	OUTDOOR TABLES
ST-MARTIN-DE-LONDRES: *Les Muscardins* $F$$F$$F$ 19 route des Cévennes. (04 67 55 75 90. A bright, cheerful restaurant with a notable list of local wines. Gourmets often return to savor the adventurous cooking of the Rousset family, who base their menu on regional produce – fish, lamb and pigeon. &	AE DC MC V		■	●	
ST-PONS-DE-THOMIÈRES: *Auberge de Cabarétou* $F$$F$ St-Pons-de-Thomières. (04 67 97 02 31. Set amid a forest with views across Haut Languedoc, this auberge is memorable for its combination of classic and modern local cuisine.	AE DC MC V	●	■	●	■
SÈTE: *Palangrotte* $F$$F$ 1 rampe Paul-Valéry. (04 67 74 80 35. A good place to go to sample a plate of oysters, for which this area is justifiably famous.	AE DC MC V		■		■
TAURINYA: *Auberge des Deux Abbayes* $F$$F$ 2 place de l'Oratoire. (04 68 96 49 53. This restaurant in a mountain setting serves regional dishes including Banyuls-style goose pâté and Collioure anchovies. &	MC V	●	■		■
VILLEFRANCHE-DE-CONFLENT: *Auberge St-Paul* $F$$F$$F$ Place de l'Eglise. (04 68 96 30 95. Originally a 13th-century chapel, this inn offers a good variety of local produce, cooked with a personal touch and Catalan influence. &	DC MC V		■	●	

PROVENCE AND THE CÔTE D'AZUR

	CREDIT CARDS	CHILDREN'S FACILITIES	FIXED-PRICE MENU	GOOD WINE LIST	OUTDOOR TABLES
AIX-EN-PROVENCE: *Mas d'Entremont* $F$$F$$F$ 315 Route Nationale 7. (04 42 17 42 42. Glass walls open onto the surrounding park, and the menu is wonderful, but with few local dishes. A good Provençal wine list. &	MC V	●	■	●	■
AIX-EN-PROVENCE: *Le Bistro Latin* $F$$F$ 18 rue de la Couronne. (04 42 38 22 88. An intimate restaurant on two floors, serving excellent meals at good prices, and imaginative local specialties like sole with lobster sauce.	AE MC V		■	●	
AIX-EN-PROVENCE: *L'Aix Quis* $F$$F$$F$ 22 rue Leydet. (04 42 27 76 16. Stylish fish and meat dishes in a restaurant that is fast becoming the culinary headquarters of Aix. Try the delicious six-course meal. &	AE MC V	●	■		
ARLES: *L'Escaladou* $F$$F$ 23 rue de la Porte-de-Laure. (04 90 96 70 43. This pretty Provençal restaurant is close to the bull ring in the center of town. Choose the good local fish with piles of fresh vegetables. &		●	■		■
ARLES: *Le Vaccarès* $F$$F$$F$ Place du Forum. (04 90 96 06 17. Provençale food in elegant surroundings. The chef here particularly enjoys putting a spin on classic dishes. The seafood and soups are especially recommended.	AE MC V		■		■
AVIGNON: *Hiély-Lucullus* $F$$F$ 5 rue de la République. (04 90 86 17 07. Avignon gastronomes have been flocking here for 60 years. Quality is as good as ever; try specialties like *foie gras* and *meringue glacée*.	MC V	●	■	●	
AVIGNON: *La Fourchette* $F$$F$ 17 rue Racine. (04 90 85 20 93. A relaxed alternative to Avignon's smarter restaurants. Prices are reasonable and there is a range of 12 mouthwatering desserts. &	MC V		■		

BIOT: *Auberge du Jarrier* ⒻⒻⒻⒻ
30 passage de la Bourgade. 🔲 *04 93 65 11 68.*
An unpretentious restaurant with an array of seafood, delicate fish and intriguing cheeses. Make reservations a week in advance in season.
AE MC V

CAGNES-SUR-MER: *Le Cagnard* ⒻⒻⒻ
Rue du Sous-barri. 🔲 *04 93 20 73 21.*
Housed in a medieval inn in the ramparts of the village, this superb restaurant offers a classic menu with delicacies such as roast pigeon.
AE DC MC V

CANNES: *Royal Gray* ⒻⒻⒻⒻ
38 rue des Serbes. 🔲 *04 92 99 79 60.*
It is difficult to eat more lavishly than at the Royal Gray, long the doyen of Cannes' restaurants. 🔲
AE DC MC V

CAVAILLON: *Restaurant Prévot* ⒻⒻⒻ
353 avenue de Verdun. 🔲 *04 90 71 32 43.*
A gastronomic treat in the heart of a pretty market town. The food is elegant and delicious; try the aubergines and langoustines. 🔲
AE MC V

CHATEAUNEUF-DU-PAPE: *La Mère Germaine* ⒻⒻⒻ
Place de la Fontaine. 🔲 *04 90 83 54 37.*
A once outstanding restaurant that is now recovering its reputation. It has superb views of the vineyards and pleasant, unobtrusive service.
MC V

CHÂTEAUX-ARNOUX: *La Bonne Etape* ⒻⒻⒻⒻ
Chemin du Lac. 🔲 *04 92 64 00 09.*
Set among lavender fields and olive groves, the flavor is Provençal, with expertly crafted dishes such as *courgettes farcies* and lamb.
AE DC MC V

COL D'EZE: *La Bergerie* ⒻⒻ
Grande Corniche. 🔲 *04 93 41 03 67.*
Winter by the fire, summer on the terrace – the hearty food includes lamb in herbs, good washed down with copious local wine. 🔲
AE MC V

CUERS: *Le Lingoustou* ⒻⒻⒻ
Route de Pierrefeu. 🔲 *04 94 28 69 10.*
Traditional Provençal specialties served in refined style, winning a Michelin star. The setting is suitably rustic, amid rolling vineyards.
AE DC MC V

GIGONDAS: *Les Florets* ⒻⒻ
Route des Dentelles. 🔲 *04 90 65 85 01.*
Locals pack the dining room, sampling the good regional food. In summer, eat on the terrace overlooking the Dentelles de Montmirail. 🔲
AE DC MC V

LA GARDE FREINET: *Auberge Sarrasin* Ⓕ
Route Nationale 98. 🔲 *04 94 43 67 16.*
A rural dining room where a fire roars in winter and flowers adorn the tables in summer. Try *cassoulet Provençal* washed down with rosé. 🔲
MC V

LES BAUX-DE-PROVENCE: *L'Oustau de Baumanière* ⒻⒻⒻⒻⒻ
Val d'Enfer. 🔲 *04 90 54 33 07.*
Two Michelin stars, views over the medieval village and a memorable menu – a blend of ancient local dishes and *nouvelle cuisine*.
AE DC MC V

LOURMARIN: *Le Moulin de Lourmarin* ⒻⒻⒻⒻ
Rue Temple. 🔲 *04 90 68 06 69.*
The millstones are still intact in this luxurious converted olive mill, and the food is delicious – especially the fish and Lubéron game.
AE DC MC V

MARSEILLE: *Dar Djerba* ⒻⒻ
15 cours Julien. 🔲 *04 91 48 55 36.*
A North African restaurant serving delicious couscous dishes in an intimate atmosphere. 🔲
MC V

MARSEILLE: *Miramar* ⒻⒻⒻⒻ
12 quai du Port. 🔲 *04 91 91 10 40.*
The *bouillabaisse* is one of the most authentic in Marseille – but at a price. There is also a huge selection of seafood. 🔲
AE DC MC V

MONACO: *Le Périgourdin* Ⓕ
5 rue des Oliviers. 🔲 *00377 93 30 06 02.*
Two minutes walk from the casino, this friendly restaurant offers all the riches of Périgord cuisine – such as *foie gras* – at bargain prices.
AE MC DC V

For key to symbols see back flap

	Average prices info	CREDIT CARDS	CHILDREN'S FACILITIES	FIXED-PRICE MENU	GOOD WINE LIST	OUTDOOR TABLES

Average prices for a three-course meal for one, including a half-bottle of house wine, tax and service:
- Ⓕ under F150
- ⒻⒻ F150–F250
- ⒻⒻⒻ F250–F350
- ⒻⒻⒻⒻ F350–F500
- ⒻⒻⒻⒻⒻ over F500

CHILDREN'S FACILITIES
Some restaurants have high chairs and offer smaller portions for children.

FIXED-PRICE MENU
A good-value fixed-price menu available at lunch, dinner or both, usually with three courses.

GOOD WINE LIST
Denotes a wide range of good wines, or a more specialized selection of local wines.

OUTDOOR TABLES
Facilities for eating outdoors, on a terrace or in a garden or courtyard, often with a good view.

	Price	Credit Cards	Children's	Fixed-Price	Wine List	Outdoor
MONTE-CARLO: *Café de Paris* Place du Casino. 【 04 92 16 20 20. A re-creation of a Belle Epoque brasserie. Among the specialties are *pavé de saumon* and Charolais beef with morels. 🕭	ⒻⒻ	AE DC MC V				▪
MOUGINS: *Le Moulin de Mougins* Notre Dame de Vie. 【 04 93 75 78 24. Now only with two Michelin stars, but still managing to stay ahead of competition. *The* restaurant for stars during the Cannes Film Festival. 🕭	ⒻⒻⒻⒻ	AE DC MC V	▪	●	▪
NICE: *Nissa Socca* 5 rue Sainte-Réparate. 【 04 93 16 18 35. Features huge servings of *socca* (chickpea bread) with pasta and carafes of red wine. Crowded, usually taking over the street in summer.	Ⓕ					▪
NICE: *Le Chanteclef* 37 promenade des Anglais. 【 04 93 88 39 51. Long the bastion of gastronomy in Nice, the restaurant retains immaculate standards established when Russian princes came to dine in the last century. Seafood and fish are featured. 🕭	ⒻⒻⒻⒻ	AE DC MC V	●	▪	●
ORANGE: *La Roselière* 4 rue du Renoyer. 【 04 90 34 50 42. Chalkboards propped against stone walls display the daily-changing menu, with every dish lovingly prepared from local produce.	Ⓕ			▪		▪
ST-AGNES: *Le Logis Sarrasin* 40 rue de Sarrasin. 【 04 93 35 86 89. A simple, family-run restaurant in the Alpine foothills behind Menton, offering six huge courses of local game and Italian specialties.	ⒻⒻ			▪		▪
ST-JEAN-CAP-FERRAT: *Le St-Jean* Place Clemenceau. 【 04 93 76 04 75. In the busy town square, this restaurant serves up simple but excellent food, such as pizzas cooked over wood, pastas and fish. The first-floor terrace is perfect for balmy summer evenings. 🕭	Ⓕ	AE MC V	●			▪
ST-JEAN-CAP-FERRAT: *Le Sloop* Nouveau port de St-Jean. 【 04 93 01 48 63. Amid the smart yachts of St-Jean's picturesque and buzzing port, Le Sloop specializes in light and delicious seafood. 🕭	ⒻⒻ	AE MC V		▪	●	▪
ST-RÉMY-DE-PROVENCE: *Le Jardin de Fréderic* 8 bd Gambetta. 【 04 90 92 27 76. This small, family-run restaurant, housed in a villa, serves local dishes such as onion tart, and poached turbot with sorrel.	ⒻⒻ	MC V		▪		▪
ST-VALLIER-DE-THIERY: *Le Relais Impérial* Route Napoléon, Route Nationale 85. 【 04 93 42 60 07. In an agreeable atmosphere, and with friendly service, this is one of the few places to offer an authentic *pissaladière* – onions, olives and anchovies cooked in dough – with superb Provençal white wines. 🕭	Ⓕ	AE DC MC V	●	▪	●	▪
SÉGURET: *La Table du Comtat* Séguret. 【 04 90 46 91 49. Truffles, pigeon and wild boar grace the menu of local produce. A memorable view forms the backdrop, and the cellar stuffed with Côtes du Rhône provides a fitting accompaniment. 🕭	ⒻⒻⒻ	AE DC MC V	●	▪		▪
TOUËT-SUR-VAR: *Auberge des Chasseurs* Touët. 【 04 93 05 71 11. Local game makes for appetizing and filling dishes at this country auberge, where the wild boar and blue trout are excellent.	ⒻⒻ	AE DC MC V	●	▪		▪

VENCE: *Auberge des Seigneurs* (F)(F) Place du Frêne. [04 93 58 04 24. Come with an appetite to this medieval auberge, complete with roaring fire and five succulent courses, including the local blue trout and tender lamb, cooked in front of you on a spit.	AE DC MC V		■			
VENCE: *Le Vieux Couvent* (F)(F) 68 av Générale Leclerc. [04 93 58 78 58. Housed in a former 17th-century convent, this restaurant is popular for Provençale fare with an inventive touch.	MC V		■	●	
VILLEFRANCHE-SUR-MER: *Mère Germaine* (F)(F)(F)(F) Quai Courbet. [04 93 01 71 39. Bouillabaisse and *sole tante marie* (sole with mushrooms) are served in this friendly restaurant overlooking the beach. &	AE MC V		■		■

CORSICA

BONIFACIO: *L'Auchivolto* (F) Rue de l'Auchivolto. [04 95 73 17 58. Part of the flea market, the chef at l'Auchivolto makes the most of fresh seasonal produce. The terrace makes outdoor dinning a pleasure.	MC V		■		■
BONIFACIO: *Stella d'Oro* (F)(F) 7 rue Doria. [04 95 73 03 63. A family institution, with steep prices and a hearty local atmosphere. Fish and chicken are prominent on the menu.	AE DC MC V		■		
CALVI: *L'Ile de Beauté* (F)(F)(F)(F) Quai Landry. [04 95 65 00 46. This restaurant is on the quayside and concentrates on perfect fish creations such as oysters with lime and lobster. The dining room on the first floor specializes in meat dishes. Neither is cheap!	AE DC MC V		■		■
CAURO: *U Barracone* (F)(F) Barracone. [04 95 28 40 55. A quiet place to eat in the countryside near Cauro. The menu includes tournedos with morel mushrooms and *crêpes* with orange coulis. &	AE DC MC V		■		
CORTE: *Auberge de la Restonica* (F)(F) Vallée de la Restonica. [04 95 46 09 58. Run by an ex-international athlete, this is a rural hillside inn with a dining room opening onto views of the forest. Simple, good food. &	MC V	●	■		■
L'ILE ROUSSE: *La Bergerie* (F)(F) Route de Monticello. [04 95 60 01 28. Dine in the shady garden of this lovely converted farmhouse. Try a sea-urchin omelette accompanied by a bottle of Corsican wine. &	MC V				■
PORTO: *Le Soleil Couchant* (F) Porto Marine. [04 95 26 10 12. On the terrace, there are wonderful views over the marina. The local fare is a very good value, the *charcuterie* and sheeps' cheeses excellent.	MC V		■		■
PORTO-VECCHIO: *Auberge du Maquis* (F)(F) Ferruccio. [04 95 70 20 39. Order kid or wild boar and it will be roasted in front of you in this peaceful country retreat, a short drive from Porto-Vecchio.		●			
PORTO-VECCHIO: *Le Regina* (F)(F) Route de Bastia. [04 95 70 14 94. A rather regal restaurant with a complicated cuisine prepared from the finest local produce. Seafood, sweetbreads and pastas are served in elaborate forms. The wine list is the best on the island.	AE DC MC V			●	
ST-FLORENT: *La Gaffe* (F)(F) Port de St-Florent. [04 95 37 00 12. Savor fresh, appetizing mussels and lobster in lemon and mint, while sitting on the shady terrace watching the boats sail by. &	AE DC MC V	●	■	●	■
SARTÈNE: *La Chaumière* (F)(F) 39 rue du Capitaine-Benedetti. [04 95 77 07 13. Carved out of the granite hillside, this Corsican inn serves traditional island cooking: *charcuterie*, tripe and wild boar, with local wines.	AE DC MC V	●	■		■

For key to symbols see back flap

SURVIVAL GUIDE

PRACTICAL INFORMATION

France is justifiably proud of its many attractions, for which it has excellent tourist information facilities. Both in France and abroad, French Government Tourist Offices are an invaluable source of reference for practical aspects of your stay. Most towns and villages in France have a tourist information office; the relevant

Tourist information logo

address and telephone number is provided for each town and area listed in this guide. Domestic tourism in France creates vacation migrations, especially between July 14 and August 31. Consequently, the hotel and restaurant trades are seasonal. A little advance planning will allow you to avoid the disappointment of seasonal closings.

MANNERS

THE FRENCH have rituals of politeness that are easy to pick up. In shops be ready to say *Bonjour* before asking for what you want, then *merci* when you receive your change, and *merci, au revoir* when you get your purchases and leave.

Shake hands when introduced to someone, or at any time when you see a hand offered. In small communities, many people may greet you with a *Bonjour* in the street even if they have never seen you before.

For other useful expressions, refer to the phrase book on pages 671–2.

VISAS

CURRENTLY THERE are no visa requirements for EU nationals or visitors from the United States, Canada or New Zealand who plan to stay in France for under three months. Visitors from most other countries, including Australia, require a tourist visa.

Visas should be obtained prior to departure from your local French consulate. Anyone planning to study or work in France should apply to their local French consulate several months in advance about visa requirements.

TAX-FREE GOODS AND CUSTOMS INFORMATION

VISITORS RESIDING outside the European Union can reclaim the sales tax TVA or VAT on French goods if they spend more than F2,000 in one shop, get a *détaxe* receipt and take the goods out of the

country within six months. The form should be handed in at customs when leaving the country. The reimbursement will be sent to you.

Exceptions for *détaxe* rebate are food and alcohol, medicines, tobacco, cars and motorcycles. Tax can be reimbursed for bicycles. More information and advice is available from the **Centre des Renseignements des Douanes**, but this is usually in French.

Sign for tourist office in smaller towns and villages

TOURIST INFORMATION

ALL MAJOR CITIES and large towns have *offices de tourisme*. Small towns and even villages have *syndicats d'initiative*. Both will give you town maps, advice on accommodations, and information on regional recreational and cultural activities.

You can also get information before you leave for France from **French Government Tourist Offices**, or by phoning or writing to local tourist offices (see headings for each town

in this guide) or the appropriate CRT (*Comité Régional de Tourisme*) – ask the FGTO for the address.

ADMISSION CHARGES

MOST MUSEUMS and monuments in France charge an entrance fee, usually from F15 to F40. This may be reduced or waived on Sundays. Those under seven and over 60 are admitted free at all times. Discounts are often available to people under the age of 26 carrying a *Carte Jeune Internationale* (International Youth Card), and students (*see facing page*).

OPENING HOURS

THIS GUIDE lists which days of the week sights are open. Generally, hours are from 10am–5:40pm with one late evening per week. Most sights close on public holidays. National museums and sights are normally closed on Tuesdays, with a few exceptions which close on Mondays. Municipal museums normally close on Mondays. Churches open every day but close at lunchtime. Check the opening hours for private museums because they do not always have standard opening times.

See page 622 for details on opening hours for shops; page 620 for banks; and pages 576–7 for restaurants.

Colonne de la Grande Armée

Sign to monument of cultural importance

Visitors taking the weight off weary feet

FACILITIES FOR THE DISABLED

Detailed listings by town are provided in *Guide Rousseau H comme Handicapés*, available from **Les Editions La Route Robert** and French bookstores. *Touristes Quand Même* details in French the services in the main towns, with translations in English and German of common phrases. It is issued free by **CNRH** (Comité National Français de Liaison pour la Réadaptation des Handicapés), and is also available from **Paris Convention and Visitors Bureau Headquarters**. The **CIDJ** (Centre d'Information et de Documentation Jeunesse) offers information for young disabled travelers. **Mobility International USA** provides information on wheelchair access, as does the **Association des Paralysés de France** (*see p539*).

FRENCH TIME

France is one hour ahead of Greenwich Mean Time (GMT). The French use the 24-hour clock, so 7pm = 19:00, for example.

Lining up for the Eiffel Tower

STUDENT INFORMATION

Students with valid ID cards (an International Student Identity Card or the French *carte jeunes*) benefit from many discounts. **CIDJ** offices provide a comprehensive service for students.

ELECTRICAL ADAPTORS

The voltage in France is 220 volts. Plugs have two round pins, or three round pins for applications which need to be earthed. Some hotels offer built-in adaptors for shavers only.

Standard French two-pin plug for electrical appliances

CONVERSION CHART

Imperial to metric
1 inch = 2.54 centimeters
1 foot = 30 centimeters
1 mile = 1.6 kilometers
1 ounce = 28 grams
1 pound = 454 grams
1 US pint = 0.47 liter
1 US gallon = 3.8 liters

Metric to imperial
1 millimeter = 0.04 inch
1 centimeter = 0.4 inch
1 meter = 3 feet 3 inches
1 kilometer = 0.6 mile
1 gram = 0.04 ounce
1 kilogram = 2.2 pounds
1 liter = 2.1 US pints

Personal Security and Health

ON THE WHOLE, France is a safe place for visitors: take normal precautions, such as sensible care of your possessions at all times, and avoid isolated and unlit urban areas at night. If you become ill during your stay, pharmacies are an excellent source of advice. Consulates and consular departments at your embassy are a good source of help and advice in an emergency *(see p617)*. For serious medical problems, this section gives the numbers of the most important emergency services.

French pharmacy sign

PERSONAL SECURITY

VIOLENT CRIME is rare in France, though there can be random incidents. If you are involved in an argument or a car accident, avoid confrontation. In potentially difficult situations you should above all stay calm and speak French if you can, to help defuse the situation.

LEGAL ASSISTANCE

IF YOU HAVE a comprehensive insurance policy that covers legal advice in France from organizations like Europ Assistance or Mondial Assist-ance, this will help with the legal aspects of insurance claims in the event of injury or accident. If you do not have this coverage, phone your nearest consulate *(see p617)*, or, as a last resort, phone the local *Ordre des Avocats* (lawyers' association) for the name of a good local lawyer.

INTERPRETERS

TRANSLATION and interpre-tation is offered by pro-fessional translators. Contact the **Société Française des Traducteurs Professionels** through Minitel *(see p624)*.

PERSONAL PROPERTY

MAKE SURE you insure your possessions before arriv-al. Beware of pickpockets, especially on the Paris metro during the rush hour. Keep all valuables securely concealed, and if carrying a purse or briefcase, never let it out of your sight. Also, only take as much cash as you think you will need. Traveler's checks are the safest method of carrying large sums of money.

Phone or visit the area police to report crimes, missing persons or stolen property, muggings or assault. The *commissariat de police* is the headquarters. In small towns and villages, go to the *mairie* (town hall), which will only be open during office hours. If your passport is lost or stolen, call your consulate *(see p617)*.

The white-gloved motorcyclists who patrol the highways are the *CRS (Compagnie Rép-ublicaine de Sécurité)*.

If you are involved in a traffic accident outside a town you may be asked to accompany the other driver to the nearest *gen-darmerie*. The *gendarmerie nationale* is a military organization that deals with all crimes outside urban areas. Making a statement (a *PV* or *procès-verbal*) can be a lengthy process. Take your

identity papers (and your vehicle papers, if relevant) with you when you go to make a statement.

MEDICAL TREATMENT

ALL TRAVELERS should consider purchasing travel insurance. Non-EU nationals are obliged to carry medical insurance, taken out before they arrive.

Discuss your medical coverage with your insurer before leaving the US. If you know that you will need to obtain prescriptions while you are abroad, find out in advance exactly how to do this. Your local consulate may be able to help.

In the case of a medical emergency call **SAMU** *(Service d'Aide Médicale Urgence)*. However, it is often faster to call **Sapeurs Pompiers** (the fire service), who offer a first-aid and ambulance service. This is particularly true in rural areas of France where the local fire department is likely to be much closer than

---

DIRECTORY

EMERGENCY NUMBERS

Ambulance (SAMU)
📞 15 or 18 (Sapeurs Pompiers).

Fire (Sapeurs Pompiers)
📞 18.

Police and Gendarmerie
📞 17.

INTERPRETERS

Société Française des Traducteurs Professionels
📞 Minitel 3616 SFTRAD.

Gendarme **Fireman**

the ambulance service based in town. The paramedics are called *secouristes*.

Emergency rooms *(service des urgences)* in public hospitals can deal with most medical problems. Your consulate should be able to recommend an English-speaking doctor in the area.

PHARMACIES

I**N FRANCE,** pharmacists can diagnose health problems and suggest appropriate treatments. They are also trained to identify mushrooms, and you can take any you are unsure about to them to eliminate the danger of poisoning.

Pharmacies have a green cross outside. A card in the window will give details of the nearest *pharmacie de garde* for night openings.

Police car

Fire engine

Ambulance

Fire hazard poster

OUTDOOR EMERGENCIES

F**OREST FIRES** are a major risk in many parts of France. High winds can make fires spread rapidly in winter as well as summer. Keep well away from an area where there is a fire, as its direction can change quickly. Make sure you do not start a fire with campfires or a cigarette butt.

When walking in the mountains or sailing, notify the relevant authority of your route and observe local regulations posted in the area.

During the hunting season (Sep–Feb and especially Sundays) dress in bright colors when out walking. Avoid areas where hunters may be concealed in blinds or stalking game in the woods *(see p629)*.

PUBLIC TOILETS IN FRANCE

Modern pay toilets are now found in many towns. Do not let children under ten use the toilets on their own as the automatic cleaning function can be dangerous. The best policy is to use toilets in cafés or restaurants where you are a customer, or go to a department store. Traditional *pissoirs* and keyhole toilets, still found in some towns, are often not very clean. Toilet facilities are provided on the *autoroute* at drive-in rest areas every 20 km (12 miles), as well as at the major service areas.

1 Put the amount indicated in the slot.

2 Press the button to open sliding door.

3 The light indicates vacant or engaged.

Banking and Local Currency

YOU MAY BRING any amount of currency into France, but if you intend to take out more than F50,000, you should declare it on arrival. Traveler's checks are the safest way to carry money abroad, but credit cards, which can be used to withdraw local currency from an automatic teller machine, are by far the most convenient. Bureaux de change are located in airports, main train stations, and in some hotels and shops, but banks usually offer the best rates of exchange.

Credit-card cash dispenser

USING BANKS

MOST FRENCH BANKS have a bureau de change, but rates can vary. Many banks now have ATMs (automatic teller machines) outside, which you can normally use with cards in the **Visa/Carte Bleue** or **Mastercard** (Access) groups. Instructions are often given in French, English and German. Bear in mind that ATMs may run out of cash before the end of the weekend.

If there is no ATM, you can withdraw up to F2,000 per day on Visa at the foreign counter of a bank showing the Visa sign. The bank will need to obtain telephone authorization for such withdrawals first.

BANKING HOURS

AS A GENERAL RULE, banks in northern France are open Mon–Fri approximately 9am–4:30 or 5:15pm. However, some are open only till noon, and many will close at noon on the working day before a holiday.

In southern France, banks are normally open Tue–Sat, approximately 8am–12 noon and from 1:30–4:30pm. Around a public holiday, they are usually closed from Friday noon to Tuesday morning.

OTHER SOURCES

GIRO BANK ACCOUNT holders can obtain cash from post offices, which are often open longer hours than the banks.

Outside Paris, independent bureaux de change are rare, but are often found in major

train stations and areas with a high density of tourists.

Privately owned bureaux de change can have variable rates: check commission and minimum charges first.

CARDS AND CHECKS

TRAVELER'S CHECKS can be obtained from **American Express**, **Thomas Cook** or your bank. If you know that you will spend most of them it is best to have them issued in French francs. American Express checks are widely accepted in France. If checks are exchanged at an Amex office, no commission is charged. In the case of theft, checks are replaced at once.

Because of the high commissions that are charged, many French businesses do not accept the American Express credit card. The most commonly used credit card is Visa/Carte Bleue. Mastercard/Eurocard (Access in UK) is also widely accepted.

Machine to read credit cards

Credit cards issued in France are now "smart cards," which means they have a *puce* (a microchip capable of storing data). Many retailers have machines designed to read both smart cards and magnetic strips. If your conventional card cannot be read in the smart card slot you will be told you have a *puce morte*. Persuade the cashier to try passing the card through the magnetic reader (*bande magnétique*). You may also be asked to punch in your PIN code (*code confidentiel*) and then

to press the green key (*validez*) on a small keypad by the cash desk.

THE EURO

THE EURO BECAME legal tender in 11 EU countries including France on Jan 1, 1999. Only paper or electronic transactions can be made in Euros until Jan 1, 2002, when bills and coins come into circulation. The Euro then replaces national currencies, and can be used in any of the 11 countries.

DIRECTORY

FOREIGN BANKS

American Express
11 rue Scribe, 75009 Paris.
Map 4 D5.
☎ 01 47 77 70 07.

Thomas Cook
25 boulevard des Capucines, 75002 Paris.
☎ 01 42 96 26 78.

Barclays
21 rue Lafitte, 75009 Paris.
☎ 01 44 79 79 79.

Midland
20 bis av Rapp, 75007 Paris.
Map 1 C4.
☎ 01 44 92 70 00.

LOST CARDS AND TRAVELER'S CHECKS

American Express
☎ 01 47 77 72 00 in Paris or (1) (800) 528 4800 in US.

VISA
☎ (1) (800) 336 8472.

Mastercard
☎ (1) (314) 275 6690 (collect).

CURRENCY

THE OUTGOING FRENCH UNIT OF CURRENCY is the franc, which is indicated by the letter "F" before or, more frequently, after the amount. It is distinguished from the Swiss or Belgian franc by the use of the letters "FF." There are 100 centimes to the franc, but their value is now so small that 1-centime coins are no longer in circulation.

Bank Notes
French bank notes are available in the denominations F20, F50, F100, F200 and F500. They increase in size progressively according to their value.

F500 note

F200 note

F100 note

F50 note

F20 note

Coins
Coins come in the following denominations: 5, 10, 20 and 50 centimes; F1, F2, F5, F10 and F20. The 5-, 10- and 20-centime coins are brass. The 50-centime , F1, F2 and F5 coins are silver-alloy. The F10 and F20 coins are bi-metal, with a silver center and a brass edge.

F20

F10

F5

F2

F1

50 centimes

20 centimes

10 centimes

5 centimes

Shopping

SHOPPING IN FRANCE is a delight. Whether you go to the hypermarkets and department stores, or seek out the small specialist stores and markets, you will be tempted by stylish French presentation and the quality of goods for sale. Renowned for its food and wine, France also offers world-famous fashion, pottery, porcelain and crystal.

This section gives guidelines on opening hours, and the range of goods stocked by the different types of stores and markets. There are also tips on how to buy wine straight from the vineyards and wine cooperatives, and a size conversion chart to make clothes shopping easier.

Olive oil
om Baux

Fresh nectarines and melons for sale at a market stall

OPENING HOURS

FOOD SHOPS open at around 7am and close around noon for lunch. After lunch most are open until 7pm or later. Bakeries often stay open until 1pm or later, serving snacks at lunchtime.

Shops that do not close at lunchtime include some supermarkets, department stores and most hypermarkets.

General opening hours for nonfood shops are around 9am–6pm Mon–Sat, often with a break for lunch. Many of these shops are closed Monday mornings.

Food shops (and newsagents) are open on Sunday mornings. Virtually every shop in France is closed on Sunday afternoon, except for the last weeks before Christmas when hypermarkets remain open all day. Smaller shops may be closed one day of the week, usually Monday. However, those in tourist regions are often open every day in the high season.

LARGER SHOPS

HYPERMARKETS (*hypermarchés* or *grandes surfaces*) can be found on the outskirts of every sizable town: look for signs indicating *centre commercial*. Among the biggest are Carrefour, Casino, Auchan and Continent. Discount gas is often sold, but you may have to pay for it in cash. Check before you fill up.

Department stores (*grands magasins*), such as the cheap and cheerful Monoprix and Prisunic, are often found in town centers. Others, like the more upscale Printemps and Galeries Lafayette, can be found both in town and out-of-town centers.

A local bakery, which will often sell pâtisseries as well as bread

SPECIALIST SHOPS

ONE OF THE PLEASURES of shopping in France is that specialist food shops still flourish despite the new large supermarkets. The *boulangerie*, for bread, is frequently combined with a *pâtisserie* selling cakes and pastries. The *traiteur* sells prepared foods. Cheese shops (*fromagerie*) and other shops specializing in dairy products (*laiterie*) may also be combined, while the *boucherie* (butcher's) and *charcuterie* (delicatessen) are often separate shops. For general groceries go to an *épicerie fine*.

Cleaning and household products are available from a *droguerie*, but hardware is bought from a *quincaillerie*. The term *Papeterie* (stationer's) covers both the expensive, specialist retailers and the colorful, seductive sections in hypermarkets.

MARKETS

THIS GUIDE LISTS the market days for every town featured. To find out where the market is, ask a passerby for *le marché*. Markets usually close promptly at noon and don't re-open in the afternoon.

Look for local producers, including those with only one or two special items to sell, because their goods are often cheaper and of better quality.

By law, price tags include the origin of all produce: *pays* means local. Chickens from Bresse are marketed wearing a red, white and blue badge giving the name of the producer as proof of authenticity. If you are visiting markets over several weeks, look for items just coming into season, such as fresh walnuts, the first wild asparagus, early artichokes or tiny *fraises des bois* (wild strawberries).

At the market, you can also buy spices, shoes and clothes, and some unusual items such as decorative cabbages.

There is a full calendar of important seasonal regional markets in France, specializing in such things as truffles, hams, garlic, *foie gras* and livestock. *Foires artisanales* may be held at the same time as the seasonal fairs, selling local produce and crafts.

REGIONAL PRODUCE

FRENCH REGIONAL specialties can be bought outside their area of origin. It is, however, interesting to buy them locally because their creation and flavor reflect the region's traditions, tastes and climate.

Provence, in the south, prides itself on the quality of its olive oil, the best of which is made from the first cold pressing and lovingly decanted every day for a week. In the temperate north, Camembert is the product of fresh Norman milk that has been cured for at least three weeks. Popular drinks are also associated with particular regions. Pastis, made from aniseed, is popular in the south, while calvados, made from apples, is from the north *(see p245)*.

Location also determines quality. Lyon's culinary importance stems from the distinctive cheeses that come from the surrounding dairy region, and the proximity of Bresse for chickens, Charolais for beef and the Alsace region for sausages.

Sausages and cheeses, regional specialties for sale in a Lyon market

WINE

IN WINE-producing areas, follow the *dégustation* (tasting) signs to vineyards *(domaines)* where you can taste the wine. You will be expected to buy at least one bottle. Wine cooperatives sell the wine of small producers. Here you can buy wine in five- and ten-liter containers *(en vrac)*, as well as in bottles. The wine is often rated AOC, *appellation d'origine contrôlée*, selling at

Pastis 51, drunk in the south

less than F10 a liter. Because wine sold *en vrac* is "duty-free," customers get a *laissez-passer* (permit) indicating their destination. Bottled wine sold by coops is duty-paid.

HOUSEHOLD AND KITCHEN GOODS

WHEN BUYING goods for the home, try the best department stores such as Alinéa, Cèdre Rouge and Habitat, whose stock is geared to the Gallic market. Despalles is good for garden furniture, and Le Roy Merlin is the home-improvement hypermarket.

It is surprisingly rare to see the whole range of kitchen goods available in a specialist shop. Try instead the kitchen

section of department stores. General hardware stores stock cast-iron cookware and cooking equipment. White china is found in specialist stores.

A good variety of pottery is available anywhere in France at reasonable prices, but particularly near the centers where it is made, such as Aubagne near Marseille, and Vallauris near Grasse *(see p512)*.

Other fine examples of French craftmanship come from Limoges, a world-famous center for porcelain since the 18th century *(see p168)*, and Baccarat, renowned for fine crystal since 1764.

CLOTHING

ELEGANT AND CASUAL clothes can be found even in quite small towns. Paris, however, remains the center for fashion; refer to pages 136–7 for details on men's and women's fashion.

Provençal dried herbs for culinary use and making teas

SIZE CHART
For Australian sizes follow the British and American conversions.

Women's dresses, coats and skirts

French	34	36	38	40	42	44	46
British	8	10	12	14	16	18	20
American	6	8	10	12	14	16	18

Women's shoes

French	36	37	38	39	40	41
British	3	4	5	6	7	8
American	5	6	7	8	9	10

Men's suits

French	44	46	48	50	52	54	56	58
British	34	36	38	40	42	44	46	48
American	34	36	38	40	42	44	46	48

Men's shirts

French	36	38	39	41	42	43	44	45
British	14	15	$15^{1}/_{2}$	16	$16^{1}/_{2}$	17	$17^{1}/_{2}$	18
American	14	15	$15^{1}/_{2}$	16	$16^{1}/_{2}$	17	$17^{1}/_{2}$	18

Men's shoes

French	39	40	41	42	43	44	45	46
British	6	7	$7^{1}/_{2}$	8	9	10	11	12
American	7	$7^{1}/_{2}$	8	$8^{1}/_{2}$	$9^{1}/_{2}$	$10^{1}/_{2}$	11	$11^{1}/_{2}$

Communications

FRENCH TELECOMMUNICATIONS are today sophisticated and efficient. They are run by France Télécom; the postal service is La Poste. Public telephones are located in most public places, including on the streets. If you are phoning abroad from France, the best way is to use a telephone card (*télécarte*).

Bureaux des postes (post offices) are identified by the blue-on-yellow La Poste sign. La Poste used to be called the PTT, so road signs often still indicate PTT.

Foreign language newspapers are available in most large towns. Some TV channels and radio stations broadcast foreign-language programs.

Sign for public telephone

TELEPHONING IN FRANCE

PAYPHONES TAKE coins (F1, F2, F5 and F10) or plastic telephone cards (*télécartes*). Cards are cheaper and more convenient to use than coins. They are sold in either 50 or 120 units and can be bought at post offices and *tabacs* (tobacconists) and some newsagents. For local calls, a unit lasts up to six minutes. Many phones now also accept credit cards (with a PIN number).

In cafés, payphones are coin-operated and are reserved for the use of patrons. Post offices have telephone booths (*cabines*) where you can telephone first and pay after the call. This is cheaper than making long-distance calls from hotels, which often add hefty surcharges.

The Minitel electronic directory can also be used free in post offices.

Home Direct calling service, or *pays directe,* lets you make the call through an operator in your country, and pay by credit card or by reversing the charges. Sometimes you can also call a third country.

In October 1996, all telephone numbers in France changed from eight to ten digits, and the old "16" code was dispensed with. For calls to and within Paris and the Ile de France, the prefix 01 is now added to the original eight-digit number; a 02 prefix is added for northwestern regions; 03 for the northeast; 04 for the southeast (including Corsica); and 05 for the southwest. When phoning from abroad, omit the initial 0 from the new area code, ie dial 33 followed by nine digits.

USING A PHONECARD TELEPHONE

1 Lift receiver and wait for a dial tone.

2 Insert the *télécarte*, arrow side up, in the direction that the arrow is pointing.

3 The display will show how many units are stored on the card and then tell you to dial.

4 Key in the number and wait to be connected.

5 If you want to make another call, do not replace the receiver; simply press the green follow-on call button.

6 When you have finished the call, replace the receiver. The card will emerge from the slot. Remove it.

7 If card runs out in mid-call, it will reemerge; remove and insert another.

French phonecards

HOW TO KEY INTO MINITEL

Minitel provides a variety of services through a screen and keyboard connected to the telephone line. To use Minitel, press the telephone symbol and enter the Minitel number and code. For directory information, press the telephone symbol and key in 3611. When beeping starts, press Connexion/Fin. Specify the service or name of supplier required. Enter town or area. Press Envoi to search. To disconnect, press Veille or Connexion/Fin. Charges vary and are displayed on the screen.

TV AND RADIO

THE ARTE CHANNEL broadcasts foreign films, documentaries and concerts every evening, dubbed in French or with French subtitles. M6 is mainly music, pop and jazz, as well as dubbed US sitcoms and detective series. Canal+ specializes in sports and films. Foreign films are first screened with subtitles and then a dubbed version is shown later in the month. Listings indicate whether the screening will be *v.o. (version originale)* or *v.f. (version française)*. Films on channels FR2 and FR3 are dubbed, except late on Friday and late on Sunday.

Radio France Internationale (738 MW) broadcasts news in English from 4–5pm daily. The French radio news station, France Inter, broadcasts news and weather and traffic reports. The BBC monthly magazine "Worldwide" gives the wavelengths and program guides for BBC World service broadcasts.

Foreign newspapers sold in France

USING A COIN-OPERATED TELEPHONE

1 Lift receiver and wait for the tone.

2 Insert F1, F2, F5 or F10 coins.

3 The digital display shows amount of credit. If more money is required, the message *Crédit épuisé* appears.

4 Key in telephone number and wait to be connected.

5 Replace receiver after call. Any unused coins will be returned.

1 Franc   **2 Francs**   **5 Francs**   **10 Francs**

NEWSPAPERS AND MAGAZINES

ENGLISH LANGUAGE newspapers printed in Europe and widely available on the day of publication are the *Financial Times*, the *Guardian International*, and the *International Herald Tribune*. The *European*, published every Friday, and English language magazines like the *Economist*, *USA Today* and *Newsweek* are easy to find, especially at *maisons de la presse* (newsagents) and railway kiosks in large towns and cities. Many other English newspapers and the major Swiss, Italian, German and Spanish titles are sold the day after publication.

The most influential French newspapers are, from right wing to left: *Le Figaro, France Soir, Le Monde, Libération* and *L'Humanité*.

Special interest magazines listing events all over France are: *Diapason*, for music; *Beaux Arts*, for art; and *Art Presse* for all the arts. See page 140 for magazines of what's on in Paris.

USEFUL FRENCH DIALING CODES

- All domestic calls require a two-digit area prefix followed by eight digits. The area codes are:
  Paris and Ile de France 01; northwest 02; northeast 03; southeast 04; southwest 05.
- For operator service, dial 13.
- For international information, dial:
  12 for Germany;
  13 for other European countries;
  14 for the rest of the world.

- To make direct international calls, dial 00, wait for the tone, then dial the country code, area code and the number.
- The front pages of the A–H telephone directory give the cost of calls per minute for each country and lists their country code.
- The country codes for the following are:
  Australia: 61; **Canada and USA**: 1; **Ireland**: 353; **France**: 33; **New Zealand**: 64; **UK**: 44. Always omit the initial 0 of the area code.

LA POSTE ➤

Road sign giving directions to the post office

USING LA POSTE

LA POSTE (the Post Office) used to be called the P.T.T. *(postes, télégraphes, téléphones)* and although the signs have been changed on post office buildings, some road signs still give directions to the P.T.T.

The postal service in France is fast and reliable. However, it is not cheap, especially when sending a parcel abroad, because all sea-mail services have been discontinued.

At La Poste, postage stamps *(timbres)* are sold singly or in *carnets* of seven or ten. Common postage stamps are also sold at *tabacs*. You can also consult telephone directories *(annuaires)*, buy phonecards, cash postchecks, send or receive money orders *(mandats)*, and call abroad.

Post offices also provide, for a small collection fee, a mail holding service *(poste restante)* so you can receive mail, care of post offices in France. As an address, the sender should write the recipient's surname in capital letters before the first name, followed by "Poste Restante," then the postcode and name of the town it is to be sent to. Unless specified otherwise, mail will go to that town's main post office *(recette principale)*.

Post offices usually open from 9am–5pm Mon–Fri, often with a break for lunch, and 9am–noon on Saturdays.

French mailboxes are a distinctive yellow

SENDING A LETTER

LETTERS ARE MAILED in yellow mailboxes that often have separate slots for the town you are in, the *département* and other destinations *(autres destinations)*.

There are eight different price zones for international mail. EU countries are the cheapest, Australasia the most expensive. You can also buy aerograms, which cost the same for all countries.

A mailman *(un facteur)*

POSTCODES

ALL FRENCH ADDRESSES have a five-digit postcodes. The first two digits represent the *département (see p627)*. If they are followed by 000, this indicates the main town in that *département*, so, for example, Bordeaux is 33000. France's largest cities, Paris, Lyon and Marseille are divided into *arrondissements*, which are shown in the last two digits of the postcode.

A variety of standard issue French stamps

carnet of seven stamps

The town hall in Compiègne

LOCAL GOVERNMENT IN FRANCE

A COMPLEX JIGSAW, France's local government operates in a three-tier system – *région*, *département* and *commune*. The country used to comprise separate semi-autonomous provinces or duchies, like Provence and the smaller Anjou. During the Revolution, these were replaced by a network of 96 *départements*. These are administrative units mostly named after rivers, for example Haute-Loire, each governed by a "prefect" appointed in Paris.

The system had its strengths, but was too state-controlled for a modern democracy. Now some of the prefect's power has gone to the *département*'s elected council. For some functions the *départements* have been grouped into 22 *régions*, each with an elected assembly. Several, like Brittany and Alsace, roughly correspond to the old provinces; others are hybrids, like Centre and Rhône-Alpes.

At a lower level, France remains split up into around 35,000 *communes* (parishes or boroughs), ranging from big cities like Paris or Lyon to tiny villages. Each *commune* has its elected mayor, a figure of great local influence, ruling from the *mairie* (town hall). This system is cumbersome, yet village communes refuse to merge, so great is the pull of local pride.

Regions of France
In 1972, France was officially divided into 22 regions. This map shows the 15 regional divisions used in this guide plus all of France's 96 départements.

The Paris and Ile de France *région* is divided into eight separate *départements.* Central Paris (*département 75*) is subdivided into 20 *arrondissements (see p144).*

THE DÉPARTEMENTS OF FRANCE

PARIS AND ILE DE FRANCE
75 Paris
77 Seine-et-Marne
78 Yvelines
91 Essonne
92 Hauts-de-Seine
93 Seine-St-Denis
94 Val-de-Marne
95 Val-d'Oise

NORTHEAST FRANCE
Le Nord and Picardy
02 Aisne
59 Nord
60 Oise
62 Pas-de-Calais
80 Somme

Champagne
08 Ardennes
10 Aube
51 Marne
52 Haute-Marne

Alsace and Lorraine
54 Meurthe-et-Moselle
55 Meuse
57 Moselle
67 Bas-Rhin
68 Haut-Rhin
88 Vosges

WESTERN FRANCE
Normandy
14 Calvados
27 Eure
50 Manche
61 Orne
76 Seine-Maritime

Brittany
22 Côtes-du-Nord
29 Finistère

35 Ille-et-Vilaine
56 Morbihan

The Loire Valley
18 Cher
28 Eure-et-Loir
36 Indre
37 Indre-et-Loire
41 Loir-et-Cher
44 Loire-Atlantique
45 Loiret
49 Maine-et-Loire
53 Mayenne
72 Sarthe
85 Vendée

CENTRAL FRANCE
Burgundy and Franche-Comté
21 Côte d'Or
25 Doubs
39 Jura
58 Nièvre
70 Haute-Saône
71 Saône-et-Loire
89 Yonne
90 Territoire de Belfort

The Massif Central
03 Allier
12 Aveyron
15 Cantal
19 Corrèze
23 Creuse
43 Haute-Loire
48 Lozère
63 Puy-de-Dôme
87 Haute-Vienne

Rhône Valley and French Alps
01 Ain
05 Hautes Alpes
07 Ardèche
26 Drôme
38 Isère
42 Loire

69 Rhône
73 Savoie
74 Haute-Savoie

SOUTHWEST FRANCE
Poitou and Aquitaine
16 Charente
17 Charente-Maritime
33 Gironde
40 Landes
79 Deux-Sèvres
86 Vienne

Périgord, Quercy and Gascony
24 Dordogne
32 Gers
47 Lot
47 Lot-et-Garonne
81 Tarn
82 Tarn-et-Garonne

The Pyrenees
09 Ariège
31 Haute-Garonne
64 Pyrénées-Atlantiques
65 Hautes-Pyrénées

THE SOUTH OF FRANCE
Languedoc-Roussillon
11 Aude
30 Gard
34 Hérault
66 Pyrénées-Orientales

Provence and the Côte d'Azur
04 Alpes-de-Haut-Provence
06 Alpes-Maritimes
13 Bouches-du-Rhône
83 Var
84 Vaucluse

Corsica
2A Corse-du-Sud
2B Haute-Corse

Special Vacations and Outdoor Activities

A COUNTRY AS RICHLY DIVERSE in culture and geography as France offers an amazing variety of sports and leisure activities. For the best in entertainment and spectator sports, festivals and annual events, see *France through the Year* on pages 32–5. Information on current leisure and sporting activities in a particular region is available from the tourist offices listed for each town in this guide. The suggestions below cover some of the most popular as well as some more unusual pursuits.

Hiking along the Gorges du Verdon in Provence *(see pp504–5)*

SPECIAL VACATIONS

F RENCH GOVERNMENT TOURIST Offices *(see p617)* have extensive information on travel companies offering special-interest vacations. Send for *The Traveler in France Reference Guide*.

Educational courses include language learning, often combined with other activities. Ask for *Cours de francais pour étudiants étrangers* from the cultural counselor's office of your **French Embassy**, or send for *Le Petit Guide* from **Ulysses International**.

Young people can enjoy a French-speaking vacation by working part-time on the restoration of historic sites with **R.E.M.P.ART** *(Association pour la Réhabilitation et Entretien des Monuments et du Patrimoine Artistique)*.

There is a wide choice of gastronomic courses available, offering classical cuisine or regional cooking. Wine appreciation courses for various levels of expertise are

also available. Craft activities include courses for tapestry, sculpture and painting.

Nature lovers can enjoy the *parcs nationaux* and can join organized bird-watching and botanical trips in many areas, including the Camargue, the Cévennes and Corsica.

The Guide des Jardins de France from **Editions Hachette** is a useful reference guide when visiting France's many beautiful gardens.

GOLF AND TENNIS

T HERE ARE golf courses all over France, especially along the north and south coasts and in Aquitaine. French players have to reach a minimum standard and obtain a license in order to play, so take your handicap certificate with you. Most top courses offer weekend or longer tutored breaks geared to any level of player. *Le Guide des Golfs de France* from **Editions Sand et Menges** will give details.

Tennis is very popular in France and courts for hourly rental can be found in almost every town. Take your own equipment with you as rental facilities may not be available.

Mountain bikes, wonderful for exploring

Escaping into the forest at Fontainebleau *(see pp170–71)*

WALKING, BICYCLING AND HORSE RIDING

M ORE THAN 30,000 km (19,000 miles) of *Grandes Randonnées* (long-distance tracks) and the shorter *Petites Randonnées* are clearly marked. The routes vary in difficulty and include long pilgrim routes, alpine crossings and tracks through national parks. *Topo Guides*, published by **Fédération Française de la Randonnée Pédestre**, describe the *GR* tracks in French with details of transportation connections, overnight stops and food shopping. They also publish a general walking guide, *Guide du Randonneur*.

Some *Grandes and Petites Randonnées* are open to mountain bikes and horses. For detailed advice on bicycling in France, contact the **CTC** (Cyclists' Touring Club) or **Fédération Française de Cyclotourisme**. Local tourist offices in France provide details about area riding facilities. *Gîtes d'étapes* *(see p539)* offer dormitory accommodations close to well-known tracks.

MOUNTAIN SPORTS

A PART FROM down-hill skiing and *ski de fond* (cross-country skiing), catered for by numerous travel operators, the mountains, especially the Alps and Pyrenees, are enjoyed in the

Canoes at St-Chély, near the Gorges du Tarn *(see pp360–61)*

summer by rock-climbers and mountaineers. Contact the **Fédération Française de la Montagne et de l'Escalade** for more information.

AERONAUTICAL SPORTS

LEARNING TO FLY in France can be much cheaper than in the US. Information on schools can be obtained from the **Fédération Nationale Aéronautique**. There are also plenty of opportunities to learn the exhilarating skills of gliding, paragliding and hang gliding. For more information, contact the **Fédération Française de Vol Libre**.

Paragliding or *parapente* off the cliffs of Chamonix *(see pp312–13)*

WATER SPORTS

WHITE-WATER rafting, kayaking and canoeing take place on many French rivers, especially in the Massif Central. More information can be obtained from The **Fédération Française de Canoë-Kayak**. The Atlantic coast around Biarritz offers some of the

best surfing and windsurfing in Europe. Sailing and water-skiing are also popular all over France. Training schools and equipment rentals are found at the coast and near lakes.

Swimming facilities are generally good, although beaches in the South of France can be very crowded *(see pp464–5)*.

FIELD SPORTS

ALTHOUGH HUNTING is a popular sport in France, a *permis de chasser* is essential. This involves passing an exam in French, which makes it difficult for visitors to take part. There are regional variations of season depending on the activity. Details are displayed in local town halls.

All kinds of fishing, for both fresh and seawater fish, are available, depending on the area. Local fishing shops sell the *carte de pêche*, which gives details of regulations.

NATURISM

THERE ARE NEARLY 50 centers in France for naturism, mostly in the south, south-west and Corsica. Information is available in English from French Government Tourist Offices or **Fédération Française de Naturisme**.

PUBLIC EVENTS

TO JOIN the French enjoying their spare time, look for football (soccer) and rugby matches, or bicycling races. Seasonal markets and local *fêtes* often combine antiques fairs and *boules* tournaments with rock and pop concerts.

USEFUL ADDRESSES

CTC
Cotterell House, 69 Meadrow, Godalming, Surrey GU7 3HS UK.
☎ *01483 417 217.*

Editions Hachette
43 quai de Grenelle, 75015 Paris.
☎ *01 43 92 30 00.*

Editions Sand et Menges
6 rue de Mail, 75002 Paris.
☎ *01 44 55 37 50.*

Fédération Française de Canoë-Kayak
87 quai de la Marne, 94340 Joinville-le-Pont. ☎ *01 45 11 08 50.*

Fédération Française de Cyclotourisme
8 rue Jean-Marie-Jego, 75013 Paris. ☎ *01 44 16 88 88.*

Fédération Française de la Montagne et de l'Escalade
8–10 quai de la Marne, 75019 Paris. ☎ *01 40 18 75 50.*
FAX *01 40 18 75 59.*

Fédération Française de Naturisme
65 rue de Tocqueville, 75017 Paris. ☎ *01 47 64 32 82.*
FAX *01 47 64 32 63.*

Fédération Française de la Randonnée Pédestre
64 rue de Gergovie, 75014 Paris.
☎ *01 45 45 31 02.*

Fédération Française de Vol Libre
4 rue de Suisse, 06100 Nice.
☎ *04 93 88 62 89.*

Fédération Nationale Aéronautique
155 av Wagram, 75017 Paris.
☎ *01 44 29 92 00.*
FAX *01 44 29 92 01.*

French Embassy
Cultural Department, 972 Fifth Avenue, New York, NY 10021.
☎ *212 439 1400.*

R.E.M.P.ART
1 rue des Guillemites, 75004 Paris. ☎ *01 42 71 96 55.*

Ulysses International
21 Avenue du Professeur Grasset, 34093 Montpellier.
☎ *04 67 04 48 24.*

TRAVEL INFORMATION

RANCE has advanced transportation systems, with Paris at the hub. Paris's two main airports, Roissy-Charles-de-Gaulle and Orly, have direct flights to North America, Africa, Japan, and the rest of Europe. The city's six major train stations connect it to some 6,000 destinations in France and provide links to all of Europe. France is also well connected by sea, with frequent ferry crossings in the English Channel and the Mediterranean.

ARRIVING BY AIR

RANCE IS SERVED by nearly all international airlines. Some airports near the border, such as Geneva, Basle, and Luxembourg, can also be used for destinations in France.

The main British airlines with regular flights to France are British Airways and British Midland, and the main French airline is **Air France**. From the United States there are regular flights through **American Airlines** and **Delta**. **Air Canada** runs flights from Canada, and **Qantas** provides connecting flights from Australia and New Zealand.

AIR FARES

AIRLINE FARES are at their highest during the peak summer season in France, usually from July to September. Different airlines, however, may have slightly different high summer season periods, so check with the airlines or an

CDG Airport *Terminals CDG1, CDG2, and T9 are linked by shuttle buses and mini-subway trains. Departures are on the lower level and arrivals on the upper.*

PARIS ROISSY-CHARLES-DE-GAULLE (CDG)

THERE ARE TWO main terminals: CDG1 and CDG2. T9 is for charter flights. Taxis to central Paris cost F200–300.

Air France buses go to Porte Maillot and Charles de Gaulle-Etoile. The journey takes about 40 minutes. Air France buses also go to Montparnasse TGV train station. The journey takes around 50 minutes. RATP buses (Roissybus) leave every 15 minutes for L'Opéra.

The journey takes about 45 minutes, depending on traffic conditions, and costs F45.

All the major car rental companies can be found at the airport. A limousine service is also available, but this must be reserved in advance, and costs F700–F900 to Paris.

A fast, reliable and cheap way to the center is by train. With a station in CDG2, and linked to CDG1 by a free shuttle bus, the RER reaches Châtelet-les-Halles, in the heart of Paris, in less than 30 minutes and the Gare de Nord in 35 minutes.

CDG2 also has its own TGV station, with direct lines to Lille (1hr) and Lyon (2hrs), and connections to other branches of the TGV network.

Major expansion is underway at CDG2, due for completion in 2003, so layouts may alter.

Airport Information
🛈 *01 48 62 22 80.*

CDG1 is used for international flights, except those of Air France.

Car-rental agencies (Doors 16 & 20)

Air France bus to Montparnasse (Door 26)

RER shuttle buses (Door 28)

Taxi stand (Door 16)

Air France bus to Porte Maillot and Etoile (Door 34)

Disneyland Paris bus (Door 30)

CDG2 is used for all Air France flights and for short-hop international flights by other carriers.

Air France buses: Orly/Montparnasse (Door 1)

Air France buses: Maillot/Etoile (Door 5)

CDG2B

Disneyland Paris bus (Door 1)

CDG2A

Air France buses: Maillot/Etoile (Door 5)

RATP buses (Door 12)

Taxi stand (Door 8)

CDG2D

RATP buses (Door 10)

CDG2C

Taxi stand (Door 8)

TGV and RER stations

CDG2F (not yet open)

Air France buses: Maillot/Etoile (Door 6)

CDG2E (under construction)

agent to find out which fares will apply when you travel.

APEX (Advance Purchase Excursion) fares are booked in advance. They cannot be changed or canceled without penalty, and there are also minimum and maximum stay requirements. Note that children often travel more cheaply than adults.

Fierce competition among airlines means there are some very attractive discounts available. Look for the best deals; reputable travel agents provide some very good ones. The addresses of a selection of recommended discount travel agents are listed on page 633. These agents offer both charter and regular scheduled flights at competitive prices. Many of them have representatives in other countries.

Getting to or from France on the national carrier, Air France

FLIGHT TIMES

FLIGHT TIMES to Paris from various cities are: London: 1 hour; Dublin: 90 minutes; Montreal: 7½ hours; New York: 8 hours; Los Angeles: 12 hours; Sydney: 23 hours.

INTERNATIONAL AIRPORTS

MAIN AIRPORTS in France serving international and domestic flights are on pages 632-3, with transportation details. Details of Paris's two main airports are listed below.

Orly Airport
The two terminals, Orly Sud and Orly Ouest, are linked by a mini-subway, but they are within walking distance of one another.

Orly Ouest is used almost exclusively for domestic flights.

Orlyrail shuttle buses (Hall 3)

Air France buses (Hall 3, ground floor)

Orlybus (Door C, ground floor)

Orlyval (Hall 2, first floor)

Taxi stand (Hall 2)

Orly Sud handles a wider range of services, including the majority of international and charter flights.

Air France buses (Door F, platform 5)

Orlybus (Door H, platform 4)

Taxi stand (Door H)

Orlyval (Doors E/F, ground floor)

Orlyrail (Door H, platform 1)

ORLY AIRPORT (ORY)

THERE ARE two terminals: Orly Sud and Orly Ouest. Taxis take 25–45 minutes to the city center, depending on the traffic, and cost about F155.

Air France buses leave the airport every 12 minutes and take around 30 minutes to reach the center of Paris, stopping at Les Invalides and Montparnasse.

The RATP Orlybus leaves every 13 minutes and takes about 25 minutes to reach the Denfert-Rochereau metro.

The Jet Bus, which connects Orly to Villejuif-Louis Aragon metro, departs from the airport every 15 minutes.

Shuttle buses link the airport with RER line C services at nearby Rungis. Trains for Gare d'Austerlitz leave every 15 minutes, and take 35 minutes.

A train service, Orlyval, links up with the Roissy Rail RER line B at Antony station nearby, with trains leaving every 4–7 minutes for Châtelet. The journey takes 30 minutes.

Car rental companies at the airport include Avis, Budget, Europcar, Hertz and National Citer. A chauffeur-driven limousine to Paris costs around F450.

Airport Information
🆔 *01 49 75 15 15.*

FRANCE BY AIR

THE MAIN domestic airline is **Air Inter Europe**. **TAT** (Touraine Air Transport) and **Air Littoral** also have routes, as does Air France, and there are many small airlines that operate within just one region.

Unless you are eligible for discounts, you may find it cheaper and faster to travel on the high-speed trains *(see p635)*, given the time taken to reach out of town airports.

Air Inter Europe, in particular, offers many discounted fares, based on the red, white and blue calendar system: peak flights are red *(rouge)*, off-peak flights are designated *bleu* (blue) or *blanc* (white). Discounts are available based on various combinations of age and frequency of travel.

Domestic flights can be booked from abroad with travel agents or Air France.

AIRPORT	INFORMATION	DISTANCE FROM CITY
Bâle–Mulhouse	☎ 03 89 90 31 11	25 km (16 m
Bastia (Poretta)	☎ 04 95 54 54 54	20 km (13 m
Bordeaux (Mérignac)	☎ 05 56 34 50 50	12 km (8 m
Lille (Lesquin)	☎ 03 20 49 68 68	8 km (5 m
Lyon (Satolas)	☎ 04 72 22 72 21	25 km (16 m
Marseille (Marignane)	☎ 04 42 14 14 14	25 km (16 m
Montpellier Fréjorgues	☎ 04 67 20 85 00	7 km (4 m
Nantes Atlantique	☎ 02 40 84 80 00	12 km (8 mi
Nice (Côte d'Azur)	☎ 04 93 21 30 30	6 km (4 m
Strasbourg	☎ 03 88 64 67 67	12 km (8 mi
Toulouse (Blagnac)	☎ 05 61 42 44 00	7 km (4 m

CROSSING THE CHANNEL

THERE ARE SEVERAL crossings between UK and Continental ports. The Channel Tunnel provides a direct link between UK and France.

Stena Sealink has 90-minute crossings from Dover to Calais and four-hour crossings from Newhaven to Dieppe. **P&O European Ferries** has a 75-minute crossing from Dover to Calais and a six-hour crossing from Portsmouth to Le Havre. It also operates a six-hour service from Portsmouth to Cherbourg. **Sally Viking Line** operates a 2½-hour service from Ramsgate to Dunkirk and a 4-hour service to Oostende. **Brittany Ferries** run a nine-hour service from Portsmouth to St-Malo. They also have a service to Santander in Spain and to Biarritz, near the French border, and sail from Cork in Eire to Roscoff.

North Sea Ferries sail from Hull to Zeebrugge in Belgium, with good road links to north-east France; P&O sail from Felixstowe to Zeebrugge.

Hoverspeed operates 35-minute hovercraft services between Dover and Calais. The high-speed catamaran is run by **Seacat** between Folkestone and Boulogne, and takes 55 minutes.

Eurotunnel logo

THE CHANNEL TUNNEL

THE CHANNEL Tunnel was inaugurated by the Queen and President Mitterrand in 1994. A car-carrying shuttle service, operated by **Eurotunnel**, runs between Folkestone and Calais. The passenger service, **Eurostar**, links London and Ashford with Paris *(see p634)*.

OTHER CROSSINGS

CAR FERRIES sail to Corsica from Marseille and Nice all year round, or from Toulon between April and October. The ferries are run by **SNCM Ferryterranée**. In the high season, SNCM also sails weekly to Sardinia from Marseille and Toulon. SNCM also goes to Tunis and Algiers from Marseille. From April to September **Corsica Marittima** (CMT) operates a three-hour car ferry service between Bastia in Corsica and Livorno in Italy, and an overnight crossing from Porto Vecchio in Corsica to Livorno. **Compagnie Marocaine de Navigation** offers a luxury two-night car ferry service between Sète and Tangier.

Plying the Mediterranean with SNCM Ferryterranée

TAXI FARE TO THE CITY	BUS DETAILS	CAR RENTAL
SF240–260	City center 30 mins	Avis, Budget, Europcar, Hertz, National Citer
F180–250	City center 25 mins	Avis, Budget, Europcar, Hertz-Filipi Auto, National Citer
F160–200	Gare St-Jean 30–45 mins	ADA, Avis, Budget, Europcar, Hertz, National Citer, Sixt-Eurorent
F100–130	Lille SNCF 20 mins	Avis, Budget, Europcar, Hertz, National Citer
F200–250	Perrache SNCF 40 mins. Also to Chambery, Geneva Apt Valence, St-Etienne and ski resorts	Avis, Budget, Century, Hertz, National Citer, Sixt-Eurorent
F200–250	St-Charles SNCF 25 mins	Avis, Budget, Europcar, Hertz, National Citer, Sixt-Eurorent
F80–100	City center 20 mins	ADA, Avis, Budget, Europcar, Hertz, National Citer, Sixt-Eurorent
F100–130	City center 20 mins	ADA, Avis, Budget, Europcar, Hertz, National Citer, Sixt-Eurorent
F100–120	Gare Routière 20 mins	Avis, Budget, Europcar, Hertz, Mattei, National Citer, Sixt-Eurorent
F150–200	City center 30 mins	ADA, Avis, Budget, Europcar, Hertz, National Citer, Sixt-Eurorent
F100–130	Gare Routière Marengo 20 mins	ADA, Avis, Budget, Europcar, Hertz, National Citer, Sixt-Eurorent, Spanghero

DIRECTORY

AIRLINES

Air Canada
(1) (800) 361 8620 (US).
01 42 18 19 20 in Paris.

Air France
0802 802 802.
(212) 247 0100 in US.

Air Inter Europe
0802 802 802.

Air Littoral
0803 834 834.

American Airlines
(1) (800) 433 7300 (US).
01 42 89 05 22 in Paris.

Delta Airlines
(1) (800) 221 1212 (US).
01 47 68 92 92 in Paris.

Qantas
01 44 55 52 00 in Paris.
(1) (800) 227 4500 (US).

TRAVEL AGENCIES

Bordeaux
Usit Voyages, 284 rue St-Cathérine, 33000 Bordeaux.
05 56 33 89 90.

Lyon
Council Travel, 35 rue Victor Hugo, 69000 Lyon.
04 78 38 78 38.

Nice
Council Travel, 37 bis rue d'Angleterre, 06000 Nice.
04 93 82 23 33.

Usit Voyages, 10 rue de Belgique, 06000 Nice.
04 93 87 34 96.

Paris
Council Travel
1 place de l'Odéon, 75006 Paris.
01 44 41 89 89.

Nouvelles Frontières, 66 bd St-Michel, 75006 Paris.
01 40 29 12 12.

O.T.U. 119 rue St-Martin, 75004 Paris.
01 40 29 12 12.

Usit Voyages, 12 rue Vivienne, 75002 Paris.
01 42 44 14 00.

Usit Voyages, 6 rue de Vaugirard, 75006 Paris.
01 42 34 56 90.

Toulouse
Usit Voyages, 5 rue des Lois, 31000 Toulouse.
05 61 11 52 42.

New York
Council Travel, 205 East 42nd St, New York, NY 10017.
(212) 822 2700.
Nouvelles Frontières, 12 East 33rd Street, New York, NY 10016.
(212) 779 0609.

Travel Cuts, University of British Columbia, Students Union Boulevard, Vancouver, British Columbia V6T 121.
(604) 822 6890.

FERRY SERVICES

Brittany Ferries
02 33 88 44 88.
01202 44 11 36 in UK.

Compagnie Marocaine de Navigation
01 45 22 27 52.

Corsica Marittima (CMT)
04 95 54 66 95.

Hoverspeed
03 21 46 14 14.
01304 240 241 in UK.

North Sea Ferries
01482 77177 in UK.

P&O European Ferries
03 21 46 10 10.
0990 980 980 in UK.

Seacat
03 21 46 78 30.
01304 240 241 in UK.

Stena Sealink
03 21 46 78 30.
01233 647 047 in UK.

SNCM Ferryterranée
0836 57 95 00 (24-hrs for all ports).

Marseille
Embark at Joliette ferry terminal.

Nice
Embark at quai du Commerce.

Toulon (SNCM/CMT)
Embark at Gare Maritime.

CHANNEL TUNNEL

Eurostar
01233 617 575 in UK.

Eurotunnel
01 43 18 62 22.
03 21 00 61 00.

Traveling by Train

SNCF logo

THE FRENCH state railway, Société Nationale des Chemins de Fer (**SNCF**), provides an excellent rail network that covers nearly all of France. Even where lines have been closed for economic reasons, SNCF runs bus services, which are free to people with rail passes. The best trains are, however, confined to the *Grandes Lignes* which radiate out of Paris. Traveling off these major lines can be slow, so it is sometimes quicker to make your way cross-country via Paris.

ARRIVING IN FRANCE

TRAINS FROM the UK through Dieppe and ports in Normandy arrive in Paris at Gare St-Lazare, or at the Gare du Nord from Boulogne and Calais. Most trains from Scandinavia, Holland and Belgium also arrive at the Gare du Nord.

The terminus for trains from Brittany ports is the Gare Montparnasse on the Left Bank. Trains from southern France, the Alps, Italy, Switzerland and Greece arrive at Gare de Lyon in eastern Paris, the city's main station. The Gare d'Austerlitz on the Left Bank serves southwest France, Spain and Portugal. The Gare de l'Est serves eastern France, Switzerland, Austria and Germany.

Eurostar's passenger service through the Channel Tunnel runs between Waterloo International and the Gare du Nord. **Hoverspeed City Link** provides connecting train travel between London and Paris, with fast Channel crossings via Folkestone.

Traveling by train and car through France with Motorail

TRAVELING AROUND FRANCE BY TRAIN

FRANCE HAS ALWAYS been known for the punctuality of its trains, and now also for a positive attitude to upgrading it's rail system. Apart from the four types of TGVs, *Trains à Grande Vitesse*, there are many other frequent train services such as the Corail express, the Motorail service (*Trains Autos Couchette* or *TAC*, sometimes called *TAA*). There are also very good local and suburban train services in the largest cities, and the excellent RER (*Reseau Express Régionale*) train network in the Paris area.

Rail traveller with luggage trolley

Services such as Train + Auto and Train + Vélo, are also available – you reserve a rental car or bike when you buy your train ticket and collect it from the station of arrival. Train + Hotel provides pre-booked accommodations at your destination. Train de Nuit/Hôtel de Jour gives sleeping-car passengers use of a hotel room and its services the following day for half-price.

Information on all these services is available from the **Rail Europe** office in London. In France, brochures are available at most stations. Overnight services are popular in France. Most long-distance trains have couchettes, which you must reserve for a fee. Not all trains have restau-

Symbol for Paris suburban trains

rant cars or bars, even on long journeys. TGV trains have bars with light meals, but reservations must be made in advance for the at-seat meal service available in first class.

Note that for Lille, Mâcon and Vendome the TGV terminus is in a different location from the main railroad station.

FARES

TICKETS BOOKED in France are normally subject to surcharges, as indicated by the *calendrier voyageurs*, a red, white and blue calendar. Red is for peak-time travel, and blue for the cheapest fares. Many of the discounts offered (up to 60 percent) for rail travel are only available on blue days. Fares are also dependent on the distance of the journey, whether you travel first/second class, a reservation fee and the station surcharge. Reservations are compulsory for all TGV trains.

SNCF issues cards that entitle holders to discount fares: *carte vermeil* for the over 60s; *carte à deux* for couples sharing an address; and *carte Kiwi* for up to four people traveling with a child. There are also 12–25 fares for those under 26; *découvertes* fares for advance booking; and *séjours* return fares for trips over 1,000 km (600 miles). Rail passes bought outside the country for use in France include Eurodomino tickets, which allow three-, five- or ten-days' travel in a month. Eurotrain fares are for travelers under 26 and are valid for two months.

Air France Rail offers a combined air and rail package that includes flights from a choice of five British airports to Charles de Gaulle and then unlimited train travel in France with a Eurodomino pass for either a 3-, 5- or 10-day period, including transfers in Paris.

Specialist agencies, such as **Council Travel** and **Wasteels**, issue the InterRail Card that allows anyone under 26 one month's unlimited travel in France and 25 other European countries. The slightly more expensive InterRail Plus 26 Card is for travelers over 26. A 10-day pass is also available. Note, you must be a resident to buy an InterRail in France. InterRail passengers must still pay reservation fees and surcharges where applicable.

PRIVATE RAILROADS

Privately run railroads are numerous but mostly serve as tourist attractions rather than as transportation. However, **Chemins de Fer de Provence** runs the Train des Pignes over the 150-km (90-mile) spectacular route from Nice to Digne. In Corsica, **Chemins de Fer de la Corse** operates two routes, Bastia-Calvi and Calvi-Ajaccio.

A high-speed TGV link

TGV RAIL SERVICE

Trains à Grande Vitesse, or high-speed trains, travel at speeds up to 300 km/h (185 mph). There are three routes. TGV Nord from Paris Gare du Nord, TGV Atlantique from Paris Gare Montparnasse and TGV Sud-Est from Paris Gare de Lyon.

KEY

- Nord
- Atlantique
- Sud-Est

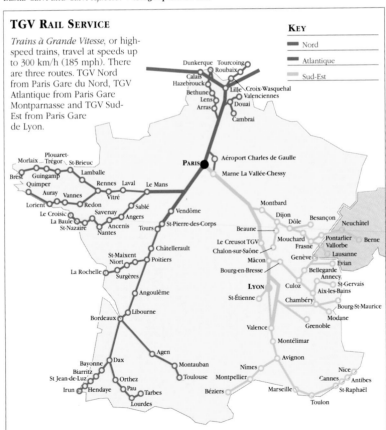

To Book in France

Aᴜᴛᴏᴍᴀᴛɪᴄ ᴛɪᴄᴋᴇᴛ and reservation machines *(billetterie automatique)* are found at main stations. They take credit cards or coins. You can also check train times and fares and make reservations by phoning **SNCF** or by using the Minitel system *(see p624)*. Tickets may be purchased by credit card, then picked up at the station.

Reservations are compulsory for travel by TGV, on public holidays, and for a *couchette* or *siège inclinable* (reclinable seat) and must be made at least five minutes before departure. Both reservations and tickets must be validated in a *composteur* machine before boarding the train *(see below)*.

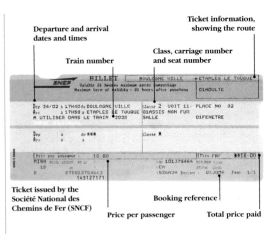

Departure and arrival dates and times

Train number

Ticket information, showing the route

Class, carriage number and seat number

Ticket issued by the Société National des Chemins de Fer (SNCF)

Price per passenger

Booking reference

Total price paid

An automatic ticket machine

To Book Abroad

Bᴏᴏᴋɪɴɢ ꜱᴇʀᴠɪᴄᴇꜱ by mail, telephone and fax for all tickets to and within France can be made through **Rail Europe Inc.** in the US, who also give information on prices and departure times. There is a small booking fee per person. Tickets are sent out by registered mail the same or next day with credit card bookings and after five days if paid for by check.

If you intend to travel by **Motorail**, it is a good idea to get their booklet *French Railways, the Expressway into Europe* first, because there

are various routes, fares, and sleeping accommodations. The Rail Europe office in London offers the full range of discount tickets *(see p634)*, including InterRail. Bookings can be made up to two months in advance and up to two days before departure.

Reservations made in the UK or US may prove difficult to change in France. You may have to buy another reservation, or in the case of Motorail, another ticket and claim a refund later after your return. If you want to change your booking, it is better to do so before leaving for France, where possible, because you will then pay only a small penalty.

Tickets for **Eurostar** can be booked direct from this company or via Rail Europe.

Timetables

Fʀᴇɴᴄʜ ʀᴀɪʟᴡᴀʏ timetables change twice a year, in May and September. French Railways sell the *Ville à Ville* timetable, which lists major routes from Paris. They also sell the regional timetables for the Atlantic coast, the southeast and the northeast.

Free leaflets give information on traveling with children, reduced fares, train travel for the disabled, and the TGV network *(see pp634–5)*. Some regions, such as Provence-Alpes-Côte d'Azur, now have a regional TER *(Transports Express Régionaux)* timetable that includes bus travel.

Bear in mind that trains in France are punctual. Your train will almost certainly leave on time!

Composteur Machine
Orange composteur *machines are located in station halls and at the head of each platform. Insert tickets and reservations separately, printed side up, in the machine. The* composteur *will punch your ticket and print the time and date on the back. A penalty may be imposed by the inspector on the train if you fail to do this.*

ARRIVING BY BUS

BUS TRAVEL is the cheapest way to get to France. The modern buses operated by **Eurolines** travel to 270 destinations in Europe, including many in France.

There are three departures daily to Paris from Victoria Coach Station in London, with stops in Bagnolet and Versailles. The trip takes about nine hours – tickets may be purchased from the **National Express** office at Victoria. Eurolines offer one-way tickets, returns and round trips throughout Europe.

Hoverspeed City Sprint uses the faster hovercraft crossing and takes about 6 hours from Victoria Coach Station to Paris, with a drop-off point 15 minutes by metro from the Gard du Nord.

TRAVELING AROUND FRANCE BY BUS

LONG-DISTANCE buses generally only operate where trains don't offer a good service (for example, Geneva to Nice). SNCF (the state railroad) operates some buses and issues regional TER *(Transports Express Régionaux)* combined timetables and tickets.

Eurolines offers a wider range of destinations than most. It also offers excursions and arranges accommodations.

There are many local buses, which run from the town's *Gare Routière* (which is often at the Gare SNCF). Timetables are geared to carry students and people going to work, so the morning departure time from a village may be very early.

TAXIS

IN THE PROVINCES prices vary from one region to another. All taxis must carry meters *(compteurs)*. The pickup charge should be about F12 plus F3.60 or more per km. You may be able to agree on a price for a long journey. Look for a *station de taxi* outside airports or train stations or in the center of town. Because hailing a taxi is only common practice in France's large cities, you have to book a taxi by telephone in rural areas.

BICYCLE TRAVEL

ALTHOUGH CYCLING is popular in France, there are not many trains on which you can take your bicycle. The ones upon which you may are indicated on the timetable by a bicycle symbol. In most instances, however, a bicycle has to be sent as a separate package. The drawback is that you may have to wait up to four days for delivery.

Alternatively, you can rent a bicycle. Through the SNCF, you can reserve a rental bike at a number of stations when you buy your ticket *(see Train + Vélo p634)*. Bicycle shops in many towns have touring bikes or mountain bikes for rent, and may also rent mopeds and light motorcycles.

Rural France is ideal for cycling due to its large network of uncrowded roads. There are, however, few bike lanes in towns. For more details on marked bicycle routes, see page 628.

HITCH-HIKING

IT IS NOT EASY to get around France by hitch-hiking. You must look clean and "normal" to have any chance of a lift, especially since it is car, rather than truck, drivers who will be your best bet. The safest and easiest way to hitch-hike long-distance is through **Allo-stop**. This organization has branches in many major towns and will set you up with rides for a very reasonable rate.

INFORMATION AND RESERVATIONS

Eurostar
℡ 01233 617 575.

Rail Europe
179 Piccadilly
London W1V 0BA.
℡ 020 7203 7000.
℡ 0990 300 003.
℡ 0990 848 848.
FAX 020 7409 1652.

SNCF, Paris
℡ 08 36 35 35 35.
Minitel 36 15 SNCF.

INTER-RAIL AGENTS

Travel Cuts
295A Regent Street
London W1R 7YA.
℡ 020 7255 1944.

Wasteels
121 Wilton Road
London SW1V 1JZ.
℡ 020 7834 7066.

PRIVATE RAILWAYS

Chemins de Fer de Provence
℡ 04 93 88 34 72.

Chemins de Fer de Corse:
Ajaccio
℡ 04 95 23 11 03.
Bastia
℡ 04 95 32 80 61.
Calvi
℡ 04 95 65 00 61.

EUROLINES

London
52 Grosvenor Gardens
Victoria, London SW1.
℡ 020 7730 8235.

Paris
28 av du Général de
Gaulle, 93170 Bagnolet.
℡ 01 49 72 51 51.

National Express
Victoria Coach Station,
164 Buckingham Palace
Road, London SW1 9WTP.
℡ 0990 80 80 80.

BUS STATIONS IN FRANCE

Paris (Eurolines)
Porte de Bagnolet.
℡ 01 49 72 51 51.

Bordeaux
Place des Quinconces.
℡ 05 56 43 68 43.

Lyon
Gare de Perrache.
℡ 04 78 71 70 00.

Marseille
Place Victor Hugo.
℡ 04 91 50 57 55.

Nice
5 boulevard Jean Jaurès.
℡ 04 93 85 61 81.

Strasbourg
Place des Halles.
℡ 03 88 32 36 97.

HOVERSPEED CITY LINK/SPRINT

Hoverspeed Ltd
International Hoverport
Marine Parade, Dover,
Kent CT17 9TG.
℡ 01304 240241 in UK.

HITCH-HIKING

Allo-stop
8 rue Rochambeau,
Paris 75009.
℡ 01 53 20 42 42.

On the Road

The classic Citroën 2 CV

FRANCE HAS one of the densest road networks in Europe, with modern highways that allow quick and easy access to all parts of the country. However, you can save money on tolls and explore France in a more leisurely way by using some of the other high quality roads that dissect the country. This section gives instructions on how to use the highway tollbooths and French parking meters (*horodateurs*), as well as explaining some of the rules governing driving in France. There are also various travel tips, such as where to buy gas, how to get weather and traffic forecasts, where to rent a car and where to find the best road maps.

A 26

S^T OMER DUNKERQUE

Highway and D-road signs

GETTING TO FRANCE BY CAR

THERE IS A GOOD choice of car-ferry operators from the UK *(see p632)*. You can profit from discount fares for short trips, a flat rate for a car with up to five passengers, or by buying tickets for the crossing in conjunction with Motorail *(see pp634 and 637)*.

You can also take the car on the **Eurotunnel** shuttle *(see p632)* via the Channel Tunnel.

WHAT TO TAKE

CHECK with your car insurance agent (and any automotive club you belong to, such as AAA) before leaving for France to determine the extent of your coverage abroad. An international driver's license is recommended but not mandatory.

If you drive your own car, you must have the original registration insurance certificate and a valid driver's license. You should also carry a passport or National ID card. A sticker showing the country

of registration should be displayed close to the rear number plate. The headlights of right-hand drive cars must be adjusted for left-hand driving. You must also carry a red warning triangle, spare headlight bulbs, a first-aid kit and a fire extinguisher. If you are caught without these you are liable to be fined. When driving around ski resorts in winter, snow chains *(chaînes)* are essential.

BUYING GAS IN FRANCE

GAS *(essence)* is expensive in France, especially on the *autoroutes*. Large supermarkets and hypermarkets sell gas at a discount.

A map *(la carte de l'essence moins chère)*, available from French Government Tourist Offices *(see p617)*, shows the location of stores that are close to highway exits. Gas coupons are not accepted in France. Filling up the tank is known as *faire le plein*.

Diesel fuel *(gazole or gas-oil)* is comparatively cheap in France and is sold everywhere, as is unleaded gas *(sans plomb)*.

Some of the most widely available car rental firms in France

RULES OF THE ROAD

UNLESS ROAD signs indicate otherwise, *priorité à droite* means that you must give way to any vehicle joining the road from the right. Most major roads outside built-up areas have the right of way indicated by *passage protegé* signs. Cars already on a traffic circle have right of way.

Contrary to convention in the US and UK, flashing headlights in France mean the driver is claiming the right of way.

Other French driving rules, including parking regulations, are summarized in the **RAC** publication *The European Motoring Guide*. Rules include the compulsory wearing of seat belts, and no passing where there is an unbroken white center line.

40 km/h (25 mph) speed limit

SPEED LIMITS AND FINES

SPEED LIMITS in France are as follows:
• On autoroutes: 130 km/h (80 mph); 110 km/h (70 mph) when it rains.
• On divided highways: 110 km/h (70 mph); 90–100 km/h (55–60 mph) when it rains.
• On other roads: 90 km/h (55 mph), 80 km/h (50 mph) when it rains.
• In towns: 50 km/h (30 mph). This applies anywhere in a village, hamlet or city, unless marked otherwise. In some places it may be lower. Normal limits may not be shown.

On-the-spot fines may be collected, especially from visitors, for speeding offenses and for drunk-driving offenses. Fines are also imposed for not carrying the proper documentation and for breaking the rules of the road.

Sign indicating one-way system

No entry for any vehicles

Passage protegé ends, *priorité à droite* starts

ROAD CONDITIONS AND WEATHER FORECASTS

LOCAL RADIO stations report on road conditions – look for highway signs listing their frequencies. **CRICR** (Centre Régional d'Information et de Coordination Routière) lines give general information on regional road conditions. The **CNIR** (Centre National d'Information Routière) line covers the whole of France.

The **RAC** sells a tailormade route-planning information service, giving scenic options and road conditions.

To get weather forecasts in English for the English Channel telephone **Marinecall**, and for selected cities in France, call the **Holiday Weatherline**.

Sign for Channel Tunnel terminal

HIGHWAYS

MOST HIGHWAYS in France have a toll system (*autoroutes à péage*), which can be expensive. There are short sections that are free, usually close to major centers. Tolls can be paid with either credit cards or cash. Where only small sums are involved, you throw coins into a large receptacle and change is given automatically.

Much of the *autoroute* network has been built in the last 20 years. It includes good and frequent rest areas and picnic spots 10–20 km (6–12 miles) apart, gas stations at every 40 km (25 miles), and emergency telephones every 2 km (1¼ miles). Service areas include shops, takeout food places and restaurants, fax and telephone facilities.

OTHER ROADS

IN FRANCE the RN (*route nationale*) and D (*départementale*) roads are a good alternative to highways. *Bis/Bison futée* signs are posted for alternative routes away from heavy traffic.

Sunday is usually a good day to travel since there are very few trucks on the road. Try to avoid traveling at the French vacation rush periods known as *grands départs*. The worst times are weekends in mid-July, and the beginning and end of August when vacations begin and end.

If you are bypassing rather than driving into Paris, it is more advisable to take the highways on either side of the city, avoiding the busy *boulevard péripherique* that encircles Paris.

USING THE AUTOROUTE TOLL

When you enter an autoroute, take a ticket from the machine. This identifies your starting point on the autoroute. You do not pay until you reach an exit toll. You are charged according to the distance traveled and the type of vehicle driven.

Highway Sign
These signs indicate the name and distance to the next toll booth. They are usually blue and white; some show the tariff rates for cars, motorcycles, trucks and caravans.

Tollbooth with Attendant
When you hand in your ticket at a staffed tollbooth, the attendant will tell you the cost of your journey on the autoroute, and the charge will be displayed. You can pay with coins, notes, credit cards or with a Eurocheque in French francs. A receipt is issued on request.

Automatic Machine
On reaching the exit toll, insert your ticket into the machine and the price of your journey will be displayed in French francs. You can pay either with coins or by credit card. The machine will give change and can issue a receipt.

USING AN HORODATEUR MACHINE

F1

F2

F5

F10

1 If using coins (F1, F2, F5 or F10), insert according to the tariff shown.

2 If using a card, insert and press the blue button for each 15 minutes required.

3 To obtain the ticket, press the green button.

4 Remove ticket when it emerges and place inside the car windshield.

Horodateurs
These parking meters operate from 9am–7pm Mon–Fri. Unless otherwise indicated, parking is free Sat–Sun, public holidays and in August.

PARKING

Parking REGULATIONS vary from town to town. Most operate pay-and-display systems *(horodateurs)*. Some machines accept a parking payment card, which can be bought at tobacconists. Provincial towns offer free parking from noon to 1:30pm. Parking is normally limited to two hours. In small towns, parking is confined to one side of the street only, alternating at different times of the month. Signs show where parking is allowed.

In larger cities, especially Paris, finding a parking space can be hard. Because space is so limited, cars frequently "bump" one another to squeeze into a space.

If you are in an area where parking permits are in use, the local tourist office will supply you with one.

CAR RENTAL

All THE MAIN international car-rental companies operate in France. It is worth making arrangements before you leave for France because discount rentals can often be booked and prepaid in the UK or USA. In France, two smaller companies offer very competitive rates.

Century Self Drive operates outside airport terminal buildings, usually from a hotel lobby in the immediate vicinity and will pick you up when you arrive. The other option is **Autos Abroad**, brokers who use cars owned by other car-rental companies, like **Budget** and **Citer**. Renting from either of these companies may be half the price of the standard rental.

For car hire booked in combination with flights, your travel agent can usually organize a good deal. SNCF (the French state railroad) offers combined train and car-rental fares called Train + Auto

(see p634) with pick-up points at 200 stations in France. Phone **Rail Europe** for information.

For non-EU residents planning to drive in France for a minimum of three weeks, the best option is the short-term tax-free purchase-and-buy-back service (sometimes called TT leasing) offered by **Citroën**, **Peugeot** and **Renault**.

Information on chauffeur-driven car rentals can be obtained from the **Automobile Club de l'Ile de France**.

MAPS

In THIS GUIDE, each chapter begins with a map of the region showing all the sights and giving useful tips on getting around. If you plan to use autoroutes extensively, *Enjoy your trip on the French Motorways* is a good foldout map of the autoroute network with useful information on the back. The more general *France Tourist Map* marks historic sites and also has useful information on the back. You can get both maps at French Government Tourist Offices *(see p617)*.

For driving shorter distances and for cycling, the best routes are the smaller D *(département)* roads marked in yellow or white on **Michelin** maps, and often quite empty of traffic. The red Michelin maps of France (scale 1:1,000,000) are useful for planning a trip. The excellent Michelin atlas of France has generously overlapping maps

Mountain cyclists in the Alps

at a scale of 1:200,000. At the same scale, a series of regional maps with yellow covers is sold in different sheet sizes. Maps showing the whole country are also available (red covers). Larger scale maps (green covers) are currently only available for the south of France and the area surrounding Paris. A new series of *Cartes Zoom*, also at 1:100,000 scale, focus on the areas round Toulouse, Bordeaux, Clermont-Ferrand and Nantes.

IGN (Institut Géographique National) is the equivalent of the British Ordnance Survey. The whole of France is available in sheets at 1:250,000, 1:100,000, 1:50,000 and 1:25,000. Their atlas is published in conjunction with the **AA** as *The Big Road Atlas to*

France. **Espace IGN**, just off the Champs-Elysées in Paris, is a haven for map lovers. For super clarity and detail use the *Daily Telegraph* (*Recta Foldex* in France) series from **Roger Lascelles**. Refer to page 628 for walking and cycling maps.

In France, all newsagents and gas stations stock the more commonly used maps. In the UK, **Stanfords** is famous for its range. In the US **Rand McNally** have a good selection. For more specialized requests try **Roger Lascelles** or World Leisure Marketing (*see p629*).

The town maps included in this guide locate all the important sights. You can

A selection of French road maps

usually get town plans free from tourist offices, although for large towns you might need the more detailed maps published by Michelin.

DIRECTORY

CAR RENTAL

ADA
[01 49 58 44 44 (Paris).

Autos Abroad
[020-7509 1900 (UK).

Avis
[(1) (800) 331 1212 (US).
[01 46 10 60 60 (Paris).

Budget
[(1) (800) 527 0700 (US).
[01 47 55 61 00 (Paris).

Century Self Drive Ltd
[0442 216512 (UK).
[01 34 29 00 08 (Paris).

Europcar
[(1) (800) 227 3876 (US).
[01 45 00 08 06 (Paris).

Hertz
[(1) (800) 654 3131 (US).
[01 39 38 38 38 (Paris).

National Citer
[01 44 38 61 61 (Paris).

Sixt-Eurorent
[01 44 38 55 55 (Paris).

TRAIN + AUTO

Rail Europe
[020-7203 7000 (UK).

TT LEASING

Citroën
19 bis rue Friant
75014 Paris.
Map 11 C5 (off "N 306").
[01 45 40 30 30.
FAX 01 45 40 30 40.

Peugeot Sodexa
[0800 44 24 44 (Paris).

Renault Eurodrive
Renault Ventes Spéciales
Exportation,
186 av Jean-Jaurès,
75019 Paris.
[0800 05 15 15 (Paris).
FAX 01 42 41 83 47 (Paris).

Australia: International Market Development
[(2) 229 33 44.
FAX (2) 290 39 63.

CAR RENTAL WITH CHAUFFEUR

Automobile Club de l'Ile de France
14 av de la Grande
Armeé,
75017 Paris.
Map 2 D4.
[01 40 55 43 00.

WEATHER FORECASTS

Holiday Weatherline
[0839 444070 forecasts for France.

Marinecall
[0839 444071 forecasts for the Channel.

NATIONAL ROAD CONDITIONS

RAC
RAC House, Bartlett Street, South Croydon, Surrey CR2 6XW.
[0345 333 222.
[0800 550 055 for guides.

REGIONAL ROAD CONDITIONS

CRICR
Bordeaux
[05 56 96 33 33.

Lille
[03 20 47 33 33.

Lyon
[04 78 54 33 33.

Marseille
[04 91 78 78 78.

Metz
[03 87 63 33 33.

Paris Region
[01 48 99 33 33.

Rennes
[02 99 32 33 33.

MAPS

AA
30–31 Haymarket
London SW1X 4EU.
[0990 989 989.

Espace IGN
107 rue la Boétie
75008 Paris. **Map** 2 F5.
[01 43 98 80 00.
FAX 01 43 98 51 08.

Michelin
[01 45 66 12 34 (Paris).
[(803) 458 6470 (US).

Rand McNally
Map and Travel Store
150 East 52nd Street,
New York, NY 10022.
[(212) 758 7488.

Roger Lascelles
47 York Road,
Brentford, Mddx
TW8 0QP.
[020 8847 0935.
FAX 020 8568 3886.

Stanfords
12–14 Long Acre
London WC2E 9LP.
[020 7836 1321.
FAX 020 7836 0189.

General Index

Acknowledgments

DORLING KINDERSLEY would like to thank the following people whose contributions and assistance have made the preparation of this book possible.

MAIN CONTRIBUTORS

John Ardagh, Rosemary Bailey, Judith Fayard, Lisa Gerard-Sharp, Alister Kershaw, Alec Lobrano, Anthony Roberts, Alan Tillier, Nigel Tisdall.

CONTRIBUTORS AND CONSULTANTS

JOHN ARDAGH is a writer and broadcaster, and author of many books on France, among them *France Today* and *Writers' France*.

ROSEMARY BAILEY has written and edited several guides to regional France, including *Burgundy*, the *Loire Valley*, and the *Côte d'Azur*.

ALEXANDRA BOYLE is a writer and editor who has worked in publishing in England and France for 20 years.

ELSIE BURCH DONALD, editor and writer, is the author of *The French Farmhouse*.

DAVID BURNIE B.Sc. has written over 30 books on natural sciences, including *How Nature Works*.

JUDITH FAYARD, an American based in Paris, was Paris bureau chief for *Life* magazine for 10 years, and is now European editor of *Town & Country*. She contributes to various publications, including the *Wall Street Journal*.

LISA GERARD-SHARP is a writer and broadcaster and author of several regional guides to France and Italy.

COLIN JONES is Professor of History at Exeter University. His books include *The Longman Companion to the French Revolution* and *The Cambridge Illustrated History of France*.

ALISTER KERSHAW is an Australian writer and broadcaster who has lived in the Loire Valley for 30 years.

ALEC LOBRANO is an American writer, based in Paris. He is the European editor of *Departures* magazine and contributes to *International Herald Tribune*, *Los Angeles Times*, and *The Independent*.

ANTHONY ROBERTS is a writer and translator who has lived in Gascony for 15 years, contributing to various publications including *The Times*, *World of Interiors*, and *Architectural Digest*.

ANTHONY ROSE is the wine correspondent of *The Independent* and co-author of *The Grapevine*.

JANE SIGAL is the author of two books on French food, *Normandy Gastronomique* and *Backroom Bistros, Farmhouse Fare*.

ALAN TILLIER is the main contributor to the *Dorling Kindersley Travel Guide to Paris*. He has lived in Paris for more than 20 years as correspondent for various journals, including the *International Herald Tribune*, *Newsweek*, and *The Times*.

NIGEL TISDALL is a travel writer and author of guides to Brittany and Normandy.

PATRICIA WELLS is food critic of the *International Herald Tribune* and author of the *Food Lovers' Guide to Paris* and the *Food Lovers' Guide to France*.

ADDITIONAL CONTRIBUTORS

Caroline Bugler, Ann Cremin, Bill Echikson, Adrian Gilbert, Peter Graham, Marion Kaplan, Jim Keeble, Alexandra Kennedy, Fred Mawer, Clive Unger-Hamilton.

ADDITIONAL PHOTOGRAPHY

Jo Craig, Michael Crockett, Mike Dunning, Philip Enticknap, Steve Gorton, Alison Harris, John Heseltine, Roger Hilton, Eric Meacher, Neil Mersh, Roger Moss, Robert O'Dea, Alan Williams, Peter Wilson.

ADDITIONAL ILLUSTRATIONS

Dinwiddie Maclaren, John Fox, Nick Gibbard, Paul Guest, Stephen Gyapay, Kevin Jones Associates, Chris Orr, Robbie Polley, Sue Sharples.

EDITORIAL AND DESIGN

MANAGING EDITOR Douglas Amrine
MANAGING ART EDITOR Gaye Allen
SENIOR EDITOR Helen Partington
SENIOR DESIGNER Annette Jacobs
EDITORIAL DIRECTOR David Lamb
ART DIRECTOR Anne-Marie Bulat
RESEARCHER Philippa Richmond
PRODUCTION Hilary Stephens
PICTURE RESEARCH Naomi Peck
DTP DESIGNER Ingrid Vienings

Louise Abbott, Peter Adams, Laetitia Benloulou, Steve Bere, Jane Branneky, Arwen Burnett, Maggie Crowley, Fay Franklin, Tom Fraser, Emily Green, Elaine Harries, Sasha Heseltine, Elaine Hewson, Paul Hines, Nicholas Inman, Gail Jones, Nancy Jones, Siri Lowe, Francesca Machiavelli, Lesley McCave, Rebecca Milner, Ella Milroy, Malcolm Parchment, Shirin Patel, Alice Peebles, Marianne Petrou, Salim Qurashi, Caroline Radula-Scott, Marisa Renzullo, Rupert Small, Andrew Szudek, Dawn Terrey, Fiona Wild.

ADDITIONAL CARTOGRAPHY

Colourmap Scanning Limited; Contour Publishing; Cosmographics; European Map Graphics; Meteo-France. Street Finder maps: ERA Maptec Ltd (Dublin), adapted with permission from original survey and mapping by Shobunsha (Japan).

CARTOGRAPHIC RESEARCH

Jennifer Skelley, Rachel Hawtin (Lovell Johns); James Mills-Hicks, Peter Winfield, Claudine Zarte (Dorling Kindersley Cartography).
MAP CO-ORDINATORS Simon Farbrother, David Pugh

Special Assistance
Mme Jassinger, French Embassy Press Department; Peter Mills and Christine Lagardère, French Railways Ltd.

Photographic Reference
Altitude, Paris; Sea and See, Paris; Editions Combier, Maçon; Thomas d'Hoste, Paris.

Photography Permissions
Dorling Kindersley would like to thank the following for their assistance and kind permission to photograph at their establishments: The Caisse Nationale des Monuments Historiques et des Sites; M. A. Leonetti, the Abbey of Mont St-Michel; Chartres Cathedral; M. Voisin, Château de Chenonceau; M. P Mistral, Cité de Carcassonne, M. D. Vingtain, Palais des Papes, Avignon; Château de Fontainebleau; Amiens Cathedral; Conques Abbey; Fontenay Abbey; Moissac Abbey; Vézelay Abbey, Reims Cathedral and all the other churches, museums, hotels, restaurants, shops, galleries and sights too numerous to thank individually.

Picture Credits
t = top; tl = top left; tc = top center; tr = top right; cla = center left above; ca = center above; cra = center right above; cl = center left; c = center; cr = center right; clb = center left below; cb = center below; crb = center right below; bl = bottom left; b = bottom; bc = bottom center; br = bottom right; (d) = detail.

Works of art have been reproduced with the permission of the following copyright holders; ©ADAGP, Paris and DACS, London 1994: 25tl, 59tl, 61tl (detail), 88c, 89ca, 95t, 109b, 514bl; ©DACS, London 1994: 24c, 24cb, 25c, 25cb, 26bl, 60–61, 84cl, 86t, 86b, 89t, 203t, 341t, 371br, 412t, 463t, 472t, 498ca, 503b, 511t, 512b, 514tr, 514bl, 519b; © J Fabris: 25c; © Succession H. Matisse/DACS 1994; 25b, 88b, 516b.

Photos achieved with the assistance of the EPPV and the CSI: 132–3; Photo of Euro Disneyland ® Park and the Euro Disneyland Paris ® 168cr; The characters, architectural works and trademarks are the property of The Walt Disney Company. All rights reserved; Courtesy of the Maison Victor Hugo, Ville de Paris: 87t; Musée National des Châteaux de Malmaison et Bois-Preau: 163b; Musée de Montmartre, Paris: 129t; Musée National de la Legion d'Honneur: 56t; © Sundancer: 138bl.

The publisher would like to thank the following individuals, companies and picture libraries for permission to reproduce their photographs:

Air France/D Toulorge: 631t; Alpine Garden Society/Christopher Grey-Wilson: 450bl, 450br; Agence Photo Aquitaine: D. Lelann 411tl; Ancient Art and Architecture Collection: 43 crb, 46c, 46cb, 48br, 53bl, 242–3b, 325bl, 372t, 424t, 428b; Photo AKG, Berlin: 41cra, 42bl, 50bc, 51crb, 392t, 393b; Archives Photographiques, Paris/DACS: 412t; Atelier du Regard/A Allemand: 432cl, 432cr, 432b.

Bibliotheque Nationale, Dijon: 45cb; F. Blackburn: 451bl; Gerard Boullay/Photola: 83bl, 83cra; Bridgeman Art Library: Albright Knox Art Gallery, Buffalo, New York 265br; Anthony Crane Collection 201br; Bibliothèque Nationale, Paris 46cr–47cl, 48t, 49cr, 65bl; British Library, London 48bl, 64br, 282c, 283br, 283tl; Bonhams, London 55tc, 58tl; Château de Versailles, France 65tr; Christies, London 25c, 503b; Giraudon 24tr, 24tl, 52cr–53cl, 53tl, 55tl, 65bc, 171b, 324c, 333c, 355t; Guildhall Library, Corporation of London 407b; Hermitage, St. Petersburg 25bl; Index 462b; Kress Collection, Washington DC 283bl; Lauros-Giraudon 42t, 65br; Musée des Beaux Arts, Quimper 233c; Musée Condé, Chantilly 46tl, 53tr, 64bl, 65tcl, 65cb, 194t, 283c; Musée d'Orsay, Paris 24cb; Paul Bremen Collection 245t; Sotheby's New York 51tl; V&A Museum, London 328b; Walters Art Gallery, Baltimore, Maryland 346t; John Brunton: 504b; Michael Busselle: 172–3.

Campagne, Campagne: 340t; C. Guy 315t; Lara 181cr; B. Lichtstein 207b, 314cl; Pyszel 180bl; CNMHS, Paris/DACS: Longchamps Delehaye 203tl; Castelet/Grotte de Clamouse: 483b; Collection CDT Gard: 315bl; CDT Lot: 429b; Cephas: Stuart Boreham 250–1; Hervé Champollion 312tr, 324t, 340b; Mick Rock 34c, 388tl, 388cl, 461t, 508–9; Jean Loup Charmet: 43b, 46br, 48clb, 54t, 58cl, 58clb, 59tl, 59tc, 60bl, 60br, 61crb, 204b, 233b, 255br, 259b, 264t, 271b, 290br, 333br, 348b, 349t, 351c, 391cr, 391br, 411b, 465t, 497t; Cité des Sciences et L'Industrie: Michel Lamoureux 133c; Pascal Prieur 132tr, 132ca; Michel Viard 132cb; Bruce Coleman: Udo Hirsch 361br; Flip de Nooyer 377br; Hans Reinhard 313tl, 313tr; Photos Editions Combier, Macon: 193t; Joe Cornish: 112, 224–5, 360br, 438.

Dansmuseet, Stockholm/Peter Stenwall: 60cr–61cl; Doherty: 235tc; E. Donard: 31tr, 31c, 31cl, 31bc; Editions d'Art Daniel Derveaux: 390cr–391cl; Photo Daspet, Avignon: 494bl.

ET Archive: 290bl; Cathedral Treasury, Aachen 4t; 44cl; Musée Carnavalet, Paris 57tl; Museum of Fine Arts, Lausanne 51br; Musée d'Orsay, Paris 57cra; Musée de Versailles 52b; 289bl; National Gallery, Scotland 54br; Victoria and Albert Museum, London 49tl; 333bl; Mary Evans Picture Library: 9c, 42br, 46bl, 47c, 49b, 50tl, 52cla, 54c, 58b, 59cr, 59br, 61br, 108c, 109cl, 167b, 173c, 181t, 187b, 225c, 269t, 281b, 283tr, 291bl, 305c, 356b, 383c, 445t, 455c, 463b, 498tl, 535c, 615c; Explorer 27b, 50clb.

Photo Flandre, Amiens: 193b; France Télécom: 624cr; M Reynard 624b; French Railways/SNCF: 634bl, 635t.

Giraudon, Paris: 8–9, 15t, 25cra, 25br, 42ca, 44tl, 44clb, 45tl, 46cl, 48cr–49cl, 52tl, 52clb, 54cl, 56cl, 56cr–57cl, 323br, 337br, 359b, 481cb MS Nero EII pt.2 fol. 20V0; Lauros-Giraudon 40tl, 40bc, 41t, 41crb, 41cb, 41br, 43tc, 45tr, 47crb, 51cr, 56clb, 56br, 341bl, 481cl; Musée d'Art Moderne, Paris

25tl; Musée de Beaux Arts, Quimper 24cl; Telarci 45cr; RONALD GRANT ARCHIVE: 17b, 62clb.

SONIA HALLIDAY PHOTOGRAPHS: Laura Lushington 299tr; ROBERT HARDING PICTURE LIBRARY: 26bl, 33tr, 35tr, 35cl, 39b, 108tl, 131bl, 230tl, 233tr, 312bl, 312br, 313br, 339t, 390cla, 427cr, 451tr, 479b, C. Bowman 442t; Explorer, Paris 35cr, 63br, 97br, 169b, 352t, 361tr, 450cb, 451tl, 474b, 487br, 617b, 628b, 640b; R.Francis 82clb, 626c; D.Hughes 382–3; W.Rawlings 45br, 63tl, 227tl, 246b; A.Wolfitt 22tr, 160, 538b; JOHN HESELTINE: 135c; HONFLEUR, MUSÉE BOUDIN: 252b; DAVID HUGHES: 2–3, 357t, 357b; THE HULTON DEUTSCH COLLECTION: 181br, 291br, 463c, 506b; FJ Mortimer 180tl.

THE IMAGE BANK: Peter Miller 362; IMAGES: 313c, 450cl, 450tr.

JACANA: F Gohier 450tl; JM Labat 451bc; TREVOR JONES: 194b.

MAGNUM PHOTOS LTD: Bruno Barbey 16b, 27tr, 32bl; R Capa 462tr; P Halsman 515b; P Zachman 15b; THE MANSELL COLLECTION: 27tl, 272t, 285b, 449b, 494tl; JOHN MILLER: 214b, 326tr, 397b; MUSÉE DE L'ANNONCIADE, ST-TROPEZ: 514tr; MUSÉE DES BEAUX ARTS, CARCASSONNE: 479tl; MUSÉE DES BEAUX ARTS, DIJON: 333tl; MUSÉE DES BEAUX ARTS DE LYON: 371tr, 371bl, 371br; MUSÉE DE LA CIVILISATION GALLO-ROMAINE, LYON: 43cr, 368cl; MUSÉE DEPARTMENTAL BRETON, QUIMPER: 264bl; MUSÉE FLAUBERT, ROUEN: 255bl; MUSEUM NATIONAL D'HISTOIRE NATURELLE, PARIS: 134c; COURTESY OF THE MUSÉE MATISSE, NICE: 516b; MUSÉE NATIONAL D'ART MODERNE, PARIS: 88clb, 89t, 89cr, 89cb, 325br; Succession Henri Matisse 88bl; MUSÉE RÉATTU, ARLES: M Lacanaud 498ca; CLICHÉ MUSÉE DE SENS/J.P. ELIE: 320tl; MUSÉE TOULOUSE-LAUTREC, ALBI: 434b.

SERVICE NATIONAL DES TIMBRES POSTE ET DE LA PHILATÉLIE: designed by Eve Luquet 626bl; NETWORK PHOTOGRAPHERS: Barry Lewis 328t; Rapho/Mark Buscail 628tl; Rapho/De Sazo 628tr; Rapho/Michael Serraillier 629b.

PICTURES COLOUR LIBRARY: 392b, 416, 534, 614–5;

MICHEL LE POER TRENCH: 26br; CENTRE GEORGES POMPIDOU: Bernard Prerost 89b; POPPERFOTO: 241c; PYRENEES MAGAZINE/DR: 390bl.

REDFERNS: William Gottlieb 60clb; RETROGRAPH ARCHIVE: M. Breese 464tl, 464tr; RÉUNION DES MUSÉES NATIONAUX: Musée des Antiquités Nationales 393c; Musée Guimet 107t; Musée du Louvre 53ca, 97bl, 98t, 98bl, 98br, 99tl, 99c, 99b; Musée Picasso 84cl, 86b, 463t; Musée de Versailles 169t; RF REYNOLDS: 235bc; REX FEATURES: Sipa 18t; ROCAMADOUR: 427t; ROGER-VIOLLET: 109tc; FOUNDATION ROYAUMONT: J Johnson 162t.

SIPA PRESS: 128bl; PHOTO SNCM/SOUTHERN FERRIES: 632b; SPECTRUM COLOUR LIBRARY: P Thompson 239b; FRANK SPOONER PICTURES: Bolcina 33b; Uzan 62br; Simon 63ca; Gamma Press 35b, 63crb; JEAN MARIE STEINLEN: 394; TONY STONE IMAGES: 312c, 316; SYGMA: 521t; C de Bare 32t; Walter Carone 140t; P Forestier 304–5; Frederic de la Fosse 510b; D Goldberg 17c; L'Illustration 104tl; Keystone 131crb; T Prat 426c; L de Raemy 63bl; Sunset Boulevard 131br.

EDITIONS TALLANDIER: 38, 40cb, 43tl, 44br, 44br–45bl, 47t, 47b, 48cl, 49tr, 50br, 54clb, 54bl, 54cr–55cl, 55crb, 55bl, 57tr, 57crb, 57br, 59bl, 59bc, 60cla, 60crb, 61tc, 61tr; TOURIST OFFICE SEMUR-EN-AUXOIS: 325t; © TMR/A.D.A.G.P, PARIS AND DACS, LONDON 1994 – COLLECTION L. TREILLARD: 61tl detail.

JEAN VERTUT: 40br–41bl; VISUAL ARTS LIBRARY: 24b.

WORLD PICTURES: 313bl.

ZEFA: 168c, 341t; O. ZIMMERMAN/MUSÉE D'UNTERLINDEN 6800 COLMAR: 217t.

Front Endpaper: All special photography except JOE CORNISH lbl; THE IMAGE BANK rcb; PICTURES COLOUR LIBRARY lcr; JEAN MARIE STEINLEIN lcl; TONY STONE IMAGES rca.

Jacket: All special photography except CEPHAS/Mick Rock front t; MICHAEL BUSSELLE front cbr; ROBERT HARDING PICTURE LIBRARY spine t.

Phrase Book

IN EMERGENCY

Help!	**Au secours!**	oh se**koor**
Stop!	**Arrêtez!**	aret-**ay**
Call a doctor!	**Appelez un médecin!**	apuh-**lay** uñ med**sañ**
Call an ambulance!	**Appelez une ambulance!**	apuh-**lay** oon oñboo-**loñs**
Call the police!	**Appelez la police!**	apuh-**lay** lah poh-**lees**
Call the fire department!	**Appelez les pompiers!**	apuh-**lay** leh poñ-**peeyay**
Where is the nearest telephone?	**Où est le téléphone le plus proche?**	oo ay luh tehleh**fon** luh ploo **prosh**
Where is the nearest hospital?	**Où est l'hôpital le plus proche?**	oo ay l'**opee**tal luh ploo **prosh**

COMMUNICATION ESSENTIALS

Yes	**Oui**	wee
No	**Non**	noñ
Please	**S'il vous plaît**	seel voo **play**
Thank you	**Merci**	mer-**see**
Excuse me	**Excusez-moi**	exkoo-**zay** mwah
Hello	**Bonjour**	boñ**zhoor**
Goodbye	**Au revoir**	oh ruh-**vwar**
Good night	**Bonsoir**	boñ-**swar**
Morning	**Le matin**	matañ
Afternoon	**L'après-midi**	l'apreh-**meedee**
Evening	**Le soir**	swar
Yesterday	**Hier**	eeyehr
Today	**Aujourd'hui**	oh-zhoor-**dwee**
Tomorrow	**Demain**	duhmañ
Here	**Ici**	ee-**see**
There	**Là**	lah
What?	**Quel, quelle?**	kel, kel
When?	**Quand?**	koñ
Why?	**Pourquoi?**	poor-**kwah**
Where?	**Où?**	oo

USEFUL PHRASES

How are you?	**Comment allez-vous?**	kom-moñ talay **voo**
Very well, thank you.	**Très bien, merci.**	treh byañ, mer-**see**
Pleased to meet you.	**Enchanté de faire votre connaissance.**	oñshoñ-**tay** duh fehr votr kon-ay-**sans**
See you soon.	**A bientôt.**	byañ-**toh**
That's fine.	**Voilà qui est parfait**	vwalah kee ay par**fay**
Where is/are...?	**Où est/sont...?**	oo ay/soñ
How far is it to...?	**Combien de kilomètres d'ici à...?**	kom-**byañ** duh keelo-metr d'ee-**see** ah
Which way to...?	**Quelle est la direction pour...?**	kel ay lah deer-ek-**syoñ** poor
Do you speak English?	**Parlez-vous anglais?**	par-**lay** voo oñg-lay
I don't understand.	**Je ne comprends pas.**	zhuh nuh kom-**proñ** pah
Could you speak slowly please?	**Pouvez-vous parler moins vite s'il vous plaît?**	poo-**vay** voo par-**lay** mwañ veet seel voo play
I'm sorry.	**Excusez-moi.**	exkoo-**zay** mwah.

USEFUL WORDS

big	**grand**	groñ
small	**petit**	puh-**tee**
hot	**chaud**	show
cold	**froid**	frwah
good	**bon**	boñ
bad	**mauvais**	moh-**veh**
enough	**assez**	assay
well	**bien**	byañ
open	**ouvert**	oo-**ver**
closed	**fermé**	fer-**meh**
left	**gauche**	gohsh
right	**droit**	drwah
straight ahead	**tout droit**	too drwah
near	**près**	preh
far	**loin**	lwañ
up	**en haut**	oñ oh
down	**en bas**	oñ bah
early	**de bonne heure**	duh bon urr
late	**en retard**	oñ ruh-**tar**
entrance	**l'entrée**	l'on-**tray**
exit	**la sortie**	sor-**tee**
toilet	**les toilettes, les WC**	twah-let, vay-**see**
free, unoccupied	**libre**	leebr
free, no charge	**gratuit**	grah-**twee**

MAKING A TELEPHONE CALL

I'd like to place a long-distance call.	**Je voudrais faire un interurbain.**	zhuh voo-dreh fehr uñ añter-oorbañ
I'd like to make a collect call.	**Je voudrais faire une communication PCV.**	zhuh voo**dreh** fehr oon komoonikah-**syoñ** peh-seh-veh
I'll try again later.	**Je rappelerai plus tard.**	zhuh rapel-**eray** ploo tar
Can I leave a message?	**Est-ce que je peux laisser un message?**	es-**keh** zhuh puh leh-**say** uñ meh**sazh**
Hold on.	**Ne quittez pas, s'il vous plaît.**	nuh kee-**tay** pah seel voo play
Could you speak up a little please?	**Pouvez-vous parler un peu plus fort?**	poo-**vay** voo par-**lay** uñ puh ploo for
local call	**la communication locale**	komoonikah-**syoñ** low-**kal**

SHOPPING

How much does this cost?	**C'est combien s'il vous plaît?**	say kom-**byañ** seel voo play
I would like ...	**je voudrais...**	zhuh voo-**dray**
Do you have?	**Est-ce que vous avez?**	es-**kuh** voo zav**ay**
I'm just looking.	**Je regarde seulement.**	zhuh ruh**gar** suhl**moñ**
Do you take credit cards?	**Est-ce que vous acceptez les cartes de crédit?**	es-**kuh** voo zaksept-**ay** leh kart duh kreh-**dee**
Do you take traveler's checks?	**Est-ce que vous acceptez les chèques de voyage?**	es-**kuh** voo zaksept-**ay** leh shek duh vwa**yazh**
What time do you open?	**A quelle heure vous êtes ouvert?**	ah kel urr voo zet oo-**ver**
What time do you close?	**A quelle heure vous êtes fermé?**	ah kel urr voo zet fer-**may**
This one.	**Celui-ci.**	suhl-wee-**see**
That one.	**Celui-là.**	suhl-wee-**lah**
expensive	**cher**	shehr
cheap	**pas cher, bon marché**	pah shehr, boñ mar-**shay**
size, clothes	**la taille**	tye
size, shoes	**la pointure**	pwañ-**tur**
white	**blanc**	bloñ
black	**noir**	nwahr
red	**rouge**	roozh
yellow	**jaune**	zhohwn
green	**vert**	vehr
blue	**bleu**	bluh

TYPES OF SHOPS

antiques shop	**le magasin d'antiquités**	maga-**zañ** d'oñteekee-**tay**
bakery	**la boulangerie**	booloñ-**zhuree**
bank	**la banque**	boñk
book store	**la librairie**	lee-**brehree**
butcher	**la boucherie**	boo-**shehree**
cake shop	**la pâtisserie**	patee-**sree**
cheese shop	**la fromagerie**	fromazh-**ree**
dairy	**la crémerie**	krem-**ree**
department store	**le grand magasin**	groñ maga-**zañ**
delicatessen	**la charcuterie**	sharkoot-**ree**
drugstore	**la pharmacie**	farmah-**see**
fish seller	**la poissonnerie**	pwasson-**ree**
gift shop	**le magasin de cadeaux**	maga-**zañ** duh kadoh
greengrocer	**le marchand de légumes**	mar-**shoñ** duh lay-**goom**
grocery	**l'alimentation**	alee-moñta-**syoñ**
hairdresser	**le coiffeur**	kwa**fuhr**
market	**le marché**	marsh-**ay**
newsstand	**le magasin de journaux**	maga-**zañ** duh zhoor-**no**
post office	**la poste, le bureau de poste, le PTT**	pohst, booroh duh pohst, peh-teh-teh
shoe store	**le magasin de chaussures**	maga-**zañ** duh show-**soor**
supermarket	**le supermarché**	soo pehr-**marshay**
tobacconist	**le tabac**	tabah
travel agent	**l'agence de voyages**	l'azhoñs duh vwayazh

SIGHTSEEING

abbey	**l'abbaye**	l'abay-**ee**
art gallery	**la galerie d'art**	galer-**ree** dart
bus station	**la gare routière**	gahr roo-tee-**yehr**

Central Paris

AVENUE FOCH

AVENUE DE LA GRANDE ARMÉE

AVENUE CARNOT

AVENUE MACMAHON

AVENUE DE WAGRAM

AVENUE HOCHE

RUE DU FAUBOURG ST HONORE

AV DE FRIEDLAND

BD DE HAUSSMANN

Arc de Triomphe

PL CHARLES DE GAULLE

AVENUE DES CHAMPS ELYSEES

RUE DE COURCELLES

RUE LA BOETIE

RUE DE MIROMESNIL

RUE TRONCHET

BD

RUE WASHINGTON

AV F.D. ROOSEVELT

PLACE VICTOR HUGO

R COPERNIC

RUE SERBIE

ROND POINT DES CHAMPS ELYSEES

AVENUE DE MARIGNY

RUE ROYALE

PLACE VENDÔME

AVENUE BUGEAUD

AVENUE VICTOR HUGO

AVENUE KLEBER

AVENUE D'IENA

AVENUE MARCEAU

PREM GEORGE V

AVENUE GEORGE V

PLACE AMIRAL DE GRASSE

PLACE FRANCOIS PREMIER

COURS LA REINE

PLACE DE LA CONCORDE

RUE DE RIV

CHAILLOT

RAYMOND POINCARE

RUE BOISSIERE

AV PIERRE

QUAI D'ORSAY

JARDIN DES TUILERIE

AVENUE D'EYLAU

AV DU PRES WILSON

La Seine

AVENUE G MANDEL

PLACE DU TROCADERO ET DU 11 NOVEMBRE

AVENUE DE NEW YORK

QUAI

DE ANATO

CIMETIERE DE PASSY

JARDINS DU TROCADERO

QUAI BRANLY

L'UNIVERSITE

INVALIDES

QUAI DE L'UNIVERSI

Mus d'Or

RUE FRANKLIN

Tour Eiffel

AVENUE DE LA BOURDONNAIS

AVENUE RAPP

RUE SAINT DOMINIQUE

RUE DES

RUE SAINT DOMINIQUE

PLACE DES INVALIDES

AVENUE DU MARECHAL GALLIENI

RUE DE BELLECHASSE

BOULEVARD SAI

Pont de Bir-Hakeim

QUAI

BOSQUET

DE GRENELLE

RUE DE GRENELLE

BOULEVARD RASPAIL

PARC DU CHAMP DE MARS

AVENUE DE LA

MOTTE PICQUET

BD DE LA TOUR MAUBOURG

JARDIN DE L'INTENDANT

BOULEVARD DES INVALIDES

RUE DE VARENNE

RUE VANEAU

PLACE JOFFRE

AV DE TOURVILLE

PRESIDENCE DU CONSEIL

AVENUE DE SEGUR

AVENUE DE SUFFREN

PLACE DE FONTENOY

AVENUE DE LOWENDAL

RUE DE BABYLONE

CHAMPS-ELYSÉES AND INVALIDES
Pages 100–111
Street Finder maps 1–3, 6, 7

THE LEFT BANK
Pages 112–123
Street Finder maps 7–9, 12, 13

KEY

Major sight

M Metro station

RER RER station

Main bus stop

P Main parking area

Hospital with emergency unit

0 meters	500
0 yards	500